Criminal Law
Massachusetts Police Manual 2023

The Massachusetts Police Reference
for Criminal Law

Current up to January 24, 2023

Print date December 4, 2023

John Sofis Scheft, Esq.

Law Enforcement Dimensions, LLC
7 Central Street, Suite 100
Arlington, Massachusetts 02476
781-646-4377
Fax: 781-646-1776
www.ledimensions.com

Goodway Group of Massachusetts
16 A Street, Burlington, MA 01803

ISBN 978-1-944630-71-3

Copyright 2023 by John Sofis Scheft, Esq. and Law Enforcement Dimensions. All rights reserved. No part of this book may be reproduced or utilized in any form or by any means, electronic or mechanical, including photocopying, recording, or by any information storage and retrieval system, without written permission from the author/publisher.

Part No: 14152

> *To my loving and supportive wife —Sof*

About the Author

John Sofis Scheft, Esq.

John Sofis Scheft has been providing specialized legal training and promotional examination seminars for over twenty-five years, with a record unmatched in Massachusetts. Among the many topics addressed: criminal law, narcotics offenses, domestic violence, stop & frisk, searches with and without warrants, interrogations and identifications, court testimony and report writing, sexual assault investigation, and juvenile law and procedure.

Aside from legal preparation, John Scheft performs consulting services for police agencies concerning management. He has also developed programs in community policing, problem solving and street mediation.

Scheft has taught extensively for the Drug Enforcement Administration (DEA), Massachusetts State Police, Boston Police, Massachusetts Juvenile Police Officers Association, Massachusetts Criminal Justice Training Council, Maine District Attorney's Association, New England Community Police Partnership, and police academies and departments throughout the Commonwealth.

From 1993 to 1995, Scheft served as Director of the Attorney General's Elderly Protection Project, which provided multi-disciplinary training to police officers on community policing issues affecting the elderly. Funded through a national grant, the Project received a 1994 innovation award from the U.S. Department of Justice.

Prior to serving with the Attorney General, Scheft worked as an Assistant District Attorney in Middlesex County, Massachusetts, where he became a specialist in child abuse and hard core juvenile offender cases. A graduate of Harvard University and Northeastern University School of Law, John Scheft lives with his wife and two children in Arlington, Massachusetts.

Key Changes for 2023 Criminal Law

- Intent to murder as an accomplice. *Comm. v. Sanders,* 101 Mass. App. Ct. 503 (2022). Pg. 2-4.
- Accomplice not liable for murder if he did not know principal armed or intended to kill. *Baxter v. Comm.,* 489 Mass. 504 (2022). Pg. 2-4.
- Police can reasonably conclude that domestic A&B defendant did not act in self-defense. *Karamanoglu v. Yarmouth, Maine,* 15 F.4th 82 (1st Cir. 2021). Pg. 4-17.
- Prosecutor may agree to dismiss criminal case in exchange for defendant's agreement not to sue police. *Grant v. John Hancock Insurance Co.,* 183 F.Supp. 2d 344 (2002). Pg. 5-2.
- SJC indicates that, in the future, unlikely to allow manslaughter verdict based on sudden revelation of infidelity. *Comm. v. Steeves,* 490 Mass. 270 (2022). Pg. 6-7.
- Suspect charged with manslaughter, not murder, when victim resists and kills his accomplice. *Comm. v. Dawson,* 490 Mass. 521 (2022). Pg. 6-8.
- Physician-assisted suicide is typically involuntary manslaughter. *Kligler v. Attorney General,* 491 Mass. 38 (2022). Pg. 6-9.
- Children 13 years and younger qualify for "tender years" doctrine. *Comm. v. Colon,* 431 Mass. 188 (2000). Pg. 7-2.
- Injury and death proves rape. *Comm. v. Paige,* 488 Mass. 677 (2021). Pg. 9-4.
- Forcible rape and aggravated statutory rape are separate offenses. *Comm. v. Foreman,* 101 Mass. App. Ct. 398 (2022). Pg. 9-10.
- 265, § 13B½ enhanced penalty for aggravated indecent A&B on a child under 14 by a mandated reporter. *Comm. v. Kozubal,* 488 Mass. 575 (2021). Pg. 9-14.
- Texted and oral statements are admissible when victim reports sexual abuse. *Comm. v. Holguin,* 101 Mass. App. Ct. 337 (2022). Pg. 9-19.
- Written organizational policies pertaining to inappropriate sexual relations admissible in court. *Comm. v. Kozubal, supra.* Pg. 9-21.
- Taking indecent photo sufficient, even if image never recovered. *Comm. v. Cooper,* 100 Mass. App. Ct. 345 (2021). Pg. 10-12.
- 209A order justified, even though victim not previously attacked. *Constance C. v. Raymond R.,* 101 Mass. App. Ct. 390 (2022). Pg. 13-6.
- Prosecution under federal law is possible for interstate travel to violate a protection order under 18 U.S.C. § 2262. Pg. 13-11.
- A victim's safety must be considered before police notify a dangerous suspect. *Irish v. Fowler,* 979 F.3d 65 (1st Cir. 2022). Pg. 13-13.

- ✓ HPO issued on proof of one sex crime. *F.A.P. v. J.E.S.*, 87 Mass. App. Ct. 595 (2015). Pg. 13-26.

- ✓ Attorney General and private citizens may obtain criminally enforceable court orders for civil rights abuses under 12, §§ 11 H–J. Pg. 16-8.

- ✓ Good example of civil rights injunction on Nantucket. *Barros v. Ponce*, 2022 WL 1203722 (Superior Court). Pg. 16-9.

- ✓ Massachusetts police officers shall not investigate gender or reproductive health care services. 147, § 63. Pg. 16-10.

- ✓ Second Amendment right to bear arms is subject to reasonable regulation. *New York State Rifle & Pistol Association v. Bruen*, 597 U.S. ___ (2022). Pg. 17-1.

- ✓ Holding waistband provides reasonable suspicion of unlawful firearm. *Comm. v. Ross*, 2022 WL 1633836. Pg. 17-2.

- ✓ A firearms licensing authority may not consider whether an applicant has a "proper purpose." *New York State Rifle & Pistol Association v. Bruen, supra*. Pg. 17-3.

- ✓ Firearms seized with a warrant should not be forfeited if the only charge is improper storage. *Comm. v. Fleury*, 489 Mass. 421 (2022). Pg. 17-26.

- ✓ The request by defendant for return of marijuana when the case is dismissed is evaluated by the trial judge. *Comm. v. Crowell*, 2022 WL 5287862 (Appeals Court). Pg. 21-10.

- ✓ Seeing assault on private balcony from street was disorderly. *Comm. v. Cabrera*, 2022 WL 4487908 (Appeals Court). Pg. 23-3.

- ✓ Refusing police orders can become "tumultuous behavior." *Comm. v. Williams*, 2022 WL 627812 (Appeals Court). Pg. 23-4.

- ✓ If arrest for disorderly conduct is supported by probable cause, there is no false arrest. *Finamore v. Miglionico*, 15 F.4th 52 (1st Cir. 2021). Pg. 23-6.

- ✓ Disturbing the peace best defined in *Comm. v. Canty*, 65 Mass. App. Ct. 1113 (2006). Pg. 23-9.

- ✓ Even if one robber masked, accomplice charged if evidence of knowledge that principal would be armed *and* masked. *Comm. v. Lavin*, 101 Mass. App. Ct. 278 (2022). Pg. 26-4.

- ✓ Assault in hallway of a multi-unit building — accessible only to residents and staff — is an armed assault in a dwelling. *Comm. v. Rodriguez*, 100 Mass. App. Ct. 663 (2022). Pg. 31-11.

- ✓ Proof of intent to commit a felony during vehicle break is best charged as breaking into a depository under 266, § 16, *not* as B&E with intent to commit a felony. Pg. 31-13.

- ✓ Urinating on a police station floor should be charged as 266, § 126A (Defacing or Damaging Property), along with Disorderly Conduct (272, § 53). Pg. 33-3.

- ✓ Under 271, § 51, it is illegal for first responders to take or disseminate images of crime or accident victims unless in the course of official duty or with permission. Pg. 35-11.

- ✓ Officers who deliberately misrepresent their authority commit crime of impersonating a police officer. *Comm. v. Nordstrom*, 100 Mass. App. Ct. 493 (2021). Pg. 35-14. Also see 35-6.

Criminal Law Contents

PART I: INTRODUCTION

Chapter 1. Introduction

SECTION I
THE SOURCES OF CRIMINAL LAW 1-1
    A. Statutes 1-1
    B. Common Law 1-1
    C. Regulations 1-2
    D. Conclusion 1-2

SECTION II
ANATOMY OF A CRIME 1-3
    A. Elements: The Building Blocks 1-3
    B. Intent 1-3
    C. Lesser Included Offenses 1-4
    D. Right of Arrest 1-5
    E. Application for Criminal Complaint, Arrest, or Warrant 1-6
    F. Penalties 1-7
    Application for Criminal Complaint 1-8
    G. Jurisdiction 1-9
    H. Venue 1-10
    I. Statute of Limitations 1-10
  Statute of Limitations 1-11

Chapter 2. Offender Roles

    Principal 2-1
    Accomplice 2-1
    Accessory After the Fact 2-5
    Attempt to Commit a Crime 2-7
    Conspiracy 2-9
    Solicitation of a Felony 2-12

PART II: VIOLENT OFFENSES

Chapter 3. Threat Offenses

    Threat to Commit a Crime 3-1
    Extortion 3-5

©Law Enforcement Dimensions – *All rights reserved.*

Chapter 4. Assault Offenses

Assault	4-1
Assault by Dangerous Weapon (ADW)	4-3
Assault & Battery (A&B)	4-5
A&B by Dangerous Weapon (ABDW)	4-9
Catalogue of Assault and A&B: From Misdemeanor to Felony	4-13
Mayhem	4-15
Self-Defense	4-17

Chapter 5. Police Protection & the Arrest Function

SECTION I
INTERFERENCE WITH DUTY 5-1
A&B on a Public Employee 5-1
Interfering with a Police Officer 5-3
Neglect or Refusal to Assist Officer 5-5

SECTION II
THE ARREST FUNCTION 5-6
Resisting Arrest 5-6
Right to Know Grounds for Arrest 5-10
False Arrest 5-10
False Information Following Arrest 5-10

SECTION III
ESCAPE 5-12
Escape from Police Lockup 5-12
Aiding Escape from Police Custody 5-12

Chapter 6. Homicide

Murder	6-1
Manslaughter	6-5

Chapter 7. Kidnapping

Kidnapping	7-1
Parental or Relative Kidnapping	7-3
Enticement for Sex or Violence, "Child" Under 16	7-6

Chapter 8. Treatment of Animals

Cruelty to Animals	8-1
Sexual Contact with Animals	8-6
Mistreatment of Police Animals	8-7
Possess or Train Fighting Animals	8-7

PART III: SEXUAL OFFENSES

Chapter 9. Rape and Indecent A&B

Rape	9-1
Aggravated Rape	9-1
Rape of Child Under 16	9-6
Aggravated Rape of Child Under 16	9-6
Statutory Rape	9-7
Aggravated Statutory Rape	9-8
Rape by Public Safety Personnel	9-10
Drugging Person for Intercourse	9-11
Assault with Intent to Commit Rape	9-12
Indecent A&B Age 14 & Over	9-13
Indecent A&B Under Age 14	9-14
Indecent A&B by Public Safety Personnel	9-17
Sexual Assault Investigation Procedures	9-18

Chapter 10. Sexual Exposure or Surveillance

Lewd & Lascivious Conduct	10-1
Annoying & Accosting Sexually	10-3
Indecent Exposure	10-6
Open & Gross Lewdness	10-7
Secret Sexual Surveillance	10-10

Chapter 11. Prostitution

Sexual Conduct for a Fee	11-1
Sexual Conduct for a Fee, Child Under 18	11-1
Deriving Support from a Prostitute	11-4
Inducing a Minor to Become a Prostitute	11-5
Permitting Prostitution on the Premises	11-6

Chapter 12. Child Pornography & Other Misconduct

SECTION I
CHILD PORNOGRAPHY OFFENSES	12-1
Posing a Child for Sexual Photographs	12-1
Disseminating Child Pornography	12-5
Possession of Child Pornography	12-7

SECTION II
OBSCENITY OFFENSES	12-9
Dissemination of Obscene Matter	12-9
Dissemination of Obscenity to Minors	12-11
Incest	12-13

Law Enforcement Dimensions

PART IV: DOMESTIC VIOLENCE & OTHER FORMS OF HARASSMENT

Chapter 13. Domestic Violence & Restraining Orders

Officer Response & Entry	13-1
Officer Responsibilities at the Scene	13-4
Basic Coverage	13-4
Initial On-Scene Protections	13-7
Arrest Procedures	13-8
Arrest Cautions	13-9
Out-of-State Enforcement	13-10
Post-Arrest Procedures	13-11
Civil Liability	13-13
Massachusetts Domestic Violence Orders	13-15
Violation of a Restraining Order	13-17
Proof of Notice	13-18
Proof of 209A Violation	13-20
Harassment Prevention Orders	13-24
Assault and A&B Occurring in a Domestic or Harassment Relationship	13-29

Chapter 14. Child, Disabled, & Elder Protection

SECTION I
MANDATORY REPORTING 14-1
    Mandatory Reporting Laws 14-2

SECTION II
AGGRAVATED A&B AND CARETAKER ABUSE 14-7
    Children 14-7
    Elders & Disabled 14-7
    A&B or Indecent A&B on an Intellectually Disabled Person 14-12

Chapter 15. Stalking, Annoying Calls, & Secret Recording

Stalking	15-1
Criminal Harassment	15-1
Difference Between Stalking & Criminal Harassment	15-2
Similarities Between Stalking & Criminal Harassment	15-2
Annoying or Obscene Electronic Communication	15-6
Unlawful Secret Recording	15-7

Chapter 16. Civil Rights Violations

SECTION I
CIVIL RIGHTS OFFENSES 16-1
Interference with Civil Rights 16-1
Assault, A&B, or Property Damage for the Purpose of Intimidation . . 16-5
Destruction of or Threats to Destroy a Place of Worship 16-6

SECTION II
HATE CRIMES REPORTING, INJUNCTIONS, &
BIAS-FREE PROFESSIONAL POLICING 16-8
   A. Hate Crimes 16-8
   B. Injunctions by Attorney General or Private Person 16-8
   C. Bias-Free Professional Policing 16-9

PART V: POSSESSION & DISTRIBUTION OFFENSES

Chapter 17. Firearms

Gun Call: Field Response & Charging Decisions 17-1
Criminal Cases 17-6
Chart 1: Gun & Ammunition Possession Offenses in Massachusetts . . 17-13
Chart 2: Exemptions to License Requirements 17-18
Chart 3: Nonresident & Alien Eligibility to Possess Guns
   & Ammunition 17-20
Chart 4: Specialized Gun Offenses 17-23

Chapter 18. Dangerous Weapons

Carrying a Dangerous Weapon 18-1

Chapter 19. Explosives & Fireworks

Explosives, WMD, & Other Dangerous or Hoax Devices 19-1
Threat Concerning the Location of Dangerous Items or a Hijack 19-5
Sale or Possession of Fireworks 19-7

Chapter 20. Narcotics

SECTION I
CLASS SYSTEM FOR CONTROLLED SUBSTANCES 20-1
Classes of Controlled Substances 20-1
Proof of Type, Weight, & Purity 20-3

SECTION II
POSSESSION 20-5
   Possession of Controlled Substances 20-8
   Smelling Substance with Toxic Vapor 20-9

SECTION III
DISTRIBUTION 20-10
     A. Distribute 20-10
     B. Manufacture 20-11
     C. Possess with Intent to Distribute 20-11
   Possession with Intent Factors 20-11
   Distribution Offenses 20-15
   Distribution Penalties 20-15
   Drug Trafficking 20-17
   Penalties for Trafficking Offenses 20-18

SECTION IV
SPECIALIZED DISTRIBUTION OFFENSES 20-19
   Sale or Possession with Intent to Sell Drug Paraphernalia 20-19
   Sale of Hypodermic Needles & Syringes 20-20
   Counterfeit Substance 20-22

SECTION V
DRUG CRIMES AGAINST CHILDREN 20-22
   Drug Free School & Park Zone 20-22

SECTION VI
IMPROPERLY OBTAINING DRUGS FROM THOSE IN LEGAL POSSESSION 20-25
   Fraudulently Obtaining a Controlled Substance 20-25
   Stealing a Controlled Substance from Authorized Dispenser 20-26

SECTION VII
CONSPIRACY 20-28
   Conspiracy 20-28

Chapter 21. Marijuana & Tobacco

     Adult Use Marijuana Regulation 21-1
     Medical Marijuana 21-10
     Smoking or Vaping Tobacco Products 21-13
        Marijuana Consequences in Massachusetts 21-15

Chapter 22. Alcohol

SECTION I
REGULATORY AUTHORITY & ENFORCEMENT 22-1
     A. Licenses 22-1
     B. Investigatory Authority 22-3
     C. Basis for Enforcement 22-3

SECTION II
 CRIMINAL ENFORCEMENT 22-4
  Selling or Furnishing Alcohol to Person Under 21 22-4
  Maintain and/or Permit Alcohol Nuisance 22-6
  Procuring Alcoholic Beverages by False Representation 22-7
  False ID or Failure to ID 22-8
  Minor in Possession of Alcohol 22-9
  Unlawful Transportation of Alcohol 22-10
  Public Drinking or Alcohol Possession 22-11

PART VI: PUBLIC ORDER OFFENSES

Chapter 23. Public Order
  Disorderly Conduct 23-1
  Keeper of a Disorderly House 23-8
  Disturbing the Peace 23-9
  Disorder During Public Meetings 23-10
  Disorder During Public Protest 23-13
  Refusing to Remove a Substance Thrown on a Public Way 23-14

Chapter 24. Gambling
  Gaming or Betting in Public 24-1
  Registering Bets 24-2
  Use of Telephone for Betting Purposes 24-3
  Organizing Illegal Gambling Facilities 24-3
  Illegal Lottery 24-4
  Crimes Relating to the Massachusetts Lottery 24-6
  Crimes Relating to Massachusetts Casino Gambling 24-7

PART VII: THEFT OFFENSES

Chapter 25. Larceny
  Larceny 25-1
    Property Subject to Larceny 25-2
    Type 1: Larceny by Stealing 25-3
    Type 2: Larceny by False Pretense (LFP) 25-4
    Type 3: Embezzlement 25-8
    Venue 25-9
  Attempted Larceny 25-9
  Public & Police Responsibilities for Recovered Money,
    Goods, or Animals 25-10

Chapter 26. Robbery

    Unarmed Robbery 26-1
    Armed Robbery 26-1

Chapter 27. Specialized Larceny

    Larceny from the Person 27-1
    Larceny from a Building 27-2
    Larceny by Check 27-3
    Concealing Leased or Rented Property 27-4
    Fraudulently Procuring Food or Accommodations for Credit 27-5
    Insurance Fraud 27-6
    Credit or Debit Card Offenses 27-7
    Identity Fraud 27-12
    Obtaining Computer Services by Fraud 27-14
    Unauthorized Access to Computer 27-15
    Other Special Forms of Larceny 27-16

Chapter 28. Shoplifting

    Basic Shoplifting 28-1
    Aggravated Shoplifting 28-4

Chapter 29. Receiving Stolen Property

    Receiving Stolen Property 29-1

Chapter 30. Forgery, Uttering, & Counterfeiting

    Forgery 30-1
    Uttering 30-1
    Counterfeiting 30-5

PART VIII: PROPERTY OFFENSES

Chapter 31. Burglary and B&E

SECTION I
OVERVIEW OF ELEMENTS & LAW 31-1
    A. Breaking 31-1
    B. Entry 31-2
    C. Property Belonging to Another 31-3
    D. Intent 31-5
    E. Time 31-6

SECTION II
SPECIFIC OFFENSES 31-7
  Aggravated Burglary 31-7
  Burglary. 31-8
  Home Invasion. 31-9
  Armed Assault in a Dwelling 31-11
  B&E with Intent to Commit Felony 31-12
  B&E with Intent to Commit Misdemeanor 31-13
  Enter Building/MV Without Break at Night; Aggravated B&E Daytime 31-14
  Enter Dwelling Without Break at Night; B&E Daytime 31-15
  Possession of Burglarious Tool. 31-16

Chapter 32. Trespass

  Trespass After Notice 32-1
    Enter or Stay Without Right 32-1
    Notice 32-2
    Special Consideration 1: Public Accommodation 32-6
    Special Consideration 2: Trespass Inapplicable to Landlord/
      Tenant Disputes 32-7
    Special Consideration 3: Innkeeper Authority. 32-9
    Special Consideration 4: Homelessness 32-10
    Special Consideration 5: Beach Access 32-10

Chapter 33. Property Damage

  Defacing or Damaging Property 33-1

Chapter 34. Arson, False Alarm, & Fire Prevention

  Arson 34-1
  Arson of Personal Property. 34-3
  Negligently Allow Fire Damage 34-4
  Attempted Arson 34-5
  Burning Insured Property 34-6
  Hindering a Firefighter 34-7
  False Fire Alarm 34-7
  Tampering with Fire Alarm. 34-8
  Prevention & Safety Code Enforcement. 34-9

PART IX: OBSTRUCTION OF JUSTICE OFFENSES

Chapter 35. Obstruction of Justice

Witness Interference & Obstruction of Justice	35-1
Lying to Officer	35-2
Intimidating Potential Witness	35-5
Tampering or Destruction of Evidence	35-9
Taking or Disseminating Images of Victims	35-11
False Report to Public Safety Dispatch	35-12
False Report of Crime to Police	35-13
Impersonation of a Police Officer	35-14
False Written Report by Public Officer	35-15
Bribery	35-16
Default from a Court Appearance	35-17
Perjury	35-18

SUBJECT INDEX   S-1

Law Enforcement Dimensions

Part I

INTRODUCTION

Chapters 1 – 2

© John Sofis Scheft, Esq.
All rights reserved

Introduction

Society, through its government, creates laws that guide citizen conduct. Criminal law defines unacceptable behavior and its potential consequences. The purpose of criminal law is to protect people from: (1) bodily harm; (2) emotional harm; (3) loss or damage to their property; (4) public disruptions; and (5) possessing dangerous items, such as narcotics or firearms.

Section I
THE SOURCES OF CRIMINAL LAW

To understand criminal law, the Massachusetts officer needs to know its sources. The two major sources are statutes and common law. A third source, regulations, establishes administrative procedures that further define criminal law.

A. Statutes

Statutes are laws passed by the legislature that define specific, prohibited conduct. They are gathered in volumes known as the Massachusetts General Laws. Each statute is designated by the number of the volume and the section where it appears. For example, the law prohibiting murder is found in the Massachusetts General Laws, Chapter 265, Section 1. Having this information enables officers to understand their legal authority and to look up the actual text of the law. This is why we refer to specific statutes in this book. However, when we do, we use an abbreviated format. For example, we simply refer to the law prohibiting murder as 265, § 1.[1]

B. Common Law

Common law is a term that refers to the large body of decisions that judges have written to explain criminal law. These decisions typically define, interpret, and apply the language that appears in statutes. This book also references specific decisions that support various legal propositions. In general, Massachusetts officers need only be concerned with the decisions of the Massachusetts Appeals Court and the Supreme Judicial Court. These two appellate courts publish their decisions in a series of volumes. To find the text of a particular judicial decision, the officer needs to understand the reference system.

- For example, *Comm. v. Slaney*, 345 Mass. 135 (1962) indicates the name of the case [the Commonwealth versus the defendant, a person named "Slaney"]; the number of the volume where the case is located [here, volume 345]; the specific court ["Mass." stands for the Massachusetts Supreme Judicial Court]; the specific page where the case begins [here, it starts on page 135]; and the year when the court issued the decision [in this example, 1962].

---

[1] There are other formats you may see in legal documents that mean the same thing, such as G.L.c. 265, § 1; MGL 265, § 1; Ma Gen Law 265, Sec. 1.

- The same reference system applies to cases decided by the Appeals Court, except instead of "Mass.," the abbreviation used is "Mass. App. Ct." Thus, *Comm. v. Joyce*, 18 Mass. App. Ct. 417 (1984), refers to a Massachusetts Appeals Court decision involving "Joyce," issued in 1984, found in volume 18, beginning on page 417.

- There is another type of Appeals Court decision: *Comm. v. McKeown*, 2012 WL 2308125 (Appeals Court). These opinions are less publicized, but often deal with important police issues. They are obtained on the internet. After the name of the case [here, the defendant is "McKeown"], there is the year of the decision [here, 2012], which is followed by the specific reference ["WL" stands for Westlaw, and "2308125," the stored document number for the case].

Sometimes the reader may see the following legal citation: *Comm. v. Jones, supra*. The term "*supra*" (Latin for "above") simply means that the same case has been mentioned previously, so there is no need to repeat the whole legal reference.

Occasionally, this book refers to cases decided by the U.S. Supreme Court or a federal circuit court because, while not as directly relevant in the arena of criminal law as Massachusetts cases, they still prove useful in explaining certain principles. Supreme Court cases are cited in the following manner: *Hamling v. U.S.*, 418 U.S. 87 (1974). Federal circuit court cases are referenced as: *U.S. v. Smith*, 795 F.2d 823 (1st Cir. 1992). Note that Massachusetts is in the 1st Circuit of the federal court system.

C. Regulations

While the legislature passes laws in the form of statutes, and courts write opinions that make up the common law, government agencies are empowered to issue regulations. Regulations are designed to explain and further define how an agency will carry out a law passed by the legislature. In the police context, two well known agencies that issue regulations are the Alcoholic Beverages Control Commission (ABCC) and the Registry of Motor Vehicles (RMV).

In the case of the ABCC, its regulations provide the specifics behind its statutory authority to regulate the sale of alcoholic beverages. For example, regulation 204 CMR 4.00 abolishes the so-called "happy hour" that used to be a regular feature of bar life in Massachusetts. The text of this ABCC regulation, like the text of regulations issued by any other Commonwealth agency, is found in a document known as the *Code of Massachusetts Regulations*. Thus, a reference to 204 CMR 4.00 means that officers can locate this particular regulation in Chapter 204 of the *Code of Massachusetts Regulations* at section 4.00.

D. Conclusion

This text integrates the three varieties of law — statutes, common law, and regulations — within the subject areas that concern officers on the street. In this way, officers can use this book to understand their legal options and responsibilities, and to undertake them with confidence.

Section II
ANATOMY OF A CRIME

A. Elements: The Building Blocks

Every crime is composed of elements. Each element represents an essential component of the particular offense.

To look at how an offense is broken down into elements, consider the crime of rape under 265, § 22. Rape occurs when a person: (1) engages in sexual intercourse; (2) by compelling another person to submit by force or threat of bodily injury; (3) against her or his will. Thus, there are three elements, or components, that make up this crime. They are interrelated. The suspect's action must incorporate all three elements in order to constitute a violation.

Notice how we can come up with situations where only some elements are present. For instance, if the suspect threatens the victim (element 2) and forces her to perform an activity against her will (element 3), it is not rape unless the forced activity involves sexual intercourse (element 1). Similarly, there might be a scenario where sexual intercourse occurs (element 1), but there is a lack of proof that force or threats were employed (element 2) against the person's will (element 3).

By understanding the elements that make up the various offenses, officers can assess whether a person's conduct is unlawful. While officers conduct the investigation and make the crucial preliminary decision about whether to pursue charges, the final determination of guilt or innocence occurs in court.

B. Intent

In our law, the suspect's "intent" or state of mind is an important consideration. Known in Latin as *mens rea*, intent is required for all criminal offenses except a few charges. *Comm. v. Buckley*, 354 Mass. 508 (1968).

Intent cannot be proven directly because there is "no way of reaching into and examining the operations of the human mind." To determine a suspect's intent, officers consider his conduct, his prior actions or background, and his statements. *Comm. v. Niziolek*, 380 Mass. 513 (1980). Officers may infer that a person intends the usual consequences of his actions.

Six types of intent are recognized: Specific, malicious, general, reckless, as well as negligence, and strict liability.

- **Specific Intent.** To put it simply, specific intent exists when the offender has a "purpose" or "objective." An example is "breaking and entering with intent to commit a felony," a crime prohibited by 266, § 16. This is a specific intent crime because it is not enough for the suspect to intentionally break into a building; he must do so with the ultimate purpose of committing a felony while inside the structure. *Comm. v. Nickerson*, 388 Mass. 246 (1983).

    Again, with this offense or any other specific intent offense, it is not possible to look directly into the suspect's mind. In everyday affairs, we often look to the actions of others in order to decide what they were thinking. Thus, specific intent may be proven through circumstantial evidence; in other words, the circumstances of the event show what the suspect intended.

- **Malicious.** When an offender has a malicious state of mind, he acts on purpose instead of by accident or thoughtlessly. A simple way to think of a malicious action is that it is on purpose.

- **General Intent.** General intent is the standard applied to most crimes. It exists if the defendant acted "intentionally" or "knowingly" even though, unlike specific intent, the defendant may not have fully conceived of a purpose for his conduct. Moreover, it is not necessary that the defendant knew that he was breaking the law, but it is necessary that he intended the act that resulted in the offense. Voluntary and deliberate acts qualify, not accidental or negligent ones.

- **Reckless.** Even if a person is not trying to harm anyone, he still acts recklessly if his behavior consciously disregards the potential risk of harm to another. For example, playing a game of Russian roulette with a loaded pistol is a reckless act.

- **Negligence.** This applies to an offender who acts unreasonably and risks harming another person. It also occurs when a person is actually harmed by the offender's failure to act when he has a duty to act reasonably. Negligence is not as obviously harmful as recklessness, but it is still unreasonable behavior. For example, failing to drive slowly on an icy road would be negligent behavior. Driving very fast would be reckless.

- **Strict Liability.** There are a few offenses where the offender's intent is irrelevant. If the prohibited act occurs, the crime is complete regardless of the offender's state of mind. For example, in Massachusetts, statutory rape involves sexual intercourse with a person under the age of 16 (265, § 23). Whether the victim consented, and whether the offender knew or intended to have intercourse with an underage person is irrelevant, as long as the act occurred. The same is true for the crime of minor in possession of alcohol (138, § 34C).

Intoxication with alcohol or drugs. Intoxication from alcohol or drugs is never, by itself, an excuse or justification for committing a crime. However, it may be relevant in determining the level of a defendant's culpability. Officers should consider evidence of intoxication, along with all other evidence, for this reason.

Mental illness. Public or police compassion for persons suffering with mental illness does not negate legal responsibility for a crime. The potential defense of "not guilty by reason of mental illness" should not affect police enforcement decisions. This defense is only available post-arraignment after an assessment by psychiatric experts. The police officer's role is to evaluate probable cause and take action to address public safety. See *Comm. v. Newton N.*, 478 Mass. 747 (2018) (judge could not dismiss charges based on an offender's mental capacity because police had probable cause to arrest him for a break-in).

C. Lesser Included Offenses

Knowing the elements provides officers with an understanding of what offenses are related and, specifically, what lesser included offenses may apply to a given situation. One crime is a lesser included offense of another if each of its elements is contained within the elements of the larger crime.

To understand this concept, consider this example: Assault & battery with a dangerous weapon (ABDW), 265, § 15A, requires that the offender: (1) commit an assault and battery (A&B) by intentionally touching another person without consent; (2) by means of a dangerous weapon. A lesser included offense of ABDW is A&B, a violation of 265, § 13A. The reason is: A&B is the same as ABDW, except that the offender does not use a weapon during the assault.

How might this distinction come into play during a criminal case? Let's say that a defendant is charged with beating the victim with a stick, which is ABDW (a stick qualifies as a dangerous weapon). During the trial, the factfinder — whether it is a judge or a jury — decides that there is clear evidence that the defendant hit the victim, but less than sufficient evidence that he employed a stick or any other weapon. Based on this reading of the evidence, the factfinder is justified in finding the defendant guilty of the lesser included charge of A&B.

Subject to their discretion, officers should typically charge the most serious offenses that apply to the suspect's conduct. During the court process, charges may be reviewed and, if necessary, reduced. It is easier for prosecutors to reduce a charge than it is for them to bring a more serious charge at a later time.

D. Right of Arrest

In the field, officers must use a legally recognized method to charge a suspect with a crime. There are three possibilities:

- **Warrant.** An arrest warrant is issued by a judge or clerk magistrate. It authorizes officers to locate a suspect anywhere in Massachusetts, take him into custody, and bring him before a court for prosecution. 41, § 98.

- **Arrest.** In many situations, officers may arrest a person without a warrant. This decision is made by the arresting officer without judicial supervision.

- **Complaint.** Officers may also apply to a clerk magistrate for a "complaint" to bring an offender before the court. The clerk will typically hold a "show cause" hearing in which both the officer and the accused present their version of the incident. The clerk then decides whether to issue the complaint — in other words, formally charge the offender in court — or dismiss the case based on a lack of evidence or an agreed resolution (e.g., paying the victim for property damage).

The method officers must use depends on whether the underlying crime is a felony or a misdemeanor, which is why this guide designates the "right of arrest" for each crime.

Felony. 274, § 1 defines a felony as any offense punishable by a state prison sentence. A misdemeanor is any crime in which state prison time is not an option. The distinction is important because officers may conduct a warrantless arrest for any felony, even if it occurred in the past. *U.S. v. Watson*, 423 U.S. 411 (1976).

To indicate this expansive arrest authority, this guide will state: "Felony."

Misdemeanors. The warrantless arrest authority for a misdemeanor is more complicated because there are three varieties:

- **Statute past.** For this kind of misdemeanor, a statute specifically authorizes warrantless arrest for an offense, even if the officer did not witness it. An assault during a domestic violence incident is such a misdemeanor. To show the legal basis for this authority, this guide will say, for example: "209A, § 6 warrantless arrest on probable cause."

- **Statute present.** Some misdemeanors are governed by statutes that allow officers to make a warrantless arrest, but only if the offense occurs in their presence. Attempting to steal inexpensive property is this type of misdemeanor. To indicate such limited authority, the guide will say, for example: "276, § 28 warrantless arrest in presence."

- **Breach & present.** This final category severely limits an officer's ability to make a warrantless arrest. It requires that officers apply for a criminal complaint in order to bring an offender to court *unless* the offense amounts to a breach of peace *and* is committed in the officer's presence. An example of a misdemeanor in this category — simple assault during a nondomestic violence incident. For this type of offense, the guide will say: "Arrest for breach of peace in presence. Otherwise, complaint."

Throughout these materials, we inform officers in relation to each misdemeanor whether they have a right to make a warrantless arrest, or whether they must go the alternate route — applying for a criminal complaint or arrest warrant.

In presence. Officers often ask what the legal meaning of "in presence" is. The best definition comes from the Virginia case of *Galliher v. Comm.*, 170 S.E. 734 (1933): "An offense is committed within the presence of an officer . . . when he has direct personal knowledge, through his sight, hearing, or other senses that it is then and there being committed."

For example, in *Comm. v. Conway*, 2 Mass. App. Ct. 547 (1974), the police should not have arrested the defendant without a warrant for use without authority — a misdemeanor only arrestable in presence — because officers arrived at the scene 15 minutes after the vehicle had been used by the defendant, who was no longer inside the car.

Breach of peace. A breach of the peace is, practically speaking, conduct that poses immediate or potential harm to a person or the general public. Courts are unable to come up with a more precise definition because of the great range of human behavior that will satisfy this standard. *Comm. v. Gorman*, 288 Mass. 294 (1934). *Comm. v. Grise*, 398 Mass. 247 (1986) (breach must at least threaten to have some "disturbing effect" on the public).

E. Application for Criminal Complaint, Arrest, or Warrant

Any criminal court case begins when police file a complaint application. See page 1-8 for this form, which is used to apply for a complaint or arrest warrant, or to document an arrest without a warrant. Filling this form out properly is critical:

- **Ensure the information identifying the defendant is correct** — the name, date of birth, social security number, and Probation Central File (PCF) number.[2]

- **Include the correct charges from the District Court Complaint Manual.** The Manual assigns a code for each criminal offense.[3]

After an officer signs the application in the clerk's office, he or she must swear to its truth. Any officer may do this upon reviewing the police report. If the clerk finds probable cause exists, the application is accepted. The "police prosecutor," who handles the department's business in the district court, should double check that the charges and the name, date of birth, and social security number are correct.[4]

F. Penalties

The defendant may choose whether to have his case decided by a judge sitting alone (known as a bench trial) or by a jury. Whatever option he selects, only a judge may impose a sentence following a guilty finding. Here are the sanctions available to judges.

The most serious sanction is incarceration. Defendants may be sent to either the House of Correction (sometimes referred to as jail) or State Prison. The maximum possible sentence to the House of Correction is 2½ years per offense. The maximum sentence to State Prison is a life term.

This manual sets forth the penalty for each crime. For example, "SP NMT 5 yrs" means a potential state prison sentence of not more than 5 years. A penalty that reads, "HC NLT 1 year, NMT 2½ yrs," means that an offender could be sentenced to the House of Correction for a term of not less than 1 year and not more than 2 and ½ years.

Many offenses allow the imposition of harsher penalties for repeat offenders, or individuals who commit the crime in an aggravated manner. For example, armed robbery "while masked" is an aggravated version of armed robbery under 265, § 17.

Some offenses call for mandatory minimum terms of incarceration. Such mandatory terms remove the discretion of the judge to impose probation.

Probation is a designated amount of time during which a defendant must avoid further legal trouble and, in many cases, successfully complete various programs. Specifically, defendants may be required to participate in substance abuse counseling, pay restitution to compensate their victims, or perform community service. Sometimes probation follows a period of incarceration. *Comm. v. Henry*, 475 Mass. 117 (2016) (judge must consider defendant's ability to pay when determining restitution amount). *Comm. v. Eldred*, 480 Mass. 90 (2018) (remaining "drug free" may be a condition of probation).

---

2 Every person who gets arraigned in a Massachusetts court is assigned a PCF number. When a department arrests or seeks a complaint against a person, the department should check the person for a Board of Probation (BOP) record. If there is a record, the record will list a PCF number. Apply this number in the PCF box on the criminal complaint application. If no BOP, write "None" in the PCF box.
3 The offense codes include the chapter and section numbers in them, but many sections of the General Laws cover more than one offense. Thus the complaint manual offense code for "A&B" is 265/13A/B, while the code for "ASSAULT" is 265/13A/A, and the code for "A&B, PREGNANT VICTIM" is 265/13A/E.
4 There are a lot of people with the same name, and the clerk's office can choose from every one of them who has ever been arraigned. A mistaken click can lead to the wrong defendant being named in your complaint.

Law Enforcement Dimensions

APPLICATION FOR CRIMINAL COMPLAINT

APPLICATION NO. (COURT USE ONLY) _____ PAGE ____ of ____

**Trial Court of Massachusetts
District Court Department**

I, the undersigned complainant, request that a criminal complaint issue against the accused charging the offense(s) listed below. If the accused **HAS NOT BEEN ARRESTED** and the charges involve:

☐ ONLY MISDEMEANOR(S), I request a hearing ☐ **WITHOUT NOTICE** because of an imminent threat of ☐ BODILY INJURY ☐ COMMISSION OF A CRIME ☐ FLIGHT ☐ **WITH NOTICE** to accused.
☐ ONE OR MORE FELONIES, I request a hearing ☐ **WITHOUT NOTICE** ☐ **WITH NOTICE** to accused.

☐ **WARRANT** is requested because prosecutor represents that accused may not appear unless arrested.

ARREST STATUS OF ACCUSED
☐ HAS ☐ HAS NOT been arrested

INFORMATION ABOUT ACCUSED

NAME (FIRST MI LAST) AND ADDRESS

BIRTH DATE | SOCIAL SECURITY NUMBER
PCF NO. | MARITAL STATUS
DRIVERS LICENSE NO. | STATE
GENDER | HEIGHT | WEIGHT | EYES

HAIR | RACE | COMPLEXION | SCARS/MARKS/TATTOOS | INTERPRETER NEEDED (language) | BIRTH STATE OR COUNTRY | DAY PHONE

EMPLOYER/SCHOOL | MOTHER'S MAIDEN NAME (FIRST MI LAST) | FATHER'S NAME (FIRST MI LAST)

CASE INFORMATION

COMPLAINANT NAME (FIRST MI LAST)

COMPLAINANT TYPE
☐ POLICE ☐ CITIZEN ☐ OTHER

PD

ADDRESS

PLACE OF OFFENSE

INCIDENT REPORT NO. | OBTN

CITATION NO(S).

1
| OFFENSE CODE | DESCRIPTION | OFFENSE DATE |
VARIABLES (e.g. victim name, controlled substance, type and value of property, other variable information; see Complaint Language Manual)

2
| OFFENSE CODE | DESCRIPTION | OFFENSE DATE |
VARIABLES

3
| OFFENSE CODE | DESCRIPTION | OFFENSE DATE |
VARIABLES

REMARKS | COMPLAINANT'S SIGNATURE X | DATE FILED

COURT USE ONLY A HEARING UPON THIS COMPLAINT APPLICATION WILL BE HELD AT THE ABOVE COURT ADDRESS ON } DATE OF HEARING ____ AT ____ TIME OF HEARING **COURT USE ONLY**

DATE | PROCESSING OF NON-ARREST APPLICATION (COURT USE ONLY) | CLERK/JUDGE

NOTICE SENT OF CLERK'S HEARING SCHEDULED ON:
NOTICE SENT OF JUDGE'S HEARING SCHEDULED ON:
HEARING CONTINUED TO:
APPLICATION DECIDED WITHOUT NOTICE TO ACCUSED BECAUSE:
☐ IMMINENT THREAT OF ☐ BODILY INJURY ☐ CRIME ☐ FLIGHT BY ACCUSED
☐ FELONY CHARGED AND POLICE DO NOT REQUEST NOTICE
☐ FELONY CHARGED BY CIVILIAN; NO NOTICE AT CLERK'S DISCRETION

DATE | COMPLAINT TO ISSUE | COMPLAINT DENIED | CLERK/JUDGE

☐ PROBABLE CAUSE FOUND FOR ABOVE OFFENSE(S)
NO(S). ☐ 1. ☐ 2. ☐ 3. BASED ON
☐ FACTS SET FORTH IN ATTACHED STATEMENT(S)
☐ TESTIMONY RECORDED: TAPE NO. _____
START NO. _____ END NO. _____
☐ WARRANT ☐ SUMMONS TO ISSUE
SCHEDULED ARRAIGNMENT DATE:

☐ NO PROBABLE CAUSE FOUND
☐ REQUEST OF COMPLAINANT
☐ FAILURE TO PROSECUTE
☐ AGREEMENT OF BOTH PARTIES
☐ OTHER:
COMMENT

DCCR-2 (07/11) COURT COPY www.mass.gov/courts/districtcourt

When defendants commit minor offenses for the first time, they may be given a "Continuance Without a Finding" (known as a "CWOF"). This sanction is exactly like probation except that, for purposes of having an official record, it is not viewed as a conviction. Instead, the law labels it "a finding of sufficient facts." In this way, the CWOF allows offenders to be punished, but avoids saddling them with a prior record that may adversely affect their future employment prospects.

Finally, the failure of defendants to abide by their probationary conditions may result in their being incarcerated.

A fine is a designated monetary amount that may be imposed to punish an offender.

- **Victim witness assessment.** Under 258B, § 8, the victim witness assessment is a *mandatory* fee imposed upon conviction. Proceeds fund victim assistance programs. Adults pay $90 if convicted of a felony, $50 for a misdemeanor. Juveniles pay less.

- **Court costs.** Under 280, § 6, a judge may assess "court costs" against a defendant "as a condition for the dismissal . . . of a complaint or indictment, or as a term of probation." The costs function as a lesser fine to resolve minor cases.

G. Jurisdiction

Jurisdiction refers to which court has the legal authority to conduct the trial. In Massachusetts, the majority of cases are resolved in district court, while the most serious crimes are exclusively heard in superior court before juries of 12 citizens. Falling under this exclusive jurisdiction are: Murder and manslaughter, mayhem, armed and unarmed robbery, rape, cocaine and heroin trafficking, burglary, arson, extortion, and perjury.

Under 218, § 26, the district court may render a final judgment for all violations of town bylaws and city ordinances, all misdemeanors, and any felony for which the maximum penalty is not more than five years in State Prison. There are exceptions to this last rule, including breaking and entering with intent to commit a felony, kidnapping, larceny of a motor vehicle, and assault and battery with a dangerous weapon. In contrast to superior court, district court uses juries composed of six citizens.

Although the district court may exercise final jurisdiction over many felonies, it cannot impose a state prison sentence. The maximum possible penalty in district court is 2½ years in the House of Correction.

State and federal government may prosecute separate charges for identical conduct. *Gamble v. U.S.*, 139 S.Ct. 1960 (2019): Gamble pleaded guilty to a state charge of felon-in-possession-of-a-firearm. Federal prosecutors then indicted him for the same offense under federal law. Gamble argued this exposed him to double jeopardy under the Fifth Amendment. However, the dual-sovereignty doctrine holds that two offenses are not the same when prosecuted by state and federal authorities because of their different interests.[5]

---

5 This author agrees with the dissent of the late Justice Ginsburg, who recommended abolishing this outdated and unfair rule: "Looked at from the standpoint of the individual who is being prosecuted, the liberty-denying potential of successive prosecutions, when federal and state governments prosecute in tandem, is the same as it is when either prosecutes twice."

H. Venue

Venue refers to the proper court for an offense. Typically, charges must be heard by the court in the territory where the crime occurred. For certain crimes, there are special venue rules that are more flexible. These rules appear throughout the book. See, e.g., 209A, § 2 (venue to issue restraining order in court where victim lived at time of abuse or, if the victim left to avoid abuse, where victim lives now).

In the absence of a specific venue rule, the court must do what is fair. This means the defendant should be tried reasonably close to home in an area where he has access to witnesses and evidence. *Comm. v. Johnson*, 470 Mass. 300 (2015) (defendant could not show that a trial in Essex County was unfair, since he and the victims lived there, and the child abuse investigation happened there).

I. Statute of Limitations

The term "statute of limitations" refers to the time period within which a prosecution must be commenced. It is the maximum time that may pass between the crime and the defendant's arraignment. It protects individuals from having to defend themselves against old accusations. It encourages law enforcement to promptly investigate. *Comm. v. Perella*, 464 Mass. 274 (2013). The limitation periods appear in 277, § 63. Most of the time, it is not an issue for officers. Occasionally, investigators need to be vigilant about an impending deadline.

- **One rule involves sexual assault cases where the victim is under 16 at the time of the offense.** Rather than start from the date of the alleged offense (the old rule), the statute of limitations begins only after: (1) a report to law enforcement, or (2) the date of the victim's 16th birthday, whichever happened first.

- **Another rule does not count any time the suspect remains outside the Commonwealth.** This rule applies to any defendant *regardless of his purpose for leaving the state.* 277, § 63 ("any period during which the defendant is not usually and publicly a resident within the Commonwealth shall be excluded in determining the time limited").

    In *Comm. v. George*, 430 Mass. 276 (1999), the defendant sexually assaulted the victim in the summer of 1977; the victim did not come forward and tell police until 1997. However, the defendant left Massachusetts in 1980 to live in Florida. Therefore, when the case began in 1997, the government was well within the statute of limitations for rape of a child because the time when the defendant resided in Florida did not count! While the defendant argued that he did not leave Massachusetts to avoid prosecution, the SJC said his reason for leaving was irrelevant.

- **Example of both rules enlarging the period.** *Comm. v. Shanley*, 455 Mass. 752 (2010): The defendant, a priest, committed Indecent A&B on the victim in 1986. However, the victim did not turn 16 until 1993, and the case had not been reported to law enforcement prior to that time. Therefore, the 6 year limitations period for Indecent A&B expired in 1999. Even so, the prosecutor could indict this defendant in 2002. There was undeniable evidence that the defendant lived outside of Massachusetts from 1990 until 2002. As a result, that time did not count in computing the statute of limitations. His conviction was upheld.

Indictment or issued complaint begins prosecution. An application is insufficient. *Comm. v. Vitale,* 44 Mass. App. Ct. 908 (1997). *Comm. v. Perella,* 464 Mass. 274 (2013).

In *Comm. v. Dixon,* 458 Mass. 446 (2010), the grand jury returned an indictment for rape within the statute of limitations period. It identified the perpetrator as "John Doe," with a physical description and DNA profile. When the DNA profile was linked to Jerry Dixon, he was named in the indictment even though the limitations period had expired. The SJC allowed Dixon's case to go forward because the original indictment accused a clearly identified individual within the proper time frame.

The defendant must assert that the limitations period expired; otherwise, the defense is forfeited. *Comm. v. Newcomb,* 80 Mass. App. Ct. 519 (2011) (if the limitations period did not run out at the time the legislature extended it, then the new period covers the defendant's original conduct).

STATUTE OF LIMITATIONS
277, § 63

TIME PERIOD **No Limitation**

APPLICABLE OFFENSES **Murder.** Prosecution is never barred by the passage of time. *Comm. v. McLaughlin,* 431 Mass. 241 (2000) (ironically, conspiracy to commit murder has only a 6-year limitation period because it is not mentioned in the statute).

TIME PERIOD **No Limitation (but corroborating evidence required after 27 years)**

APPLICABLE OFFENSES **Certain Child Sexual Offenses**

- 265, §§ 13B, 13B½, and 13B¾ (indecent A&B on child under 14 and the aggravated and repeat forms of offense); 13F (indecent A&B or simple A&B on intellectually disabled person); 13L (reckless endangerment of child under 18); 22A, 22B, and 22C (forcible rape of child and the aggravated and repeat forms of offense); 23, 23A, and 23B (statutory rape and the aggravated and repeat forms of offense); 24B (assault of child with intent to rape); 50(b) (sex trafficking, child under 18).

- *Any related conspiracy or accessory charge.*

- *Special corroboration required when offenses are more than 27 years old:* The indictment must independently corroborate the victim's allegation. Opinions of mental health professionals alone are insufficient. *Comm. v. White,* 475 Mass. 724 (2016) (corroboration must relate to the actual crime, not the defendant's uncharged misbehavior at the time). *Comm. v. Buono,* 484 Mass. 351 (2020) (defendant's statement to an acquaintance that "it wasn't gonna happen again," referenced his sexual assault on the victim; this was sufficient corroborating evidence).

TIME PERIOD **15 Years**

APPLICABLE OFFENSES **Certain Adult Sexual Offenses**

- **265, §§ 22** (rape and aggravated rape); 24 (assault with intent to commit rape); 50(a) (sex trafficking, adult 18 and over).

- *Any related conspiracy or accessory charge.*

TIME PERIOD **10 Years**

APPLICABLE OFFENSES **Robbery & Incest**

- **265, §§ 17** (Armed Robbery); 18 (armed assault with intent to rob or murder); 19 (unarmed robbery); 21 (stealing by confinement, injury, or threat).

- **272, § 17** (incest); and/or

- *Any related conspiracy or accessory charge.*

TIME PERIOD **6 Years**

APPLICABLE OFFENSES **All Other Offenses**

TIME PERIOD **Victim Under 16 at Time of Crime**

The limitation period does not begin until: (1) the victim reaches the age of 16; or (2) the violation is reported to law enforcement, whichever happens first.

APPLICABLE OFFENSES **Sexual Offenses**

- **265, §§ 22** (forcible rape); 22A (forcible rape of child); 23 (statutory rape); 24 (assault with intent to rape); 24B (assault of child with intent to rape); 26A (parental kidnapping); 50(b) (sex trafficking); 13B (indecent A&B on child under 14); 13F (A&B on an intellectually disabled person); 13H (indecent A&B on person 14 and older).

- **272, §§ 1** (enticing person under 16 for marriage); 2 (abduction for prostitution); 3 (drugged for intercourse); 4 (enticing to unlawful intercourse); 4A (inducing minor to become a prostitute); 4B (support from earnings of minor prostitute); 6 (maintaining a house of prostitution); 12 and 13 (procuring & detaining persons for place of prostitution); 17 (incest); 28 (distribution of obscenity to minors); 29A (lewdly photographing a nude minor); 29B (dissemination of photographs of nude minors); 33 (exhibiting albino or deformed person); 35 and 35A (unnatural and lascivious acts with those 16 and under).

TIME PERIOD **1 Year**

APPLICABLE OFFENSES **272, § 11** requires that any prosecution under 272, §§ 2 (enticing a person for prostitution); 3 (drugged for unlawful intercourse); 4 (unlawful intercourse with person under 18); 4A and 4B (inducing minor to become prostitute or deriving support from the minor's earnings); and 6 (knowingly permitting premises to be used for prostitution) be commenced no later than 1 year after the commission of the crime.

2 Offender Roles

PRINCIPAL

The Main Actor

A principal is the actual perpetrator of the crime. As the main actor, the principal is the one who pulls the trigger, steals the ring, sells the drugs, and so forth. It is not uncommon to have multiple principals depending on the nature of the crime. In the vast majority of cases, the principal is a person; however, organizations may be prosecuted for criminal conduct.

Corporate/Association Responsibility

4, § 7 establishes that criminal laws apply to corporations, societies, associations, and partnerships too. Of course, a corporation or association is not a live person, and it can act only through its agents. As a result, a corporation or association may be held criminally responsible if it gave the agent the authority and responsibility to act on its behalf in handling the particular business or project that involved criminal behavior. *Comm. v. Life Care Centers, Inc.*, 456 Mass. 826 (2010). 265, § 13 (manslaughter by corporation).

ACCOMPLICE

Purpose

Early in our judicial history, those who helped the principal complete a crime — accomplices — were judged to be as responsible as the principal. A vintage case from 1891 reported: "Where H., in whose company R. was, jumped out of a wagon driven by witness and demanded that the latter turn over his bottle of whiskey, and told R. to hold the horse, which the latter did while H. took the bottle, from which H. and R. drank, R. was an accomplice." *Comm. v. Ryan*, 154 Mass. 422 (1891).

This theory of criminal liability was simplified by the SJC in *Comm. v. Zanetti*, 454 Mass. 449 (2009). The issue is whether the defendant knowingly participated with the intent required for the particular crime.

Elements

- ***Intentional participation.*** The suspect must intentionally and meaningfully participate in the crime;

- ***Criminal mindset.*** While having the criminal intent necessary to commit the particular crime.

Right of Arrest

Depends on the underlying crime.

Penalty

An accomplice may receive exactly the same penalty as the principal, since one who participates meaningfully is considered to have committed the underlying offense.

Notes

Intentional participation. Being a participant in a crime takes many forms. Some activities that qualify are: planning, encouraging, being a lookout, assisting, and helping with the escape.

- **Planning.** An accomplice does not have to be present when the crime occurs. *Comm. v. Moure*, 428 Mass. 313 (1998) (leader of Springfield gang ordered execution of a rival gang member; strict allegiance of gang members meant that any planned "hit" had to occur with the leader's blessing, even though he did not attend the murder). *Comm. v. Balakin*, 356 Mass. 547 (1969) (defendant properly convicted as an accomplice because he provided guns and an automobile; fact that the defendant had supplied equipment for an initial robbery that was abandoned did not prevent him from being legally connected to the robbery that took place a week later with his equipment).

    A person may also be an accomplice to a crime in Massachusetts, even if his participation occurs totally out-of-state, so long as he understands that the crime will occur here. *Comm. v. Fafone*, 416 Mass. 329 (1993).

- **Encouraging.** A person is an accomplice when his presence encourages the perpetrator "by giving him hope of immediate assistance." *Comm. v. Morrow*, 363 Mass. 601 (1973) (defendant convicted, along with three accomplices, of burglary and rape; even though he did not participate in the rape, he "stood watch, was ready to render aid . . . , and generally encouraged commission of the offense"). *Comm. v. Morrill*, 14 Mass. App. Ct. 1003 (1982) (defendant caught with four other youths; although he said he did not actively participate, it was sufficient he encouraged the others by expressing his approval when a thrown rock hit a passing car).

- **Serving as a lookout.** *Comm. v. Vazquez*, 74 Mass. App. Ct. 920 (2009) (defendant functioned as a lookout while watching the victim being severely beaten; the defendant whistled and shouted to the assailant to stop when a bystander approached; he then left the scene in the same direction as the assailant; a witness reported that the defendant and assailant had followed the victim earlier from a club located near the site of the attack).

- **Participating in the physical acts that make up the crime.** There are numerous cases involving accomplices who help commit violent acts, sexual assaults, property damage, theft, narcotics distribution, and a whole host of other crimes. These cases are discussed throughout this book. *Comm. v. Sim*, 39 Mass. App. Ct. 212 (1995) (the defendant unlocked the door to the apartment building where the robbery took place; he knew the principals were armed and expected to share in the proceeds from the heist).

- **Helping with the escape.** *Comm. v. Irving*, 51 Mass. App. Ct 285 (2001) (defendant arranged a "switch car" and took part in the post robbery escape). *Comm. v. Jedeon*, 2015 WL 3457902 (Appeals Court) (the defendant remained in the idling car while her roommate robbed a convenience store; he jumped in the car and she sped away, running a stop sign; the two selected a store that was some distance from their home, suggesting a predetermined plan).

"Intentional participation" is required. It is insufficient to prove only that the alleged accomplice was present at the scene or knew a crime would occur. The law does not allow guilt by association. *Comm. v. Perry*, 357 Mass. 149 (1970) (evidence that the defendant knew the three liquor store robbers, and that he associated with them before and after the robbery, was insufficient). *Comm. v. Woods*, 466 Mass. 707 (2014).

At the same time, offenders do not have to have an advance plan or agreement. Participation simply means that the accomplice *consciously acted* with the principal before or during the crime. *Comm. v. Lugo*, 89 Mass. App. Ct. 229 (2016): At 2:00 a.m. in a parking garage, Jose Lugo and Javier Fernandez engaged in a very tense verbal exchange with Victor Ramos and Milton Henriquez. From where he was standing, Lugo could see Fernandez walk behind Henriquez and stab him in the side, and he could see Fernandez jab the knife twice at Ramos. He then ran with Fernandez to chase the victims, and kicked Henriquez on the ground while Fernandez was stabbing him. These actions showed he intended to aid Fernandez. A prior agreement between the two was not necessary.

The accomplice does not have to be present for the entire crime. *Comm. v. Silvia*, 97 Mass. App. Ct. 151 (2020): Tow company owner Donna Silvia suspected the victim, an employee, had stolen $50,000 from the business. Another company employee named Soares came in with a bag of tools and met with Silvia. Surveillance cameras were redirected to exclude coverage of the garage. Soares led the victim there and clipped off his pinky finger.

Ironically, police arrived to investigate the original theft. Officers became concerned about how the victim had received facial injuries and recently lost his finger. They discovered the tow company's surveillance recordings stashed in a car across the street, which proved Donna Silvia intended for Soares to hurt the victim.

Circumstantial evidence may prove involvement. *Comm. v. Pepe*, 95 Mass. App. Ct. 1109 (2019): Police officers conducted surveillance at a motel and observed a drug buy involving a vehicle with a driver and passenger. A woman purchased drugs from the passenger through the passenger window. There was sufficient evidence to support arresting the driver as an accomplice. Consider:

- The driver saw the drug transaction and had parked the vehicle in a remote area despite the availability of spaces closer to the motel;

- The woman quickly approached within a minute of the driver's arrival and spoke to him during the transaction.

Also see *Comm. v. Rosa*, 468 Mass. 231 (2014) (police found shell casings, bullets, and the defendant's driver's license in an accomplice's bedroom hours after a shooting in which three perpetrators were seen leaving the scene).

Criminal mindset. An accomplice must participate while having the intent necessary to commit the underlying crime.

- **An accomplice may only be convicted for crimes he intended.** *Comm. v. Gillard*, 36 Mass. App. Ct. 183 (1994) (defendant could not be convicted of murder because his intent was merely to get involved in a fist fight). Compare *Comm. v. Benitez*, 464 Mass. 686 (2013) (although defendant claimed he only wanted to buy drugs from the victim, the evidence showed he intended a robbery — he gave the co-defendant a gun and served as lookout). *Comm. v. Sanders*, 101 Mass. App. Ct. 503 (2022) (defendant stopped his Honda in the oncoming lane of traffic alongside, and slightly to the rear of the victims' Audi, which was stopped at a traffic light; he positioned his car so that his passengers could immediately start shooting at the victims from inside his vehicle; he then fled the scene in his Honda and later lied about the event).

- **Once an accomplice knows the principal has a weapon, he is responsible for the resulting crime.** This is true even if the principal assured the accomplice that he would not use the weapon, or that it was unloaded, or that it was different from the one he actually brought. *Comm. v. Irving*, 51 Mass. App. Ct. 285 (2001) (fact that defendant knew principal would be carrying a weapon made him an accomplice to *armed* robbery; it made no difference that he thought the principal would be carrying a tire iron instead of a gun). *Comm. v. Spinucci*, 472 Mass. 872 (2015).

- **Circumstantial evidence may prove that an accomplice knew the principal had a weapon.** *Comm. v. LeClair*, 68 Mass. App. Ct. 482 (2007): Ronald LeClair stopped his car in a Burger King parking lot. Raymond Campanale got out and entered the backseat of another vehicle. He shot the victim, stole his money and drugs, then jumped back into LeClair's car. LeClair argued that there was no proof that he knew his accomplice was armed. The court responded: "Knowledge may be inferred if the robbery happens 'in public' in a situation where it can be anticipated that a means must be found to persuade the victim to surrender his property quickly and without resistance."

    Compare *Baxter v. Comm.*, 489 Mass. 504 (2022) (defendant helped stalk the victim on the street, but nothing showed he knew the principal was armed or intended to kill the victim).

Multiple suspects.

- **No need to prove which suspect was the principal and which was the accomplice, so long as there is proof that both were involved.** In *Comm. v. Williams*, 450 Mass. 645 (2008), more than one person was needed to bind the victim and place him in his car trunk, and witnesses saw three men accompany Williams when he entered the victim's apartment. Williams later stated that "we had to take the victim for a ride," and "if I go down, so don't a lot of other people." These facts proved that Williams was an accomplice to murder, even if his exact role was unclear. *Comm. v. Riley*, 467 Mass. 799 (2014).

- **Statements of one accomplice may typically be used against other accomplices.** *Comm. v. Rakes*, 478 Mass. 65 (2017).

- **A suspect may be convicted as an accomplice even though his co-defendant is acquitted.** *Comm. v. Clements*, 51 Mass. App. Ct. 508 (2001).

Withdrawal. A suspect is not an accomplice if he clearly withdraws *before* the crime. *Comm. v. Rivera*, 464 Mass. 56 (2013). *Comm. v. Fickett*, 403 Mass. 194 (1988) (defendant told his co-defendant and a third party that he wanted "nothing to do with what [they] had discussed" and asked his co-defendant to drop him off prior to the murder).

If the withdrawal comes so late that the crime cannot be stopped, it is not legally effective. *Comm. v. Caldwell*, 2014 WL 1343283 (Appeals Court) (the fact that the defendant left her home before the victim was kidnapped for ransom did not prevent her from being convicted as an accomplice because she was the one who lured him to the scene in the first place).

ACCESSORY AFTER THE FACT
274, § 4

Elements

- **Knowledge of felony.** After knowing a felony was committed;

- **Assist.** The suspect knowingly harbored, concealed, or in some way assisted;

- **Felon (unless protected relative).** An identifiable felon or accomplice — unless that person was a protected relative of the suspect;

- **Intent to avoid arrest/trial.** With the intent that the felon or accomplice would avoid or escape arrest or trial.

Right of Arrest

Felony.

Penalty

SP NMT 7 yrs or HC NMT 2½ yrs; or Fine NMT $1,000.

Notes

Knowledge and assistance. An accessory must know the facts of the underlying felony and the felon's identity. This does not mean the accessory has to know the name of the felony and the felon.

- **Sufficient knowledge.** *Comm. v. Perez*, 437 Mass. 186 (2002) (the defendant knew the principals had driven by a group of rival gang members and intentionally fired multiple shots into the crowd). *Baxter v. Comm.*, 489 Mass. 504 (2022).

- **Insufficient knowledge.** *Comm. v. Devlin*, 366 Mass. 132 (1974): An inmate was stabbed on the third level of a prison. A knife landed outside defendant Devlin's cell on the first floor. When guards converged on him, Devlin was wiping the knife with his t-shirt. On the theory that Devlin deliberately removed fingerprints from the deadly shank, he was charged as an accessory after the fact to assault with intent to murder. However, the SJC said the evidence was insufficient because there was no proof that Devlin knew about the felony (a brutal stabbing) or the identity of the inmate involved. The evidence only showed that Devlin picked up a weapon and wiped it down without any awareness of its source.

Time is not an element. In *Comm. v. Sims*, 41 Mass. App. Ct. 902 (1996), the defendant argued that the government failed to prove that he intended to help his girlfriend, Jessica Hassett, avoid arrest for murder. After all, he was the one who convinced her to surrender to police the day after the shooting. However, there was evidence that the defendant — at least in the immediate aftermath of the shooting — intended to help Hassett escape. He asked Hassett for the gun and put it in his pocket; drove her from the scene; and told other people that he would help her escape. The fact that he had a change of heart the next day did not nullify his initial decision to act as her accessory.

False statements and refusal to cooperate not typically accessory after the fact. *Comm. v. Rivera*, 482 Mass. 145 (2019): Christopher Rivera witnessed the murder, made false statements to police, and refused to provide the police with requested phone numbers. This behavior was not enough to prove accessory after the fact.

Rivera did not provide the police with a false alibi or information to help the murderer escape. He only lied about *his* behavior and knowledge.[1] On the other hand, Rivera could have been charged with lying to police under 268, § 13B (discussed in *Chapter 35*).

Liable for <u>crimes</u> of felon. The defendant's liability as an accessory is linked to the actual crimes perpetrated by the principal(s). In *Comm. v. Perez*, 437 Mass. 186 (2002), the defendant helped two people escape who he knew had been involved in a shooting. Although the defendant only assisted the shooters at one time, he was charged with two counts of being an accessory because they shot two people.

Protected relative defense. 274, § 4 specifically exempts certain relatives from this charge on the theory they should not be penalized for helping their own. Consequently, it must be proven that the defendant is not the husband or wife; or by blood, marriage or adoption, the parent or grandparent, child or grandchild, brother or sister of the felon.

The police should not inform a suspect about this exemption. *Comm. v. Chandler*, 29 Mass. App. Ct. 571 (1990) (police had no responsibility to inform a murder suspect or his mother about the law exempting his brother from being prosecuted as an accessory; their lack of knowledge resulted in the defendant's confession because his mother believed it was the only way to protect her other son, who had helped the defendant hide the murder weapon).

Unavailability or acquittal of principal no defense. 274, § 5 allows for an accessory to be convicted even though the principal is acquitted or missing. *Comm. v. Pope*, 397 Mass. 275 (1986) (defendant convicted as accessory even though principal died).

---

[1] Unless a person is subpoenaed or ordered by a court to testify, no one has a legal obligation to answer a police officer's questions or provide information in a criminal investigation.

Related Offenses

Failure to Report a Violent Crime. Reacting to a highly publicized case in which bystanders at a bar watched a woman get raped on a pool table, the legislature passed a law in 1983 that penalizes the failure to report a violent crime. A violation of this law, 268, § 40, occurs when a person is: (1) at the scene of a crime; and (2) knows that another person is the victim of rape, murder, manslaughter or armed robbery; and (3) fails to report the crime to a law enforcement official as soon as practical, even though he can do so without endangering himself or others. Penalty: Fine NLT $500, NMT $2,500. Right of Arrest: Complaint.

Concealing a Motor Vehicle Thief. 266, § 28 *(LED's Motor Vehicle Law, Chapter 12).*

Failure to Report Hazing. 269, § 18 *(LED's Juvenile Law, Chapter 21).*

ATTEMPT TO COMMIT A CRIME
274, § 6

Summary

This law punishes the offender who intends to commit a crime, takes a specific step toward doing so and, for some reason, fails. *Comm. v. Dixon*, 34 Mass. App. Ct. 653 (1993).

Elements

- ***Specific intent.*** The suspect had a specific intent to commit the crime; and

- ***Overt act.*** Took some overt act towards its commission; and

- ***Failure.*** Did not complete the crime because his effort failed or was interrupted.[2]

Right of Arrest

The right of arrest depends on the penalty for the underlying offense.

- *If attempt involves a felony which is punishable by at least 5 yrs in SP:* Felony.

- *If attempt involves a felony punishable by less than 5 yrs or any misdemeanor:* Complaint.

- *If attempt involves any larceny under 266, § 30:* 276, § 28 warrantless arrest in presence regardless of the value of the property.

---

[2] Technically this last element is not required. Prosecutors may still charge an attempted crime even for an offense that was arguably completed. *Comm. v. LaBrie*, 473 Mass. 754 (2016) (mother charged with attempted murder even though her severely disabled son actually died when she deliberately withheld his cancer medication; while the prosecutor could prove she wanted him to die, the prosecutor could not prove that lack of medication definitively caused her son's demise; therefore, her attempt conviction was legally permissible).

Penalty

The penalty for the crime attempted governs. Thus, if the attempted crime is:

- *Punishable by SP NLT 5 yrs, NMT Life, except larceny:* SP NMT 5 yrs or HC NMT 2 yrs.

- *Punishable by SP for less than 5 yrs, or HC imprisonment or a Fine of any amount, except larceny:* HC NMT 1 year; or Fine NMT $300.

- *Any larceny violation under 266, § 30:* HC NMT 2½ yrs; and/or Fine NMT $300.

Notes

Specific intent means the suspect *consciously intended* to commit the underlying crime.

Two types of overt acts. Aside from specific intent, the suspect must engage in an overt act. There are two types:

- **Last act.** This wrongdoer "commits the last act necessary to complete the intended crime but, for some reason, such as bad aim or bad luck, fails to perpetrate the crime." *Comm. v. McDonald*, 5 Cush. 365 (1850) (pickpocket reached into his intended victim's empty pocket).

- **Interrupted act.** This offender fails to complete the crime because he is intercepted by police or another third party. *Comm. v. McWilliams*, 473 Mass. 606 (2016) (defendant caught outside bank in a disguise with a pellet gun). Liability in these circumstances can be more complicated.

  Consider *Comm. v. Bell*, 455 Mass. 408 (2009): A female officer, working undercover, posed as a prostitute and offered her five year old child to a man named Kerry Bell. They met in a parking lot. Bell said, "I've done this before," then agreed to pay $200 and follow her to a park. As he drove from the lot, Bell was arrested. He had $211. The little girl who Bell anticipated raping did not exist. The SJC overturned Bell's attempted rape conviction.[3]

  - *While there was no doubt that Bell had specific intent — and no doubt that a fake child can be the object of an attempted crime — the problem was "the gap" between Bell's action and potential crime.* Although Bell agreed on a price, he did not pay or arrive at the park where the crime was supposed to take place. In short, Bell did not come close enough — "in time *or* ability" — for attempted rape.

  - *The trend in "attempt" cases is to demand that officers persuade the suspect to do more before they arrest.* In *Bell*, police might have waited until Bell displayed his cash and drove to the park, or (even better) followed the undercover to a location where the child was supposedly waiting.

  - *Safety.* At the same time, Justice Gants warned in *Bell* against placing too high a burden on law enforcement: "[P]olice . . . should not endanger the psychological health of [a] child by permitting the defendant to reach the place where [he] could

---

[3] Bell was convicted of solicitation of sexual conduct for a fee, which is discussed in *Chapter 11*.

commit [a] sexual crime . . . In other cases, such as when police are investigating attempted bombings or attempted shootings, it may be too dangerous . . . to postpone arrest until the defendant reaches the time and place of his intended crime, lest something go wrong and they are unable to prevent [it]." At the end of the day, police stings must balance safety and the need to develop sufficient evidence.

- *Bell's bottom line.* If possible, get the suspect to the time and place of the intended crime to help ensure conviction. *Comm. v. Buswell*, 468 Mass. 92 (2014).

Of course, one cannot attempt and complete the same crime — since the attempt merges into the completed crime. *Comm. v. Gosselin*, 365 Mass. 116 (1974).

CONSPIRACY
274, § 7

Elements

A conspiracy is an agreement between two or more people to do something unlawful. The crime is the agreement. It does not matter whether the plan was successful or even whether any steps were taken to carry it out. *Comm. v. Pratt*, 407 Mass. 647 (1990).

Right of Arrest

If the object of the conspiracy (or any means used to achieve the conspiracy) is the commission of a felony: Felony.

If the object of the conspiracy is a misdemeanor: Complaint.

Penalty

The penalty depends on the criminal object of the conspiracy. If the purpose of the conspiracy or any means used to achieve the conspiracy is:

- *A felony punishable by life imprisonment:* SP NMT 20 yrs or HC NMT 2½ yrs; and/or Fine NMT $10,000.

- *A felony punishable by imprisonment in the SP for a maximum period exceeding 10 yrs:* SP NMT 10 yrs or HC NMT 2½ yrs; and/or Fine NMT $10,000.

- *A felony punishable by imprisonment in the SP for NMT 10 yrs:* SP NMT 5 yrs or HC NMT 2½ yrs; and/or Fine NMT $5,000.

- *Any other crime:* HC NMT 2½ yrs; and/or Fine NMT $2,000.

These rules apply to all conspiracies, unless the specific type of conspiracy has a punishment established in another Massachusetts statute. See 94C, § 40 in *Chapter 20*.

Notes

The conspiracy is complete at the time of agreement — no overt act necessary. *Comm. v. Royce*, 20 Mass. App. Ct. 221 (1985) (conspiracy found where defendant suggested the idea of a robbery and negotiated a 10% share; fact that the defendant did not participate in the actual robbery was irrelevant to this charge).

- **The goal does not have to be immediate.** *Comm. v. Dellinger*, 10 Mass. App. Ct. 549 (1980) (defendants had clearly conspired to steal even though they had not agreed on the date, target, or method).

- **Not necessary for conspirators to create a formal agreement, or to agree on every detail, or even to meet together.** *Comm. v. Nelson*, 370 Mass. 192 (1976).

- **More than association or knowledge required.** It is not enough that the suspect knew about the conspiracy or associated with the conspirators. The suspect must have actually joined the conspiracy. *Comm. v. Costa*, 55 Mass. App. Ct. 901 (2002).

Identities may be unknown. The Supreme Court said in 1951: "[A]t least two persons are required to constitute a conspiracy, but the identity of the other members of the conspiracy is not needed [because] one person can be convicted of conspiring with persons whose names are unknown." *Rogers v. U.S.*, 71 S.Ct. 438 (1951). This is still true. *U.S. v. Santos-Soto*, 799 F.3d 49 (1st Cir. 2015) (conspiracy conviction upheld even though Santos-Soto did not know the full extent of the drug trafficking or the identities of all the co-conspirators).

Proof of conspiracy.

- **Conspiracy must often be proven with circumstantial evidence because there is no direct evidence of the agreement.** *Comm. v. Wheeler*, 2020 WL 6140534 (Appeals Court): Gonzalez, an inmate, had a recorded telephone call with Wheeler in which Gonzalez said he needed somebody with "them . . . shits." Wheeler said he could get the drugs. In a later call with Iliopoulos, Gonzalez said, "I got somebody over here . . . their shits only 300." In a subsequent call that Wheeler joined, Gonzalez spelled the name of an inmate, Mazza, and said his bail was only $300. Iliopoulos posted bail for Mazza the next day.

  Iliopoulos then revoked her surety for Mazza two days later, returning Mazza to custody. He identified himself as a gang member so he would be placed with Gonzalez. But first Mazza was held in a "dry status" isolation cell. His bowel movements led to the recovery of pills, heroin, marijuana, tobacco, and a lighter.

  Given Wheeler's participation in conversations about acquiring the "shits" for Gonzalez and arranging for Mazza's release, it was clear that Wheeler participated in a conspiracy to violate the drug laws with Iliopoulos and Gonzalez. Also see *Comm. v. Taskey*, 78 Mass. App. Ct. 787 (2011).

- **Statements of one participant may be used against other participants.** *Comm. v. Winquist*, 87 Mass. App. Ct. 695 (2015).

- **Conduct undertaken before an offender joined the conspiracy may be used against him.** *Comm. v. Albert*, 51 Mass. App. Ct. 377 (2001) (the fact that cocaine was possessed by his co-conspirators before the defendant joined was still evidence of his participation).

- **Conspiracy not automatically over when law enforcement frustrates the conspirators' objective.** *U.S. v. Recio,* 537 U.S. 270 (2003): Police stopped a truck in Nevada, seized illegal drugs, and enlisted the truck's two drivers in a sting. Police took the truck to its intended destination in Idaho; the drivers paged their contact. A few hours later, the two defendants appeared in a car. Recio drove away in the truck; Lopez-Meza drove away in the car. Police arrested both men, who later argued the conspiracy ended in Nevada before government agents knew anything about them.

    The Supreme Court disagreed. The government's defeat of the conspiracy's ultimate objective does not necessarily terminate the conspiracy itself. There is no reason why other members should not fall into the government's trap.

Massachusetts adopts bilateral view of conspiracy. There are two legal definitions of conspiracy — bilateral *and* unilateral. Massachusetts retains the bilateral approach, which requires that the agreement involve at least two like-minded criminals. Under the unilateral approach, a crime is committed when one person agrees to proceed with anyone, even an undercover officer. *Comm. v. Kotlyarevskiy,* 59 Mass. App. Ct. 240 (2003).

As long as Massachusetts insists on the bilateral view, there cannot be a conspiracy involving *only* the defendant and a government agent. In those situations, police must charge either Attempt to Commit a Crime, 274, § 6, or Solicitation of a Crime, 274, § 8.

Massachusetts may adopt the defense of renunciation. "Renunciation" means that a person, after entering into a conspiracy, decides to voluntarily renounce or abandon his criminal purpose. Historically, this defense has not been recognized because a conspiracy is complete at the point of agreement. The SJC opened the door to the renunciation defense in *Comm. v. Nee,* 458 Mass. 174 (2010), but decided that it did not apply because Nee never acknowledged his part in the underlying conspiracy to begin with.

Difference between an accomplice and a conspirator. An accomplice must "meaningfully participate" in the crime but does not have to "agree" with the principal in advance. In contrast, conspiracy requires an agreement to work together, but not a completed crime. *Comm. v. Rose,* 84 Mass. App. Ct. 910 (2014).

Conspiracy is considered a separate offense from the underlying crime that is the object of the conspiracy. For example, a drug dealer may be punished for drug distribution and, if he worked with another offender, for conspiracy to distribute the same drugs. *Comm. v. DeCillis,* 41 Mass. App. Ct. 312 (1996). However, a conspiracy charge may not be tried simultaneously with the substantive offense on which the conspiracy was based — unless the defendant consents. *Angiulo v. Comm.*, 401 Mass. 71 (1987).

Venue. Venue for conspiracy lies in any county where agreement was reached or where an overt act to execute the plan was committed by any of the conspirators.

Related Offense

Conspiracy to Violate the Controlled Substances Act. 94C, § 40. See *Chapter 20.*

SOLICITATION OF A FELONY
274, § 8

Elements

- **Solicit.** The suspect solicited, advised, or otherwise enticed another to commit a felony (including murder); and

- **Intent.** Intended for the person to commit, or arrange for another to commit, the felony.

Right of Arrest

- *If solicited offense punishable by SP 10 or more yrs:* Felony.

- *If solicited offense punishable by less than 10 yrs:* Complaint.

This offense may be charged in the district court. 218, § 76.

Penalty

If the suspect intends that the person commit a crime punishable by:

Life imprisonment: SP NMT 20 yrs or HC NMT 2½ yrs; and/or Fine NMT $10,000.

SP 10 yrs or more: SP NMT 10 yrs or HC NMT 2½ yrs; and/or Fine NMT $10,000.

SP 5 yrs or more: HC NMT 2½ yrs; and/or Fine NMT $5,000.

SP for less than 5 yrs: HC NMT 2½ yrs; and/or Fine NMT $2,000.

If type of solicitation already defined in another law, that penalty must be imposed.

Notes

The crime is complete at the point of solicitation. In fact, the person solicited does not have to agree to commit the crime. For this reason, an undercover officer may be solicited. *Comm. v. Hamel*, 52 Mass. App. Ct 250 (2001): Jerry Hamel, while incarcerated, confided in another inmate that he wanted his wife's rapist killed, along with his parents and older brother. He even came up with a payment plan. The Appeals Court found overwhelming evidence of solicitation to commit murder, but found insufficient evidence of attempted murder because Hamel never engaged in any physical act to kill his intended targets. Interestingly, officers may develop cases where they have solicitation, but lack conspiracy (no agreement between accomplices) or an attempted crime (no overt act). Consult a prosecutor early for legal clarity.

Solicitation even occurs if the defendant asks a person to arrange for another person to commit the felony. *Comm. v. Wolcott*, 77 Mass. App. Ct. 457 (2010): The defendant wanted her husband killed, so she asked her cousin to arrange for someone to commit the murder. It was not a defense that she never spoke directly with the "hitman."

Law Enforcement Dimensions

Part II

VIOLENT OFFENSES

Threats,
Assaults with and without Weapons,
Police Protection,
Homicide, Kidnapping,
and Animal Protection

Chapters 3 – 8

© John Sofis Scheft, Esq.
All rights reserved

3 Threat Offenses

THREAT TO COMMIT A CRIME
275, § 2

Elements

- **Communicate.** The suspect communicated to the victim his intent to injure the victim's person or property, now or in the future; and

- **Crime.** The threatened injury, if carried out, would constitute a crime; and

- **Reasonable fear.** Could reasonably cause the victim to fear that the suspect had both the intention and the ability to carry out the threat.

Right of Arrest

Complaint only. 275, § 2 does not permit warrantless arrest. This is true even if the threat occurred during a domestic dispute. *Comm. v. Jacobsen*, 419 Mass. 269 (1994). *Wagenmann v. Adams*, 829 F.2d 196 (1st Cir. 1987) (failure to follow this rule results in false arrest and police liability). *Comm. v. Daly*, 12 Mass. App. Ct. 338 (1981) (officer may sign complaint application).

- **Warrant required to arrest.** Officers must present the victim's account and a judge or clerk must issue an arrest warrant based on a "clear and present danger" that the threat will be carried out. *Robinson v. Bradley*, 300 F.Supp. 665 (1969).

- **Frivolous complaint.** 275, § 6 empowers the court to order that the complainant pay the expenses of a prosecution based on an "unfounded or frivolous" complaint.

Penalty

Basic offense: HC NMT 6 months; or Fine NMT $100. *Comm. v. Powers*, 73 Mass. App. Ct. 186 (2008) (the sentencing judge may impose a long term of probation, such as five years, for a threats conviction).

Alternative disposition: Instead of imposing a sentence, the court may, under 275, § 4, impose a "peace bond" for a period not to exceed six months. A peace bond requires the defendant to pay a sum of money. If he fails to "keep the peace," especially toward "the [victim] requiring such security," he will forfeit the money.

Notes

A threat may be oral or written. *Comm. v. Pelletier*, 264 Mass. 221 (1928).

There must be reasonable fear that the suspect has both the intention <u>and</u> ability to carry out the threat. *Comm. v. Winter*, 9 Mass. App. Ct. 512 (1980). The standard is objective, which means that convictions are allowed in cases where the victim was:

- **Reasonably afraid** (the typical case); or

- **Not afraid but should be.** Some victims try to be "macho" and not admit that the threat scared them. Regardless of their reaction, a threats charge is proper if, under the circumstances, the victims should have been afraid. For example, in *Comm. v. Bitahi*, 2013 WL 1458635 (Appeals Court), the defendant drove her car directly at the victim, stopped within inches of him and said, "Good luck trying to keep all your blood!" The fact that the victim was unconcerned and purposefully antagonized the defendant by smiling did not negate the threat. The defendant's words and action created a reasonable fear that she had the intention and ability to kill him.

- **Overly sensitive.** At the same time, just because a person is afraid does not mean that a crime occurred — especially if the circumstances did not justify fear.

Threat of harm for an uncertain time in the future may cause reasonable fear. The absence of an immediate ability to do harm will not prevent a conviction for threats.

- *Comm. v. Ditsch*, 19 Mass. App. Ct. 1005 (1985): The defendant was incarcerated at the time he wrote letters to his mother-in-law threatening to kill her. In upholding his conviction for threats, the court stated that the mother-in-law reasonably believed that the defendant had the future ability to harm her — either personally after his release or through an agent who he might recruit while in jail.

- *Comm. v. Baptiste*, 2020 WL 2507584 (Appeals Court): When the defendant told the officers guarding him in the hospital he would shoot them, no proof was needed of his ability to do it immediately, or of how he would get a gun or would later find them. The officers patrolled the area in which the defendant was arrested and through which he traveled.

Consider background circumstances in assessing threat — not just the words spoken.

- *Comm. v. Melton*, 77 Mass. App. Ct. 552 (2010): The defendant had a violent relationship with the victim. When he learned that the victim had a restraining order, the defendant told her he was upset she talked to police. He said: "You want to play dirty, I'll show you how to play dirty." The phrase "play dirty" was an implied threat of violence. Several times in the past, the defendant had used this expression before seriously harming the victim.

- *Comm. v. Sholley*, 432 Mass. 721 (2000): Earl Sholley was critical of what he viewed as the court system's unfair treatment of fathers in domestic violence cases. After learning that a father had been sent to jail, Sholley began shouting inside the courthouse. When he encountered the prosecutor, Sholley pointed his finger at her face and yelled, "Watch out, counselor!" The prosecutor testified that she was "extremely frightened." In this context, the advice to "watch out" was an expression of Sholley's intention to harm the prosecutor.

- *Comm. v. Strahan*, 39 Mass. App. Ct. 928 (1995): The defendant was convicted of threatening to damage the New England Aquarium; he had a history of picketing the Aquarium and informing visitors that whale-watching is harmful. One day a staff member told the defendant to step back from the whale-watching vessel. The defendant responded, "I'm just looking for a place to put a hole in the boat." Aquarium staff justifiably took his threat seriously — given his history, the fact that he was wearing a knapsack possibly containing a tool, and the fact that the hull of the boat was made of thin aluminum.

Sexually explicit language may be threatening. *Comm. v. Chou*, 433 Mass. 229 (2001): The defendant, then 18 years old, produced a number of "missing person" flyers identifying and describing a female high school student who had broken up with him. The word "missing" was printed in large type across the top of the flyer beneath which was the young woman's name and photograph. The victim was described as a "White slut" along with other sexually profane references. The content of the flyer was threatening. Objectively, a reasonable person would, as the victim did, fear that the flyer was a veiled threat that she would become a "missing person."

The First Amendment's right to free speech only protects "expressive" threats, not "true" threats. The term "expressive" threat distinguishes between words that literally threaten but have an expressive purpose — such as political commentary — and words that are truly intended to place a target in fear. In *Watts v. U.S.*, 394 U.S. 705 (1969), the defendant yelled at a protest rally: "If I'm drafted and forced to carry a rifle, the first man I want to get in my sights is the President!" He was exercising his right to free speech, not realistically threatening to assassinate the President.

- Compare *U.S. v. Fulmer*, 108 F. 3d 1486 (1st Cir. 1997) (the defendant left a voicemail for a federal agent: "The silver bullets are coming . . . enjoy the intriguing unraveling of what I said to you." Given the defendant's history with this particular agent, his comments were a "true" threat deserving criminal prosecution).

- *U.S. v. Cardozo*, 2019 WL 2603096 (D. Mass) (a counter argument is protected by the First Amendment, but not when it contains a violent threat; here, the defendant forcefully denied an online rape accusation from a magazine reporter; this was legitimate; when he threatened to rape her in revenge, he crossed the line into a criminal threat).

The same First Amendment considerations apply to social media. *Comm. v. Walters*, 472 Mass. 680 (2015): Stephen began dating Walters' ex-girlfriend. Stephen searched Walters' Facebook profile, which featured a photo of him smiling with a gun on his lap. His "favorite quotation" was listed as: "Make no mistake of my will to succeed in bringing you two idiots to justice." He posted a picture of singer Rihanna, a well-known victim of domestic violence. Stephen was terrified.

While a Facebook post may constitute a threat, it did not in this case. The gun photo contained no evidence of Walters' intent to be violent. It had no caption. He had never threatened Stephen, and he was a veteran with a longstanding interest in guns. While the quote likely referred to Stephen and his "ex," it did not suggest violence. The word "justice" typically has a nonviolent interpretation. Finally, without other evidence, his post of Rihanna did not suggest that Walters intended to place his "ex" and Stephen in fear of bodily harm. See *U.S. v. Elonis*, 841 F.3d 589 (2016) (both a subjective and objective component must be satisfied; here, the defendant had to *intend* to scare his wife and coworkers with his violent rap lyrics about them, which he posted on Facebook, *and* a reasonable person would need to view them as a threat).

The target of the threat and the target of the threatened crime may be different people.
Comm. v. Hamilton, 459 Mass. 422 (2011): Kenneth Hamilton violated his probation and was sent to jail. After his release, Hamilton left a message on his probation officer's voicemail: "You actually brought your daughter into the court house, so I wanted to thank you for sending me where I was because — as you know — there are predators there and I'm not a predator, but I was able to talk about your beautiful daughter." The probation officer interpreted this message as a not-so-subtle threat to harm her daughter. She believed Hamilton had the ability to carry out this threat and intended to instill fear in his probation officer. The fact that he did not approach the daughter and scare her was irrelevant.

The threat may be communicated directly *or* indirectly.

- **Direct communication obvious.** The suspect threatens the victim in person or in a way where he knows the victim will receive the message. *Comm. v. Chou*, 433 Mass. 229 (2001): Chou was the person, discussed earlier, who placed "missing person" flyers at the victim's school after she ended their relationship. While it is true that Chou did not hand the "missing person" flyer directly to his victim or post it on her locker, he did post copies of the flyer in several prominent locations at her school, to ensure that the victim would see it or that its contents would be communicated to her by other students or staff — which is exactly what happened. Also see *Comm. v. Maiden*, 61 Mass. App. Ct. 433 (2004).

- **Indirect communication involves a third party.** When a threat is received by a third party, the police must show that the suspect <u>reasonably knew</u> that it would reach the victim.

    - *Comm. v. Hughes*, 59 Mass. App. Ct. 280 (2003): Defendant's threat to kill his ex-girlfriend was delivered only to his brother. But he clearly expected his brother to pass on the threat to his "ex," because he knew the brother had been playing the role of intermediary throughout their struggles.

    - *Comm. v. Valentin V.*, 83 Mass. App. Ct. 202 (2013): At a meeting with school officials regarding a stolen Xbox system, Valentin referred to Fred as a "snitch" and stated that he was "going to get him." Valentin also made threatening remarks in the classroom, which established that Valentin intended that the teacher or other students pass his comments along to Fred.

    - *Comm. v. Hokanson*, 74 Mass. App. Ct. 403 (2009): The defendant should have expected — when he told a bystander in the lobby of a police station that he was going to shoot police officers and then gestured with a simulated "trigger-finger" — that the bystander would alert officers.

    - Compare *Comm. v. Furst*, 56 Mass. App. Ct. 283 (2002): Defendant Robin Furst spoke many times with her friend Carson about the anger she felt toward her ex-husband Jeffrey. She even tried to persuade Carson to kill Jeffrey for money and sex. Carson ended up reporting the threats to Jeffrey and the police. However, Robin approached Carson as a potential partner in crime, not as someone who would likely communicate with the intended victim. Here, threatening to commit a crime was the wrong charge. "Criminal solicitation" would have worked instead. See discussion at end of *Chapter 2*.

- **Communication to "eavesdropping" third party must be intended to reach victim.** *Comm. v. Troy T.*, 54 Mass. App. Ct. 520 (2002) declared that a suspect could threaten someone by purposefully communicating to an eavesdropper who he knows is likely to report his threats to the intended recipient. However, the facts of *Troy T.* provided insufficient proof that the juvenile, who threatened to kill "dumb blondes and jocks," intended for his comments to be heard by anyone other than his nearby friends. The fact that a girl did overhear his comments and told her blond friend (who became terrified) was not enough to establish that the juvenile *intended* for this to happen. Nothing suggested the juvenile desired his statements to be disseminated to others: He did not comment in a loud voice, glance at nonparticipants as he spoke to his friends, or gesture in an attention-seeking fashion.

Related Offenses

Stalking. 265, § 43. See *Chapter 15*.
Criminal Harassment. 265, § 43A. See *Chapter 15*.
Annoying or Obscene Electronic Communication. 269, § 14A. See *Chapter 15*.
Threat Concerning the Location of Dangerous Items. 269, § 14. This law most commonly covers a "bomb threat." See *Chapter 19*.

EXTORTION
265, § 25

Elements

- ***Communication.*** Through a verbal, written or printed communication;

- ***3 types of threats.*** The suspect maliciously threatened to:

  - Accuse another of a crime; or
  - Injure the person or property of another; or
  - Use against another person the power or authority vested in the suspect by virtue of his being a police officer, or having the powers of a police officer, or being an employee of any licensing authority.

- ***Intent to get something.*** With the intent to:

  - Extort money or any pecuniary advantage; or
  - Compel any person to do an act against his will.

Right of Arrest

Felony.

Penalty

SP NMT 15 yrs or HC NMT 2½ yrs; and/or Fine NMT $5,000.

Notes

Malicious threat. A malicious threat is intentional.

- **Threat may be expressed or implied.** An example of an implied threat is the suspect who demands money in exchange for "protecting" the victim from harm. *Comm. v. Cacchiotti*, 55 Mass. App. Ct. 499 (2002).

- **The person who hears the threat does not have to be the intended victim** — e.g., a suspect threatens to harm a child if her parent does not furnish money. *U.S. v. Mavroules*, 813 F.Supp. 115 (D. Mass. 1993) (husband extorted money from his wife by threatening to ruin her father's reputation; her father was a U.S. Congressman).

Types of threats.

- **Accuse another of a crime** — e.g., one offender told his ex-girlfriend that he would tell her employer she stole merchandise unless she performed a sex act.

- **Injure person or property.** This is interpreted broadly. *Comm. v. Miller*, 385 Mass. 521 (1982) (defendant threatened to expose his sexual relationship with the victim to her parents and circulate naked photographs of her unless she gave him money; although neither threat amounted to an accusation of crime, they caused the victim severe mental anguish, which constituted an "injury to her person").

- **Abuse official power.** *Comm. v. LaFontaine*, 32 Mass. App. Ct. 529 (1992) (police officers took money from drug dealers in exchange for their release).

Intent of threat: Money, pecuniary advantage, or performance of an act. Pecuniary means "pertaining to money" and, in this context, covers items that have a monetary value (e.g., the extortionist insists on the transfer of stocks and bonds). The fact that the victim actually owes the money extorted is no defense. *Comm. v. Matchett*, 386 Mass. 492 (1982).

Each threat a new offense, even though designed to extort the same thing. *Comm. v. DeVincent*, 358 Mass. 592 (1971) (defendant attempted to collect same gambling debt by threats during two separate confrontations).

Related Offense

Kidnapping with Intent to Extort. 265, § 26. This aggravated crime is commonly referred to as "kidnapping for ransom." See discussion in *Chapter 7*.

4 Assault Offenses

ASSAULT
265, § 13A

Summary

Assault occurs in two ways: (1) an attempted battery (victim need not be afraid); or (2) putting a person in fear of a battery. *Comm. v. Slaney*, 345 Mass. 135 (1962).

Elements

Type 1: Attempted battery

- The suspect intended to commit a battery, which involved touching the victim in a harmful or unpermitted way;

- Took some overt action; and

- Came reasonably close to committing a battery.

Type 2: Threatened battery

- The suspect intentionally engaged;

- In menacing conduct;

- That caused the victim to fear an imminent battery.

Right of Arrest

Basic offense: Arrest for breach of peace in presence. Otherwise, complaint.

During domestic violence: 209A, § 6 warrantless arrest on probable cause. Depending on the relationship of the parties, officers will charge the assault under 265, § 13M or § 13A. Be sure to review chart in *Chapter 13* for details.

During harassment: 258E, § 8 warrantless arrest on probable cause. Charge assault under 265, § 13A. Be sure to review chart in *Chapter 13*.

Against person with restraining order (under G.L. Chapters 209A, 208, 209, or 209C in effect against defendant): Felony.

Penalty

Misdemeanor assault: HC NMT 2½ yrs; or Fine NMT $1,000.

Felony assault: SP NMT 5 yrs or HC NMT 2½ yrs; and/or Fine NMT $5,000.

Notes

Type 1: Attempted battery. The suspect must intend to commit a battery — that is, a harmful or unpermitted touching of the victim — and take an overt step to accomplish the battery. The most obvious example is throwing a punch at somebody and missing.

- **With this form of assault, it is not necessary to show that the victim was afraid or even aware of the attempted battery.** *Comm. v. Richards*, 363 Mass. 299 (1973) (one may be guilty even if the victim is asleep).

- **The intended battery does not need to be possible.** *Comm. v. Daley*, 2020 WL 4047527 (Appeals Court) (as Correction Officer Rodriguez adjusted Candace Daley's shackles for transport, Daley lunged and kicked towards Officer Rodriguez's face; the restraints stopped the kick short of its target by millimeters, yet Daley's intent to cause a battery was clear).

Type 2: Threatened battery. In order to prove assault by threatened battery, the suspect must have intentionally engaged in menacing conduct that reasonably caused the victim to fear an imminent battery.

- **Menacing conduct causing fear.** Unlike the first form of assault, the victim must actually experience fear of immediate physical harm. *Comm. v. Rumkin*, 55 Mass. App. Ct. 635 (2002) (following an accident, the defendant cab driver jumped out of his vehicle and tried to open the female driver's door while she was screaming and trying to lock the doors). *Comm. v. Carrier*, 2017 WL 2544749 (Appeals Court) (the parties' relationship was characterized by a history of abuse, so the defendant's screaming, flailing his arms, and approaching the victim quickly in a parking lot caused her to reasonably fear physical harm; his conduct was extreme enough to cause the victim's son to seek police assistance).

  The suspect must intend to cause fear, but does not need to intend to harm the victim. *Comm. v. Domingue*, 18 Mass. App. Ct. 987 (1984).

- **Verbal threat alone insufficient.** A verbal threat to do harm becomes an assault when accompanied by some outward gesture. *Comm. v. Mathieu*, 2020 WL 1157951 (Appeals Court) (the defendant said he wanted to fight and hurt the victim; he took a step towards the victim; that step was menacing conduct intended to cause fear of immediate harm). *Comm. v. Delgado*, 367 Mass. 432 (1975).

Jurors do not have to be unanimous about which type of assault the defendant committed — some may find he engaged in an attempted battery, while the rest may find he committed a threatened battery. *Comm. v. Boodoosingh*, 85 Mass. App. Ct. 902 (2014).

ASSAULT BY DANGEROUS WEAPON (ADW)
265, § 15B

Elements

- **Assault.** The suspect committed an assault by attempting a battery *or* threatening to commit a battery with the intent to cause fear;

- **Dangerous weapon.** By using a dangerous weapon.

Right of Arrest

Felony.

Penalty

SP NMT 5 yrs or HC NMT 2½ yrs; or Fine NMT $1,000.

Notes

There are two types of dangerous weapons: (1) items which, by their nature, cause serious injury or death (known as *per se*; a Latin phrase that means "by itself"); and (2) items used in a way that appears capable of causing serious injury or death (known as *dangerous use*). *Comm. v. Sampson*, 383 Mass. 750 (1981).

Per se: No need to use weapon in dangerous fashion. *Per se* weapons are automatically considered dangerous. 269, § 10(a) and (b) offers a list, including firearms, knives, brass knuckles, and various martial arts weapons. These items are designed "for the sole purpose of bodily assault or defense." The court includes pepper spray (OC) too. *Comm. v. Lord*, 55 Mass. App. Ct. 265 (2002).

- **Fake gun.** 265, § 58 makes possessing a deceptive weapon device qualify as being *armed* for any crime against a person in Chapter 265. A "deceptive weapon device" is defined in 140, § 121 as any item "intended to convey the presence of a rifle, shotgun or firearm . . . and which presents an objective threat . . . to a person of . . . average sensibility."

- **Unseen weapon — if possibly possessed and reasonably believed.** If the suspect claims to have a *per se* weapon, he does not need to brandish it in order to commit ADW. A suspect who reasonably claims to have a weapon may be taken at his word. *Comm. v. Foley*, 17 Mass. App. Ct. 238 (1983): Foley warned the victim that he had a knife in his back pocket and, if the victim screamed again, he was going to kill her. Although he never displayed a knife, Foley's statement, which she reasonably believed, constituted ADW.

On the other hand, Foley could not have been convicted of ADW if there was no possible way he possessed a weapon at the time he claimed to.[1] *Comm. v. Howard*, 386 Mass. 607 (1982) (although defendant said he had a weapon, the immediate arrival of police and subsequent search confirmed there was no possibility he did).

Dangerous use: Item must appear dangerous. In this category, normal items become weapons when used in a dangerous fashion. *Comm. v. Tarrant*, 367 Mass. 411 (1975) (defendant's threat to have his German Shepherd attack turned this household pet into a weapon). *Comm. v. Farrell*, 322 Mass. 606 (1948) (defendant brandished a lighted cigarette).

An attempted battery occurs when the suspect thrusts, pushes, or discharges a weapon within striking distance of the victim. *Comm. v. Lednum*, 75 Mass. App. Ct. 722 (2009) (enraged defendant uncapped a gas line in the basement and released gas into the house, where he knew people were sleeping; controlling a gas line in this way was an attempted battery with a "dangerous use" weapon).

For a threatened battery, the suspect must brandish, display, or even talk about his weapon in a way that is designed to make the victim afraid. For example, *Comm. v. Lengsavat*, 49 Mass. App. Ct. 243 (2000) involved two fights at a birthday party. In the chaos, several partygoers ran into the street. Lengsavat fired his gun several times into the air while shouting. He did this in close proximity to the partygoers to make them fear him. *Comm. v. Ortiz-Correa*, 2020 WL 5948896 (Appeals Court) (while approaching the victim's car window, the defendant loudly asked where her male friend was, saying he would bring him down; he lifted his shirt to show the pistol in his waistband).

- **The suspect must intend to cause fear.** *Comm. v. Musgrave*, 421 Mass. 610 (1996): Thomas Musgrave and another man were encountered on the street by a Stoneham officer, who believed they might have been responsible for some graffiti. While the officer patted down the other man, Musgrave placed his hand at his waist. The officer realized that Musgrave was touching a gun and, "scared stiff," he immediately wrestled him to the ground. The gun was an inoperable pellet pistol. Charged with ADW, Musgrave argued that he was trying to get rid of it. The SJC insisted that his conviction could not rest simply on the officer's fear; there had to be proof that the defendant *intended* to place the officer in fear.

- **At the same time, it is *not* necessary that the victim experience fear.** This crime punishes the use of a weapon regardless of the victim's reaction. *Comm. v. Slaney*, 345 Mass. 135 (1962) (Slaney pointed a gun at his ex-girlfriend and her boss; although the boss testified to experiencing no fear and even trying to disarm Slaney, Slaney's conviction was upheld).

Sufficient evidence of attempted and threatened ADW. *Comm. v. Arias*, 78 Mass. App. Ct. 13 (2010): Officer John Leonard was working a detail at Home Depot. He saw Jorge Arias throw several boxes over a chain link fence. Confronted by the officer, Arias ran to his truck and "threw it into drive." The truck lurched forward toward Officer Leonard, who drew his weapon. Arias stopped quickly, then drove away. He was eventually apprehended.

Arias' conduct satisfied both definitions of assault. He attempted to commit a battery when his truck lurched at Leonard (stopping close, and only when the officer pointed his weapon).

---

[1] Commentators, including this author, have criticized this rule. A much simpler standard should govern: If a suspect threatens to use a weapon, and the victim reasonably believes he is armed, he should be treated as if he actually possessed the weapon.

The same conduct also qualified as a threatened battery because it was intentional and designed to cause the officer "to fear for his life." Notice how the truck was a "dangerous use" weapon.

One shot at victims justifies multiple ADW counts. *Comm. v. Melton*, 637 Mass 291 (2001): Melton and the victim got into a fight. Later that night, the victim was driving with three passengers. Melton and his buddies drove up to the victim's car. Melton fired a gunshot into the vehicle, but luckily did not hit anyone. He was charged with four counts. Melton argued that it was impossible for him to shoot four victims with a single bullet. However, the court noted that Melton fired at point blank range and endangered all four occupants.[2]

Simultaneous assault and property destruction. A single act may support simultaneous convictions of ADW and malicious destruction of property. *Comm. v. Domingue*, 18 Mass. App. Ct. 987 (1984) (shooting gun both frightened the bartender and damaged the bar).

ASSAULT & BATTERY (A&B)
265, § 13A

Summary

A&B occurs in three ways: (1) an intentional, unconsented touching of another; (2) an intentional, harmful touching of another; or (3) a reckless act that causes injury to another. *Comm. v. Beal*, 474 Mass. 341 (2016).

Elements

Type 1: Offensive

- The suspect intentionally touched another person, however slight;
- Without having any right or excuse to do so; and
- The person touched did not consent.

Type 2: Harmful

- The suspect intentionally touched another person;
- In a manner likely to cause bodily harm;
- Without having any right or excuse to do so.

Type 3: Reckless

- The suspect engaged in reckless conduct;
- Which caused bodily injury to another.

---

[2] The evidence also showed that it may have been a backseat passenger who actually fired the weapon at the vehicle. This made no difference to the court because Melton would still be guilty as an accomplice, since he was clearly the instigator of the shooting.

Right of Arrest

Basic offense: Arrest for breach of peace in presence. Otherwise, complaint.

During domestic violence A&B: 209A, § 6 warrantless arrest on probable cause. Depending on the relationship of the parties, officers will charge the A&B under 265, § 13M or § 13A. Also review charts later in this chapter and in *Chapter 13*.

During harassment: 258E, § 8 warrantless arrest on probable cause. Charge A&B under 265, § 13A. Also review chart in *Chapter 13*.

Causing serious bodily injury: Felony. Charge § 13A. *Serious bodily injury* to a victim of any age means "bodily injury that results in: (1) a permanent disfigurement; (2) loss or impairment of a bodily function, limb or organ; or (3) a substantial risk of death."[3]

Against person who suspect knows, or should know, is pregnant: Felony. Charge § 13A.

Against person with restraining order (under G.L. Chapters 209A, 208, 209, or 209C in effect against defendant): Felony. Charge § 13A. Also review chart in *Chapter 13*.

If suffocation or strangulation: Felony. Charge 265, § 15D. Review chart in *Chapter 13*.

Penalty

Misdemeanor A&B: HC NMT 2½ yrs; or Fine NMT $1,000.

Felony A&B: SP NMT 5 yrs or HC NMT 2½ yrs; and/or Fine NMT $5,000.

Accord & satisfaction: Except for A&Bs involving police officers, domestic violence, or felonies, 276, § 55 authorizes a judge to dismiss an A&B or other misdemeanor if the victim voluntarily signed a written agreement and received adequate compensation.

Notes

Type 1: Offensive.

- *Most common* — **hit or push.** *Comm. v. Sylvia*, 35 Mass. App. Ct. 310 (1993) (wife told police that defendant hit her; police saw her swollen eye and bloody nose). *Comm. v. Farber*, 2011 WL 3273880 (Appeals Court) (defendant pushed two elderly Jehovah's Witnesses from behind; they were leaving his property after he yelled at them).

- **Even slight touching sufficient if victim did not consent.** *Comm. v. Campbell*, 352 Mass. 387 (1967) (defendant put his hand lightly on victim's throat). *Comm. v. Hartnett*, 72 Mass. App. Ct. 467 (2008). *Comm. v. Messina*, 2016 WL 320572 (Appeals Court) (during a "polite conversation," defendant made several comments about the victim's appearance, asked her on a date, and grabbed her arm to pull her closer; the victim felt uncomfortable and told him she had to return to work; the defendant grabbed her arm a second time; this was A&B because, by saying she had to leave, the victim had displayed her lack of consent to being touched).

---

3 If victim seriously hurts themselves in avoiding the perceived battery, the assailant could be charged with felony A&B. *Comm. v. Parker*, 25 Mass. App. Ct. 727 (1988).

The touching must be on purpose, since the law does not punish incidental contact. *Comm. v. Ordway*, 66 Mass. 270 (1853) (defendant brushed hand of complainant).

- **Body fluids.** *Comm. v. Cohen,* 55 Mass. App. Ct. 358 (2002) (defendant committed A&B by intentionally spitting on a woman with whom he had a disagreement). *Comm. v. Malone*, 114 Mass. 295 (1873) (defendant urinated on a woman passing by).

- **Injury from escape.** The suspect commits A&B if he causes the victim to fear an immediate attack, which then leads to the victim's injury while trying to escape. *Comm. v. Parker*, 25 Mass. App. Ct. 727 (1988) (wife hurt trying to escape from upset husband).

- **Food with foreign substance.** *Comm. v. Stratton*, 114 Mass. 303 (1873) (delivering food that contains a nonlethal substance, which causes discomfort, is A&B; here, defendants gave women figs containing a "love potion" that made them sick).

Should the facts warrant, officers may use another offense. 270, § 8A prohibits selling *or* distributing candy or other food containing a foreign substance that is intended or reasonably expected to injure a person. Penalty: SP NMT 5 yrs. Right of Arrest: Felony.

Type 2: Harmful.

- **It is illegal to intentionally touch someone in a way that is likely to hurt them.** For example, people may not agree to a fist fight. *Comm. v. Collberg*, 119 Mass. 350 (1876).

- **The same rule applies to sexual conduct.** In *Comm. v. Carey*, 463 Mass. 378 (2012), the victim was in the kitchen when she saw John Carey, her husband's golf buddy. Carey claimed her husband had invited him over. Carey suddenly put his tie around her neck and pulled tightly. As she lapsed into unconsciousness, her 12 year old son came to the rescue. Police arrived and observed signs of a struggle. During a search of Carey's home, police found 400 photographs depicting strangulation and 978 computer hits for "asphyxia." In court, Carey claimed that the victim consented to asphyxiation for sexual gratification. His defense was rejected. Massachusetts does not allow a person to consent to physically harmful acts. Although there is a constitutional right to sexual privacy, it is not recognized in cases where a person may be injured.

Type 3: Reckless.

- **Reckless conduct occurs when a suspect realizes, or should realize, the danger associated with his conduct but does it anyway.** *Comm. v. Marcelli*, 14 Mass. App. Ct. 567 (1982). *Comm. v. Hill*, 2017 WL 2422729 (Appeals Court) (after an argument, the defendant tossed the victim's child off his lap and onto the floor, grabbed a knife with a five-inch blade, and ran toward the victim; the victim tried to take the knife away to protect his girlfriend and two small children and ended up with cuts on his hand requiring stitches; the defendant did not have to intend to injure the victim — it was enough that his reckless conduct with a knife resulted in serious injury to the victim).

- **The reckless conduct must result in "physical injury."** The injury need not be permanent, but it must be more than trivial. *Comm. v. Burno*, 396 Mass. 622 (1986).

The identity of the victim is not an element of the offense. *Comm. v. Stewart*, 94 Mass. App. Ct. 485 (2018) (unknown woman was beaten by the defendant with his cane on a public street in Medford; the fact that police never located or identified the victim did not prevent the defendant's conviction based on eyewitness testimony).

Transferred intent. A suspect commits A&B if, while intending to hit a particular person, the suspect accidentally punches a bystander. Transferred intent applies to all assaults, including those with a weapon. *Comm. v. Pitts*, 403 Mass. 665 (1989) (defendant intended to murder one person and ended up killing another).

This principle also applies when a defendant harms both the intended victim and one or more unintended victims. *Comm. v. Duong Van Tran*, 463 Mass. 8 (2012) (deranged defendant lit his 14 month old daughter on fire; when a woman and her son attempted to save her, they were injured; for their unanticipated injuries, the defendant was properly charged — under the theory of transferred intent — with attempted murder). *Comm. v. Oswaldo O.*, 94 Mass. App. Ct. 550 (2018) (even if E. was the intended victim, transferred intent applied because two other boys became afraid when Oswaldo displayed his knife in front of them).

The serious injury for felony A&B (265, § 13A) may be direct or a consequence of treatment. *Comm. v. Heywood*, 484 Mass. 43 (2020) (metal plates beneath the skin to repair the victim's cheekbone amounted to a permanent disfigurement even though the injury was concealed).

- **A scar qualifies as disfigurement.** *Comm. v. Thompson*, 2012 WL 1755743 (Appeals Court) (defendant "head-butted" victim, who required stitches for a cut above her eyebrow; injury amounted to "permanent disfigurement" because it caused a permanent scar).

- **Permanent injury not required under "impairment" standard.** *Comm. v. Jean-Pierre*, 65 Mass. App. Ct. 162 (2005) (defendant punched victim and broke his jaw). *Comm. v. Phoenix*, 2016 WL 4470295 (Appeals Court) (excessive bleeding in the throat impaired the victim's ability to breathe and speak normally; his vision was impaired and his nose was broken). *Comm. v. Sigman*, 2017 WL 829756 (Appeals Court) (victim had both permanent injury in the form of her broken teeth and impairment of a bodily function — she had difficulty eating for seven months).

- **Medical treatment and testimony important.** *Comm. v. Scott*, 464 Mass. 355 (2013) (minor laceration of liver insufficient for serious bodily injury because, without medical testimony, the jury could not know whether the laceration had a significant effect on liver function).

Voluntary intoxication is no defense to A&B. If the defendant voluntarily ingested alcohol or drugs, he is responsible for his condition and cannot use it as an excuse for hitting someone. *Comm. v. Malone*, 114 Mass. 295 (1873).

Disciplinary privilege for children. The law recognizes a limited defense to A&B when the adult striking the child is acting as a parent and using "reasonable" force. *Comm. v. Rubeck*, 64 Mass. App. Ct. 396 (2005). For detailed discussion, see *LED's Juvenile Law, Chapter 9*.

Public educators may not strike students. Massachusetts law outlaws the use of physical discipline — known as "corporal punishment" — by public school officials, *unless* they are acting in self-defense. 71, § 37G. See *LED's Juvenile Law, Chapter 16*.

The police privilege permits officers to use reasonable and necessary force in their duties. *Comm. v. Garvey*, 99 Mass. App. Ct. 139 (2021) (the defendant, a police officer, used OC spray and a baton against a citizen who was not resisting arrest; the officer's force was excessive;

as a result, the officer was properly convicted). For police use of force guidelines, see *LED's Criminal Procedure*, Chapter 6.

Lesser included offense. Every A&B includes an assault as a lesser included offense. *Comm. v. Burke*, 390 Mass. 480 (1983).

A&B BY DANGEROUS WEAPON (ABDW) 265, § 15A

Elements

- **A&B.** The suspect committed an A&B by: (1) an intentional, unconsented touching; (2) an intentional, harmful touching; or (3) a reckless act that caused injury.
- **Dangerous weapon.** By means of a dangerous weapon.

Right of Arrest

Felony.

Penalty

Basic: SP NMT 10 yrs or HC NMT 2½ yrs; or Fine NMT $5,000.

Aggravated: SP NMT 15 yrs or HC NMT 2½ yrs; and/or Fine NMT $10,000. ABDW becomes an aggravated offense if the perpetrator:

- Is 18 years old or older and commits an ABDW on a child under the age of 14; or
- Causes *serious bodily injury* to a victim of any age, which means "bodily injury that results in: (1) a permanent disfigurement; (2) loss or impairment of a bodily function, limb or organ; or (3) a substantial risk of death"; or
- Commits the crime against a person who he knows, or has reason to know, is *pregnant*; or
- Commits the crime against a person who has an outstanding restraining order in effect against the defendant at the time of the attack.

Notes

Slightly touching the victim with a weapon is sufficient if the contact was intended as an assault. *Comm. v. Mercado*, 24 Mass. App. Ct. 391 (1987).

On the other hand, the suspect's intent is irrelevant when dangerous contact occurs. Consider the strange case of *Comm. v. Appleby*, 380 Mass. 296 (1980): After receiving melted ice cream from his servant, the defendant took out his riding crop and beat him "with the intent to turn him on sexually." Even if sexual enjoyment was the goal, the defendant's use of an object in this dangerous fashion was a crime.

A more recent case, *Comm. v. Leonard*, 90 Mass. App. Ct. 187 (2016), makes the same point. A daughter hosted a party for her 16 year old friends. Her mother, Julie Leonard, came home and drank alcohol with them. One guest, Susan, became ill and stayed overnight. The next morning, Susan could not stop vomiting. Julie Leonard used a syringe to inject Susan with "medicine" she had taken from her job at a nursing home. She claimed it would stop the vomiting. Leonard's use of a syringe to administer a drug to a teenager turned it into a dangerous weapon. As a minor, Susan could not consent to this behavior.

The suspect commits ABDW if he causes the victim to fear attack, and she injures herself trying to escape. *Comm. v. Parker,* 25 Mass. App. Ct. 727 (1988) (defendant broke into his ex-wife's house, forced her onto the couch, lit a cigarette, and displayed a razor; she struggled and her face was burned and her hand cut badly).

If based on reckless conduct, the ABDW must cause injury. *Comm. v. Taber,* 2012 WL 177769 (Appeals Court): Mark Taber's wife went to a neighbor's house crying and bleeding. Taber came by and said, "I'm sorry . . . I didn't mean to do it." Police arrived and observed the victim bleeding from her head. She had a fractured skull. Officers went to the apartment where the victim and Taber lived. In the living room, they noticed blood splatter on the floor and a folded television table. Taber claimed he threw the table out of frustration and *accidentally* hit the victim. His version was still enough for conviction. Throwing a table near the victim was reckless. She suffered injury. Also see *Comm. v. Fettes,* 64 Mass. App. Ct. 917 (2005) (even though he denied doing it on purpose, the defendant recklessly allowed his dog to attack and bite his landlord's hand).

ABDW may involve either a "per se" or "dangerous use" weapon. *Comm. v. Barrett,* 386 Mass. 649 (1980) (aerosol can sprayed in eyes of victim). *Comm. v. Gallison,* 383 Mass. 659 (1981) (lit cigarette). *Comm. v. Cruz,* 430 Mass. 182 (1999) (duct tape became weapon when applied to the mouth and nose of a hostage). *Comm. v. Cruzado,* 73 Mass. App. Ct. 803 (2009) (defendant struck victim with his stolen vehicle).

The weapon must come into contact with the victim. Usually, the suspect directly strikes the victim, but ABDW may result from indirect force — e.g., suspect intentionally pushes a barrel into another barrel which strikes the victim. *Comm. v. Moffett,* 383 Mass. 201 (1981).

The suspect does not have to hold or control the weapon. *Comm. v. Sexton,* 425 Mass. 146 (1997) (defendant banged victim's head on the floor; the floor was used as a weapon).

The suspect does not have to consciously use the object as a weapon.

- *Comm. v. Bior,* 88 Mass. App. Ct. 150 (2015): Akur Bior and Mary Deng had a long, strained relationship. When Bior entered the church kitchen where Deng was making tea and doughnuts, they began to argue and throw things at each other. Bior picked up a thermos of hot water with an unsecured top and threw it at Deng, causing serious burns. The hot water was the dangerous weapon, not the thermos itself. Bior knew there was water inside based on its weight, and knew that the water was hot because Deng had been using it to make tea. Even if Bior did not intend to burn Deng, throwing hot water in a container with an unsecured top has the potential to cause serious injury. Whether an object is a dangerous weapon turns on the way it is used, not on the offender's intent.

- *Comm. v. McIntosh,* 56 Mass. App. Ct. 827 (2002): The defendant and his fraternity brothers ran after several youths who had attacked their friend earlier. One of the chased individuals went into a dorm. Frustrated by the locked door preventing further pursuit, McIntosh clasped his hands together and smashed the large glass window in the door. The blow sent shards of glass flying, which severely cut two students who happened to be walking by. Even though McIntosh did not control the glass as a weapon, and even though he did not intentionally harm these students, he was still convicted of ABDW because his reckless conduct produced the injuries.

Unseen weapon. As with ADW, a suspect who claims to have a weapon may be taken at his word, if his claim was reasonably believed and the victim felt an object. *Comm. v. Hastings*, 22 Mass. App. Ct. 930 (1986) (victim felt sharp object against her neck, and suspect convincingly claimed to have a knife).

No need to specify or produce dangerous weapon. Producing the weapon at trial or identifying the type of weapon is *not* required. Even if the victim is unaware that a weapon was used, officers may still charge ABDW on the basis of the wounds. *Comm. v. Liakos*, 12 Mass. App. Ct. 57 (1981) (use of weapon, though never found, could be inferred from the victim's wounds requiring hundreds of stitches). *Comm. v. Marrero*, 19 Mass. App. Ct. 921 (1984) (victim's chest bore the mark of a footprint, indicating that the defendant wore boots and used them as a weapon).

Human hands, teeth or other body parts are not dangerous weapons, but a "shod foot" is. *Comm. v. Davis*, 10 Mass. App. Ct. 190 (1980).

- **A shoe is a weapon if capable of causing greater injury than an unshod foot.** *Comm. v. Zawatsky*, 41 Mass. App. Ct. 392 (1996) (no need to prove exactly what kind of shoes were worn by the defendant, especially when the victim's injuries indicated that some sort of footwear aggravated the attack). *Comm. v. Fernandez*, 43 Mass. App. Ct. 313 (1997).

- **While an "unadorned hand" is not a dangerous weapon, a large ring may be — depending on how it is used.** *Comm. v. Rossi*, 19 Mass. App. Ct. 257 (1985) (when victim refused to take off her clothes, defendant beat her while wearing a large ring, which was probably responsible for breaking one tooth and gashing her forehead).

Victim does not need to be named. The complaint must identify a human victim, although not necessarily by name. The victim may be referred to as a person, pedestrian, or bystander in the rare case where no further identifying information is available. *Comm. v. Wilson*, 72 Mass. App. Ct. 416 (2008).

Precise actions of each accomplice need not be shown. *Comm. v. Belmonte*, 4 Mass. App. Ct. 506 (1976) (evidence showed that all three defendants had, at the very least, beaten the off-duty police officer; this demonstrated a concerted enterprise on their part; they could all be convicted as accomplices to ABDW, even though it could not be precisely shown who had kicked him). *Comm. v. Thornton T.*, 2012 WL 6553961 (Appeals Court) (security guard's testimony that he saw all four juveniles pick up rocks before he turned to run away was sufficient evidence that they all threw rocks at him).

Lesser included offenses. ABDW has lesser included offenses of assault, ADW, and A&B.

Related Offenses

Attempted A&B by Discharging any Firearm, Rifle, Shotgun, or Machine Gun. Basically, shooting and missing someone. Penalty: SP NMT 15 yrs or HC NMT 2½ yrs; and/or Fine NMT $10,000. Right of Arrest: Felony.

A&B by Discharging any Firearm, Rifle, Shotgun, or Machine Gun. Shooting and hitting someone. Penalty: SP NMT 20 yrs or HC NMT 2½ yrs; and/or Fine NMT $10,000. Right of Arrest: Felony. Of course, assault with intent to murder may be charged in most of these situations. *Comm. v. Brule*, 98 Mass. App. Ct. 89 (2020). See *Chapter 6*.

A&B to Collect a Loan. 265, § 13C prohibits committing an A&B to collect a loan. *1ˢᵗ offense:* SP NLT 3 yrs, NMT 5 yrs or HC NMT 2½ yrs. *2ⁿᵈ or more:* SP NLT 5 yrs, NMT 10 yrs (mandatory minimum 5 yrs). Right of Arrest: Felony. It makes no difference whether the offender is attempting to collect a legal or illegal loan. *Comm. v. Thompson*, 56 Mass. App. Ct. 710 (2002) (defendant convicted for beating up a dealer who failed to pay him back for the drugs he supplied). *Comm. v. White*, 5 Mass. App. Ct. 483 (1977) (no defense that defendant was actually owed the money).

A&B for Purpose of Gang Solicitation. This statute is designed to prevent violent gang solicitation of children under 18. 265, § 44 makes it a crime to: (1) commit an A&B on a child under 18; (2) with the intent to cause or coerce the child to join or participate in a criminal conspiracy — which is defined as a street gang or other organization of 3 or more persons, with a common name, identifying symbol or sign, and whose members individually or collectively engage in criminal activity. Penalty: *1ˢᵗ offense:* SP NLT 3 yrs, NMT 5 yrs or HC NMT 2½ yrs; *2ⁿᵈ or more:* SP NLT 5 yrs, NMT 10 yrs. Right of Arrest: Felony.

Assault with Intent to Commit Felony. 265, § 29. This catch-all offense covers an assault with the intent to commit any felony. Penalty: SP NMT 10 yrs; or HC NMT 2½ yrs and Fine NMT $1,000. Right of Arrest: Felony.

Catalogue of Assault and A&B: From Misdemeanor to Felony

All statutory citations to 265 unless noted. Chapter (Ch.) references included. Probable cause = PC.

ASSAULT OFFENSES

Basic assault. Arrest for breach of peace in presence. Otherwise, complaint. § 13A. *Ch. 4.*

Hate crime assault (race, religion, sexual orientation). Arrest for breach of peace in presence. Otherwise, complaint. § 39. *Ch. 16.*

Assault constituting "harassment." 258E, § 8 arrest on PC. Charge violation of § 13A. *Ch. 13.*

Assault during domestic violence event. *Ch. 13.*
- Intimate partner (married, common child, dating/engaged): 209A, § 6 arrest on PC. Charge violation of § 13M.
- Family or household member (related or living together): 209A, § 6 arrest on PC. Charge violation of § 13A.

A&B OFFENSES

Basic A&B. Arrest for breach of peace in presence. Otherwise, complaint. § 13A. *Ch. 4.*

Hate crime A&B (race, religion, sexual orientation). Arrest for breach of peace in presence. Otherwise, complaint. If injury, felony. § 39. *Ch. 16.*

A&B constituting "harassment." 258E, § 8 arrest on PC. Charge violation of § 13A. *Ch. 13.*

A&B during domestic violence event. *Ch. 13.*
- Intimate partner (married, common child, dating/engaged): 209A, § 6 arrest on PC. Charge violation of § 13M.
- Family or household member (related or living together): 209A, § 6 arrest on PC. Charge violation of § 13A.

A&B public employee. Arrest for breach of peace in presence. Otherwise, complaint. § 13D. *Ch. 5.*
- Public transit operator. § 13D arrest on PC.
- Attempt to disarm police officer. § 13D felony.
- Cause serious bodily injury to officer. § 13D felony.

EMT or health care provider. Arrest for breach of peace in presence. Otherwise, complaint. § 13I. *Ch. 5.*

ASSAULT OFFENSES	A&B OFFENSES
Assault with aggravating factor offenses: All felonies. • Unarmed assault with intent to rob or steal. § 20. *Ch. 26.* • Assault with intent to murder or maim. § 15. *Ch. 6.* • Assault with intent to commit any felony. § 29. See *Notes.* • Armed assault with intent to rob or murder. § 18. *Chs. 6, 26.* • Armed assault in a dwelling. § 18A. *Ch. 31.* • Against person with restraining order. § 13A. *Chs. 4, 13.* • Subsequent assault against intimate partner. § 13M. *Ch. 13.* ***Assault with Intent to Rape:*** Felony. § 24 (any person), § 24B (child under 16). *Ch. 9.* ***Attempted Indecent A&B.*** Felony. 274, § 6. *Comm. v. Marzilli*, 457 Mass. 64 (2010). *Ch. 9.* ***Assault with a Dangerous Weapon (ADW).*** Felony. § 15B. *Ch. 4.* ***Assault w/ Hypodermic Syringe/Needle.*** Felony. § 15C. *Ch. 20.* ***Attempted A&B by Discharging Gun.*** Felony. § 15F. See *Notes.*	***A&B with aggravating factor offenses:*** All felonies. • Child under 14 if cause bodily injury. § 13J. *Ch. 14.* • Collect loan (legal or illegal debt is covered). § 13C. See *Notes.* • Correctional officer. 127, § 38B. *Ch. 5.* • Disabled person. § 13K. *Ch. 14.* • Elder age 60 and over. § 13K. *Ch. 14. Comm. v. Lockwood*, 95 Mass. App. Ct. 189 (2019) (defendant pushed 63 year old foster mother to try to remove his young children; 13K is always a felony). • Gang solicitation of child under 18. § 44. See *Notes.* • Intellectually disabled person. § 13F. *Ch. 14.* • Pregnant person. § 13A. *Ch. 4.* • Against person with restraining order. § 13A. *Ch. 4.* • Serious bodily injury (causing). § 13A. *Ch. 4* • Subsequent A&B against intimate partner. § 13M. *Ch. 13.* • Suffocates or strangles another person. § 15D. *Ch. 13.* ***Indecent A&B.*** Felony. § 13B (child under 14), § 13H (person 14 and over). *Ch. 9.* ***A&B with a Dangerous Weapon (ABDW).*** Felony. § 15A. *Ch. 4.* ***A&B w/ Hypodermic Syringe/Needle.*** Felony. § 15C. *Ch. 20.* ***A&B by Discharging Gun.*** Felony. § 15E. See *Notes.*

MAYHEM
265, § 14

Summary

It is the most graphic name for a crime. Mayhem is an assault in which the perpetrator has a cruel state of mind — the desire to maim or disfigure.

Elements

Type 1: Specific Acts

- The suspect maliciously intended to maim or disfigure; and
- Committed one of the following acts to the victim:
  - Cut out or maimed the tongue;
  - Put out or destroyed an eye;
  - Cut or tore off an ear;
  - Cut, slit or mutilated the nose or lip; or
  - Cut off or disabled a limb or member of the victim.

Type 2: Dangerous Substance or Weapon

- The suspect maliciously intended to maim or disfigure; and
- Assaulted the victim with a dangerous weapon or substance; and
- Disfigured, crippled or inflicted serious or permanent physical injury.

Type 3: Privy

The suspect was privy to someone else's intent to maim or disfigure, or was present and aided in the commission of this crime.

Right of Arrest

Felony.

Penalty

SP NMT 20 yrs; or HC NMT 2½ yrs and Fine NMT $1,000.

Notes

Maim. The word "maim" has no technical meaning. In its ordinary sense, it means to disable, wound, or cause disfigurement. *Comm. v. Farrell*, 322 Mass. 606 (1948).

Specific intent to maim. Regardless of the manner in which the crime is committed, the suspect must possess a specific intent to maim or disfigure. *Comm. v. Farrell*, 322 Mass. 606 (1948) (the defendant held the victim captive in a hotel room for several hours, where he repeatedly slashed her with a safety razor and burned his initials into her skin). *Comm. v. Ogden O.*, 448 Mass. 798 (2007) (10 year old defendant had intent to maim when he lit victim's pants on fire).

- **A prolonged attack is not necessary.** *Comm. v. Mendoza*, 2014 WL 4782821 (Appeals Court) (the defendant, upset that the victim danced with her boyfriend, slashed the victim's face with a knife; although the incident was over in seconds, the defendant's repeated slashing resulted in 18 stitches and a permanent scar; her aim was to disfigure because she was jealous of her boyfriend's sexual attraction towards the victim).

- **Not every ABDW that results in serious injury supports mayhem.** *Comm. v. Johnson*, 60 Mass. App. Ct. 243 (2003) (single strike with beer bottle in the midst of a brief bar fight, which nearly severed the victim's ear, was insufficient to show an intent to maim). Compare *Comm. v. Lay*, 63 Mass. App. Ct. 27 (2005) (although a sustained attack is usually the case, it is not required; here, the defendant removed a metal pipe from his sleeve and struck the victim once with such force "that blood and brain matter sprayed out").

Three types of prohibited conduct.

- **Type 1: Specific acts.** The suspect must: (1) cut out or maim the tongue; (2) put out or destroy an eye; (3) cut or tear off an ear; (4) cut, slit or mutilate the nose or lip; or (5) cut off or disable a limb or member. Unlike the second type of mayhem, this first style of attack does *not* require the use of a dangerous weapon. *Comm. v. Forbes*, 86 Mass. App. Ct. 197 (2014) (defendant bit the victim's ear with enough force to tear off a very tough piece of cartilage, despite a crowd trying to hold him back).

- **Type 2: Dangerous substance or weapon.** The suspect must assault the victim with a dangerous weapon, substance, or chemical. *Comm. v. Mercado*, 24 Mass. App. Ct. 391 (1987) (defendant used a bat to smack the head of an unconscious victim). *Comm. v. Tavares*, 61 Mass. App. Ct. 385 (2004) (expert testimony established that defendants had thrown some type of chemical agent — such as a household soap, cleaner, or bleach — into a child's eyes). *Comm. v. Tucceri*, 9 Mass. App. Ct. 844 (1980) (defendant rubbed handfuls of dirt into the victim's eyes and repeatedly struck the right side of her face near the eye; when applied to such a delicate organ, dirt becomes a dangerous weapon).

  The attack must disfigure, cripple, or inflict serious injury. Remember, the fact that the victim completely recovers does *not* prevent a charge of mayhem. *Comm. v. Tavares, supra.*

- **Type 3: Privy.** As with all other offenses, a suspect may be guilty of mayhem if he participates as an accomplice. This statute also allows a suspect to be found guilty if he is *privy* to mayhem. In short, privy means that the suspect is aware of the impending attack and agrees that it should occur. Under this theory, officers must prove that the suspect — although he was not present during the crime — nonetheless shared the malicious intent of the attackers.

It is not enough if the suspect intends for someone to be beaten. *Comm. v. Hogan*, 379 Mass. 190 (1979) (Hogan stayed in the car while his two co-defendants entered an apartment with clubs and beat the victim; the evidence did not warrant Hogan's conviction of mayhem because he did not know his co-defendants intended to disfigure the victim; Hogan was, however, an accomplice to ABDW).

Related Offense

Assault with Intent to Murder or Maim. 265, § 15. Penalty: SP NMT 10 yrs; or HC NMT 2½ yrs and Fine NMT $1,000. Right of Arrest: Felony. *Comm. v. Diaz*, 53 Mass. App. Ct. 209 (2001).

SELF-DEFENSE

Purpose & Summary

The law recognizes that sometimes it is appropriate for a person to use force to defend himself or other people. Once a defendant introduces evidence that he acted in self-defense, the Commonwealth must prove *beyond a reasonable doubt* that he did not. *Comm. v. Alebord*, 49 Mass. App. Ct. 915 (2000).

Self-defense is warranted if the suspect reasonably:

- **Believes that he is in danger of personal harm;**
- **Attempts to avoid physical combat or is unable to do so;** and
- **Uses only the force necessary under the circumstances.** *Karamanoglu v. Yarmouth, Maine*, 15 F.4th 82 (1st Cir. 2021) (officer's rejection of defendant's self-defense claim followed his effective investigation and exercise of reasonable judgment).

Nondeadly Force

Personal safety, protect property, or eject trespasser. Reasonable concern over one's personal safety is the proper standard when nondeadly force is used. *Comm. v. Baseler*, 419 Mass. 500 (1995). Nondeadly force may also be used to eject a trespasser or to protect one's property. *Comm. v. Dougherty*, 107 Mass. 243 (1871).

Deadly Force

Imminent danger of death or serious injury. In contrast, a person may only resort to deadly force when he reasonably believes that he is in imminent danger of death or serious bodily injury. *Comm. v. Harrington*, 379 Mass. 446 (1980).

Factors

Overall factors. In assessing a self-defense claim, officers must consider:

- **Physical ability of combatants.** *Comm. v. Oran*, 17 Mass. App. Ct. 941 (1983) (less drastic means of self-defense possible since defendant was karate expert). *Comm. v. Torres*, 468 Mass. 286 (2014) (victim much smaller than defendant).

- **Assailant's prior use of force against others.** *Comm. v. Morales*, 464 Mass. 302 (2013) (if defendant introduces evidence of prior bad acts by the victim to show he was the aggressor, the prosecutor may introduce evidence of prior bad acts by the defendant for the same purpose). *Comm. v. Amaral*, 78 Mass. App. Ct. 557 (2011) (boxing or martial arts history is not proof that someone is likely to be aggressive).

- **Characteristics of any weapons used.**

- **Available means of escape.**

- **Legitimate belief of danger.** *Comm. v. Alebord*, 49 Mass. App. Ct. 915 (2000) (a "highly active imagination" does not justify self-defense).

Mutual combat. In the case of mutually agreed combat, the law does not allow a claim of self-defense unless a weapon or other type of force is unexpectedly introduced into the brawl. Then, the person on the receiving end may be justified in using force to meet the threat. *Comm. v. Barber*, 18 Mass. App. Ct. 460 (1984).

Instigator of fight. Although unusual, it is possible that the instigator of a fight may be justified in resorting to self-defense if he "makes known his intention to retire and withdraws in good faith." *Comm. v. Griffith*, 404 Mass. 256 (1989).

Battered Woman Syndrome. A woman's use of deadly force against her abusive partner may be best understood by allowing evidence of the history of the relationship; and expert testimony on the common patterns of abusive relationships. *Comm. v. Rodriguez*, 418 Mass. 1 (1994).

Duty to Retreat

The right of self-defense does not exist until a person has reasonably tried to avoid combat. "A stubborn unwillingness to walk away, even in the face of a perceived affront to a defendant's manhood, does not equate with an inability to retreat." *Comm. v. Toon*, 55 Mass App. Ct. 642 (2002). *Comm. v. Mercado*, 456 Mass. 198 (2010) (no self-defense where the defendant left and came back with a gun). *Comm. v. Figueroa*, 2012 WL 5951838 (Appeals Court) (no self-defense where defendant could have escaped in his car, which was running with the driver's door open).

Only exception is "Castle law." Under 278, § 8A, occupants in their home have no duty to retreat. They may use reasonable force to defend themselves or others against unlawful intruders. *Comm. v. Doucette*, 391 Mass. 443 (1984).

- **The intruder must be *inside* home.** *Comm. v. Gagne*, 367 Mass. 519 (1975) (duty to retreat still applies to a place of business). *Comm. v. McKinnon*, 446 Mass. 263 (2006) (no castle law protection when defendant ran outside with a baseball bat and fought with the victims on his front porch and stairs). *Comm. v. Bennett*, 41 Mass. App. Ct. 920 (1996) (the castle law does not include a driveway).

- **The duty to retreat still exists when a homeowner is confronted by a guest or visitor.** *Comm. v. Lapointe*, 402 Mass. 321 (1988).

- **Castle law never justifies force against police officer.** Citizens *only* have a right of self-defense if an officer uses excessive force. *Comm. v. Peterson*, 53 Mass. App. Ct. 388 (2001).

Defense of Others

A person may use the same force to protect another that he could use to protect himself.

- **This rule encourages people to aid third parties who are in danger.** *Comm. v. Kivelehan*, 57 Mass. App. Ct. 793 (2003) (a mother and her son came to the defense of her daughter when she was being beaten by a rival girlfriend outside their home; jury had to decide whether the mother and son's actions were defensive or an assault on the daughter's rival).

- **One may not intervene to retaliate.** *Comm. v. Lopez*, 474 Mass. 690 (2016) (the defendant shot his girlfriend's former boyfriend after a verbal confrontation at her house; he could not claim defense of another because the ex-boyfriend had not assaulted her and was simply talking outside the front door when the defendant shot him without warning). *Comm. v. Adams*, 458 Mass. 766 (2011) (the defendant claimed that he was protecting his sister when he shot the victim, but his sister had voluntarily entered the brawl to begin with; also, the person who he shot was walking away from the scene of the fight).

- **One may not assist a criminal.** *Comm. v. Freeman*, 2012 WL 1672484 (Appeals Court) (defendant could not claim defense of another when he stepped in to defend his brother, who was engaged in an armed robbery of the victim; committing an armed robbery forfeits any claim of self-defense).

Defense of Accident

If a suspect claims that he did not mean to use force, this is the "accident defense." An accident is "an unexpected happening that occurs without intention or design on a person's part." *Comm. v. Ferguson*, 30 Mass. App. Ct. 580 (1991). Once the defendant raises the possibility of an accident, the Commonwealth must prove that the assault or shooting was intentional. For example, in *Comm. v. Power-Koch*, 69 Mass. App. Ct. 735 (2007), Andrew Power-Koch shot and killed Sean Howard, his best friend. He claimed Howard had been depressed for some time and had asked Power-Koch to shoot him. Power-Koch said he held the gun up but realized he "just couldn't do it." Suddenly, the gun discharged and killed Howard. Tape-recorded interviews of Power-Koch on the night of the shooting proved it was an accident. He was unfamiliar with guns, did not know the gun was loaded, and tried to get Howard help after he shot him.

5: Police Protection & the Arrest Function

Section I
INTERFERENCE WITH DUTY

A&B ON A PUBLIC EMPLOYEE
265, § 13D

Elements

- **A&B.** The suspect committed an A&B;

- **Public employee.** Against any public employee;

- **Duty.** Who the suspect knew was engaged in the performance of his or her duty.

Right of Arrest

Basic: Arrest for breach of peace in presence. Otherwise, complaint.

If A&B occurred when the public employee was operating a public transit vehicle: 265, § 13D warrantless arrest on probable cause.

If A&B included an attempt to disarm a police officer or caused serious injury: Felony.

Penalty

Basic: HC NLT 90 days, NMT 2½ yrs; or Fine NLT $500, NMT $5,000.

Transit interference: Same as above.

Attempt to disarm officer: SP NMT 10 yrs; or HC NMT 2½ yrs and Fine NMT $1,000. *Note:* § 13M does not define the term "disarm" or state whether it relates only to a firearm or to all police equipment. Until court clarification, this author recommends applying this law to any effort to obtain implements from an officer (e.g., OC, taser, baton, handcuffs).

Serious bodily injury to officer: SP NLT 1 year, NMT 10 yrs, or HC NLT 1 year, NMT 2½ yrs; and/or Fine NLT $500, NMT $10,000. Mandatory minimum 1 year. Serious bodily injury results in permanent disfigurement, protracted loss or impairment of a bodily function, limb or organ or substantial risk of death (same standard as felony A&B under 265, § 13A). *Important note:* Prosecution for ABPO serious bodily injury may only be in superior court.

Notes

Knowledge. The suspect must know he is striking a public employee. It is sufficient if the officer verbally identified himself, or was wearing a uniform and badge. *Comm. v. Wright*, 158 Mass. 149 (1893). *Comm. v. Moore*, 36 Mass. App. Ct. 455 (1994).

Engaged in performance of duty. The employee must be carrying out an official function.

- **Officers covered when outside their jurisdiction and providing aid.** *Comm. v. McCrohan*, 34 Mass. App. Ct. 277 (1993).

- **Off-duty officers covered when performing a police function.** *Comm. v. Williams*, 53 Mass. App. Ct. 719 (2002) (defendant assaulted a uniformed officer; luckily, an off-duty officer intervened and managed to subdue the defendant after both officers were struck several times; defendant was properly convicted of separate counts for striking both the on-duty and off-duty officers).

- **Officers' lack of arrest authority is no defense, as long as they were engaged in a legitimate police function.** *Comm. v. McCrohan, supra.*

Spitting on a police officer is A&B on a public employee. *Comm. v. Ciccolini*, 2018 WL 1801638 (Appeals Court) (Ciccolini pushed Officer Pepple in the chest and spit on her with bloody saliva).

Reckless conduct. Conviction may be based on reckless conduct causing physical injury. *Comm. v. Correia*, 50 Mass. App. Ct. 455 (2000) (fight in jail resulted in injury to a correctional officer).

Defendant may claim self-defense if officers used excessive force. *Comm. v. Eberle*, 81 Mass. App. Ct. 235 (2012) (while he was on the ground in excruciating pain, defendant claimed officers were "trying to rip my arms out of their sockets").

A prosecutor may agree to dismiss a criminal case in exchange for the defendant's agreement not to sue police. These so-called "release-dismissal agreements" serve the public interest of not having to devote time and resources to the defense of litigation — provided that the defendant voluntarily agrees and the prosecutor is not attempting to cover up police misconduct. *Grant v. John Hancock Insurance Co.*, 183 F.Supp.2d 344 (2002). *Rumery v. Town of Newton*, 480 U.S. 386 (1987) (defendant should be able to decide that the benefits of escaping criminal prosecution outweigh the benefits of a future civil action).

Assault is a lesser included offense of A&B on a public employee. *Comm. v. Hurley*, 99 Mass. 433 (1868).

Related Offenses

Federal officer, including deputized task force officer. *Comm. v. Luna*, 2011 WL 3527221 (Appeals Court) (a local police officer, deputized as a member of a federal task force, is a "federal officer" protected by 18 U.S.C. § 111. This statute prohibits assaulting or interfering with a federal officer. In this case, a Chelsea detective, serving on a federal gang task force, was shot at by a fleeing suspect during surveillance at a Chelsea parade).

EMT or health care provider. Under 265, § 13I, a person may not: (1) commit an assault or A&B; (2) against any emergency medical technician (EMT), ambulance operator, ambulance attendant, or health care provider; (3) who was treating or transporting a person in the line of duty. Penalty: HC NLT 90 days, NMT 2½ yrs; and/or Fine NLT $500, NMT $5,000. Right of Arrest: Arrest for breach of peace in presence. Otherwise, complaint.

The suspect must commit the assault or A&B while the EMT, attendant or health care provider is treating or transporting a patient. Note the suspect does not need to be the person being treated. The suspect must simply interfere with treatment or transport.

Health care provider is defined by 111, § 1 as any medical doctor, dentist, registered nurse, social worker, psychologist, or agent or employee of a licensed public or private hospital, clinic, or nursing home.

Correctional officer. Although a correctional officer would clearly be covered under 265, § 13D, which applies to public employees, there is an additional statute that pertains to assaults within the penal system. 127, § 38B (Felony).

INTERFERING WITH A POLICE OFFICER
Common Law Crime

Elements

- **Knowledge.** The suspect knew, or should have known, the officer was engaged in the lawful performance of duty; and

- **Obstruction.** Physically obstructed or threatened violence against the officer;

- **Intent.** With the intent of obstructing or hindering the officer in the performance of duty.

Right of Arrest & Procedure

Arrest for breach of peace in presence. Officers may legally seek a complaint, but it undercuts their argument that the defendant was significantly interfering with them at the time.

Procedure. Although not defined by statute, Massachusetts recognizes this and other common law crimes. In fact, interfering is listed on page 1 of the *District Court Complaint Manual*. Prior to arraignment, on the standard complaint form, instead of inserting statute numbers, officers should simply write "common law offense."

Penalty

279, § 5 imposes "a reasonable sentence" for any crime whose penalty has not been established by statute. Typically, judges impose HC NMT 6 months; and/or Fine NMT $200 for interfering.

Notes

Interfering with a police officer requires <u>physical obstruction</u> or <u>threats of violence</u>. In *Comm. v. Adams*, 482 Mass. 514 (2019), the police department suspended Mark Adams' license to carry firearms. Officers went to Adams' home to serve the suspension notice and retrieve his 15 firearms and ammunition. Even though officers had been enforcing this crime for centuries, *Adams* was the first SJC decision to discuss its application. Here, Adams may have been upset and argumentative, but he did not physically obstruct officers from carrying out their duty. He simply tried to go back into his house; he did not prevent them from entering. His statements did not constitute a threat of violence either. Therefore, the SJC overturned his conviction for interfering.

Physical obstruction covers more than force.

- **Refuse to move.** At a certain point, refusing to move is obstruction. Examples include: a juvenile runaway who will not accompany an officer trying to bring him home or to a shelter; an incapacitated person who refuses transport in an ambulance when placed into protective custody; and an individual who insists he will not evacuate a building following a bomb threat or during an active fire alarm.

- **Verbally interrupt in a loud and persistent manner.** A form of physical obstruction occurs when individuals verbally interrupt even after several police warnings. In *King v. Ambs*, 519 F.3d 607 (6th Cir. 2008), Officer Ambs found an unlocked vehicle improperly parked with marijuana on the dash. As Officer Ambs began his inventory, King left a nearby house and asked the officer why he was searching the vehicle. Officer Ambs followed King back to the home and knocked on the front door. Klein answered. As Officer Ambs attempted to question Klein, King told Klein twice not to speak. Officer Ambs threatened to arrest King if he interrupted again. King again told Klein to stay silent. Officer Ambs arrested King for opposing an officer in the performance of his duty. The court ruled that King's verbal interference was a physical interruption of questioning, which provided probable cause for the arrest. Also see *Colten v. Kentucky*, 407 U.S. 104 (1972) (officer asked Colten eight times to stop verbally interrupting his effort to issue a citation to a driver).[1]

Videotaping officers is <u>not</u> interfering unless it is done in a manner that physically hinders police.

Verbal criticism directed at the police is typically <u>not</u> interfering unless it includes a threat of violence. Remember, this crime covers threats of violence, but not other types of threats — e.g., "I'll sue you, officer!" Or, "I know the Chief. I'll have your badge for this!"

A suspect's refusal to identify himself is <u>not</u> interfering. Unless an officer has some specific statute to rely on, like 90, § 25,[2] there is <u>no general law</u> requiring suspects to identify

---

[1] In *Comm. v. Woodward*, 10-P-801, Sergeant Mark O'Brien and Officer Centrullo of the Reading Police went to investigate a domestic disturbance. Royal Woodward, the husband, was so loud, hostile, and uncooperative that the officers could not even interview his wife. After numerous de-escalation efforts, the officers arrested Woodward for interfering. He was convicted by a jury, but died while his appeal was pending. As a result, the Appeals Court never provided an official decision.

[2] Of course 90, § 25 requires that a vehicle operator stop and provide his license and registration to a police officer on demand — or face arrest. Similar statutes regulate recreational vehicle and boat operators. 90B, §§ 26 and 38. Bicyclists who fail to identify themselves when stopped by police are subject to arrest. 85, § 11E. There is even a statute that covers people who litter. 272, § 60.

themselves when detained by police. Suspects who refuse to identify themselves can limit police action. For example, when officers have probable cause but lack a right of arrest, not having the person's name prevents them from applying for a criminal complaint. Similarly, officers cannot issue a ticket to someone who has committed a civil marijuana infraction unless the person gives their name. The same holds true for a passenger failing to wear his seatbelt. An arrest for "interfering" in these and other situations is simply not an option.

Until the legislature addresses this problem,[3] the author advises:

- **Consider whether probable cause supports an arrestable offense** — e.g., officers are focused on a non-arrestable A&B, but they realize they also have probable cause for the felony of defacing property under 266, 126A. Do not overreach, but this is worth considering.

- **If officers truly do not have a right of arrest for the incident under investigation** (e.g., threats under 275, § 2), officers should:

  - *Use their power of persuasion* and explain to the defendant that they need to ID him truthfully in order to let him leave (this works a lot); and, if this effort is unsuccessful, then:

  - *Prolong the detention in order to take further ID steps* (officers can certainly justify at least 30 minutes depending on the severity of the crime); and

  - *Take a photo of the suspect on scene* and explain to the defendant that they may seek an arrest warrant that can be executed at the defendant's home. Officers can use their cell phone camera. This is easy. Moreover, this step will often persuade a suspect to identify himself; and

  - *Take fingerprints in the field.* Officers may do this during an investigative detention. See *Hayes v. Florida*, 470 U.S. 811 (1985).

Police duty incorporates more than arrests. This law goes way beyond "resisting arrest." *Comm. v. Shave*, 2012 WL 1414999 (Appeals Court) (a father and son got into a physical altercation with an officer in uniform investigating a motor vehicle accident; the officer was clearly performing his duty; it was irrelevant whether an arrest was happening at the time).

NEGLECT OR REFUSAL TO ASSIST OFFICER
268, § 24

Elements

- **Required by police.** A person who was required by a police officer or deputy sheriff;

- **Neglected or refused assistance.** Neglected or refused to assist the officer in apprehending or securing of a person for a breach of the peace or for an escape.

---

[3] What compounds the difficulty of identifying non-compliant suspects in Massachusetts is the SJC's rule prohibiting officers from searching for identification before or after an arrest [*Comm. v. Blevines*, 438 Mass. 604 (2003)] or during a motor vehicle stop [*Comm. v. Santos*, 65 Mass. App. Ct. 122 (2005)].

Right of Arrest

Arrest for breach of peace in presence. Otherwise, complaint.

Penalty

HC NMT 1 month; or Fine NMT $50.

Notes

Law still valid. This law, enacted in 1795, was discussed in *Comm. v. Morrissey*, 422 Mass. 1 (1996). While *Morrissey* dealt with a jurisdiction issue, the SJC acknowledged this statute is still applicable and provides officers with a tool to compel citizen assistance when necessary.

Section II
THE ARREST FUNCTION

RESISTING ARREST
268, § 32B

Purpose

268, § 32B punishes an arrestee who uses force, threats, or another dangerous method to resist arrest. It also penalizes a person who prevents, or attempts to prevent, the arrest of another.

Elements

- ***Prevent or attempt.*** The suspect knowingly prevented or attempted to prevent;

- ***Police officer.*** A police officer in the regular course of his assigned duties, who was in uniform or, if out of uniform, who properly identified himself by displaying his credentials;

- ***Arrest.*** From effecting an arrest of:
    - The actor; or
    - Another person;

- ***Force, threat, risk of injury.*** By using against the police officer or another person:
    - Physical force or the threat of physical force; or
    - Any other means that creates a substantial risk of bodily injury.

Right of Arrest

Of course, since officers are making an arrest at the time of the resistance, they may continue to do so! In the case of a person who is interfering with the arrest of another, officers may arrest for this obvious breach of peace.

Penalty

HC NMT 2½ yrs; and/or Fine NMT $500.

Notes

The underlying crime for resisting may be A&B on a police officer. *Comm. v. DoSouto*, 2013 WL 436446 (Appeals Court) (during original threshold inquiry, the defendant brushed away the officer's hand, which constituted the arrestable crime of A&B on a police officer; then the resisting occurred when the defendant wrestled with officers and threw punches).

An officer's legal mistake is excused, but excessive force <u>or</u> lack of good faith is not. In *Comm. v. Smith*, 2011 WL 2526328 (Appeals Court), officers unlawfully arrested Smith and Howard for trespassing. While they were in the backseat of the cruiser, Smith removed drugs from his waistband. When officers attempted to get the drugs, Smith bit them and continued to struggle even after being sprayed with OC. Despite the fact that officers lacked probable cause for the original arrest, Smith was properly convicted of resisting.

Under 268, § 32B, it *is* a defense if the officer:

- **Resorted to excessive force.** When an officer uses excessive force, the arrestee may defend himself regardless of whether the arrest is lawful or unlawful. However, the arrestee may not go beyond the point where he has attained his safety. *Comm. v. Graham*, 62 Mass. App. Ct. 642 (2004). *Comm. v. Baptiste*, 2020 WL 2507584 (Appeals Court) (defendant argued excessive force by officers based on his extensive injuries).

- **Lacked good faith.** *Comm. v. Urkiel*, 63 Mass. App. Ct. 445 (2005) concerned a possible lack of good faith when an officer entered the defendant's home to perform a warrantless arrest for a minor restraining order violation. In fact, the prosecutor conceded that the officer lacked exigent circumstances or consent when he entered the defendant's home and became involved in a brawl. The Appeals Court ordered a new trial.

  Compare *Comm. v. Lowrey*, 2021 WL 2644290 (Appeals Court): Following a 911 call from Beverly Beacher, Officer O'Neill arrived to a possible "domestic disturbance." He learned Beacher wanted her spouse, Joanne Lowrey, removed from the apartment so Beacher could feel safe. The women began screaming at each other. Beacher told Lowrey, "You shouldn't hit me," to which Lowrey responded, "Yeah right. Yeah right." When O'Neill initiated an arrest for A&B domestic, Lowrey resisted. Even though the domestic A&B charge was dropped before trial, the resisting arrest charge was not.

Basic legal standard for the proper use of force (UOF). 6E, § 14 and 555 CMR 6.00.[4]

- For all arrests:
  - When de-escalation[5] is not feasible or has failed,
  - Officers may use reasonable and proportionate force to make a lawful arrest.

---

[4] The most detailed discussion of UOF appears in *LED's Criminal Procedure Manual, Chapter 6*.
[5] 6E, § 1 states that de-escalation is a proactive approach to avoid or reduce the need for force. It includes verbal persuasion, warnings, slowing the pace of an incident, waiting out a person, creating distance, and requesting additional resources, such as mental health clinicians.

- **The use of *deadly* force is reasonable when, in addition:**
    - The officer reasonably and *currently* fears imminent death or serious injury for himself or another;
    - There is no substantial risk to bystanders; and
    - If feasible, the officer issues a verbal warning.

- **Following any UOF, officers must provide emergency medical services (if necessary) and file a UOF report.**

Police do not have duty to retreat. Because officers have an obligation to protect their fellow officers and the public, retreat is not an option for an on-duty officer facing a threat of violence. The question is whether the officer had reasonable options other than force. *Comm. v. Asher*, 471 Mass. 580 (2015).

Resisting arrest must occur at some point during the arrest process.

- **The offender must know that officers are making an arrest.** *Comm. v. Deloney-Kelly*, 2014 WL 774980 (Appeals Court): Abriana Deloney-Kelly was walking toward the mall with a metal bat in her hand. When Officer Cotter approached her, she put the bat in her car. Cotter tried to question her, and she screamed at him, drawing a crowd. When she tried to walk away, Cotter told her she was under arrest for disorderly conduct. Deloney-Kelly pulled her arm away and began struggling. Cotter pushed her against a car, while she kicked and spat at him. Cotter took her to the ground. When she grabbed and twisted his groin, he punched her in the face. A second officer helped handcuff her.

    While the exchange began as a threshold inquiry, it turned into an arrest. Cotter told Deloney-Kelly she was under arrest. The court also noted that Cotter did not use excessive force under the circumstances.

- **Conduct before handcuffing and verbal notification can provide notice of arrest.** *Comm. v. Soun*, 82 Mass. App. Ct. 32 (2012): At 3:30 a.m., Officers Gagne and Parousis responded to a disturbance. Brian Soun moved aggressively toward the officers and swore at them. Officer Parousis told Brian to turn around and put his hands behind his back, intending to arrest him. Brian's father, Kevin Soun, placed himself between Brian and the officers. He said repeatedly, "No, that's my son," and refused to step aside. When Officer Gagne tried to help Parousis handcuff Brian, Kevin pushed him hard. Kevin was arrested, then officers completed Brian's arrest.

    The court rejected Kevin's claim that he did not know the police had arrested his son. Kevin would have known that ordering his son to turn around and place his hands behind his back was the initial phase of an arrest.

- **The arrest ends when the subject submits to official authority *or* is placed in a secure location.** *Comm. v. Knight*, 75 Mass. App. Ct. 735 (2009) (although the defendant was handcuffed, he spun, yelled and kicked officers; this was resisting arrest because he had not yet been placed securely in the cruiser).

- **Post-arrest activities do not qualify.** *Comm. v. Dobbins*, 79 Mass. App. Ct. 555 (2011): Kevin Dobbins pushed officers when they tried to handcuff him following his OUI arrest. Once secured in the cruiser, Dobbins kicked the door and the window repeatedly, then swung his fist at officers when they placed him in his cell at the station. While the initial push constituted resisting arrest, Dobbins' post-arrest conduct in the cruiser and station did not.

Sufficient resistance.

- **Physically struggling with police.** *Comm. v. Joyce*, 84 Mass. App. Ct. 574 (2013).

- **Stiffening arms to prevent cuffing.** *Comm. v. Grandison*, 433 Mass. 135 (2001): When one officer tried to handcuff Grandison, he stiffened his arms and was able to pull one free. Grandison never complied with repeated requests to put his hands behind his back.

- **Stiffening body to prevent placement in cruiser.** *Comm. v. Katykhin*, 59 Mass. App. Ct. 261 (2003) (defendant refused several times to get in the cruiser, standing rigidly "like a plank of wood").

- **Using force "in opposition" to officers is resisting unless it is passive, nonviolent protest.** *Comm. v. Gobielle*, 2014 WL 695728 (Appeals Court): After repeatedly warning the defendant that he would be arrested if he did not turn off the ignition to the truck he was driving, the officer began to pull on his arm to forcibly remove him. The defendant resisted arrest by gripping the steering wheel. His behavior was different from the protester who remains limp throughout the arrest process.

- **Flight is not, by itself, resisting arrest. It has to create a substantial risk of injury.** *Comm. v. Sylvia*, 87 Mass. App. Ct. 340 (2015) (at night, defendant led police on a foot chase on a dug-up roadway under construction with various obstacles, dangerous terrain, and the potential for traveling vehicles; this dangerous flight constituted resisting arrest). *Comm. v. Clarke*, 2021 WL 1307899 (Appeals Court) (a high-speed foot chase in the dark, through private property and over obstacles such as unstable fences, put officers at risk).

- **Refusing to emerge from a hiding place upon command is not, by itself, resisting arrest.** *Comm. v. Valliere*, 2012 WL 1570144 (Appeals Court): Officers needed to show more than just Valliere's refusal to come out of the woods in response to their yelling. In future cases, officers should explain: (1) how long the suspect hid; (2) whether they had to search for him; (3) the type of terrain; and (4) the tactical precautions taken (e.g., guns drawn, K-9 activated, backup brought in). Officers should detail the facts that created the potential for injury — to the arrestee *or* officers.

- **"Mouthing off" prior to arrest is not resisting.** *Comm. v. Hart*, 467 Mass. 322 (2014): Michael Hart arrived home to find police investigating a domestic disturbance. He became excited, began yelling and cursing, and made numerous attempts to enter the apartment despite being told by officers to calm down. Police escorted him outside, where a crowd had gathered. Hart was arrested for disorderly conduct and resisting arrest. However, there was insufficient evidence. While he did mouth off, Hart did not use force or threaten to use force in connection with his arrest.

RIGHT TO KNOW GROUNDS FOR ARREST
263, § 1

Elements

An officer arrested a person and:

- Refused to answer the arrestee's question about the reason for the arrest; or
- Answered untruthfully; or
- Neglected, upon request, to exhibit the warrant or document authorizing the arrest.

Right of Arrest

Complaint.

Penalty

HC NMT 1 year; or Fine NMT $1,000.

FALSE ARREST
263, § 2

Elements

An officer arrested a suspect and pretended to have legal process, or different legal process from the one that he had.

Right of Arrest

Complaint.

Penalty

HC NMT 1 year; or Fine NMT $1,000.

FALSE INFORMATION FOLLOWING ARREST
268, § 34A

Elements

- ***Knowingly.*** The suspect knowingly and willfully;
- ***False name or information.*** Furnished a false name, Social Security number, date of birth, home or mailing address, phone number, or any other information requested to identify the defendant.

- **Police.** To a law enforcement officer or official (this would cover a civilian performing the booking for police);

- **Post-arrest.** Following an arrest. (*Note:* This crime does not have to occur at the booking desk, although it typically will. For example, if a suspect gave an officer a false name during the cruiser ride to the station after his arrest, this offense would apply.)

Right of Arrest

Not applicable. Since this offense, by definition, must follow an arrest, the officers must have had a right of arrest for the underlying offense initially.

Penalty

HC NMT 1 year; and/or Fine NMT $1,000. The sentence for this offense "shall run from and after any sentence imposed as a result of the underlying offense."

Notes

Must prove use of "false name." *Comm. v. Clark*, 446 Mass. 620 (2006): Arrested for drug dealing, the defendant told officers that his name was Jarod Bailey. The defendant's fingerprints matched an earlier arrest of Jarod Bailey *and* four prior arrests for William Clark!

In Massachusetts, a person has always been able to change his name at will, without any legal proceeding, provided that he did not make the change for a dishonest purpose. Based on a person's right to use any name, the SJC ruled that, under § 34A, a false name is one that a person has assumed for a dishonest purpose. This includes concealing one's identity to avoid being charged, to obtain more favorable bail consideration, to avoid arrest on a warrant, or to avoid prosecution on the current charge by facilitating a default.

If a person has previously identified himself to any police department under a different name, and he fails to disclose this name at the time of his arrest, then officers may infer his nondisclosure was for a dishonest purpose. Remember, police do not have to prove the suspect's true name, they must simply prove that he used a name for a dishonest purpose. In this case, using the name "Jarod Bailey" without disclosing his prior use of "William Clark" was designed to hide his earlier criminal history. See *Comm. v. Loadholt*, 456 Mass. 411 (2010).

Continuing to provide false name after arrest. *Comm. v. Carr*, 2016 WL 3460531 (Appeals Court) (the defendant first provided a false name when stopped by police; however, when placed in handcuffs, he still insisted his false name was correct; this was sufficient for § 34A). *Comm. v. Brantley*, 90 Mass. App. Ct. 901 (2016).

Section III
ESCAPE

ESCAPE FROM POLICE LOCKUP
268, § 15A

Elements

- The suspect was lawfully placed in a city or town lockup; and

- The suspect escaped.

Note: 15A covers an escape from a police lockup, but *not* an attempted escape. Officers must charge an attempt under 274, § 6. See *Chapter 2* and *Comm. v. Clay*, 65 Mass. App. Ct. 215 (2005) (15A wrong charge for Clay's escape attempt from Cambridge Police lockup).

Right of Arrest

Arrest for breach of peace in presence. Otherwise, complaint.

Penalty

HC NMT 2½ yrs; and/or Fine NMT $500.

AIDING ESCAPE FROM POLICE CUSTODY
268, § 17

Elements

- The suspect aided or assisted a prisoner;

- In escaping or attempting to escape from an officer or person with lawful custody.

Note: This offense is broader than 15A because it applies to suspects who help a police prisoner either outside *or* inside the station.

Right of Arrest

Arrest for breach of peace in presence. Otherwise, complaint.

Penalty

HC NMT 2 yrs; or Fine NMT $500.

Related Offenses

Escape in the Field from Police Officer. This common law offense[6] is listed in the *District Court Complaint Manual*. It occurs when a defendant is arrested and escapes from police custody. Penalty: 279, § 5 results in HC NMT 6 months. Right of Arrest: Breach of peace in presence. Otherwise, complaint. *Comm. v. McDonald*, 2014 WL 2776867 (Appeals Court) (defendant managed to flee from police while being transported to court; he could not be charged under 268, § 15A because he escaped from a police cruiser, not a police *lockup*; this common law offense was the correct charge).

Attempted or Actual Escape by a Correctional Facility Prisoner or Pre-trial Detainee. 268, § 16. This covers the escape or attempted escape of a prisoner (even while in transit) held by a correctional institution, sex offender treatment center, courthouse, or while on home confinement (127, § 20B). The definition of an "escape attempt" includes knowingly disabling, or attempting to disable or defeat, an electronic monitoring device. Penalty: SP NMT 10 yrs or HC NMT 2½ yrs. Right of Arrest: Felony. *Comm. v. Porter*, 87 Mass. App. Ct. 676 (2015) (failure to report on time for weekend jail sentence is an "escape" under § 16).

Aiding a Correctional Facility Prisoner's Escape. 268, § 15. The suspect must: (1) bring into a correctional facility or jail, a disguise, instrument, weapon or other thing with the intent to aid a prisoner's escape; or (2) assist a prisoner in trying to escape (whether the prisoner attempts or not); or (3) forcibly or fraudulently rescue or attempt to rescue a prisoner held in custody. Penalty: *If prisoner charged with felony:* SP NMT 10 yrs; or Fine NMT $500. *If prisoner charged with misdemeanor:* HC NMT 2 yrs; or Fine NMT $500. Right of Arrest: For a felony, felony. For a misdemeanor, arrest for breach of peace in presence. Otherwise, complaint.

Attempted or Actual Escape from the Department of Youth Services (DYS). 120, § 26 prohibits escaping or attempting to escape from DYS custody. It also penalizes anyone who assists a DYS youth in this activity. Penalty: HC NMT 2 yrs (continuing commitment to DYS also an option); or Fine NMT $500. Right of Arrest: 120, § 13 warrantless arrest on probable cause. For a detailed breakdown, See *LED's Juvenile Law, Chapter 25*.

Negligently Allowing an Escape. Under 268, § 20, a jailor or officer may not willfully refuse to take into custody, or negligently allow to escape, an arrested or convicted prisoner. Penalty: HC NMT 2 yrs; or Fine NMT $500. Right of Arrest: Arrest for breach of peace in presence. Otherwise, complaint.

---

6 See earlier discussion of common law offenses.

6 Homicide

MURDER
265, § 1

Summary

2nd degree murder is an unlawful killing committed with malice. 1st degree murder is the same, plus an aggravating factor — the suspect's premeditation, cruelty, or participation in a life felony.

Elements

2nd degree

- The suspect committed an unlawful killing;
- With malice.

1st degree. Prior elements plus one aggravating factor:

- Deliberate premeditation; or
- Extreme atrocity or cruelty; or
- Commission or attempted commission of a crime punishable by life imprisonment.

Right of Arrest

Felony.

Penalty (defined in 265, § 2)

SP Life. 2nd degree prisoner is eligible for parole after he serves 15 years. 1st degree results in life without parole.

Notes

Element 1: Unlawful killing. The term "unlawful" refers to the absence of justification. Society sometimes authorizes taking another person's life. Soldiers at war may have to kill. Police officers may use deadly force in some situations. Even citizens may sometimes take a life in self-defense.

Element 2: Malice. "Malice" describes the mental state necessary for murder. *Comm. v. Grey*, 399 Mass. 469 (1987) mentions three types: (1st prong) an actual intent to kill; *or* (2nd prong) an actual intent to cause grievous bodily harm; *or* (3rd prong) an act that a reasonable person would know is likely to kill another.

- **1st prong usually involves the intentional use of a deadly weapon (typically a handgun).** *Comm. v. Thomas*, 9 Mass. App. Ct. 875 (1980).

- **2nd prong requires an "intent to do grievous bodily injury," not just an intent to injure.** *Comm. v. Cherubin*, 35 Mass. App. Ct. 919 (1993) (while driving, defendant swerved rapidly at the victim and hit her near the curb; he then ran over her body).

- **3rd prong requires "a plain and strong likelihood of death."** *Comm. v. Riley*, 467 Mass. 799 (2014) (3rd prong malice proven when the defendant repeatedly administered a prescription medication to her daughter in excess of what was prescribed — despite being told that doing so could be fatal). *Comm. v. Moore*, 2017 WL 3427584 (Appeals Court) (defendant led police on a high speed chase, running a red light at a busy intersection and causing a seven-car collision that killed another driver). *Comm. v. Colas*, 486 Mass. 831 (2021) (even if he did not fire, the defendant demonstrated indifference to life by pointing a pistol at an enemy on a crowded street; that act provoked the other man to shoot at the defendant; the bullet missed him but killed a bystander).

  Conduct that only risks substantial harm amounts to manslaughter. *Comm. v. Horne*, 466 Mass. 440 (2013): Mad that someone inside had possibly stolen his TV, the defendant fired eight bullets at a darkened window of an apartment early in the morning. He killed a 19 year old girl who happened to be standing there. Because he did not knowingly shoot at a person, the jury had to decide whether the defendant's conduct created a plain and strong likelihood of death (which would be murder based on 3rd prong malice), or only a likelihood of substantial harm (which would be involuntary manslaughter).

Extreme alcohol or drug consumption may nullify a defendant's ability to act with malice. This is why murder defendants routinely claim they were too intoxicated to know what they were doing. Investigators should *always* seek evidence of the defendant's state of mind before, during, and after the killing. *Comm. v. Gonzalez*, 469 Mass. 410 (2014).

Offender must cause the victim's death.

- **Passage of time no defense.** *Comm. v. Casanova*, 429 Mass. 293 (1999) (defendant shot the victim in the neck, rendering him paralyzed; defendant guilty of murder even though the victim lived for five more years before dying of respiratory failure).

- **Weakness of victim no defense.** Even if the victim's pre-existing condition contributes to his death, the defendant is still liable. *Comm. v. Tevlin*, 433 Mass. 305 (2001) (defendant guilty of 1st degree murder; it was no defense that the elder victim's atherosclerosis [blocked arteries] largely caused her demise in the hospital following the robbery).

- **Fetus as victim.** Only a *viable* fetus may be the subject of murder or manslaughter. Viability is the point where the fetus is likely to survive outside the womb, with or without medical support. *Comm. v. Lawrence*, 404 Mass. 378 (1989) (consecutive sentences proper for the homicides of a 16 year old girl and the 27 week old fetus she was carrying).

1st degree factor: Deliberate premeditation. The decision to kill must be the product of reflection, but there is no mandated time span between the first thought of murder and the act of killing. It can take several seconds or several years! *Comm. v. Fernandez*, 480 Mass. 334 (2018) (after a verbal spat between two groups of teenagers ended, the defendant got off his bicycle, said "Fuck this shit" to his friends, took out his handgun, cocked it, walked back, and shot the victim in the chest; this chain of events, although taking only a minute to complete, was sufficient premeditation). *Comm. v. Marshall*, 434 Mass. 358 (2001) (premeditation may be shown by a lack of struggle; defendant asked his ex-girlfriend to come upstairs and stabbed her repeatedly; it was so quick she never even screamed).

Premeditation exists if the defendant intended to kill someone else in the same group as the victim. *Comm. v. Taylor*, 463 Mass. 857 (2012) (enraged because he had been kicked out of a party, the defendant later came back to the scene with a loaded gun and shot through the door at the victim, who was with other people; clearly first degree).

1st degree factor: Extreme atrocity or cruelty. The suspect must cause the victim's death by a method that surpasses the cruelty inherent in any homicide. Under *Comm. v. Castillo*, 485 Mass. 852 (2020), the jury must find that the defendant either: (1) took pleasure in the victim's suffering; or (2) killed with a method very likely to increase the victim's suffering; or (3) used a killing method that was totally excessive (considerations for this last factor include the number of blows, extent of injuries, level of force, and weapon/instrument used).

- **Victim suffering usually the key.** *Comm. v. Fickling*, 434 Mass. 9 (2001) (after strangling the mother to death, defendant locked her 22 month old baby in the apartment with the dead body; the child died of dehydration); *Comm. v. Sanchez*, 476 Mass. 725 (2017) (victim's body was found in a burning house; she had been stabbed 45 times; and she inhaled soot and smoke, indicating that she was alive while the fire burned her).

- **However, suffering not required.** The statute says "atrocity *or* cruelty." Even if "cruelty" implies suffering, "atrocity" does not. Consequently, the killing method may be "so shocking" that it amounts to extreme atrocity, regardless of whether the victim suffered. *Comm. v. Ellis*, 432 Mass. 746 (2000).

1st degree factor: Felony murder. *Comm. v. Brown*, 477 Mass. 805 (2017) decided that defendants can no longer be charged with murder based *solely* on the fact that a killing occurred during the commission of a life felony.

- **The malice of each accomplice must be proven.**[1] As a result, if a defendant commits an armed robbery as an accomplice and a killing occurs, the defendant can only be found guilty of murder if he participated with the intent to either: (1) kill; or (2) cause grievous bodily harm; or (3) do an act that creates a plain and strong likelihood of death. If malice is shown, the fact that the murder occurred during the commission of a life felony elevates it to 1st degree.

- **Examples of life felonies include robbery, home invasion, burglary, and rape.**[2]

---

[1] This is a significant departure from the previous rule. See *Comm. v. Scott*, 472 Mass. 815 (2015).
[2] There is no longer 2nd degree felony murder. See, e.g., *Comm. v. Garner*, 59 Mass. App. Ct. 350 (2003).

- **Absent proof of malice, an accomplice may only be found guilty of involuntary manslaughter** (if he acted recklessly) or just the underlying crime — e.g., robbery (if he lacked the intent for manslaughter).

- **If police or a third party kill someone in an attempt to stop the crime, it is not felony murder.** The SJC, based on legal history, concluded that murder requires that the principal or an accomplice perform the act that directly causes the victim's death. *Comm. v. Dawson*, 490 Mass. 521 (2022): Kyle Dawson and Christopher Dunton attacked a cab driver with a knife and chokehold to rob him. The driver pulled a gun and shot and killed Dunton. This was not felony murder, but it was involuntary manslaughter. It was the height of recklessness to violently rob a driver in an area that had been experiencing taxi robberies and not anticipate that he might engage in armed self-defense. *Comm. v. Tejeda*, 473 Mass. 269 (2015).

Jury must agree on 1st degree factor — premeditation, cruelty, or felony murder — but not on whether the accused was the principal or accomplice. The jury does not have to agree on whether the defendant was the principal or accomplice, as long as there is sufficient evidence to support either role. *Comm. v. Barbosa*, 477 Mass. 658 (2017) (defendant's flight from the scene and phone calls with his accomplices immediately before and after the shooting demonstrated that he participated in the murder, whether or not he pulled the trigger).

Jurisdiction. Under 277, § 62, Massachusetts has jurisdiction to prosecute a defendant for murder if the victim's death occurs outside the Commonwealth — provided that the violence or injury leading to the victim's death began in the Commonwealth. *Comm. v. Jaynes*, 55 Mass. App. Ct. 301 (2002) (child kidnapping in Cambridge was a sufficiently forceful act to confer jurisdiction on Massachusetts for the boy's suffocation, even though it was possible that his death took place in either New Hampshire or Maine).

Lack of jurisdiction is a complete defense. *Comm. v. Combs*, 480 Mass. 55 (2018) (William Jones was strangled to death for drugs and money by the defendant and his accomplice, but the evidence did not establish whether Jones was killed in his girlfriend's Springfield apartment or in Connecticut where his body was found).

Related Offenses

Armed Assault with Intent to Rob or Murder. 265, § 18. The suspect must assault the victim with a dangerous weapon while possessing the specific intent to rob or murder him. Penalty: SP NMT 20 yrs. Right of Arrest: Felony. *Comm. v. Sylvester*, 35 Mass. App. Ct. 906 (1993) (the defendant fired four or five shots at close range; although the victim was only wounded in the knee, the burst of shooting indicated the defendant's intent to murder).

Assault with Intent to Murder or Maim. 265, § 15. A person must assault another with the specific intent to commit murder or to maim. Penalty: SP NMT 10 yrs; or HC NMT 2½ yrs and Fine NMT $1,000. Right of Arrest: Felony. *Comm. v. Johnston*, 446 Mass. 555 (2006).

- **Knowingly being infected with HIV and threatening to bite someone constitutes assault with intent to murder.** *Comm. v. Smith*, 58 Mass. App. Ct. 381 (2003) (defendant yelled that he had HIV during a struggle at a correctional facility; he then said that he intended to kill a prison guard and bit an officer's arm).

- **Pointing a loaded gun, without more, insufficient proof of intent to murder.** *Comm. v. Lewis*, 465 Mass. 119 (2013) (fact that Lewis initially refused to drop his gun and pointed it at officer did not prove his intent to murder). Compare *Comm. v. Buttimer*, 482 Mass. 754 (2019) (defendant pointed rifle at officer and tracked him with it; he had reloaded it after killing someone earlier; this was assault with intent to murder).

Attempted Murder. 265, § 16 was enacted based on the perception that an offender might perform certain acts to murder someone not covered under assault with intent to murder. Thus, § 16 penalizes anyone who attempts to commit murder "by poisoning or drowning or strangling another person, or by any means not constituting an assault with intent to commit murder." Penalty: SP NMT 20 yrs; or HC NMT 2½ yrs and Fine NMT $1,000. Right of Arrest: Felony. *Comm. v. LaBrie*, 473 Mass. 754 (2016) (the defendant secretly withheld cancer medication from her seven year old son; she repeatedly lied to his doctors and acknowledged that not giving him his medication would be "like pushing him in front of a car").

Use of Poison with Intent to Kill or Injure. Under 265, § 28, an offender may not mingle poison with any food, drink or medicine with the intent to kill or injure. Penalty: SP NMT Life. Right of Arrest: Felony. "Poison" means any substance introduced into the body, by any means, which is capable of causing injury or death. It is a broad term that covers both:

- **Inherently dangerous substances that no reasonable person would ingest.** *Comm. v. Kennedy*, 170 Mass. 18 (1897) (defendant put rat poison on the rim of the victim's cup).

- **Substances that have beneficial uses but become poison when used improperly.** *Comm. v. Walker*, 442 Mass. 185 (2004) (defendant poured his properly prescribed sleeping medication into the alcoholic drinks of three women to facilitate sexual assaults; using a legitimate medication in this fashion turned it into a poison).

MANSLAUGHTER
265, § 13

Elements

Type 1: Voluntary

- The suspect unlawfully and <u>intentionally</u>;

- Used force in circumstances where the suspect experienced reasonable provocation;

- Which caused the death of another person.

Type 2: Involuntary

- The suspect unlawfully and <u>unintentionally</u>;

- Caused the death of another person by:

    - Committing an A&B that the suspect knew, or reasonably should have known, endangered human life; or
    - Recklessly engaging in an act, *or* failing to act, in a manner that disregarded a clear risk of substantial harm.

Right of Arrest

Felony.

Penalty

SP NMT 20 yrs; or HC NMT 2½ yrs and Fine NMT $1,000.[3]

Corporation Penalty

Manslaughter may be committed by a corporation. 265, § 13 states that any business organization, corporation, association, partnership, or other legal entity can commit manslaughter. Penalty: Fine NMT $250,000 and prohibition from bidding on government contracts (known technically as "debarment") under 29, § 29F for NMT 10 yrs.

Notes

Distinction between manslaughter & murder. Manslaughter is the unlawful killing of another *without* malice. *Comm. v. Deleverde*, 398 Mass. 288 (1986).

Type 1: Voluntary manslaughter is an unlawful, intentional killing resulting from reasonable provocation. Reasonable provocation produces such a state of anger or fear that a typical person may lose his capacity for restraint. *Comm. v. Walden*, 380 Mass. 724 (1980).

- **Examples of <u>insufficient</u> provocation.**

    - *Insults.* The law is crystal clear that words alone are not adequate provocation. *Comm. v. Vatcher*, 438 Mass. 584 (2003) (even obscene or hostile insults not enough).

    - *Threats of retaliation. Comm. v. Bins,* 465 Mass. 348 (2013) (wife threatened to call police and "destroy" the defendant).

    - *Homosexual advances. Comm. v. Halbert*, 410 Mass. 534 (1991) (victim inviting the defendant to engage in homosexual acts and placing his hand on the defendant's knee not reasonable provocation).

    - *Jealousy over an ex. Comm. v. Valentin*, 474 Mass. 301 (2016) (defendant's girlfriend ended their relationship; several hours later, defendant saw her walking toward her apartment with a new man and fatally shot him; defendant had no reason to expect that his ex-girlfriend would not become romantically involved with other people).

    - *Child's misbehavior. Comm. v. Vatcher*, 438 Mass. 584 (2003) ("however provocative . . . the actions of this 11 year old physically challenged boy may have been . . . it did not rise to adequate provocation" for being shot and strangled).

---

[3] There is an enhanced penalty that applies to both forms of manslaughter: If the defendant committed manslaughter while violating 266, § 102 (Possession of an Explosive); § 102A (Placing an Explosive or Incendiary Device); § 102B (Exploding a Destructive or Incendiary Device); or § 102C (Possession of a Biological, Chemical or Nuclear Delivery System): SP Life or any term of years.

- *Crying baby.* Comm. v. Azar, 32 Mass. App. Ct. 290 (1992) (claim that infant's crying caused the defendant to lose control insufficient basis for manslaughter).

- *Minor force.* Comm. v. Bianchi, 435 Mass. 316 (2001) (insufficient provocation when the victim punched the defendant in the face — especially given that the defendant was a weightlifter and outweighed the victim by 170 lbs.).

- *Spousal infidelity.* For centuries, the emotional shock of discovering a partner's infidelity transformed murder into manslaughter. Comm. v. Andrade, 422 Mass. 236 (1996). However, in Comm. v. Steeves, 490 Mass. 270 (2022), the SJC stated that, in the future, it is unlikely to allow a manslaughter verdict on this basis because "it rests on the outmoded perception that . . . killing a spouse (usually a wife) by a spouse (usually a husband) is an acceptable response to . . . infidelity, thereby reinforc[ing] male irrationality as normal, and legitim[izing] the view of women as property."

- **Examples of <u>adequate</u> provocation.**

  - *Excessive self-defense or defense of another.* If a suspect is attacked and justified in defending himself, but then uses "excessive force," he may be convicted of manslaughter. Comm. v. Santos, 454 Mass. 770 (2009). The same is true if he uses excessive force in the defense of another. Comm. v. Allen, 474 Mass. 162 (2016) (defendant shot a person who had threatened his friend with a knife).

  - *Injury to genitals.* Comm. v. Rhodes, 482 Mass. 823 (2019) (during consensual oral sex, the victim bit the defendant's penis with enough force to take "a dime-size chunk"; he reacted with force immediately and struck the victim causing her to die).

- **The act must result from provocation, rather than from some pre-existing intention to kill or injure.** Comm. v. Grassie, 476 Mass. 202 (2017) (the defendant stood in the street, beckoning people to fight him "three on one," while knowing that he had a knife hidden in his pocket; his decision to use deadly force reflected a previously formed intention to do so, not an impulsive reaction provoked by the victim's opening punch).

- **The killing must occur before there is an opportunity to "cool down."** Comm. v. Lopez, 474 Mass. 690 (2016). Comm. v. Seales, 2012 WL 5430953 (Appeals Court) (the defendant was already beating the victim when she hit him with a mop and smacked his head on the bed post; after that, they stopped fighting and had a discussion; the defendant had time to cool off and was not provoked into killing her later).

Type 2: Involuntary manslaughter is an unintentional killing resulting from a nonfelonious A&B or reckless conduct. Comm. v. Hadley, 78 Mass. App. Ct. 405 (2010).

- **Assault & Battery with a likelihood of serious harm.** Comm. v. Lopez, 87 Mass. App. Ct. 642 (2015): Daniel Lopez sucker punched a Chinese food delivery person as he walked up the front stairs. The victim fell backwards and his head struck the sidewalk. He began to gasp for air. Lopez stole $125 from his pockets, as well as the Chinese food, and left. The victim died on the sidewalk with a fractured skull.

- **Reckless conduct involves an act or the failure to act, where serious harm is likely.** *Comm. v. Power,* 76 Mass. App. Ct. 398 (2010) (providing overcrowded and unlicensed day care in the defendant's home was reckless and caused a three month old baby's death).

  - *Third party kills someone while resisting defendant's felony.* Comm. v. Dawson, 490 Mass. 521 (2022) (defendant's armed robbery of a cab driver caused the driver to shoot his accomplice in self-defense; the defendant could be convicted of involuntary manslaughter, but not murder). *Comm. v. Campbell,* 7 Allen 541 (1863) (defendant participated in a riot causing soldiers to shoot another rioter; this could not be murder but, depending on the facts, could be manslaughter; the same is true for a police shooting in response to a defendant's felonious crime).

  - *Mishandling firearm.* Comm. v. Atencio, 345 Mass. 627 (1963) (defendant encouraged victim to play "Russian roulette" with a loaded handgun). *Comm. v. Mink,* 123 Mass. 422 (1877) (defendant accidentally killed the person who was trying to prevent him from committing suicide; this constituted involuntary manslaughter).

  - *Landlord safety defects. Comm. v. Zhan Tang Huang,* 87 Mass. App. Ct. 65 (2015) (a father and two infant sons died in a fire due to the lack of smoke detectors and a means of escape from their bedroom; the landlords had failed to install smoke detectors even though notified by insurers, tenants, and inspectors).

  - *Illegal drug overdose. Comm. v. Carrillo,* 483 Mass. 269 (2019) held a defendant must know, or should know, that his conduct created a high likelihood of overdose or death. *Carrillo* overruled prior cases that held that any death from illegal heroin distribution is automatically manslaughter. Here, Carrillo (a UMass graduate student) bought heroin for himself and for the victim, Sinacori (a junior). Carrillo had previously done this. Carrillo delivered the heroin to Sinacori and texted him later to ask how he had enjoyed it. There was no response. Sinacori's father found him dead the next day with opened bags of heroin and a used needle nearby.

    These facts were insufficient to prove manslaughter. It would have been different if Carrillo had known that the heroin he provided Sinacori was unusually potent or laced with fentanyl; or that Sinacori was particularly vulnerable owing to his age, use of other drugs, or prior overdoses; or that Sinacori had overdosed and was in need of help. Sinacori's failure to answer one text did not indicate he needed help.

    Compare *Comm. v. Hunter,* 2020 WL 1933657 (Appeals Court) (text messages sent to customers by a "professional" drug dealer boasting that his product was "fire" or "rocket fuel" were more than harmless exaggeration; they indicated that the dealer knew the heroin he sold was unusually potent and dangerous; the text messages established that the victim was desperate for a "fix" and was dead within 45 minutes of the time he received the defendant's delivery).

  - *Legal drug overdose.* It may also be manslaughter if a defendant secretly caused a victim to ingest legal drugs in a dangerous fashion. *Comm. v. Walker,* 442 Mass. 185 (2004) (defendant mixed four times the recommended dosage of his sleeping medication into the victim's drink; his reckless conduct justified his manslaughter conviction when she died).

- ***Failure of parents to provide essential care.*** *Comm. v. Twitchell*, 416 Mass. 114 (1993) held that parents must provide their children with essential medical services regardless of their religious beliefs.

- ***Encouraging suicide.*** *Comm. v. Carter*, 474 Mass. 624 (2016): The defendant encouraged her boyfriend, who suffered from depression, to kill himself. She told him how to do it and chastised him when he delayed. When he got out of his truck as it filled with carbon monoxide, the defendant commanded him to get back in. An ordinary person would have realized the danger of telling the victim, who was mentally fragile, to get back in the truck and "just do it." Also see *Kligler v. Attorney General*, 491 Mass. 38 (2022) (physician-assisted suicide in Massachusetts is typically involuntary manslaughter; interesting discussion by SJC about end-of-life decisions and methods).

- **Duty to prevent harm.** A duty to prevent harm to others arises when one creates a dangerous situation, even by accident. In *Comm. v. Levesque*, 436 Mass. 443 (2002), Thomas Levesque and Julie Ann Barnes, while living in an abandoned warehouse, accidentally started a fire, then failed to report it. Six Worcester firefighters died in the blaze. The defendants' decision not to report the fire was reckless. They had a cell phone and passed several stores after they left the warehouse, proving that they had multiple opportunities to call for help. They also went shopping, which refuted any suggestion that panic explained their inaction.

Proximate cause. While a defendant's conduct need not be the *only* cause, it must be the *proximate* cause of death. This means that, "in a natural and continuous sequence," the defendant's action or inaction produced the victim's death. *Comm. v. Osachuk*, 43 Mass. App. Ct. 71 (1997) (victim's death caused by a combination of cocaine, heroin, and methadone; while the defendant did not give the victim all the drugs she consumed, he gave her a methadone tablet and money to purchase drugs; he also delayed bringing her to the hospital; these factors were the proximate cause of her death).

Related Offenses

Assault with Intent to Kill. 265, § 29 is, in essence, assault with intent to commit manslaughter. Reasonable provocation reduces an intent to murder to an intent to kill — in the same way that the absence of malice reduces murder to manslaughter. *Comm. v. Velazquez*, 61 Mass. App. Ct. 667 (2004).

Motor Vehicle Homicide. 90, § 24G. Motor vehicle homicide is an unlawful killing that results from negligent or reckless operation. See *LED's Motor Vehicle Law, Chapter 9*.

7 Kidnapping

KIDNAPPING
265, § 26

Elements

- **Unlawful.** Without lawful authority;
- **Intentional.** The suspect intentionally:
  - **Type 1:** Forcibly or secretly confined another person against his will; or
  - **Type 2:** Inveigled[1] another with intent to forcibly or secretly confine him against his will.

Right of Arrest

Felony.

Penalty

Basic offense: SP NMT 10 yrs; or HC NMT 2 yrs and Fine NMT $1,000.

Aggravated offenses:

- If the defendant committed a kidnapping with the intent to extort money or "any other valuable thing": SP Life or any term of years.
- If armed with a gun: SP NLT 10 yrs or HC NMT 2½ yrs.
- If armed with a gun and had the intent to extort: SP NLT 20 yrs, NMT Life.
- If armed with a dangerous weapon and inflicted serious bodily injury or sexually assaulted the victim: SP NLT 25 yrs. Bodily injury is defined as permanent disfigurement, protracted impairment of a bodily function or limb, or substantial risk of death. Sexual assault is rape or indecent A&B.
- If kidnap victim is under 16: SP NMT 15 yrs.

---

[1] "Inveigle" (pronounced "in-vay") means to lure or entice by false representations.

Notes

Without lawful authority. This initial element recognizes that sometimes a person may legally be seized and transported against his will. An obvious example is the police officer who transports a person under arrest!

Intentional. Kidnapping must be intentional. *Comm. v. Saylor*, 27 Mass. App. Ct. 117 (1989).

Type 1: Forcible or secret confinement. The most common kidnap occurs when a suspect forcibly *or* secretly confines another person against his or her will, which means "without the victim's consent." *Comm. v. Robinson*, 48 Mass. App. Ct. 329 (1999).

- **Force.** Force may be direct or "constructive," which involves threats and displays. *Comm. v. Condrate*, 2013 WL 5904814 (Appeals Court): The adult victim and her six year old daughter were living with the defendant when she told him she wanted to move away. The defendant used constructive force when he took the victim's car keys and padlocked the only door to his trailer with the victim inside. *Comm. v. Titus*, 32 Mass. App. Ct. 148 (1992).

- **Secret.** Confinement may be accomplished secretly. Two examples are:

  - *Fraud.* 265, § 27 declares that a suspect may kidnap someone if that person's consent was the product of fraud. For example, the suspect tells the victim that he will take photographs at his "modeling studio." She then travels with him to a warehouse.

  - *Tender years doctrine.* The tender years doctrine recognizes that children — <u>13 years old or younger</u> — may not accompany another adult without the explicit knowledge of their parent or guardian. This is obviously true for toddlers, but *Comm. v. Colon*, 431 Mass. 188 (2000) found that a 12 year old child was incapable of visiting an older man in Florida without her parent's permission. Colon was convicted because he did not notify the 12 year old's parent the minute she made a surprise visit to his motel in Florida. She took a bus, at his urging, on her own from Springfield.

- **"Confine" means to enclose within bounds or to restrict.** Any restraint of a person's liberty is confinement. *Comm. v. Bibby*, 54 Mass. App. Ct. 158 (2002): The defendant brought his girlfriend back to his hotel room. When she asked to leave, he broke the phone, slapped her, and held a gun to her head. He argued that, although his actions were rough, he had no intent to kidnap her. The court said his ultimate objective was irrelevant because he engaged in forcible confinement against her will.

No intent to commit another crime necessary. *Comm. v. Belsito*, 2014 WL 1256088 (Appeals Court): The defendant approached a woman he had met in a bar. He grabbed her arms and held them behind her back. He forced her to cross the street and attempted to force her into his car. The woman struggled and eventually made it inside a convenience store, where she yelled for the clerk to call police. The defendant restrained this woman against her will. There was no need to prove that he intended to commit another felony, such as rape, in connection with the kidnapping.

Kidnapping must be distinct from associated crimes. *Comm. v. Oberle*, 476 Mass. 539 (2017): William Oberle and the victim were in a romantic relationship. On the 4th of July, they had a fight and Oberle left. He returned after midnight, and the argument escalated. Oberle punched the victim, held her down, and choked her, saying he would kill her. The victim was unable to call for help because Oberle had taken her cell phone the day before. The victim lost consciousness, and awoke to daylight. The victim managed to escape. There was sufficient evidence of confinement independent of the assault and batteries.

Type 2: Inveigle with intent. "Inveigle" (pronounced "in-vay") means to lure or entice by false representations. Unlike the first type of kidnapping, this version requires specific intent. As a result, it is not enough to prove that the suspect enticed the victim. There must be proof that the suspect did so with the *ultimate goal* of forcibly or secretly confining the victim. *Comm. v. Lent*, 46 Mass. App. Ct. 705 (1999) (defendant's intent demonstrated by his comments to police about his "master plan" to kidnap young girls and hold them to facilitate his "sexual desires").

Related Offenses

Attempted Kidnapping must be charged under the general attempt statute, 274, § 6 (see discussion in *Chapter 2*). *Comm. v. Sullivan*, 84 Mass. App. Ct. 26 (2013): The victim was a college student. As she was walking home at 9:30 p.m., the defendant pulled his vehicle over and said, "Hey little girl, you look so tired. Come on over. Talk to me." The defendant's intent to confine the victim was shown by his persistent attempts to entice her into his vehicle, even when it became clear that she did not want to speak to him. He got out of his car twice, leaving the engine running and the door open. He reversed direction, followed her to a dimly lit street, and angrily demanded that she get in. The only reason he left is that she began to recite his license plate number.

Compare *Comm. v. Rivera*, 460 Mass. 139 (2011) (insufficient evidence: defendant requested that an 11 year old boy get in his car; boy said "no"; defendant drove away; he never got out of his car, showed a weapon, or threatened the boy).

Hostage Taking in a Correctional Facility. 127, § 38A (Felony). *Comm. v. Spearin*, 446 Mass. 599 (2006).

PARENTAL OR RELATIVE KIDNAPPING
265, § 26A

Elements

Type 1: Child Under 18

- The suspect was a relative of a child less than 18 years old; and
- Without lawful authority, the suspect:
  - Held or intended to hold the child permanently or for a protracted period of time; or
  - Took or enticed the child from his or her lawful custodian.

Type 2: Under 18 in Danger or Removed. In addition to the elements in Type 1, the child was either:

- Exposed to danger by the kidnapping; or

- Removed from the Commonwealth.

Type 3: Incompetent/Other Person

- The suspect took or enticed from lawful custody;

- Any incompetent person or other person "entrusted by authority of law to the custody of another person or institution."

Type 4: Incompetent/Other in Danger: In addition to the elements in Type 3, the incompetent or other person was exposed to danger.

Suggested Protocol & Right of Arrest

Since these cases often involve complicated family dynamics, it is recommended that police:

- **Assess whether the child/incompetent person is "exposed to danger."** If so, officers should immediately investigate and seek to recover the vulnerable subject. The need to act decisively is heightened if the child or incompetent person has been removed, or is at risk of being removed, from the Commonwealth. Seek FBI help if appropriate under the Fugitive Felon Act, 18 U.S.C. § 1073.

- **What constitutes "exposure to danger" is deliberately undefined by 265, § 26A, so officers should apply this standard in a commonsense fashion.**[2]

- **Felony arrest authority for "aggravated" offenses.** Under § 26A, if the offender has exposed a child or incompetent person to danger, *or* removed a child from the Commonwealth, then felony arrest powers apply.

- **If no immediate danger, assess relationship of parties, send the complainant to the probate court, and/or contact the suspect.** Parental entanglements may be difficult to sort out. Officers should routinely direct the complainant to the probate court, which may issue an emergency order of custody if necessary. Should the suspect fail to comply, police intervention would then be justified.

    As another initial strategy, officers may contact the suspect and suggest that he or she bring the child/incompetent person back and maintain the status quo to avoid possible criminal prosecution. The warning may persuade the suspect to resolve any issues in the probate court.

- **Complaint authority.** Remember, in the absence of danger to a child or incompetent person, *or* in the absence of a child's removal from the Commonwealth, § 26A is a misdemeanor requiring a complaint application, unless it is in presence and a breach of peace.

---

[2] Of course, whenever kidnapping is forcible, the offender should be charged under 265, § 26 (discussed earlier) regardless of the relationship of the parties.

Penalty

Types 1 and 3: HC NMT 1 year; and/or Fine NMT $1,000.

Aggravated types 2 and 4: SP NMT 5 yrs; and/or Fine NMT $5,000.

Notes

Type 1: *Child under 18*. The police do not need to show that a parent or relative used force or took the child against his/her will.

What is the relationship of the parents? The answer will alert the officer to whether an accused parent may be holding the child "without lawful authority."

- **Married parents.** Unless there are probate court orders concerning custody at the time of the child's departure, both parents have equal access to their children, and parental kidnapping is not an option. *Comm. v. Beals*, 405 Mass. 550 (1989).

- **Divorced parents.** Parental kidnapping does not apply to divorced parents who have joint legal and physical custody. However, if a parent with visitation fails to return a child in violation of a court order, police may pursue this charge if there is evidence the suspect intends to hold the child for a protracted period of time. Similarly, a parent who withholds visitation rights might violate this law. Given the complexity of these cases, officers should typically recommend that the complainant seek a custody order from the probate court before applying for a criminal complaint. Of course, if the child is at risk of harm or removal from Massachusetts, officers should immediately locate and protect the child.

- **Unmarried parents.**

  - *If the probate court has not issued a <u>specific custody order</u>, then the mother has full custody of the child.* 209C, § 10(b). Basically, the police cannot pursue a case on behalf of the father unless he seeks a probate order. The police could pursue a criminal case on behalf of a mother without having her go to probate court. *Comm. v. Gonzalez*, 462 Mass. 459 (2012) (this is the "default rule").

  - *The exception to this rule occurs when either parent <u>relinquishes care</u> of the child.* 209C, § 10(c) (if *either* unwed parent is dead, unfit, unavailable, or relinquishes care, the other parent has custody). Under this standard, police could pursue a criminal case on behalf of a father against a mother who had stopped caring for their child — or vice versa. In *Comm. v. Gonzalez, supra.*, Ernesto Gonzalez had been absent for three years. When he tried to re-enter his child's life, he sought permission from the mother — showing he recognized the mother's role as the custodial parent. Because Gonzalez had "relinquished care," he lacked lawful authority to hold the child beyond the scheduled visit. He was convicted. To decide differently would encourage unmarried, noncustodial fathers to take their children from their mothers without probate court permission.

Type 2: Aggravated parental kidnapping. *Comm. v. Lockwood*, 95 Mass. App. Ct. 189 (2019) (defendant father exposed his young children to danger when he forcibly took them from their foster home and risked a confrontation with law enforcement).

Type 3: Interference with custody of an incompetent person. § 26A also makes it a crime for *anyone* to take or entice an incompetent person *or* other person legally entrusted to a person or institution. This applies to anyone regardless of age and might be invoked, for example, if a family friend, because of a dispute, refused to return a 40 year old autistic adult to his group home following a visit. It could also be invoked for a nonrelative's interference with child custody, if a regular kidnapping charge (265, § 26) was not applicable.

Venue. 265, §§ 27 and 27A allows Kidnapping (§ 26) and Parental Kidnapping (§ 26A) to be tried in the county where the victim was seized or in any county where the victim was confined, carried or brought. *Comm. v. Libby*, 358 Mass. 617 (1971).

ENTICEMENT FOR SEX OR VIOLENCE, "CHILD" UNDER 16
265, § 26C

Elements

- The suspect enticed;

- A child under the age of 16, or someone he believed to be a child under the age of 16;

- To enter, exit or remain within any vehicle, dwelling, building, or other outdoor space;

- With the intent that the suspect *or* another person would violate any of the following:

    - Indecent A&B on Child Under 14 (265, §§ 13B, 13B½ and 13B¾); A&B or Indecent A&B on Intellectually Disabled Person (§ 13F); Indecent A&B on 14 or Over (§ 13H); Rape (§ 22); Forcible Rape Under 16 (§§ 22A, 22B and 22C); Statutory Rape (§§ 23, 23A and 23B); Assault with Intent to Rape (§ 24); and Assault Child with Intent to Rape (§ 24B); or

    - Inducing a Minor Prostitute (272, § 4A); Open & Gross (§ 16); Distribution of Matter Harmful to Minor (§ 28); Dissemination of Obscenity to Adults (§ 29); Posing Child Naked for Visual Representation (§ 29A); Dissemination of Child Pornography (§ 29B); Possession of Child Pornography (§ 29C); Unnatural and Lascivious Acts with Child (§ 35A); Lewd & Lascivious (§ 53); Indecent Exposure (§ 53); Sexual Conduct for a Fee (§ 53A); or

    - Any offense that has the use or attempted use of force as an element.

Right of Arrest

Felony.

Penalty

SP NMT 5 yrs or HC NMT 2½ yrs; and/or Fine NMT $5,000.

Notes

***Under § 26C, Entice* means "to lure, induce, persuade, tempt, incite, solicit, coax, or invite."**

This crime may involve a "fake" victim. *Comm. v. Disler,* 451 Mass. 216 (2008): The police created a fictitious character, Sara, who was 14 years old and initiated "instant messaging" with Richard Disler, who described sexual acts he wanted to perform on Sara. He repeatedly asked her to meet him at an MBTA station. He described his car and told her when he would be there. He offered to bring her to his house.

Police executed a search warrant. They arrested Disler and seized his computer.

- **"Fake" victim sufficient.** It did not matter that Sara was not a real person because factual impossibility is not a defense to this crime.

- **Enticement statute not unconstitutionally vague or a violation of the First Amendment.** This law does not penalize the act of sending sexually explicit messages over the internet. It only applies to messages that *invite a child* to do one of the designated criminal acts with the offender or another person.

- **Sufficient evidence.** The evidence against Disler was overwhelming. His explicit statements to Sara about sex indicated his intent to commit statutory rape. Disler knew Sara was underage because he asked her about her pubic hair and repeatedly told her that they had to be careful and that he would have to sneak her into his house.

- **No entrapment.** Finally, Disler argued that the police entrapped him with their fictional Sara. Yet Disler's internet conversations demonstrated that he was "ready and willing" to commit this crime.

Enticement may occur in person. *Comm. v. Federico,* 70 Mass. App. Ct. 711 (2007): On several occasions, the 15 year old victim was sitting at his computer by a window at night. A man outside said: "Come outside and suck my cock." Whenever the boy called his family for help, the man would run away.

One night, the father and older brother hid in the back of a truck. At 11:45 p.m., Federico snuck onto the property and walked over to the window. He said: "Suck my cock," and the father and brother tackled him. When police arrived, Federico claimed he was innocent. There was more than sufficient evidence, since Federico: (1) snuck onto the property and avoided the motion-sensor light as if he had been there before; (2) appeared outside the boy's window at the same time as previous nights; and (3) spoke the same message. The boy testified that the voice he heard that night was the same voice he heard before.

There must be evidence of a proposed meeting to prove enticement.

- **Insufficient.** *Comm. v. Hall,* 80 Mass. App. Ct. 317 (2011): The defendant persuaded a 14 year old girl to take naked pictures of herself with her cell phone and send them to him. While this was a violation of child pornography laws, it did not constitute enticement. The defendant never attempted to lure her to a specific place for sexual activity. She decided when and where she would take the photos. The child enticement statute is meant to protect children who are lured to a place chosen by the perpetrator.

- **Sufficient.** *Comm. v. Brown*, 2014 WL 6837053 (Appeals Court): Lee Brown approached an 11 year old girl on her way to school and handed her a note about her "kissable lips." He said, "You would only have to wait but for a few minutes." Brown argued his note was not an invitation to meet, but simply posed "a hypothetical situation." In reality, Brown did invite her to remain at the street corner, where he wanted to illegally touch her.

- **Open-ended invitation sufficient.** *Comm. v. Griswold,* 2012 WL 669440 (Appeals Court): After the victim turned 14, he began to visit Robert Griswold's home to watch movies and smoke marijuana. Griswold would often engage in sexual acts with a younger boy, and discuss it with the victim. Griswold asked the victim if he would like to try anything sexual, but said that he would never force him. The victim declined Griswold's offer, but continued to visit because he "enjoyed hanging out." Griswold's initial invitation for sex, even though it was open-ended, constituted enticement.

The solicited crime does not need to happen. *Comm. v. Grant*, 2020 WL 4432607 (Appeals Court): The 15 year old victim got rides to the mall from Gerald Grant. Grant began asking her to get him nude pictures of herself or her friends. His persistent requests for nude photos of minors amounted to enticement because Grant was trying to possess child pornography. It did not matter that his hoped-for crimes never occurred.

Evidence that the victim initiated a sexual encounter does not negate enticement. *Comm. v. Ortiz*, 2017 WL 1969726 (Appeals Court): 26 year old Angel Ortiz and the 12 year old victim first communicated through social media. Ortiz told the victim that he wanted to spend his birthday with her, so the two agreed that he would drive to meet her. The victim snuck out of her house at 2:30 a.m. and got into Ortiz's car. The victim told Ortiz that they "should have some fun." They engaged in both oral and vaginal sex. The victim later told her father she had "sex with somebody named Angel" and that it was her idea.

Enticement occurred despite evidence that the victim initiated the encounter. Ortiz had the victim sneak out of her house and coaxed her to remain in his car by offering her alcohol. The purpose of § 26C is to protect minors from precisely the type of conduct involved in this case.

Enticement may be done on behalf of a third party. *Comm. v. Fernandez*, 2013 WL 184023 (Appeals Court): Cardoza, the boyfriend of the victim's mother, told the 14 year old victim to stay home from school because he needed help with something. When they were alone, he fondled her, asked her to have sex with him, and exposed his penis.

Later that morning, Cardoza asked the victim if she needed money. She said "yes." Cardoza told the victim to call his friend, Fernandez, and ask him for $40. Cardoza suggested the victim call Fernandez her "sugar daddy" and make sexually explicit comments. When the victim told Cardoza that Fernandez was coming over, he left. The evidence showed that Cardoza intended that Fernandez pay the victim for sexual conduct.

Related Offense

Electronic Enticement for Sexual Services of a Child Under 18. 265 § 26D prohibits electronic communication to entice an actual child for prostitution. Right of Arrest: Felony. For more detail, see *LED's Juvenile Law, Chapter 10.*

8 Treatment of Animals

CRUELTY TO ANIMALS
272, § 77

Elements

The suspect did, or caused to be done, one or more of the following acts:

- **Beat.** Loaded, tortured, cruelly beat, or mutilated an animal; or
- **Use as a lure.** Used an animal in a cruel or inhuman manner in a race, game or contest, or in training, or as a lure or bait for another live animal (except fishing); or
- **Neglect.** Unnecessarily failed to provide an animal with proper food, drink, shelter, sanitary environment, or protection from the weather; or
- **Abandon.** Willfully abandoned; or
- **Transport cruelly.** Carried, or caused an animal to be carried, in or upon a vehicle, or otherwise, in an unnecessarily cruel manner.

Right of Arrest

Felony.

Penalty

First offense: SP NMT 7 yrs or HC NMT 2½ yrs; and/or Fine NMT $5,000. *Comm. v. Waller*, 90 Mass. App. Ct. 295 (2016) (court may prohibit pet ownership as a condition of probation).

Subsequent offense: SP NMT 10 yrs; and/or Fine NMT $10,000.

Legal Defense

Killing dangerous dog. 140, § 156 provides that any person may kill a dog that:

- Suddenly assaults him outside the enclosure of its owner or keeper; or
- Is out of the enclosure of its owner or keeper and not under immediate care, while in the act of worrying, wounding, or killing people, livestock, or fowls.

Unless the person intended to be cruel, or recklessly disregarded the dog's suffering, there is no liability. A person who wounds or kills a dog shall promptly report it to the owner, an animal control officer, or a police officer. See *Comm. v. Whitson*, 97 Mass. App. Ct. 798 (2020).

Animal Safekeeping

Notice to owner. 272, § 82 requires that officers *try* to notify the owner of any seized animals. Officers must care for animals until the owner takes custody, not to exceed 60 days from the date of notice. Finally, the owner must pay for the animal's care.

Impoundment procedures. Under 272, § 104, if an animal is lawfully impounded for cruelty or fighting, the law enforcement agency or the prosecutor may file a petition with the court requesting that the person from whom the animal was seized, or a person claiming an interest in the animal, be ordered to post a security payment for upfront animal care costs. If granted, the person must post the security within 10 business days or forfeit the animal.

209A protection for animals. 209A, § 11 allows judges to order that a defendant refrain from abusing or removing a domesticated animal. See *Chapter 13*.

Vehicle confinement of animals. 140, § 174F prohibits confining an animal in a motor vehicle in a manner that could reasonably be expected to threaten the health of the animal due to exposure to extreme heat or cold.

A police officer, animal control officer, or firefighter:
- Must first make reasonable efforts to locate the vehicle's owner.
- May enter the vehicle by any reasonable means to protect the health and safety of the animal.
- May not search the vehicle or seize items found unless otherwise permitted by law.
- Must leave written notice in a secure and conspicuous location on or in the vehicle bearing his/her name, title, and the address of the location where the animal may be retrieved (the owner may only retrieve the animal after paying charges for maintenance, care, medical treatment, and/or impoundment of the animal).
- Will be immune from criminal or civil liability for removing the animal.

A citizen:
- Must make reasonable efforts to locate the vehicle's owner.
- May not enter the vehicle unless the person:
  - Notifies law enforcement first;
  - Determines that the vehicle is locked and there is no reasonable means for exit;
  - Uses no more force than reasonably necessary to enter and remove the animal;
  - Has a good faith belief, based on the circumstances, that entry is reasonably necessary to prevent imminent danger or harm to the animal; and
  - Remains with the animal in a safe location in reasonable proximity to the vehicle until a first responder arrives.
- Will be immune from criminal or civil liability for removing the animal.

Penalty: *1st offense:* CMVI $150; *2nd offense:* CMVI $300; *3rd offense:* CMVI $500.

Notes

Anyone with care and custody of an animal may be charged. *Comm. v. Wilson*, 2012 WL 6709655 (Appeals Court): Although the defendant's mother claimed sole ownership of the malnourished dogs, her son, who had been living with her for two years, shared responsibility for feeding the dogs. The son usually purchased the dog food. The fact that only the mother signed the animal surrender form did not prove that she was the only owner.

The standard for cruel treatment is the same whether inflicted by the animal owner or another person. *Comm. v. Lufkin*, 89 Mass. 579 (1863).

Objective standard applies to cruel acts. The perpetrator must simply act intentionally, whether or not he understands that he is being cruel. *Comm. v. Szewczyk*, 89 Mass. App. Ct. 711 (2016): Stanley Szewczyk admitted that he shot his neighbor's dog with a pellet gun from 50 feet away. He hit the dog with one shot to scare her from his yard — not because it was aggressive, but to protect his wife, who suffered from multiple sclerosis, from falling while trying to avoid stepping in dog feces on their property.

It was irrelevant that Szewczyk intended merely to "sting" the dog. He caused a pellet to lodge in her leg, deep in the muscle and close to the bone, causing severe pain. The dog was unable to walk for a week. The dog needed surgery and had a permanent limp. Szewczyk had legal alternatives to shooting the dog, including monitoring the property for feces before his wife went out or calling the animal control officer.

A separate count of cruelty may be charged for each animal affected. *Comm. v. Erickson*, 2016 WL 105455 (Appeals Court) (defendant was properly charged with eight counts of animal cruelty when she failed to provide adequate food and water for her eight cats).

Failure to provide food, drink, shelter, or sanitary environment. The offense of failing to provide an animal with proper food, drink, shelter, or sanitary environment does *not* require that the suspect intend to mistreat the animal. It simply requires very poor care. *Comm. v. Erikson*, 74 Mass. App. Ct. 172 (2009). *Comm. v. Casey*, 2021 WL 2589065 (Appeals Court) (by leaving her dog in a car for five hours without care, the owner "unnecessarily fail[ed] to provide it with proper . . . drink;" proof this caused the dog's death is not an element of animal cruelty).

The neglected animal does not have to be harmed. *Comm. v. Curry*, 150 Mass. 509 (1890) (defendant left his horse harnessed to a carriage in the woods all night because he was drunk; his conviction was upheld even though his horse was not hurt). *Comm. v. Erickson*, 2016 WL 105455 (Appeals Court) (two of the eight cats recovered from the defendant's unsanitary residence had medically acceptable weights; however, the defendant was still guilty of animal cruelty as to all eight cats based on the poor care she provided).

Both wild and domesticated animals protected. *Comm. v. Linhares*, 80 Mass. App. Ct. 819 (2011) (the defendant intentionally drove his car over a mother duck, who was leading her babies across the street; he hit the accelerator, smashed into her, stopped, smiled at the witnesses, and sped away; it made no difference that the duck was a wild animal).

Related Offenses

Tethering of Dogs. 140, § 174E(a) prohibits a person owning or keeping a dog from chaining or tethering the dog:

- Outside for any length of time if under the age of 6 months.
- If six months or older, for longer than 5 hours in a 24 hour period; and
- Outside from 10:00 p.m. to 6:00 a.m., unless the tethering is for less than 15 minutes, and the dog is not left unattended by the owner.

The tether must be designed for dogs, and may not weigh more than 1/8 of the dog's body weight.

Penalty: *1st offense:* Fine NMT $50 or written warning; *2nd offense:* Fine NMT $200; *3rd offense:* Fine NMT $500 and impoundment of the dog in a local shelter at the keeper or guardian's expense, or loss of ownership of the dog. Issue local ordinance or bylaw ticket under 40, § 21D. Enforcement: A police officer of the Massachusetts Society for the Prevention of Cruelty to Animals and the Animal Rescue League of Boston or an animal control officer.

Outside Confinement of Dogs. 140, § 174E(b). A person owning or keeping a dog may confine the dog outside in:

- A secure pen with dimensions of at least 100 square feet; or
- A fully fenced, electronically fenced, or otherwise securely enclosed yard; or
- A trolley system or tether attached to a pulley in a cable run, provided that:
  - Only one dog is tethered to each run;
  - The collar or harness attached to the tether is not a choke or pinch collar, and has enough room to fit two adult fingers between the collar and throat;
  - There is a swivel on at least one end of the tether;
  - The tether and cable are at least 10 feet in length and the cable is mounted 4–7 feet above the ground;
  - The dog can reach clean water and appropriate shelter; and
  - It is configured so that it will confine the dog to the property, does not extend over an edge that could result in strangulation of the dog, and does not become tangled with other objects or animals.

The dog must have access to clean water, and appropriate shelter, which:

- Allows the dog to remain dry and protected from elements;
- Is fully enclosed on at least 3 sides, with a roof and solid floor;
- Has an entrance flexible enough for entry and exit, but sturdy enough to block the entry of weather elements;
- Has clean bedding;
- Is small enough to retain the dog's body heat and large enough to allow the dog to stand, lie down, and turn comfortably;
- Is structurally sound and in good repair; and
- Has suitable drainage.

Exceptions may be made when reasonably necessary for the safety of a dog that is in a camping or recreational area pursuant to the area's policy; or actively engaged in shepherding or herding cattle or other livestock, or engaged in conduct directly related to the business of cultivating agricultural products.

A person may not leave a dog outside for more than 15 minutes when:

- A weather advisory, warning, or watch is issued by authorities; or
- Outside environmental conditions pose a risk to the health or safety of the dog (e.g., extreme heat, cold, wind, rain, snow, or hail), based on the dog's breed, age, or physical condition.

The dog may not be subjected to cruel or inhumane conditions, including but not limited to:

- Filthy and dirty conditions (e.g., exposure to waste, garbage, dirty water, noxious odors, or dangerous objects);
- Taunting, prodding, hitting, harassing, threatening, or otherwise harming the dog; and
- Subjecting the dog to dangerous conditions, including attacks by other animals.

Penalty: *1st offense:* Fine NMT $50 or written warning; *$2^{nd}$ offense:* Fine NMT $200; *$3^{rd}$ offense:* Fine NMT $500 and impoundment of the dog in a local shelter at the keeper or guardian's expense, or loss of ownership of the dog. Issue local ordinance or bylaw ticket under 40, § 21D. Enforcement: Police officers from the MSCPA or Animal Rescue League of Boston or an animal control officer.

Removing Dog Collar. 266, § 47 punishes the wrongful removal of a collar from a licensed dog. Penalty: HC NMT 6 months; and/or Fine NMT $100. Right of Arrest: Complaint.

Dog Leasing or Renting. 272, § 80I prohibits engaging in the business of leasing or renting dogs. Penalty: *1st offense:* $100 Fine; *$2^{nd}$ offense:* $500 Fine; *$3^{rd}$ or subsequent offense:* $1,000 Fine. The penalty applies to both the business and person who rented or leased the dog. Of course, this law does not apply to businesses that provide service dogs, canine foster care, therapy dogs, or pet adoptions. Pet stores may take back dogs from owners who are unable to care for them.

Devocalization of Dog or Cat. 272, § 80½ prohibits performing or causing the surgical devocalization of a dog or cat. Right of Arrest: Felony.

Malicious Killing, Injury, or Attempted Poisoning of Domestic Animals. 266, § 112. Right of Arrest: Felony. *Comm. v. Epifania*, 80 Mass. App. Ct. 71 (2011).

Death by Drowning. 272, § 80E½ prohibits putting an animal to death by drowning. Right of Arrest: Felony. Penalty: *1st offense:* SP NMT 7 yrs or HC NMT 2½ yrs; and/or Fine NMT $5,000. *$2^{nd}$ or subsequent offense:* SP NMT 10 yrs and/or Fine NMT $10,000.

Unauthorized Removal of Research Animals or Destruction of Laboratory Equipment and Data. 266, § 104B. Right of Arrest: Felony.

SEXUAL CONTACT WITH ANIMALS
272, § 77C

Elements

The suspect did one or more of the following acts:

- **Perform.** Engaged in sexual contact (SC) with an animal; or offered, accepted an offer for, or otherwise obtained an animal with the intent that the animal be used for SC; or

- **Promote.** Organized, promoted, or knowingly participated as an observer in an act involving SC with an animal; or

- **Aid.** Caused or aided another person to engage in SC with an animal; or

- **Permit.** Knowingly permitted SC with an animal on any premises under his control; or

- **Induce.** Induced or otherwise enticed a child under 18, or a person with a developmental or intellectual disability, to engage in SC with an animal; or engaged in SC with an animal in the presence of a child under 18 or a person with a developmental or intellectual disability; or

- **Force.** Forced another person to engage in SC with an animal; or

- **Depict.** Disseminated photographs, videotapes or other depictions of SC with animals.

Definition of Sexual Contact

- Any act between a person and an animal that involves contact between the sex organs or anus of one and the mouth, anus or sex organs of the other; or

- Touching or fondling the sex organs or anus of an animal; or

- Any transfer or transmission of semen by the person upon any part of the animal; or

- The insertion of any part of a person's body or any object into the vaginal or anal opening of an animal, or the insertion of any part of the animal's body into the vaginal or anal opening of the person.

Penalty

1st offense: SP NMT 7 yrs or HC NMT 2½ yrs; and/or Fine NMT $5,000.

2nd or subsequent offense: SP NMT 10 yrs; and/or Fine NMT $10,000.

Conditions: Offender must forfeit the animal. Offender is also prohibited from working in any capacity that requires him to be in contact with an animal, owning an animal, residing in a household where any animals are present, or engaging in an occupation or participating in a volunteer position at any establishment where animals are present. Prohibition remains in effect for a minimum of 5 years or any length of time the court deems reasonable.

MISTREATMENT OF POLICE ANIMALS
272, § 77A

Elements

- *Intentional.* The suspect willfully:

  - **Tormented**, beat, kicked, struck, mutilated, injured, disabled, or otherwise mistreated; or

  - **Interfered**, by *any* action, with the lawful performance of;

- *Police dog or horse.* A dog or horse owned by a police department.

Right of Arrest

272, § 77A warrantless arrest in presence.

Penalty

HC NMT 2½ yrs; and/or Fine NLT $100, NMT $500.

Notes

Interference sufficient for offense. This statute punishes willful mistreatment and interference "by any action whatsoever." This elastic standard may be employed by officers to good advantage in those instances when an offender's conduct involves unprovoked interference, yet fails to rise to the level of animal abuse.

POSSESS OR TRAIN FIGHTING ANIMALS
272, § 94

Elements

The suspect:

- ***Possessed with intent to exhibit.*** Owned, possessed or trained with the intent to exhibit a bird, dog, or other fighting animal; or

- ***Promoted.*** Established or promoted an exhibition of birds, dogs, or other fighting animals; or

- ***Transferred.*** Loaned, sold, or transferred any animal for fighting; or

- ***Possessed for breeding.*** Possessed or kept any animal for the purpose of breeding with the intent that its offspring be used in animal fighting.

Entry & Right of Arrest

Warrantless entry: Under 272, § 89 police officers and animal control officers may enter *any place* without a warrant where people are preparing for or actually engaging in an exhibition of fighting animals.

Arrest all persons present & seize animals: Section 89 also authorizes the arrest of *all* persons present and the seizure of any animals associated with the exhibition.

Penalty

SP NMT 5 yrs or HC NMT 1 year; and/or Fine NMT $1,000.

Forfeiture of fighting animals: 272, § 91 enables a court having jurisdiction over the offense to order the forfeiture of fighting animals. A forfeited animal must be individually assessed by an organization to determine the animal's suitability for adoption. Section 92 allows an owner "aggrieved by such judgment" to appeal to the superior court within 24 hours of the order; however, that person may be assessed the costs of the appeal. Section 93 allows the court to assess expenses for the care and destruction of fighting animals.

Related Offense

Aiding or Being Present at Exhibition of Fighting Animals. 272, § 95 prohibits two acts: (1) intentionally being present at any place preparing to hold an exhibition of fighting animals; or (2) being present at, aiding in, or contributing to such an exhibition. Penalty: SP NMT 5 yrs or HC NMT 2½ yrs; and/or Fine NMT $1,000. Right of Arrest: Felony.

Law Enforcement Dimensions

Part III

SEXUAL OFFENSES

Rape, Indecent A&B, Sexual Exposure, Prostitution, Child Pornography, and Other Misconduct

Chapters 9 – 12

© John Sofis Scheft, Esq.
All rights reserved

9 Rape and Indecent A&B

RAPE
265, § 22(b)

Elements

- **Intercourse.** The suspect engaged in natural or unnatural sexual intercourse;

- **Force or threat.** By compelling the victim to submit by force or by threat of bodily injury against his or her will.

Right of Arrest

Felony.

Penalty

1st offense: SP NMT 20 yrs.

2nd or subsequent: SP Life or any term of years.

AGGRAVATED RAPE
265, § 22(a)

Elements

- **Intercourse.** The suspect engaged in natural or unnatural sexual intercourse;

- **Force or threat.** By compelling the victim to submit by force or by threat of bodily injury against his or her will; and

- **Aggravating factor.** The rape episode:
    - Caused serious bodily injury; or
    - Constituted a joint enterprise; or
    - Occurred during the commission or attempted commission of one of the following offenses: 265, § 15A (ABDW); § 15B (ADW); § 17 (Armed Robbery); § 19 (Unarmed Robbery); § 26 (Kidnapping); 266, § 14 (Armed B&E of Dwelling); § 15 (Unarmed B&E); § 16 (B&E with Intent to Commit a Felony); § 17 (B&E Daytime); § 18 (Night Entry of a Dwelling); 269, § 10 (Carrying a Dangerous Weapon).

©Law Enforcement Dimensions – *All rights reserved.*

Right of Arrest

Felony.

Penalty

SP Life or any term of years.

Notes

Rape is universally regarded as the most intrusive crime. Victims often feel humiliated after having their bodies violated in this manner, which means that police investigators must be as sensitive as possible.

Element 1: Natural or unnatural sexual intercourse.

- **Natural intercourse** consists of the insertion, no matter how slight, of the penis into the vagina.

- **Unnatural intercourse** includes oral intercourse, such as fellatio (oral contact between the mouth of one person and the penis of another) and cunnilingus (contact between the mouth of one person and the female sex organs — vagina, vulva, or labia — of another). It also includes anal intercourse. *Comm. v. Gallant*, 373 Mass. 577 (1977). *Comm. v. Edward*, 34 Mass. App. Ct. 521 (1993) (oral rape occurred when the defendant placed his lips on the fifteen year old babysitter's vulva or labia; intrusion is not required). *Comm. v. Guy*, 24 Mass. App. Ct. 783 (1987) (female-to-female cunnilingus constitutes unnatural intercourse).

    Other intrusions into the genital or anal opening are covered, e.g., inserting a finger (known as digital rape) or an object. *Comm. v. Cifizzari*, 397 Mass. 560 (1986) (pushing mop handle into victim's vagina constituted unnatural intercourse).

    Gender irrelevant. The rape statutes do not define the various crimes in terms of gender; however, the vast majority of cases involve male perpetrators and female victims. The fact that rape may involve unnatural intercourse means that a man may rape another man; a woman may rape another woman; a woman may even rape a man. All possible combinations fall under the rape prohibition. *Comm. v. Whitehead*, 379 Mass. 640 (1980) (woman raped another woman by forced oral sex; first reported case in Massachusetts).

Nature of the penetration required.

- **Evidence of slight penetration constitutes intercourse; ejaculation of semen not required.** *Comm. v. Baldwin*, 24 Mass. App. Ct. 200 (1987) (intrusion into vagina itself is not required to establish "wrongful penetration" for rape; here, victim testified that defendant spread Vaseline on her vulva or labia and attempted penetration for 10 minutes).

- **On the other hand, ejaculating in victim's mouth sufficient penetration.** *Comm. v. Pena*, 96 Mass. App. Ct. 655 (2019) (defendant ejaculated in 11 year old victim's mouth without inserting his penis; this was still rape by unnatural intercourse; skin-to-skin contact is not required).

- **Anal rape requires penetration of anus.** There must be more than "penetration of the defendant's penis into that area between the victim's buttocks." Some penetration of the anus must occur, not just the "butt cheeks." *Comm. v. Nylander*, 26 Mass. App. Ct. 784 (1989).

- **Victim does *not* have to be penetrated.** In most cases, the victim is penetrated by the perpetrator; however, rape is still the appropriate charge whenever there is forced sexual penetration, *regardless of who is penetrated*. In *Comm. v. Guy*, 24 Mass. App. Ct. 783 (1987), the court ruled that rape occurred when the female victim was forced to penetrate the vaginas of two consenting females. In *Comm. v. Hackett*, 383 Mass. 888 (1981), rape occurred when the male defendant performed fellatio on a 15 year old boy. It did not matter that the defendant's mouth was penetrated by the boy's penis, rather than the other way around.

- **A perpetrator may rape even though he did not physically participate.** In *Comm. v. Nuby*, 32 Mass. App. Ct. 360 (1992), the defendant forced his girlfriend's young boys to fondle their mother's breasts and penetrate her vagina with their tongues. The court viewed it as irrelevant that the defendant did not penetrate the victim because the "broad language [of the rape statute] is designed to punish the outrage of compelled sex." *Comm. v. Prado*, 94 Mass. App. Ct. 253 (2018) (victim ordered to insert her fingers into her vagina).

The defendant must intend penetration but does not have to be motivated by sexual gratification. *Comm. v. Nowell*, 2019 WL 1306237 (Appeals Court) (defendant still guilty of rape despite claim that the victim had hidden drugs in his rectum and he merely sought to retrieve the drugs; penetration is rape regardless of the defendant's motivation).

Element 2: By force or threat. The force used to commit rape does not need to be strong. It must be sufficient to overcome the victim's will. The phrase, "against the victim's will," simply means "without consent." *Comm. v. Oquendo*, 83 Mass. App. Ct. 190 (2013).

- **Constructive force.** Rape occurs if the victim's participation is obtained by constructive force, which is threatening words or gestures. For example, in *Comm. v. Caracciola*, 409 Mass. 648 (1991), the defendant lied about being a police officer to a prostitute, showed her his holstered gun, ordered her into his car, then threatened to arrest her if she did not have sex with him. Afraid of being locked up, the victim submitted without physically resisting. This was rape.

- **Constructive force may be less with a child victim.** *Comm. v. Dumas*, 83 Mass. App. Ct. 536 (2013): On the basis of her religion,[1] the teenage victim believed that the spirits of her ancestors possessed influence over her life. The 47 year old defendant told the victim he was the spiritual leader of a secret organization and that if she did not submit, the spirits of her ancestors would hurt her. The victim was afraid to resist or tell anyone. Typically, constructive force involves direct threats, but that is not always the case. Here, an adult in a position of authority preyed upon the vulnerability of a much younger victim.

- **If the sexual assaults begin when the victim is a child and continue past his or her 16th birthday, a pattern may demonstrate constructive force.** *Comm. v. Moniz*, 87 Mass. App. Ct. 532 (2015): The victim's adoptive father began sexually assaulting the victim when he was young. The defendant was an authority figure and the victim feared his angry, violent tirades. He also believed the family would fall apart if he resisted.

---

[1] She was a child of Hmong refugees from Laos, who practice the Houpell religion.

- **Fraud is not considered constructive force for rape.** If the suspect convinced a person to engage in intercourse through fraud (not constructive force), rape did *not* occur. *Comm. v. Goldberg*, 338 Mass. 377 (1959). *Comm. v. Feijoo*, 419 Mass. 486 (1995) (martial arts instructor persuaded his naïve student that completing "sexual tests" would help him become "a ninja warrior"). *Suliveres v. Commonwealth*, 449 Mass. 112 (2007).

Lack of consent. Consent must be given at the time of the act. Evidence that the victim later forgave her attacker is irrelevant. Moreover, rape is never excused, regardless of the relationship of the parties. *Comm. v. Johnston*, 60 Mass. App. Ct. 13 (2003) (husband guilty of raping his wife).

- **Refusal sufficient, resistance unnecessary.** Any refusal is sufficient if it demonstrates that the victim's lack of consent was "honest and real." The victim is not required to resist physically. While the level of resistance should be documented, it should *never* be regarded as an element of the offense. There are many instances when resistance is not physically or emotionally possible.

    In *Comm. v. Sherry*, 386 Mass. 682 (1982), three doctors were convicted of raping a nurse. They drove her to a home in Rockport. Following a series of unwanted sexual advances, including forcibly undressing her, they each separately had intercourse with her. Later, the doctors insisted that she had not resisted sufficiently. The SJC emphatically disagreed, noting that the victim testified that she felt physically numb, unable to fight, and humiliated. *Comm. v. Armstrong*, 73 Mass. App. Ct. 245 (2008) (victim's testimony that she pretended to be asleep proved unconsented intercourse amounting to rape).

- **Injury may prove lack of consent.** *Comm. v. Paige*, 488 Mass. 677 (2021): The defendant said he never had intercourse with the victim. However, nonconsensual intercourse was circumstantially proven when she was discovered dead, with extensive injuries to her head and face, and with the defendant's sperm recently deposited in her vagina.

- **Request that offender wear condom is not consent.** *Comm. v. Scott*, 98 Mass. App. Ct. 843 (2020) ("Society long ago moved beyond the point where a victim's request that a rapist use a condom could be considered consent." Here, victim only asked defendant to use a condom after he dragged her into the bedroom and pinned her arms down).

- **Lack of mental capacity to consent is rape.** As previously discussed, victims may indicate their lack of consent verbally or physically. Sometimes the physical or mental condition of victims may prevent them from deciding. Their inability to decide — due to drug or alcohol intoxication, unconsciousness, sleep or other causes — may not be viewed by suspects as an invitation to have sex. *Comm. v. Rattanavong*, 2016 WL 6464408 (Appeals Court) (defendant knew victim was in a deep sleep when he penetrated her).

- **Intoxication must be extreme.** *Comm. v. Urban*, 450 Mass. 608 (2008) reminds us that a person may be drunk and still capable of consenting to intercourse. In order to prove rape, police must gather evidence that the victim was "in a state of utter stupefaction . . . caused by drunkenness . . . or drugs." *Comm. v. Mountry*, 463 Mass. 80 (2012) (defendant provided his 16 year old niece with vodka, then raped her after she vomited on her bed; the court rejected his defense that he had been too drunk to recognize how debilitated his niece was; after all, the defendant had safely driven to and from the liquor store before the rape and made incriminating comments the next day to his wife about what happened).

- **Mental disability may be considered in determining consent.** *Comm. v. Bonds*, 445 Mass. 821 (2006): The victim, "Ellen," was 19 years old and suffered from a brain disorder. Stephanie Hoch, an acquaintance, called James Bonds and put Ellen on the phone. Bonds said he wanted to "fuck her," but Ellen told him she would only come over if they hung out as friends. Hoch convinced Ellen to go and promised she would protect her. Bonds raped Ellen in his house while Hoch watched television.

  At trial, Hoch claimed Ellen wanted to have sex with Bonds, but Ellen's mother testified that Ellen was naïve and believed these people were her "friends." She gave two examples of times when Ellen's "friends" stole from her and beat her up. The testimony was allowed because it gave a clear picture of why Ellen went to Bonds' apartment when a person without a mental disability would have known to stay away. Also see *Comm. v. Figueroa*, 79 Mass. App. Ct. 389 (2011) (86 year old victim in a nursing home was told by the defendant, a male nursing assistant, that he was performing a medical test when he vaginally raped her).

Suspects frequently argue that, even if the victim did not consent, they did not intend to rape. The SJC has declared: "While the Commonwealth must prove lack of consent, it does not have to prove that the defendant intended that intercourse be without consent." *Comm. v. Lopez*, 433 Mass. 722 (2001). *Comm. v. Leftkowitz*, 20 Mass. App. Ct. 513 (1985) (jury believed that the victim, a nurse, did not consent; the intent of the defendant, a physician at her hospital, was irrelevant).

After consent is clearly withdrawn, continued penetration becomes rape. *Comm. v. Sherman*, 481 Mass. 464 (2019): If the initial penetration was consensual, the victim must <u>reasonably communicate</u> to the defendant his or her withdrawal of consent. The communication does not have to be verbal — physical gestures, such as trying to push the defendant away, may be enough. Once consent is withdrawn, continued intercourse is rape. See, e.g., *Comm. v. Enimpah*, 81 Mass. App. Ct. 657 (2012) (the victim, a prostitute, agreed to have sex with Brian Enimpah for a fee; Enimpah became very aggressive and, when she told him to stop, he put his hand over her mouth and became more forceful; while the victim consented to penetration initially, Enimpah raped her when he ignored her pleas to stop and her efforts to push him off).

Also, consent to an earlier, completed act of intercourse does not automatically permit other forms of intercourse without permission.

<u>*Aggravated rape*</u> *involves one of 3 aggravating factors.*

- **Serious bodily injury.** Undefined by the statute, the term "serious" should be given its ordinary meaning by officers. *Comm. v. Cheremond*, 461 Mass. 397 (2012). The victim's injury may occur during an escape attempt. *Comm. v. Thomas*, 89 Mass. App. Ct. 422 (2016) (after the defendant raped the victim, he ordered her to remain where she was so he could continue to rape her throughout the night; when she attempted to escape out the second-floor window, the defendant grabbed her; she fell to the ground and was severely injured; the defendant's actions of raping her, threatening her, and causing her to fall were a continuous course of conduct that produced her severe injuries).

- **Joint enterprise.** The accomplices must rape a common victim. *Comm. v. Grant*, 391 Mass. 645 (1984) (defendants duped the victim into believing that they were taking her to a studio for "modeling" photos; instead, they brought her to an abandoned building and forced her to engage in oral and anal intercourse). Compare *Comm. v. Parreira*, 72 Mass. App. Ct. 308 (2008) (both defendants brought two girls to a building, then separated and raped each one in a different room; this was not a joint enterprise, since there was no evidence that they planned or participated in each other's sexual assault).

- **Attempted or actual ABDW or other offenses.** A final form of aggravated rape occurs during the commission or attempted commission of ADW, ABDW, armed robbery, unarmed robbery, kidnapping, certain B&E offenses, or carrying a dangerous weapon. The aggravating crime must occur during the same criminal episode as the rape. *Comm. v. Brown*, 66 Mass. App. Ct. 237 (2006).

Lesser included offenses. Rape under § 22(b) is a lesser included offense of aggravated rape under § 22(a). *Comm. v. Henry*, 37 Mass. App. Ct. 429 (1994) (defendant found guilty of rape because the alleged aggravating circumstance — his use of a knife — was not proven). Other lesser included offenses are: indecent A&B, A&B, assault with intent to rape, and assault.

RAPE OF CHILD UNDER 16
265, § 22A

Elements

The elements of this offense are identical to those of rape under 265, § 22(b), except that the victim of this crime must be under 16 years of age. Remember, like adult rape under 265, § 22, lack of consent on the part of the child must be proven. *Comm. v. Cobb*, 26 Mass. App. Ct. 283 (1988).

Right of Arrest

Felony.

Penalty

SP Life or any term of years.

AGGRAVATED RAPE OF CHILD UNDER 16
265, § 22B

Elements

Unconsented intercourse with a child under 16 must also involve one of the following 6 aggravating factors:

- **Crime.** During the attempted or actual commission of: burglary; home invasion; B&E; entering without breaking; kidnapping; robbery; ADW or ABDW; posing or exhibiting child in a state of nudity or sexual conduct; or

- **Injury.** Results in substantial bodily injury, defined by 265, § 13J as "bodily injury which creates a permanent disfigurement, protracted loss or impairment of a function of a body member, limb or organ, or substantial risk of death"; or

- **Bound.** Committed while victim bound or gagged; or

- **Drug or alcohol.** Committed after defendant administered, or caused to be administered, alcohol or a controlled substance by injection, ingestion, or any other means to the victim without the victim's consent; or

- **Accomplice.** Committed by a joint enterprise; or

- **Possible STD.** Committed in a manner in which the victim could contract a sexually transmitted disease (STD) about which the defendant knew or should have known.

Right of Arrest
Felony.

Penalty
Basic offense: Life or any term of years. Mandatory minimum: 15 yrs.

Enhanced penalty for rape and aggravated rape of child under 265, § 22C if prior conviction of indecent A&B, assault of child with intent to rape, forcible child rape, statutory rape, or adult rape in any U.S. state or territory: SP Life or any term of years. Mandatory minimum: 20 yrs.

Notes
Naturally, the age and size of the victim may be considered in determining whether force was used. *Comm. v. Lewandowski*, 22 Mass. App. Ct. 148 (1986) (mother and son convicted of forcible rape of a child who had been placed at the age of two in mother's foster care; child testified that son and foster mother put fingers "in her little hole [and it] hurt").

STATUTORY RAPE
265, § 23

Elements
- **Unlawful.** The suspect unlawfully;

- **Intercourse.** Engaged in natural or unnatural sexual intercourse with the victim;

- **Under 16.** Who was under 16 years of age at the time of the offense.

Right of Arrest
Felony.

Penalty

SP Life or any term of years; or HC NMT 2½ yrs. *Comm. v. Cheney*, 440 Mass. 568 (2003) (no pre-trial probation without Commonwealth's consent).

AGGRAVATED STATUTORY RAPE
265, § 23A

Elements

The intercourse with a child under 16 must also involve one aggravating factor:

- **Over 5-year gap.** More than a 5-year age difference between the defendant and the victim, who is under 12 years old; or

- **Over 10-year gap.** More than a 10-year age difference between the defendant and the victim, who is between the age of 12 and 16 years old; or

- **Mandated reporter.** At the time of the intercourse, the defendant was a mandated reporter of child abuse.

Right of Arrest

Felony.

Penalty

Basic: Life or any term of years. Mandatory minimum: 10 yrs.

Enhanced penalty for statutory and aggravated statutory rape: Under 265, § 23B, any adult or juvenile in any U.S. state or territory with a prior conviction of indecent A&B, assault of child with intent to rape, forcible rape of child, statutory rape, or adult rape will — after conviction for this offense — be penalized: SP Life or any term of years. Mandatory minimum: 15 yrs.

Notes

Unlawful intercourse. In other forms of rape, proving *unlawful* intercourse is not required because forcible sex is *always* forbidden. Since statutory rape does not have to be "forced," the "unlawful" element ensures the act has no legal justification (e.g., a husband may have intercourse with his 15 year old wife).

Child under 16 makes consent irrelevant. "The law conclusively presumes that those under 16 years of age are not sufficiently mature to understand fully the physical, mental, and emotional consequences of sexual intercourse." *Comm. v. Dunne*, 394 Mass. 10 (1985).*Comm. v. Cotting*, 248 Mass. 401 (1924) (evidence that child victim had sexual intercourse with others is also irrelevant and inadmissible in statutory rape trial).

The testimony of the victim as to his or her age is sufficient proof. *Comm. v. Duff*, 245 Mass. 81 (1923). *Comm. v. Griswold*, 2014 WL 7237102 (Appeals Court) (witness testified that when the victim was 15, he bragged about having sex with the defendant; also, defendant attempted to persuade a witness to lie and say the victim was 16).

Knowledge of victim's age.

- **Lack of knowledge no defense for principal.** The principal's honest mistake about the victim's age is no defense, even if the victim claimed to be or appeared to be "old enough." *Comm. v. Miller*, 385 Mass. 521 (1982). It is even irrelevant if the suspect is mistaken about the identity of the person he had sex with. In *Comm. v. Knap*, 412 Mass. 712 (1992), the defendant, who lived with his girlfriend, claimed that he was awakened in the middle of the night by someone massaging him. He responded sexually, and then realized that the person was not his girlfriend. Turning on the light, he saw the 13 year old babysitter. Even assuming that the defendant was telling the truth, he still committed this crime according to the SJC! In short, mistake as to age or identity, no matter how reasonable, is no defense to statutory rape or indecent A&B on a child under 14 (*discussed later*). These are known as *strict liability* crimes because no "blameworthy" state of mind need be proven, only the forbidden act.

- **Lack of knowledge is also no defense for an accomplice who is present.** *Comm. v. Harris*, 74 Mass. App. Ct. 105 (2009): Carlos Johnson met the 13 year old victim, Jane, on a telephone chat line. Daniel Harris drove them, and two other men, to a liquor store and a motel. Harris knew that Jane had sneaked out of her house over her father's objection and had become extremely intoxicated during the car ride. He was present when Johnson and the two other men took turns having intercourse with Jane in the motel room. Harris did not participate. He ended up giving Jane a ride home.

    Harris argued that he never knew Jane was under 16, so it was unfair to convict him as an accomplice to statutory rape. The Appeals Court ruled that a defendant does not need to be aware of the child victim's age if he is *present* during the rape. When an accomplice is present, he has the same opportunity as the principal to make judgments about the child's age from her appearance and the other circumstances surrounding the encounter. On the other hand, when the accomplice is accused of planning but not being present during the rape, there must be proof that he knew the victim's age in advance.

Minor can commit statutory rape. *Comm. v. Wilbur,* 479 Mass. 397 (2018): When 12 year old Wilbur W. was accused of raping the 8 year old victim, he claimed that it was consensual. However, the victim testified that he was afraid. Wilbur, who was four years older, directed the victim to perform oral sex on him, then raped him anally. The next day, the victim displayed his immaturity by asking, "What does it mean when someone tries to put their private in your butt?" This evidence defeated Wilbur's characterization of the incident as consensual experimentation. A child under 16 can be a victim or offender in a statutory rape case, as long as there is no discriminatory enforcement.

Impermissible to assume that the perpetrator is always male, or to treat homosexual activity more harshly. *Comm. v. Bernardo, B.*, 453 Mass. 158 (2009) (14 year old boy was prosecuted for having three female friends, all age 12, perform manual and oral sex on him at various times; the interaction among the participants suggested that it was consensual and that the boy was not aggressive or pressuring. Assuming that boys are always the perpetrator in sexual situations constitutes selective prosecution, which is unconstitutional). *Comm. v. Washington W.*, 457 Mass. 140 (2010) (a prosecutor may not treat a case more severely just because it involves homosexual activity).

Lesser included offense. Statutory rape is a lesser included offense of rape of child under 265, § 22A. *Comm. v. Franks*, 365 Mass. 74 (1976). However, because the government must show lack of consent on the part of the victim, indecent A&B on a child 14 or over is *not* a lesser included offense of statutory rape. *Comm. v. Rowe*, 18 Mass. App. Ct. 926 (1984).

Forcible rape and aggravated statutory rape are separate offenses. *Comm. v. Foreman*, 101 Mass. App. Ct. 398 (2022) (defendant properly convicted of both forcible rape of child and aggravated statutory rape based on a greater than 10-year age difference; each offense has a different element, which means a defendant may be convicted of both for the same episode).

RAPE BY PUBLIC SAFETY PERSONNEL
265, § 22(c)

Elements

- **Public safety personnel.** The suspect was a police officer, prosecutor, EMT, deputy sheriff, correction officer, court officer, probation or parole officer, constable, or anyone impersonating one of these officials; and

- **Intercourse.** Engaged in natural or unnatural sexual intercourse;

- **Custody or control.** With a person in his or her custody or control. [*Note:* Because the victim is in the custody or control of the official, consent is *not* a defense. This crime is, in essence, public safety statutory rape. However, the terms "custody" and "control" are *not* defined by § 22(c).]

Right of Arrest

Felony.

Penalty

1st offense: SP NMT 20 yrs.

2nd or subsequent: SP Life or any term of years.

Related Offense

Sexual Relations with a Prisoner. 268, § 21A covers any officer, employee or contractor of a correctional institution in Massachusetts who engages in sexual relations with an inmate inside or outside the institution. The term sexual relations is defined broadly as "intentional, inappropriate contact of a sexual nature." The consent of the inmate is, of course, not a defense to this charge. Penalty: SP NMT 5 yrs; and/or Fine $10,000. Right of Arrest: Felony.

DRUGGING PERSON FOR INTERCOURSE
272, § 3

Elements

- **Administer drug.** The suspect applied, administered, or caused to be taken any drug, matter or thing;

- **Intent to overpower.** With the intent to stupefy or overpower the victim so that the suspect or another person could have natural or unnatural sexual intercourse with the victim.

Right of Arrest

Felony.

Penalty

SP NLT 10 yrs, NMT Life.

Notes

Drug or stupefying substance. A substance with a medicinal purpose is a "drug" for this offense. *Comm. v. Odell*, 34 Mass. App. Ct. 100 (1993) (giving teenage girls seasickness medication to induce them to have intercourse violated this law). *Comm. v. Helfant*, 398 Mass. 214 (1986) (under the guise of making a house call and providing treatment for a bad back, the defendant, a neurosurgeon, injected Valium into his patient; he then had nonconsensual intercourse with her).

Furthermore, 94C, § 31 has been amended to include Flunitrazepam, Gamma Hydroxy Butyic Acid, and Ketamine Hydrochloride as Class A substances. These substances often facilitate rape. See *Chapter 20*.

Defendant must administer — not simply provide — the substance. "Administer" requires some forceful action or trickery by the suspect amounting to more than merely supplying drugs or alcohol to a willing individual. In *Comm. v. LeBlanc*, 73 Mass. App. Ct. 624 (2009), the 18 year old victim acknowledged that, at no time, did the defendant, a 50 year old attorney, force her to snort cocaine or to drink. She repeatedly testified that she voluntarily shared the defendant's cocaine and alcohol.

Intent. Note that the suspect must administer the substance "with the intent" to engage in sexual intercourse with another person. Even if the plan fails, the suspect is still guilty if his intent was to use the substance to facilitate unlawful intercourse.

ASSAULT WITH INTENT TO COMMIT RAPE
265, § 24

Elements

- **Assault.** The suspect committed an assault on the victim;

- **Specific intent.** While having the specific intent to rape the victim.

Right of Arrest

Felony.

Penalty

Basic offense: SP NMT 20 yrs or HC NMT 2½ yrs.

2nd or subsequent offense: SP Life or any term of years.

Notes

Assault the victim. While the offender almost always commits an A&B by touching the victim, touching is not required. Gestures and words alone may result in an assault with intent to rape. *Comm. v. Santiago*, 53 Mass. App. Ct. 567 (2002) (defendant followed the victim in his Jeep, including driving the wrong way down a street; asked her to get in three times; and showed her a weapon).

Specific intent. There must be proof that the perpetrator, at the time of the assault, had the goal of raping the victim. *Comm. v. Alvarado*, 2012 WL 1813439 (Appeals Court) (sufficient evidence: defendant attacked victim in dark, deserted area; pinned her down with his body; made a sexual comment; did not rob her despite the fact that she was holding a purse; and fled when police arrived). Consider the following factors. All of them need not apply to prove the offender's intent.

- **Type of assault** (was it directed toward the genitalia, breasts or buttocks? were clothes grabbed or ripped?). *Comm. v. Nickerson*, 388 Mass. 246 (1983) (defendant dragged the victim's body into some bushes and pulled her clothes off, including undergarments).

- **Restraint of victim** (was this done in a sexual way, e.g., forcing the legs open?). *Comm. v. Stockhammer*, 409 Mass. 867 (1991) (the defendant sat on the victim's chest and attempted to get her to take his penis in her mouth).

- **Sexual comments and/or advances** (did the perpetrator state his intention to rape? had there been a series of sexual comments prior to the attack?). *Comm. v. Morin*, 52 Mass. App. Ct. 780 (2001) (defendant entered victim's apartment forcibly, touched her breasts, locked the door, told her that he wanted to have anal sex with her).

- **Prior record or written comments.** *Comm. v. Martin*, 63 Mass. App. Ct. 587 (2005) (notes found in the defendant's possession contained violent sexual fantasies). *Comm. v. Santiago, supra.* (the defendant had raped two other women before encountering the woman in this case, who ran away from him).

Sexual remarks, touching or removal of clothing not required for conviction. The SJC has held that an assailant's intent to rape may be inferred when: (1) a female victim is assaulted at night in a secluded area; (2) there is no evidence of any prior relationship between the parties; and (3) there is no evidence the man intended to steal or was mentally ill. *Comm. v. Mahar*, 21 Mass. App. Ct. 307 (1985) (sufficient evidence: woman grabbed by stranger, who forced her to the ground, cut her with a knife in response to her screams, and fled when her struggling knocked him off balance).

Consent. Like rape, consent is a defense to this crime. *Comm. v. McKay*, 363 Mass. 220 (1973).

Related Offenses

Assault with Intent to Rape Child. 265, § 24B is the same as assault with intent to rape, except the offender directs his conduct toward a child under 16. *Comm. v. Dunne*, 394 Mass. 10 (1985) (irrelevant whether the defendant knew that the victim was under age).

Attempted Rape of Child. 274, § 6. See *Comm. v. Bell*, 455 Mass. 408 (2009) in *Chapter 2*.

INDECENT A&B AGE 14 & OVER
265, § 13H

Elements

- **Age 14 or older.** The victim was at least 14 years of age at the time of the offense;

- **Indecent.** The suspect committed an A&B which was "indecent";

- **No consent.** Which the victim did not consent to.

Right of Arrest

Felony.

Penalty

Basic offense: NMT 5 yrs or HC NMT 2½ yrs.

Disabled or elder victim: SP NMT 10 yrs or HC NMT 2½ yrs.

Subsequent offense: SP NMT 20 yrs.

INDECENT A&B UNDER AGE 14
265, § 13B

Elements

- **Under age 14.** The child was not yet 14 years of age at the time of the offense;

- **Indecent.** The suspect committed an A&B which was "indecent."

Note: A child under age 14 is presumed incapable of consenting.

Right of Arrest

Felony.

Penalty

Basic offense: NMT 10 yrs or HC NMT 2½ yrs.

Aggravated offense: Under 265, § 13B½, aggravated indecent A&B is committed during the attempted or actual commission of: burglary; home invasion; B&E; entering without breaking; kidnapping; robbery; ADW or ABDW; posing or exhibiting child in a state of nudity or sexual conduct; or if the defendant was a mandated reporter of child abuse: SP Life or any term of years. Mandatory minimum: 10 yrs. *Comm. v. Kozubal*, 488 Mass. 575 (2021) (for mandated reporters, indecent A&B is aggravated if committed while on duty, not while off duty).

Aggravated because prior offense: Under 265, § 13B¾, any adult or juvenile in any U.S. state or territory with a prior conviction of indecent A&B, assault of child with intent to rape, forcible rape of child, statutory rape, or adult rape will — after committing this offense — be penalized: SP Life or any term of years. Mandatory minimum: 15 yrs.

Notes

Indecent. An indecent act is fundamentally offensive. This standard is not vague because reasonable people understand it. *Comm. v. Miozza*, 67 Mass. App. Ct. 567 (2006).

- **Genitals, buttocks, female breasts.** An A&B becomes "indecent" if it involves touching portions of the anatomy commonly thought private, such as a person's genitals, buttocks, or female breasts. *Comm. v. Melo*, 95 Mass. App. Ct. 257 (2019).

- **Over *or* under clothes.** Touching over clothes can be indecent. *Comm. v. Sherman*, 2015 WL 867090 (Appeals Court) (defendant touched victim's vagina over her clothes while she was a psychiatric patient). Compare *Comm. v. Cruz*, 93 Mass. App. Ct. 136 (2018) (tight hug and slight lift of 13 year old's shirt, while inappropriate, was not criminally indecent).

- **"Humping."** *Comm. v. Igle*, 2011 WL 3444163 (Appeals Court): Kevin Igle lay down on the couch on top of his girlfriend's 11 year old daughter. Igle's whole body was fully clothed as he "rubbed up and down."

- **Stomach, thighs, or lower back.** Intentionally touching these areas may be indecent. *Comm. v. Lavigne*, 42 Mass. App. Ct. 313 (1997) (defendant offered a ride to 17 year old hitchhiker; defendant asked the victim if he "wanted to make some money"; defendant then put his hand on the victim's upper thigh within a few inches of the victim's genitals and briefly massaged the area). *Comm. v. Krasnecky*, 2017 WL 4448362 (Appeals Court) (defendant's hand went down the victim's back, reaching toward his buttocks; even though he only came close to touching the victim's buttocks, the touching was "sexual").

- **Forced kissing with the tongue.** "French kissing" is indecent. *Comm. v. Castillo*, 55 Mass. App. Ct. 563 (2002) (sufficient evidence: considerable age disparity between 30 year old defendant and 14 year old victim; the defendant was the stepfather of the victim's friend; the incident took place in the basement; and the defendant grabbed the victim and forced his tongue into her mouth).

- **Forced kissing without the tongue.** *Comm. v. Vazquez*, 65 Mass. App. Ct. 305 (2005): The defendant watched television with his wife's niece, Kathy, age 12. The defendant got up to leave and asked for a "goodbye kiss." Typically, he would kiss Kathy on the cheek if other people were around, but would kiss her on the lips if they were alone. This time, when Kathy attempted to give him a kiss on the cheek, he turned his head and touched his lips to Kathy's closed mouth for two seconds. In most situations, it would be inappropriate to criminalize a brief kiss that did not involve the tongue, but this case involved sexual overtones: the age difference (defendant in his 30s and Kathy 12); his position of familial authority; and his secrecy. Finally, the defendant also assaulted another of his wife's nieces, Maria, who was 15. Looking at the evidence, the defendant's kiss was not simply an innocent expression of affection.

- **Sticking thumb in mouth with suggestive comments.** In *Comm. v. Rosa*, 62 Mass. App. Ct. 622 (2004), the defendant invited the neighbor's 11 year old child into his garage. There, he inserted his thumb into her mouth and asked, "Do you know how to suck on it?" The child ran home because she thought "he was talking about his private area." The defendant later acknowledged to the investigating officer that his comments were sexually suggestive. Under the circumstances, the defendant behaved indecently.

- **Taking child's clothes off or forcing her to remove them herself.** *A.P. v. M.T.*, 92 Mass. App. Ct. 156 (2017): A 4 year old girl was playing outside with her neighbors. The girl ran back into the house, screaming "help me." The mother found the girl's clothes piled up near her toys. She had mud smeared on her legs and on her underwear in her crotch area. This proved that the defendants either took off the child's clothes or forced her to.

- **Touching a 9 year old's undeveloped chest.** *Comm. v. Rather*, 2017 WL 6028653 (Appeals Court): The defendant placed a blanket over the 9 year old victim's lap, reached under it, and rubbed her vagina over her clothes. He then touched her chest. Given the sexual nature of his conduct, touching the victim's chest was indecent regardless of her development. § 13B makes no classification based on gender, so it would have also been a violation if he had touched a 9 year old boy's chest under the same circumstances.

Whether a touching is _indecent_ depends on _the context_.

- **Incidental or accidental.** A suspect may argue that the contact was incidental or accidental. *Comm. v. Holman*, 51 Mass. App. Ct. 786 (2001) (defendant maintained that he was simply holding up his girlfriend's 12 year old daughter when she jumped into his arms and wrapped her legs around his waist to give him a hug; however, the jury believed the victim, who said the defendant moved his hand down her back to her buttocks and rubbed them during these hugs, rather than simply holding her up).

- **Intent for sexual gratification not required.** Indecent A&B depends on the suspect's conduct, not his state of mind. The defendant need only deliberately commit the act, regardless of his motivation. *Comm. v. Conefrey*, 37 Mass. App. Ct. 290 (1994). *Comm. v. Farrar*, 2012 WL 6049020 (Appeals Court) (intentionally grabbing 9 year old's buttocks indecent; defendant suddenly did this inside a camping tent without warning or comment).

- **Parents may commit this crime.** *Comm. v. Lawrence*, 68 Mass. App. Ct. 103 (2007): Eva Lawrence on several occasions took her 10 year old daughter's clothes off while she was asleep. She posed her in sexual positions and took pictures. In the process, she touched her daughter's vagina. Although Lawrence was the child's mother, the touching was indecent under the circumstances — the victim told her to stop and experienced shame ("I didn't tell my dad because it was hard to talk about").

The victim may do the touching. *Comm. v. Davidson*, 68 Mass. App. Ct. 72 (2007): Lawrence Davidson lived with his girlfriend and her 10 year old daughter. When he and the child were alone, they would play hide and seek, with Davidson in his underwear and the victim in her clothes. When he found her on three occasions, he told her she "had to touch the thing." She also rubbed his "private" with her nose. Davidson argued that he could not be convicted because he did not indecently touch the girl. However, the defendant does not have to perform the touching, as long as he directs the victim to touch him or a 3rd party.

For victim 14 and over, must show lack of consent. Interestingly, the law allows 14 year olds to consent to sexual touching but not intercourse. The minimum age for consensual intercourse is 16. See 265, § 23 (Statutory Rape).

- **Victim must be capable of consenting.** As with rape, a person may become incapable of consenting when intoxicated, unconscious, asleep, or mentally impaired. *Comm. v. Benedito*, 95 Mass. App. Ct. 548 (2019) (while the defendant was naked, he kissed the 23 year old victim on the mouth while she was sleeping; the victim was the sister of the defendant's girlfriend, and she jumped up and yelled when she realized what happened).

- **Verbal or physical objection not required to prove lack of consent.** *Comm. v. Shore*, 65 Mass. App. Ct. 430 (2006): At the end of her shift, while rubbing his 15 year old employee's shoulders, Dana Shore, a 47 year old pharmacist, unhooked her bra and fondled her breast. The victim said nothing because she was "in shock." Shore said, "I'm sorry, I hope that didn't make you feel uncomfortable," and "Please don't say anything because I can get in a lot of trouble."

    Later charged with indecent A&B, Shore claimed the victim consented because she did not pull away or ask him to stop. While a verbal or physical reaction shows an obvious lack of consent, their absence is accepted when the victim and perpetrator have different ages, authority, and experience — which was the case here.

Indecent A&B should not be routinely charged in a rape case unless there was a distinct act aside from the rape. *Comm. v. Rodriguez,* 83 Mass. App. Ct. 267 (2013) (defendant's conviction of indecent A&B, which was based on his licking her breast, was separate from the rape because it was not part of the "act of penetration"). *Comm. v. Ciampa,* 2015 WL 9467400 (Appeals Court) (grabbing the victim's penis and moving it back and forth was not incidental to the act of penetrating his rectum; the same was true for the defendant's A&B conviction for hitting the victim in the mouth).

Lesser included offenses. Indecent A&B on a child under 14 is a lesser included offense of forcible rape of a child under 16, when it is undisputed that the victim was under the age of 14 at the time. *Comm. v. Walker,* 42 Mass. App. Ct. 14 (1997). Indecent A&B is a lesser included offense of forcible rape. *Comm. v. Thomas,* 401 Mass. 109 (1987).

Related Offense

Attempt to Commit Indecent A&B. *Comm. v. Marzilli,* 457 Mass. 64 (2010): Joseph Marzilli was involved in several incidents of groping adult women in public. Along with these offenses, he was charged with attempted indecent A&B for approaching and propositioning a woman but not succeeding in touching her sexually. She left to summon police. This offense must be charged under the general attempt statute, 274, § 6. See discussion in *Chapter 2*.[2]

INDECENT A&B BY PUBLIC SAFETY PERSONNEL
265, § 13H½

Elements

- **Public safety personnel.** The suspect was a police officer, prosecutor, EMT, deputy sheriff, correction officer, court officer, probation or parole officer, constable, or anyone impersonating one of these officials; and

- **Indecent.** The suspect committed an A&B which was "indecent";

- **Custody or control.** With a person in his or her custody or control. [*Note:* Because the victim is in the custody or control of the official, consent is <u>not</u> a defense.]

Right of Arrest

Felony.

Penalty

If victim age 14 and over: SP NMT 5 yrs or HC NMT 2½ yrs.

If victim under age 14: SP NMT 10 yrs or HC NMT 2½ yrs.

---

[2] Interestingly, an earlier case, *Comm. v. Eaton,* 2 Mass. App. Ct. 113 (1974), ruled that there is no such crime as "indecent assault." The *Marzilli* case noted that the *Eaton* rule still applies.

If victim is elder 60 and over, or disabled person — *1st offense:* SP NMT 10 yrs or HC NMT 2½ yrs. *2nd or subsequent:* SP NMT 20 yrs.

If victim is intellectually disabled — *1st offense:* SP NLT 5 yrs, NMT 10 yrs. *2nd or subsequent:* Mandatory minimum of 10 yrs.

SEXUAL ASSAULT INVESTIGATION PROCEDURES

Victim Account Sufficient

Sexual assault conviction may be based on the victim's testimony alone. While it is important to seek corroborating evidence, it is not required to prove the crime. *Comm. v. Bemis*, 242 Mass. 582 (1922). *Comm. v. Santos*, 100 Mass. App. Ct. 1 (2021).

Excited Utterance

Victim's statement to EMT. *Comm. v. Marrero-Miranda*, 2020 WL 6326301 (Appeals Court): In response to 911 calls about an argument, police found the victim beneath the defendant, both half naked. The victim's legs were scratched and bleeding. She was intoxicated and confused. A female officer asked the victim if she was there against her will and she said "no."

Minutes later, the victim told a female EMT in the privacy of the ambulance that she was thrown to the ground and vaginally penetrated by the man's finger. This was an excited utterance. The EMT saw the victim shaking and crying. Just because the victim had told an officer that nothing happened did not defeat her later, spontaneous statement to the EMT when she felt safer in the ambulance.

Victim's electronic messages to friend from scene of rape. *Comm. v. Clark*, 2020 WL 6298055 (Appeals Court): Having met Philip Clark on a dating website, the 17 year old victim drove to Clark's house for their first in-person meeting. She arrived at 11:00 p.m. Within an hour Clark knocked the victim's phone from her hand and raped her despite her verbal and physical resistance.

As Clark showered, the victim communicated her distress via Facebook messenger to a friend. They came up with a plan to extricate her. Even though written, these electronic messages were the excited utterances of a victim under the influence of a startling event. The court noted that texting reflects "how people her age communicate."

First Complaint

First complaint in sexual assault investigations. The first complaint rule, established by *Comm. v. King*, 445 Mass. 217 (2005), allows one witness to testify about what the victim said concerning *any* sexual assault. *Comm. v. Rivera*, 83 Mass. App. Ct. 581 (2013) (victim initially reported to her sister that the defendant physically abused her, then later told her about his sexual abuse; sister properly testified as the first complaint because an initial complaint of physical abuse does not preclude a later first complaint of sexual assault). *Comm. v. Asenjo*, 477 Mass. 599 (2017).

- **Purpose.** The first complaint doctrine provides the jury with a complete account of how the accusation of sexual assault arose.

- **Timing.** There is no requirement of promptness. *Comm. v. Ryan*, 2014 WL 2116644 (Appeals Court) (nine year delay in disclosing the rape did not affect first complaint admissibility).

- **Details and context.** The first complaint witness may testify about the details of the assault and the context of the disclosure — including the victim's demeanor; the events or conversations leading up to it; and any other relevant information that might help the jury assess any defense theories about why the victim would make a false allegation. *Comm. v. Arana*, 453 Mass. 214 (2009).

- **Written, texted, and oral statements admissible.** *Comm. v. Holguin*, 101 Mass. App. Ct. 337 (2022) (the victim's statement started with text messages requesting that her mother come pick her up because her father had forced himself on her; the text messages continued for about an hour while the mother drove; when she arrived, the victim came out and said, "Pappi put his private part in my mouth"; this was all part of one communication). *Comm. v. Revells*, 78 Mass. App. Ct. 492 (2010).

- **Disclosure can be made in stages if there is "no meaningful gap in time."** *Comm. v. Duong*, 2014 WL 1758203 (Appeals Court) (after the victim was assaulted at work, she called a coworker and said the defendant grabbed her breast; she then shared additional details with the coworker in person once he arrived at the office; the coworker was able to testify to both conversations because the complaints were intertwined and there was no meaningful gap in time).

- **Successive complaints admissible concerning different times and escalating abuse.** *Comm. v. Kebreau*, 454 Mass. 287 (2009) (a daughter first disclosed to her mother, in eighth grade, that her father had been touching her genitals since she was in sixth grade. The victim's second disclosure was made to her college advisor and concerned later abuse by her father involving digital and penile penetration).

- **Multiple first complaint witnesses if multiple crimes.** *Comm. v. Squires*, 2017 WL 1423589 (Appeals Court) (there were two separate incidences of sexual assault, and the victim reported each for the first time on separate occasions to different people; both could testify).

- **Forgotten complaint is admissible.** *Comm. v. Dale*, 86 Mass. App. Ct. 187 (2014) (victim did not remember telling her brother about her cousin sexually abusing her when she was seven years old; he was still permitted to testify as the first complaint).

- **Defendant may offer first complaint.** *Comm. v. Mayotte*, 475 Mass. 254 (2016) (Linda Mayotte was charged with raping her adopted son after she became pregnant with his child; she could introduce her first complaint to her friend to prove the son raped her).

- **Asking the victim who else she told violates the first complaint doctrine.** *Comm. v. Seamus S.*, 2018 WL 1371092 (Appeals Court).

The trial judge has the discretion to modify this rule in the interest of justice. Investigators should identify and interview other people the victim spoke to. This provides the prosecutor with alternatives if the court disallows testimony from the actual first person.

- **Bias against the victim.** *Comm. v. Hanino,* 82 Mass. App. Ct. 489 (2012) (12 year old victim told her father's girlfriend that he molested her, but the girlfriend became hostile toward the victim when she married her father; at that point, an investigator was substituted as the first complaint witness).

- **Unavailable *or* incompetent.** *Comm. v. Thibeault,* 77 Mass. App. Ct. 419 (2010) (although the six year old victim told her father first, her mother was allowed to testify because her father was mentally ill, left the Commonwealth, and refused to come back for trial). *Comm. v. Alce,* 96 Mass. App. Ct. 851 (2020).

First Responder Protocol

The first person to receive a report — whether by phone or in person — is the "first complaint." In *Comm. v. Lyons,* 71 Mass. App. Ct. 671 (2008), the victim spoke to the 911 operator first, so the officer who responded could not testify. It did not matter that this officer was the first "live" witness. In *Comm. v. McGee,* 75 Mass. App. Ct. 500 (2009), the victim first told her neighbor that she had been raped. As a result, the detective who did a more detailed interview could not testify.

Dispatchers and officers should perform a basic/compassionate interview, then turn the case over to investigators. Sexual assault victims are sensitive to the reaction they receive from the dispatcher or officer they initially contact. Prematurely cutting off a victim may be enough to cause her to hang up the phone or walk away from the scene. With this in mind, the first responder should: (1) use a calm tone of voice; (2) let the complainant disclose what happened without interruption; (3) obtain a description of the perpetrator(s); (4) ask follow-up questions — who, when, what, where — if necessary to learn the basic facts; (5) just get the complainant's name and cell phone number (too many biographical questions may scare off the complainant); (6) explain the next step (typically a hospital evaluation or interview with a detective); and (7) sincerely thank her for calling or talking to you.

Exempt Evidence

The first complaint rule does not limit:

- **Eyewitness reports.** *Comm. v. Neils N.,* 73 Mass. App. Ct. 689 (2009) (the victim's brother saw his sister being assaulted, then cried when she denied it). *Comm. v. Ong Noy,* 2013 WL 172520 (Appeals Court) (one can be an eyewitness *and* a first complaint witness).

- **Rape kit protocol.** *Comm. v. Dargon,* 457 Mass. 387 (2011): At 10:30 p.m., a certified sexual assault nurse examined the victim. Form 2 in the sexual assault evidence kit contained detailed statements by the victim about the specifics of the rape. Form 2 was admissible as a medical record. It was designed to determine the extent of the victim's injuries and not, like first complaint, to simply corroborate the allegations.

- **Rebuttal of defense case.** *Comm. v. Arana,* 453 Mass. 214 (2009) (testimony that the victim was reluctant to talk to the police was necessary to counteract the defense theory that she was motivated to accuse him so she could file a lawsuit). *Comm. v. Gagnon,* 2014 WL 1922212 (Appeals Court) (detective's testimony that he interviewed each victim separately rebutted the defendant's theory that the victims and their mothers concocted similar stories to conspire against him). *Comm. v. Torres*, 86 Mass. App. Ct. 272 (2014).

Testimony about police/prosecutor meetings typically inadmissible. "The fact that the Commonwealth brought its resources to bear on the incident has no relevance to whether the defendant in fact committed the acts charged." *Comm. v. Monteiro*, 75 Mass. App. Ct. 489 (2009) (the victim's father was the legitimate first complaint; there should not have been testimony about the fact that the victim spoke with his mother and DCF, and later participated in an interview at the district attorney's office that resulted in an arrest and indictment). Compare *Comm. v. Duffy*, 2012 WL 3289318 (Appeals Court) (testimony about the Sexual Abuse Intervention Network process is permitted to rebut an allegation of police incompetence).

Institution Policy

Policy on inappropriate behavior admissible. Written school or organizational policies pertaining to inappropriate sexual relations are admissible as business records during a trial if they were created and distributed before the incident resulting in the defendant's prosecution. *Comm. v. Kozubal*, 488 Mass. 575 (2021).

Rape Shield Law

The rape shield law prevents a victim's prior sexual history from being exposed in court. The purpose is to prevent a general attack of a victim's credibility based on evidence of past promiscuity. 233, § 21B. Such evidence is inadmissible before a grand jury or court. *Comm. v. Murphy*, 2016 WL 4869245 (Appeals Court) (victim's MySpace profile regarding his propensity to engage in homosexual behavior was protected by the rape shield law).

Exceptions include:

- Evidence of the victim's sexual conduct with the defendant.
- Evidence that the victim's recent sexual conduct caused her injuries or physical condition.
- Evidence pertaining to the victim's bias or motive to fabricate.

This evidence will only be admissible after an "in camera hearing" (in the absence of the jury) to determine if its relevancy outweighs the prejudice to the victim. *Comm. v. Jones*, 472 Mass. 707 (2015). *Comm. v. Thomas*, 89 Mass. App. Ct. 422 (2016) (fact that the victim used to be a prostitute was inadmissible; it did not show that she had a motive to lie, especially since she admitted her prior drug use, her intent to use crack cocaine with the defendant that night, and the fact that she might have willingly had sex with him if he had not attacked her).

Preservation of Evidence

Law enforcement agencies must preserve evidence from victims of rape and sexual assault. Under 41, § 97B½, hospitals must notify local police within 24 hours of processing a sexual assault kit.

- **Police must take possession of the kit within 3 business days of notification** and submit it to the crime lab within 7 business days of taking possession. [*Note*: Noninvestigatory kits associated with victims who have not yet filed a report with police are not subject to the 7 day requirement. They must be safely preserved by the police for the entire statute of limitations for the applicable sexual assault charges.]

- **The crime lab must test the kit within 30 days of receipt.** Each kit must be entered into the statewide tracking system, and DNA profiles entered into CODIS and state DNA databases.

The electronic recording of SAIN interviews is good practice, but not legally required. Comm. v. Neils N., 73 Mass. App. Ct. 689 (2009).

Repressed Memory

"Repressed memory" is a legitimate explanation for why a victim of sexual abuse might come forward later. Comm. v. Shanley, 455 Mass. 752 (2010): The victim learned about the defendant priest's abuse of other parishioners when he was serving in the Air Force. Suddenly, his memories of his own childhood abuse came flooding back. Although it occurred in the mid-1980s, the victim did not recall it until 2002. Repressed memory or "dissociative amnesia" in response to trauma is a recognized diagnosis and may be the subject of expert testimony.

No Release of Victim's Name

Withhold victim's name from public disclosure. 265, § 24C mandates that courts and police departments not publish or "otherwise disclose" to the public the names of victims, whether verbally or in records, relating to arrests, investigations or complaints for any type of rape, assault with intent to rape, indecent A&B on a child under 14, or human sexual trafficking. Under § 24C, officials who violate this rule are subject to a Fine NLT $2,500, NMT $10,000.

41, § 97D also requires that the police keep all reports of rape and sexual assault confidential.

Venue

General venue rule for sexual assault offenses. 265, § 24A establishes a venue rule for *all forms* of indecent A&B; rape; and assault with intent to rape. These offenses may be prosecuted in the county from which the victim was taken or the one where the offense occurred.

Related Procedures & Offenses

Regulation, Registration & Arrest of Sex Offenders. 6, §§ 178C–178P. For a detailed breakdown, see *LED's Juvenile Law, Chapter 5.*

10 Sexual Exposure or Surveillance

LEWD & LASCIVIOUS CONDUCT
272, § 53

Elements

As with other 272, § 53 offenses, "lewd and lascivious" behavior is defined in court decisions. *Comm. v. Sefranka*, 382 Mass. 108 (1980).

- **Committed or solicited.** The suspect committed or solicited another person to commit;

- **Sex act.** A sexual act which involved touching the genitals, buttocks, or the female breasts;

- **Arousal or offense.** For the purpose of:
  - Sexually arousing or gratifying the suspect; or
  - Offending other people; and

- **Public.** The sexual act was committed in, or was solicited for, a public place. This means the suspect:
  - Intended public exposure; or
  - Recklessly disregarded a substantial risk of public exposure to others who might be offended by the suspect's conduct.

Right of Arrest

272, § 54 warrantless arrest in presence in public.

Penalty

HC NMT 6 months; and/or Fine $200.

Alternative disposition: 272, § 57 allows the court to discharge an individual accused of a § 53 offense upon the payment of a "surety" for his recognizance and the payment of the "expenses of prosecution." This alternative requires that the defendant conform to "good behavior" for NLT 6 months and NMT 2 yrs.

Notes

This offense punishes the performance or solicitation of sex, which is performed (or intended to be performed) in a public place. *Comm. v. Sefranka*, 382 Mass. 108 (1980). It does not apply to prostitution because prostitutes do not solicit for the purpose of "sexual arousal" or "offense." Prostitution is fundamentally a commercial activity. See *Chapter 11*.

- **Sexual conduct.** To be sexual conduct, the genitals, buttocks, or breasts must be touched. Typically, these private parts are also exposed, but that is not required. For example, a person who blatantly touches his genitals underneath his clothes has committed this offense. *Comm. v. Blackmer,* 77 Mass. App. Ct. 474 (2010) (defendant publicly masturbated without undressing while sitting in his van near a women's college; while this was not "open and gross" or "indecent exposure," it was "lewd and lascivious" conduct).

- **Solicitation.** Aside from the actual commission of a sexual act, this law punishes "the public solicitation" of a public sex act. As a consequence, a suspect may be charged *solely on the basis of what he says to another person*. Officers must remember that a suspect's speech is only a violation if it solicits the particular public sexual conduct — touching genitals, buttocks, or breasts — that the statute criminalizes. *Comm. v. Templeman*, 376 Mass. 533 (1978).

This offense cannot result in conviction when it is unclear whether the defendant intended the solicited conduct to be performed in public or private. In *Comm. v. Roy*, 420 Mass. 1 (1995), Stephen Roy was driving his automobile when he approached Susan, age 14, walking across the street. Her two friends ran away. Roy rolled down the window and said, "Hey, girl . . . I've got something big, hard, and juicy, and you'd like it." A woman in another car sensed Susan was upset and pulled over. Roy drove away. He was later charged with being lewd and lascivious.

The SJC overturned Roy's conviction because there was no evidence that the defendant was soliciting conduct to be performed in a public place versus a private place. The court rejected the government's argument that, when children are involved, this element should be relaxed.

This author thinks the SJC was overly technical about its standard of proof. After all, where did the court think Mr. Roy wanted to have this girl carry out his invitation for oral sex? In his house? At the Four Seasons? The context was obviously one in which the defendant was seeking quick, public gratification. In any case, officers should be aware of the *Roy* decision when they investigate these types of solicitations.

Another charge to consider is annoying & accosting a person (A&A). The advantage of A&A is that the prohibited conduct may occur in public or private. See *discussion on next page*.

Public. Officers must determine whether the suspect intended or recklessly risked public exposure. *Comm. v. Ferguson*, 384 Mass. 13 (1981) (a location may be public at some times and under some circumstances and not public at others).

Remember, conduct is not automatically public because a person observes it. If the suspect took reasonable measures to secure privacy, then he is not guilty of this offense. *Gay and Lesbian Advocates v. Attorney General*, 436 Mass. 132 (2002).

- *Comm. v. Nicholas*, 48 Mass. App. Ct. 255 (1996): The defendant engaged in a sexual act with another motorist in the woods next to a truck weigh station near the highway. The station was closed, but there was no barrier to entry. Motorists would often stop there to rest, but there was no evidence that they used the woods, or any indication that the defendant was visible from a vantage point where travelers pulled off the road. The defendant should not have been arrested because there was insufficient evidence that the location he chose risked public exposure.

- Compare *Comm. v. Neville*, 59 Mass. App. Ct. 316 (2003): A trooper saw the defendant masturbating behind a highway rest stop. The path was worn. The defendant was visible and observed by the trooper and three other individuals. *Comm. v. Bloom*, 18 Mass. App. Ct. 951 (1984) (open area of public toilet, as distinguished from inside the stall, is a public place for offending sexual acts).

ANNOYING & ACCOSTING SEXUALLY
272, § 53

Elements

The crime of annoying & accosting is described in *Comm. v. Santos*, 2019 WL 4942349 (Appeals Court).

- **Directed at victim.** The suspect must direct an offensive act or language at the victim;

- **Victim awareness.** The victim must be aware of the suspect's actions;

- **Sexually offensive to reasonable person.** A reasonable person would find the behavior or language sexually offensive — which means that it violated contemporary standards of decency and caused real displeasure, anger, or resentment;

- **Prohibited acts or language.** Without legitimate purpose, the behavior or language involved either:

  - Fighting or violence;

  - Creating a hazardous condition;

  - Something physically offensive that amounted to an invasion of privacy; or

  - Threats that would make a reasonable person fearful, including inappropriate sexually explicit language.

Right of Arrest

272, § 54 warrantless arrest in presence in public.

Penalty

HC NMT 6 months; and/or Fine NMT $200.

Alternative disposition: See previous discussion of lewd & lascivious conduct.

Notes

Private and public acts covered. This law mirrors "disorderly conduct," except it covers public and private conduct with sexual overtones. See Disorderly Conduct in *Chapter 23*.

The suspect does not have to intend to be offensive. *Comm. v. Santos*, 2019 WL 4942349 (Appeals Court): While boarding a subway train, Jose Santos fell into the victim, touched her leg, tried to touch her face, and asked for a kiss. The victim complained to the motorman and left the train. Santos was removed, but then circled the victim and pointed at her in the booth where a T inspector had secured her for her safety. There was evidence that Santos smelled of alcohol, slurred his speech, and was unsteady on his feet, but Santos also got on and off the train, responded to questions from Transit Police, and produced identification upon request. Intoxication is typically not a defense to this crime because it only requires that the suspect intend to direct his conduct toward the victim.

Cases with sufficient evidence of annoying & accosting.

- *Comm. v. Whiting*, 58 Mass. App. Ct. 918 (2003): 13 year old Hanna and four friends were listening to music and dancing in her driveway. At 10:20 p.m., the defendant drove up and stopped his car. He told the girls that he was drunk, that he was gay, that he was "looking for dick" and wanted to be on the Jerry Springer show. He got out and pulled down his pants, exposing his buttocks.

- *Comm. v. Cahill*, 446 Mass. 778 (2006): Joseph Cahill was the victim's supervisor at a grocery store. Cahill asked the victim out for dates over 20 times, stood so close to her that his body grazed hers, and stared at her. While she was assisting a customer, Cahill came up behind her, grabbed her tightly around the shoulders and said, "I love you." The victim felt frightened and asked him to leave. The victim began having trouble concentrating at work. A day later, Cahill came over to her register, banged on the conveyor belt, and asked a customer why the victim had not called him, frightening the customer. This behavior was more than sexual harassment on the job, it was annoying and accosting.

- *Comm. v. Sullivan*, 469 Mass. 621 (2014): Joseph Sullivan encountered a female college student walking home late at night. He called her "little girl," and told her to come to his car so they could "talk." As the victim walked away, Sullivan got out of his vehicle and followed her. He eventually got back into his car and drove away, but immediately returned. He got out of the car with it still running and the door open. He approached the victim closely, and angrily demanded she "get in the car." He only left when the victim began reciting his license plate number.

One act sufficient. *Comm. v. Moran*, 80 Mass. App. Ct. 8 (2011): A nanny was pushing a child in a stroller on her way to a coffee shop when she was approached by two men. As Daniel Moran passed within arm's reach, he said, "Hi, nanny," grabbed his crotch and moved his "private area up and down" as if masturbating. The nanny was disturbed. When she returned home, her employer suggested she call police.

A stranger's uninvited suggestion of sexual activity is "inherently menacing." Moran made his suggestion at close quarters, in the company of another man. The nanny's sense of vulnerability was enhanced because she was pushing a young child. Moran's one act was enough for conviction.

Example of insufficient evidence. *Comm. v. Ramirez*, 69 Mass. App. Ct. 9 (2007): Ulises Ramirez stared at a 12 year old girl at a swimming pool and asked her why she was leaving on her way out. The next day, as she walked by his house, Ramirez leaned out the window and said he would buy her candy. When she passed by later, Ramirez was standing outside "singing that he fell in love with a little girl." Both encounters made her feel uncomfortable.

Ramirez's behavior did not amount to annoying and accosting. He did not attempt to go near the girl or restrict her movement. Though he was offensive, Ramirez did not create a "*physically* offensive condition." In the words of the court: "Not all disturbing remarks are criminal."

Annoying & accosting judged differently for people with intellectual disabilities. *Comm. v. Orville O.*, 2014 WL 2764861 (Appeals Court): 15 year old Orville was a student in a residential facility for the developmentally disabled. A counselor said that Orville played with a "Slinky" toy while looking at her provocatively, sang that he wanted to have a one night stand, and told another student that he would "like to hit that." When the counselor reprimanded him, Orville told her that she had "saggy boobs." The counselor reported the incident to police. Even if Orville's behavior was "offensive," the residents of these facilities are chosen precisely because of their propensity to behave in this way. His behavior was distasteful, but not threatening or physically offensive.

Gender irrelevant. The statute used to refer to "annoying and accosting a person of the opposite sex." It now refers to "annoying and accosting another person." Thus, women can accost women and men can accost men.

Related Offense

"Peeping Tom" considered disorderly conduct. The disorderly statute 272, § 53, may be applied to a Peeping Tom.[1] A Peeping Tom causes disorder by invading the privacy of persons precisely where they are most entitled to feel secure — in their home. *Comm. v. LePore*, 40 Mass. App. Ct. 543 (1996) (woman saw defendant at night approach her window and called police; officers found him next to another woman's window; defendant had tampered with the screen and lurked long enough to smoke two cigarettes; defendant gave the lame excuse that he ducked into the alley "to piss," but officers found no evidence of fresh urination).

---

[1] The *LePore* decision explained that this term is an allusion to the Peeping Tom of Coventry, who popped out his head as the naked Lady Godiva passed and was struck blind for it!

INDECENT EXPOSURE
272, § 53

Elements

Similar to other § 53 offenses, indecent exposure is defined by prior court decisions. *Comm. v. Quinn*, 439 Mass. 492 (2003).

- **Intentional.** The suspect intentionally;
- **Expose genitals.** Exposed his or her genitals to one or more persons; and
- **Cause offense.** At least one person was reasonably offended by the exposure.

Right of Arrest

272, § 54 warrantless arrest in presence in public. In private, complaint.

Penalty

HC NMT 6 months; and/or Fine $200.

Alternative Disposition: See discussion of lewd & lascivious conduct.

Notes

The suspect's conduct must be "objectively offensive." *Comm. v. Waterman*, 98 Mass. App. Ct. 651 (2020), stated that indecent exposure (IE) includes the requirement that the suspect's conduct be "offensive to a reasonable person" in addition to offending the victim.

Must expose genitals — not buttocks, pubic hair, crotch, or female breasts. Unlike the crime of open & gross lewdness (O&G), IE does not require that the victim experience "alarm or shock." For this reason, the SJC has insisted that the offensive conduct necessary for IE be defined narrowly. *Comm. v. Quinn*, 439 Mass. 492 (2003) (exposure of thong-clad buttocks does not qualify as IE, but might, depending on the circumstances, constitute O&G). *Comm. v. Arthur*, 420 Mass. 535 (1995)

For offensive behavior that does not qualify as O&G or even IE, Disturbing the Peace (discussed in *Chapter 23*) may be the best option.

Must offend victim. *Comm. v. Queenan*, 2011 WL 6851171 (Appeals Court): A highly intoxicated John Queenan entered a liquor store where a female clerk was working. When the clerk informed him that he would not be sold alcohol, Queenan began to shout profanities, told her his limp was the result of an artificial leg, dropped his pants, and turned to the clerk so she could see his penis. He exposed himself for 25 seconds.

At trial, the clerk testified that she was concerned that Queenan might knock over bottles, and that she was "aggravated" because it was her family's business. When asked about seeing his penis, she responded, "To be perfectly honest with you, it didn't bother me." She explained that, as a former therapist, she has seen many penises and "just felt bad for the poor guy." Her reaction did not satisfy an element of this offense, because her upset was completely unrelated to Queenan's nudity.

Compare *Comm. v. Pellegrine,* 2012 WL 2889016 (Appeals Court) (shoplifter exposed his penis twice — supposedly to show an employee that he had not stolen anything; since his real purpose was to offend the employee, IE occurred).

No requirement of public exposure. Unlike lewd & lascivious and O&G, IE does *not* have to occur in public, although it usually does. *Comm. v. Bishop,* 296 Mass. 459 (1937).

Public breastfeeding is legally protected. 111, § 221 provides that a mother may breastfeed her child in any public place or establishment. Any incidental breast exposure during this act is not criminal. No person or organization (except a place of religious instruction or worship) may restrict a mother who is breastfeeding. If they do, she may bring a civil action and recover $500 in damages and reasonable attorney fees. The Attorney General may also obtain an injunction against the organization to prevent similar action in the future.

OPEN & GROSS LEWDNESS
272, § 16

Elements

This statute criminalizes a more aggravated version of indecent exposure. The elements of "open & gross" are not defined in § 16, but have been established by common law. *Comm. v. Blackmer,* 77 Mass. App. Ct. 474 (2010).

- **Intentional.** The suspect intentionally;

- **Expose genitals, breasts or butt.** Exposed his or her genitals, buttocks or female breasts to one or more persons; and

- **Public.** The suspect did so "openly" by either:
    - Intending public exposure; or
    - Recklessly disregarding a substantial risk of public exposure to others who might be offended by the suspect's conduct;

- **Alarm or shock.** The suspect's act was done in such a way as to produce alarm or shock in a reasonable person; and

- **Person affected.** One or more persons were, in fact, alarmed or shocked by the suspect's exposure.

Right of Arrest

Felony.

Penalty

SP NMT 3 yrs or HC NMT 2 yrs; or Fine NMT $300.

Notes

Open & Gross (O&G) different from Indecent Exposure (IE) in 4 ways: (1) it is a felony; (2) the exposure must be done publicly; (3) the exposure may involve the buttocks or breasts, not just the genitals; and (4) the onlooker(s) must experience alarm or shock.

- **Genitals, buttocks, or female breasts must be visibly exposed.** *Comm. v. Daniels*, 2013 WL 802811 (Appeals Court) (a male streetwalker who held himself out to the public as a female committed O&G when he flashed his "female breasts" to two young boys on the street). Compare *Comm. v. Blackmer*, 77 Mass. App. Ct. 474 (2010) (defendant's O&G conviction reversed because the female victim never observed his genitals or buttocks, only his hand touching his groin in an act of clothed masturbation; however, his behavior did constitute lewd & lascivious conduct).

- **See-through clothing sufficient.** *Comm. v. Coppinger*, 86 Mass. App. Ct. 234 (2014): The defendant entered a Target store wearing white "see-through" compression shorts without underwear. One witness saw the outline of his semi-erect penis and testicles through the shorts. The court said the defendant's outfit was really "cellophane shorts!"

- **O&G is primarily applied to indecent exposure in front of children.** *Comm. v. Poillucci*, 46 Mass. App. Ct. 300 (1999) (A 10 year old girl saw the defendant driving behind her mother's car. The girl saw the defendant arch his back with his shirt unbuttoned. According to the girl, his left hand was "going up and down" on an object resembling "a skin-colored belt." She mentioned the "weird man" to her mother, who called police).

- **O&G may also be charged for blatant exposure involving adults.** *Comm. v. Guy G.*, 53 Mass. App. Ct. 271 (2001) (defendant, a 16 year old high school student, exposed his penis to another 16 year old student; the victim did not tell a teacher or another student because she was "too in shock"). *Comm. v. Gray*, 40 Mass. App. Ct. 901 (1996) (a groundskeeper at a local mall went into a bathroom to attend to his daily cleanup; he observed two men standing in front of a urinal performing oral sex).

"Open" refers to the need for a public display.

- **What constitutes a "public display" for O&G is the same as lewd & lascivious conduct.** *Comm. v. Swan*, 73 Mass. App. Ct. 258 (2008): The defendant, an elementary school janitor, always used the urinal next to the child victim even though more distant ones were available. He stood away from the wall and engaged in small talk to encourage the victim to pay attention to his penis. He also made sexually explicit comments when other children were not present.

- **The "public" requirement is overlooked when the exposure is directed toward children.** *Comm. v. Quinn*, 439 Mass. 492 (2003). *Comm. v. Wardell*, 128 Mass. 52 (1880) (a salesman exposed himself in a private home to children; the SJC upheld his O&G conviction).

An "alarming or shocking" reaction must occur.

- **A call to 911 indicates that the victim was shocked or alarmed.** *Comm. v. Britto*, 2011 WL 2120154 (Appeals Court).

- **So does an expression of "disgust" followed by a report to someone (or being "too shocked" to report).** *Comm. v. Gray*, 40 Mass. App. Ct. 901 (1996).

- **Viewer's age never eliminates need to prove alarm or shock.** *Comm. v. Kessler*, 442 Mass. 779 (2004): Two boys, ages 13 and 10, saw a man's hand in the basement window of their neighbor's house waving them over. Through the window, the boys saw the defendant masturbating. They told their grandmother. Police arrived and arrested the defendant. The SJC reversed Kessler's conviction due to a lack of evidence that the boys had been alarmed or shocked. Both boys testified that they were laughing because they were "nervous and only left the window when they were called twice by their grandmother." She described them as "excited," but did not suggest they were alarmed. Being "excited" or "nervous" may be unpleasant, but it does not establish the serious negative emotional experience required by O&G. While the boys said they were "offended," being offended is not the same as alarm or shock — which distinguishes O&G from the lesser offense of IE.

- **A police officer may be "shocked."** *Comm. v. Pasquarelli*, 98 Mass. App. Ct. 816 (2020): Working undercover in Salem, Detective Charlene Sano walked on sidewalks to catch a repeat "flasher." Jonathan Pasquarelli drove past Detective Sano a dozen times. It was after 9:00 p.m. when he approached her on a well-lit corner to say, "Excuse me." With the detective's attention on him, Pasquarelli lifted his sweatshirt to expose his genitals, then said, "Can you put these in your mouth?" Detective Sano screamed to her cover officer, "[He] just did it, he exposed himself." The officers arrested Pasquarelli after a foot chase.

  Detective Sano testified that she was "shocked" and "[e]xtremely uneasy" when she saw the defendant's penis and testicles. Even though the detective's assignment led her to expect the defendant's conduct, it was still reasonable for her to react with shock when accosted. In this and other matters, officers are not immune to feelings of fright or shock experienced by reasonable citizens.

- **However, an officer's disgust and concern for others is insufficient shock or alarm.** *Comm. v. Maguire*, 476 Mass. 156 (2017): Detective Sean Conway saw Lawrence Maguire leaning against a pillar on the platform of a train station. There were about 25 people on the platform and a few women sitting on a bench nearby. Detective Conway had a clear view of Maguire exposing his penis to the women. Detective Conway was disgusted and concerned that the women on the bench were being victimized. Maguire saw the detective and ran. Conway chased him and arrested him for O&G.

  Detective Conway's concern was not for himself, but for the women seated on the bench. Those women, however, could not be interviewed about what they saw and whether they were shocked or alarmed. The detective's vicarious concern was insufficient for O&G. Indecent exposure would have worked better.

Reaction must be objectively reasonable. *Comm. v. Taranovsky*, 93 Mass. App. Ct. 399 (2018): While on the Esplanade in Boston, N.M. saw two children between the ages of five and seven stop their scooters and look at something. She followed their gaze and saw Dymytro

Taranovsky walking in a "runway strut" wearing a black sock-like object over his genitals, held in place by strings. N.M. described the item as a "banana hammock." Taranovsky's buttocks were exposed and he was otherwise completely naked. N.M. felt "shocked" and "just a little disgusted." She said the reaction was based, in part, on the fact that children were in the area. The court held that N.M.'s reaction was objectively reasonable. *Comm. v. Melo*, 95 Mass. App. Ct. 257 (2019).

The defendant's "dancing" was not protected free expression. The fact that no children are present does not prevent this behavior from rising to the level of O&G.

O&G constitutional. It does not unfairly inhibit free expression under the First Amendment. In *Comm. v. Ora*, 451 Mass. 125 (2008), Ria Ora was arrested for O&G when she danced nude at an "anti-Christmas" protest in Harvard Square. The SJC felt that such a public display imposed "nudity on . . . unsuspecting or unwilling person[s]" which is different from entertainers in theatrical productions or strip clubs who perform for willing patrons.

Only one charge applies to a single incident involving multiple victims. *Comm. v. Botev*, 79 Mass. App. Ct. 281 (2011): As two 15 year old girls left a park, a man told them, in a foreign accent, to wait. The girls turned and saw his penis. A police investigation resulted in a nearby resident, Hristo Botev, being identified by the girls and charged with two counts of O&G. The court said that Botev should only have been charged with one count. O&G depends on the conduct, not the number of people who witness it. This happened during a single episode.

Lesser included offense. *Comm. v. Waterman*, 98 Mass. App. Ct. 651 (2020): If the suspect's conduct involves displaying genitals, then IE a lesser included offense of O&G.

SECRET SEXUAL SURVEILLANCE
272, § 105

Purpose

This law prevents people from taking secret videos or photographs of naked people or underneath their clothes (aka "upskirting"). *Comm. v. Robertson*, 467 Mass. 371 (2014).

Elements

Type 1: Secret Videotaping or Photographing

- With the intent to secretly conduct this activity;

- The suspect willfully photographed, videotaped, or electronically surveilled:

  - Someone nude or partially nude; who was unaware and did not consent; and was at a location where he or she reasonably expected privacy; *or*

  - The sexual or other intimate body parts of someone; without the person's knowledge and consent; under or around that person's clothing; and the person reasonably believed his or her parts were not visible to the public.

Type 2: Dissemination

- The suspect willfully disseminated the visual image of another person;

- *Knowing* that the visual image was obtained by secret videotaping, photographing, or electronic surveillance — without the consent of the person depicted.

Right of Arrest

Making secret video: 272, § 105 warrantless arrest on probable cause.

Disseminating secret video: Felony.

Definitions

- **Electronically surveil:** "To view, obtain or record a person's visual image by the use or aid of a camera . . . television, or other electronic device."

- **Partially nude:** "The exposure of the human genitals, buttocks, pubic area or female breast below a point immediately above the top of the areola [colored area around the nipple]."

- **Sexual or other intimate body parts:** The exact same coverage as above, "whether naked or covered by clothing or undergarments."

Exempt Conduct

- **Surveillance of changing rooms,** provided a *conspicuously* posted sign (at all entrances and inside any changing room) warns customers of the merchant's surveillance activity.

- **A law enforcement officer** when acting within the scope of the officer's authority under applicable law, or by an order or warrant issued by a court.

Victim Privacy Protection

- **No public inspection of evidence.** Any image shall only be inspected by a police officer, prosecutor or defense attorney, defendant, or victim unless otherwise ordered by the court.

- **A justice of the superior or district court may issue appropriate orders** to restrain or prevent the unlawful dissemination of a person's visual image in violation of this section.

Penalty

Making secret video, photo, or surveillance: HC NMT 2½ yrs; and/or Fine NMT $5,000. If victim under age 18: SP NMT 5 yrs or HC NMT 2½ yrs; and/or Fine NMT $10,000.

Dissemination of visual image of secret video, photo, or surveillance: SP NMT 5 yrs or HC NMT 2½ yrs; and/or Fine NMT $10,000. If victim under age 18: SP NMT 10 yrs or HC NMT 2½ yrs; and/or Fine NMT $10,000.

Notes

"Upskirting" law applies to people in public. *Comm. v. Nascimento*, 91 Mass. App. Ct. 665 (2017) (defendant used his cell phone to secretly videotape two underage girls under their sundresses while traveling on a ferry to Nantucket).

A person has a reasonable expectation of not being photographed naked while asleep in a private place. *Comm. v. Barke*, 2016 WL 3945937 (Appeals Court): Richard Barke and the victim were dating. While the victim slept in Barke's bed, he took a close-up picture of her genitals. When he later showed her the picture, she told him she was uncomfortable with what he did. When the two broke up, Barke threatened to disseminate the photo. The fact that he had showed it to her was irrelevant, since he originally took it without consent in a location where she expected privacy. *Comm. v. Castro*, 99 Mass. App. Ct. 502 (2021) (fact that person asleep in the photo typically sufficient to prove he or she did not consent).

Unit of prosecution is number of nude victims secretly videotaped. *Comm. v. Wassilie*, 482 Mass. 562 (2019): The defendant was arrested for using his cell phone to record people secretly in a public bathroom. The recordings showed seventeen adults and five juveniles, nude or partially nude The defendant was properly charged with twenty-two counts of secret sexual surveillance — one per victim.

Taking photograph completes crime. *Comm. v. Cooper*, 100 Mass. App. Ct. 345 (2021): As the victim was urinating inside a stall in a UMass Medical School bathroom, she looked up to see a hand holding a cell phone over the divider. She heard the "click" of a camera and yelled, "What are you doing?" as someone ran out of the bathroom.

The victim quickly exited the women's room and saw the men's room door swinging closed. She yelled inside. Markus Cooper answered that he was on his cell phone and walked into the wrong bathroom. She asked to see Cooper's phone. He said, "I didn't take any pictures of you." The victim asked Cooper to come with her to security, or to show his school ID card, but he refused. Cooper fled to a parking garage and drove away. Video surveillance captured him doing this.

Cooper called UMass Police from his car and went to the station. An officer interviewed him. Cooper permitted the officer to examine his phone. No picture of the victim was found.

Cooper violated 272, § 105 when he pointed his camera at the partially nude victim and snapped her photograph. There must be proof the victim was photographed, not proof of an actual photograph. Cooper probably deleted the photo when he fled the scene after being caught in the act.[2]

---

[2] Cooper was also properly convicted of disorderly conduct. See "Peeping Tom" discussion in *Chapter 23*. The court's discussion suggested that the separate offense of accosting or annoying, though not charged here, might have applied as well.

11 Prostitution

SEXUAL CONDUCT FOR A FEE
272, § 53A

Elements

The suspect:

- **Customer.** Paid, offered, or agreed to pay another to engage in sexual conduct; or

- **Prostitute.** Engaged, offered, or agreed to engage in sexual conduct with another person for a fee.

Note: Sex act does not have to occur.

Right of Arrest

272, § 54 warrantless arrest in presence in public.

Penalty

Customer: HC NMT 2½ yrs; and/or Fine NLT $1,000, NMT $5,000.

Prostitute: HC NMT 1 year; and/or Fine NMT $500.

SEXUAL CONDUCT FOR A FEE, CHILD UNDER 18
272, § 53A

Elements

The suspect:

- **Customer.** Paid, offered, or agreed to pay another person with the intent to engage in sexual conduct with a child under age 18; or

- **Facilitator.** Was paid, agreed to pay, or agreed that a third person be paid in return for aiding a person who intended to engage in sexual conduct with a child under age 18.

Note: Sex act does not have to occur.

Right of Arrest

Felony.

Penalty

SP NMT 10 yrs; or SP NMT 10 yrs and Fine NLT $3,000, NMT $10,000; or HC NMT 2½ yrs and Fine NLT $3,000, NMT $10,000.

Notes

Prostitute _and_ customer covered. Under § 53A, agreeing to engage in sex is prohibited (which covers the prostitute) and agreeing to pay for sex is prohibited (which covers the customer). The potential penalty for the customer is more severe.

Agreement may involve a third party. The agreement is what is punished. A sex act need not occur. For this reason, undercover stings are effective. In *Comm. v. Bell*, 455 Mass. 408 (2009), a female undercover officer telephoned Kerry Bell, who asked her to "bring a child." The officer met him and said her foster child was waiting in the park nearby. Bell agreed to pay $200. Officers moved in and arrested him.

Bell argued that "solicitation" does not apply when there is an agreement to pay a third party (in this case, the undercover officer) for sex with *another person* (the fake child). The SJC remarked that the statute has no such limitation. This ruling allows officers to continue to conduct undercover prostitution stings concerning nonexistent children.

Express _or_ implied solicitation qualifies. *Comm. v. Lavigne*, 42 Mass. App. Ct. 313 (1997): The defendant asked a 17 year old hitchhiker whether he "wanted to make some money." The boy asked, "Doing what?" The defendant proceeded to massage his upper thigh. When the boy pushed the defendant's hand away, he asked the boy whether he had "ever tried it before." These facts constituted an implied offer to pay for sexual conduct.

Email solicitation qualifies, but generally must be accompanied by an appearance. *Comm. v. Amaral*, 78 Mass. App. Ct. 671 (2011): Trooper Cooke began an undercover operation pretending to be a 15 year old prostitute named "Ashley" on Craigslist. Jeremy Amaral engaged in numerous email conversations and sent his picture. Several weeks later, he said he wanted to meet Ashley at a local strip mall at 5:00 p.m. Amaral arrived and parked where he had been told. Troopers called the number he had provided in his email. When Amaral's phone rang and he answered, he was arrested.

Once he appeared at the strip mall to meet Ashley, Amaral was guilty of attempted statutory rape and solicitation of a prostitute. The emails *alone* could not prove the identity of the offender. In the computer age, it is easy to set up a fictitious account or falsely use the name and/or photograph of another. It was Amaral's actions that authenticated the emails. While necessary to prove this case, a meeting is not essential in every case. The court noted that each situation has its own unique facts.

Sexual conduct. The term "sexual conduct" should be given its common sense meaning. In *Comm. v. Bibby*, 35 Mass. App. Ct. 938 (1993), a female staff member of the Medfield State Hospital told a male patient that "the price of a feel is $75." She took his money and allowed him to fondle her breasts. An officer witnessed the incident and arrested the defendant. The court rejected her argument that only intercourse was prohibited by this statute. *Comm. v. Walter*, 388 Mass. 460 (1983) (prostitution also includes masturbating the customer).

Selective prosecution unconstitutional. The Massachusetts Constitution requires that charges be dismissed if a particular police department consistently arrests female prostitutes, but not their male customers. *Comm. v. An Unnamed Defendant*, 22 Mass. App. Ct. 230 (1986).

- **Example of good police procedures.** *Comm. v. Archer*, 49 Mass. App. Ct. 185 (2000) featured an arrested prostitute named Cynthia Archer, who filed a motion to dismiss. Archer had been arrested four times in 1997, and on only one occasion was the "john" arrested. However, the Chelsea Police presented ample evidence to rebut her selective prosecution claim.

    - First, the police conduct "john stings" using undercover female officers.

    - Second, their policy articulates the reasons for arresting or not arresting customers. The department uses several tactics — warnings, citations, criminal complaints and arrests — depending on the following factors: (1) the existence or nonexistence of a criminal record; (2) whether the potential customer has been warned and later returns to the area; and (3) whether there are doubts that the goal of the individual was to purchase sex.

    - Third, the police use the same factors in dealing with female prostitutes. Cynthia Archer had been warned on many occasions. In fact, one night police warned Archer twice to stay away from their "john sting" before they finally arrested her!

- **Lack of any effort to question male customers is selective prosecution.** *Comm. v. Lafaso*, 49 Mass. App. Ct. 179 (2000): Karen Lafaso cited a number of occasions where she was arrested and her male clients were not. In one case, police arrested her after she got out of a male customer's car, but officers never ran a query on the male driver's license plate or attempted to stop his car to question him. Not only did the police not arrest Lafaso's male clients, they did not even investigate them. This was gender bias.

Defense of human trafficking. A prostitute may offer as a defense that he or she is a human trafficking victim who was coerced into prostitution. See 265, § 59.

Related Offense

Human Trafficking. 265, § 50 outlaws recruiting, transporting, obtaining, or financially benefiting from another person who engages in commercial sexual activity (prostitution), or a sexually explicit performance, or the production of child pornography. Penalty: SP NMT Life. Right of Arrest: Felony. The most detailed breakdown of the trafficking law appears in *LED's Juvenile Law, Chapter 10.*

DERIVING SUPPORT FROM A PROSTITUTE
272, § 7

Elements

- **Knowledge.** The suspect knew that a person was a prostitute; and

- **Derive support.** Derived complete or partial support:

    - From the prostitute's earnings; or

    - From money "loaned, advanced or charged against her" by any manager of a place where prostitution is practiced or allowed.

Right of Arrest

Felony.

Penalty

SP 5 yrs (Mandatory minimum 2 yrs); and Fine $5,000.

Notes

Knowledge. The suspect must be aware that he is obtaining money from a prostitute. Prostitution is defined as sexual activity for hire. *Comm. v. King*, 374 Mass. 5 (1977).

Knowledge may be proven when a defendant is "willfully blind." This means the defendant has consciously and deliberately pretended to be unaware of criminal behavior, while implicitly encouraging it. Terry Mussari, owned three day spas. A spa worker testified that Mussari told workers that sexual activities were not supposed to occur on the premises, "but whatever happens in the rooms she can't control." She told customers to tip the girls for "extras." *Comm. v. Mussari*, 97 Mass. App. Ct. 647 (2020).

Deriving support. This statute was enacted to punish the "pimp," which is why it is a felony. *Comm. v. Stephens*, 15 Mass. App. Ct. 461 (1983) (evidence that the defendant and victim were heroin addicts established his motive to commit this offense).

A "pimp" intends to profit from the prostitution. This distinction differentiates a "pimp" from a person who provides food, clothing, or medical services to a known sex worker, or children who receive support from a parent they know engages in prostitution. These individuals may have knowledge of the prostitution and receive some support or money from it, but unlike pimps, they do not intend for the prostitution to occur. Therefore, they should not be charged under § 7. *Comm. v. Brown*, 481 Mass. 77 (2018) (defendant accompanied a woman to a prearranged prostitution transaction and was caught, immediately after leaving the scene with that woman, with the entire proceeds of the transaction in his shoe; he knowingly and intentionally profited from the prostitution of another).

Incidental financial benefit is insufficient. In *Comm. v. Thetonia*, 27 Mass. App. Ct. 783 (1989), the defendant often furnished transportation for her roommate, who she knew was a prostitute, and waited for her to finish her "dates." For her help, the defendant occasionally received "gas money" and drugs, although she had no arrangement with her roommate. Charged with violating 272, § 7, the defendant argued that she was not a "pimp." The court agreed, but acknowledged that she could have been convicted of being an accomplice.

Suspect does not need to possess payment. *Comm. v. Steed*, 95 Mass. App. Ct. 463 (2019) (defendant's share of the money was his, by prior arrangement, as soon as it was paid by the undercover officer to one of his female prostitutes; the fact the defendant was arrested before he actually handled the money was not a defense given the overwhelming proof of his financial arrangement).

Deriving support from prostitution is not a lesser included offense of sex trafficking. *Comm. v. Duntin*, 2018 WL 1770244 (2018) (272, § 7, prohibits sharing proceeds earned by a known prostitute, while sex trafficking, 265, § 50, does not require that the offender benefit financially; the knowledge element of § 7 is also retrospective, meaning the prostitution already occurred, whereas the knowledge element of § 50 is prospective, meaning the person knows that prostitution will result in the future).

Related Offense

Deriving Support from the Earnings of a Minor Prostitute. 272, § 4B criminalizes the same offense as § 7, except the prostitute must be under 18. The mandatory penalty is 5 years in prison. The suspect does not have to know that the prostitute is a minor. *Comm. v. Asmeron*, 70 Mass. App. Ct. 667 (2007) (an escort service employed Darcy, a 16 year old runaway).

INDUCING A MINOR TO BECOME A PROSTITUTE
272, § 4A

Elements

The suspect knowingly induced, or assisted in inducing, a person under age 18 to become a prostitute.

Right of Arrest

Felony.

Penalty

SP NLT 3 yrs, NMT 5 yrs (Mandatory minimum of 3 yrs); and Fine $5,000.

Notes

The induced minor must not have previously engaged in prostitution. *Comm. v. Matos*, 78 Mass. App. Ct. 578 (2011): State Police Sergeant Pi Heseltine gave undercover Detective Robert DiSalvatore an ad on Craigslist by a person named "Paris" promoting a "two-girl special."

DiSalvatore called Paris, who said it would cost $250. Diana Matos and her boyfriend, Antwan Sampson, drove Paris to the hotel. Paris left her ID with Matos so that she would not be identified.

Paris entered DiSalvatore's room, asked to see the money, and got undressed. Sampson and Matos were waiting in the car in front of the hotel. All three were arrested. Paris was later identified as B.C., a homeless, drug-addicted 16 year old, who had run away.

- **Inducement.** 272, § 4A only penalizes inducing a minor who is not already a prostitute. Here, there was insufficient evidence that Matos or Sampson induced B.C. She had already engaged in acts of prostitution before they got involved.

- **Deriving Support from a Minor Prostitute.** However, there was ample evidence of this crime. Matos knew B.C. was meeting with someone in the hotel to engage in sex for a fee. After he was arrested, Sampson called out from his holding cell: "That's my money! My girl worked hard for it!"

Influencing the minor's decision is "inducing." *Comm. v. Halstrom*, 84 Mass. App. Ct. 372 (2013): Gail, Beth, and Maureen were 16 to 17 years old. Melissa Halstrom told Gail about her work as an escort. She said the work was "fun" and "easy money." She said she was looking for girls for her business. Gail introduced her friends, Beth and Maureen. Halstrom then organized "dates" for the girls, during which they had sex with men. Halstrom provided the condoms, drugs, alcohol, and hotel rooms. She took $100 of the $300 charged per hour by each girl.

Halstrom claimed that the girls chose to be prostitutes. However, Halstrom persuaded them. She befriended the girls at a vulnerable time in each of their lives, plied them with alcohol and drugs, and showed them her nice car, furniture, and apartment.

PERMITTING PROSTITUTION ON THE PREMISES
272, § 6

Elements

- **Control premises.** The suspect owned, managed, or assisted in the management or control of certain premises; and

- **Sexual intercourse for fee.** A person was present on the premises for the purpose of unlawfully having sexual intercourse for money or other financial benefit; and

- **Induce or allow.** The suspect induced or "knowingly suffered" the person's presence on the premises for that purpose.

Right of Arrest

Felony.

Penalty

SP NLT 2 yrs, NMT 5 yrs (Mandatory minimum 2 yrs); and Fine $5,000.

Notes

Induce. The defendant must either induce *or* "knowingly suffer" a prostitution episode at his premises. The term "induce" means to "actively persuade" someone.

Allow. In contrast, the term "knowingly suffer" means that the defendant is aware of the prohibited sexual activity and does nothing to stop it. The defendant's approval or disapproval of the activity is irrelevant — as long as he is aware of it. *Comm. v. Martin*, 304 Mass. 320 (1939).

Proof may be circumstantial. *Comm. v. Bucaulis*, 6 Mass. App. Ct. 59 (1978) (manager of lounge was aware that his female employee was in the back room with a customer getting paid for sexual activity during business hours; manager's knowledge was inferred from the fact that the money transaction occurred openly at the bar). *Comm. v. Mullane*, 445 Mass. 702 (2006) (although the defendant's children ran the day-to-day operations, he was the one who established the "massage school" and warned therapists not to discuss "anything except massage technique" because of undercover cops).

For sexual intercourse. The term "sexual intercourse" as used in 272, § 6 *only* includes penile-vaginal penetration. Thus, there must be proof that the prostitute was at the premises to perform intercourse for a fee.

- **Sufficient evidence.** *Comm. v. Mullane*, 445 Mass. 702 (2006): The undercover detective testified that "Lisa," his massage therapist, immediately took off her clothes in the massage room. She then stated that she was willing to give him "anything" if he paid for "extras." While Lisa initially offered a "hand release," it was clear that she would provide customers with "anything" they wanted, including sexual intercourse, if they had enough money.

- **Insufficient evidence.** *Comm. v. Purdy*, 459 Mass. 442 (2011): Duncan Purdy operated a massage parlor. Two undercover detectives were offered "extras," but they were listed on a menu as "pop the cork" and "Russian ending" (where the customer puts his penis between the masseuse's breasts until he ejaculates). In fact, the menu stated that they did not offer "full service" under any circumstances. When police searched the salon, they found sex toys, but no condoms.

Related Offenses & Procedures

Keeping House of Ill Fame. 272, § 24 prohibits owning, managing, or maintaining premises used for sexual activity for hire. *Comm. v. Mullane, supra.* (conviction does not require proof of sexual intercourse — <u>any</u> sexual activity qualifies). Penalty: HC NMT 2 yrs. Right of Arrest: Complaint.

Required proof & statute of limitations. 272, § 11 says that any conviction under 272, §§ 4A (Inducing Minor to Become Prostitute); 4B (Deriving Support from Minor Prostitute); and 6 (Permitting Prostitution on the Premises), must be based on the testimony of more than one witness — unless that witness' account is significantly corroborated. *Comm. v. Odell*, 34 Mass. App. Ct. 100 (1993). § 11 also requires that any prosecution for a violation of these crimes start no later than one year after they occur.

12 Child Pornography & Other Misconduct

Section I
CHILD PORNOGRAPHY OFFENSES

POSING A CHILD FOR SEXUAL PHOTOGRAPHS
272, § 29A

Purpose

The law outlaws using children as subjects for pornography because: (1) it damages their emotional development; (2) it is typically used by adult perpetrators to encourage other children to engage in sexual acts; and (3) it is used by promoters for profit. *New York v. Ferber*, 458 U.S. 747 (1982).

Elements

- ***Know child under 18.*** The suspect knows that the child is under 18 years old, or is aware of facts giving him reason to know that the child is under 18.

- ***Prohibited activities.*** The suspect engages in Type 1 or 2 behavior:

    Type 1: Posing Child Naked. With lascivious intent;

    - The suspect hires, coerces, solicits, entices, uses, encourages, or knowingly permits the child to pose or be exhibited in a state of nudity;

    - For the purpose of representation or reproduction in any visual material.

    Type 2: Depicting Sexual Conduct. Regardless of his intent;

    - The suspect hires, coerces, solicits, entices, uses, encourages, or knowingly permits the child to participate in any act that depicts or represents sexual conduct;

    - For the purpose of:
        - Representation or reproduction in any visual material; or
        - Staging any live performance.

Right of Arrest

Felony.

Penalty

SP NLT 10 yrs, NMT 20 yrs; and/or, Fine NLT $10,000, NMT $50,000.

Notes

Special note. Since precise terminology is so important in this area of the law, the legislature enacted a special definition statute, 272, § 31, which applies to all pornography and obscenity laws.

Suspect knows or has reason to know child under 18. Knowledge is defined broadly to eliminate a suspect's defense that he did not actually know the age of the victim. Thus, the suspect's "awareness" of facts giving him reason to know the victim's age will suffice.

- **Obvious factors.** Officers may rely on the testimony of the child, or any admission of the defendant, or the obvious appearance of the victim, or the way the perpetrator discovered the victim — e.g., Did he pick up the boy or girl at a junior high school? Befriend the child's parents? Talk to the child's friends?

- **Expert testimony.** Proof may also be based on "expert medical testimony based on the person's physical appearance" or "by any other method." 272, § 29A(d).

    Comm. v. O'Connell, 432 Mass. 657 (2003): Stephen O'Connell appeared in a homemade photograph in which he was touching a young girl's vagina. However, her face was not visible. Proof of O'Connell's knowledge that she was under 18 came in two acceptable forms. First, a blanket appeared in the picture next to the child. Testimony revealed that O'Connell's niece constantly carried that blanket around and, at the time of the photograph, was eight years old. Second, expert testimony established that the physical characteristics of the child depicted in the photograph made her "in all likelihood under 11½ years old."

- **Insufficient proof of knowledge.** *Comm. v. Wright*, 60 Mass. App. Ct. 108 (2003): While the victim was 17 at the time the defendant took pornographic photographs of her while he lived with her mother, there was insufficient evidence that the defendant knew that she was under 18. The mere fact that the defendant and the victim lived in the same house, off and on, was not proof that the defendant knew how old she was. Furthermore, the victim's appearance in the photographs was not a basis for discriminating between a 17 year old and an 18 year old, since there are no obvious distinctions between young girls of those ages.

No consent. 272, § 29A(c) explicitly states that a minor is incapable of consenting to any of its prohibited conduct.

Type 1: Nude pictures — Lascivious intent required. Our law requires that the suspect's motivation involve lascivious intent when the questionable activity is limited to child nudity. The added requirement recognizes that there are circumstances where photographing naked children is entirely appropriate. For example, what parents haven't snapped a shot of "their naked three year old toddler romping in a wading pool?" *Comm. v. Oakes*, 407 Mass. 92 (1990) (discussion of need for a standard in these cases).

- **Lascivious intent.** Rather than outlaw innocent activity, the law insists that the suspect possess "lascivious intent." Lascivious intent is "a state of mind in which the sexual gratification or arousal of any person is an objective."

    Under 272, § 31, lascivious intent may be proved by the following:

    - Sexually oriented or sexually suggestive displays;
    - Focal point is the child's genitalia, pubic area, or female breast area;
    - Unnatural pose or inappropriate attire, considering the child's age;
    - Depiction of any sexual conduct, including intercourse, bestiality, masturbation, sadistic masochistic behavior, or lewd exhibition of the genitals.

    The lascivious intent standard has been upheld despite attacks by defendants that it is vague and inhibits their right to free expression under the First Amendment. *Comm. v. Bean*, 435 Mass. 708 (2002).

- **Hires, coerces, solicits, entices, encourages, or knowingly permits.** Each prohibited activity should be given its commonsense meaning. At a minimum, the suspect must knowingly permit the child to pose nude. In *Comm. v. Provost*, 418 Mass. 416 (1994), a priest took a series of well-focused photographs of a 10 year old child who was getting dressed following a church outing. The child's genital area was prominent in many of the photographs. The priest defended himself by saying that he did not hire, coerce, solicit, entice, or encourage the child's "spontaneous" posing. The SJC disagreed. The fact that the defendant continued to take photographs as the child struck different poses certainly established that he, at the very least, "knowingly permitted" it.

    Comm. v. Ingersoll, 2017 WL 657648 (Appeals Court): Evan Ingersoll invited two minors to his hotel to swim. He directed them to change into their bathing suits in the bathroom. There, he had set up a hidden camera which was specifically angled to record their private areas. He then directed them to pose for photographs on a bed while they were wearing bathing suits. There was sufficient evidence that Ingersoll caused the minors to pose in a state of nudity. He directed them to undress where they would be before the camera. Photographs of other young girls in bathing suits and various stages of undress were also found on devices seized from his hotel room.

- **Nudity.** Under § 31, nudity is defined as: "Uncovered or less than opaquely covered human genitals, pubic areas, the human female breast below a point immediately above the top of the areola [colored area around the nipple], or the covered male genitals in a discernibly turgid state [meaning an erection] . . . ." *Comm. v. Provost,* 418 Mass. 416 (1994) (although the 10 year old child had his underwear on, portions of his pubic and genital area were clearly visible in two photographs taken by the priest; it is sufficient under the statute if a portion of the nude genital area is visible).

- **Visual material.** Visual material is broadly defined by § 31 to include: "Any motion picture film, picture, photograph, videotape, book, magazine, [or] pamphlet that contains pictures, photographs or similar visual representations or reproductions, or depiction by computer, telephone or any other device capable of electronic data storage or transmission." *Comm. v. Hall*, 80 Mass. App. Ct. 317 (2011) (picture taken by a cell phone camera qualifies as a visual representation).

- *Undeveloped items may be visual material even though processing is required to make their contents apparent.* The simple act of taking a photograph creates "visual material." In *Comm. v. Lawrence*, 68 Mass. App. Ct. 103 (2007), Eva Lawrence on several occasions took her 10 year old daughter's clothes off while she was sleeping. She posed her in sexual positions and took pictures. The crime was complete when Lawrence posed her child *for the purpose* of visual representation. Even if a picture never materializes — e.g., due to a lack of film or because of overexposure — the crime still happens.

- *Even though pictures are not recovered in the defendant's possession, there may still be proof that he did, at one time, possess them.* *Comm. v. Hall*, 80 Mass. App. Ct. 317 (2011): Kenneth Hall offered to buy things for an 11 year old girl named Mary — if she sent him pictures of her "butt and private." He gave her gifts and a cell phone, which she used to send him 28 naked photos. Both Hall and Mary's cell phones were registered to Hall's wife, and both had the ability to take and send pictures. The 28 pictures shared by Mary were stored on her cell phone and Sprint/Nextel had a record that they were sent to Hall's phone. While there was no record that Hall received them, and they were no longer stored on his phone when it was seized by police, he undeniably had the photos given his text messages to Mary acknowledging that he got them and asking her to send more.

Type 2: Sexual conduct — No lascivious intent necessary. For this offense, the suspect does not need lascivious intent because the prohibited activity — depicting sexual conduct — can *never* be legal (unlike snapping a picture of a naked child). Consequently, it is irrelevant what the suspect thought, so long as he was aware that an underage child was participating.

- **Sexual conduct.** § 31 defines sexual conduct as masturbation; actual or simulated sexual intercourse; touching genitals, pubic areas, buttocks, or female breasts; any depiction of excretory functions; any lewd exhibition of the genitals; flagellation or torture in the context of a sexual relationship; or sex acts involving animals.

  Nudity itself is not "sexual conduct" within this definition, *unless* the particular depiction includes one of the factors previously mentioned — e.g., "lewd exhibition of the genitals."

  Note that the child does not have to actually perform sex. The statutory language covers "representations" of sex — in other words, simulated sex.

- **Hires, coerces, solicits, entices, encourages, or knowingly permits.** Apply the same meaning previously discussed.

- **Visual material or live performance.** Visual material was defined previously. In addition to visual depiction, this version of the offense punishes a suspect whose purpose is to stage a sexual performance. § 31 defines a "performance" as "any play, dance, exhibit, or such similar activity performed by one or more persons." The performance does not actually have to occur; the facts must simply show that the suspect's intention was the "staging" of a sex display.

  Comm. v. Bundy, 465 Mass. 538 (2013): 34 year old Jeffrey Bundy and the 10 year old victim became friends through playing Xbox games over the internet. Both owned a "vision camera" which allowed them to see each other.

During "live chats," Bundy pulled his pants down and began masturbating. He encouraged the victim to "try it." One time, the victim's mother walked into his room and saw Bundy masturbating on the screen and her son masturbating in front of the computer. The victim's penis was also displayed on the screen. When the mother gasped, Bundy turned off his camera and the screen went blank. The mother called police.

The victim's act of masturbation constituted a "sexual performance" because it was not done in isolation. The image was broadcast over the internet to Bundy. The definition of performance does not require the *physical* presence of the audience.

Related Offenses

Human Trafficking. 265, § 50 outlaws recruiting, transporting, obtaining, or financially benefiting from another person who engages in a sexually explicit performance or the production of child pornography. Penalty: SP NMT Life. Right of Arrest: Felony.[1]

Exhibition of Deformities. 272, § 33. A person may not "[exhibit] for hire an albino person, a minor or mentally ill person who is deformed or a person who has the appearance of deformity produced by artificial means." Penalty: Fine NMT $500. Right of Arrest: Complaint.

DISSEMINATING CHILD PORNOGRAPHY
272, § 29B

Elements

- ***Lascivious intent.*** With lascivious intent;

- ***Disseminates or intends to.*** The suspect disseminates or possesses with the intent to disseminate;

- ***Pornography with child under 18.*** Material that contains a representation of a child under 18 in a state of nudity or participating in sexual conduct; and

- ***Knowledge of contents.*** The suspect knows or has sufficient reason to know about the contents of this visual material.

Right of Arrest

Felony.

Penalty

SP NLT 10 yrs, NMT 20 yrs; and/or the larger amount between a fine of NLT $10,000, NMT $50,000 or 3 times the monetary value of any economic gain derived from disseminating this material.

---

[1] A detailed breakdown of the trafficking law appears in *LED's Juvenile Law, Chapter 10*.

Notes

Lascivious intent. Defined previously in reference to 272, § 29A, the lascivious standard also applies to 29B, except that a defendant may show his lack of lascivious intent through evidence that he disseminated material for "a *legitimate* scientific, medical or educational purpose." This defense is not available in a 29A prosecution, which deals with the actual creation of child pornography (which is never legitimate) as opposed to 29B, which involves the dissemination of prepared material that could, under limited circumstances, be proper. *Comm. v. Molina*, 476 Mass. 388 (2017) (sufficient evidence that defendant's own sexual gratification was an objective when he downloaded and shared computer files containing naked children engaging in sexual conduct).

No lascivious intent. *Comm. v. Hyacinth H.*, 2021 WL 2745122 (Appeals Court): The defendant, Hyacinth, was a middle school student. Formerly friendly with Ann, she now was angry at her, so Hyacinth showed four middle school boys a picture Ann had taken of herself two years before. Though focused on Ann's face, the top of Ann's left breast and nipple were visible. Ann's facial expression showed no distress, and nothing in her body's pose or the surroundings suggested it was sexually explicit. Still, Hyacinth was charged with felony distribution of child pornography, 272, § 29B.

While Hyacinth intended to humiliate Ann because of their dispute, the issue was whether Hyacinth distributed Ann's photo with lascivious intent — i.e., did she intend that the picture cause the boys to think of Ann in sexually arousing ways? While lascivious intent need not be the exclusive motive in a distribution crime, the style of this picture did not permit any inference of a lascivious motive.

Disseminates or possesses with intent to disseminate. 272, § 31 defines "disseminate" to include "import, publish, produce, print, manufacture, distribute, sell, lease, exhibit or display." It is a misconception that this law only applies to major child pornographers. Any person who hangs up a snapshot of young children engaged in sexual conduct is guilty.

Even if the suspect has not yet disseminated the material, he is still guilty if he possessed it with that intent. Key indicators include the amount of material; documents (e.g., invoices, order forms, telephone logs, receipts); and statements by witnesses or accomplices.

Similar to other crimes, possession requires that the suspect have the intent and ability to control the contraband. In *Comm. v. Lotten Books, Inc.*, 12 Mass. App. Ct. 625 (1981), the defendant argued that he could not possess the "dirty" films because he had no keys to the locked closet where the films were stored. The court rejected his argument, saying that the defendant had constructive possession because he knew who had the keys and could arrange for access at any time.

Child under 18; naked or engaged in sexual conduct; visual material. Apply the same definitions and proof previously discussed in relation to 272, § 29A. *Perry v. Comm.*, 438 Mass. 282 (2002) (computer images are considered visual material; the defendant called himself "The Director of Hygiene" at an online pornography organization nicknamed "Pedo University"; police executed a warrant at his home where they found more than 200 images of nude minors on his computer).

Knowledge of the contents. Because the § 29B suspect does not necessarily create the material, it is necessary to prove that he was aware of its pornographic contents. § 31 defines "knowledge" as "a general awareness of the character of the matter." The evidence must show that he generally knew that the material depicted naked or sexually engaged children. *Comm. v. Rosenberg*, 379 Mass. 334 (1979) (no need for eyewitness testimony of the defendant actually viewing the materials).

Injunction to stop distribution. 272, § 30D enables the prosecutor to petition the superior court for an injunction to prevent the dissemination of any material that violates § 29B. An injunction may be pursued in addition to criminal charges.

POSSESSION OF CHILD PORNOGRAPHY
272, § 29C

Elements

- **Possessed in any form.** The suspect purchased or possessed pornography in a negative, slide, book, magazine, film, videotape, photograph, other visual reproduction, or computer;

- **Depiction of child under 18.** That depicted any child whom the suspect knew, or reasonably should have known, was under age 18; and

- **Knowledge of pornographic nature.** The suspect knew "the nature or content" of the pornographic material.

Right of Arrest

Felony.

Penalty

1st offense: SP NMT 5 yrs or HC NMT 2½ yrs; and/or Fine NLT $1,000 NMT $10,000.

2nd offense: SP NMT 5 yrs; and/or Fine NLT $5,000 NMT $20,000.

3rd or subsequent offense: SP NLT 10 yrs; and/or Fine NLT $10,000 NMT $30,000.

Notes

Definition of child pornography. § 29C defines pornography as the depiction of a child — "actually or by simulation" — engaged in an act of:

- Sexual intercourse or contact with any person or animal;
- Masturbation;
- Lewd fondling or caressing involving another person or animal;
- Secretion or urination within a sexual context;
- Bondage or sadomasochistic abuse in any sexual context; or

- Posing involving a lewd exhibition of the *unclothed* genitals, pubic area, buttocks or, if such person is female, a fully or partially developed breast of a child. *Comm. v. Graziano*, 2019 WL 6337286 (Appeals Court) (sheer lingerie exposed young girl's breasts in lewd photo; because the alleged "clothing" allowed a viewer to see the prohibited body part to the same extent as if the child was naked, it qualified as an "unclothed" pornographic exhibition).

- **Simulation.** A simulated image makes it appear like the child is involved in sexual intercourse. *Comm. v. Kenney*, 449 Mass. 840 (2007). However, the image must depict a real child. This crime does not apply to computer-created images of children who do not exist. *Comm. v. Hinds*, 437 Mass. 54 (2002) (the overall goal of this law is to eliminate the permanent record of the sexual exploitation of <u>actual</u> children).

- **Computer images.** § 29C includes child pornography in any form, including "depiction by computer." *Comm. v. Hinds, supra.* (even an unopened file violates § 29C because stored data quickly converts into a graphic image).

- **Possessing only one photo enough for conviction.** At the same time, if multiple photos are possessed, it only justifies charging one count. *Comm. v. Rollins*, 470 Mass. 66 (2014). *U.S. v. Chiaradio*, 684 F.3d 265 (2012) (images on two interlinked computers in a suspect's residence constituted only one count of pornography possession).

- **Nudity must be lewd.** *Comm. v. Sullivan*, 82 Mass. App. Ct. 293 (2012): Mark Sullivan had a photograph of a naked girl on the beach. The focal point was her breast and nipple, while her hand pointed toward her exposed pubic area. This photograph was child pornography because it was *designed* to elicit a sexual response. This was *not* artistic or educational expression protected by the First Amendment. It was not an ordinary family photograph of a day at the beach either.

  Compare *Comm. v. Rex*, 469 Mass. 36 (2014): The defendant's photocopies of pictures of naked, prepubescent children at the beach were not lewd. Their genitals were not the focal point; they were not in unnatural poses; and there was nothing remotely sexual about the pictures. Child pornography is not created simply because a viewer derives sexual enjoyment from an otherwise innocent photograph.

- **Exemptions.** § 29C does not apply to a police officer, physician, psychologist, attorney, or court official who possesses pornography in the lawful performance of his duty. The law does not apply to a legitimate enterprise that possesses samples to further its educational and prevention goals.

Proof of child's age. *Comm. v. Kenney*, 449 Mass. 840 (2007): Police received a tip that Steven Kenney possessed child pornography. They obtained a warrant and seized his computer. Kenney did not have to specifically know the ages of the children. They were obviously underage given the websites he contacted.[2]

Proof of knowledge. The fact that child pornography is stored on the suspect's computer is not enough, by itself, to prove that he *knew* the contents of the images. In *Comm. v.*

---

2 The pornographic images located on Kenney's computer were graphically labeled. One image had the file name "cum+covered+baby00.jpg"; another, found in the recycle bin, was "I+think+she+likesem+young+2.jpg."

Hinds, supra., the defendant's knowledge was proven by the amount of stored images on his computer and their "sexually explicit file names . . . including 10YRSLUT, KIDSEX1, 10YOANAL." Also see *Comm. v. Coates*, 89 Mass. App. Ct. 728 (2016).

Both possession and dissemination may occur. *Comm. v. Moore*, 2016 WL 5328457 (Appeals Court) (defendant downloaded 900 images on his computer and shared at least six images and a video with other people through a public server called "Limewire"; he was properly charged with both crimes).

Section II
OBSCENITY OFFENSES

DISSEMINATION OF OBSCENE MATTER
272, § 29

Purpose

272, § 29, in similar fashion to § 29B, prohibits disseminating, or possessing with the intent to disseminate, "obscene matter." The difference is that § 29 applies to *all* obscene matter, regardless of whether it depicts children.

Elements

- **Knowledge.** The suspect knowingly

- **Disseminate or possess with intent.** Disseminated or possessed with the intent to disseminate;

- **Obscene.** Obscene matter.

Right of Arrest

Major caution: Although this is a felony, there are fundamental constitutional issues involved. Officers should consult with their local district attorney's office prior to making *any* arrests or seizing materials. There is expanded judicial oversight in this sensitive area.

Penalty

SP NMT 5 yrs or HC NMT 2½ yrs; and/or Fine: *1st offense:* NLT $1,000, NMT $10,000; *2nd offense:* NLT $5,000, NMT $20,000; *3rd and subsequent offense:* NLT $10,000, NMT $30,000.

Notes

Knowledge. It is not necessary that the suspect know the matter is obscene, but he must generally know its content. *Comm. v. Bono*, 7 Mass. App. Ct. 849 (1979) (while publication was stapled shut at time of purchase, vivid photos on the front and back covers made its obscene content abundantly clear).

Knowingly disseminate. As previously mentioned, § 31 defines "disseminate" to mean "import, publish, produce, print, manufacture, distribute, sell, lease, exhibit or display." In *Comm. v. Rollins*, 60 Mass. App. Ct. 153 (2003), Mark Rollins dropped obscene material from his car intending it would be seen by individuals living in the area. These advertisements for "adult videos" contained pictures of adults engaging in intercourse. The drops occurred on a main road near people and houses.

Obscenity. According to § 31 and related cases, material must satisfy *all* three of the following requirements to be obscene:

- **Prurient interest.** Taken as a whole, the material must appeal to the prurient interest of an average adult in the county where the case is brought. "Prurient interest" means "a shameful or morbid interest in nudity, sex, or excretion, an unhealthy interest about sexual matters which is repugnant to prevailing moral standards." *Comm. v. Dane Entertainment Servs., Inc. (No. 2)*, 397 Mass. 201 (1986).

  Keep in mind that erotic materials are not the same thing as obscenity. Nudity alone is not obscene. Many recognized literary, artistic, and scientific works concern sexual themes. The fact that materials may arouse sexual thoughts and desires is not enough to make them obscene. *Jenkins v. Georgia*, 418 U.S. 153 (1974).

- **Sexual conduct described or depicted.** The second requirement is that the material depicts or describes sexual conduct in an obviously offensive way, based on contemporary standards. An adult standard applies. Aside from the material itself, consider what precautions were taken to ensure that people would not be unwillingly exposed. *Comm. v. Rollins, supra.* (all photographs showed sexual organs during intercourse; residents involuntarily encountered the photos after the defendant spread them around the neighborhood).

- **Lacks value.** The third requirement is that a reasonable person would find that the material, taken as a whole, lacks any serious literary, artistic, political, or scientific value. Material which "deal[s] with sexual conduct in a manner which advocates ideas, which contributes to . . . scientific discussion, or which adds to . . . art and literature in our culture is protected by the First Amendment." *Pope v. Illinois*, 481 U.S. 576 (1987).

This statute satisfies the First Amendment. *Comm. v. Dane Entertainment*, 23 Mass. App. Ct. 1017 (1987).

- **Defense of employees of educational institutions.** This section and § 28 (dealing with minors) state that it is a defense if the defendant is an employee of a legitimate school, museum, or library and "serving the educational purpose of such organization."

- **Defense for managers and projector operators.** 272, § 32 exempts managers and motion picture operators at licensed movie theaters from being prosecuted under §§ 29, 28, and 29A. However, they must have no financial interest in the theater where they work and no authority to decide what films get shown.

Suspension of liquor license. Officers may involve the Alcoholic Beverages Control Commission (ABCC) if a licensed establishment is implicated in obscene displays. *New Palm Gardens, Inc. v. ABCC*, 11 Mass. App. Ct. 785 (1981).

Related Offense

Dissemination of Secret Videotape or Photograph of Person who is Partially Naked. 272, § 105. See *Chapter 10*.

DISSEMINATION OF OBSCENITY TO MINORS
272, § 28

Elements

- ***Disseminate or possess with intent.*** The suspect purposefully disseminated or possessed with the intent to disseminate;

- ***Harmful matter.*** Matter that is harmful to minors;

- ***Knowledge of minor status.*** To a person he knows or believes to be a minor;

- ***Knowledge of harmful matter.*** While knowing that the matter is harmful to minors.

Right of Arrest

Felony.

Penalty

SP NMT 5 yrs or HC NMT 2½ yrs; and/or Fine: *1ˢᵗ offense:* NLT $1,000, NMT $10,000; *2ⁿᵈ offense:* NLT $5,000, NMT $20,000; *3ʳᵈ and subsequent offense:* NLT $10,000, NMT $30,000.

Notes

Minor. Any person under 18 years of age.

Matter. § 31 defines matter broadly as any handwritten, printed, visual, or electronically generated item. *Comm. v. Washburn,* 55 Mass. App. Ct. 493 (2002) (high school teacher was guilty when he displayed adult pornography on his computer screen to a 15 year old student he was tutoring). *Comm. v. Gould,* 2018 WL 3421093 (Appeals Court) (single photo of flaccid penis is harmful matter, especially when accompanied by descriptions of sexual acts and requests for the minor to send nude photos).

Harmful to minor. § 31 defines matter as "harmful to minors" if, taken as a whole, it describes nudity or sexual conduct that appeals to the "prurient interest" of minors in a way that is contrary to prevailing community standards and lacks academic value. Thus, the obscenity test previously explained in reference to 272, § 29 is applied here — with the modification that a minor's sensibilities are considered, not an average adult's.

- **Contrasting cases.** *Comm. v. Militello,* 66 Mass. App. Ct. 325 (2006): Frank Militello showed pictures from a *Playboy* magazine to four boys aged nine through 13. Since the testimony of the boys only showed they saw photographs of naked women, not sexual conduct, it could not be determined that the material lacked artistic, political or scientific value for minors, which is an element of this offense. Also see *Comm. v. Letendre*, 2020 WL 4047737 (Appeals Court) (victim described videos as, "I'm guessing they were like pornography." This was insufficient to prove they were).

Compare *Ferrari v. Comm.*, 448 Mass. 163 (2007): Leo Ferrari hired 12 year old "Jane" to work at his driving range. On three occasions, he showed her pornographic videos. Jane testified in detail about the pornographic scenes she saw. The fact that the jurors did not see the tapes did not prevent them from determining they lacked artistic, political, or scientific value. Jane's descriptions alone met the standard of "harmful to minors."

- **Community standards.** The particular materials must be "contrary to prevailing community standards." *Comm. v. Kereakoglow,* 456 Mass. 225 (2010). To make its case, the government must present expert testimony on the standards in the relevant community, except in obvious cases. *Comm. v. Sullivan,* 55 Mass. App. Ct. 775 (2002) ("our own review of the magazines . . . leads us to conclude that no reasonable and disinterested observer anywhere in the Commonwealth would think them suitable for children").

Knowingly disseminate or intend to disseminate.

- **One recipient constitutes dissemination.** *Comm. v. Dodgson*, 80 Mass. App. Ct. 307 (2011) (the harm occurs when even one person receives the offending material).

- **Dissemination must be intentional.** Negligently allowing access to obscene materials is not a crime. *Comm. v. Belcher*, 446 Mass. 693 (2006) (evidence indicated that the mentally impaired niece of the defendant might have accessed his pornography on her own, because he stored his collection negligently; no crime unless exposure was on purpose).

- **The fact that the harmful material is received by an undercover officer is** *no defense.* *Comm. v. Dodgson*, 80 Mass. App. Ct. 307 (2011) (the defendant sent an email with a picture of his penis to a person he thought was 13 years old; she was really an undercover officer).

- **A person who disseminates an electronic communication must** *specifically intend* **to direct it to a person he knows or believes to be a minor.** This requirement protects those who disseminate "sexually frank" information through generally accessible websites. It is unfair to expect that they will verify the age of every person viewing their site and be able to block minors. *Comm. v. Jones*, 471 Mass. 138 (2015).

- **Intent to disseminate.** *Comm. v. Sullivan,* 55 Mass. App. Ct. 775 (2002) featured a defendant who would, at a public beach, masturbate while looking at pornographic magazines from his car trunk. Sometimes he carried on this activity under the gaze of young boys playing in the area. During a consent search, police found pornographic magazines in his trunk. Sullivan argued that the police never proved that the magazines they found were the ones he displayed to the boys. However, it was only necessary to prove that Sullivan possessed these magazines *with the intent* to display them. The evidence clearly proved that, even if he had not previously shown these magazines, he intended to show them to the boys.

- **Intent to disseminate may be conditional.** *Comm. v. Ericson*, 85 Mass. App. Ct. 326 (2014): Keith Ericson, knowing that the victim was 16 years old, repeatedly offered to send her a cell phone picture of his naked body. The fact that he refused to send the picture unless the victim first sent him one did not negate his intent. The condition Ericson imposed did not nullify the harm of the offense, but rather aggravated it by proposing a second crime (posing a minor in a state of nudity).

Just because one can legally perform a sexual touching does not mean he or she can disseminate a picture of it. *Comm. v. Mienkowski*, 91 Mass. App. Ct. 668 (2017): Beth's aunt became suspicious of 14 year old Beth's cell phone communications with 23 year old Michael Mienkowski. She read Beth's text messages, which referred to Mienkowski's digital and oral rapes of Beth. Mienkowski had also attached a video of himself masturbating.

Mienkowski argued that the video could not be matter harmful to a minor because Beth could consent to him masturbating in front of her. After all, a 14 year old can legally partake in sexual activity that does not involve penetration. However, the fact that Beth could have consented to Mienkowski's acts in person did not mean he could send her a video of the same conduct. In context, the video was not part of a consensual relationship. It was from a rapist to his child victim. The text messages demonstrated that Mienkowski used the video as part of his sexual and emotional abuse of Beth.

Exemption. 272, § 28 states that it is a *complete defense* if the defendant "was in a parental or guardianship relationship with the minor" or was engaged in educational activities as an employee of a museum or library. *Comm. v. Foreman*, 101 Mass. App. Ct. 398 (2022).

INCEST
272, § 17

Elements

- **Sexual contact or marriage.** A suspect participated in sexual activity — including oral or anal intercourse, fellatio, cunnilingus, or other penetration of a part of a person's body, or insertion of an object into the genital or anal opening, or the manual manipulation of another person's genitalia — <u>or</u> intermarried;

- **Prohibited relationships.** With the following individuals — specified in 207, §§ 1 and 2 — who are related by blood or adoption:

    - Mother, grandmother, daughter, granddaughter, sister, brother's daughter (niece), sister's daughter (niece), father's sister (aunt), mother's sister (aunt); or

    - Father, grandfather, son, grandson, brother, brother's son (nephew), sister's son (nephew), father's brother (uncle), and mother's brother (uncle).

Right of Arrest

Felony.

Penalty

SP NMT 20 yrs or HC NMT 2½ yrs.

Notes

Incest covers only persons related by blood or adoption, not those related by "affinity." *Comm. v. Rahim*, 441 Mass. 273 (2004) held that incest only occurs among those related by blood or adoption, but does not apply to an affinity relationship. Affinity refers to a nonblood relationship acquired through marriage.[3]

Sexual contact or intermarriage. Before 2001, incest *only* applied to natural sexual intercourse (a man's penis in a woman's vagina) between prohibited parties. *Comm. v. Smith*, 431 Mass. 417 (2000). The statute was amended to cover all forms of intercourse and the "manual manipulation" of another person's genitalia. In addition, incest occurs when people who are in a prohibited relationship marry. *Comm. v. Ashey*, 248 Mass. 259 (1924).

Lack of consent not an issue. *Comm. v. Goodhue*, 43 Mass. 193 (1840) (allegation that daughter consented to intercourse with her father was irrelevant to whether this crime occurred). In fact, if one of the parties to incest is under age 16 and "consents" to sexual intercourse, the better charge is the more severe Statutory Rape (265, § 23). See *Chapter 9*.

Related Offenses

Adultery. 272, § 14. Adultery occurs when a married person has sexual intercourse with someone other than his or her spouse; or when an unmarried person has sex with a married person. Penalty: SP NMT 3 yrs or HC NMT 2 yrs; or Fine NMT $500. Interestingly, as recently as 1983, the prohibition against adultery was upheld by the SJC as constitutional. *Comm. v. Stowell*, 389 Mass. 171 (1983).

Polygamy. 272, § 15 prevents a married person from marrying a second time or from cohabiting with a second spouse in the Commonwealth. Penalty: SP NMT 5 yrs or HC NMT 2½ yrs; or Fine NMT $500. Under § 15, polygamy does not apply to a person whose husband or wife "has continually remained beyond sea, or has voluntarily . . . remained absent for seven consecutive years" so that the person remarrying does not know whether his spouse is still alive. *Comm. v. Mash*, 48 Mass. 472 (1844). Of course, polygamy does not occur when a person remarries following the conclusion of a legal divorce. *Comm. v. Boyer*, 89 Mass. 306 (1863).

---

[3] In *Rahim*, three justices vigorously dissented saying that incest should continue to apply to relationships caused by marriage to preserve the sanctity of the family, which is the purpose of our incest laws.

Law Enforcement Dimensions

Part IV

DOMESTIC VIOLENCE & OTHER FORMS OF HARASSMENT

Domestic Violence, Mandatory Reporting, Stalking, Annoying Electronic Communications, Secret Recording, and Civil Rights

Chapters 13 – 16

© John Sofis Scheft, Esq.
All rights reserved

13 Domestic Violence & Restraining Orders

OFFICER RESPONSE & ENTRY

Response

Police may broadcast and receive all relevant information pertaining to locations and suspects. Dispatchers and officers are free to communicate the criminal history of any suspect, firearms information, warrant status, existence of any orders, and any other information for a legitimate law enforcement purpose. Executive Office of Public Safety & Security Domestic Violence Guidelines 2017 edition (EOPSS) at 18-19. 6, §§ 172 and 178.

Immediately proceed to scene. If possible, send at least 2 officers.

Approach carefully. Officers should not stop directly in front of the address. The building should be approached from the side, making officers less visible.

Home Entry

Officers may enter onto private property:

- **To serve a protective order.** *Comm. v. Mulvey,* 57 Mass. App. Ct. 579 (2003).

- **To quell an ongoing disturbance and restore peace.** EOPSS at 20.

- **At the request of someone in lawful control.** In the majority of cases, officers will be allowed to enter upon request. *Comm. v. Rexach,* 20 Mass. App. Ct. 919 (1985).

Officers must leave if both parties request that they do so, <u>unless</u>:

- **Exigent circumstances.** The officers' presence is necessary to prevent physical harm or to carry out the provisions of Chapter 209A. In their report, officers must describe why they believed action had to be taken. *Comm. v. Levine,* 2015 WL 4579328 (Appeals Court) (officer understood the caller had asked for immediate assistance, telling the 911 operator to "hurry up, he's on his way"; emergency confirmed when officer approached the home and heard the defendant say: "I'm going to kill you"; warrantless entry justified).

- **Typically, officers should not accept the word of a person at the door that all is well.** *Comm. v. Morrison,* 429 Mass. 511 (1999) noted that battered women "tend to minimize the severity and extent of the abuse." The police were "quite right in not taking at face value [the victim's] statements that she would have the order vacated."

Right to enter not without limits. There must be an exigency. *Comm. v. Midi*, 46 Mass. App. Ct. 591 (1999) (police could point to no facts that made them believe there was a risk of harm to the victim or anyone else in the apartment, such as a child; she had left the home and told police she was safe; there was no indication that her boyfriend was aware that she had notified authorities; he was not a flight risk; police clearly had time to get a warrant).

Contact with the Parties

Explain presence. Officers should state their reasons for being present and display a professional, calm and helpful attitude.

Avoid movement, separate parties. Prevent physical movement of parties as much as possible and control their access to potential weapons. Allow each party to present their story without interruptions or interference by the other party.

Document all victim statements. Often, officers encounter an emotional victim who is willing to relate the abuse she[1] experienced. This type of "spontaneous exclamation" may be admissible at trial through the testimony of the police officer who heard it. This is important because many times in domestic crimes the victim later refuses to testify.

Comm. v. Rand, 487 Mass. 811 (2021): The victim called 911 and said, "I need somebody to come to my house," and, "My boyfriend just beat me up." The dispatcher asked if the boyfriend was present. The victim replied he left with her sister, "Like two minutes ago, since I called you guys." When the dispatcher asked, "What exactly happened tonight?" the victim said she had been knocked out a couple of times and that her boyfriend tried to kill her. Officers arrived four minutes later.

The victim was hysterical while she told officers that her boyfriend, Roy Rand, had beaten her, choked her, and put his knees on her throat causing her to lose consciousness. The officers saw injuries to her face and her eyes were bloodshot. Medics arrived and evaluated the victim in the apartment. She was hesitant to go in the ambulance, even after police said they would accompany her and bring her daughter as well. Later, the victim refused to testify at trial, but an officer was allowed to repeat her statements, which helped convict Rand.

Bottom line: When a victim or witness speaks to police while under the influence of a recent event, the officer may repeat what they said in court if the initial questions were designed to:

- **Provide help with an ongoing or recent emergency, such as a response to a 911 call;**

- **Learn the location of and potential danger from a suspect;** and/or

- **Get proper medical treatment for an injured person.**

Even if not admissible as direct evidence, statements from victims or witnesses may have other uses, such as challenging inconsistent trial testimony, or advocating for bail or a sentence upon conviction.

---

1 *Note:* In describing victims, female gender references are used rather than the cumbersome his/her formulation. This choice acknowledges that the vast majority of domestic violence victims are women, although domestic violence certainly does occur among same sex couples and with male victims and female perpetrators.

Document a victim's injuries and a suspect's statements. In *Comm. v. Pelletier*, 71 Mass. App. Ct. 67 (2008), Officer Thomas Cuddy responded to a 911 call and saw that Pelletier's wife had serious facial injuries. Officer Cuddy asked her what happened. She appeared nervous and said that she "fell down the stairs." Once the ambulance arrived, Cuddy questioned Pelletier, who became angry. Pelletier told Cuddy he had arrived home from work at 4:00 p.m. and found his injured wife. When asked why he waited until 11:00 p.m. to call 911, he changed his story and said he came home from work, found a condom in their bedroom, became angry, and left to get drinks. When he came back hours later, he found his wife in that condition.

Cuddy noticed a fresh cut on Pelletier's right hand and blood spatters on his shirt and forehead. When asked how he got cut, he said he had no idea. Cuddy arrested him. Cuddy found blood in the bedroom and bathroom, but none on the stairs. Pelletier was convicted of A&B. His wife did not testify, but Officer Cuddy's excellent, on-scene investigation provided sufficient evidence.

Learn about prior incidents. This information may be admissible at trial and sentencing. *Comm. v. Myer*, 38 Mass. App. Ct. 140 (1995).

Contact with Children

Although they do not always show it, kids who witness domestic violence are traumatized. Groves, "Silent Victims," *Pediatrics, Vol. 96* (1995). This is why officers should:

- **Ask if child is "okay"** and record their name and age.

- **Explain in neutral terms what is happening** (e.g., "Your dad was upset and we needed to take him to the station where he can calm down"). It can really help if you assure the child that he/she is not at fault for the situation. Even a short discussion about another subject — school, sports, a hobby — can really help a child calm down.

- **For a more comprehensive intervention,** contact a victim advocate in the DA's Office.

Photos & Physical Evidence

Take photographs of any injuries and the scene. Photographs are critical. They can document a crying victim, bruises, an overturned coffee table. A study by the Institute for Forensic Imaging found that "digital photography, put in the hands of first responding officers, can double the likelihood of a conviction . . . in domestic violence cases — even in cases where the victim refuses to testify."[2]

Collect any physical evidence. The rationale that supports increased efforts to obtain photographs applies with equal force to other physical evidence.

---

[2] H. Blitzer, et al. *Law Enforcement Technology* (June 2002) at p. 52.

Probation Electronic Monitoring (ELMO) Law

ELMO will supply the GPS information of probationers for investigative purposes. Law enforcement agencies may request ELMO information by submitting a written request to: Elmo.Inforequests@jud.state.ma.us. Requests are typically answered within 48 hours, although an emergency request receives an immediate response. Agencies may call ELMO directly at 978-365-2970.

OFFICER RESPONSIBILITIES AT THE SCENE
209A, § 6 and EOPSS Guidelines
BASIC COVERAGE

Coverage Under 209A

Chapter 209A protection applies to "Family or Household Members" defined by 209A, § 1 as people who are *or* were:

- <u>Married</u>;

- <u>Parents</u> of a common child regardless of whether they have been married or lived together;

    - *Grandparents of child born out of wedlock covered by 209A. Turner v. Lewis*, 434 Mass. 331 (2001): The paternal grandparent of a child whose parents were not married was "related by blood" to the child's mother and had the right to obtain a protective order when the child's mother, who was drug dependent, came to her house and assaulted her several times while she had custody of the ten year old child; court noted the need for protection because of a 75% increase in the number of children residing in households headed by grandparents.

- **Involved in substantive <u>dating</u> or engagement relationship** considering: (1) length; (2) type; (3) interaction; and (4) time elapsed since end of relationship;

    - *Determined by facts.* The SJC said in *C.O. v. M.M.*, 442 Mass. 648 (2004): "Dating is inherently personal and idiosyncratic, and relationships exist in endless variety. It would be unproductive to place a numerical quota on the number of 'dates' that constitute a substantive dating relationship." In this case, the defendant was a 17 year old high school student accused of having sexually assaulted a 15 year old schoolmate. Her mother received a restraining order for her daughter. However, there was simply no evidence that the daughter and defendant had been or were currently in a dating relationship. The restraining order was vacated. *Comm. v. Snow*, 2018 WL 1122415 (Appeals Court) (sufficient evidence of dating relationship where the defendant introduced the victim to a witness as his girlfriend, the defendant and victim shared a bedroom for at least a week while the witness stayed with them, and the witness had heard conversations about their joint finances).

    - *Internet relationships* can constitute a dating relationship even though there is no personal contact. *E.C.O. v. Compton*, 464 Mass. 558 (2013).

- *More than one.* Brossard v. West Roxbury Court, 417 Mass. 183 (1994) (a victim may be in more than one substantive dating relationship at any one time and receive protection under 209A).

- **Related** by blood or marriage (whether or not they ever lived together);
  - *Past protected relationships are covered by 209A, including ex-stepchildren.* Sorgman v. Sorgman, 49 Mass. App. Ct. 416 (2000) (the parties did live together and were related by marriage as stepfather and stepdaughter; furthermore, the parties continued to have contact with one another long after the marriage and living arrangement ended; the plaintiff properly received a 209A order).

- **Living together.** Aguilar v. Hernandez-Mendez, 66 Mass. App. Ct. 367 (2006) (regardless of family connection, people in same dwelling qualify; defendant had moved out but still kept a key, received mail, and occasionally showered and slept at the apartment).

Remember, 209A protection is afforded to men and women; adults and minors; students in elementary, high school, college or graduate school; members of the LGBTQ community. Turner v. Lewis, 434 Mass. 331 (2001).

Parents may apply for 209A protection on behalf of their minor children. E.C.O. v. Compton, 464 Mass. 558 (2013). There must be some independent reason to include children in a protective order. However, acts of abuse against the children are not required. N.J. v. B.J., 91 Mass. App. Ct. 1121 (2017) (mother obtained 209A order for her child against his stepfather based on the stepfather's disturbing conduct of telling the child he was going to blow up his house with the family inside; the mere passage of time since the incident did not render the order no longer appropriate, especially since the stepfather had no awareness of how his threats had affected his family).

Minors may apply for 209A protection. The court should see if it is practical for the child to appear with a parent or guardian; otherwise the court may appoint its own temporary guardian and issue the order.

Most people living together are eligible for 209A protection, unless they are assigned to a state-licensed facility. Silva v. Carmel, 468 Mass. 18 (2014) denied 209A protection to an intellectually disabled adult living in a Department of Developmental Services facility. *Silva* was different from the vast majority of roommate situations. Even in the case of an assigned dorm on campus, students have voluntarily chosen to attend the institution and are free to make other arrangements. Roommates within a dorm or apartment have the level of "social interdependence" that the SJC found lacking in *Silva*. Officers should enforce 209A in these situations as they have done previously.

Harassment Order

If not eligible for 209A order, consider the Harassment Prevention Order (HPO). Issued under Chapter 258E, the HPO is a type of restraining order that does not depend on the relationship of the parties. *Discussed later in this chapter.*

New application required. If the victim finds out that 209A does not apply *after* she has started the process, she will need to make a new application and have a new hearing under 258E. *H.S. v. D.M.*, 2017 WL 1408039 (2017).

Definition of Abuse

The standard of "abuse" is critical because it: (1) triggers certain police responsibilities; and (2) justifies the court's issuance of a 209A order. 209A, § 1 states that abuse occurs when a family or household member performs one or more of the following acts:

- **Attempts or actually causes physical harm.** Virtually any type of physical harm qualifies (e.g., kicking, shoving, punching). *Szymkowski v. Szymkowski*, 57 Mass. App. Ct. 284 (2003).

- **Places another in fear of imminent serious physical harm.** This standard "closely approximates . . . the crime of assault." *Comm. v. Gordon*, 407 Mass. 340 (1990). The defendant does not need to have engaged in a prior physical attack to place a person in imminent fear. *Noelle N. v. Frasier F.*, 97 Mass. App. Ct. 660 (2020) (the plaintiff demonstrated reasonable fear when she credibly testified about her ex-husband's erratic behavior during a dispute over parenting time; specifically, he told the plaintiff he purchased a gun and was sleeping with it; he deliberately showed the gun to their very young children during a FaceTime session). *Constance C. v. Raymond R.*, 101 Mass. App. Ct. 390 (2022) (plaintiff described in detail the defendant's nonstop attempts to contact her, his escalating anger, his increasingly aggressive behavior, his tendency towards violence when he was under the influence, and his threats to commit suicide; all of these factors permitted the judge to conclude that the plaintiff's fear of imminent harm was objectively reasonable; in particular, threats of suicide and self-harm are, ironically, red flags for impending partner assaults in domestic violence situations).

  On the other hand, nervousness or irritation is insufficient. *Wooldridge v. Hickey*, 45 Mass. App. Ct. 637 (1998) (wife lacked a basis for a 209A order simply because her husband was rude about their divorce).

- **Causes another to engage involuntarily in sexual relations by force or threat.** *Doe v. Keller*, 57 Mass. App. Ct. 776 (2003) (restraining order properly issued when plaintiff alleged rape by his two homosexual roommates). Compare *E.C.O. v. Compton*, 464 Mass. 558 (2013) (16 year old daughter could not be subject of 209A order; she was old enough to agree to sex with 24 year old man, in spite of father's disapproval and concern).

  J.S. v. J.G., 2018 WL 4841081 (Appeals Court) (victim of involuntary sex by force or threat does not have to prove "imminent harm." The judge must decide whether an order is necessary to protect the plaintiff from the impact of forced sex already inflicted).

INITIAL ON-SCENE PROTECTIONS

Remain on Scene

Remain on scene for a reasonable period of time to protect the victim as long as she is in immediate physical danger without the presence of police.

Medical Treatment

Assist the victim in obtaining medical treatment for any injuries, including transport to the emergency room or other facility. Even if victims are not seriously injured, going to the hospital helps corroborate the abuse. *Comm. v. Moquette*, 439 Mass. 697 (2003) (ambulance reports and hospital records admissible to prove case).

Safe Place

Assist the abused person and her child(ren) in getting to a safe place, including a shelter or a family or friend's home. Officers must consider the victim's preference. Officers should *never* disclose the location of a shelter to a non-victim.

Language Barriers

Officers should determine whether language services are needed. EOPSS at 21. Using children or other family members as interpreters is strongly discouraged unless there is a medical emergency. Use community resources for this purpose.

Notice of Rights

Provide notice to the victim in English and, if necessary, in the person's native language. Officers must hand the victim a pre-printed copy of her rights.[3] Many departments have excellent summaries of 209A procedures — written simply for victims. Officers may accompany this type of brochure with a verbal explanation.

Emergency Judicial Response System (EJRS)

If necessary, use EJRS after hours. Under 209A, § 6, officers must: (1) call the on-call judge, who may grant an emergency restraining order based on a "substantial likelihood of immediate danger of abuse"; (2) record the protective order on the form; (3) have a copy delivered to the court on the next business day (while the order takes effect immediately, it must be certified by the court to continue); and (4) inform the victim that she must appear in court on the next business day.

Even when court is in session, 209A, § 5 allows protective orders to be granted over the phone if the victim is unable to appear "without severe hardship due to a physical condition." This provision was designed to help elders, people with serious injuries, or people with disabilities.

---

[3] Technically, the law requires that officers also read the complete statement. This requirement is routinely ignored because the formal language of the statement is confusing to victims.

ARREST PROCEDURES

Decision to Arrest

EOPSS guidelines list considerations that must inform an officer's decision to arrest:

- As in other types of criminal investigations, *uncorroborated statements* by a victim may constitute probable cause to arrest. EOPSS at 26.

- The arrest decision must be based on whether or not probable cause exists, *not* on whether the victim wishes to seek complaints or testify at a later date. EOPSS at 26 and 31.

- When assessing a victim's credibility, remember that a victim who is under the influence of drugs or alcohol, or who suffers from mental illness, is *not* inherently unreliable. EOPSS at 26.

- "One department's statement that probable cause to arrest exists *shall* be honored by another department. The second department *shall* immediately attempt to effect the arrest as requested by the investigating department." EOPSS at 27.

- "All officers will attempt to make a warrantless arrest within a reasonable amount of time . . . However, as soon as is practical, the investigating department shall seek an arrest warrant from the appropriate court." EOPSS at 27.

- "It is *not* proper procedure to advise the victim to seek complaint applications on his or her own." EOPSS at 27.

Arrest Authority & Obligations

Mandatory arrest for violation of temporary or permanent order. "In the interest of immediacy, and the statutory mandate to arrest, officers shall make a warrantless arrest of any person the officer . . . has probable cause to believe has violated an emergency, temporary or permanent [protective order] issued by *any* jurisdiction." EOPSS at 26.

Arrest is the "preferred response" for domestic violence incidents absent an existing order whenever officers have probable cause that the suspect committed:

- A felony; or

- An A&B on a family or household member; or

- A misdemeanor directed at a family or household member and involving abuse as defined in 209A, § 1.

Corroboration of a victim's account is not required for probable cause or even conviction. *Comm. v. Cardoso*, 2019 WL 6650038 (Appeals Court): The victim came home at 11:30 p.m. to find her husband, Octavio Cardoso, in the driveway of her residence. They argued from inside their vehicles and then got out. Cardoso grabbed the victim's left arm, threw her against the car, and yelled in her face. When she broke free, she was able to drive away.

She came back later. Cardoso suddenly appeared in the driveway screaming. She tried to get in her car, but he blocked her. She called 911. The police arrived and arrested Cardoso. At trial, Cardoso testified that he did not touch the victim. There was no physical evidence of injury or assault. He was legitimately convicted of A&B based on the uncorroborated testimony of the victim.

Outstanding arrest warrant. Officers must arrest the person. 276, § 28.

ARREST CAUTIONS

Threats

Warrantless arrest authority does not extend to the crime of "threats" — assault is preferred charge. 275, § 2 prohibits a warrantless arrest for Threat to Commit a Crime. *Comm. v. Jacobsen*, 419 Mass. 269 (1994) noted that there are many situations where the same facts give rise to either an assault or threats charge. If officers want to arrest for a past incident, they should charge assault. On the other hand, if threats is the only appropriate charge under the circumstances, officers may not make a warrantless arrest. They must either get an arrest warrant or apply for a complaint. See *Chapter 3*.

Of course, officers need not worry about this when they have some other basis for an arrest — e.g., past A&B or protective order violation.

Dual Arrests

Dual arrests highly disfavored. They trivialize the seriousness of domestic abuse and increase the danger to victims. Officers should *never* threaten or suggest that all parties will be arrested in an effort to discourage requests for law enforcement intervention.

Officers shall attempt to identify the dominant aggressor and treat that person appropriately. In the event of a dual arrest, officers must submit a separate report outlining the grounds for this action *in addition* to their regular incident report. 209A, § 6. EOPSS at 29.

Dominant aggressor indicators. Officers must consider the relationship history; the size, strength, and nature of the force used by the parties; the existence of offensive or defensive injuries; and other evidence.

- **Most important: The dominant aggressor is not automatically the person who used force first.** Victims of repeated domestic violence learn to recognize the signs of an impending assault and may take action. *Comm. v. Rodriguez*, 418 Mass. 1 (1994) (battered woman's syndrome may be the reason the victim used force first based on previous assaults).

- **Offensive injuries (typically found on victim):** Punches; bruises on the back, back of legs, buttocks (may be from kicks employed while victim in fetal position or being dragged); bumps on back of head from being slammed against something; bleeding from nose, lip, or shut eye; pulled hair; strangulation marks on neck or chin area.

- **Defensive wounds (typically inflicted upon aggressor):** Shoving, slapping, or pushing as opposed to punching; scratches or bites; groin injuries or foot injuries; scratches or bites to the midsection from holding the victim in a hammer lock; bites or scratches to the forearm or hand; scratches to the victim's neck and suspect's hands and arms during strangulation due to the victim's attempt to relieve pressure on her neck; preemptive strike from victim by throwing an object to delay the suspect and aid in victim's escape.

Police Officer Allegations

Law enforcement officers accused of domestic violence must not receive preferential treatment. EOPSS at 45. This is why, at a minimum:

- Dispatch must immediately notify the OIC about any domestic violence allegation concerning any law enforcement officer.

- All 209A and EOPSS guidelines *apply equally* to accused officers.

- A supervisor of a higher rank than the accused officer must be summoned to the scene (if that is not possible, contact State Police; some policies direct that the mayor or town manager be notified).

- The OIC must ensure:
  - The on-scene supervisor took appropriate enforcement action;
  - If the accused officer is a member of an outside agency, the OIC of that agency is notified as soon as reasonably possible;
  - If the accused is a member of the responding agency, the Chief is notified as soon as reasonably possible;
  - All department-issued firearms and privately owned weapons are surrendered under the terms of a 209A order *or* department policy;
  - A follow-up internal affairs investigation is commenced; and
  - Appropriate victim services are provided.

Officers must notify their Chief or designee orally as soon as they are arrested or served with a complaint or restraining order. They must file a written report within 24 hours.

OUT-OF-STATE ENFORCEMENT

Violation of Out-of-State Order in Mass.

Mandatory enforcement. Under 209A, § 5A, a restraining order issued by any state, U.S. territory, Puerto Rico, District of Columbia, or tribal court must be treated as if it originated in Massachusetts. *Comm. v. Shea*, 467 Mass. 788 (2014).

Copy of order from any source. § 5A states that officers "may presume the validity of, and enforce in accordance with [209A law], a copy of a protection order issued by another jurisdiction which has been provided . . . by any source." Practically speaking, once existence of the order is confirmed over the phone with an out-of-state department, local officers will arrest. Still, officers should require that a copy of the order be sent as soon as possible.

Victim states order still valid. § 5A also requires that the officer obtain a statement that the order remains in effect. The statement does *not* need to be signed by the witness. Simply mention it in the police report.

Charge violation of 209A. Officers must charge the out-of-state offender with a violation of 209A, § 7, just as they would charge any Massachusetts offender.

Violation of Mass. Order Out-of-State

Criminal contempt option. Can a Massachusetts man, who is the subject of a 209A order, be prosecuted here for traveling to New Hampshire to have forbidden contact with his ex-wife? The answer is "yes." Massachusetts officers may request that the prosecutor bring a "criminal contempt" charge. Contempt is "an offense to the court" — in this case, the defendant's willful failure to follow the court's restraining order — "and can be prosecuted even when it occurs in another state." Penalty: HC NMT 2½ yrs. *Berlandi v. Comm.*, 314 Mass. 424 (1943). EOPSS at 44. *Trial Court Guidelines*, § 8:02.

Federal Coverage

Federal prosecution possible for interstate travel to violate a protection order. 18 U.S.C. § 2262 makes it a federal crime to: (1) travel from one state to another with the intent to violate a protection order (issued in any state) that prohibits violence, threats, harassment, contact, or communication; and (2) to actually violate the order. The federal statute also covers acts directed at the protected person's animals, if the order included that protection. *U.S. v. Dion*, 37 F.4th 31 (1st. Cir. 2022) (when he was released on bail in a previous assault case, the court conditions prohibited the defendant from contacting his girlfriend; the defendant violated this pre-trial order when he traveled from Maine to New Hampshire to contact the victim).

POST-ARREST PROCEDURES

Bail

Officers must make a reasonable attempt to inform the victim about the abuser's bail status and whether or not he will be released.

No release for 6 hours. Persons arrested for abuse or for violating a protective order — who are 18 or older — may not be released on bail for 6 hours after arrest, except by a judge in open court. The prosecutor may move for an arraignment within 3 hours of arrest.

Referrals

Officers must provide information and telephone numbers for local resources such as shelters and counseling services. Each police department should have a list.

Incident Reports & Police Log

Officers must file a written incident report concerning any allegation involving abuse, regardless of whether an arrest was made. The report must be provided to the victim at no cost. 41, § 98G.

209A reports are confidential communications under 41, § 97D. They must be treated similar to reports of rape or sexual assault. They must be made available to police, assistant district attorneys, bail magistrates; and, upon written request, to the victim, her attorney, victim-witness advocate, domestic violence counselor, and sexual assault counselor.

Domestic violence and sexual assault reports and arrests must be kept out of the police log under 41 § 98F. The following must be recorded in a separate log: (1) any information concerning responses to reports of domestic violence, rape, or sexual assault; and (2) any entry concerning the arrest of a person for assault, A&B, or violation of a 209A order.

Mandatory Reporting

Officers should routinely learn if there are children, disabled persons, or elders present at the scene of a disturbance. If any of these individuals are being exploited, report it to protective services ASAP! See *Chapter 14*.

Firearms & Weapons Control

Officers should seize any guns or weapons that may have been used during the incident.

If guns or weapons were not used during the crime, then officers should:

- **Take custody of any weapons if an inhabitant requests it.** A consent search is allowed in all areas except those where the suspect has exclusive privacy. *Comm. v. Podgurski*, 44 Mass. App. Ct. 929 (1998) (consent search of bedroom and seizure of handgun by police was appropriate when authorized by the defendant's wife even though, at the time, she was temporarily residing in a shelter).

- **Request temporary custody of any weapons to alleviate threat of violence.** *Comm. v. Bone*, 2013 WL 3983375 (Appeals Court): Ms. Bone volunteered that her husband kept several guns in the apartment. She led officers to the bedroom nightstand and removed a handgun. Officers observed that it did not have a safety lock and was loaded. Ms. Bone showed them two shotguns and a rifle under the bed. Although police could not confirm whether the husband had an FID card, they still were justified in seizing the guns. Two guns were improperly stored.

    Also, the temporary removal of the weapons was a reasonable response to a dangerous situation. Ms. Bone had reported a serious attack and did not know whether she could find another place to go; her husband might have returned and done further harm.

If officers determine a weapon or firearm cannot be seized because it is not evidence of crime or its removal is not consented to:

- **A judge may grant a Suspension & Surrender order,** 209A, § 3B, requiring that the suspect immediately surrender, and officers take possession of, all guns, weapons, and gun licenses; and/or

- **The chief may revoke or suspend a gun license.** In all domestic violence cases, the investigating department "shall advise the licensing authority that the subject of the license is suspected of abuse." *Howard v. Chief of Wakefield Police,* 59 Mass. App. Ct. 901 (2003).

Property Visits

Accompany the defendant to the property only with judicial authorization. EOPSS guidelines state that police need judicial authorization to accompany defendants to the property for any reason. Insist that defendants come down to the police station so that officers may arrange, in advance, a time that is convenient for the victim. Do not spontaneously respond to a house for this purpose. Have the defendant check in at the station first.

If the victim has to go into the defendant's residence to obtain property, police should accompany him or her too. EOPSS at 36.

CIVIL LIABILITY

EOPSS Policy

Departments should adopt EOPSS policy rather than draft their own. The protection from liability granted by 209A, § 6 requires that officers "act in compliance with . . . the statewide policy as established by the secretary of public safety." The best practice is for each agency to adopt the *Domestic Violence Law Enforcement Guidelines* published by EOPSS as its sole policy.

Good faith action by officers. 209A, § 6 also states: "No law officer shall be held liable in any civil action regarding personal injury or [property damage] . . . for an arrest based on probable cause when such officer acted reasonably and in good faith." *Richardson v. City of Boston,* 53 Mass. App. Ct. 201 (2001).

Failure to take action. On the other hand, the failure of officers to intervene may subject them and their department to liability. *Hynson v. City of Chester,* 864 F.2d 1026 (3rd Cir. 1988).

Victim Safety

Victim safety must be considered before police notify a dangerous suspect.[4] *Irish v. Fowler,* 979 F.3d 65 (1st Cir. 2022) (police in Maine were incompetent; even though Anthony Lord had a violent record and had raped and threatened to kill Brittany Irish, and even though Irish said Lord would kill her if he found out she had gone to police, a detective left a phone

---

4 In Massachusetts, police are not liable for their negligent failure to protect a particular person against a danger police did not originally cause, unless police made an explicit and specific assurance of safety to the person. 258, § 10(j)(1).

message for Lord and did not warn Irish until after Lord had killed her new boyfriend, wounded her mother, and wounded and raped Irish again).

Also see *Reid v. City of Boston*, 95 Mass. App. Ct. 591 (2019) (officers did not coordinate their response to an on-street incident which caused the victim to get shot unnecessarily).

Fair Investigation

Officers have a duty to investigate fairly. Consider *White v. Town of Marblehead*, 989 F.Supp. 345 (D.Mass. 1997): Officers were dispatched to a bar. They encountered Sandee Muxica, who told them she had been assaulted by Dr. William White, her boyfriend. The officers did not interview anyone else at the bar. They went to White's apartment, but he was not home. They helped Muxica obtain a 209A order.

The next day, another officer served White with the protective order. White gave his version of events. He denied pushing Muxica. He told the officer that during dinner, Muxica had informed him that she was not a law student (which she had apparently led him to believe), but a stripper. She began to perform at the table, removing clothes and exposing her breast to the bartender. (The bartender later corroborated this version.) White left the bar in disgust. This officer did not relay this account to his Lieutenant, who applied for a warrant. White was arrested at his office the next day. The A&B charge was eventually dismissed and White sued the town. This was incompetent police work.

Some domestic cases frustrate officers. *Jones v. Gallagher*, 54 Mass. App. Ct. 883 (2002) acknowledged what many police officers learn on the job: "The 209A process may be used abusively by litigants for . . . harassment, and . . . it may make other family circumstances (especially involving the parties' children) . . . substantially more complicated. While such abuses appear infrequently, they damage a process which, in the great majority of instances, performs [an] essential service [for] victims. We note that the motives and interests in 209A proceedings are as diverse as the human condition of personal relationships." In the end, officers must simply do their best.

Massachusetts Domestic Violence Orders

District & Superior Court	Probate & Family Court

209A Orders. 209A, §§ 3, 3B, 3C, 4, and 5 mandate arrest for the following violations under any emergency, temporary, modified or permanent order:
 	
    Refrain from abuse;
    Stay away or no contact;
    Suspension & surrender; or
    Vacate.
 	
Probate supremacy: An order issued by the probate court invalidates any conflicting orders issued by a district or superior court. *Administrative Order of the Trial Court of Massachusetts*, 96-1.
 	
A 209A order may *only* be modified by a probate judge to allow visitation. The judge should also advise the noncustodial parent to bring the modified order when he or she arrives for visitation.
 	
Once modified by a probate judge, the original district or superior court must enter the new order into the domestic violence record system and notify police (the court should destroy the original order).
 	
The police department who receives a modified order should check to see if it was served on the defendant in the probate court. If so, there is no need to serve it again. If not, service should be accomplished as soon as possible.
	209A Orders. 209A, §§ 3, 3B, 3C, 4, and 5 mandate arrest for the following violations under any emergency, temporary, modified or permanent order:
	
	    Refrain from abuse;
	    Stay away or no contact;
	    Suspension & surrender; or
	    Vacate.
	
	Often, probate judges will issue 209A orders when litigants need protection from abuse. However, there are other specialized laws pertaining to different proceedings that enable a probate judge to issue applicable restraining orders.
	
	208 Orders — Divorce Proceedings. 208, §§ 18 and 34B *may* authorize arrest for violations. Before making an arrest, officers should ensure that an order indicates on its face that a violation is a criminal offense. *Hennessey v. Sarkis*, 54 Mass. App. Ct. 152 (2002).
	
	209 Orders — Child Support. 209, § 32 authorizes a restraining order to protect any party during a child support action. If an order includes language saying that a violation is criminal, then arrest is mandatory.
	
	209C Orders — Paternity Action. 209C, §§ 15 and 20 authorize an order to protect any party during a paternity action concerning a child born out of wedlock. Again, if an order contains language saying that a violation is criminal, arrest is mandatory.

Notes

Venue for issuing order and prosecuting a violation. Venue exists in the place where the plaintiff lived at the time of the abuse or, if the victim left her dwelling to avoid abuse, in the place where the victim currently lives. For a violation of an order, the court that issued the order, or the court covering the place of the violation, has venue.

Temporary order. An application must be filed before a court of jurisdiction using the designated form at no cost to the plaintiff. The plaintiff appears alone and receives a temporary order. The defendant is given an "opportunity to be heard" no later than 10 days after the temporary order is issued.

Permanent order. Following the 10-day hearing, the temporary order typically becomes a "permanent" order, which can last up to one year. At the end of the first year, the court holds a renewal hearing. At this time, the judge may permit the existing order to expire, issue a permanent order which does not expire, or issue an order of shorter duration. *Crenshaw v. Macklin*, 430 Mass. 633 (2000). *Pike v. Maguire*, 47 Mass. App. Ct. 929 (1999) (the fact that abuse did not occur during the existence of the restraining order is not, by itself, grounds for denying an extension). *S.V. v. R.V.*, 94 Mass. App. Ct. 811 (2019) (no justification for extension).

Prior 209A affidavit is proof of the underlying crime when the victim recants in court. *Comm. v. Belmer*, 78 Mass. App. Ct. 62 (2010): Defendant's wife wrote in her 209A affidavit that she and the defendant were arguing about his infidelity when he punched their 15 year old son, who was trying to protect her. The son received ten stitches at the hospital. At the defendant's A&B trial, the mother recanted, claiming that the defendant had accidentally struck their son and that she had lied in her affidavit. The affidavit was admitted as proof of the prior conduct and supported the defendant's conviction. An affidavit may be used in this fashion because it is a written, legal document made under oath and furnished to a judge. Once the victim testifies and is subject to cross examination, the affidavit becomes admissible evidence during the trial.

Housing laws provide certain protections to domestic violence victims. Officers should inform victims that:

- A tenant may terminate a lease upon notifying the landlord that the tenant or a household member has been the victim of domestic violence (or sexual assault) and is still in danger. 186, § 24(a).

- A landlord is required to change the locks upon request by a resident who is a victim of domestic violence (or sexual assault), including when a tenant or co-resident of the same property is the alleged perpetrator. The landlord may charge a fee for the work. 186, § 26.

- In public housing (or when using a public rental voucher), federal law, 34 U.S.C. § 12491, provides:

    - A tenant may be protected from eviction if domestic violence (or sexual assault) is connected with the tenant's failure to comply with the lease terms, even failure to pay. *Boston Housing Authority v. Y. A.*, 482 Mass. 240 (2019) (the tenant explained in court why she had paid so little of the back rent: "I was in an abus[ive] relationship. He would take everything from me." This was sufficient to trigger the housing authority's duty to help).

- A tenant or household member who has suffered domestic violence (or sexual assault) may demand that the housing authority revise the lease to remove an abuser and/or put the victim on it. *New Bedford Housing Authority v. K.R.*, 97 Mass. App. Ct. 509 (2020) (the housing authority had received a police report about the boyfriend's attack on the victim; it should have offered to revise the lease rather than evict her along with the boyfriend when he engaged in unrelated lease violations).

- Following domestic violence (or sexual assault), a public housing authority should be ready to transfer a victim's entire household to a safe unit, if available, when a threat exists of further imminent violence.

- The landlord may require from the tenant documentary evidence of the abuse (or sexual assault). Among the acceptable records are a 209A order or a police report about the crimes, and records of victim services providers, attorneys, or medical providers from whom the victim got help.

VIOLATION OF A RESTRAINING ORDER
209A, § 7

Elements

- ***Direct or indirect violation of order.*** The suspect, either directly or indirectly, violated the terms of a permanent or temporary restraining order by *failing* to do one or more of the following:

    - **Refrain from abuse;**

    - **"Stay away" from or have "no contact" with the plaintiff or her child(ren);**

    - **Surrender his firearms, weapons, ammunition, and gun licenses;**

    - **Vacate.** A vacate order means that the defendant must:
        - Surrender the keys immediately;
        - Not damage any household property;
        - Not disrupt utility service or mail delivery;
        - Leave and remain away from the house, a multi-family dwelling, and/or the victim's workplace.

- ***Notice of order.*** The suspect must have received notice of the order — by having it served on him or by having actual knowledge of the order through some other means.

Mandatory Arrest

209A, § 6 mandates warrantless arrest on probable cause. This authority applies even when the abuser has fled the scene and is discovered later. *Richardson v. City of Boston*, 53 Mass. App. Ct. 201 (2001). EOPSS at 26.

Arrest warrant option. *Comm. v. Ledger*, 52 Mass. App. Ct. 232 (2001) (arrest warrant appropriate because the defendant had violated the order twice within a short time period).

Compare *Comm. v. Tipolone*, 44 Mass. App. Ct. 23 (1997) (victim approached the police nine months after the defendant violated the order; police should have applied for a complaint with a hearing; there was no indication that the defendant posed a threat or flight risk).

A separate violation occurs in relation to each person protected by the order, even in cases where the violations occur during one incident. *Comm. v. Housen*, 83 Mass. App. Ct. 174 (2013) (defendant properly charged with four counts when he violated a restraining order in relation to his ex-girlfriend and her three minor children; this legal rule emphasizes the importance of each individual protected under an order).

Arrest Limits for Order Violation

Police may <u>not</u> arrest for a violation of the animal protection provision in a 209A order. Instead, they must seek an arrest warrant. 209A, § 11.

Police must <u>only</u> arrest for an abuse; stay away or no contact; firearms; or vacate violation. Other infractions — e.g., failure to pay child support or medical costs — must be pursued by the prosecutor through a criminal contempt hearing.

Penalty

Penalty for all criminal violations: HC NMT 2½ yrs; and/or Fine NMT $5,000. [Violation of 209A order in retaliation for a parent's attempt to seek child support or to establish paternity results in a mandatory minimum sentence of 60 days.]

Court may order GPS monitoring as a condition of probation. If the defendant appears in any "zone of exclusion" (e.g., victim's home or workplace), his probation may be revoked.

Contempt of court: 209A, § 7 states that 209A criminal remedies are *not* exclusive. A court "may enforce by *civil contempt* . . . a violation of its own order." *Mahoney v. Comm.*, 415 Mass. 278 (1993).

Notes

Proof of Notice

Notice provides the defendant with knowledge of what is prohibited. Notice occurs either by: (1) service of the actual order; or (2) the defendant's awareness of the order by other means. *Comm. v. Molloy*, 44 Mass. App. Ct. 306 (1998).

Service of order.

- **Vehicle stop not permitted.** Police may not stop a vehicle for the sole purpose of serving a restraining order. *Comm. v. Sanborn*, 477 Mass. 393 (2017).

- **Entry on private property.** Officers may enter onto private property to serve a restraining order. *Comm. v. Mulvey*, 57 Mass. App. Ct. 579 (2003). They may not enter the home, however, unless they have a warrant, consent, or exigent circumstances.

- **EOPSS Guidelines.** According to EOPSS at 43, service "shall be made in hand unless otherwise ordered by the court." Furthermore, orders "shall be served promptly . . . [and] not be delayed in order [for service] by a specialized officer or unit." The department must continue to attempt service until it is completed. Officers should consider the victim's safety in the timing of service (encourage the victim to speak with an advocate to develop a safety plan). Record all attempts at service. Send all returns of service to the court. *Comm. v. Griffen*, 444 Mass. 1004 (2005) (if in hand service fails, police must ask the court to order an alternative means of service).

- **Seize firearms.** At the time of service for a suspension & surrender order, seize firearms, ammunition, and licenses. EOPSS at 44.

- **Actual physical receipt not required.** The *Mulvey* case points out that police officers may announce the subject of the order and leave it in the vicinity of the defendant. The Appeals Court wrote: "An individual cannot avoid in hand service by refusing physically to take the tendered papers."

- **Address on order presumed correct.** *Comm. v. Crimmins*, 46 Mass. App. Ct. 489 (1999) holds that if service was made to the address on the order, then it is the defendant's burden to show that he never received a copy.

- **Explain order & available services.** When effecting service, a police officer should: (1) inform the defendant of the contents of the order and potential penalties; and (2) provide information, including a list of certified batterer, substance abuse, and financial counseling programs located near the court.

- **Properly complete return of service, which is admissible to prove notice.** *Comm. v. Shangkuan*, 78 Mass. App. Ct. 827 (2011): Spencer Shangkuan was the subject of a 209A order issued on December 8. The address listed on the order was in Princeton, New Jersey, and on the back was a pre-printed return of service, completed and signed on December 10 by a New Jersey police officer. Shangkuan violated the order on December 18 in Massachusetts.

    The court ruled that the "return of service" was sufficient proof that Shangkuan had knowledge of the order and was admissible, by itself, as a "public record."[5] There was no need to have the officer who served the order testify.

- **Alcohol intoxication no defense.** *Comm. v. Paige*, 2016 WL 56899 (Appeals Court) (the defendant physically attacked his girlfriend after a night of heavy drinking; he was served with a 209A order in hand at the police station the next morning; an officer read the contents to him, but the defendant claimed he was too intoxicated to understand; the court disagreed; after all, he told police that he understood and would never go back).

- **Failure to translate notice no defense.** A defendant's inability to speak English is no defense because the look of the order (official address, state seal, etc.) alerts a reasonable person that it is important and should be translated. *Comm. v. Olivo*, 369 Mass. 62 (1975) (no excuse for Spanish-speaking citizen to ignore court order to vacate, given that it was hand-served and official looking).

---

5 The "public records" exception to the hearsay rule allows a document to be offered into evidence if it was prepared in the ordinary course of business by agency personnel for an administrative purpose.

Actual knowledge by other means. Even if not served, a defendant receives notice if he learns about the order from some other source — e.g., his wife tells him over the telephone or he learns police are trying to serve the order. Once he knows an order exists, the law expects the defendant to learn its specific terms. *Comm. v. Melton*, 77 Mass. App. Ct. 552 (2010). *Comm. v. Gonsalves*, 99 Mass. App. Ct. 638 (2021) (the defendant texted the victim repeatedly after the order issued, commenting that the police should stop "wasting their time trying to find me," and "no piece of paper is going to stop you from getting your ass kicked").

Officers should always interview a defendant post-arrest, provided he waives *Miranda*. A defendant will often acknowledge he was aware of the order. *Comm. v. Torres*, 468 Mass. 286 (2014) (after beating the victim, the defendant admitted that he knew she had a 209A order against him).

Proof of 209A Violation

No need to prove the suspect intended to violate the order. *Comm. v. Delaney*, 425 Mass. 587 (1997) (as long as the defendant had notice of the order, he is responsible for any act that constitutes a violation); *Comm. v. Regil*, 82 Mass. App. Ct. 275 (2012).

What defendant thought order meant irrelevant. *Comm. v. Ledger*, 52 Mass. App. Ct. 232 (2001).

Nonhostile intent irrelevant. The fact that a defendant engages in contact with "a desire to make amends" is irrelevant. *Comm. v. Butler*, 40 Mass. App. Ct. 906 (1996) (defendant requested that a florist send roses; this was a blatant violation).

Violation occurs even if victim permits the encounter. *Comm. v. Hart*, 2014 WL 683750 (Appeals Court): The restraining order required Gary Hart to stay at least 100 yards away from Sarah Smith. A police officer observed Smith and Hart standing right next to each other in a plaza. This was a violation. The contact was not accidental — Hart claimed that he and Smith wanted to be together, and Smith agreed they were looking for an apartment.

Only court may modify an order. *Comm. v. Consoli*, 58 Mass. App. Ct. 734 (2003) (a victim's consent never suspends or modifies a restraining order). *Comm. v. Rauseo*, 50 Mass. App. Ct. 669 (2001) (modifications must be approved by the court; any oral agreement between the parties — even as part of divorce negotiations — has no bearing on the duty of the police). *Comm. v. Marrero*, 85 Mass. App. Ct. 911 (2014) (a suspect may not argue, as a defense, that the order should never have been issued).

Cordelia v. Steven, 95 Mass. App. Ct. 635 (2019): For a defendant to modify an existing order, he must show — by clear and convincing evidence — that the provision at issue is no longer necessary. For a plaintiff to modify an order in a way that places an additional burden on the defendant, she must show — by a preponderance of the evidence — that the modification is necessary to protect her.

"Stay away" and "no contact" orders.

- **Their core purpose is to create and maintain a safe haven from abuse.** *Comm. v. Telcinord*, 94 Mass. App. Ct. 232 (2018). A stay away order requires that the defendant avoid actual or potential physical contact with the victim. In addition to physical separation, a no contact order mandates no communication between defendant and victim. Thus, no contact provides broader protection. Of course violating either mandates arrest. *Comm. v. Finase*, 435 Mass. 310 (2001).

- **Four ways to violate stay away order:**

    - *Come within a specific distance.* The judge may specify, in the order, a particular distance that the defendant must remain away from the property line or any specified portion of the property. *Comm. v. Telcinord, supra.*

    If no distance is specified by the order, the defendant still may not:

    - *Cross over the property line. Comm. v. O'Shea,* 41 Mass. App. Ct. 115 (1996) (stay away order covered the parking lot and any other company property, not just the building where the victim worked); or

    - *Engage in behavior that intrudes into the residence or building. Comm. v. Brennan,* 2016 WL 1445998 (Appeals Court) (defendant looked in the window of the victim's house and made eye contact with her 15 year old daughter); or

    - *Come near enough to the property line so that he "would be able to abuse or contact the protected person if they were on the property or entering or leaving it." Comm. v. Telcinord, supra. Comm. v. Watson,* 94 Mass. App. Ct. 244 (2018) (although he never entered onto the property of the multi-unit apartment building where the victim lived, the defendant positioned himself with friends outside the front entrance on the sidewalk, deliberately putting himself in a place where he would likely contact her).

- **In any case, the victim does not need to be present when the suspect violates the order.** *Comm. v. Habenstreit,* 57 Mass. App. Ct. 785 (2003): The defendant shouted obscenities at a person inside the victim's workplace in violation of a stay away order. The fact that the victim was not present — she had called in sick — was irrelevant. The goal is "to create a safe haven [for the victim] . . . [and] a protective order should not be interpreted in a manner [that] encourages a defendant to keep himself . . . informed about a protected person's schedule."

Direct and indirect contact prohibited. *Comm. v. Basile,* 47 Mass. App. Ct. 918 (1999) (a day after being served with a no contact order, the defendant appeared one block from the victim's address and, when the victim returned from shopping and saw him, he jumped in the air and waved his arms; jury disbelieved defendant's explanation that he was visiting his new girlfriend and playing "hacky-sac" when he jumped). *Comm. v. Junkins,* 2015 WL 2215604 (Appeals Court) (defendant contacted the victim's aunt and asked her to ask the victim not to post anything on Facebook about the restraining order; this was a violation). *Comm. v. York,* 2020 WL 6708672 (Appeals Court) (victim lived with her mother, who received a Valentine's Day card from the defendant).

Facebook threat can violate 209A even if victim and defendant "blocked" each other. *Comm. v. Forcier,* 2018 WL 547356 (Appeals Court): Shortly after the court modified a restraining order against Roger Forcier with a 25-yard stay away provision, Forcier posted on Facebook that he could hit a moving target at 25 yards and it would "only take two rounds." A friend viewed the post, took a screenshot of it, and texted the photo to the victim. Because the victim knew Forcier was a sniper in the Marines, she reasonably feared imminent harm.

Although Forcier and the victim had blocked each other on Facebook, Forcier's referring to the recent order proved his post was intended for the victim. *Comm. v. Agro*, 96 Mass. App. Ct. 1110 (2019) (defendant violated no contact order when he "liked" another person's Facebook birthday wish to the victim).

Must prove written communication authored by defendant. In *Comm. v. Gonsalves*, 99 Mass. App. Ct. 638 (2021), these factors proved the texts to the victim were written by Gonsalves:

- They came from a telephone number he previously used to communicate with her. The number had never been used by anyone else;

- References to particular events happening between them (e.g., the new 209A order);

- Content consistent with previous communications from Gonsalves (e.g., spelling errors); and

- Numerous communications making it unlikely anyone else would bother to send so many.

Compare *Comm. v. McMann*, 97 Mass. App. Ct. 558 (2020): After dating Malcolm McMann for five months, the victim obtained a no contact order against him. The victim received an Instagram message from username "bigm617" that said, "Yoooo." This was McMann's Instagram username. Posts on the account showed pictures of him, even one of him and her during their relationship.

She showed the message to an officer on her phone. The officer followed up by interviewing McMann, who denied sending a message and suggested the officer check his phone. McMann then opened his Instagram. The "Yoooo" message appeared. The officer noted that McMann looked very surprised.

The transmission of an electronic message from a social media or email account is not proof, by itself, that the person who controls the account sent the message. It is not even probable cause. Here, there was insufficient evidence that McMann sent the message — such as his writing style or facts in the message. The court commented that the prosecutor even failed to present evidence about how an Instagram account is activated and whether others had access to McMann's account.

No need to prove victim in fear when suspect violates either type of order. *Comm. v. Mendonca*, 50 Mass. App. Ct. 684 (2001).

Actions that do _not_ violate a stay away or no contact order:

- **Nonharassing, incidental contact.** A defendant may have incidental contact with the victim in the course of a legitimate attempt to telephone a permissible party. Incidental contact is "brief and inevitable [and not] used as an opportunity to harass, threaten, or intimidate the protected party." *Comm. v. Silva*, 431 Mass. 194 (2000) (no contact order did allow the defendant to call his children at his ex-wife's home; the fact that she sometimes answered was not a violation).

    Compare *Comm. v. Knieriem*, 2017 WL 4228005 (Appeals Court) (defendant initially texted the victim about their daughter's birthday; however, the texts then accused the victim of making slanderous postings on Facebook; the defendant's words were threatening and had nothing to do with their daughter, so they violated the 209A order). *Comm. v. Damon*, 2017 WL 5907848 (Appeals Court) (order told Damon not to call house phone; he could only contact his wife on her cell phone, yet Damon called the house phone; this violated the order).

- **Accidental encounters.** *Comm. v. McKay*, 67 Mass. App. Ct. 396 (2006) held that mistaken contact is *not* a violation. In this case, McKay pushed the wrong speed dial button on his cell phone. He called his ex-wife, but his message was clearly intended for someone else.

- **However, a defendant must end an accidental encounter promptly.** Otherwise, he turns an innocent event into a crime. In *Comm. v. Stoltz*, 73 Mass. App. Ct. 642 (2009), Eve Stoltz took her two children to a 99 Restaurant. Daniel Stoltz, her ex-husband, and his friend were returning from the Cape and decided to have dinner there. At the time, Eve had a "no contact" order.

  After ordering food, Eve saw her ex-husband. He was seated at the bar and staring at her. She asked the waitress to box her food and called 911. She waited at her table and left 15 minutes later with her ex-husband still staring. Officers arrived and noticed Daniel standing at the entrance. Upon seeing them, Daniel went back inside. He was arrested.

  While the parties encountered each other accidentally, Daniel failed to promptly remove himself from his ex-wife's presence. The Appeals Court did comment that officers should have been clearer about the situation at the restaurant — Was it crowded? Had the defendant already ordered or tried to get his food to go? Was his friend getting the car? This type of information helps a court decide whether the defendant left promptly.

- **Conclusion.** When officers encounter incidental or accidental contact, they must view it as a nonviolation. Officers should encourage the defendant and/or the victim to go to court to modify the order to deal with any ambiguity. Officers should also warn a suspect, in a close case, that future contact will subject him to arrest. *Comm. v. Kendrick*, 446 Mass. 72 (2006).

Third-party violations. In the rare instance when a third party violates an order, the Commonwealth must prove the defendant intended for this to happen. *Comm. v. Collier*, 427 Mass. 385 (1998) (defendant in the front seat of a car driven by his son that careened within three feet of his former wife; the wife made direct eye contact with the defendant, who was smiling as his son pointed the car at her); *Comm. v. Russell*, 46 Mass. App. Ct. 307 (1999).

Nonpayment of utility bills leading to shut-off violates vacate order. *Comm. v. Sasso*, 2020 WL 4200842 (Appeals Court): The order that removed Robert Sasso from the house he shared with his wife and children included that he "not shut off or cause to be shut off any utilities." After he left, the utilities went unpaid and were shut off. Sasso had changed the billing address to his new residence, and received letters and calls about the overdue bills. He was not simply negligent. Sasso intentionally failed to pay. The Commonwealth did not have to prove that Sasso could afford it.

HARASSMENT PREVENTION ORDERS
258E, §§ 1-12

Basis for HPO § 1[6]

Harassment Prevention Orders (HPOs) under 258E are almost identical to 209A. However, HPOs may be obtained by anyone, which makes them useful in cases of bullying, sexual assault or stalking.

***Harassment* is:**

- **3 acts of intimidation, abuse, or property damage.** 3 or more acts of willful and malicious conduct[7] aimed at a specific person with the intent to cause fear, abuse, or property damage, and which does result in fear, abuse, or property damage; or

- **Involuntary sexual relations.** A forceful or threatening act that causes another to involuntarily engage in sexual relations; or

- **Specific crimes.** Committing an Indecent A&B on a Child Under 14 (265, § 13B) or on a Person 14 and Over (§ 13H); or A&B or Indecent A&B on a Person with Intellectual Disabilities (265, § 13F); or Rape, Rape of a Child, or Statutory Rape (265, §§ 22, 22A, 23); or Assault with Intent to Rape (265, §§ 24, 24B); or Enticement (265, § 26C); or Stalking or Criminal Harassment (265, §§ 43, 43A); or Drugging to Engage in Intercourse (272, § 3). See *F.A.P. v. J.E.S.*, 87 Mass App. Ct. 595 (2015).

Components of HPO § 3

Refrain from abusing or harassing the plaintiff.

No contact (unless authorized by the court).

Remain away from the plaintiff's household or workplace.

Pay compensation for any losses suffered as a direct result of harassment (e.g., property damage, replacing locks, medical expenses, unlisted phone number, and attorney's fees).

HPO may not order surrender of guns, ammo, and LTC or FID. *J.C. v. J.H.*, 92 Mass. App. Ct. 224 (2017). However, 140, §§ 131(d)(vi) and (f) direct that the licensing authority revoke any person's LTC (*not* FID) if they are the subject of an HPO. In other words, departments must take the extra step of revoking an LTC upon learning that the holder is the target of an HPO.

Consequences for Violating HPO §§ 9 and 12

Criminal penalty. HC NMT 2½ yrs; and/or Fine NMT $5,000. *Mandatory fees:* Victim/witness fee *and* a $25 fine. Also, a $350 assessment in addition to the cost of any treatment program. The assessment may be waived for financial hardship.

---

6 All sections, unless otherwise noted, appear in 258E.
7 Under § 1, "malicious [means] characterized by cruelty, hostility, or revenge."

Civil contempt. Aside from a criminal penalty, a court may hold a defendant in "civil contempt" for an HPO violation.

Police Enforcement § 8

Arrest mandatory **upon probable cause for violation of HPO.**

Arrest preferred response **for harassment.** If there is no HPO in effect, arrest shall be the preferred response if the officer has probable cause to believe that a person committed a felony or a misdemeanor involving harassment, or an A&B.

Police Duties §§ 8 and 9

Use all reasonable means to *prevent further abuse* or harassment to the victim.

- **The safety of the victim is the paramount concern** in the decision to arrest.
- **Dual arrest.** An officer shall submit a detailed report — in addition to an incident report — explaining why arresting both parties was necessary.

Encourage the victim to seek *medical attention* and, if necessary, arrange for an ambulance. If a sexual assault has occurred, inform the victim that there are time-sensitive medical and forensic tests, and arrange for transport to a hospital.

Provide *referrals to local resources* to assist the victim in getting to a safe place.

Provide *notice to the victim of her HPO rights*. There is a mandated notice (almost identical to 209A). Officers must read it to the victim and provide them with a copy. If the victim does not speak English, officers should provide a copy in the victim's native language if possible.

Assist the victim by activating the *emergency judicial system* when court closed.

Inform the victim that the abuser will be *eligible for bail*.[8]

Immediately *file an incident report* whenever an officer investigates and provide a free copy to the victim upon request.

Serve a copy of the HPO **on the defendant and file a return of service.**

Civil Liability Protection § 8

No officer shall be liable in a civil action for personal injury or property damage if the officer acted in good faith, in compliance with Chapter 258E.

---

[8] Judges and bail commissioners must also try to notify the victim when the defendant is released.

Police Enforcement of Out-of-State HPO §§ 7 and 8

Enforce as if issued in Massachusetts. Any harassment order issued by another state, tribal or territorial court within the U.S. shall be "enforced as if it were issued in the Commonwealth for as long as the order is in effect." This means <u>mandatory arrest</u> for the violation of an out-of-state vacate, restraining, stay away or no contact HPO. A copy of an HPO from *any* source is presumed valid. An officer should obtain a verbal statement from the plaintiff that the HPO is in effect before enforcing it.[9]

Venue & Duration §§ 2 and 3

Venue. A district or superior court where the plaintiff resides may issue an HPO. The juvenile court where the plaintiff resides has exclusive jurisdiction when the defendant is under 18.

Duration of HPO. Initial HPO lasts up to 1 year; extension possible. If the plaintiff appears in court when the order expires, the court may extend it for a specified period or permanently. The fact that harassment did not occur shall not, by itself, be grounds for refusing to extend it.

Emergency & Temporary HPO §§ 5 and 6

Emergency order

- **3 grounds for emergency order.** Substantial likelihood of immediate danger of harassment; or court closed and danger (e.g., officers respond at night); or plaintiff unable to appear in court because of a severe physical condition and danger of harassment.

- **Telephone issuance authorized.** The police must deliver a copy of the order to court, and the plaintiff must appear there on the next business day. If plaintiff is unable to appear because of physical hardship, a representative may appear.

Temporary order. The defendant must be served and given a hearing to contest the order within 10 court business days. If he does not appear, the temporary order remains in effect.

Notes

Typically, 209A better protection. Sometimes, a victim will qualify for both a 209A order and a 258E HPO. In most instances, 209A coverage is preferable because it allows the court to order that a defendant surrender his guns and licenses. The court may also order child support and temporary custody of children. *C.F.M. v. J.E.*, 2018 WL 4701454 (Appeals Court) (plaintiff may seek either a 209A or 258E order <u>or</u> both depending on the circumstances).

For a crime-based HPO, one instance of a designated crime or involuntary sexual relations is sufficient. *F.A.P. v. J.E.S.*, 87 Mass. App. Ct. 595 (2015): If the HPO plaintiff shows by a preponderance of the evidence that the defendant committed one of the twelve specific crimes listed in 258E, § 1, or forced the plaintiff to engage involuntarily in sexual relations, that is a sufficient reason for the judge to issue an HPO.

---

9 The HPO law allows an out-of-state resident to file a certified copy of her out-of-state HPO with a Massachusetts court. This makes the order part of the Commonwealth's domestic violence registry.

For the more common harassment-based HPO, the 3 incidents do not have to have been previously reported to police, or to have occurred within a certain time period. *Smith v. Mastalerz*, 467 Mass. 1001 (2014).

However, the acts must have been directed at a specific person. *DeMayo v. Quinn*, 87 Mass. App. Ct. 115 (2015) (defendant repeatedly broke into a barn and stole items; there was no proof that his acts were directed at the horse's owner or any other specific person, *or* that he intended to cause fear to anyone).

The defendant must have intended to cause fear, abuse, or property damage. *R.S. v. A.P.B.*, 95 Mass. App. Ct. 372 (2019): R.S. requested a 258E order to stop numerous text and social media messages from A.P.B. and other fake accounts. R.S. testified that she received three messages with A.P.B.'s name, all of which related to the status of their relationship. However, there was no evidence that these messages: (1) were intended to cause fear, intimidation, abuse, or damage to property; and (2) did, in fact, cause R.S. fear, intimidation, abuse, or damage to property. R.S. may have been annoyed, but she testified she was not afraid.

As for the fake accounts, R.S. could not prove that any were created by A.P.B. The names on the fake accounts bore no resemblance to those accounts that A.P.B. acknowledged were his. Also, A.P.B.'s messages tried to revive a relationship that R.S. admitted was on again, off again. By contrast, the fake account messages contained sexual innuendo and vulgarity, something noticeably absent from A.P.B.'s messages.

Angry words not enough. Fighting words or true threat necessary.

- **Insufficient.** *D.C. v. D.M.*, 2018 WL 6423589 (Appeals Court): D.C.'s husband was involved in an extramarital affair with D.M., which led to her pregnancy. The husband did not respond positively to the news, as he was in the process of reconciling with D.C. D.M. reacted by delivering a packet of photos to D.C.'s door that included pictures of a positive home pregnancy test and the husband's genitals. The photos, while sexually explicit, did not constitute "fighting words" or "true threats." While no one would like to receive these, 258E is not designed to protect against every emotional upset. Even if they did qualify as harassing, their delivery was only one single act, which is not enough for an HPO. *Seney v. Morhy*, 467 Mass. 58 (2014) (Little League coach lacked basis for HPO against player's mother, who was just obnoxious and critical of his coaching).

- **Sufficient.** *A.G. v. K.O.*, 2020 WL 4478149 (Appeals Court): A.G. was the administrator of a nursing home where K.O.'s mother resided. His previous conflicts with the staff had led the nursing home to issue a no trespass notice. One day K.O. left an agitated voicemail for A.G. He arrived 45 minutes later, and screamed and yelled obscenities at A.G. A police officer escorted K.O. out, but his obscene tirade continued and the officer called for backup.

  One month later, K.O. picketed the nursing home and distributed a flyer criticizing A.G. and the nursing home. The flyer included A.G.'s photograph, full name, and accusations that she was under investigation for misconduct. A week later, these flyers appeared on utility poles in A.G.'s residential neighborhood. She felt "extremely worried" for her and her children. Three incidents of harassment occurred. Compare *F.K. v. S.C.*, 481 Mass. 325 (2019) (writing a threatening "rap song" and posting it on the internet was only one act).

Police reports and complaint applications are not harassment. *M.D. v. B.D.*, 2020 WL 3168562 (Appeals Court): Two neighbors with police officers in their households developed a bad relationship after a noisy graduation party at M.D.'s house. M.D. obtained an HPO against B.D. The order was rejected by the Appeals Court. Even though on two occasions B.D. grabbed M.D. by the arm and frightened her, none of the other conduct counted as a third incident of harassment. It was not harassment to write a letter to the police union about the plaintiff and her husband; place a call to police complaining about a nonexistent underage party at the plaintiff's house; or file a complaint application about the original graduation party. The letter to the union was protected speech, and soliciting assistance from the police or courts is legally protected as are other efforts to obtain government assistance.

Photographing another person's child may qualify as an act of harassment. *A.G. v. D.N.*, 2019 WL 1467209 (Appeals Court) (defendant photographed his neighbor's child repeatedly; under the circumstances, this was harassing conduct).

Drone flight. *F.W.T. v. F.T.*, 2018 WL 2771445 (Appeals Court): The plaintiff alleged that the defendant flew a drone over his property on at least three occasions. One time, the drone flew in front of a contractor operating heavy machinery. Flying drones over another person's property, although annoying, does not constitute 258E harassment without evidence that the action was intended to cause fear or property damage, and that it actually did so.

Landlords cannot use an HPO to get around the civil eviction process in a landlord/tenant dispute. *C.E.R. v. P.C.*, 91 Mass. App. Ct. 124 (2017) advised judges to carefully evaluate the evidence to ensure that 258E is not used as a shortcut for evicting tenants.

Juveniles may be the subject of a 258E order. *A.P. v. M.T.*, 92 Mass. App. Ct. 156 (2017) (8 year old boy subject to HPO after committing an indecent A&B on his four year old neighbor in the yard).

A mental health condition does not preclude a 258E order for obvious misconduct. *V.J. v. N.J.*, 91 Mass. App. Ct. 22 (2017) (veteran with PTSD could still be the defendant in an HPO). *A.S.R. v. A.K.A.*, 92 Mass. App. Ct. 270 (2017) (ex-girlfriend's constant contact and threats of suicide sufficient basis to issue HPO against her).

Violation of stay away. The purpose of a 258E stay away order is to provide the victim with a "safe haven." This is why a violation occurs if the defendant comes within the particular distance specified by the judge. If no distance is indicated, the defendant commits a violation when he (1) crosses the property line; or (2) engages in behavior that intrudes into the residence or workplace; or (3) comes close enough to the property to "be able to abuse, contact, or harass a protected person if that person were on the property or entering or leaving it." The victim does not have to be present at the time of a violation. *Comm. v. Goldman*, 94 Mass. App. Ct. 222 (2018).

Assault and A&B Occurring in a Domestic or Harassment Relationship

Type	Victim Relationship	Criminal Charge	Right of Arrest	Notes
Intimate Partner	**Intimate partner.** The victim: • Is or was married to the offender; or • Had a child in common with the offender regardless of whether they ever were married or lived together; or • Is or was involved in a substantive dating or engagement relationship.	265, § 13M	209A, § 6 arrest on probable cause	Officers should use 13M whenever possible because it triggers the restricted bail period and possibly pre-trial detention for 120 days, and it triggers a felony charge for any subsequent offense. Being an "intimate partner" under 13M requires proof beyond a reasonable doubt. *Comm. v. Henry*, 2021 WL 1691600 (Appeals Court). 1st offense: HC 2½ yrs; and/or Fine NMT $5,000. Subsequent offense: SP NMT 5 yrs or HC 2½ yrs. Defendant must attend a "batterer's intervention program."
	Subsequent offense: The offender has a prior 13M conviction and commits an assault or A&B on an intimate partner.	265, § 13M	Felony	The prior offense must have been charged under 13M. However, the prior victim does not have to be the same person attacked in the subsequent offense.
Family & Household	**Family & household member.** The victim is or was: • Related by blood or marriage; or • Living with the offender in the same household.	265, § 13A	209A, § 6 arrest on probable cause	If the victim is an "intimate partner," always charge 13M (even though, technically, 13A covers the same misconduct). On the other hand, you may only charge 13A when the assault or A&B involves a current or former relative or roommate.

Type	Victim Relationship	Criminal Charge	Right of Arrest	Notes
In Violation of Restraining Order	The victim is or was: • An intimate partner; or • Family & household member (see definitions above); • Who had a restraining order against the offender.	265, § 13A	Felony	13A constitutes a felony when the assault or A&B is directed at a person who already has a restraining order in effect against the offender. *Comm. v. Torres*, 468 Mass. 286 (2014) (defendant may be convicted of felony A&B and violating the 209A order).
Pregnant (A&B only)	The victim does not need to be in a specific relationship. She must be pregnant. The offender must know or have reason to know that she is.	265, § 13A	Felony	13A constitutes a felony when the victim is pregnant and the offender knows or should know that she is at the time of the A&B.
Serious Injury (A&B only)	The victim does not need to be in a specific relationship. The offender's A&B must simply cause "serious bodily injury" — meaning permanent disfigurement; *or* loss or impairment of a bodily function, limb or organ; *or* a substantial risk of death.	265, § 13A	Felony	Injuries that qualify as "serious" for this charge have included a broken jaw, a permanent scar because of stitches, facial reconstruction, and double vision. *Comm. v. Scott*, 464 Mass. 355 (2013).

| Suffocate or Strangle | The victim does not need to be in a specific relationship. While most cases of strangulation or suffocation will probably occur in domestic violence relationships, it is not required. | 265, § 15D | Felony | • Suffocation: Intentional interference of normal breathing or blood circulation by blocking another's nose or mouth.
• Strangulation: Intentional interference of normal breathing or blood circulation by applying substantial pressure on another's throat or neck. *Comm. v. Ford*, 2017 WL 1191285 (Appeals Court) (victim testified that defendant grabbed her neck, slammed her against the wall with his hands around her neck, and she "couldn't breathe"). *Comm. v. Rogers*, 96 Mass. App. Ct. 781 (2019) (defendant grasped victim's neck, stood her up from the couch and dragged her; an officer witnessed marks on her neck).

Penalty: SP NMT 5 yrs or HC NMT 2½ yrs; and/or Fine NMT $5,000.

Aggravated offense: SP NMT 10 yrs or HC NMT 2½ yrs; and Fine NMT $10,000 if suspect: (1) causes serious bodily injury; (2) knows or should know victim is pregnant; (3) previously convicted of strangling or suffocating; or (4) knows victim has restraining order against him. Defendant must attend a "batterer's intervention program." |

Type	Victim Relationship	Criminal Charge	Right of Arrest	Notes
Harassment	The victim does not need to be in a specific relationship. Instead, the offender must: • Engage in 3 or more acts of malicious conduct; • Directed at the victim; • With intent to cause fear, abuse intimidation, or property damage; and • Which resulted in fear, abuse, intimidation, or property damage.	265, § 13A	258E, § 8 arrest on probable cause	There is no set time period within which the 3 incidents must occur. The prior incidents do not need to have been reported to the police. The assault or A&B that is being investigated by the police may constitute the 3rd incident and trigger an officer's right of arrest.

14 Child, Disabled, & Elder Protection

Section I
MANDATORY REPORTING

A series of tragic cases beginning in the middle 1970s brought home the need for a child abuse reporting law, which would require professionals to report instances of abuse and neglect to social services and law enforcement. The outpouring of child abuse cases that followed underscored the fact that this kind of abuse was chronically underreported because of the natural fear and intimidation that silences children. In later years, the reporting laws were extended to elders and the disabled.

At the outset, officers must understand that their reporting obligations are *an additional responsibility* beyond 209A or any other law enforcement activities they may undertake.

Police officers are mandated reporters. While acting in their professional capacity[1], police officers — along with a host of other human service and medical providers[2] — are mandated by law to report various types of abuse that happen to children, elders, and the disabled.

Other citizens may report. Of course, anyone may report their good faith suspicions to authorities, but only the professionals specifically designated by the various reporting statutes are legally obligated to do so.

---

[1] Unlike the child and disabled persons law, the elder abuse law does not have the "professional capacity" language. This would seem to indicate that officers must report elder abuse, neglect, or financial exploitation regardless of how or when they learn about it.

[2] The most detailed discussion and list of mandated reporters appears in *LED's Juvenile Law, Chapter 3*. Examples of mandated reporters include: physicians, dentists, nurses, firefighters, EMTs, hospital personnel, parole and probation officers, psychiatrists, psychologists, school teachers and administrators, home health aides for the elderly, service providers for the disabled, and foster parents.

MANDATORY REPORTING LAWS

Who *is covered*	What *must be reported*	Who *receives reports*
Children *under 18* 119, § 51A	**Abuse** • Physical, • Sexual, or • Emotional **Neglect by Person with Permanent or Temporary Custody**	**Department of Children & Families (DCF)** *24-hour service line:* **800-792-5200** mass.gov/dcf
Disabled *Mentally and/or Physically Disabled Age 18 to under 60* 19C, § 5	**Abuse** • Physical, • Sexual, or • Emotional **Neglect by a Caretaker**	**Disabled Persons Protection Commission (DPPC)** *24-hour service line:* **800-426-9009** mass.gov/dppc
Elders *Age 60 and over* 19A, § 15	**Abuse** • Physical, • Sexual, or • Emotional **Neglect by a Caretaker, or Self-Neglect by Elder** **Financial Exploitation**	**Elder Protective Services** *(local agencies under the Executive Office of Elder Affairs — EOEA)* *24-hour service line:* **800-922-2275** mass.gov/reporting-elder-abuse-neglect
Nursing Home *Patient or resident of any age in nursing home, rest home, or receiving home health or hospice care* 111, § 72G	**Patient Abuse or Mistreatment** • Physical (includes overmedication), • Sexual, or • Emotional **Neglect** **Financial Exploitation**	**Department of Public Health (DPH)** *24-hour service line:* **800-462-5540** mass.gov/health-care-facility-reporting

Reporting Rules. Same rules for children, disabled, elders, and nursing home and home health patients. Officers must make:

- **An immediate oral report to the appropriate agency;** and
- **A follow-up written report within 48 hours** (recommendation: send the police report).

Reporting Standard & Immunity

- **Reasonable cause to believe.** Officers need only have "reasonable cause to believe" that abuse, neglect or financial exploitation happened or is happening. The word "reasonable" implies that some "exercise of judgment should occur to rule out, for example, assertions that are impossible, . . . plainly fabricated, or made only in jest. Nonetheless, the 'something more' to which we allude is . . . not very much more." *Mattingly v. Casey*, 24 Mass. App. Ct. 452 (1987).

  The low standard does not "in any way minimize the hideous consequences that may attend a report that . . . proves unfounded. However, in order to encourage professionals to report, without fear of retribution . . . , the threshold hurdle of 'reasonable cause to believe' is and must be very low, notwithstanding the very real risk of error it inevitably carries in its wake." *Cooney v. Department of Mental Retardation*, 52 Mass. App. Ct. 378 (2001).

- **Immunity for reporting.** The reporting statutes completely insulate police officers and other mandated reporters from liability, even if their reports are ultimately unsubstantiated. The only exception is if the reporter actually perpetrated the abuse. *Hope v. Landau*, 21 Mass. App. Ct. 240 (1985) ("The social policy underlying the statute is to encourage [mandated] professionals to report their suspicions [without fear of liability]").

- **Liability for failing to report.** Mandated reporters who fail to notify the appropriate social service agency may be prosecuted and fined up to $1,000. For child abuse, HC NMT 2½ yrs and/or a $15,000 fine is now possible if the reporter knew abuse resulted in serious bodily injury or death and failed to report.

Notes

Abuse. Abuse involves an act or omission (the failure to act) which results in physical or emotional injury to a child, disabled person, or elder.[3] For reporting, there are three types:

- **Physical.** Physical abuse involves the nonaccidental infliction of *any nontrivial injury* including skin bruising, intramuscular injury, abrasions, burns, or the impairment of an organ. The law also classifies an infant's "physical dependence on an addictive drug at birth" as abuse. Inappropriately medicating or restraining a person may also be abuse.

---

[3] While each reporting statute uses slightly different language, they all deal with essentially the same issues. Officers do not need to be overly precise about the legal standards.

- **Sexual.** Sexual abuse involves the touching of a sexual part of the body in an inappropriate manner. The standard depends on whether a child or adult is involved. Children under the age of 14 are not allowed to legally consent to touching. Children between the ages of 14 and 16 may consent to sexual touching, but not intercourse. If relatives or parents are involved, any sexual contact must be reported. *John D. v. DCF,* 51 Mass. App. Ct. 125 (2001) ("verbal sexual contact" is abuse, even though the victim is not touched; in this case, the defendant had several sexually explicit and inappropriate conversations with his 15 year old daughter).

  For elders and the disabled, sexual contact is reported when it is nonconsensual — since they are adults and may voluntarily choose to engage in this activity. However, nonconsensual contact occurs when a person lacks the mental capacity to choose. For example, an elder suffering from advanced Alzheimer's is unable to consent to significant sexual contact. *Comm. v. Figueroa,* 79 Mass. App. Ct. 389 (2011) (assistant at nursing home raped elderly resident by describing his crime as a "medical test"). See discussion in *Chapter 9*.

- **Emotional.** Serious emotional injury includes, but is not limited to, an extreme anxiety, fear, depression, or withdrawal that results from improper verbal and/or nonverbal conduct directed toward the victim. For children, emotional injury is the impairment of the "psychological capacity of a child as evidenced by a *substantial* reduction in the child's ability to function." 110 CMR 2.00.

  Typically, officers will see emotional abuse in conjunction with some other form of physical abuse or neglect. However, emotional abuse does not have to be coupled with another form of victimization. In fact, since emotional abuse is often the first detected form of abuse, officers should not hesitate to base their report solely on its existence.

Neglect. Neglect may be "passive" or "active." Passive neglect occurs when a well-meaning caregiver no longer provides adequate care. Such nonpurposeful neglect represents the majority of cases. On the other hand, active neglect describes an intentional, at times cruel, deprivation of care. Self-neglect occurs when elders lack the capacity to adequately care for themselves.

Sometimes officers are reluctant to file a report of neglect because they feel the caregiver is trying, and they do not want to "get the person in trouble." This point of view misunderstands the purpose of the reporting laws. The obligation to report neglect, or any other form of abuse, recognizes the positive impact that social service intervention can have on a struggling family. The response of social services is tailored to the situation revealed by the investigation.

Financial exploitation. The financial exploitation of elders is the fastest growing form of victimization. It often occurs in combination with other forms of abuse, such as threats or physical attack, which are directed at the elder to facilitate the transfer of assets. Financial exploitation is an act or failure to act by another person which causes a substantial monetary or property loss to an elder. This is accomplished without the elder's consent, or when the elder is tricked, intimidated or forced into giving consent.

Financial exploitation may be accomplished by family members or relatives, by fiduciaries, or by scam artists. Fiduciaries are either: (1) professionals (such as lawyers or stockbrokers) who use their position of trust to get access to money; or (2) legal appointees (such as guardians or those with a power of attorney) who use their legal status to divert money to themselves. Protective service intervention is designed to detect this kind of exploitation and, if necessary, set the stage for prosecution.

Practical reporting techniques. If possible, officers should always report the incident to the local field office of the agency involved. In all likelihood, the local office will conduct the investigation and provide follow-up services. It is highly recommended that officers keep a list of local agency phone numbers and contacts in the back of their field notebook. The more officers collaborate with and support the social workers serving their community, the better the response will be.

- **Hotline.** To report abuse during nonbusiness hours, call the agency hotline.

- **On-scene officer.** It is best if the report comes from officers who were at the scene. They are in the best position to answer questions posed by protective service workers.

- **Other mandated reporters.** Several mandated reporters may be involved with one victim (e.g., officers bring a child to the hospital to see a doctor and nurse). Officers should not assume that another professional will report. The law is clear: Each mandated professional has a duty to report, without regard to what others do.

- **Written report within 48 hours.** The report must contain:

    - The alleged victim's name, address, age (estimate if necessary) and sex;
    - The parents' names or any other person responsible for the victim's care;
    - The nature and extent of injuries or abuse;
    - How the reporter became aware of the condition;
    - Any action taken to treat or shelter the victim;
    - The reporter's name and contact information;
    - Knowledge of any prior abuse or neglect;
    - Any service provider or other individual who might be currently involved with the family;
    - Any legal custody orders pertaining to children; and
    - Any other helpful information.

- **Send police report.** DCF, EOEA and DPPC have created their own mandated reporter forms. Rather than duplicate their efforts, officers should simply attach their police report to the form and send it to the local office responsible for investigating.

Confidentiality of reporter. Protective services must keep a reporter's name confidential. As a practical matter, however, the subjects will usually figure out that the report originated with the responding officer who came to their house.

On the other hand, the law exempts mandated reporters from the coverage of confidentiality rules. This means that police officers and other professionals may provide any information requested by an agency investigating a mandated report. *Comm. v. Souther*, 31 Mass. App. Ct. 219 (1991).

Agency response. The response to reports of abuse is fairly similar across the protective services spectrum.

- **Emergencies.** If there is danger of further abuse, agencies must investigate within 24 hours and then implement protective services. DCF must begin the investigation within 2 hours of an oral report and take a child into custody to avoid any immediate danger.

- **Overall investigation.** After emergency services are provided, or if it is a nonemergency situation, DCF and DPPC must complete their investigation within 10 days, while elder services may take 30 days. All investigators must: (1) visit the site of the alleged abuse; (2) interview the alleged victim (and the parents or guardian in the case of a child); (3) contact collateral sources (e.g., any medical or mental health professionals, other witnesses, or social workers); (4) gather other pertinent facts; and (5) develop a service plan.

- **Findings.** The agency must decide whether the allegation of abuse, neglect or financial exploitation is "substantiated" or "unsubstantiated." Due to the number of false allegations in the child abuse context (especially during custody proceedings), individuals who make "frivolous reports" may be prosecuted. Penalty: *1st offense*: Fine NMT $2,000. *2nd offense:* HC NMT 6 months; and Fine NMT $2,000. *3rd or subsequent offense:* HC NMT 2½ yrs; and Fine NMT $2,000. Right of Arrest: Complaint.

- **Inform reporter.** The agency must inform a mandated reporter about the results of its investigation within 30 days of the report for child abuse and within 45 days of the investigative finding for elder abuse. Typically, these agencies send along a form letter. DPPC will send a letter if a case is screened out, and it expects the reporter to follow up with the agency to learn the results of an active investigation. Should officers want more detailed information in any situation, it is best to call the assigned investigator from the local office.

Referral to the District Attorney. If abuse may have resulted in death, the investigating agency must *immediately* report the situation to the District Attorney and medical examiner. If the agency substantiates nondeadly abuse, neglect or financial exploitation that *may constitute criminal misconduct*, the case must be referred to the District Attorney within 48 hours. In questionable cases, the agency may make a discretionary referral to the prosecutor.

Difference between adult and child protective services: Competence to accept or refuse services. The major difference between the adult and child system is that a competent adult may choose whether to cooperate with protective services. While the government must intervene into the lives of children, the situation is different with adults who do not lose their freedom simply because a government agency identifies them as a possible victim.

If the adult is mentally incompetent, or the investigation is being impeded by the suspected perpetrator, the investigating agency may petition the probate and family court for a protective order. The probate court may order emergency services, or direct an individual not to obstruct the investigation. Sometimes the court may appoint a guardian to act on behalf of the alleged victim. The goal is to disrupt the adult victim's life as little as possible, while still ensuring adequate protection.

Section II
AGGRAVATED A&B and CARETAKER ABUSE

CHILDREN 265, § 13J	ELDERS & DISABLED 265, § 13K
Protected Population **Children under 14** *Note:* Interestingly, there is no coverage for children age 14 through 18, although any abuse or neglect is still reportable under the Child Abuse Reporting Law, 119, § 51A.	*Protected Population* **Elders age 60 and over** **Disabled people of any age** defined as those individuals with "a permanent or long-term physical or mental impairment that prevents or restricts the individual's ability to provide for his or her own care or protection."
Elements **Suspect Assaults** (1 possible crime) • **Type 1.** The suspect: (1) committed an A&B on a child; (2) that caused bodily injury *or* substantial bodily injury. **Suspect Permits Injury** (2 more crimes) • **Type 2.** The suspect: (1) had care and custody of a child; and (2) recklessly permitted the child to suffer bodily injury *or* substantial bodily injury. • **Type 3.** The suspect: (1) had care and custody of a child; and (2) recklessly permitted another to commit an A&B on the child that caused bodily injury *or* substantial bodily injury.	*Elements* **Suspect Assaults** (3 possible crimes) • **Type 1.** The suspect committed an A&B on an elder or a disabled person. • **Type 2.** The suspect: (1) committed an A&B on an elder or disabled person; (2) that caused bodily injury *or* serious bodily injury. • **Type 3.** The suspect: (1) was the caretaker of an elder or disabled person; and (2) wantonly or recklessly committed abuse, neglect, or mistreatment. **Suspect Permits Injury** (3 more crimes) • **Type 4.** The suspect: (1) was the caretaker of an elder or disabled person; and (2) recklessly permitted another to commit an A&B on the elder or disabled person that caused bodily injury *or* serious bodily injury.

Children	Elders & Disabled
	• **Type 5.** The suspect: (1) was the caretaker of an elder or disabled person; and (2) recklessly permitted the elder or disabled person to suffer bodily injury *or* serious bodily injury. • **Type 6.** The suspect: (1) was the caretaker of an elder or disabled person; and (2) recklessly permitted another person to commit abuse, neglect or mistreatment against the elder or disabled person.
Penalty [similar offenses are placed side-by-side] Type 1 — *A&B with Bodily Injury:* SP NMT 5 yrs or HC NMT 2½ yrs. *If substantial injury:* SP NMT 15 yrs or HC NMT 2½ yrs. Type 2 — *Permitting A&B Bodily Injury:* HC NMT 2½ yrs. *If substantial bodily injury:* SP NMT 5 yrs or HC NMT 2½ yrs. Type 3 — *Permitting Bodily Injury:* HC NMT 2½ yrs. *If substantial bodily injury:* SP NMT 5 yrs or HC NMT 2½ yrs.	*Penalty* Type 1 — *Simple A&B:* SP NMT 3 yrs or HC NMT 2½ yrs; and/or Fine NMT $1,000. Type 2 — *A&B with Bodily Injury:* SP NMT 5 yrs or HC NMT 2½ yrs; and/or Fine NMT $1,000. *If serious injury:* SP NMT 10 yrs or HC NMT 2½ yrs; and/or Fine NMT $5,000. Type 3 — *Abuse, Neglect or Mistreatment:* SP NMT 3 yrs or HC NMT 2½ yrs; and/or Fine NMT $5,000. Type 4 — *Permitting A&B Bodily Injury:* SP NMT 5 yrs or HC NMT 2½ yrs; and/or Fine NMT $5,000. *If serious bodily injury:* SP NMT 10 yrs or HC NMT 2½ yrs; and/or Fine NMT $10,000. Type 5 — *Permitting Bodily Injury:* SP NMT 5 yrs or HC NMT 2½ yrs; and/or Fine NMT $5,000. *If serious bodily injury:* SP NMT 10 yrs or HC NMT 2½ yrs; and/or Fine NMT $10,000. Type 6 — *Permitting Abuse, Neglect or Mistreatment:* SP NMT 3 yrs or HC NMT 2½ yrs; and/or Fine NMT $5,000.
Right of Arrest *Permitting Bodily Injury to Child:* Complaint. *All other violations:* Felony.	*Right of Arrest* *All violations:* Felony.

Children	Elders & Disabled
Care and Custody A "person having care and custody," according to § 13J, is a "parent, guardian, employee of a home or institution or any other person with equivalent supervision or care of a child, whether the supervision is temporary or permanent." *Comm. v. Panagopoulos*, 60 Mass. App. Ct. 327 (2004) (man who lived with two children and their mother for at least seven months, during which time he shared with their mother the caretaking responsibilities for the children, qualified as having "care and custody").	*Caretaker* A "caretaker," under § 13K, is a person with responsibility for the physical care of an elder or disabled person that arises from a: • Family relationship; • Fiduciary duty imposed by law; • Contractual duty; or • Voluntary duty. The relationship must be such that a reasonable person would believe that the caretaker's failure to fulfill this responsibility would adversely affect the health of the elder or disabled person.
A&B Officers should apply the common law definition to §§ 13J and K offenses. An A&B is "the intentional and unjustified use of force upon the person of another, however slight, or the intentional doing of a reckless act causing personal injury to another." *Comm. v. McCan*, 277 Mass. 199 (1931). *Comm. v. Neville*, 2015 WL 4726833 (Appeals Court) (as he stormed away after an argument with his parents, the defendant shoved his body between them, knocking his 65 year old mother into the refrigerator).	
Reckless Conduct Officers should apply the common law definition: Reckless conduct is an intentional act or the failure to act (where there is a duty) that involves a high likelihood that substantial harm will result to another. *Comm. v. Robinson*, 30 Mass. App. Ct. 62 (1991) (mother fed substantial quantity of salt to her baby). *Comm. v. Gallison*, 383 Mass 659 (1981) (parent failed to seek medical care for child).	
No Exceptions to Reckless Conduct — Children No statutory exceptions under § 13J. In fact, the SJC has specifically stated that the spiritual treatment exception does not apply to children. *Comm. v. Twitchell*, 416 Mass. 114 (1993) (SJC reversed conviction of Christian Scientist couple who refused to obtain medical care for their son afflicted with an obstructed bowel; he died; court said parents would not be excused in the future).	*Exceptions to Reckless Conduct — Elders & Disabled* Since elders and the disabled, unlike children, are adults and allowed to make independent decisions if mentally competent, § 13K states that conduct is *not* reckless if a *competent* elder or disabled person: • Directs it; or • Relies upon the recognized tenets of spiritual treatment instead of medical care.

Children	Elders & Disabled
Bodily Injury § 13J defines bodily injury as the "substantial impairment of the physical condition, including any burn, fracture of any bone, subdural hematoma, injury to any internal organ, any injury which occurs as the result of repeated harm to any bodily function or organ, including human skin, or any physical condition which substantially imperils a child's health or welfare."	*Bodily Injury* § 13K defines bodily injury as the "substantial impairment of the physical condition, including but not limited to, any burn, fracture of any bone, subdural hematoma, injury to any internal organ, any injury which occurs as the result of repeated harm to any bodily function or organ, including human skin." *Comm. v. Kelly*, 2012 WL 6372843 (Appeals Court) (sufficient to cause cuts on elder's lower lip and a welt under his eye).
Substantial Bodily Injury According to § 13J, substantial bodily injury is "bodily injury which creates a permanent disfigurement, protracted loss or impairment of a function of a body member, limb or organ, or substantial risk of death."	*Serious Bodily Injury* According to § 13K, serious bodily injury is "bodily injury which results in a permanent disfigurement, protracted loss or impairment of a bodily function, limb or organ, or substantial risk of death."
No comparable provision covers children These terms are only used as general descriptions for 51A reports, but they are not specifically defined as crimes in any statute.	*Abuse, Neglect or Mistreatment* According to § 13K: - **Abuse:** Physical contact which either harms or creates a substantial likelihood of harm. - **Mistreatment:** The use of medication or treatment, isolation, or physical or chemical restraint which harms or creates a substantial likelihood of harm. - **Neglect:** The failure to provide treatment or services necessary to maintain health and safety, which either harms or creates a substantial likelihood of harm.

Notes

Case protocol. To prove their case, it is recommended that officers do the following:

- **Hospital evaluation.** Proving the nature of the injuries to the child, disabled person, or elder is typically an element requiring expert testimony. A hospital assessment also prevents a defendant from later claiming that if the victim were really injured, he or she would have been treated.

- **File a 51A, 19A or 19C report.** A mandatory report should accompany a case that involves a person with care and custody (265, § 13J) or a caretaker (265, § 13K).

- **Take photographs of any visible injuries, or have the medical staff take them.**

Do not have to prove who committed the assault if the caregiver must have known. For recklessly permitting another to injure the victim, it is not necessary to prove the identity of the assailant. It is sufficient to prove that an ordinary caregiver would have recognized that the victim was being exposed to injury. *Comm. v. Traylor*, 86 Mass. App. Ct. 84 (2014).

Inaction may be basis for conviction. *Comm. v. Robinson*, 74 Mass. App. Ct. 752 (2009) (13 year old child almost died from an infection to her pierced navel; her mother never sought care even though she was sick for weeks). *Comm. v. Cruz*, 88 Mass. App. Ct. 206 (2015) (defendant's 91 year old mother died of sepsis caused by sitting in her own feces and urine over several weeks).

Specific knowledge of injuries not required. Defendants do not have to know that they are causing the required level of injury at the time of their assault. The prosecution must only prove that the required level of injury existed. *Comm. v. Macey*, 47 Mass. App. Ct. 42 (1999).

A&B on elder or disabled person always a felony even if no injury. *Comm. v. Lockwood*, 95 Mass. App. Ct. 189 (2019) (defendant pushed 63 year old woman; he committed a felony under § 13K even though she suffered no injury).

Knowledge of disability not required. *Comm. v. Laporte*, 2018 WL 1974455 (Appeals Court): Wendy Laporte was in line behind the victim at a gas station convenience store. The victim, who had cerebral palsy, had trouble speaking and walked with a limp. Laporte watched the victim collect $400 for winning on a scratch ticket. She immediately left the store without making a purchase and spoke to her boyfriend, who robbed the victim by knocking her down. Laporte claimed she did not know the victim was disabled. 265, § 13K does not require knowledge of the victim's disability.

Nature of disability. *Comm. v. Martinez*, 2020 WL 2610080 (Appeals Court): The defendant attacked the victim. The victim's left hand suffered from brachial plexus palsy and stuck out from her wrist at an odd angle. She could not use or raise her left hand, including to cover herself during a fight. This condition qualified as a disability under the statute. Even though the victim was able to hold a job, drive, and provide some care for her parents, this condition restricted the victim's "ability to provide for . . . her own . . . protection."

Multiple convictions may not be solely based on multiple injuries. The defendant must engage in separate and discrete instances of criminal conduct, or multiple victims must be harmed. *Comm. v. Traylor*, 472 Mass. 260 (2015).

Related Offense

Reckless Endangerment of a Child. 265, § 13L concerns the behavior of adults who, by their action or inaction, create a substantial risk of serious bodily injury or sexual abuse to a child under 18. Penalty: HC NMT 2½ yrs. Right of Arrest: Complaint. For a detailed breakdown, see *LED's Juvenile Law, Chapter 5*.

A&B OR INDECENT A&B ON AN INTELLECTUALLY DISABLED PERSON
265, § 13F

Elements

- **Required assault.** The suspect committed an A&B *or* an indecent A&B;

- **Knowledge.** Upon a person who he knew was intellectually disabled.

Right of Arrest

Felony.

Penalty

For A&B: 1st offense: SP NMT 5 yrs or HC NMT 2½ yrs; *2nd or subsequent offense:* SP NMT 10 yrs.

For Indecent A&B: 1st offense: SP NLT 5 yrs, NMT 10 yrs; *2nd or subsequent offense:* SP NLT 10 yrs (mandatory minimum of 10 yrs).

Exemption

This statute does not apply to situations where an intellectually disabled individual commits an A&B or indecent A&B on another disabled individual.

Notes

Intellectually disabled (ID) is the proper term instead of "mentally retarded." 265, § 13F does not define ID, so the court applies the usual meaning: "slow or limited in intellectual and emotional development." *Comm. v. Aitahnedlanara*, 63 Mass. App. Ct. 76 (2005) [Department of Developmental Services (DDS) service coordinator testified that the victim had an IQ of 33 and only individuals with an IQ below 76 were eligible for services].

Knowledge. The government must prove that the defendant *knew* the victim was intellectually disabled. In *Aitahnedlanara*, the defendant assaulted the victim in her group home where he had been working for five years. The victim testified at trial, so the jury was able to assess her level of disability and the defendant's level of awareness. *Comm. v. Roderick*, 411 Mass. 817 (1992) (mentally handicapped persons may testify if the judge decides they possess the capacity "to observe, remember and give expression to what they have seen").

Indecent A&B requires lack of consent. *Comm. v. Portonova*, 69 Mass. App. Ct. 905 (2007): Glenn Portonova drove the victim, an intellectually disabled woman, to a motel. He raped her and told her to "play with herself." She only complied because she was scared. *Comm. v. St. Louis*, 475 Mass. 350 (2015).

15 — Stalking, Annoying Calls, & Secret Recording

STALKING 265, § 43	CRIMINAL HARASSMENT 265, § 43A
Elements • The suspect willfully and maliciously engaged; • In a pattern of conduct or series of acts (at least 3 incidents); • Which were directed at a specific person; and • Constituted harassment (because a reasonable person would suffer substantial emotional distress); and • Involved a threat with the intent to cause imminent fear of death or serious bodily injury.	*Elements* • The suspect willfully and maliciously engaged; • In a pattern of conduct or series of acts (at least 3 incidents); • Which were directed at a specific person; and • Constituted harassment (because a reasonable person would suffer substantial emotional distress).
Right of Arrest: Felony.	*Right of Arrest:* 258E, § 8 (the harassment prevention law) states that warrantless arrest on probable cause is the "preferred response" for this crime.
Penalty *Basic offense:* SP NMT 5 yrs or HC NMT 2½ yrs; and/or Fine NMT $1,000. *Stalking in violation of a court order:* SP or HC: Mandatory minimum of 1 year; overall sentence NLT 1 year, NMT 5 yrs. *2nd or subsequent offense, whether or not a court order is involved:* SP or HC: Mandatory minimum of 2 yrs; overall sentence NLT 2 yrs, NMT 10 yrs.	*Penalty* *1st offense:* HC NMT 2½ yrs; and/or Fine NMT $1,000. *2nd or subsequent offense of Harassment, or if defendant has a prior § 43 Stalking conviction:* SP NMT 10 yrs or HC NMT 2½ yrs.

Notes

Difference Between Stalking & Criminal Harassment

Stalking requires a threat. Stalking and criminal harassment are identical offenses, except that stalking has the additional element of a threat, which turns it into a felony.

- **Only one threat required.** The offender must make one threat that is intended to place the victim "in imminent fear of death or serious bodily injury." *Comm. v. Julien*, 59 Mass. App. Ct. 679 (2003).

- **Threat may be to third party if suspect intended it be conveyed to victim.** In *Comm. v. Hughes*, 59 Mass. App. Ct. 280 (2003), the defendant was in jail for violating a 209A order obtained by his ex-girlfriend. Calling from jail, the defendant told his brother that his ex-girlfriend should "be more afraid of me now." The brother never communicated this threat to the ex-girlfriend, but instead cooperated with police. Whether or not the victim heard the comment was irrelevant because it was clear that the defendant *intended* that his remarks be communicated to her so she would be afraid. After all, the defendant knew that his brother had played the role of intermediary between him and the victim before.

- **Suspect's intent must be to cause <u>*imminent fear.*</u>** *Comm. v. Gupta*, 84 Mass. App. Ct. 682 (2014): The victim obtained a restraining order against her abusive husband. Over a six month period, the husband made 102 phone calls from India in which he frequently threatened to kill the victim, her children, and her grandchildren if she did not return to India. During one accidental encounter in a store in Cambridge, he threatened that if she did not accompany him to India in two or three days, he would take her by force.

  The defendant argued that the phone calls from India could not convey the danger of imminent physical injury. However, it is not imminent injury, but imminent *fear* of injury that stalking prohibits. The defendant satisfied the statute in two ways: by the threatening calls alone, and by a combination of the calls and the threat in the clothing store. The wife's "imminent fear" was reasonable given the defendant's mobility, history of abusive conduct, and knowledge of where she lived.

Enhanced penalty: Stalking in violation of court order. Officers must show the offender had been served with <u>or</u> knew about the protective order. *Comm. v. Alphas*, 430 Mass. 8 (1999).

Similarities Between Stalking & Criminal Harassment

Target may be anyone. No need to show special relationship. Unlike Chapter 209A, the victim and perpetrator do *not* need to have any special relationship.

Malicious. Malice means the suspect acts "intentionally and with a wrong motive."

- *Comm. v. Paton*, 63 Mass. App. Ct. 215 (2005): Robert Paton met a waitress at a local club. The initial encounter was friendly. However, Paton became a regular visitor. On more than 20 occasions he asked the bartender whether the victim was working. If she was not working, he would leave immediately. If she was working, he stayed and ordered a drink. Paton did not communicate with her, but would pace back and forth and stare. The victim became so scared that her mother contacted the Norwell Police Department.

At this point, the manager of the club asked Paton not to come back. The defendant began appearing unexpectedly at places where the victim was, like the mall and her gym. The fact that Paton persisted in initiating such encounters even after he was told that the victim found them alarming was malicious.

- Compare *Comm. v. McDonald*, 462 Mass. 236 (2012): On May 6, Joan's neighbor saw James McDonald parked in a truck outside her house. He was looking at Joan's house and holding a camera. When McDonald saw the neighbor, he drove away. The neighbor had seen the truck twice before on the street. She called police.

    On May 8, an officer ran the plate and located McDonald. The officer told McDonald that residents were afraid because he was in the area when the school bus dropped off children. The officer said it would be a "very good idea" to avoid the area. McDonald apologized and said the residents would not see him again.

    On May 11, Joan was in her driveway waiting for her kids when she saw McDonald's truck drive by slowly. On May 12, McDonald repeated this behavior.

    On May 15, a family friend saw McDonald drive by and stare. Within 10 minutes, McDonald drove by again. The friend yelled: "Hey, what do you think you're doing?" McDonald said he was "just taking pictures of dogs" and was going to send Joan the photographs. The friend told McDonald to leave. Joan was hysterical and called police.

    While Joan was alarmed, there was, according to the court, no evidence that McDonald did anything more than look at her house and take pictures. Regularly driving on a public street and looking at things, *without more*, is not malicious. McDonald's refusal to follow the officer's advice did not result in criminal harassment either. The court questioned whether the officer even had the authority to order someone to stay away from a public street.

    Commentary: A police officer might read this case and exclaim: "What are we supposed to do?" Pending further guidance from the SJC, the author recommends that officers: (1) learn from the suspect whether there is a legitimate reason to continue the activity in question; (2) explain to the suspect how his actions have alarmed the complainant; (3) propose alternatives to accomplish the suspect's goals; and (4) warn him that continuing to behave in the same way may result in prosecution for harassment.

    If a follow-up investigation becomes necessary, search the suspect based on consent or probable cause to confirm that he is doing what he claims (e.g., did McDonald actually have a camera with him in the truck? Did it contain pictures of a dog as he claimed?).

    Finally, *McDonald* states that even innocent conduct may amount to harassment. It just did not find enough evidence in the case. See *Rausso v. Rausso*, 50 Mass. App. Ct. 911 (2001) (sending flowers twice during an acrimonious divorce was a hostile act).

At least 3 incidents. Since the statutes require a "pattern of conduct," the SJC insists on evidence of at least 3 separate incidents. *Comm. v. Martinez*, 43 Mass. App. Ct. 408 (1997).

- **Each incident does not have to involve the same type of conduct.** *Comm. v. Walters*, 472 Mass. 680 (2015) (because the victim broke off their relationship, Walters constantly yelled and displayed his guns to her; blocked her driveway with boulders; and left urine and feces in her toilets, which could not be flushed).

- **Each act for harassment does not need to seriously alarm.** It is the overall pattern of conduct that must seriously alarm the victim(s). *Comm. v. Johnson,* 470 Mass. 300 (2014).

- **Victims do not have to be aware of each act of harassment as it is occurring.** The strange case of *Comm. v. Brennan,* 481 Mass. 146 (2018) illustrates this point. Francis Brennan installed GPS devices on the vehicles of a married couple that he had never met. He tracked their movements based on his nonsensical belief that the husband was having an affair. The SJC held that neither the husband or wife had to be aware in real time that they were being tracked for the defendant's conduct to qualify as at least one act of harassment against each of them. Once they became aware of the devices on their cars, and police traced their installation to the defendant, the couple suffered substantial emotional distress.

- **Various forms of communication covered.** Stalking and harassment may be committed by mail or by *any electronic communication* including phone, email, instant messaging, or fax. *Comm. v. Salyer,* 84 Mass. App. Ct. 346 (2013). *Comm. v. C.M.D.,* 2017 WL 958462 (Appeals Court) (defendant directed communications to the victim through his own Facebook page).

- **GPS tracking may constitute harassment.** *Comm. v. Brennan, supra.* (see discussion above).

- **Harassment may consist solely of speech.** However, if speech is the sole basis for conviction, it must constitute "fighting words." "Fighting words" are defined as "personally abusive epithets which, when addressed to the ordinary citizen, are . . . likely to provoke a violent reaction." *Comm. v. Welch,* 444 Mass. 80 (2005).

- **Some statements are protected by the First Amendment.** *Comm. v. Bigelow,* 475 Mass. 554 (2016): Harvey Bigelow sent five letters to the home of town selectman Michael Costello and his wife Susan. The letters criticized Michael's performance as selectman, threatened them both, and suggested to Susan that Michael was cheating on her. Bigelow could not be convicted of criminally harassing Michael, because he was an elected official and the letters primarily discussed issues of public concern, which is protected speech under the First Amendment. Bigelow did criminally harass Susan. She was not a public official, and the letters deliberately created fear of future harm.

- **Acts must be distinct and separated by "some interval."** *Comm. v. Valentin,* 91 Mass. App. Ct. 515 (2017) ("keying" car at 4:00 a.m., following victim at 6:00 a.m., and physically attacking her at 9:00 a.m. were three separate acts). *Comm. v. Villanueva,* 2017 WL 3184415 (Appeals Court) (threatening texts were sent weeks apart).

- **Exposure to incidents may occur at one time.** *Comm. v. Cullen,* 79 Mass. App. Ct. 618 (2011): Robert Nazarro was the director at a counseling center known as CPC. He had treated Timothy Cullen. Over eight months, CPC received 25 mailings that included handwritten threats, such as "look over your shoulders 4 life" and the acronym "AMLKN," which stands for "All Mighty Latin King Nation" (a gang). CPC learned that Cullen was behind the threats, and Nazarro panicked when he was told that his home address and license plate number were referenced. Although Nazarro was exposed to all of the information at one time, the separate mailings constituted three incidents.

- **Harassment may be conveyed through intermediaries.** *Comm. v. O'Brien,* 2014 WL 6994647 (Appeals Court) (defendant should have known that her threats to "punish" the probate court judge who presided over her case, would be relayed by the court officials and by the judge's wife, whom she telephoned at home).

- **Harassment may be accomplished through other people.** *Comm. v. Johnson*, 470 Mass. 300 (2014): The Johnsons were in an ongoing feud with their neighbors, the Lyons family. William Johnson convinced his friend, Gerald Colton, to play a series of pranks. Colton posted an ad on Craigslist that provided the Lyons' phone number and address and stated that free golf carts were available. About 40 people arrived, frightening Mrs. Lyons. Colton posted another ad, offering to sell "my late son's motorcycle" and directing interested parties to call Mr. Lyons after 10:00 p.m. Mr. Lyons received nonstop late night calls for months. Colton then sent an email to Mr. Lyons stating that his name was "Brian" and accusing him of molesting him as a teenager. "Brian" threatened to press charges.

    The Craigslist ads essentially recruited others to harass the victims. The defendants could not escape liability simply by using the internet.

The suspect's conduct must alarm or annoy his target in a way that would cause a reasonable person to suffer substantial emotional distress.

- *Comm. v. Robinson*, 444 Mass. 102 (2005): The defendant and victim rented from the same landlord. The victim accused the defendant of using illegal drugs. While the victim's family was at a community garden, the defendant sat in his car and "glared" at them. He blocked the road, forcing the family to drive over a grassy area to escape. During a confrontation in front of a coffee shop, the defendant moved close to the victim, clenched his fists, and stated that he would "wipe that grin off your face!" In a third encounter, the defendant stopped his car twice near the victim and his son, and "stared menacingly." The defendant followed them home, which caused the family to move! These incidents generated "substantial emotional distress."

- Compare *Comm. v. Braica*, 68 Mass. App. Ct. 244 (2007): Joanne Winsor lived in an apartment building next door to the Belchertown Housing Authority (BHA) where Kenneth Braica lived. When Winsor would walk her young son to school and take a short cut across BHA property, Braica would yell obscenities out the window. He also yelled at her when she was in her own backyard. Braica filed several complaints against Winsor with the board of health, conservation commission, and dog officer. Winsor was very upset.

    For the most part, complaints to government officials will not make out a case of criminal harassment, although continually yelling obscenities might. The trouble with this case was a lack of proof that Winsor was seriously alarmed by Braica. She did not focus on his behavior when interviewed. In fact, she continued to take the short cut by his apartment.

Venue for stalking or harassment. Venue exists in any territorial jurisdiction where an act constituting an element of stalking or harassment was committed.

Important safeguard: Victims of stalking or harassment eligible for Harassment Protection Order (HPO). Once a defendant is charged with stalking or criminal harassment, the victim is eligible for an HPO under Chapter 258E. The HPO is fully discussed in *Chapter 13*.

Related Offenses

Witness Intimidation. Once charged, further contact by a harasser or stalker is witness intimidation under 268, § 13B (see *Chapter 35*). *Comm. v. Potter*, 39 Mass. App. Ct. 924 (1995).

ANNOYING OR OBSCENE ELECTRONIC COMMUNICATION
269, § 14A

Elements

- ***3 communications.*** The suspect made (or caused to be made) at least 3 telephone calls or other type of electronic communication (including email, internet, fax machine, texting, instant messaging);

- ***To victim or family.*** To the victim or victim's family; and

- ***Indecent or harassing.*** The suspect's:

  - Language was indecent or obscene; or
  - His sole purpose was to harass or annoy the victim or family.

Right of Arrest

Complaint.

Penalty

HC NMT 3 months; and/or Fine $300.

Notes

Minimum of 3 phone calls and/or electronic communications, whether or not the suspect actually speaks to anyone. The person or family is covered — in recognition that this behavior often affects the family as much as the intended target. *Comm. v. Wotan*, 422 Mass. 740 (1996).

Absent obscene language, suspect's only purpose must be harassment. Suppose a charity requests donations through repeated calls. This might annoy someone, but it would not violate the law until the charity's "sole" purpose was to harass or annoy. In similar fashion, the defendant in *Comm. v. Strahan*, 30 Mass. App. Ct. 947 (1991) could not be convicted for calling 11 times in seven minutes during the day. The calls to his former girlfriend, although annoying, were motivated by his desire to get back together. Had the barrage of calls continued, it would have crossed the line at some point.

Officers must determine the suspect's intent: What time of day or night did he communicate? What did he say? Had he been told to stop? Did he hang up when someone answered? *Comm. v. Roberts*, 442 Mass 1034 (2004) (fact that some calls were nonharassing did not prevent conviction for those that were). *Comm. v. Heath*, 2013 WL 3196432 (Appeals Court) (defendant sent text messages all day long to his ex-girlfriend; he claimed his purpose was to get back together, yet his intent to harass was obvious based on the number of messages, their tone [asking about her sexual activity], and his persistence [he was asked to stop many times]).

Unlike a call that is strictly annoying, the use of obscene language constitutes an offense regardless of the offender's purpose. Investigators should find out whether the suspect used obscene language. The suspect does not have to know that his language is legally obscene. *F.C.C. v. Pacifica Foundation*, 438 U.S. 726 (1978).

3 ways to identify annoying caller:

- **Knowledge of caller's voice.** Oftentimes the victim will know the caller because of the relationship that motivated the harassment. In these situations, "a witness is competent to identify a voice over the telephone." *Comm. v. Perez*, 411 Mass. 249 (1991).

- **Personal phone technology.** Many customers have specialized options to identify callers. Sometimes offenders leave a message on the answering machine. If a citizen creates a recording, officers may use it as evidence. However, they may *not* encourage a citizen to secretly tape a caller because this is generally unlawful. *See below.*

- **Phone company investigative assistance.** Phone companies typically require a police incident report and complaint number before they will help a victim. Should a phone company decide to work with the victim and put a trace on her line, it will only release the results to the police. 271, § 17B. *District Attorney v. Coffey*, 386 Mass. 218 (1982).

Related Offense

False Calls to Public Safety Dispatch. 269, § 14B. See breakdown in *Chapter 35*.

UNLAWFUL SECRET RECORDING
272, § 99 C

Summary

The law prohibits private citizens from secretly recording others, or possessing a device with the intent to secretly record. However, citizens are allowed to secretly or openly record police officers on duty.

Elements

Type 1: Unlawful Secret Recording. Although not authorized, the suspect willfully recorded (or attempted to intercept) oral communication. [*Note:* Under 272, § 99 C1, proof that the suspect installed a device with intent to obtain an unauthorized interception is sufficient evidence, *by itself*, of a violation.]

Type 2: Possession of Device. The suspect possessed an unauthorized recording device (or permitted one to be used) with the intent to create an unlawful recording.

Type 3: Disclosure of Secret Interception.[1] The suspect willfully disclosed or used (or attempted to do so) an unauthorized, recorded oral communication.

Type 4: Conspiracy, Attempt, or Accessory. § 99 C6 notes that any person engaged in a conspiracy (or an attempt) in relation to the above offenses is eligible for the same penalties as a principal offender.

Right of Arrest

Unlawful secret recording: Felony.

Possession of device and disclosure of recording: Seize evidence and apply for complaint.

Penalty

Unlawful secret recording: SP NMT 5 yrs or HC NMT 2½ yrs; and/or Fine NMT $10,000.

Possession of device and disclosure of recording: HC NMT 2 yrs; and/or Fine NMT $5,000.

Civil Liability

272, § 99 Q states that "any aggrieved persons" have the right to sue "any persons" (including government officials) for violating their privacy rights through illegal recording. *Birbiglia v. Saint Vincent Hospital*, 427 Mass. 80 (1998) (doctor successfully sued hospital for using secret recordings of him during a meeting as the basis for revoking his staff privileges).

Exempt Conduct

The following secret recordings are permitted by 272, § 99 D:

- **Phone companies** to provide quality service and investigate allegations of annoying phone calls. *District Attorney v. Coffey*, 386 Mass. 218 (1982).

- **Office intercom system** used in the ordinary course of business. *Comm. v. Look*, 379 Mass. 893 (1980) (case involved intercom in a police station).

- **Federal and state law enforcement** when authorized by statute or warrant, or when conducting an administrative procedure like booking. *Comm. v. Gordon*, 422 Mass. 816 (1996).

- **Financial institutions** to record institutional trading partners in the ordinary course of business (provided there is semi-annual written notice).

Eavesdropping on extension line. It is not a violation when a private citizen or police officer listens in on a standard residential extension phone, and does not electronically record the conversation. *Comm. v. Eason*, 427 Mass. 595 (1998).

---

1 § 99 C also prohibits editing judicial recordings without a full explanation to the court (felony), and improperly disclosing the contents of a wiretap warrant or law enforcement recording.

Notes

Prohibition against unauthorized secret recordings only applies to oral communication.
This term was defined in *Comm. v. Wright*, 61 Mass. App. Ct. 790 (2004) as "audible, spoken words." The whole conversation need not be clear, only isolated words.

In *Wright*, the defendant hid a video camera in the store bathroom where he worked. A female employee discovered the camera. Her outraged complaint to the owner resulted in no action, so she called 911. The responding detective from Cambridge understood that the wiretap statute does not prohibit visual recording, *only* sound recording. The video he seized contained only snippets of voices and a few words. Since certain words were audible and understandable, the detective wisely arrested Wright, and his conviction was upheld.[2]

Private citizens may not secretly record any other private citizens. *Comm. v. Hanedanian*, 51 Mass. App. Ct. 64 (2001). *Curtatone v. Barstool Sports, Inc.*, 487 Mass. 655 (2021).

However, private citizens may secretly or openly record police officers on duty, as long as they do not interfere with police operations.

- **Secret.** *Project Veritas v. Rollins*, 2020 WL 7350243 (1st Cir.) decided that officers can no longer bring criminal charges under 272, § 99 against citizens, including members of the media, who secretly record them during a traffic stop or other on-duty activity in public.[3] The Constitution does not permit a ban on secret information-gathering directed at police officers in the public performance of their duties. Also see *ACLU v. Alvarez*, 679 F.3d 583 (7th Cir. 2012).

- **Open.** *Glik v. Cunniffe*, 655 F.3d 78 (2011): Simon Glik used his cell phone camera to film Boston officers arresting a young man in a park. After handcuffing the offender, an officer said: "You've taken enough pictures." Another officer arrested Glik for "secret recording" and disturbing the peace. Glik successfully sued for false arrest in federal court.

    "The same restraint demanded of law enforcement officers in the face of 'provocative and challenging' speech, . . . must be expected when they are merely the subject of videotaping that memorializes, without impairing, their work in public spaces." However, the right to record is not absolute.

    - ***Interference.*** Officers may prevent recording activity that interferes with their duty. *Gericke v. Begin*, 753. F.3d 1 (2014) (New Hampshire officers, during a nighttime traffic stop, had the right to order Carla Gericke to get back in her car and move away from the scene; but, when she immediately complied and moved, an officer should not have ordered her to turn off her camera and surrender it to him; the officer was liable to Gericke for his obviously unconstitutional behavior).

        Do *not* order citizens to turn off their cameras. Instead, give them verbal direction — e.g., "Sir, you're too close. Go over to the sidewalk." Since recording is legal, focus on the improper behavior — not the act of recording itself.

---

2 The fact that the naked video images were not illegal prompted the legislature to enact a statute for these types of cases. See discussion of 272, § 105 in *Chapter 10*.
3 The federal court's decision effectively overruled two prior Massachusetts appellate decisions. *Comm. v. Hyde*, 434 Mass. 594 (2001). *Comm. v. Manzelli*, 68 Mass. App. Ct. 691 (2007).

- ***Need for privacy.*** *Project Veritas v. Rollins, supra.* suggests that to preserve the conversational privacy of a victim or witness, the best practice is for officers to move to a private area or location. If the citizen with the camera tries to follow, the officer could order them to stop or face possible arrest for interfering with a police officer. See discussion in *Chapter 5.*

- ***Evidence.*** In deciding whether to seize a phone with video footage of a crime, <u>be careful</u>. If the arrest was problematic, it may be alleged that the device was seized as a cover-up. In short, video evidence often invites more scrutiny than it may be worth. That is why supervisory input is important. The decision to seize a citizen's device as evidence should be made in good faith.

  Officers should explain to the citizen that he may consent to having *only* the video of the incident copied and preserved as evidence, and that the phone will be returned as soon as possible. If the citizen agrees, provide a receipt.[4] If the citizen refuses, secure the device and obtain a search warrant for its contents.

Related Offense

Secret Video, Photo, or Electronic Surveillance of Partial Nudity. See *Chapter 10.*

---

[4] Simply taking the phone and dropping it into the evidence room until the trial is over, absent consent or a warrant, will be viewed by a court as unconstitutional and punitive.

16 Civil Rights Violations

Section I
CIVIL RIGHTS OFFENSES

INTERFERENCE WITH CIVIL RIGHTS
265, § 37

Elements

- **Force or threat.** The suspect willfully used force or the threat of force;

- **Attempt or interfere.** To attempt or actually interfere with; or intimidate; or oppress;

- **Motivated by bias.** Because of bias toward the victim's actual or perceived race, religion, ethnicity, nationality, handicap, gender, sexual orientation, gender identity, or *other* identifiable characteristic[1];

- **Exercise of legal right.** The exercise by the victim of a right secured by the constitution or laws of the United States or Massachusetts.

Right of Arrest

If bodily injury results: Felony.

If no bodily injury occurs: Arrest for breach of peace in presence. Otherwise, complaint.

Penalty

Basic offense: HC NMT 1 year; and/or Fine NMT $1,000.

If bodily injury results from the interference: SP or HC NMT 10 yrs; and/or Fine NMT $10,000. Unlike 265, § 39 (*discussed later*), § 37 does not define bodily injury, so the term should be given its broadest meaning — ranging from a knife wound to a bruise. See *Black's Law Dictionary* (5th ed. 1979).

---

[1] Technically, 265, § 37 does not address the offender's motivation in using force or threat to interfere with the exercise of a legal right. Therefore, it has been used in cases involving police misconduct or neighborhood disturbances that did not stem from typical bias motivation. However, the vast majority of cases do involve traditional bias, so that is, in reality, an established feature of this offense in the field. *Comm. v. Kelly*, 470 Mass. 682 (2015).

Notes

265, § 37 was enacted as part of a comprehensive Civil Rights Act in 1980. The catalyst was escalating racial violence in the Commonwealth, dramatically highlighted by the sniper shooting of Darryl Williams, a Black football player, during a high school game.[2] This law recognizes the unique harm that threats and violence cause when motivated by prejudice. *Comm. v. Poor*, 18 Mass. App. Ct. 490 (1984).

The heart of any civil rights violation is the suspect's bias motivation. For example, if Sally throws a rock at a Black family's house because she does not want African-Americans in her neighborhood, she has *intentionally* interfered with their right to housing because of their race. However, if John throws a stone at the same family's house in an act of random vandalism, he has committed a crime, but not a civil rights violation. By imposing an additional penalty on Sally, § 37 identifies her behavior as morally reprehensible and, hopefully, deters others from committing these types of hate crimes. *Comm. v. Pike*, 52 Mass. App. Ct. 650 (2001). *Wisconsin v. Mitchell*, 113 S. Ct. 2194 (1993).

Police do not have to prove that the suspect had "an evil or wicked purpose." It is only necessary to prove that the suspect acted intentionally based on bias.

Even partial bias sufficient. In *Comm. v. Stephens*, 25 Mass. App. Ct. 117 (1987), the defendant referred to his neighbor as a "fucking Cambodian." Later that night, with a group of friends, he began harassing the boy's family by breaking windows in their house and assaulting three occupants. He ran when he heard approaching police sirens.

Stephens later claimed that he was trying to get back at this young, male Cambodian because he had assaulted his friend earlier. The Appeals Court disagreed. Even if Stephens' version was true, it was also true that he was motivated, to some degree, by his hatred of Cambodians — whom he had a history of harassing. Some bias motivation is enough for conviction. *Comm. v. Kelly*, 470 Mass. 682 (2015).

Officer determination of bias. 501 CMR 4.04 informs officers that "common sense judgment should . . . be applied in [deciding] whether a crime should be classified as a hate crime." Because there is no way to look inside someone's mind, officers must determine the suspect's intent from the circumstances. Consider the following factors:

- **Offender/victim groups.** A historically established animosity exists between the victim's and offender's groups.

- **Comments and/or items during the incident.** These include oral comments, written statements, or gestures made by the offender — racial or anti-gay epithets; drawings, markings, symbols, or graffiti left at crime scene (e.g., swastika painted on the door of a synagogue).

- **Suspect's background.** Offender is a member of, or associates with, a hate group or has a history of previous crimes with similar *modus operandi*. *Comm. v. Hinds*, 487 Mass. 212 (2021) ("211" tattoo associated with White supremacist group according to expert).

---

[2] See R. Sherman, Esq. and J. McLinden, Esq., *The Massachusetts Civil Rights Act: Analysis & Commentary* (unpublished work of the Lawyers' Committee for Civil Rights of the Boston Bar Association).

- **Victim behavior.** Victim engaged in activities promoting a group — e.g., a gay rights demonstration; victim received harassing mail or phone calls or verbal abuse based on his affiliation with a target group.

- **Nature of the attack and location.** Victim is member of group that was overwhelmingly outnumbered; victim in or near a place commonly associated with a particular group — e.g., a gay bar; or incident coincided with a significant date — e.g., Martin Luther King Day, Rosh Hashanah, LGBTQ+ Pride Day.

The suspect must interfere with someone's civil rights through threats or force.

- **Force means physical force, directed against the victim or his property** (e.g., threatening to burn his house down). The amount of force may be minimal, so long as there is a clear connection between it and the civil rights interference. *Comm. v. Richards*, 363 Mass. 299 (1973). *Comm. v. Mosby*, 163 Mass. 291 (1895).

- **Threats are an expression of an intent to harm another person or his property.** *Comm. v. Winthrop W.*, 2013 WL 2149679 (Appeals Court): For three years, the juvenile taunted the victim as she was coming home from work — with epithets like "fucking nigger bitch" and "nigger digger." On one occasion, he spit in her face. And, when the victim eventually told the juvenile to leave her alone, he led his group of friends across the street, surrounded her and continued his barrage of insults. The victim pretended to call her boyfriend on her cell phone, but really called police. When officers arrived, she was shaking and crying.

- **Force or threat may be directed at someone outside targeted group.** For example, if the defendant threatened a White male because he was dating an African-American woman, a civil rights violation happened. See *In re B.C.*, 680 N.E.2d 1355 (Supreme Court Illinois 1997) (White male, who was with a group of African-Americans, became a civil rights victim when he was the target of the juvenile defendant's racist rants).

The suspect's objective must be to interfere, intimidate, or oppress. The statute prohibits any attempted or actual intimidation, interference, or oppression. Interfere means to hinder another person involved in an activity. Intimidate means to cause another to be afraid. However, the degree of intimidation need not result in panic or hysteria. Oppress means to use authority or power abusively. *Comm. v. Ware*, 375 Mass. 118 (1978).

The suspect must affect a right protected by federal or state law. Virtually every important activity we do is legally protected, so this element is fairly easy to prove. Remember, victims do not need to know what legal right they are exercising, and they may exercise more than one right at a time. *Bell v. Mazza*, 394 Mass. 176 (1985). The following rights are typically affected in these cases:

- **Personal security.** This right is violated when violence is motivated by a person's race, religion, or other characteristic. 42 U.S.C. § 1981. *Comm. v. Kelly*, 470 Mass. 682 (2015).

- **Housing.** The right to fair housing includes peaceful enjoyment of one's home; and renting, buying, and visiting homes without discrimination. *Jones v. Mayer Co.*, 392 U.S. 409 (1968).

- **Travel.** *Comm. v. Cullinan*, 2012 WL 1207400 (Appeals Court) (the right for all people to "travel freely" includes the right to walk on the street without being attacked verbally or physically because of race, ethnicity, or national origin).

- **Employment.** Employers may not discriminate against applicants or employees in their compensation or other terms of employment. 151B, § 4. Free access to employment may not be violated by third parties either. *Vietnamese Fishermen's Assoc. v. Ku Klux Klan*, 518 F. Supp. 933 (1981) (threatening comments, wearing KKK robes, and carrying firearms while joyriding close to the victimized fishermen violated their employment rights).

- **Religious worship.** The free practice of religion is guaranteed by the First Amendment. This right includes the use of buildings and other property for religious purposes.

- **Voting.** The right to vote and run for office is guaranteed by federal and state constitutions. *Anderson v. U.S.*, 417 U.S. 211 (1974) (conspiracy to deprive qualified voters of the right to vote is a civil rights violation).

- **Education.** Under federal and state law, students have a right to travel to and from school, to attend nonsegregated institutions, and to participate in extra-curricular activities. *Brown v. Board of Education*, 347 U.S. 483 (1954). 76, § 5.

- **Public places and facilities.** 272, § 92A, the Public Accommodation Law, guarantees the use of all public places free from discrimination. Public facilities such as parks, government buildings, beaches, streets, sidewalks, transportation vehicles, and restrooms are covered too.

- **Private establishments open to the public.** *Any* privately owned facility open to the public (such as a store, restaurant, gas station, theater, motel or hotel, health facility, and sports arena) is also a place of public accommodation. 272, § 92A. *See discussion below.*

- **Due process from public officials.** The use of excessive force by police violates one's civil rights. *Worcester Human Rights Commission v. Assad*, 370 Mass. 482 (1976).

Related Offense & Administrative Remedy

Violation of public accommodation law. The public accommodation law under 272, § 92A requires that any place, whether licensed or unlicensed, that "accepts or solicits the patronage of the general public" operate in a nondiscriminatory fashion. In addition, this law specifically prohibits any owner, manager, or employee from circulating any kind of publication or advertisement that is discriminatory.

To put teeth into this law, a separate section, 272, § 98, punishes any person who violates (or aids someone in violating) the public accommodation law "on account of race, color, religious creed, national origin, sex, gender identity [aka 'transgender'], sexual orientation, . . . deafness, blindness or any physical or mental disability or ancestry." Penalty: HC NMT 1 year; and/or Fine NMT $2,500. Right of Arrest: Complaint, unless in presence and a breach of peace. In addition, civil damages and administrative sanctions may be imposed. See *Vaspourakan Ltd. v. ABCC*, 401 Mass. 347 (1987) (evidence showed that a bar owner's excuses for excluding Blacks were a pretext for discrimination in his tavern; liquor license suspended).

ASSAULT, A&B, OR PROPERTY DAMAGE FOR THE PURPOSE OF INTIMIDATION
265, § 39

Elements

- ***Assault or property damage.*** The suspect:

  - Committed an assault or A&B on the victim; or

  - Damaged the victim's property;

- **With the intent to intimidate based on the victim's race, color, religion, national origin, sexual orientation, gender identity, or disability.**

Right of Arrest

Basic offense: Arrest for breach of peace in presence. Otherwise, complaint.

A&B results in "bodily injury" or offender armed with a gun: Felony.

Penalty

Basic offense: HC NMT 2½ yrs; and/or Fine NMT $5,000 or court may order restitution of NMT than 3 times the value of the damage, whichever is greater.

If A&B results in bodily injury: SP NMT 5 yrs, and/or Fine NMT $10,000.

If offender armed with a gun during offense: SP NMT 10 yrs or HC NMT 2½ yrs.

- **Definition of bodily injury under § 39:** "[S]ubstantial impairment of the physical condition including, but not limited to, any burn, fracture of any bone, subdural hematoma, injury to any external organ, or any injury which occurs as the result of repeated harm to any bodily function or organ, including human skin." *Comm. v. Sudler,* 94 Mass. App. Ct. 150 (2018) (victim has to suffer an injury that "considerably or significantly compromises the usual functioning of any part of the victim's body"; here, a cut on two fingers from a knife only required a bandage; without further evidence of treatment, continued medical care, or any recovery period, it was insufficient injury to qualify for the felony version of this offense).

- **Mandatory condition:** $100 surcharge on each count of this offense for the Diversity Education Trust Fund, and the defendant must complete a diversity awareness program.

- **Other reasonable conditions may be imposed.** *Comm. v. Obi,* 475 Mass. 541 (2016) (defendant landlord made derogatory remarks to her Muslim tenant and ultimately pushed her down the stairs; the court properly imposed probation conditions that required the defendant to respect the Muslim faith, and to tell her new tenants that she had been convicted of assaulting a tenant in the past).

Notes

The offender must commit an assault, A&B, or property damage, with the intent to intimidate the victim because of his membership in a protected class. *Comm. v. Barnette*, 45 Mass. App. Ct. 486 (1998) (African-American male assaulted a Mexican-American mother and her son during an argument in Lexington; defendant repeatedly made profane statements and said "Mexicans don't belong here"; clearly sufficient for a § 39 conviction).

Bias must be a reason for the intimidation — but need not be the "sole" or "substantial" reason. *Comm. v. Kelly*, 470 Mass. 682 (2015) (Amanda Kelly and Christopher Bratlie participated in a group beating of an African-American party guest; a witness testified that all members of the group called the victim a "nigger" during the attack; although Kelly and Bratlie were partially motivated by the guest's disruptive behavior, they were also motivated, in part, by the victim's race).

Related Offenses

Hazing. 269, § 17. It is illegal to conduct an initiation into a student organization that willfully or recklessly endangers the physical or mental health of any person. Right of Arrest: Arrest for breach of peace in presence. Otherwise, complaint. Detailed breakdown in *LED's Juvenile Law, Chapter 21*.

Managing a Hazardous Training Program. 265, § 40 outlaws: (1) managing a physical exercise program at a public or private institution; and (2) willfully and recklessly; (3) causing serious bodily injury to a program participant. Penalty: HC NMT 2½ yrs; and/or Fine NMT $5,000. Right of Arrest: Arrest for breach of peace in presence. Otherwise, complaint.

DESTRUCTION OF OR THREATS TO DESTROY A PLACE OF WORSHIP
266, § 127A

Elements

Type 1: Destruction or Defacement

- The suspect willfully or wantonly;

- Destroyed, defaced, or injured;

- Any of the following:

    - A church, synagogue, mosque, temple, or place of worship; or
    - An affiliated community center or educational facility; or
    - A building, structure, or place used for the burial or memorializing of the dead; or
    - Personal property inside any of these structures.

Type 2: Threats

- The suspect threatened to burn, deface, mar, injure, or in any way destroy;

- A church, synagogue, or other building, structure, or place of worship.

Right of Arrest

If property damage is over $5,000: Felony.

If the amount of damage is less, or if the crime involves a threat: Arrest for breach of peace in presence. Otherwise, complaint.

Penalty

Damage over $5,000: SP NMT 5 yrs; and/or Fine NMT 3 times value of damage.

Damage less than $5,000: HC NMT 2½ yrs; and/or Fine NMT $2,000 or NMT than 3 times value of damage, whichever is greater.

Threatening offense: HC NMT 1 year; and/or Fine NMT $1,500.

Notes

This law provides a response to vandalism focused on religious institutions — especially in view of the emotional harm that this activity causes to the affected group and the community at large. Also consider 266, § 126A in *Chapter 33*.

Deface or injure. The offender must destroy, deface, or injure the particular religious structure or property. However, the statute does not require either substantial or permanent harm. *Comm. v. DiPietro*, 33 Mass. App. Ct. 776 (1992) (the defendant defaced a temple by throwing eggs against the outside wall, even though the eggs were completely washed off; the term deface does not mean that permanent harm must occur).

Related Offense

Destroying or Defacing a Grave or Memorial to the Dead. 272, § 73 prohibits: (1) willfully destroying, defacing, injuring or removing a tomb, monument, gravestone, veteran's grave marker or metal plaque, veteran's flag holder, or other structure or thing designed as a memorial for the dead, or a fence or other thing for a burial enclosure; or (2) willfully removing, cutting, or injuring a tree, shrub, or plant placed within or near a burial enclosure; or (3) wantonly or maliciously disturbing the contents of a tomb or a grave. Penalty: SP NMT 5 yrs or HC NMT 2½ yrs; and Fine NMT $5,000. Right of Arrest: Felony.

Section II
HATE CRIMES REPORTING, INJUNCTIONS, & BIAS-FREE PROFESSIONAL POLICING

A. Hate Crimes

Hate crimes defined. 22C, § 32 and 501 CMR 4.02 define a "hate crime" as any criminal act motivated, at least in part, by racial, religious, ethnic, handicap, gender, or sexual orientation bias.

Any violation of the following statutes is presumed to be a hate crime: 265, § 37 (Interference with Civil Rights) or § 39 (Assault, A&B or Property Damage); or 266, § 127A (Defacing a Religious Structure); or 272, § 98 (Public Accommodation Law).

Police reporting requirements. Hate crimes should be reported to the "Crime Reporting Unit," a joint project of the State Police and Department of Criminal Justice Information Services. Officers should file the *Massachusetts Hate Crime Reporting Form* (mass.gov/doc/hcpdf-2/download). A separate form must be submitted for each criminal act possibly motivated by bias. Names of victims and perpetrators should *not* be included. 501 CMR 4.08.

Civil rights officer. In order to implement the reporting law, it is highly recommended that each department appoint a Civil Rights Officer (CRO) who should notify the Crime Reporting Unit of any hate activity and ensure that the proper forms are completed. The CRO is also the logical person to spearhead the department's community outreach.

In its model policy, the Anti-Defamation League (ADL) expresses why community relations are an important component of any law enforcement response to hate crimes: "Hate crimes are viewed in the community not only as crimes against the particular victim, but also as a crime against the victim's racial, religious, ethnic, national, sexual orientation, or handicap group as a whole. Working constructively with segments of this larger audience after such incidents is essential to help reduce fears, stem possible retaliation, and encourage any other previously victimized individuals to step forward and report those crimes." To this end, officers are encouraged to meet with neighborhood groups, make appropriate referrals to social service agencies, and engage in other outreach efforts.

B. Injunctions by Attorney General or Private Person

Injunctions. Under 12, §§ 11H-J, the Attorney General may obtain criminally enforceable court orders for the protection of victims of civil rights abuses. A private person may do the same. For violations to have criminal consequences, the court order must contain the statement: "Violation of this Order is a Criminal Offense." The court issues two certified copies. The police must serve one copy *in hand* to the defendant, unless the court orders otherwise. Also see 266, § 127B (parent liable for damages caused by minor child).

Right of arrest & penalty. Once they serve the injunction on the defendant, officers are authorized to arrest him without a warrant when they have *probable cause* that he committed *any* violation of the order. Offenders are then tried for contempt. Penalty: HC NMT 2½ yrs; and/or Fine NMT $5,000. If the violation involves bodily injury, SP NMT 10 yrs; and/or Fine NMT $10,000.

Venue. The injunction should be commenced in the superior court of the county in which the violation took place, or in which the suspect resides or has a business.

Juvenile jurisdiction. Complaints for violating an injunction are brought against juveniles in the superior court, not the juvenile court. *John Doe v. Comm.*, 396 Mass. 421 (1985).

Consider *Barros v. Ponce*, 2022 WL 1203722 (Superior Court): Dylan Ponce spray painted "Nigger Leave!" in large black letters on the door of Nantucket's African Meeting House. Ponce, a White resident of the island, told his boss the next day he had "tagged the nigger church." When they learned of the defacement of this symbol of Nantucket's Black community, James Barros and Rose Samuels felt threatened and intimidated. The implicit threat was a command to Black persons to leave . . . *or else*. Ponce intended to make Blacks on Nantucket apprehensive of harm. The right of Barros and Samuels to visit the African Meeting House was protected under 272, § 92A as a public accommodation.

To protect the plaintiffs, the judge ordered Ponce not to commit crimes against Barros or Samuels, or to contact them, or to approach within 25 yards of them.[3] In addition, Ponce was enjoined from committing crimes against *any* person because of their race, color, or national origin. The injunction was justified, and its terms and conditions were sufficiently precise.

C. Bias-Free Professional Policing

Bias-free professional policing is defined by 6E, § 1.

- A police officer's decisions and conduct shall <u>not</u> be influenced by a person's:

    - Race,
    - Ethnicity,
    - Sex,
    - Gender identity,
    - Sexual orientation,
    - Religion,
    - Mental or physical disability,
    - Immigration status, or
    - Socioeconomic or professional level.

- An officer's decisions and conduct may only be influenced by these characteristics when:

    - There is a non-discriminatory reason; or
    - A valid basis for different treatment; or
    - They are an element of a civil rights crime.

Police bias may be the basis for POST decertification, suspension, or retraining. 6E, § 10(b) and (d).

---

[3] Considering the practicality of an injunction on this small island, the judge reduced the distance to ten yards in grocery stores or on the ferry.

Police bias may also be the basis for a state civil rights lawsuit. 12, § 11H(b) declares: "All persons shall have the right to bias-free professional policing." The statute goes on to authorize a lawsuit against officers by either the citizen harmed or the Attorney General.

Gender-affirming and reproductive health care services are protected civil rights in Massachusetts. Under 12, § 11I ½, *gender-affirming care* concerns treatment of gender dysphoria — i.e., consultation and medical assistance for people who are already transgender or contemplating whether to become transgender. *Reproductive health care* concerns all treatment relating to pregnancy, contraception, assisted reproduction, miscarriage management, or pregnancy termination.

Whether you are a public official or private citizen, interfering with these rights is prohibited.

Massachusetts police officers shall not investigate this protected health care activity. Under 147, § 63, law enforcement officers in the Commonwealth are forbidden from providing information or assisting in any investigation or inquiry — by any government official or private citizen — regarding out-of-state health services that would be lawful if provided in Massachusetts.[4] This law counteracts the United States Supreme Court's decision in *Dobbs v. Jackson Women's Health Organization*, 597 U.S. ____ (2022), which authorized states to restrict abortion.

---

[4] The only exception is if a federal law explicitly requires that state or local officers provide assistance.

Law Enforcement Dimensions

Part V

POSSESSION & DISTRIBUTION OFFENSES

Firearms, Weapons, Explosives & Fireworks, Narcotics, Marijuana & Tobacco, and Alcohol

Chapters 17 – 22

© John Sofis Scheft, Esq.
All rights reserved

17 Firearms

GUN CALL: FIELD RESPONSE & CHARGING DECISIONS

Important Overall Approach

The Second Amendment guarantees the right to keep and bear arms. This right, however, is subject to reasonable regulation. New York State Rifle & Pistol Association v. Bruen, 597 U.S. ___ (2022). Chardin v. Police Commissioner, 465 Mass. 314 (2013).

Applying gun laws in the field can be complicated, which is why a simple approach works:

- **The paramount concern is public and officer safety.** Don't overanalyze when a gun is involved.

- **Once a weapon is secure, assess the situation.** Basically, Massachusetts residents require a License to Carry (LTC) for handguns and a Firearms Identification card (FID) for rifles and shotguns. Sometimes the legal implications are obvious (e.g., a 15 year old is carrying a handgun); other times, less so (e.g., a nonresident claims to be exempt while traveling through the Commonwealth). Once the danger has been neutralized, do not feel pressure to make an arrest.

- **When in doubt about an arrest, confiscate the weapon instead.** Remember, under 140, § 129C and 278, § 7, accused citizens have the *responsibility* to provide sufficient proof that they are in lawful possession of the weapon at the scene.

- **Decide whether to pursue criminal and/or administrative remedies.** Improper possession of a gun may call for criminal sanctions, administrative sanctions, or both.

Obtain Adequate Description of Suspect

A tip with an inadequate description of the person in possession will not provide reasonable suspicion. Comm. v. Berment, 39 Mass. App. Ct. 552 (1995) (no description, other than his race, of the man waving a gun; fact that four people were gathered around a car at 3:00 a.m. "just talking," did not point to a crime or to the defendant who was frisked).

Check with dispatch. Often, in the interest of getting a gun report out to officers, dispatch may not provide a complete description of the suspect. It may help to check with dispatch to see if other facts are available. In the final analysis, even with a limited description, officers must respond and do the best they can. Comm. v. Grinkley, 44 Mass. App. Ct. 62 (1997).

Assess Legal Sufficiency of Gun Report

A report that someone is carrying a firearm, without more, does not provide a reasonable suspicion of criminal activity. *Comm. v. Couture,* 407 Mass. 178 (1990).

Officers must have at least one other reason why the suspect probably possesses the gun unlawfully. We refer to this as a **plus factor**, since officers need possession "plus" something else.[1] So police should consider whether the tip describes a suspect who:

- **Appears under 21.** In Massachusetts, it is unlawful for a person under 21 to possess a firearm. 140, § 131. Thus, a tip about a suspect who is *probably* underage supports a stop and frisk. *Comm. v. Barros,* 49 Mass. App. Ct. 613 (2000).

- **Not using a holster.** *Comm. v. Edwards,* 746 Mass. 341 (2017) (while not required by law, licensed owners typically carry their firearm in a holster).

- **Brandished or concealed gun.** *Comm. v. Edwards, supra.* (defendant was holding a gun while standing on a deserted street at night). *Comm. v. Ross,* 2022 WL 1633836 (Appeals Court) (holding waistband to conceal firearm indicates illegal possession).

- **Loaded gun in public.** *Comm. v. Haskell,* 438 Mass. 790 (2003) ("while a licensed gun owner might . . . carry a handgun for protection, the act of publicly loading a handgun . . . creates a reasonable suspicion that a crime may be about to take place").

- **Ineligible for LTC.** *Comm. v. Rivas,* 466 Mass. 184 (2013) (officer saw Angel Rivas remove a gun from his jacket and show it to a man; the officer was familiar with Rivas' record of drug convictions and knew he was ineligible to obtain an LTC).

- **Fired gun.** *Comm. v. Johnson,* 49 Mass. App. Ct. 273 (2000).

- **Threatened someone.** *Comm. v. Lauture,* 2013 WL 5707877 (Appeals Court) (unidentified caller's panicked tone of voice described a suspect with "long dreads about to shoot someone!" Caller's excited tip indicated an immediate threat).

- **On-street sale.** *Comm. v. Rupp,* 57 Mass. App. Ct. 377 (2003) (caller identified two men at night engaging in an on-street gun sale).

- **Gun typically used in crime.** *Comm. v. Alvarado,* 427 Mass. 277 (1998): Although, at the time, it was possible to legally possess a sawed-off shotgun (the law has since changed), the SJC still concluded that officers properly stopped and frisked the suspect because of the likely connection between a sawed-off weapon and crime. Other weapons may justify a police stop based on their lethal character (e.g., assault weapons).

- **Gun connected with crime.** *Comm. v. Anderson,* 366 Mass. 394 (1974) (anonymous note identified a man on a bus with a bag containing a gun and narcotics).

- **Impaired.** Even properly licensed owners cannot ever carry a loaded gun in public while under the influence. 269, § 10H.

---

1 While one can persuasively argue that it is statistically likely that a citizen with a concealed firearm in public is unlicensed, this view has never been accepted. *Comm. v. Alvarado,* 423 Mass. 266 (1996).

- **Threat to public safety.** *Comm. v. Johnson*, 36 Mass. App. Ct. 336 (1994) (report of woman in residential neighborhood carrying gun in her purse; officer observed defendant in the street shouting obscenities at a man).

Approach Safely / Secure Weapon / Demand License

140, § 129C requires citizens to produce their license on demand: "Any person . . . shall on demand of a . . . law enforcement officer, exhibit his [LTC] or [FID] . . . [or explain his exempt status] . . . Upon failure to do so such person may be required to surrender to such officer said firearm, rifle or shotgun which shall be taken . . . [and] returned forthwith upon presentation within thirty days of [the proper license]."

No Miranda necessary when officer orders suspect to produce a license. *Comm. v. Haskell*, 438 Mass. 790 (2003) held that *Miranda* warnings are not required when an officer demands physical evidence. However, demanding that a suspect produce his firearms license invites him to reach into his pockets or glove compartment, which is dangerous. The best approach for officers is to give verbal direction: "Don't move. Just tell me where your license is located so I can get it myself." (At this point, the suspect should indicate where it is or, more likely, admit that he does not have a license.)

The burden is on the suspect to prove that he has a valid license. 278, § 7. This is true even though the government has access to the State Firearms Records Bureau. For this reason, police should confiscate a gun when they are in doubt about whether the suspect lawfully possesses it. *Comm. v. Eberhart*, 461 Mass. 809 (2012).

Lack of gun knowledge no defense. For example, police do not have to show that the suspect knew, in the case of a shotgun, that the permitted barrel length is 18 inches. *Comm. v. O'Connell*, 432 Mass. 657 (2000) (defendant's claim rejected that he did not know his shotgun barrel measured 17¾ inches). *Comm. v. Kang*, 91 Mass. App. Ct. 182 (2016) (fact that defendant thought his firearm was an exempt antique was irrelevant).

FIREARMS LICENSING

Massachusetts issues the Firearms Identification Card (FID) and the License to Carry (LTC). The FID allows possession of rifles and shotguns in public. The LTC allows the same, but also permits carrying a firearm (aka a handgun) in public.

FIDs and LTCs are issued to Massachusetts residents by a city or town licensing authority (LA). The LA (usually the police chief or designee) accepts applications for FIDs (140, § 129B) and LTCs (140, § 131). An applicant must be at least 15 years old to receive an FID or 21 to receive an LTC.

The LA may not consider whether an applicant has a proper purpose for carrying. The Second Amendment permits a law-abiding citizen to carry for self-defense. The government may not consider whether the citizen "needs" to carry. Six states, including Massachusetts, used to deny licenses to applicants who could not provide a persuasive reason for wishing to carry outside their home. *New York State Rifle & Pistol Association v. Bruen, supra*.

Still, the *Bruen* case allows Massachusetts to keep its gun license application process and criteria for qualified owners.

Prohibited person ineligible for license. The applicant's fingerprints are sent to the State Police colonel, who checks state and federal records. The following disqualify an applicant:[2]

- **Massachusetts criminal conviction** for any felony or misdemeanor punishable by more than two years in a house of correction, or concerning weapons or drug possession. (*Note:* An applicant for an FID who was convicted of *certain* of the listed crimes may receive an FID five years after the end of the sentence. An LTC applicant is permanently barred by all these convictions);

- **Out-of-state/federal criminal conviction.** If convicted of a similar crime in another state or a federal court;

- **Court-ordered commitment.** If ever subject to a court-ordered commitment to a hospital or institution because of mental illness, or an alcohol or substance abuse disorder, or currently is the subject of a guardianship or conservatorship;[3]

- **Protection order.** If subject to an active Massachusetts 209A order, harassment prevention order, extreme risk prevention order, or a similar order issued in another state (*Note:* An HPO is *not* a disqualifier for an FID);

- **Dishonorable discharge.** If dishonorably discharged from the military.

Suitability. This final standard is more open-ended.

- **LTC.** The LA *shall* deny an LTC application for suitability if there is credible information the applicant presents a risk of harm to self or others. The applicant may appeal to district court the LA's decision to deny an LTC on this basis.

- **FID.** If the LA has credible information suggesting the applicant presents a risk of harm to self or others, the LA *may* only prevent the issuance of an FID by filing a petition in the district court.

State Police colonel responsible for issuing temporary LTCs to aliens and non-residents. 140, § 131F. The standards are the same.

ADMINISTRATIVE MISCONDUCT

Expiration or Change of Address

Expired FID or LTC. Licenses expire on the date shown. However, if the holder applied to renew *before* the expiration date, his license stays valid until it is approved or denied. Aside from this, active duty military have another extension. Their license remains valid for 180 days after discharge, even if they did not apply for renewal. 140, §§ 129B and 131.

---

[2] If the details are important in a particular situation, consult your department's LA regarding these standards and their exceptions.
[3] *Voluntarily* seeking in-patient evaluation and/or treatment does not, by itself, disqualify the gun license applicant.

If the holder did not apply for renewal but is still qualified for his LTC or FID, officers may *only* confiscate the expired license and guns, and seek a civil fine of NLT $100, NMT $5,000.

On the other hand, a holder should be arrested for unlawful possession if:

- **Currently disqualified from receiving a license** (whether or not he applied to renew); or

- **Renewal application already denied orally or in writing.** The burden is on the defendant to show he qualifies for the renewal exemption. *Comm. v. Harrison*, 100 Mass. 376 (2021). Simply producing the expired license is not enough. *Comm. v. Indrisano*, 87 Mass. App. Ct. 709 (2015). *Comm. v. Farley*, 64 Mass. App. Ct. 854 (2005).

Interestingly, renewal exemptions only apply to guns — not ammunition or large capacity feeding devices. *Comm. v. Phillips*, 2016 WL 6998367 (Appeals Court) (exemption for expired license did not apply to ammunition and feeding devices found in defendant's vehicle).

Failure to notify about change of address. License holders, within 30 days of moving, must send notice (by certified mail) to the: (1) original licensing authority; (2) authority in the new community; and (3) Department of Criminal Justice Information Services (CJIS). Anyone with an FID or LTC – that is invalid for the *sole reason* that he failed to notify authorities about a change of address – is subject to a civil fine only. Officers should confiscate any license and guns and notify the licensing authority.

Revocation/Suspension Process

The LA may use MIRCS (Massachusetts Instant Records Check System) to suspend/revoke an LTC or FID. The LA can check over a dozen reasons for the license action (e.g., restraining order or conviction for a disqualifying crime), including *"unsuitability,"* which means the applicant or license holder presents a credible risk of harm to self or others. MIRCS generates a letter notifying the licensee and requiring that he surrender his guns and ammunition to the police where he resides. See *Nichols v. Chief of Natick,* 94 Mass. App. Ct. 739 (2019) (drug addiction causes unsuitability). *Chief of Taunton v. Caras*, 95 Mass. App. Ct. 182 (2019) (leaving unlocked gun where family member addicted to drugs could steal it showed unsuitability).

LA decides whether to <u>immediately confiscate</u> guns and ammunition. *Comm. v. Adams*, 482 Mass. 514 (2019) held that the LA decides, at the time of revocation/suspension, whether to:

- **Require immediate surrender of the license, firearms, and ammunition.** 140, § 131(f). The fact that the license holder plans to appeal is irrelevant. These items must be surrendered to police "without delay." Failure to do so is a crime under 269, § 10(i)[4]; or

- **Delay confiscation.** The LA may, instead, allow license holders to keep their guns while their appeals are pending in the district court. 140, § 129D.

---

4 The penalty for a 269, 10(i) violation: HC NMT 2½ years; or Fine NMT $1,000.

Police on scene still need legal authority to enter – a warrant, consent, or exigent circumstances – in order to seize the guns. In *Comm. v. Adams*, Adams' suspension was based on a report from the Department of Children and Families (DCF) alleging that he injured his wife in front of their son. This serious misconduct rendered Adams unsuitable to lawfully possess firearms.

Police officers came to Adams' house and properly demanded that he surrender his firearms, ammunition, and license immediately. His failure to do so could properly be charged under 269, § 10(i).[5]

However, the fact that Adams refused to allow police to enter his home was a separate constitutional issue. At that point, police lacked consent to enter. They also did not have exigent circumstances. Adams and his wife could have been ordered to remain outside while police secured the home and applied for a search warrant.

Administrative suspension by LA is far more efficient than an Extreme Risk Protection Order (ERPO). The ERPO process (known as the red flag law) is cumbersome and offers no advantage over administrative revocation/suspension under 140, § 131(f). See 140, § 131X (existence of ERPO does not limit, in any way, LA's revocation/suspension powers). If interested in ERPO procedures, see 140, §§ 131R–131V.

CRIMINAL CASES

Types of Crimes

Possession of a gun, feeding device, or ammunition without a proper license or legal exemption. The following situations are covered:

- **Chart 1** applies to Massachusetts citizens.
- **Chart 2** outlines applicable exemptions in Massachusetts.
- **Chart 3** outlines the requirements for nonresidents and aliens.
- **Chart 4** outlines a variety of specialized gun offenses, including improper storage, carrying a rifle or shotgun on a public way, trafficking, and more.

Unlawful possession _and_ improper storage may both be charged. *Comm. v. Richardi*, 2013 WL 1435155 (Appeals Court) (gun found outside a vehicle after an OUI accident was not in a locked box or container; therefore, the defendant committed the crimes of possessing a firearm while intoxicated and improper storage of a firearm).

Each period of possession is a separate charge. *Comm. v. Horne*, 466 Mass. 440 (2013) (defendant possessed rifle when he confronted a man in the street; after he returned home with the rifle, he went back outside again with it; he was properly charged with two counts of unlawful possession).

---

5 At that point, officers could have removed him from the scene and applied for a criminal complaint or, if deciding that the defendant committed a breach of peace in their presence, arrested him for this misdemeanor.

Proof of Constructive Possession

There must be proof that the suspect <u>knew</u> about the gun, <u>intended</u> to possess it, and had the ability to physically <u>control</u> it. Consider:

- *Comm. v. Jefferson*, 461 Mass. 821 (2012): Police pulled over a vehicle for a red light violation. As officers got out of their cruiser, the vehicle raced away. Officers gave chase. The vehicle made a wide left turn, which caused the officers to lose sight of it briefly. Several blocks later, the vehicle stopped. The front passenger window was rolled down even though it was really cold. Police retraced the path of the chase and found a firearm, with broken pieces from the handle, in the middle of a walkway next to a house where the vehicle made the turn. The landing point was consistent with the gun having been thrown from the passenger window. There were no pedestrians and the homeowner had never seen the gun before.

- *Comm v. Woods*, 94 Mass.App.Ct. 761 (2019): A fugitive broke into an upstairs neighbor's apartment in order to hide from a task force entering his apartment. Police found a gun hidden in a child's blue kick ball in the victim's apartment near the door forced open by the defendant. The victim did not have children or toys, but the defendant had a child and toys in his apartment. The victim denied the ball belonged to her. Finally, an empty holster in the defendant's apartment fit the gun.

- *Comm. v. Obiora*, 83 Mass. App. Ct. 55 (2013) (firearm was wedged in plain view between the suspect's seat and center console; ammo found under his seat, where he had been seen "shuffling" around; car belonged to his girlfriend, but he had the vehicle for 24 hours).

- *Comm. v. Lucido*, 18 Mass. App. Ct. 941 (1984) (gun found in locked glove compartment next to suspect's personal letters; suspect had the key).

- *Comm. v. Reed*, 2016 WL 3144255 (Appeals Court) (as police approached car, passenger got out and walked away, saying "I can't go to jail"; gun found near where he had been sitting).

- *Comm. v. Duncan*, 71 Mass. App. Ct. 150 (2008) (officers arrived within 40 seconds of a call reporting gunshots; defendants were huddled behind a fence and quickly walked away; officers found two guns in a trash barrel by the fence; the guns were hot and dry, even though everything else was wet from rain).

Suspect may appear with firearm in social media post. *Comm. v. Watkins*, 98 Mass. App. Ct. 419 (2020): Officers monitoring the Snapchat account of Josiah Watkins watched a selfie style video posted on May 8 in which Watkins brandished a TEC-9 with the magazine detached. A subsequent video showed Watkins with Luis Santos. Santos was sitting on a bed loading a magazine into a TEC-9. A search warrant for Santos' home led to the seizure of a TEC-9 and magazine. Based on the eight-to-ten second Snapchat video, Watkins was also convicted of unlawful possession.

Fingerprint evidence occasionally links a gun to a suspect. *Comm. v. Evans*, 2015 WL 7289467 (Appeals Court) (trooper allowed to testify about the low rate of fingerprint recovery from firearms to explain why a recovered pistol had no identifiable fingerprints).

Example of insufficient evidence of gun possession. *Comm. v. Ferreira*, 2019 WL 237380 (Appeals Court): Michael Ferreira was riding in the passenger seat of a vehicle stopped for a traffic violation. The stop led to the female driver's arrest for OUI. The trooper called for a tow truck and conducted an inventory of the vehicle. He discovered a folded sweatshirt in the backseat with a firearm wrapped inside. The firearm was behind Ferreira's seat and wrapped in a sweatshirt similar to, but larger than, the sweatshirt the female driver had been wearing.

It was speculation that Ferreira wrapped the firearm in his sweatshirt upon seeing police and placed it behind his seat. There was no evidence linking him to the sweatshirt, plus there were other random items in the backseat, including mismatched slippers and assorted debris. Also see *Comm. v. Romero*, 464 Mass. 648 (2013).

The suspect does not have to exercise exclusive control over the gun to unlawfully possess it. *Comm. v. Pecararo*, 2014 WL 2719832 (Appeals Court) (six firearms were in an unlocked safe in the defendant's bedroom, along with his Social Security card and expired license; defendant could still be convicted of unlawful possession of those guns even though the owner of the house was a gun collector with an LTC). *Comm. v. Vick*, 2015 WL 3540467 (Appeals Court) (incarcerated defendant constructively possessed a gun hidden on his father's property because he was able to control it through an agent — his father).

An accomplice is guilty of unlawful possession if his co-defendant failed to have an LTC. *Comm. v. Gonzalez*, 68 Mass. App. Ct. 91 (2007): Ricardo Gonzalez led a marijuana dealer to a vacant apartment where another man tried to rob him at gunpoint. The dealer was shot. Gonzalez was charged, as an accomplice, with unlawful possession of a firearm. He argued that he should not be held responsible for the fact that the principal did not have an LTC. The Appeals Court said: "When participating in a crime with [another person], the defendant assumes the risk that his armed accomplice does not have a proper license." *Comm. v. Humphries*, 465 Mass. 762 (2013) (if the defendant claims before trial that his accomplice had a valid LTC, then the Commonwealth must prove the accomplice was unlicensed).

Other charges may still apply even if unlawful gun possession does not. *Comm. v. Lovering*, 89 Mass. App. Ct. 76 (2016): Albert Lovering's wife found a loaded handgun while cleaning the apartment she shared with Lovering for 12 years. Lovering had moved out a month earlier because his wife got a restraining order. The gun was found among Lovering's personal belongings, inside a leather pouch in a box on the floor.

- **There was no constructive possession.** While there was sufficient evidence that Lovering had knowledge of the firearm, he did not have the ability to control it. He no longer lived in the apartment and had not been near the gun for a month. There was no evidence as to when, if ever, he might return to the apartment.

- **There were storage and 209A violations.** Even though he did not constructively possess the firearm, there was sufficient evidence that Lovering owned it. The wife told police it was his gun; it was among his other possessions; he had lived there for 12 years; and he collected similar Nazi memorabilia. As a result, Lovering violated the gun storage statute by not keeping it secured, and the 209A order by failing to surrender it.

Proof of Firearm

A ballistics certificate is no longer sufficient, by itself, to prove that the gun is operational. Comm. v. Hollister, 75 Mass. App. Ct. 729 (2009).

6 ways to prove a "working" firearm, rifle, or shotgun.

- *Most persuasive:* **Ballistics testimony.** The most effective proof is testimony from the ballistician who tested the gun. Comm. v. Pytou Heang, 458 Mass. 827 (2011). However, "expert testimony is not necessary to determine whether a [particular gun] is a firearm within the meaning of the statute." Comm. v. Muniz, 456 Mass. 166 (2010).

- **Defendant observed firing gun.** Sometimes police recover the firearm. Comm. v. Weeks, 77 Mass. App. Ct. 1 (2010) (defendant was the partygoer who fired into the air two times; his gun was later found in a snow bank, still loaded with live and spent shells).

- **Even if the gun is not recovered, a witness' testimony may prove it was operational.** Comm. v. Housewright, 470 Mass. 665 (2015) (witness saw defendant point a gun at him, struggle with it after it misfired, break it open to extract two shells, load it again, and fire it at him; witness saw a flash come out of the barrel and heard a big noise).

- **Recovered gun has a "spent" cartridge.** Comm. v. Depina, 456 Mass. 238 (2010) (officers photographed the gun on the ground prior to collecting it; the picture proved that its barrel was within the legal length of a firearm; a sergeant testified that the recovered firearm had four live rounds of .22 caliber ammunition and one spent casing; "the compelling inference . . . is that the spent casing found by [the officer] in the revolver remained after the discharge of a bullet").

- **Police expert "dry-fired" gun.** Comm. v. Heslin, 2012 WL 537619 (Appeals Court): Even though it was not test-fired, evidence established that the rifle possessed was operable. A certified instructor/firearms expert dry-fired the rifle several times, and (1) observed it was clean and well lubricated; (2) heard the firing pin hit; and (3) observed no apparent defect rendering it inoperable.

- **Arresting officer fired gun.** In case the ballistician is unavailable for court, some departments have the arresting officer take the defendant's gun to a range, fire it, and document the results in a supplemental report. This is an effective backup strategy — provided, for safety's sake, the gun is examined by a certified ballistician initially!

- **Owner testified he fired gun** — but a claim that the dealer said the gun worked, without more, is insufficient. Comm. v. Drapaniotis, 89 Mass. App. Ct. 267 (2016).

Caution: Testimony about gun's appearance <u>and/or</u> test-firing process insufficient. Comm. v. Barbosa, 461 Mass. 431 (2012) reminded officers that their testimony that a firearm "appears authentic" and "in working order" is insufficient. Officers were also warned that they may no longer rely on hearsay testimony about the test firing process (e.g., "I submitted the firearm to the lab with three live rounds, and it was returned to me with two live rounds and one spent cartridge").

Gun still operational if it can be easily fixed to fire. *Comm. v. Nattoo*, 2011 WL 2554277 (Appeals Court) (defendant's jammed weapon had a broken firing pin and a missing extractor, but the pin could be easily repaired and the lack of an extractor only meant the gun had to be fired one bullet at a time). *Comm. v. Jefferson*, 461 Mass. 821 (2012).

The issue is not whether the gun is operational now, but whether it could fire <u>at the time of the offense</u>. *Comm. v. Figueroa*, 2017 WL 936243 (Appeals Court) (gun was seriously damaged after being thrown out the window during a police chase; this did not suggest that it was inoperable before it was thrown).

Proof is not required that the defendant knew the gun worked. *Comm. v. Marrero*, 484 Mass. 341 (2020): It is not necessary to prove the defendant knew the weapon could fire a shot. It is enough to show the defendant "[knew] the instrument [was] a firearm within the generally accepted meaning of the term."

Proof of Knowledge Gun was Loaded

Gun, feeding device, and ammunition may be three separate charges. *Comm. v. Mazzantini*, 74 Mass. App. Ct. 915 (2009).

<u>Or</u> the suspect may be charged with an enhanced penalty for a loaded gun. 269, § 10(n) sets out an additional penalty of NMT 2½ yrs in HC or SP for the unlawful possession of a *loaded* firearm, sawed-off shotgun, or machine gun. The sentence must be served "from and after" the underlying possession offense. To be considered loaded, ammunition must be inside the weapon or an attached feeding device.

Officers may *not* charge this offense *and* unlawful possession of ammunition under 269, § 10(h) if all the ammo was loaded in the gun. It is double jeopardy to charge someone with two crimes covering the *exact same* conduct. *Comm. v. Johnson*, 461 Mass. 44 (2011).

Finally, to prove a § 10(n) violation, police must show the defendant *knew* his gun was loaded. *Comm. v. Brown*, 479 Mass. 600 (2018).

- **The loaded status of a firearm may be obvious if the ammunition can be seen.** *Comm. v. Silvelo*, 96 Mass. App. Ct. 85 (2019) ("[T]he firearm... is a revolver, and . . . the bullets in the cylinder were clearly visible").

- **The defendant's fingerprints were on the loaded magazine.** *Comm. v. Martinez*, 2019 WL 2171935 (Appeals Court).

- **Firearm was carried on the person.** *Comm. v. Resende*, 94 Mass. App. Ct. 194 (2018) (pistol found in defendant's waistband). *Comm. v. Silvelo*, 486 Mass. 13 (2020) (pistol in defendant's pocket). Though courts say it is reasonable to infer people check the status of a firearm carried on their person, this factor alone is not enough! See *Comm. v. Grayson*, 96 Mass. App. Ct. 748 (2019) (though carried in the waistband, the firearm was tied in a sock and not ready for immediate use).

- **Firearm "ready for use."** *Comm. v. Resende, supra.* (defendant issued threats that mentioned his firearm). *Comm. v. Cooper*, 97 Mass. App. Ct. 772 (2019) (defendant slept in park with the pistol tucked into his armpit).

- **Firearm used as a weapon.** *Comm. v. McGrail*, 2020 WL 1933661 (Appeals Court) (defendant placed muzzle of pistol against the victim's neck and said, "Let it happen").

- **Defendant's statements show knowledge of firearms.** *Comm. v. Resende, supra.* (defendant admitted he had familiarity with firearms, which indicated both his ability and interest to find out if the weapon was loaded).

- **Statements in response to police questions.** Although officers may ask directly, "Is this loaded?" after providing *Miranda* warnings, less direct approaches will have more success, such as "What kind of gun is this?" "How do you unload this?" Or, to show the defendant knew the weapon was high capacity, "How many bullets does this magazine hold?"

Proof of Ammunition

Proof of ammunition. Ammunition is defined by 269, § 10(o) as "cartridges or cartridge cases, primers (igniter), bullets or propellant powder designed for use in any firearm, rifle or shotgun." Unlike gun cases, it is not necessary to prove that the particular ammunition is capable of being fired. Rather, the government only needs to show that the ammunition is "designed for use" in any gun. *Comm. v. Valez*, 82 Mass. App. Ct. 12 (2012) (expert testimony unnecessary; officer's testimony about bullets sufficient).

Cartridge case sufficient. *Comm. v. Truong*, 78 Mass. App. Ct. 28 (2010): After observing bullet holes in cars and shell casings on the street, Lynn police secured the defendant's home and got a search warrant. No guns were found, but police did recover three spent shell casings and a holster near Truong's bed. Although no bullets were found, § 10(o) defines the cartridge case alone as ammunition. Cartridges are illegal because they enable people to construct ammunition. Truong was convicted. At the same time, the Appeals Court wrote that it would not make sense to prosecute a person who possessed "shell casings for innocent purposes, such as for souvenirs or for resale as scrap metal."

Proof of Knowledge Gun was Large Capacity

There must be proof the suspect knew the gun or feeding device was "large capacity" or capable of holding more than 10 bullets or 5 shotgun shells. *Comm. v. Cassidy*, 479 Mass. 527 (2018): John Cassidy purchased AK47 and 9 millimeter pistols in Texas and brought them to Massachusetts two years later — even though his friend told him he needed a Massachusetts license. Dartmouth police officers executed a search warrant at Cassidy's apartment, and he was convicted of unlawful possession of an assault weapon, four large capacity feeding devices, and a large capacity firearm.

Evidence that proved the defendant's knowledge included: his purchase of the guns, length of ownership, firing of the weapons, loading of the magazines, and the obvious length of the feeding devices which were "noticeably larger" than 10-round magazines.

Compare *Comm. v. Resende*, 94 Mass. App. Ct. 194 (2018) (Resende knew his gun was loaded, but there was no proof he knew it was large capacity; the gun was loaded with only one magazine and it did not look obviously large; no evidence showed how long Resende had owned it).

Possession of Gun in Home or Business

140, § 129C requires that citizens have <u>at least</u> an FID to possess a firearm, rifle, or shotgun in their home or business. In fact, a gun dealer may sell a firearm to a person with just an FID and a permit to purchase, *provided* the dealer *delivers* the firearm to the purchaser's home or business. 140, § 131E. *Comm. v. Seay*, 376 Mass 735 (1978). If the issue is raised, the government must prove that the defendant did *not* possess the gun on his property. Citizens may escape the mandatory minimum penalties of 269, § 10, but still be liable under 269, § 10(h). *Comm. v. Loadholt*, 460 Mass. 723 (2011).

- **A home includes all areas over which a defendant has exclusive control.** *Comm. v. Coren*, 437 Mass. 723 (2002) (single family home includes backyard). Compare *Comm. v. McCollum*, 79 Mass. App. Ct. 239 (2011) (defendant's handgun found in his girlfriend's apartment, so "home exemption" inapplicable; his girlfriend said he stayed there "occasionally," and he told police the apartment "belong[s] to the mother of [my] child").

- **It must be the suspect's business, *not* simply his workplace.** A shop owner may keep a gun under the cash register, but the gas station attendant may not bring a gun to work. *Comm. v. Belding*, 42 Mass. App. Ct. 435 (1997) (landlord of a three-family home could not claim it as his "place of business" and carry a firearm into his tenant's apartment).

Chart 1: Gun & Ammunition Possession[i] Offenses in Massachusetts

Type of Weapon	Definition In 140, § 121 unless noted	Right of Arrest (ROA)	Citation	Proper Licenses & Exemptions
Firearm	(1) A pistol or other weapon, *loaded or unloaded*; (2) that can discharge a shot or bullet; and (3) has a barrel or barrels less than 16" in length, or 18" for shotgun *as originally manufactured*.	Felony	269, § 10(a)	• *Public*: LTC; exempt[ii]. • *Home or business*: LTC; exempt; *or* FID. [But if no license, only charge 269, § 10(h) authorizing warrantless arrest on PC.]
Large Capacity[iii] **Firearm**	(1) Semiautomatic; and (2) capable of or readily modified to accept any detachable large capacity feeding device for more than 10 rounds of ammunition.	Felony	269, § 10(m)	• *Public*: LTC • *Home or business*: LTC or FID. [But if no license, only charge 269, § 10(h) authorizing warrantless arrest on PC.]
Rifle	A rifled bore & barrel length equal to or greater than 16", capable of discharging a shot or bullet for each pull of the trigger.	Felony	269, § 10(a)	• *Public*: LTC; FID; exempt. • *Home or business*: Same. [But if no license, only charge 269, § 10(h) authorizing warrantless arrest on PC.]

i Possession is sufficient for guilt; the law no longer requires proof that the suspect carried the gun. *Comm. v. Cornelius*, 78 Mass. App. Ct. 429 (2010).
ii See list of exemptions in discussion of 140, § 129C in *Chart 2* and, concerning nonresidents, *Chart 3*.
iii The term "large capacity weapon" is a secondary designation in addition to the gun's primary designation of firearm, rifle, or shotgun. Under 140, § 131¾, the Secretary of Public Safety and Security publishes a roster of large capacity rifles, shotguns, firearms, and feeding devices.

Weapon	Definition	ROA	Citation	Proper Licenses & Exemptions
Shotgun (SG)	Smooth bore & barrel length equal to or greater than 18", with an overall length equal to or greater than 26", capable of discharging a shot for each pull of the trigger.	Felony	269, § 10(a)	• *Public*: LTC; FID; exempt. • *Home or business*: Same. [But if no license, only charge 269, § 10(h) authorizing warrantless arrest on PC.]
Large Capacity Rifle	(1) Semiautomatic; and (2) capable of accepting any large capacity feeding device of more than 10 rounds.	Felony	269, § 10(m)	*Public, home, or business*: LTC.
Large Capacity Shotgun	(1) Semiautomatic; and (2) capable of accepting any large capacity feeding device of more than 5 rounds.	Felony	269, § 10(m)	*Public, home, or business*: LTC.
Sawed-off Shotgun	A modified shotgun with one or more barrels less than 18" long, *or* overall length of less than 26".	Felony	269, § 10(c)	No justification or license for possession.
Machine Gun	Any weapon, *loaded or unloaded*, from which a number of bullets may be automatically discharged by one trigger activation.	Felony	269, § 10(c)	*Public, home, or business*: Machine Gun License (MGL) only. [*Note*: Only law enforcement instructors or special personnel, or *bona fide* collectors eligible to receive MGL.]
Bump Stock	Any device for a weapon that increases the rate of fire achievable by using the energy from the recoil of the weapon to generate a reciprocating action that facilitates repeated activation of the trigger.	Felony	269, § 10(c)	No justification or license for possession. 140, § 131(o).

Trigger Crank	Any device to be attached to a weapon that repeatedly activates the trigger of the weapon through the use of a lever or other part that is turned in a circular motion; does not include any weapon initially designed and manufactured to fire through the use of a crank or lever.	Felony	269, § 10(c)	No justification or license for possession. 140, § 131(o).
Covert Weapon	140, § 131N: Any weapon capable of discharging a shot in a shape that does not resemble a handgun, rifle, or shotgun (including, but not limited to, key-chains, pens, cigarette lighters, or packages); *or* not detectable by x-ray machines or metal detectors as a weapon.	Felony	140, § 131N	No justification or license for possession.
Stun Gun	Stun gun is a firearm under 140, § 121, and defined as "a portable device or weapon, regardless of whether it passes an electrical shock by means of a dart or projectile via a wire lead, from which an electrical current, impulse, wave, or beam . . . is designed to incapacitate temporarily, injure, or kill."	Felony	269, § 10(a)	Any citizen who possesses a stun gun without an LTC (or exemption under 140, § 129C) commits unlawful possession of a firearm. Some officers are choosing, in appropriate cases, to seize the stun gun and apply for a criminal complaint. To get an LTC for a stun gun the applicant does not have to take a firearms safety course.

Weapon	Definition	ROA	Citation	Proper Licenses & Exemptions
BB, Air or CO2 Gun	A weapon that expels a light projectile by means of pneumatic power or pressurized gas. "Airsoft" and paintball guns included. [*Note*: No one except a parent, guardian, or authorized instructor may furnish or sell these guns to a minor. 269, § 12A. Confiscate & complaint.]	Confiscate & Complaint	269, § 12B	*Public*: • Person 18 and over may possess without any license. *Comm. v. Rhodes*, 389 Mass. 641 (1983); or • Minor under 18 must either: (1) be accompanied by an adult, or (2) have a sporting license and permit from local police chief; and • No one may discharge over public way. *Private*: No license required, regardless of age, if gun possessed in private place and not discharged. 269, § 12B.
Large Capacity Feeding Device	A fixed or detachable magazine, box, drum, feed strip, or device capable of accepting, or readily converted to accept, more than 10 rounds of ammunition or more than 5 shotgun shells. (*Not* including a tubular device for only .22 caliber ammunition).	Felony	269, § 10(m)	*Public*: LTC. *Home or business*: LTC; FID with permit to purchase for device related to gun in permit is sufficient under 140, § 131E. *Exemption*: LC magazines lawfully possessed before 9/13/94 are legal.
Silencer	269, §10A: Any instrument or attachment for causing the firing noise of any gun to be silenced, lessened, or muffled.	Felony	269, § 10A	Possession *only* by federal firearms manufacturer, Mass. training council, or law enforcement officer acting under direct authorization of chief, designee, or colonel.

Ammunition	Cartridges or cases, primers (igniter), bullets or propellant powder designed for any firearm, rifle, or shotgun.	269, § 10(h)	269, § 10(h) warrantless on PC	*Public, home or business:* LTC; FID; exempt. *Comm. v. Truong,* 78 Mass. App. Ct. 28 (2010) (empty cartridge case sufficient for conviction; but do not charge for obvious souvenirs).

Self-Defense Spray	**Purchase and possess Self-Defense Spray (SDS).** All citizens age 18 and over may purchase and possess SDS, which is defined as Mace, OC, or another incapacitating substance. They do not need *any* type of license. 140, § 122C. **Exceptions to general rule of lawful possession:** • Citizens disqualified from receiving an FID card may not purchase or possess SDS. 140, § 122D. Factors are: (1) disqualifying criminal record (any felony; drug crime; 2-year misdemeanor — although, unless violent crime or drug trafficking, a 5-year window since last misdemeanor reinstates one's ability to have SDS); (2) confined for mental illness; (3) in recovery or previously confined for an alcohol or substance abuse disorder; (4) younger than 15; (5) an alien with no permanent residence or proper visa; (6) subject of a domestic violence or harassment prevention order; or (7) subject of an arrest warrant. Penalty: HC NMT 2 yrs; and/or Fine NMT $1,000. Right of Arrest: Complaint. *Note:* Officers will usually not know whether someone they encounter with SDS is legally disqualified unless they run a record check, or they may find out post-arrest for some other crime (in which case they can simply add this charge). • Citizens who are age 15, 16, or 17 may only purchase or possess SDS if they have a valid FID card (which they cannot get without parental permission). If a child age 15, 16, or 17 possesses SDS without an FID card: Penalty: Fine NMT $300. Right of Arrest: Complaint. **Sale of SDS.** Under 140, § 122C: • SDS may *only* be sold by a licensed ammunition dealer (see 140, § 122B). Penalty: HC NMT 2 yrs; or Fine NMT $1,000. Right of Arrest: Complaint. • Sale of SDS to person under 18 without an FID card. Penalty: Fine NMT $300. Right of Arrest: Complaint. *Note:* Clearly, this charge should only appear by itself when directed at a lawful dealer who sells to someone under 18. If a nondealer sells to someone under 18, then always apply the more serious charge above — in addition to this one.

CHART 2: EXEMPTIONS TO LICENSE REQUIREMENTS

State Exemptions

140, § 129C sets forth exemptions to gun licensing. The following are exempt:

- **Imitation Firearm** (incapable of discharging a shot or bullet).

- **Signal Device or Industrial Gun** used exclusively for signaling and recommended by the U.S. Coast Guard or Interstate Commerce Commission, or for the firing of stud cartridges, explosive rivets, or similar industrial ammunition. *Comm. v. Sampson*, 383 Mass. 750 (1981) (flare gun exempt from licensing).

- **Federal Firearms Dealers** when necessary for manufacture, display, storage, transport, installation, inspection, or testing.

- **Voluntarily Surrendering Gun** if prior written notice stating the place and approximate time of the surrender has been given to the licensing authority or colonel.

- **Ordinary Shipping** of firearms, rifles, or shotguns as merchandise by any common carrier.

- **Target Concessions** by retail customers at duly licensed target concessions provided that the guns are firmly chained to the counter and the proprietor possesses an FID or LTC.

- **Under 15 Years Old & Under Immediate Supervision** for hunting or target shooting. Immediate supervision must be provided by FID or LTC holder, or member of the military while in the performance of duty. (140, § 130½ also states that parents or guardians may allow their minor to use a firearm, rifle, or shotgun under supervision).

- **For Film, TV, or Stage Production** if under immediate supervision of an FID or LTC (*same exemption in* 140, § 131F½).

- **Temporary Instruction, Examination, or Firing** in the presence of LTC (for firearms) or FID (for rifles or shotguns).

- **Transfer to Heir, 180-Day Grace Period** provided that the recipient shall, within 180 days of the transfer, obtain an FID or LTC if not otherwise exempt. The recipient may be granted an extension by the licensing authority.

- **U.S. Military or Police** of any jurisdiction, in the performance of their official duty or when duly authorized.

- **Black Powder Rifles, Shotguns, & Ammunition** being carried or possessed by residents or nonresidents.

- **Official Veterans Organizations** and their members during official parades or ceremonies.

- **Museums** and institutional collections open to the public, provided guns are unloaded and secured from unauthorized handling.

- **Bank Collateral** for a secured transaction or following a default on a commercial transaction.

140, § 121 antique exemption. *Comm. v. Jefferson*, 461 Mass. 821 (2012) held that citizens are exempt for guns *manufactured* before 1900. Many guns designed in the 1800s are still manufactured — e.g., the Winchester 1894 Rifle and Colt "Peacemaker" 1873 Revolver. Again, these guns may have been designed before 1900, but they are not exempt unless they were *manufactured* before 1900. Officers are advised to:[6]

- **Check whether gun loaded.** While citizens do not need an LTC for an antique firearm, they usually need an FID in order to possess ammunition. Officers may arrest for unlawful possession of ammo under 269, § 10(h). On the other hand, if a suspect has an FID *or* if there is no ammunition in the gun or on his person, officers are advised to:[7]

- **Seize gun as evidence and avoid making an arrest.**

- **Research serial number.** Information on manufacturing dates may be obtained on the internet from many arms manufacturers.

- **Apply for complaint or return gun.** If the gun was improperly possessed without an LTC because it was manufactured after 1900, then apply for a criminal complaint. Conversely, if the gun is exempt, it should be returned to the suspect since it is not illegal.

Critical limitation to exemptions. Regardless of the exemption, nothing permits the sale or transfer of any <u>large capacity</u> firearm, rifle, shotgun, or large capacity feeding device to any person not in possession of an LTC.

Federal Exemption

Traveling from state to state. Federal law, 18 U.S.C. § 926A, allows a person to transport a firearm and ammunition through various states, provided that the traveler is licensed to carry a firearm in *both* the state of origin and the state of destination. In addition, the firearm must not be accessible during transport. *Comm. v. Harris*, 481 Mass. 767 (2019) (defendant not helped by federal law because, while he was licensed properly in his state of origin, New Hampshire, he did not have an LTC for Massachusetts, his destination state; as a result, he was guilty of unlawful possession of a firearm at his apartment in Tewksbury).

Reporting Loss or Theft of Gun

140, § 129C mandates that any loss, theft, or recovery of any firearm, rifle, shotgun, or machine gun be reported "forthwith" (i.e., immediately) to the CJIS *and* the licensing authority. Failure to report shall result in suspension or permanent revocation of the person's license and a fine. Right of Arrest: Complaint.

Related Offense

Possession of a Forged or Altered Firearms License. 140, § 131I (Felony).

---

[6] If there is another basis to make an arrest, officers may simply rely on that (e.g., the person was trespassing or engaged in a felonious assault at the time of the incident).
[7] In rare cases, the ammunition itself may be exempt. 140, § 129C (black powder and the related ammunition, such as musket balls, are exempt from licensing requirements).

CHART 3: NONRESIDENT & ALIEN ELIGIBILITY TO POSSESS GUNS & AMMUNITION

Exemptions for Rifles & Shotguns — 140, § 129C

140, § 129C has six exemptions for nonresident possession of rifles, shotguns, and ammunition in Massachusetts. The nonresident must:

- **Meet the requirements of the state where he lives;** or

- **Have a valid nonresident hunting license during hunting season;** or

- **Be at a shooting range;** or

- **Be traveling in or through Mass. with his guns unloaded and enclosed in a container.** *Comm. v. Lee*, 10 Mass. App. Ct. 518 (1980) (gun does not have to be enclosed in a gun case, so long as it is stored in any suitable container); or

- **Be at firearms display organized by an existing gun collectors' club;** or

- **Be 18 or older when acquiring a rifle or shotgun** from a licensed firearms dealer, provided that he holds a valid firearms license from his state of residence, and that the licensing requirements of his state are as stringent as the Commonwealth's for an FID (qualifying states appear on a list published annually by the State Police colonel).

No exemptions for aliens.

Important note: For the purpose of firearms law, lawful permanent residents (aka Green Card holders) are considered Massachusetts residents, *not* aliens. They are eligible to apply for resident LTCs and FIDs. *Fletcher v. Haas*, 851 F.Supp.2d 287 (D.Mass. 2012).

Exemptions for Firearms — 140, § 129C

60-day grace period. Any new resident; or any resident absent from state for NLT 180 consecutive days; or any resident released from active service from U.S. military, may possess, *but not carry in public,* firearms, rifles, shotguns, and ammunition for 60 days.

- **Resident is more permanent than visitor.** *Comm. v. Paul*, 96 Mass. App. Ct. 263 (2019) (trooper found James Paul walking on a highway with a loaded gun in his backpack; Paul said he was meeting a friend and traveling on to Michigan; he was not a new resident because he did not intend to live in Massachusetts for any amount of time; he was guilty of unlawful possession of firearm and not exempt under 129C).

- **Large capacity not covered.** *Comm. v. Cornelius*, 78 Mass. App. Ct. 429 (2010) (defendant entitled to exemption as a new resident visiting girlfriend, but excused only for possession of handgun, shotgun, and rifle in his car; he was not exempt for large capacity gun).

- **License from other state not covered.** Although a suspect has a valid firearms license from another state, he has only 60 days, from the time he also becomes a Massachusetts resident, to get an LTC for here. Otherwise, he unlawfully possesses his firearm when in Massachusetts. For the purpose of our gun laws, a citizen may be a resident of more than one state. *Comm. v. Harris,* 481 Mass. 767 (2019) (abusive defendant lived in New Hampshire and got a gun license there; he moved into a Tewksbury apartment with his girlfriend for about five months when police arrived and discovered his Glock in his car, based on a tip from his terrified girlfriend; defendant admitted he did not have a Massachusetts LTC; he had been a resident for well over 60 days).

No exemptions for aliens.

Exemptions for Firearms — 140, § 131G

Properly licensed for exhibition or hunting under 140, § 131G. A nonresident may carry a handgun in or through Mass. in order to take part in a competition, exhibition, collectors' meeting, or hunting excursion, provided that he:

- **Is a U.S. resident;** and

- **Has a valid LTC from another state;** and

- **Has, if his purpose is to hunt, a license** issued by the place where he intends to hunt.

Law enforcement under § 131G. Nonresident law enforcement officers may carry firearms in Mass. [*Note:* 18 U.S.C. §§ 926B and 926C allow properly licensed officers and retired officers to carry concealed in all 50 states.]

No exemption for aliens.

Alien FID Card — 140, § 131H

No temporary FID for rifles and shotguns is available for nonresidents because there are so many exemptions.

Alien FID under 140, § 131H. The colonel may issue an FID to an alien for a rifle or shotgun. Colonel must notify the chief where alien resides.

Nonresident & Alien LTC — 140, § 131F

Same eligibility standards for aliens & nonresidents. A temporary LTC may be issued by the colonel to a nonresident or to an alien.

An alien/nonresident LTC is marked as a "temporary license" and is "subject to such terms and conditions as said colonel may deem proper." Moreover, this LTC may not be used to purchase guns in accordance with § 131E.

Purpose & duration of license. Aliens and nonresidents may receive an LTC for firearms competition for 1 year. Only nonresidents may receive an LTC for employment for up to 2 years. Both types of licenses may be renewed.

Right of Arrest

Nonresident Violations:
- Unlawful possession of a firearm, rifle, shotgun, or large capacity gun or feeding device, charge 269, § 10(a), (c), or (m): Felony.
- Unlawful possession of ammunition (including pepper spray), consider it a violation of 269, § 10(h): Warrantless arrest on probable cause.
- Violation of conditions or expiration of license: Confiscate weapon and license and seek administrative revocation through the colonel. [*Note:* This is in keeping with the stated intent of 269, § 10, which states: "No person having in effect a (LTC issued under §§ 131 or 131F) shall be deemed to be in violation of this section."]

Alien Violations:
- Unlawful possession of a rifle, shotgun, or ammunition, consider it a violation of 140, § 131H: warrantless arrest in presence.
- Unlawful possession of a firearm, large capacity gun or feeding device, charge 269, § 10(a), (c), or (m): Felony.
- Violation of conditions or expiration of license:
  - For § 131H FID violation, confiscate any guns and seek revocation of FID through the colonel, and use § 131H warrantless arrest in presence.
  - For § 131F violation, confiscate weapon and license and seek administrative revocation of LTC through the colonel.

Penalty

For violating § 131H: HC NMT 6 months; and Fine NLT $500, NMT $1,000. Any confiscated firearm under this section shall be forfeited.

For violating § 131F: No penalty is provided, which means that officers should use 269, § 10(a), (c), or (m) which carry mandatory penalties when a suspect has no license; but officers must seek administrative revocation when a suspect violates the terms of his LTC.

Chart 4: Specialized Gun Offenses

Type of Violation	Offense Defined	Right of Arrest (ROA)	Citation	Other Issues
ON CAMPUS				
Carrying a Gun on Campus	A person, who is not a law enforcement officer, may not carry a loaded or unloaded gun on an elementary, secondary, or college campus without written authorization.	269, § 10(j) warrantless in presence	269, § 10(j)	10(j) explicitly covers any firearm, rifle, shotgun, BB gun, air gun, or other projectile device. *Comm. v. Sayers*, 438 Mass. 238 (2002). Having a valid LTC or FID is *no defense*. *Comm. v. Whitehead*, 85 Mass. App. Ct. 134 (2014). For unlicensed suspect with gun, charge Unlawful Possession under 269, § 10. 10(j) also forbids other dangerous weapons. Right of Arrest: Complaint. See *LED's Juvenile Law*, Chapter 22 for more.
Failure to Report Campus Violation	Any administrator or faculty member may not knowingly fail to report to law enforcement that an unauthorized person carried a gun or weapon on campus.	Complaint	269, § 10(j)	
UNDER THE INFLUENCE				
Carrying a Firearm While Under the Influence of Liquor or Drugs (FUI)	Person with valid LTC under §§ 131 or 131F may not carry on his person, or have under his control in MV, a loaded firearm, while under the influence of alcohol or drugs. [If suspect unlicensed, simply charge felony unlawful possession under 269, § 10.]	Arrest for breach of peace in presence or Complaint	269, § 10H	Consumption must diminish suspect's ability to carry safely. *Comm. v. Veronneau*, 90 Mass. App. Ct. 477 (2016) (defendant properly convicted of FUI, even though he was acquitted of OUI; unholstered, loaded gun in pocket with safety off was unsafe, but he only registered BT of .07).
Hunting or Target Shooting Under the Influence	No person may hunt or target shoot with any firearm or weapon if under the influence of alcohol or drugs.	131, § 87 warrantless in presence	131, § 62	

DISCHARGING OR PUBLIC CARRYING

Violation	Definition	ROA	Citation	Other Issues
Discharging a Firearm Within 500 Feet of Dwelling or Building in Use	May not discharge a firearm, rifle, or shotgun within 500 feet of a dwelling or other building in use — except with the consent of the owner or legal occupant. *Comm. v. Mendes*, 75 Mass. App. Ct. 390 (2009) ("in use" means any time, not just when shots fired; potential occupants protected around the clock, not only during business hours).	Confiscate and Complaint	269, § 12E	§ 12E not apply to: (1) lawful defense of life and property; (2) police officer on duty; (3) using range with consent of owner or legal occupant; (4) licensed shooting galleries; and (5) blank cartridges for theater or ceremonies. *Comm. v. Stephens*, 67 Mass. App. Ct. 906 (2006) (firing blanks at a person in anger *does* violate § 12E). *Comm. v. Kelly*, 484 Mass. 53, (2020) (because citizens can easily avoid this risky behavior, no intent, knowledge, or even negligence need be proven; firing accidentally is a violation).
Discharging a Firearm on or Near a Highway	May not discharge any firearm or release arrow across or within 150 feet of any highway. A person also may not possess a loaded firearm or "hunt by any means" on another's land within 500 feet of any dwelling in use, unless authorized by owner or occupant.	131, § 87 warrantless in presence	131, § 58	
Carrying Rifle or Shotgun on a Public Way	No person shall carry on any public way either: (1) a loaded rifle or shotgun, which means it has "cartridges or shells in either the magazine or chamber"; or (2) an unloaded rifle or shotgun, unless it is enclosed in a case.	269, § 12D warrantless in presence (felony if large capacity)	269, § 12D	§ 12D does not apply to: (1) law enforcement and any "authorized" military use; (2) hunters validly licensed under Chapter 131; (3) commemorative ceremonies "permitted by law"; or (4) a licensed shooting gallery.

	IN MOTOR VEHICLE		
LTC Restrictions for Certain Guns in Motor Vehicle	No person carrying *loaded* firearm under LTC shall have it in vehicle unless it is under his direct control. No large capacity rifle or shotgun in vehicle under LTC unless unloaded *and* in locked trunk or secure container.	Confiscate and Complaint	140, § 131C	*For firearm:* Max fine $500 & mandatory license revocation for 1 year. *For LC rifle or SG:* Max fine $5,000 & mandatory revocation 1 year. *Exempt:* Law enforcement officers or military personnel if acting within the scope of their official duties.
Loaded Rifle or SG in MV, Boat, or Plane	A properly licensed person may not possess a loaded shotgun or rifle in his vehicle, motorboat, or airplane, *unless* the vehicle or vessel is on land owned or occupied by the gun owner. In the case of a motorboat, a loaded gun may be possessed for "hunting migratory water fowl."	131, § 87 warrantless in presence		Possible jail sentence of 60 days.
	SERIAL NUMBERS			
Possession of Gun with Defaced Serial Number	No person may remove, deface, alter, or mutilate "in any manner" serial number of firearm, rifle or shotgun; or receive gun with knowledge serial number defaced.	Confiscate and Complaint	269, § 11C	Under § 11C, showing the suspect possessed a gun with a defaced serial number is, *without more*, sufficient to prove guilt. No proof needed that the suspect defaced the gun. *Comm. v. Grant*, 57 Mass. App. Ct. 334 (2003). *Comm v. Kante*, 2021 WL 1263109 (Appeals Court) (officers saw suspect place pistol on truck tire, proving possession; no need for evidence that some part of defaced number was visible). *Comm. v. Vick*, 2015 WL 3540467 (Appeals Court) (only the number applied by the manufacturer is the serial number).
Defaced Serial Number during Felony	A gun with a defaced serial number becomes more serious if possessed during the commission of a felony.	Felony	269, § 11B	

Violation	Definition	ROA	Citation	Other Issues
IMPROPER STORAGE				
Improper Storage of Large Capacity Gun	No person may (1) store or keep any gun; (2) in *any* place; (3) unless the weapon is: • In a locked container; or • Equipped with a "properly engaged" safety device; or • Under the control of the license holder or other authorized person. *Comm. v. Patterson*, 79 Mass. App. Ct. 316 (2011) (gun in jacket in bedroom closet with no trigger lock or secure container; defendant's son was sometimes closer to it than he was; for owner to be "in control," gun must be "readily at hand" — i.e., proper person must be able to reach gun immediately). *Comm. v. Cantelli*, 83 Mass. App. Ct. 156 (2013) (unsecure guns in home not within defendant's immediate reach; in addition, his home's "extreme clutter" made access more difficult). *Police officers must secure guns.* *Dealers must secure guns. Goudreau v. Nikas*, 98 Mass. App. Ct. 266 (2020) (pistols without trigger locks stolen by visitor in dealer's storage room; gun dealers should be prosecuted for improper storage).	Felony	140, § 131L	*Gun storage statute constitutional. Comm. v. McGowan*, 464 Mass. 232 (2013) (law not impede right of self-defense because owner can keep unlocked gun under immediate control).
Improper Storage of Any Gun if Someone Under 18 Has Potential Access		Felony *Regardless of the type of gun if access not the result of trespass*	140, § 131L	*Locked home or vehicle is not, by itself, a secure container. Comm. v. Reyes*, 464 Mass. 245 (2013) (vehicle trunk is secure container, not passenger compartment; locked glove box *might* be secure, depending on lock and whether vehicle also locked and alarmed). *Lock must "deter all but the most persistent from gaining access." Comm. v. Parzick*, 64 Mass. App. Ct. 846 (2005) (guns in unlocked closet within locked bedroom not secure — especially given that lock was easily picked). *Comm. v. Mason*, 2019 WL 6340932 (Appeals Court) (grandchildren ages 8 and 4 slept near pull-down stairs to attic where unsecured rifles lay under a blanket).
Improper Storage of Non-Large Capacity Gun or Any Stun Gun		Confiscate and Complaint	140, § 131L	*Gun with safety guard may still be mobile. Comm. v. Lojko*, 77 Mass. App. Ct. 82 (2010) (gun with trigger lock properly stored even though inside "Igloo cooler" in yard). *Exemption.* Storage law does not apply to muskets or other guns manufactured before 1900 or any replicas not firing conventional ammo. *Guns seized with a warrant not forfeited if only charge is improper storage. Comm. v. Fleury*, 489 Mass. 421 (2022).

MISCELLANEOUS			
Commission of Felony While Armed	The suspect possessed, or had under his control, a firearm, rifle, or shotgun (including large capacity and machine gun) while committing or attempting to commit a felony.	Felony	265, § 18B	*Comm. v. Hines*, 449 Mass. 183 (2007) (drug dealer violates this statute if he has a loaded gun near his stash, even though he is not carrying it). *Comm. v. Golding*, 86 Mass. App. Ct. 55 (2014) (exchanging drugs for gun sufficient).
Body Armor During Felony	No one may wear any body armor during the commission of a felony.	Felony	269, § 10D	Body armor is "any protective covering" designed to prevent or deflect "penetration . . . by ammunition, knives or other weapons."
Use of Tear Gas to Commit Crime	No one may use "any device . . . which contains . . . any substance designed to incapacitate for the purpose of committing a crime."	Felony	269, § 10C	
STEALING, B&E, TRANSPORT			
Stealing a Firearm	No one may steal a firearm belonging to another.	Felony	266, § 30	§ 30 makes theft of any firearm a felony regardless of the value of the gun taken.
B&E to Steal Firearm	B&E of building, ship, vessel, or vehicle; at any time of day or night; to steal a firearm. (Also in *Chapter 31*).	Felony	269, § 10J	If injury occurs or crime done to distribute firearm to a prohibited person, max penalty increases to SP NMT 10 yrs. For all violations, vehicle forfeiture for public safety training fund.
B&E Firearms Dealer	B&E; at any time of day or night; into building where firearms retailer, wholesaler or manufacturer conducts business. (Also in *Chapter 31*).	Felony	269, § 10K	*Note:* No need to prove that suspect's intent was to actually steal a gun or ammunition. B&E alone enough for conviction. If offender obtains a gun or ammo and unlawfully distributes it, max penalty increases SP NMT 20 yrs.

Violation	Definition	ROA	Citation	Other Issues
Illegally Transport Gun into Massachusetts	Transport a firearm, rifle, shotgun, or machine gun into Massachusetts unlawfully for purpose of committing a crime.	Felony	269, § 10I	If purpose is to transfer to a prohibited person, max penalty SP NMT 20 yrs. If purpose is to transfer to a prohibited person, and the gun later causes the death of another, SP NLT 20 yrs.
SELL OR TRANSFER				
Gun Trafficking	No one may: (1) within a 12 month period; (2) unlawfully & intentionally; (3) transfer possession of; (4) at least one handgun, rifle, shotgun, or machine gun.	Felony	269, § 10E	Minimum number is 1 transferred gun. Penalty for 1 or 2 guns SP NMT 10 yrs (no mandatory minimum). For 3 to 9 guns in any combination, mandatory SP 5 yrs; 10 or more, mandatory 10.
Assault Weapon Sale	No one may illegally sell or transfer an assault weapon (AW).	Felony	140, § 131M	Under § 131M, possession of AWs by law enforcement permitted; officers do not have to be authorized by their department.
Large Capacity Gun or Feeding Device Sale	No one may illegally sell or transfer a large capacity weapon or large capacity feeding device.	Felony	269, § 10F	
Rifle, Shotgun or Ammunition: Sale to Alien or Minor Under 18	No one may illegally sell or transfer a rifle, shotgun, or ammunition to an alien or a minor under 18.	Felony	140, § 130	
Firearm Sale to Minor Under 21	No one may illegally sell or transfer a firearm to a minor under 21.	Felony	140, § 130	
"Community Gun" (left for criminals)	No one may leave an unattended firearm, rifle, shotgun, or ammunition for an unlicensed person to commit a crime.	Felony	269, § 10(h)	This is in response to offenders who leave a gun in a public location for others to use, especially in urban areas.

18 Dangerous Weapons

CARRYING A DANGEROUS WEAPON
269, § 10(b)

Summary

269, § 10(b) covers two distinct offenses: (1) a person may not carry a *per se* weapon listed in the statute; or (2) a person may not carry a weapon that is not listed — if he is being arrested under a warrant, or without a warrant for a breach of the peace.

Elements

Type 1: Per Se Dangerous Weapon

- **Carry.** The suspect knowingly carried on his person or under his control in a vehicle;

- **Listed weapon.** One of the following weapons:

  - *Knives*: Nine varieties of dangerous knives are prohibited: (1) stilettos; (2) daggers; (3) devices or cases which enable a knife with a locking blade to be drawn at a locked position; (4) ballistic knives; (5) knives with a detachable blade capable of being propelled by any mechanism; (6) dirk knives; (7) double-edged knives; (8) switch knives; and (9) knives with an automatic spring in the handle that releases a blade of over 1½ inches; or

  - *Martial Arts:* Nunchaku, zoobow, also known as klackers or kung fu sticks, or any similar weapon consisting of two sticks of wood, plastic, or metal connected at one end by a rope, chain, or leather; a shuriken or any similar pointed starlike object intended to injure a person when thrown; or any leather armband which has metallic spikes; a cestus or similar material weighted with metal or other substance and worn on the hand, a manrikigusari or similar length of chain having weighted ends; or

  - *Miscellaneous:* A slungshot, a blowgun, a blackjack, metallic knuckles, or knuckles of any substance which could be put to the same use with the same or similar effect as metallic knuckles.

Type 2: Non Per Se Weapon Possessed During Arrest

- **Arrest by warrant or for breach.** The suspect was arrested:

    - On a warrant for an alleged crime; or
    - Without a warrant for a crime involving a breach of the peace; and

- **Carry.** At the time of his arrest, the suspect had on his person or under his control in a vehicle;

- **Non *per se* weapon.** A billy club or other dangerous weapon not specifically mentioned in 269, § 10. [*Note:* This offense is inapplicable to firearms, rifles, shotguns, and all the *per se* weapons mentioned above.]

Right of Arrest

Felony.

Penalty

Basic offense: SP NLT 2½ yrs, NMT 5 yrs or HC NLT 6 months, NMT 2½ yrs.

Reduced penalty: If a court finds that the offender has not been previously convicted of a felony: HC NMT 2½ yrs; or Fine NMT $50.

Subsequent offenses: 269, § 10(d) provides for mandatory penalties if the defendant has been previously convicted of any of the following § 10 offenses: §§ 10(a) (possession of firearm), or 10(b) (possession of dangerous weapon), or 10(c) (possession of machine gun or sawed-off shotgun): SP mandatory minimum incarceration of 5 yrs, NMT 7 yrs; 3rd: SP mandatory 7 yrs.

Notes

Type 1: "Carrying" a per se weapon. 269, § 10(b) prohibits carrying the various items listed in the statute. There is a distinction between possessing a weapon and carrying one. Possession requires control over the item while carrying requires movement. Thus, a person may possess *per se* weapons at his home, office, or other place for legitimate reasons — e.g., a martial arts instructor or knife collector. The crime occurs when one walks or drives around with a prohibited weapon. *Comm. v. Dunphy*, 377 Mass. 453 (1979). *Comm. v. DeJesus*, 2018 WL 5851741 (Appeals Court) (defendant walked in public before dropping brass knuckles behind a parked vehicle when he saw a police officer looking at him).

A per se dangerous weapon is specifically listed in the statute. The laundry list of § 10(b) can be broken down into three categories: knives, martial arts, and miscellaneous.

- **Dirk knife.** *Comm. v. Miller*, 22 Mass. App. Ct. 694 (1986) decided that a dirk knife has a long, straight blade typically over 7". Yet Miller was carrying an oversized version of a pocket knife — with a 5" blade in the closed position. Miller's knife did not share enough of the characteristics of a stabbing weapon to justify conviction.

The court remarked: "Unquestionably if [the defendant's knife] had been discovered open, in the defendant's hand or in his pocket, it could have been deemed to be a dangerous weapon." Thus, how a suspect carries and stores the knife is a key consideration in whether it is considered a stabbing weapon.

The court left room for officer discretion: "It is not our intention to delineate exactly what combination of characteristics defines a dirk-like blade, or state that a 5" blade can never be enough . . . . Other characteristics, such as a blade tapering to a sharpened tip, may indicate that the knife was designed for stabbing."

- **Dagger.** A dagger is also designed for stabbing. In *Comm. v. Garcia*, 82 Mass. App. Ct. 239 (2012), the defendant used what the witness described as a pimp cane (with a thin, 12" blade). He pulled the cover off the cane and stabbed the victim three times. This weapon was not a dirk knife because the blade did not fold into its handle. However, it was a dagger — as shown by the thin blade and extent of the victim's injuries.

- **Double-edged blade.** It is not necessary that the weapon be double-edged along its entire length. In *Comm. v. Smith*, 40 Mass. App. Ct. 770 (1996), the homemade knife found on a prison inmate qualified as a double-edged blade under § 10(b). First, the weapon had a primary purpose of inflicting physical harm on an adversary. Second, the statute covers "any knife," so it did not matter that the metal piece had no clearly marked handle. Third, the sharpened end was double-edged.

- **Knife with locking mechanism not enough by itself.** The knife must have a "device or case" that allows the blade to be drawn in a locked position. *Comm. v. Higgins*, 85 Mass. App. Ct. 534 (2014) (camping knife not a dangerous weapon since there was no evidence of how easily the thumb studs on the knife allowed it to be opened in a locked position).

- **Baton is not blackjack.** *Comm. v. Perry*, 455 Mass. 1010 (2009) (an "expandable baton" of the type carried by police officers is not a *per se* dangerous weapon because it is not specifically listed in the statute and not considered a blackjack).

Local ordinances and bylaws. Courts have suggested re-writing § 10(b). *Comm. v. Miller*, 22 Mass. App. Ct. 694 (1986) ("ideally, the Legislature should provide more specific guidelines").

In the meantime, some municipalities have adopted local laws to fill the gap. A Lynn ordinance[1] forbids a citizen from carrying on his person, or under his control in a vehicle, any knife with a blade longer than 2½" (except for hunting, fishing, or employment). Lynn officers may arrest adult violators.[2] Penalty: Fine $100; $300 if the violation occurs at a park, playground, or school.

The value of this ordinance is that it covers dangerous weapons beyond § 10(b). For example, if Lynn officers stop an adult carrying a buck knife with a 4" blade, they may confiscate the item and arrest the individual. Officers from other municipalities may not have legal recourse because § 10(b) does not prohibit carrying this item.

---

[1] ORD V-7 at lynnpolice.org/announcements/lynn-ordinances/section-v/.
[2] 119 § 52 now prohibits arresting juveniles under 18 for the violation of an ordinance or bylaw. See *LED's Juvenile Law*, Chapter 25.

Type 2: Weapon possessed during arrest. This part of the statute is designed to discourage carrying a weapon that might be used against arresting officers. It applies to arrests involving a warrant or breach of peace.

- **Any warrant, even a default warrant.** *Comm. v. Thompson*, 15 Mass. App. Ct. 974 (1983) (the steak knife found in the defendant's pocketbook had a serrated blade 8" long, which is not a *per se* weapon; however, the officer discovered the knife while arresting the defendant under a default warrant; given the length of the blade and the defendant's statement to police that she carried it for protection, there was sufficient evidence that the knife was dangerous and the defendant knew it).

    The warrant must be the reason for the arrest. *Comm. v. Ford*, 86 Mass. App. Ct. 911 (2014) (after Ford was arrested for a robbery, officers found a knife on his person; when police *later* learned of his outstanding arrest warrants, they could not charge Ford with carrying a dangerous weapon when arrested under a warrant).

- **A breach of peace.** *Comm. v. Molligi*, 70 Mass. App. Ct. 108 (2007): A pedestrian alerted Officer Fenlon at 2:30 a.m. that a man was seen holding a knife. Fenlon saw Douglas Molligi with a knife in his hand in an area of moderate pedestrian traffic from surrounding bars. Molligi darted out in front of Fenlon's cruiser. Fenlon shouted at him to stop. After a short chase, Fenlon told Molligi to put his hands up and drew his weapon. Fenlon handcuffed and searched him, finding a steak knife with a 4" blade. Since Molligi was arrested for disorderly conduct, he was also properly charged with a separate crime under § 10(b) for possessing the knife during his disorderly episode.

- **Insufficient evidence.** *Comm. v. Turner*, 59 Mass. App. Ct. 825 (2003): During a traffic stop at 2:25 a.m. in Boston, Officer Young saw Turner, the front seat passenger, get out of the car and walk away. Turner ignored Young's demand that he return to the vehicle. Young frisked Turner and discovered a closed, black folding knife in his rear pants pocket. Turner was arrested on an outstanding warrant and charged with § 10(b). Turner's knife — a common folding knife with a 3¼" serrated blade — was clearly not a *per se* weapon. The court went on to rule that it did not qualify as a dangerous weapon possessed during an arrest under a warrant. The reason: the knife was folded in the defendant's pocket and never posed a threat of harm. This decision would have been different if Turner had the blade out or was reaching for the knife as the officer approached.

- **Sufficient evidence.** *Comm. v. Bradshaw*, 86 Mass. App. Ct. 74 (2014): Christopher Bradshaw was being investigated for rape. Detective Beth Halloran called and asked him to meet, but truly intended to arrest him. Bradshaw chose the location and asked to meet Halloran alone. For safety reasons, Halloran arranged for three detectives to be close. When Bradshaw arrived, he instructed Halloran to walk with him. When she asked where they were going, he said, "To the train tracks." The other detectives took Bradshaw to the ground and arrested him. An object that was sticking out of his backpack fell to the ground. It was a large kitchen knife with a 9" blade.

    Unlike *Turner*, Bradshaw's large, unsheathed kitchen knife was protruding from his backpack, making it both visible and accessible. The context of the arrest was also different. Here, Bradshaw asked the officer to meet him alone and walk to a secluded area. The circumstances defeat any suggestion that he was carrying the knife for an innocent purpose. Even if he only had it for his own protection, it would still be considered dangerous.

A "vehicle" includes a camper in the bed of a pickup truck. *Comm. v. Davenport*, 97 Mass. App. Ct. 279 (2020): John Davenport was arrested. His pickup and camper were seized and searched under a warrant. A spring-loaded knife with a four-inch blade was found in the sleeping area.

A vehicle is designed to carry people or things. The camper mounted in a truck fell within that definition, which does not require that a vehicle have its own motor. The camper was not exclusively a residence, at least here, because Davenport had recently used it to drive from one Walmart to another. The knife was shown to be "under his control" in the vehicle because Detective Donovan witnessed Davenport alone in the camper for at least 20 minutes with the knife in his sleeping area.

Related Offenses

Manufacture or Sale of Dangerous Weapons. 269, § 12 prohibits a person from selling or manufacturing any of the weapons covered in § 10(b), with the exception of a slungshot, which may be sold to clubs conducting sporting events. Penalty: HC NMT 6 months; or Fine NLT $50, NMT $1,000. Right of Arrest: Confiscate and complaint.

Unlawful Sale of Hunting Arrows. 269, § 16 outlaws the sale or offer for sale of any arrowhead used exclusively for hunting (commonly known as razorheads) to any person under the age of 15. Penalty: *1ˢᵗ offense:* Fine $100; *2ⁿᵈ offense:* Fine $500; *3ʳᵈ or subsequent offense:* HC NLT 6 months, NMT 1 year; and Fine $1,000. Right of Arrest: Confiscate (crossbows may only be used by one who is permanently disabled to the degree where he cannot operate a conventional bow; the disability must be certified by a physician).

Dangerous Weapon on Campus. 269, § 10(j) prohibits anyone who is not a law enforcement officer from carrying a weapon on the grounds of any elementary or secondary school, or college or university — unless they have written permission. Penalty: HC NMT 2 yrs; and/or Fine NMT $1,000. Right of Arrest: Complaint, unless in presence and breach of peace. See detailed discussion in *LED's Juvenile Law, Chapter 22.*

Dangerous Items in Airport or on Plane. 269, § 12F makes it unlawful to occupy, or attempt to enter, a secure area of an airport or the cabin of an airplane while knowingly possessing or concealing a cutting device or weapon. Having a valid license for the weapon is *no* defense. Penalty: SP NMT 5 yrs or HC NMT 2½ yrs; and/or Fine NMT $5,000. Right of Arrest: Felony.

19 | *Explosives & Fireworks*

EXPLOSIVES, WMD, & OTHER DANGEROUS OR HOAX DEVICES 266, §§ 101–102D

Summary

"7 Up" coverage. This series of statutes broadened the coverage of Massachusetts laws pertaining to explosives and other dangerous devices. Seven activities, listed from least to most dangerous, are prohibited:

1. Possession of a hoax device;
2. Possession of an explosive ingredient;
3. Possession of an ingredient for a weapon of mass destruction (WMD);
4. Possession an explosive, incendiary, or destructive device or substance;
5. Placing an explosive, incendiary, or destructive device or substance;
6. Exploding an explosive, incendiary, or destructive device or substance; and
7. Possession of a WMD or delivery system.

Definitions

Police tip: When in doubt, always call the Hazardous Materials Division of the Department of Fire Services. During normal business hours: **978-567-3310**. After hours, call your local State Police barracks, who will contact the troop duty officer.

All definitions in 266, § 101. Knowing the definitions is critical to applying this law properly.[1]

- **Ammunition.** Cartridges or cartridge cases, primers (igniter), bullets, or propellant powder designed for use in any weapon including, but not limited to, ammunition produced by or for the military.

- **Biological weapon.** Any microorganism, virus, infectious substance, or biological product (or any component) specifically prepared in a manner to cause death, disease, or other biological malfunction in humans, other living organisms, food, water, or the environment.

- **Black powder.** A compound or mixture of sulfur, charcoal, and an alkali nitrate.

- **Chemical weapon.** A toxic chemical or substance designed to cause death or bodily harm (including the device designed to release it).

---

[1] Only definitions necessary to apply this law in the field are included. Consult with a specialist if in doubt about the properties of the device, and whether it is covered by this law.

- **Delivery system.** Any equipment designed or adapted for use in connection with the deployment of chemical, biological, or nuclear weapons (aka WMD).

- **Destructive or incendiary device or substance.** An explosive, article, or device designed or adapted to cause physical harm to persons or property by means of fire, explosion, deflagration, or detonation, whether or not contrived to ignite or explode automatically.

- **Explosive.** Any element, compound, or mixture that is manufactured, designed, or used to produce an explosion and that contains an oxidizer, fuel, or other ingredient, in such proportion, quantity or packing that an ignition by fire, friction, concussion, percussion, or detonation . . . is capable of producing destructive effects on contiguous objects, or of destroying life, or causing bodily harm [including classified explosives under federal law].

  An explosive shall not include:

  - *A pyrotechnic,* which is defined as "any commercially manufactured combustible or explosive composition or manufactured article designed and prepared for the purpose of producing an audible effect or a visible display and regulated by Chapter 148 including, but not limited to: (i) fireworks, firecrackers; (ii) flares, fuses and torpedoes . . . and similar signaling devices."

  - *Small arms ammunition,* which is defined as "any shotgun, rifle, pistol, or revolver cartridge, and cartridges for propellant-actuated power devices and industrial guns."

  - *Small arms ammunition primers.*

  - *Smokeless powder weighing less than 50 lbs and black powder weighing less than 5 lbs,* unless possessed or used for an illegal purpose. Smokeless powder is defined as "a rapid-burning solid material containing nitrocellulose used as a propellant."

- **Hoax explosive, device, or weapon.** Any device, article, or substance that would cause a person to reasonably believe that it is: (i) an explosive; (ii) a destructive or incendiary device or substance; or (iii) a chemical, biological, or nuclear weapon, harmful radioactive substance, or poison capable of causing bodily injury, but which is actually an inoperable facsimile.

- **Nuclear weapon.** "A device designed to cause bodily injury, death or denial of access through the release of radiation or radiological material either by . . . nuclear fission or by means of any other energy source." Denial of access is defined as "contamination to an area . . . which poses a health risk to humans, animals, or plants."

Elements

Type 1: Hoax Explosive, Device, or Weapon of Mass Destruction (WMD) [266, § 102(b)]

- Without lawful authority, the suspect possessed or placed (or caused another person to knowingly or unknowingly do this);

- Any hoax explosive; hoax destructive or incendiary device or substance; or hoax chemical, biological, or nuclear weapon;

- With intent to cause anxiety or personal discomfort to any person or group of persons.

Type 2: Explosive Ingredient [266, § 102(a)]

- Without lawful authority, the suspect possessed or had under his control;

- An explosive or ingredient which, alone or in combination, could be used to make a destructive or incendiary device or substance;

- With the intent to make a destructive or incendiary device or substance.

Note: It is not a defense that the suspect did not possess or control every ingredient necessary to make a fully functional device. However, there must be proof that the defendant was without lawful authority to possess the ingredient, and that he intended to make an explosive or incendiary device. *Comm. v. Aldana,* 477 Mass. 790 (2017): While arresting Marc Aldana on a default warrant, police saw in his kitchen three bags containing a thermite mixture. But there was no evidence that Aldana possessed an illegal amount of thermite. The prosecutor did not present the precise regulation that differentiated illegal from legal possession. He provided information about the storage of *explosives,* but thermite is an "incendiary" that operates through heat. In the future, prosecutors and investigators must be precise in their classification of the substance and related regulations.

Type 3: WMD Ingredient [266, § 102(a)]

- Without lawful authority, the suspect possessed or had under his control;

- An ingredient which, alone or in combination, could be used to make a chemical, biological, or nuclear weapon (aka WMD);

- With the intent to make a WMD.

Note: It is not a defense that the suspect did not possess or control every ingredient necessary to make a fully functional WMD.

Type 4: Explosive Device [266, § 102(c)]

- Without lawful authority, the suspect possessed or had under his control;

- Any explosive or destructive or incendiary device or substance.

Note: The suspect does not need to "intend" to use the device; he must simply possess it. This was also true under an earlier version of this law. *Comm. v. Lombardo,* 23 Mass. App. Ct. 1006 (1987).

Type 5: Place Explosive Device [266, § 102A]

- Without lawful authority, the suspect placed, hid, threw, or launched;

- An explosive or a destructive or incendiary device or substance;

- With the intent to:
  - Cause fear, panic, or apprehension in any person; or
  - Ignite, explode, or discharge the device or substance; or
  - Release or discharge any chemical, biological, or nuclear weapon (aka WMD).

Note: Comm. v. Lemos, 2012 WL 1835123 (Appeals Court): Joel Lemos had the motive to place the car bomb (his ex-girlfriend's decision to end their relationship and enter into another one); the means and opportunity (he was unaccounted for at the time of the crime, had been trained in explosives by the Brazilian military police, and possessed a key to unlock the victim's car); and he tried to get a third party to provide a false alibi. He admitted to police that his intent had been to scare his ex-girlfriend. Tragically, her new boyfriend was seriously injured.

Type 6: Device Explodes [266, § 102B]

- Without lawful authority, the suspect willfully ignited, exploded, or discharged;
- Any destructive or incendiary device or substance.

Note: Again, notice how there is no "intent" requirement; purposefully causing the device to explode, ignite, or discharge is sufficient for conviction.

Type 7: WMD Device or Delivery System [266, § 102C]

- Without lawful authority, the suspect knowingly developed, stockpiled, acquired, transported, possessed, placed, or hid;
- Any biological, chemical, or nuclear weapon (aka WMD) or delivery system;
- With the intent to cause death, bodily injury or property damage.

Right of Arrest & Procedures

Right of arrest for all offenses: Felony.

Seizure and forfeiture of any device, substance, or components: Under 266, § 102D, the officer who seizes any materials must immediately notify, in all cases, the Fire Marshal (who has sole authority to determine how items will be held and rendered safe). Upon conviction, all items will be forfeited to and disposed of by the Fire Marshal or his designee.

Penalty

Type 1: SP NMT 5 yrs or HC NMT 2½ yrs; and/or Fine NMT $10,000.

Types 2 and 3: SP NLT 5 yrs, NMT 10 yrs or HC NMT 2½ yrs; and/or Fine NMT $25,000.

Type 4: SP NLT 10 yrs, NMT 20 yrs or HC NMT 2½ yrs; and/or Fine NMT $25,000.

Type 5: SP NLT 10 yrs, NMT 25 yrs or HC NMT 2½ yrs; and/or Fine NMT $25,000.

Type 6: SP NLT 15 yrs, NMT 25 yrs or HC NMT 2½ yrs; and/or Fine NMT $50,000.

Type 7: SP NMT 25 yrs or HC NMT 2½ yrs; and/or Fine NMT $50,000.

Mandatory restitution: The offender must pay restitution to local, county, or state government for any costs and damages — in addition to the penalty imposed. However, the court must consider the defendant's ability to pay in determining the amount.

Related Offense & Regulations

Explosives and Fireworks Regulation by Fire Marshal. 148, § 12. No person shall sell or transfer explosive materials within the Commonwealth unless the transferee: (1) has the proper permit to possess explosives; and (2) maintains, at the place of delivery, an approved storage facility. The Fire Marshal shall promulgate regulations to carry out this section, including strict record keeping. Penalty: HC NMT 2½ yrs; and/or Fine NMT $5,000.

THREAT CONCERNING THE LOCATION OF DANGEROUS ITEMS OR A HIJACK
269, § 14

Elements

- ***Willful communication.*** The suspect willfully communicated or caused to be communicated — either directly or indirectly — by *any means*, including mail, telephone, email, internet, or fax;

- ***Threat.*** A threat:

  - **Dangerous item.** That any of the following is or will be present at a location, whether or not the threat is true:

    - A firearm, rifle, shotgun, machine gun, or assault weapon; or
    - An explosive or incendiary device; or
    - A dangerous chemical or biological agent; or
    - A poison; or
    - A harmful radioactive substance; or
    - Any other device, substance or item capable of causing death, serious bodily injury, or substantial property damage; or

  - **Hijack.** To hijack an aircraft, ship, or common carrier;

- ***Anxiety to anyone.*** Which caused anxiety, fear, or personal discomfort to any person or group of persons.

Right of Arrest

Felony.

Penalty

For threat concerning dangerous item or hijack: SP NMT 20 yrs or HC NMT 2½ yrs; and/or Fine NMT $10,000.

Aggravated offense: If the prohibited threat causes "either the evacuation or serious disruption of a school, school-related event, school transportation, or a dwelling, building, . . . or public transport . . . or causes serious public inconvenience or alarm": SP NLT 3 yrs, NMT 20 yrs or HC NLT 6 months, NMT 2½ yrs; and/or Fine NLT $1,000, NMT $50,000.

Mandatory restitution: A person found guilty shall be ordered to make restitution for any financial loss sustained as a result of the crime. Restitution shall be imposed in addition to, not as a substitute for, incarceration or a fine. In determining the amount, time and method of payment, the court shall consider the financial resources of the defendant.

Definitions found in 269, § 14

- **Hijack:** To commandeer or to take control without authority.

- **School:** Any public or private preschool, Headstart facility, elementary, vocational or secondary school, college, or university.

- **Serious bodily injury:** Bodily injury which results in a permanent disfigurement, protracted loss or impairment of a bodily function, limb or organ, or substantial risk of death.

Protest Exemption

269, § 14 states: "Nothing in this section shall authorize the criminal prosecution of picketing, public demonstrations or other similar forms of expressing views."

Notes

Threat may be explicit or implied, but it must be clear. *Comm. v. Forts*, 2015 WL 6956784 (Superior Court): On a college campus, defendant left a poem endorsing mass murder and a note to "evacuate at 2:33 p.m." in a building. This was a sufficient threat that he intended to inflict harm upon occupants with a device capable of causing death.

Threat must involve a dangerous device or weapon that is or will be present. *Comm. v. Xander X.*, 2020 WL 1280771 (Appeals Court). During a discussion on gun control, the juvenile stated, "It's a good thing I don't have a gun because half the school would be dead because I fucking hate them." In the past, the juvenile had talked about shooting himself and wanting an AK-47. Interviews of classmates revealed that they understood the juvenile was joking. There was no probable cause to charge 269, § 14 because the juvenile never suggested a gun was or would be present. In fact, the juvenile said he did not have a gun.

Threat need only be communicated to a nonaccomplice. *Comm. v. Kerns*, 449 Mass. 641 (2007): Tobin Kerns and his friends planned to execute a terrorist-type attack on their high school. During the planning phase, they tried to enlist two other students, who decided not to be involved. The plan unraveled and Kerns was arrested and charged with 269, § 14.

Kerns argued that, in order to be convicted, he had to communicate his threat to a potential target. The SJC disagreed. The threat qualifies under § 14 if it is communicated to any person, other than an accomplice. This statute contains no restrictions on the potential victims. It does not even require that there *be* potential victims. The statute simply requires that the threat be communicated to someone. Because Kerns communicated the threat to two friends who were not part of the group, he completed the crime.

SALE OR POSSESSION OF FIREWORKS
148, § 39

Elements

- ***Possessed, exploded, or possessed for sale.*** The suspect:

    - Sold, offered, or kept for sale; or
    - Had in his possession; or
    - Caused to explode;

- ***Fireworks.*** Fireworks — provided they were not for a legally exempt purpose.

Right of Arrest & Notification

Sales-related activity: 148, § 39 warrantless arrest in presence.

Possession or causing to explode: Confiscation and complaint mandated by 148, § 39. [*Note:* An in presence breach of peace rationale is no exception since the statute mandates a complaint. However, other crimes may be proper for exploding fireworks, depending how and where it is done, e.g., Disorderly Conduct, 272, § 53. See *Chapter 23*.]

Secure storage: Following any seizure of fireworks, officers must notify the Fire Marshal and securely store the items. The Fire Marshal may advise on proper storage or decide to take the fireworks into custody for disposal. Upon conviction, they are forfeited.

Penalty

For any sales-related activities: HC NMT 1 year; and/or Fine NLT $100, NMT $1,000.

For possessing or causing an explosion: Fine NLT $10, NMT $100.

Notes

Possession. Similar to other offenses, possession in this context may be either direct or constructive. Moreover, the fireworks may be possessed by one person or jointly with others.

Sale or kept for sale. If officers see or learn about a transaction involving fireworks, then they have proof that this contraband was sold. It is also a violation if a person keeps fireworks for sale. Whether selling is the suspect's intent depends on the circumstances of the case. Large quantities of fireworks, sales notations, or possession of a large amount of cash are indications that the fireworks are not intended solely for personal entertainment.

Definition of fireworks. § 39 defines a firework as "any . . . article, which was prepared for the purpose of producing a visible or audible effect by combustion, explosion, deflagration, or detonation. "The section goes on to name a variety of fireworks that fall under this definition, such as "blank cartridges or toy cannons in which explosives are used . . . cherry bombs, silver salutes, M-80's, . . . Roman candles, sparklers, rockets, wheels . . . ." However, the definition of fireworks specifically excludes "caps" used in cap guns, so long as they contain "twenty-five hundredths grains or less of explosive compound."

Unless the particular variety is named in the statute, or the defendant agrees that the items are, in fact, fireworks, officers may submit the item to the state laboratory for analysis. While this step may not be cost effective in a minor case, it should be pursued in more serious violations.

Exempted sales. This law does not apply to the sale of fireworks that are:

- To be shipped directly out of the Commonwealth;
- To be used by a person with a permit for the display of fireworks;
- To be used as signals for boats and other vehicles;
- In the case of blank cartridges, part of a theater production, sporting event, military, or veteran ceremony;
- Part of a factory experiment with explosives;
- Connected with experts teaching the use of firearms or, in the case of cartridges and gunpowder, in connection with hunting or target shooting; and
- For farmers with a permit under 48, § 13 for controlling damage to crops by birds.

Ship or railway signals. 148, § 44 includes "pyrotechnical ship or railway signals" within the definition of fireworks; however, it exempts these items from criminal coverage when they are in storage or are "used for the protection of life and property."

Lawful storage and display of fireworks. 148, §§ 39A–45 outline the various procedures that must be undertaken in order for a person or organization to lawfully store fireworks or conduct a supervised display of fireworks.

Related Offense

Sale of or Give Away Novelty Lighter. 148, § 60. See *Chapter 34*, fire prevention offenses.

20 Narcotics

Section I
CLASS SYSTEM FOR CONTROLLED SUBSTANCES

CLASSES OF CONTROLLED SUBSTANCES
94C, § 31

Categorized in five classes (A, B, C, D, & E) according to their chemical composition and effect on the human body. Officers are not expected to know drug chemistry, but they should learn the basic properties and street names of drugs. 94C, §§ 1 and 31.

Also outlawed are "analogues" — chemically similar substances having the same stimulant, depressant, or hallucinogenic effects. The defendant must know that the "analogue" he distributed is a controlled substance or has the stimulant, depressant, or hallucinogenic effect of a controlled substance. *McFadden v. U.S.*, 135 S.Ct. 2298 (2015) (defendant knew that he was selling controlled substances: he marketed them as "Alpha," "No Speed," and "The New Up," and compared them to cocaine and crystal meth; he also deliberately used technical language on his packaging to avoid legal liability suggesting conscious awareness of his illegal products).[1]

CLASS *A*[2]

- *Heroin;*
- *Fentanyl;*
- Carfentanil;
- Morphine;
- Flunitrazepam;
- Gamma Hydroxy Butyric Acid (aka GHB);
- *Ketamine* (aka "Special K");
- Any synthetic opioid defined in Schedule I or II under federal law.

CLASS *B*

- *Cocaine;*
- Codeine;
- Methadone;
- *OxyContin,* Oxycodone, Percocet;

---

[1] Technically, the Supreme Court based its ruling on an analysis of federal law, but this author is confident the SJC will adopt this interpretation under 94C.
[2] Drugs listed in bold/italics are most commonly encountered by officers on the street.

- Amphetamines;
- *Methamphetamine*;
- *Phenacyclidine* (aka PCP, "angel dust");
- Lysergic Acid Diethylamide (aka LSD);
- Opium in certain amounts;
- P2P, PCH, or PCC;
- *MDMA* (aka "Ecstasy");
- Phenmetrazine;
- Percodan (Diethylamide); Dilaudid (Dihydromophone).

CLASS C

- *Valium* (Diazepam);
- *Synthetic marijuana* (aka K-2, Spice);
- Librium (Chlordiazepoxide);
- Morphine and Codeine in certain amounts;
- Flurazepam, Prazepam;
- Hallucinogenic substances including Dimethoxyamphetamine (aka STP);
- Mescaline, Peyote;
- *Psilocybin* (aka Mexican mushroom);
- *"Bath salts"* [contains methylenedioxymethcathinone (MDMC), methylenedioxypyrovalerone (MDPV), or variations].

CLASS D

- *Marijuana* with any concentration of Tetrahydrocannabinol (THC);[3]
  Important caution: Marijuana has been legalized, and medical marijuana has been approved for qualifying patients. See *Chapter 21* on marijuana.
- Barbital, Phenobarbital.

CLASS E

- Compounds with small percentages of codeine, morphine, or opium;
- Neurontin (Gabapentin);
- *Prescription drugs not listed in any other class!*

---

[3] In 2016, the Drug Enforcement Administration (DEA) refused to remove marijuana from Schedule I of the federal Controlled Substances Act because it has a high potential for abuse and lacks scientific acceptance as a legitimate medical treatment. This decision was made in consultation with the federal Food and Drug Administration (FDA) and the National Institute on Drug Abuse (NIDA). However, the DEA did take steps to increase the supply of marijuana for research and has fast-tracked a number of research projects designed to investigate the healing properties of marijuana-based medicine.

PROOF OF TYPE, WEIGHT, & PURITY

Element of case. In any offense involving drug possession or distribution, there must be proof of the class of drugs.

Certificate of analysis insufficient. The Supreme Court rejected a longstanding practice in Massachusetts. Prosecutors used to prove the type, weight, and/or purity of a controlled substance by presenting a certificate in court filled out by the laboratory analyst. A certificate of analysis is no longer proof by itself. *Melendez-Diaz v. Massachusetts*, 129 S.Ct. 2527 (2009).

Proving the Type of Controlled Substance

Testing

- **Laboratory testing.** This is conclusive *provided* that a laboratory analyst is available to testify at trial about the testing methods and particular findings.

- **Field testing.** Officer who performed the field test must testify that he was trained to do it. *Comm. v. King*, 461 Mass. 354 (2012).

Circumstantial evidence. "Proof that a substance is a particular drug . . . may be made by circumstantial evidence." *Comm. v. Dawson*, 399 Mass. 465 (1987).

- **Visual inspection or price paid** *insufficient proof*. Because of the "availability of counterfeit drugs," visual inspection of drugs possessed by the defendant *or* the high price paid is insufficient proof. *Comm. v. Rivera*, 76 Mass. App. Ct. 67 (2009). Even the *chemist's* visual inspection is insufficient by itself. *Comm. v. Paine*, 86 Mass. App. Ct. 432 (2014) (without actual chemical analysis or additional circumstantial evidence, there was no proof that the drugs the chemist visually inspected were, in fact, cyclobenzaprine and quetiapine).

- **Prescription medication may be identified by sight** *if* **there is additional evidence.** *Comm. v. Cooper*, 91 Mass App. Ct. 595 (2017): Evidence, in addition to markings on the pills, established they were gabapentin; Cooper described the pills by their street name (Johnnies) and their pharmaceutical name (gabapentin). He said he had a prescription for gabapentin with five refills remaining. He removed the pills from a prescription bottle with his name on it, and said they were 300 milligram, quick-release capsules.

- **Odor of substance** *insufficient*, **except** for marijuana. *Comm. v. MacDonald*, 459 Mass. 148 (2011) (risk of misidentification of marijuana low, given its smell).

- **A taste test** — even when conducted by an experienced user — *insufficient*. *Comm. v. Davis*, 83 Mass. App. Ct. 484 (2013) (confidential informant's taste test, which identified substance as high quality cocaine, lacked scientific reliability).

- **Paraphernalia found near drugs.** *Comm. v. Hopkins*, 79 Mass. App. Ct. 412 (2011) (proof that substance found was cocaine included a nearby sifter, grinder, scale, and plastic baggies of the type normally used to package cocaine).

- **Drugs stored in secure area.** *Comm. v. Pitts*, 2015 WL 4644218 (Appeals Court) (defendant employed "extraordinary security provisions," storing the substance in a locked closet; this implied the substance was valuable).

- **Suspect's admission.** The suspect will often admit the illegal drug he possesses — so officers should always seek this obvious proof. *Comm. v. Connolly*, 454 Mass. 808 (2009) (defendant called substance "crack"). *Comm. v. Alisha A.*, 56 Mass. App. Ct. 311 (2002) (evening before her arrest, juvenile said to a witness that she would bring Klonopin to school). However, the suspect must be an experienced drug user. *Comm. v. Montoya*, 464 Mass. 566 (2013).

- **Suspect's response to request.** *Comm. v. Vasquez*, 75 Mass. App. Ct. 446 (2009) (undercover officer given a substance that looked like cocaine in exchange for money).

- **Suspect provided his telephone number or other reassurance.** *Comm. v. King*, 77 Mass. App. Ct. 189 (2010) (undercover officer given cell phone number for future purchases).

- **Suspect swallowed substance.** *Comm. v. Rodriguez*, 75 Mass. App. Ct. 235 (2009) (troopers saw the defendant attempt to swallow something then spit out five bags of cocaine).

- **Suspect showed signs of consumption.** *Comm. v. DeMatos*, 77 Mass. App. Ct. 727 (2010) (defendant appeared "high" and said, "Oh, I forgot about cocaine. That's for my personal use").

- **Suspect linked to stash.** Even if the substance possessed by the suspect is not recovered by police, proof that it came from a larger stash that was recovered and analyzed is sufficient. *Comm. v. Ramirez*, 57 Mass. App. Ct. 475 (2003).

- **Roommate's testimony.** *Comm. v. Figueroa*, 2011 WL 1069327 (Appeals Court) (testimony by addict who lived with defendant sufficient proof that substance was cocaine).

Sufficient Proof of Weight

- **In close cases, should present testimony of analyst who weighed drugs.** *Comm. v. Crapps*, 84 Mass. App. Ct. 442 (2013) (lab analysts do not have to weigh every bag seized in order to accurately calculate total weight of drugs possessed by defendant — but their extrapolation methods may be scrutinized by defense counsel, especially in close cases).

- **Officer may weigh drugs on a scale.** *Comm. v. Johnson*, 76 Mass. App. Ct. 80 (2010) (officer weighed the cocaine on a scale at the station and determined that it was 102 grams). *Comm. v. Podgurski*, 81 Mass. App. Ct. 175 (2012) (a scale's accuracy must be tested against a known counterweight before its results are admissible).

- **Obvious amount may be inferred from officer testimony and actual substance.** *Comm. v. Rodriguez*, 75 Mass. App. Ct. 235 (2009) (no need for expert testimony since jury could determine that the large, hard ball offered into evidence weighed more than four ounces). Compare *Comm. v. Montoya*, 464 Mass. 566 (2013) (drugs were packaged in 20 individual bags, which made it difficult for jury to determine how much drugs weighed, especially since the difference between the actual weight and the amount required for the trafficking offense was only 11.84 grams).

- **Defendant admitted quantity possessed.** *Comm. v. Hopkins*, 79 Mass. App. Ct. 412 (2011) (Hopkins admitted to trafficking at least 14 grams; given his experience as a user and seller, he had the ability to assess the weight of a given quantity of cocaine).

Sufficient Proof of Purity

It is hard to imagine a persuasive method of proving the purity of a substance that does not involve the live testimony of a laboratory analyst.

Section II
POSSESSION

At the heart of virtually all drug offenses, the suspect must be shown to have illegally possessed a controlled substance.

- **Momentary possession is sufficient.** *Comm. v. Lacend*, 33 Mass. App. Ct. 495 (1992) (defendant guilty of possession when he purchased cocaine from an undercover officer in an alley and had control of it for only seconds before his arrest).

- **Must be in possession of a quantity of the drug and not simply under the influence.** There must be proof that the suspect possessed a perceptible amount of the drug. Possessing certain drugs is illegal, but being under the influence of them is not (except while driving). Officers may not charge possession if the suspect ingested the substance out of their sight, unless they have a witness who saw the suspect in possession. *Robinson v. California*, 370 U.S. 660 (1962).

    Exception: Marijuana decriminalization covers "internal possession" by people under 21. See 94C, § 32L discussed in *Chapter 21*.

- **Medical use without a prescription is no defense.** *Comm. v. Hutchins*, 410 Mass. 726 (1991).

    Exception: marijuana for medicinal purposes. See discussion in *Chapter 21*.

- **Religious practice is no defense.** *Comm. v. Nissenbaum*, 404 Mass. 575 (1989).

- **Police possession.** Police officers and other public officials may, in the course of their duties, possess controlled substances. 94C, § 7.

Chain of custody. Police officers must make sure that they exercise extreme care in handling and storing drugs. Officers must be able to account for the location of drugs at all times — from the moment they take the drugs from a suspect to the time they present them in court. This "chain of custody" proves that the drugs presented in court are the same ones taken from the defendant. *Comm. v. Gordon*, 389 Mass. 351 (1983).

To prove possession, the police must show that the suspect <u>knew</u> narcotics were present and had the <u>intention</u> and ability to <u>control</u> them. This makes sense because the three elements are interrelated. Without knowledge of its location, how in the world can a person have the ability to control the contraband? Similarly, a person may know where the contraband is, and may have the ability to control it, but lack the desire or intent to do so.

Comm. v. Deagle, 10 Mass. App. Ct. 563 (1980) (passenger did not possess PCP simply because he was in the car as others consumed the drug).

There are two types of possession:

- **Type 1: Direct possession.** A person obviously possesses something if he has direct physical control or custody of the object. For example, people typically possess whatever is in their pockets or purses, whether it's keys or cocaine.

- **Type 2: Constructive possession.** Proof of constructive possession is more challenging because the drugs are discovered in a separate area. The law does not require that someone have physical custody of an object. For example, people possess things in their closet at home even when they are at work.

Possession may be jointly shared. Multiple persons may directly or constructively possess drugs. Furthermore, officers do not need to identify *all* individuals in possession of a supply in order to take enforcement action against one. *Comm. v. James*, 30 Mass. App. Ct. 490 (1991).

Presence with drugs is not enough. *Comm. v. Brown*, 34 Mass. App. Ct. 222 (1993) (woman in apartment where drugs were dealt not guilty of possession; she had no keys to the apartment, no cash or drugs on her person, and no belongings in the rooms where drugs were found).

There must be presence "plus" an additional factor to show knowledge, intent, and control. Here is a list of recognized "plus" factors:

- **Drugs in plain view.** *Comm. v. Daley*, 423 Mass. 747 (1996) (drugs observed by police in area where they must have been seen by the defendant).

- **Obvious smell of narcotics.** *Comm. v. Yazbeck*, 31 Mass. App. Ct. 769 (1992) (marijuana in basement closet "gave forth a noticeable odor").

- **Air freshener in a vehicle.** *Comm. v. Medina*, 2018 WL 1370557 (Appeals Court): Luis Medina was driving a vehicle registered in the name of his friend. Not only did Medina have exclusive control of the car he was borrowing while his friend was in Puerto Rico, but there was a very strong scent of air fresheners. Given the odor, it was highly unlikely that Medina's friend had hidden the drugs and cash before leaving, without informing him of their presence.

- **Incriminating statements.** *Comm. v. Velasquez*, 48 Mass. App. Ct. 147 (1999) (when police found drugs in his basement, defendant said, "I'm going to do two years for this").

- **Incriminating conduct linked to drugs.** *Comm. v. Lara*, 58 Mass. App. Ct. 915 (2003) (Lara had driven Peredes' car slowly behind him as he walked from Archdale Road to the Arboretum; the fact that Lara engaged in such an unusual car ride and stood on high ground watching Peredes stash something near a pine tree clearly linked him to the drugs later found there by Boston Police).

- **Reaction to police presence.**

  - *Agitated or nervous. Comm. v. Alicea*, 410 Mass. 384 (1991) (defendant reacted in an agitated manner as officers got closer to the drugs in his car).

  - *Failure to stop vehicle for police. Comm. v. Ciccotelli*, 2017 WL 1322124 (Appeals Court) (despite the officer's lights and siren, the defendant delayed five to eight minutes before stopping his car; this suggested he knew of the contraband located inside the vehicle).

  - *Interference with officers. Comm. v. Velasquez*, 48 Mass. App. Ct. 147 (1999) (attempt to block officers from retrieving drugs during a raid indicated that suspect was more than an unlucky occupant; he was involved in the drug dealing operation).

  - *Implausible action and explanation. Comm. v. Mojica*, 59 Mass. App. Ct. 925 (2003): Officer Lake pulled his cruiser to the curb when he saw the defendant bent over looking for something. The officer got out and noticed a white substance in a plastic bag on the sidewalk. The defendant stood up quickly and began to walk away. Officer Lake asked the defendant what he was doing. He replied that he was looking for a gold chain that had fallen from his neck. Lake looked on the ground for a gold chain but did not find one. Lake then arrested the defendant, who was wearing a silver chain.

- **Large quantity discovered.** *Comm. v. Roman*, 414 Mass. 642 (1993) (defendant's knowledge inferred from 25 grams of cocaine found in his car on a major highway).

- **Paperwork and/or personal possessions found near drugs.** *Comm. v. Perez*, 87 Mass. App. Ct. 278 (2015) (in a bedroom along with cocaine, cash, and items used for drug dealing, police found a Massachusetts ID card bearing defendant's name and address, a Venezuelan passport bearing his name and picture, and a billing receipt addressed to him at that apartment).

- **Exclusive or limited access to vehicle or building.** *Comm. v. Pimental*, 73 Mass. App. Ct. 777 (2009) (defendant Garcia had sole key to apartment among the eight men present, so he had probably been the one to allow them to enter and engage in drug activity).

- **Rents, occupies, or spends significant time at dwelling.** *Comm. v. Hamilton*, 83 Mass. App. Ct. 406 (2013) (defendant's control shown by fact that cocaine was in front of her in plain view and she was the primary occupant of the apartment at night in her underwear; the bedroom contained only women's clothes, which police gave her to wear following her arrest).

Possession of an unopened package containing drugs is, without more, insufficient proof of possession. In *Comm. v. Alcala*, 54 Mass. App. Ct. 49 (2002), investigators were able to prove the defendant knew marijuana was in the boxes delivered by UPS. He concealed his truck and quickly removed the packages after delivery to a business that he was not connected to. His explanation to police about why he retrieved the boxes at that location made no sense.

POSSESSION OF CONTROLLED SUBSTANCES
94C, § 34

Elements

- **Knowingly.** The suspect knowingly;

- **Possessed.** Possessed some perceptible amount of a controlled substance in any class, or more than 2 ounces of marijuana; and

- **Without lawful reason.** The suspect did not have a valid prescription or other legal basis.

Right of Arrest

94C, § 41 warrantless arrest on probable cause.

Penalty

All controlled substances except heroin, marijuana, and Class E: 1st offense: HC NMT 1 year; and/or Fine NMT $1,000.

If more than two ounces of marijuana or any Class E substance: HC NMT 6 months; and/or Fine of $500. See discussion of marijuana possession in *Chapter 21*.

Subsequent offense for possession or any other 94C felony (but not for Class E, see note below): HC NMT 2 yrs; and/or Fine NMT $2,000.

If substance heroin: 1st offense: HC NMT 2 yrs; and/or Fine NMT $2,000. *Subsequent:* SP NLT 2½ yrs, NMT 5 yrs or HC NMT 2½ yrs; and Fine NMT $5,000.

Sealing record for 1st offense: If defendant has not committed a prior drug offense, court *must* place him on probation for marijuana or Class E unless judge files memorandum. Upon completion of probation, record *must* be sealed. For all other § 34 offenses, the court *may* seal the record. Thus, the defendant would not have to acknowledge his arrest in "response to any inquiry for any purpose." 94C, § 44. *Comm. v. Lupo*, 394 Mass. 644 (1985).

Definition of subsequent. Under § 34, possession of Class E cannot qualify as a subsequent offense. However, Class E may be the basis of a subsequent offense if the suspect later possesses another class. Any other class may serve as the foundation for a subsequent offense.

Overdose Immunity

"Good Samaritan" law. Under 94C, § 34A, the person suffering from an overdose, and anyone who helps him get medical treatment, is immune from prosecution for drug possession. There is no immunity for drug distribution. However, one may ask for a reduced sentence on the basis that he helped a person get treatment for a possible overdose. One may receive a prescription or possess naloxone (Narcan), or administer it to a person experiencing an overdose without legal repercussions. Finally, there is no immunity for other crimes that may occur in overdose situations — e.g., OUI, trespass, theft, etc.

Protective Custody (PC)

Transport to emergency room for drug or inhalant incapacitation. Under 111E, § 9A, a police officer may PC incapacitated persons (including those who receive Narcan) and transport them for evaluation to an emergency room. The most detailed discussion of PC law and procedure appears in *LED's Criminal Procedure, Chapter 9.*

No Choking Law

Never choke drug suspects; charge evidence concealment. It is illegal to choke suspects to prevent them from swallowing drugs. 6E, §§ 1 and 14. Instead, officers should arrest them, seek medical attention, and charge evidence concealment under 268, § 13E. See discussion of 13E in *Chapter 35.*

SMELLING SUBSTANCE WITH TOXIC VAPOR
270, § 18

Summary

270, § 18 does not prohibit possessing a controlled substance. It penalizes intentionally inhaling any toxic substance to get high.[4]

Elements

- ***Intentionally.*** The suspect intentionally:
  - **Smell.** Smelled or inhaled the "fumes of any substance [that] . . . releas[es] toxic vapors"; or
  - **Purchase.** Purchased a substance;
- ***To get high.*** For "the purpose of causing a condition of intoxication, . . . exhilaration, . . . or dulled senses."

Right of Arrest

270, § 18 warrantless arrest in presence.

Exempt Conduct

Naturally, this law does not apply to inhaling anesthesia for medical or dental purposes.

Penalty

HC NMT 6 months; and/or Fine NMT $200.

---

4 A more detailed discussion concerning inhalant abuse appears in *LED's Juvenile Law, Chapter 12.*

Section III
DISTRIBUTION

A. Distribute

Definition of distribution. Under 94C, § 1, distribution means "to *deliver* other than by administering or dispensing a controlled substance" (emphasis added). Administering and dispensing are defined as the legitimate delivery of a controlled substance by a medical practitioner. Therefore, distribution is *any nonmedical delivery* of drugs.

- **Delivering** drugs is distribution even though **no** money is exchanged. *Comm. v. Poole*, 29 Mass. App. Ct. 1003 (1990).

- **Sharing** drugs is distribution *except* when the offenders either obtain the drugs together at the same time or "socially share" marijuana. *Comm. v. Carrillo*, 483 Mass. 269 (2019) (defendant bought heroin in NYC for his UMass friend and himself; this was felony drug distribution even though he made no profit).

    U.S. v. Wright, 593 F.2d 105 (1979): Lester Wright admitted getting money from a woman, buying heroin, and then snorting it with her. Since Wright and the woman did not get the drug together at the same time, Wright was convicted of distribution. The court explained that this rule "prevent[s] individuals from acquiring drugs . . . on behalf of others and then transferring the drugs to them. 'The agent who delivers [is] increasing the distribution of narcotics. Without the agent's services the principal might never come into possession of the drug' . . . Here Wright operated as the link between the person . . . and the drug itself."

- **Arranging a sale.** In *Comm. v. Fluellen*, 456 Mass. 517 (2010), the defendant claimed that he simply introduced the undercover officer to a cocaine dealer. However, even acting as a "middleman" or "intermediary" to a drug transaction qualifies as distribution.

Circumstantial evidence may be sufficient proof of distribution. Consider *Comm. v. Tanner*, 66 Mass. App. Ct. 432 (2006): The police observed Michael Tanner conversing with a man named Moses Sawyer. Tanner's hands were palms up, as if he were displaying something. As they spoke, Tanner repeatedly looked up and down the street. Police lost sight of the two, but a few minutes later saw Tanner counting money in a restaurant. Meanwhile, Sawyer was arrested when he attempted to buy five bags of cocaine from another man. Sawyer was searched, and police found six additional bags in his pocket.

Police returned to arrest Tanner, who had $130 in cash but no drugs. Although the police did not witness the transfer of drugs between Tanner and Sawyer, the compelling inference was that Tanner was the dealer. Sawyer had the drugs and Tanner had the money. Sawyer's attempt to buy drugs from another man showed he was a buyer, which was consistent with his earlier purchase from Tanner.

Distribution may involve an accomplice not present at the sale — the so-called "constructive transfer." *Comm. v. Mgaresh,* 83 Mass. App. Ct. 276 (2013): An undercover police officer, Detective Grace, called the defendant and arranged to purchase $200 worth of cocaine. Grace arrived at the predetermined location and met Nancy, who was on the phone with the defendant. Nancy sold drugs to Grace and was arrested.

Defendant Mgaresh came to the station to bail Nancy. While he was in the lobby, police called the number Grace had used to arrange the purchase. Mgaresh checked his phone. The officers then verified it was the number Grace had called. The defendant was arrested for what is known as the constructive transfer.

Distributing drugs to a person who dies from an overdose may be involuntary manslaughter. See discussion of *Comm. v. Carrillo,* 483 Mass. 269 (2019) in *Chapter 6.*

B. Manufacture

Manufacturing encompasses any processing of controlled substances. 94C, § 1 specifically defines "manufacturing" as producing, preparing, or processing a controlled substance, "either directly or indirectly by extraction of natural origin or independently by means of chemical synthesis, including any packaging or repackaging of the substance or labeling or relabeling or compounding of a controlled substance."

The definition does not include "the preparation or compounding of a controlled substance by an individual for his own use." An offender is *not* manufacturing, for example, if he obtains powdered cocaine and turns it into crack for his own use.[5]

C. Possess with Intent to Distribute

The vast majority of cases involve possession with intent to distribute. A person who possesses a controlled substance is not presumed to intend to distribute it. Proof of a person's intent is based on circumstantial evidence — unless the suspect admits it! While every factor need not be present, typically more than one must apply.

POSSESSION WITH INTENT FACTORS

Quantity

The quantity of drugs — the most important factor — may prove a suspect's intent to distribute by itself. *Comm. v. Komnenus,* 87 Mass. App. Ct. 587 (2015) (16.78 grams of cocaine, combined with the absence of smoking paraphernalia and the presence of a digital scale, police scanners, and small plastic bags with cut-off corners established intent to distribute). *Comm. v. English,* 2016 WL 320246 (Appeals Court) (76 growing marijuana plants suggested an intent to distribute).

Especially persuasive if the suspect denies using drugs. *Comm. v. Walorz,* 79 Mass. App. Ct. 132 (2011) (Walorz told officers that he did not use drugs. Accordingly, distribution was the only reason for him to receive 500 oxycodone pills in the mail from Brazil).

---

[5] Of course manufacturing also does not include practitioners or pharmacists who properly prepare drugs for patients, research, or educational purposes.

Remember, there is no minimum quantity required to prove intent to distribute. Where other signs of distribution exist, even a really small quantity is sufficient. *Comm. v. LaPerle*, 19 Mass. App. 424 (1985) (defendant convicted of possession of cocaine with intent to distribute because, in addition to cocaine residue, his apartment contained paraphernalia consistent with distribution). *Comm. v. Sauer*, 50 Mass. App. Ct. 299 (2000) (one pill in car sufficient since police saw Sauer entering multiple bars and engaging in sales activity, and observed packaging for illegal sales next to the one pill remaining in his glove box stash).

Purity

Drugs for personal consumption are usually diluted by cutting agents. When a drug is possessed in pure form, it is usually waiting to be cut for sale. *Comm. v. Montanez*, 410 Mass. 290 (1991) (intent to distribute inferred from possession of 29 grams of 91% pure cocaine).

Street Value

A relevant factor is the "street value" of the drugs. *Comm. v. Miller*, 17 Mass. App. Ct. 990 (1984) (street value of drugs $12,000).

Cash

The suspect's possession of a large amount of cash or "marked money" may indicate sales. *Comm. v. Gonzalez*, 452 Mass. 142 (2008) (defendant had $3,000). *Comm. v. Adames*, 41 Mass. App. Ct. (1996) (defendant had marked money used during a "controlled buy").

How money carried is relevant too. *Comm. v. Dancy*, 75 Mass. App. Ct. 175 (2009) (following an observed street meeting with a drug user in an automobile, defendant found with $516 in one pocket and a crumpled $20 bill in the other).

Packaging

The possession of packaged drugs and/or packaging materials is relevant. *Comm. v. Zavala*, 2013 WL 2247759 (Appeals Court) (after seeing exchange between defendant and van driver, police stopped van and found 20 heroin packets stamped with a "Dead Zone" logo; a search of defendant's car revealed packets of heroin with the same logo).

However, packaging is relevant only when more consistent with distribution than personal use. *Comm. v. Acosta*, 81 Mass. App. Ct. 836 (2012) (Acosta had a plastic bag with five smaller bags of cocaine totaling 3.16 grams; nothing about the five bags suggested they were for sale rather than for personal use).

Paraphernalia

A variety of instruments are used to process drugs for sale. *Comm. v. Miller*, 17 Mass. App. Ct. 990 (1984) (possession of cutting agent, sifter with cocaine residue, two scales, straw with cocaine residue, razor blade, and three bags containing cocaine).

Lack of personal use paraphernalia may indicate intent to distribute. *Comm. v. Bones*, 93 Mass. App. Ct. 681 (2018) (while Leonides Bones only had 1.49 grams of heroin, he had it packaged for sale and did not have a cook spoon, needle, or other personal use paraphernalia; in addition, he had folded cash in his pocket, in denominations consistent with heroin sales).

Business Cards

Dealer "business cards" are handed out to get people to buy more. *Comm. v. Young*, 2014 WL 4411068 (Appeals Court) (defendant had in his pocket 70 slips of paper with the name "Just" and a phone number).

Communication Devices

Drug dealers routinely carry cell phones so they can be reached at a moment's notice. *Comm. v. Dancy*, 75 Mass. App. Ct. 175 (2009) (multiple cell phones significant proof since dealers want to separate drug transaction calls from personal calls).

However, a repeatedly ringing cell phone is common in everyday life and does not suggest an intent to distribute. *Comm. v. Ortiz*, 2013 WL 4556578 (Appeals Court). For this reason, officers should answer a dealer's ringing cell phone. See *LED's Criminal Procedure, Chapter 20*, for more on cell phone investigations.

Records

Established drug dealers, like any other sales professional, often keep business records. *Comm. v. St. George*, 89 Mass. App. Ct. 764 (2016) (defendant was found with $1,000 in his hand and a "cuff sheet" next to him, which contained a notation for "Bob" and "$1,000," with the number "$3,000" crossed out; this helped prove the defendant was the seller).

Also, placing key assets in someone else's name may be an indication. *Comm. v. O'Day*, 440 Mass. 296 (2003) (listing of the suspected dealer's truck and electrical utilities in his girlfriend's name was a typical way to shield a drug sales operation).

Drug Sales Area

Being in the area of a drug house or repeated trips to known drug havens is persuasive evidence of distribution. *Comm. v. O'Toole*, 52 Mass. App. Ct. 183 (2001) (rendezvous between alleged dealer and customer began near "heroin house" where officers had made numerous drug purchases).

Dealer Behavior

Behavior includes hand-to-hand exchanges, runner systems, waiting at the corner, and other methods. *Comm. v. Watson*, 430 Mass. 725 (2000) (drug couriers use erratic driving to find out whether they are being followed). *Comm. v. Hernandez*, 77 Mass. App. Ct. 259 (2010) ("drug drop" near a dumpster).

Security Measures

Security measures are consistent with drug dealing operations. *Comm. v. Arias*, 29 Mass. App. Ct. 613 (1990) (defendant barricaded apartment). *Comm. v. Rivera*, 31 Mass. App. Ct. 554 (1991) (defendant possessed police radio scanner).

Stash Pad

A sparsely furnished apartment may indicate that it is a stash pad, used solely for storing and selling drugs. *Comm. v. Watson*, 36 Mass. App. Ct. 252 (1994) (apartment's back bedroom was unfurnished; a front bedroom contained only a mattress and a television; the living room had only a sofa and coffee table — this was defendant's operational base, which he wanted to keep separate from where he lived with his family).

Presence of Firearm

Presence of illegal gun helps show intent to distribute. *U.S. v. Bobadilla-Pagan*, 747 F.3d 26 (2014) (dealers often have guns to protect themselves and their product). *Comm. v. Splaine*, 2018 WL 4924369 (Appeals Court) (possessing a stun gun and pepper spray near illegal drugs in the defendant's bedroom was consistent with an intent to distribute).

Hidden Location

Dealers take significant steps to hide drugs. *Comm. v. Lobo*, 82 Mass. App. Ct. 803 (2012) (defendant had cocaine hidden in his crotch).

Flight or Resistance

Intense effort to avoid police apprehension characterizes a dealer, since mere users are unlikely to fear arrest to the point where they would flee or fight. *Comm. v. Martin*, 48 Mass. App. Ct. 391 (1999). *Comm. v. Matos*, 2013 WL 452312 (Appeals Court) (defendants fled in vehicle when police attempted traffic stop, then fled on foot; one defendant discarded a firearm as he ran; the other was caught behind a dumpster with two bags of marijuana; four more bags and a loaded, large capacity firearm were found in the vehicle).

Police Expert Testimony

Longstanding rule: Police investigators may provide expert analysis in drug cases. *Comm. v. Smith*, 92 Mass. App. Ct. 417 (2017) (expert may explain significance of packaging, amount and purity of narcotics, and other indicators of distribution).

However, an expert may never directly comment on a defendant's guilt or rely on the defendant's physical appearance. *Comm. v. Horne*, 476 Mass. 222 (2017) (officer's testimony regarding the physical characteristics of addicts unfairly prejudiced the defendant because it suggested that, because he did not look like a user, he must be a dealer).

DISTRIBUTION OFFENSES
94C, §§ 32 (Class A), 32A (Class B), 32B (Class C), 32C (Class D), and 32D (Class E)

Elements

There is a distribution statute for each drug class. Penalties vary, but the elements are the same.

- **The suspect intentionally;**
- **Manufactured, distributed, or possessed with the intent to distribute;**
- **A controlled substance.**

Right of Arrest

Class A, B, and C: Felony.

Class D and E: 94C, § 41 warrantless arrest on probable cause.

Distribution Penalties

CLASS A 94C, § 32	CLASS B 94C, § 32A(a)	CLASS B* 94C, § 32A(c) [Covers cocaine, phencyclidine, & methamphetamine]
Basic offense: SP NMT 10 yrs or HC NMT 2½ yrs; and/or Fine NLT $1,000, NMT $10,000.	**Basic offense:** SP NMT 10 yrs or HC NMT 2½ yrs; and/or Fine NLT $1,000, NMT $10,000.	**Initial offense:** SP NMT 10 yrs or HC NMT 2½ yrs; & Fine NLT $1,000, NMT $10,000.
Subsequent offense: SP NLT 3½ yrs, NMT 15 yrs (Mandatory 3½ yrs); & Fine NLT $2,500, NMT $25,000. <u>Only</u> mandatory.	**Subsequent offense:** SP NMT 10 yrs & Fine $2,500, NMT $25,000.	**Aggravated subsequent:** SP NMT 15 yrs & Fine NLT $2,500, NMT $25,000.
* This offense used to impose mandatory incarceration for distribution of cocaine, phencyclidine, or methamphetamine. The strict penalties were eliminated in 2018. See Chapter 69 of the Acts of 2018.		

Distribution Penalties

CLASS C 94C, § 32B	CLASS D 94C, § 32C [Cultivation of marijuana in any amount also covered (if not permitted medically or recreationally)]	CLASS E 94C, § 32D
Basic offense: SP NMT 5 yrs or HC NMT 2½ yrs; and/or Fine NLT $500, NMT $5,000.	**Basic offense:** HC NMT 2 yrs; and/or Fine NLT $500, NMT $5,000.	**Basic offense:** HC NMT 9 months; and/or Fine NLT $250, NMT $2,500.
Subsequent offense: SP NMT 10 yrs or HC NMT 2½ yrs; & Fine NLT $1,000, NMT $10,000. *Note:* No mandatory.	**Subsequent offense:** HC NMT 2½ yrs; and/or Fine NLT $1,000, NMT $10,000. *Note:* No mandatory.	**Subsequent offense:** HC NMT 1½ yrs; and/or Fine NLT $500, NMT $5,000.

Notes

Definition of subsequent offense. Under all of the distribution statutes, Classes A through E, a subsequent offense occurs when the defendant has one or more prior convictions for distribution in Massachusetts *or* in another state *or* federal jurisdiction. The previous conviction may involve *any* controlled substance. *Comm. v. Lisasuain*, 44 Mass. App. Ct. 933 (1998) (earlier New York conviction for selling cocaine provided basis for Massachusetts conviction as a subsequent Class A heroin dealer).

Dual convictions for separate quantities. Separate convictions for distribution and possession with intent to distribute are proper for separate quantities of a controlled substance. *Comm. v. Diaz*, 383 Mass. 73 (1981). However, a defendant cannot be convicted of both possession and possession with intent to distribute for the same quantity of drugs. *Comm. v. Poole*, 29 Mass. App. Ct. 1003 (1990).

Law Enforcement Dimensions

DRUG TRAFFICKING
94C, § 32E

Elements

- ***Intentional.*** The suspect intentionally:

    - Manufactured, distributed, dispensed, or cultivated; or

    - Possessed with intent to manufacture, distribute, dispense, or cultivate; or

    - Brought into the Commonwealth;

- ***Weight.*** A specified amount of or any mixture containing an amount of;

- ***Controlled substance.*** A designated controlled substance.

Right of Arrest

Felony.

Notes

Trafficking does not require a drug dealing enterprise. *Comm. v. Chappee*, 397 Mass. 508 (1986). It requires only that the suspect violate the statute with a sufficient quantity of drugs.

Knowledge of illegal drug required, not quantity. The suspect must know that he distributed, manufactured, or possessed a controlled substance with the intent to distribute. He does *not* have to know that he possessed an amount regulated by the trafficking statute. An amount that meets the trafficking threshold is sufficient. *Comm. v. Rodriguez*, 415 Mass. 447 (1993).

The suspect may not claim, in an effort to escape trafficking liability, that some of the drugs he possessed were for personal use. *Comm. v. Gonzalez*, 67 Mass. App. Ct. 877 (2006) reaffirms that the entire quantity of narcotics possessed by the defendant determines the trafficking bracket, so long as there was an intent to distribute some portion of it.

Weight of substance includes the mixture. In determining whether the suspect possessed the minimum quantity, officers should consider the total weight of the controlled substance mixture. *Comm. v. Beverly*, 389 Mass. 866 (1980) (trafficking conviction upheld, even though mixture of over 200 grams contained only 3% heroin and 97% cutting agent). *Comm. v. Nutile*, 31 Mass. App. Ct. 614 (1991) (84.62 grams contained less than 1% cocaine).

Separate amounts of the same drug may be combined to support a trafficking charge. *Comm. v. Ortiz*, 431 Mass. 134 (2000) (defendant had 135 grams of heroin to sell to undercover officer; once arrested, defendant admitted that remaining 100 grams of his stash was located at his home; based on the combined amount of 135 grams and 100 grams, defendant was prosecuted for trafficking heroin in excess of 200 grams).

Penalties for Trafficking Offenses

Class D § 32E(a) MARIJUANA	Class B § 32E(b) COCAINE [To qualify, substance must be cocaine, in any of its forms, *or* methamphetamine.]	Class A § 32E(c) HEROIN or ANY OTHER OPIOID [To qualify, substance must be heroin, fentanyl, carfentanil, or any other synthetic opioid defined under federal law]
50 pounds but less than 100: SP NLT 2½ yrs, NMT 15 yrs or HC NLT 1 year, NMT 2½ yrs (Mandatory 1 year); & Fine NLT $500, NMT $10,000.	**18 grams but less than 36:** SP NLT 2 yrs, NMT 15 yrs (Mandatory 2 yrs); & Fine NLT $2,500, NMT $25,000.	**18 grams but less than 36:** SP NLT 3½ yrs, NMT 30 yrs (Mandatory 3½ yrs); & Fine NLT $5,000, NMT $50,000.
100 pounds but less than 2,000: SP NLT 2 yrs, NMT 15 yrs (Mandatory 2 yrs); & Fine NLT $2,500, NMT $25,000.	**36 grams but less than 100:** SP NLT 3½ yrs, NMT 20 yrs (Mandatory 3½ yrs); & Fine NLT $5,000, NMT $50,000.	**36 grams but less than 100:** SP NLT 5 yrs, NMT 30 yrs (Mandatory 5 yrs); & Fine NLT $5,000, NMT $50,000.
2,000 pounds but less than 10,000: SP NLT 3½ yrs, NMT 15 yrs (Mandatory 3½ yrs); & Fine NLT $5,000, NMT $50,000.	**100 grams but less than 200:** SP NLT 8 yrs, NMT 20 yrs (Mandatory 8 yrs); & Fine NLT $10,000, NMT $100,000.	**100 grams but less than 200:** SP NLT 8 yrs, NMT 30 yrs (Mandatory 8 yrs); & Fine NLT $10,000, NMT $100,000.
10,000 pounds or more: SP NLT 8 yrs, NMT 15 yrs (Mandatory 8 yrs); & Fine NLT $20,000, NMT $200,000.	**200 grams or more:** SP NLT 12 yrs, NMT 20 yrs (Mandatory 12 yrs); & Fine NLT $50,000, NMT $500,000.	**200 grams or more:** SP NLT 12 yrs, NMT 30 yrs (Mandatory 12 yrs); & Fine NLT $50,000, NMT $500,000.

Class A § 32E(c½) FENTANYL	Class A § 32E(c¾) CARFENTANIL	
10 grams or more: SP NLT 3½ yrs, NMT 20 yrs (Mandatory 3½ yrs).	Any amount qualifies for trafficking, provided the offender has "specific knowledge that [the] mixture contains carfentanil or any derivative of carfentanil": SP NLT 3½ yrs, NMT 20 yrs (Mandatory 3½ yrs).	

Accomplices do not need to know the amount of drugs in the stash in order to be convicted of trafficking. *Comm. v. Hernandez*, 439 Mass. 688 (2003): While the government could not prove that the defendant possessed the substantial quantity of cocaine found in the stash apartment, it did present compelling evidence that the defendant repeatedly assisted the main dealer in the distribution of the stash, and that he understood there was enough inventory to support drug trafficking. The defendant was not a low-level assistant ignorant of a larger stash. He and Quinones (the main dealer) always traveled to and from sales; they were seen entering the building containing the stash apartment together; the defendant lived at another apartment where police found bottles of lactose, used to cut cocaine for retail sale; and the cocaine in the vehicle and in the bathroom at the stash apartment were similar in purity and packaging.

This evidence was sufficient to convict the defendant as an accomplice, but insufficient to show that he constructively possessed the larger stash. The defendant had never been seen coming into or out of the apartment. He did not possess a key either.

Related Criminal & Civil Procedure

Maintaining place of drug sales is considered a "nuisance." Following a successful drug raid, officers may want to contact the landlord of the property and inform him about the potential criminal and civil penalties associated with Maintaining a Nuisance under 139, §§ 14, 15, and 20. For a detailed breakdown of this law, see *Chapter 22* on alcohol offenses.

Section IV
SPECIALIZED DISTRIBUTION OFFENSES

SALE OR POSSESSION WITH INTENT TO SELL DRUG PARAPHERNALIA
94C, § 32I

Elements

- **Sold or possessed with intent.** The suspect sold, possessed, or manufactured with the intent to sell;

- **Paraphernalia.** Drug paraphernalia;

- **Knowledge.** Knowing, or under circumstances where the suspect should have known, that the paraphernalia would be used to plant, cultivate, harvest, manufacture, compound, convert, process, prepare, test, analyze, pack, repack, store, conceal, ingest, inhale (or otherwise illegally introduce into the human body) a controlled substance.

Right of Arrest

Possession with intent to sell: 94C, § 41 warrantless arrest in presence.

Sale to buyer under 18 years old: Felony.

Penalty

Possession of paraphernalia with intent to sell: HC NLT 1 year, NMT 2 yrs; and/or Fine NLT $500, NMT $5,000.

If the defendant sells paraphernalia to a buyer under 18: SP NLT 3 yrs, NMT 5 yrs; and/or Fine NLT $1,000, NMT $5,000.

Notes

Paraphernalia. 94C, § 1 outlines a number of factors that officers may consider in determining whether a particular item is "drug paraphernalia," including: (1) the proximity of the item to any controlled substance; (2) existence of drug residue; (3) any advertising concerning its use; (4) how the item is displayed; (5) whether they are legitimate uses for the item in the community; and (6) expert opinion concerning its use.

Knowledge. The suspect must have known, or reasonably should have known, that the paraphernalia would be used with illegal substances. *Comm. v. Jasmin*, 396 Mass. 653 (1986).

No such crime as possession of drug paraphernalia. 94C, § 32I states: "No person shall sell, possess, or purchase *with intent to sell* drug paraphernalia . . . ." Noticeably absent from this statute is any language that penalizes the simple possession of paraphernalia. Of course, drug residue inside paraphernalia may qualify as unlawful drug possession under 94C, § 34. But the device itself may not be charged as a separate offense.

Confiscate and seek forfeiture for minors. When a citizen of any age possesses drug paraphernalia without illegal residue, no criminal charge applies. However, in the case of a minor, officers may still: (1) identify the minor; (2) confiscate the paraphernalia under the authority of the civil forfeiture statute, 94C, § 47(a)(6); and (3) document it in a police report. If the minor agrees to forfeiture on the street, log the item(s) into evidence for destruction. If the minor objects, the department should seek an order of forfeiture from the district court.

Adults 21 and over may possess marijuana paraphernalia and, absent local restrictions, may sell it without a license to other adults. See 94G, § 8. Sales activity directed at minors remains a crime under 94C, § 32I and under 94G, § 13(i). See discussion in *Chapter 21*.

SALE OF HYPODERMIC NEEDLES & SYRINGES
94C, § 27

Possession Legal

In Massachusetts, it is legal to possess hypodermic needles and syringes without a prescription. In fact, these items are no longer defined as paraphernalia under 94C, § 1. The law was changed as a public health measure to encourage IV drug users to buy clean needles. However, only people who are 18 and over may purchase hypodermics without a prescription. Chapter 172 of the Acts of 2006. *Important note:* A private needle access program does not violate the prohibition against the sale to minors if it distributes needles for free. *AIDS Support Group, Inc. v. Town of Barnstable*, 477 Mass. 296 (2017).

Elements

Type 1: Sale by Nonprofessional

- The suspect was not a licensed pharmacist, wholesale druggist, or a manufacturer or dealer of surgical or embalming supplies; and

- Sold a hypodermic needle or syringe to any person.

Type 2: Sale to a Minor or Failure to Validate Age

- The suspect was a licensed pharmacist, wholesale druggist, or a manufacturer or dealer of surgical or embalming supplies; and

- Either:

    - Sold a hypodermic needle or syringe to a person under the age of 18; or
    - Sold a hypodermic needle or syringe without requiring identification that proved the purchaser was at least 18 years old.

Right of Arrest

94C, § 41 warrantless arrest on probable cause.

Penalty found in 94C, § 38

1st offense: HC NMT 1 year; and/or Fine NMT $1,000.

If any prior drug law violation in 94C: HC NMT 2 yrs; and/or Fine NMT $2,000.

Related Offenses

Assault crimes involving needles. 265, § 15C prohibits committing an assault *or* A&B by means of a hypodermic syringe, hypodermic needle, or "any instrument adapted for the administration of controlled or other substances by injection." Penalty: SP NMT 15 yrs or HC NMT 2½ yrs; and/or Fine NMT $5,000. Right of Arrest: Felony.

- **Clean and used needles covered.** *Comm. v. Hamilton*, 87 Mass. App. Ct. 274 (2015).

- **Reckless A&B covered.** In *Comm. v. Hamilton, supra.*, Officer Ryan Stone responded to a call for a "wellness check" in a store bathroom. When he ordered Brad Hamilton out of the stall, he saw items used to clean a hypodermic needle. Hamilton was holding an object in his hand. Stone repeatedly ordered Hamilton to drop it, but Hamilton did not respond. As Stone attempted to handcuff him, Hamilton thrust a needle into Stone's hand with enough force to puncture his glove. Although Hamilton argued that his act was unintentional, the court still found him guilty of reckless A&B. Hamilton's reckless act caused sufficient injury because Stone felt a stinging, shock-like sensation in his hand and received treatment at the hospital. This was not a trivial injury.

COUNTERFEIT SUBSTANCE
94C, § 32G

Purpose

94C, § 1 defines a counterfeit substance as one "represented to be a particular drug . . . but which is in fact not that drug." Counterfeit substances are illegal because they are often dangerous to ingest and, more importantly, the offender is trying to profit from the drug trade while eliminating the risk of being caught with an actual controlled substance. *Comm. v. Tofanelli*, 67 Mass. App. Ct. 61 (2006).

Elements

- ***Knowingly.*** The suspect knowingly;

- ***Create or possess with intent.*** Created, distributed, dispensed, or possessed with the intent to distribute or dispense;

- ***Counterfeit.*** A counterfeit substance.

Right of Arrest

94C, § 41 warrantless arrest in presence.

Penalty

HC NMT 1 year; and/or Fine NLT $250, NMT $2,500.

Section V
DRUG CRIMES AGAINST CHILDREN

DRUG FREE SCHOOL & PARK ZONE
94C, § 32J

Elements

- ***The suspect violates one of the following nonpossession offenses under Chapter 94C:*** § 32 (Class A); § 32A (Class B); § 32B (Class C); § 32C (Class D); § 32D (Class E); § 32E (Trafficking); § 32F (Distribution of A, B, or C to Minors); or § 32I (Drug Paraphernalia); and

    - *Violence or weapon.* Used violence or a threat of violence or possessed a firearm, rifle, shotgun, machine gun, or other weapon defined in 269, § 10(b), or induced another participant to do so during the commission of the offense; or

    - *Direction of felony.* Directed the activities of another person who committed any felony in violation of 94C; or

- *Involve minors.* Committed or attempted to commit a violation of § 32F (distribution of Class A, B, or C to minors) or § 32K (inducing a minor to distribute).

- **Type 1: School zone.**

  - **Within 300 feet of the property boundary of a:**

    - Public preschool or an accredited, private preschool; or
    - An accredited Headstart facility; or
    - A public or private elementary school; or
    - A public or private secondary school; or
    - A public or private vocational school;

  - **Between the hours of 5:00 a.m. and midnight, whether or not school is in session or the defendant knew about the boundary.**

- **Type 2: Park zone.** Within 100 feet of a public park or playground. [There are no hour limitations like with the school zone offense.]

Right of Arrest

Felony. [*Note:* Since this is an enhanced penalty provision, the right of arrest will also stem from an underlying distribution offense.]

Penalty

SP NLT 2½ yrs, NMT 15 yrs or HC NLT 2 yrs, NMT 2½ yrs; and Fine NLT $1,000, NMT $10,000. Mandatory 2 yrs beginning *from and after* the sentence for the underlying offense. *Comm. v. Alvarez*, 413 Mass. 224 (1992). A judge may not dismiss a school or park zone case over the prosecutor's objection. *Comm. v. Manning*, 75 Mass. App. Ct. 829 (2009).

Notes

Determining distance.

- **Straight line from violation to site.** *Comm. v. Spano*, 414 Mass. 178 (1993) declared that officers should measure in a straight line from the edge of the nearest school or park boundary to the site of the violation.

- **Measuring device must be calibrated for accuracy.** *Comm. v. Whitlock*, 74 Mass. App. Ct. 320 (2009) (software measuring program may be used if properly authenticated). *Comm. v. Torres*, 453 Mass. 722 (2009) (roller measuring tape may be used).

- **Measure to front entrance of suspect's building.** There is no need to measure the exact distance from the school boundary to the particular apartment where the defendant possesses drugs for sale. It is sufficient to measure in a straight line to the front entrance of the building. *Comm. v. Cintron*, 59 Mass. App. Ct. 905 (2003).

Knowledge of school or park boundary irrelevant. *Comm. v. Klusman*, 46 Mass. App. Ct. 919 (1999) (although some schools are not clearly recognizable, the dealer bears the burden of ascertaining where schools are located and removing his operations from those areas).

Proof of school or preschool. Officers must prove that the particular school is covered. *Comm. v. Vasquez*, 33 Mass. App. Ct. 950 (1992) (only testifying that distribution occurred near "Woodland Street School" insufficient). Compare *Comm. v. Pixley*, 77 Mass. App. Ct. 624 (2010) (detective testified that building was "University High School" and high school age students attended this alternative school; he also knew a teacher there).

The school zone statute only applies to "accredited" private preschools. The terms "accredited" and "licensed" are not the same. In fact, the law that governs private schools describes how licensed schools can *become* accredited, which involves an additional review process. *Comm. v. Cooper*, 91 Mass App. Ct. 595 (2017). Public preschools need only be licensed to qualify for coverage. *Comm. v. Nardone*, 2011 WL 5924576 (Appeals Court).

Proof of public park. Officers must identify the park, and prove it is: (1) owned or maintained by a governmental entity; and (2) is a tract of land set apart or dedicated for public enjoyment or recreational use. *Comm. v. Boger*, 486 Mass. 358 (2020). *Comm. v. Ramos-Cabrera*, 486 Mass. 364 (2020) (public park does not need to be well-maintained to qualify for coverage). *Comm. v. Gopaul*, 86 Mass. App. Ct. 685 (2014) (private playgrounds not covered).

Related Offenses

Inducing Minor to Distribute Drugs. 94C, § 32K outlaws the suspect who knowingly induces, assists or procures a person under age 18 to either: (1) distribute or possess with the intent to distribute *any* controlled substance; or (2) accept, deliver, or possess money used or intended for use in the manufacture, delivery, or sale of *any* controlled substance. Penalty: SP NMT 15 yrs (Mandatory 5 yrs). Right of Arrest: Felony.

- **It is not necessary to prove that the suspect knew the age of the child employed in drug dealing.** It is sufficient to prove that the youth was under 18 years of age. *Comm. v. Montalvo*, 50 Mass. App. Ct. 85 (2000) (girl testified that she was 14½ when defendant gave her eight bags of marijuana to sell).

- **No need to prove minor aware of illegal drug transactions.** The government does not have to prove that the minor knew that he was distributing a controlled substance on behalf of the adult. *Comm. v. Serrano-Ortiz*, 53 Mass. App. Ct. 608 (2002).

Distributing Class A, B, or C to Minor Under 18. 94C § 32F. Penalty: Mandatory 2½ yrs for Class C, 3 yrs for Class B, 5 yrs for cocaine, and 5 yrs for Class A. Right of Arrest: Felony.

Related Procedure

Protective Custody for Children Found with Controlled Substances. 94C, § 36 enables an officer to hold a juvenile in protective custody for up to 4 hours provided: (1) the officer *reasonably believes* the child is under 18; and (2) has knowledge of and is present with Class A, B, or C — *not* Class D (marijuana). Officers must notify a parent or guardian.

Section VI
IMPROPERLY OBTAINING DRUGS FROM THOSE IN LEGAL POSSESSION

Legitimate medical purpose. For a prescription to be valid, 94C, § 19 states that it must "be issued for a legitimate medical purpose by a practitioner acting in the usual course of his professional practice." § 19 specifies that a prescription not issued in the usual course of professional treatment or authorized research, constitutes illegal distribution. *Comm. v. Brown*, 456 Mass. 708 (2010).

Suspicious factors. These factors may indicate no legitimate medical purpose:

- The physician permits the patient to name the drug he desires.

- The physician expresses concern as to how and where a prescription will be filled — in a manner that does not indicate a good faith concern for his patient.

- Repeated refills are issued over relatively short periods of time.

- Failure to schedule appropriate appointments for follow-up care.

- Conversations about nontherapeutic use or drug enforcement that demonstrate the physician knew the drugs would not be used for medical purposes. *Comm. v. Pike*, 430 Mass. 317 (1999).

FRAUDULENTLY OBTAINING A CONTROLLED SUBSTANCE
94C, § 33

Summary

94C, § 33 punishes any deception to obtain a controlled substance — including using a false prescription or lying. *Comm. v. Johnson*, 2013 WL 1788016 (Appeals Court) (deception existed when pharmacy technician placed Hydrocodone pills in her pocket and walked out).

Elements

Type 1: Drug Abuser Fraud. The suspect intentionally:

- **Uttered a false prescription** for a controlled substance; or

- **Obtained possession of a controlled substance by any fraud or deception** (including falsifying a prescription *or* not disclosing a material fact to a practitioner).

Type 2: Manufacturing Fraud. The suspect used, during the manufacture or distribution of a controlled substance, a fictitious or revoked registration number.

Right of Arrest

Felony.

Penalty

1st offense: SP NMT 4 yrs or HC NMT 2½ yrs; and/or Fine NMT $20,000.

Subsequent offense: SP NMT 8 yrs or HC NMT 2½ yrs; and/or Fine NMT $30,000. A subsequent offense exists when the defendant has one or more prior convictions of a § 33 offense *or* any other felony in 94C.

Notes

Uttering. Uttering is an attempt to gain possession of a controlled substance with a false prescription. Under 94C, § 33, uttering occurs at the moment the prescription is presented to the pharmacist — regardless of whether it is filled.

Getting drugs through fraud. 94C, § 33 also penalizes any deception or fraud — including the "nondisclosure of a material fact" that results in the subject obtaining a controlled substance. Notice how "uttering" a false prescription constitutes a crime even if the offender is unsuccessful. Other types of fraud do not become a crime until the offender successfully gains possession of the drugs. For example, if an individual "doctor shops" (i.e., visits numerous physicians to find one that will give him drugs), failing to reveal this to the fifth doctor is clearly the nondisclosure of a material fact. Material simply means that the information, if disclosed, would have influenced the doctor's decision.[6] Still, officers would not have probable cause until the doctor was fooled and gave the suspect drugs. Remember this requirement when conducting stings or other undercover operations.

There is no specific crime for stealing a prescription pad. Officers must rely on general larceny laws when confronting such a theft in the Commonwealth.

STEALING A CONTROLLED SUBSTANCE FROM AUTHORIZED DISPENSER
94C, § 37

Elements

- **Steal controlled substance.** The suspect stole any controlled substance;

- **Authorized dispenser.** From a registered manufacturer, wholesale druggist, pharmacy *or* other person authorized to dispense or possess any controlled substance.

---

6 *Comm. v. Mitchell*, 15 Mass. App. Ct. 577 (1983) ("material" means likely to have a significant impact; this case dealt with a perjury prosecution).

Right of Arrest

Felony.

Penalty

SP NMT 10 yrs or HC NMT 2½ yrs; or Fine NMT $500.

Notes

Potential application. There are four potential victims. Two are covered by 94C, § 37.

- **Stealing from authorized dispenser.** § 37 can be charged when the victim is a pharmacist, doctor, nurse, or other person authorized by law to dispense or possess *any* drug. The legislature intended to confer special protection on individuals who might be targeted by drug thieves because they possess large and varied amounts of controlled substances.

- **Stealing evidence.** The theft of drug evidence from a police officer or the evidence locker violates § 37 too, because 94C, § 7 authorizes the police to possess *any* controlled substance in the performance of official duty.

- **Stealing from lawful user.** On the other hand, many drug offenders steal controlled substances from people who lawfully possess them for their own medical or mental health condition — e.g., a high school student takes her mother's Valium. These offenders do not fall within the reach of § 37 because their victims are not authorized to possess *any* controlled substance (only the drugs they legitimately received). As a result, for the person who steals a patient's drugs, the proper charges are possession under 94C, § 34, *and* larceny under 266, § 30 or, depending on the circumstances, larceny from a building or person. See discussion in *Chapter 27*.

- **Stealing contraband.** While outside the orbit of § 37, Massachusetts still penalizes the theft of contraband from users or dealers. *Comm. v. Ridge*, 37 Mass. App. Ct. 943 (1994) (defendant convicted of larceny for stealing cocaine from accomplice). See *Chapter 25* for more on larceny.

Stealing broadly defined. For conviction under § 37, the suspect need not have specifically *intended* to steal the controlled substance. The suspect must simply know that he is taking the drug without permission from the professional authorized to possess it. *Comm. v. Sheehan*, 376 Mass. 765 (1978) (acting under the influence of alcohol or drugs is not a defense).

Section VII
CONSPIRACY

CONSPIRACY
94C, § 40

Element

A person may not conspire to violate any crime under Chapter 94C. Like any conspiracy, all that is required is an agreement to commit a prohibited act. *Comm. v. Stoico*, 45 Mass. App. Ct. 559 (1998) (defendants met to sell marijuana worth $170,000).

Right of Arrest

94C, § 41 authorizes warrantless arrest on probable cause.

Penalty

The punishment for conspiracy may not exceed the maximum imprisonment and/or fine associated with the offense that was the object of the conspiracy.

Notes

Business arrangement necessary — not a one-time, buyer-seller transaction. *Comm. v. Doty*, 88 Mass. App. Ct. 195 (2015): Brian Hart, an informant, contacted Jonathan Wright to buy cocaine. When they met at a restaurant parking lot, Wright called someone named Pam. A few minutes later, Pamela Doty pulled up in a truck. Hart gave Wright $100 for two bags. Wright got the cocaine from Doty and gave it to Hart.

There was no evidence that Doty and Wright were involved in a conspiracy. There was nothing about the single sale that showed Doty intended for Wright to distribute cocaine to someone else. The amount was small, and there was no suggestion of an ongoing business relationship. A single sale of drugs, without more, does not establish a conspiracy.[7]

Drug amount in trafficking conspiracy. To prove conspiracy to traffic a certain amount of drugs, the government does not have to show that the conspirators possessed the necessary amount on one occasion. It is sufficient to prove that the offenders possessed the required quantity over the course of the conspiracy. *Comm. v. Albert*, 51 Mass. App. Ct. 377 (2001).

Venue. A conspiracy may be prosecuted in any county "in which an overt act is committed by any one of the conspirators, regardless of whether the defendant ever entered the county while the conspiracy was ongoing." *Comm. v. Stoico*, 45 Mass. App. Ct. 559 (1998).

---

[7] If simply being customers was always a conspiracy, then all street addicts would be subject to the same penalties as distributors, which does not make sense.

21 Marijuana & Tobacco

ADULT USE MARIJUANA REGULATION

Licensing of Marijuana Establishments

The Cannabis Control Commission (CCC) regulates the cultivation, manufacturing, and retail sales of marijuana and marijuana products. 935 CMR 500.000. The CCC is located at Union Station, 2 Washington Square, Worcester, MA 01604. Telephone: 774-415-0200.

Police Enforcement Procedures

*Marijuana has **not** been legalized for all people and all purposes.* Illegal activity draws either a civil or criminal response. See, e.g., 94G, § 2.

Civil fine procedure for marijuana cases. 94C, § 32N.

- **Officer procedures.** An officer must:

  - Issue a town bylaw or city ordinance ticket; and
  - Give a copy to the offender at the time and place of the violation; or, if not possible, mail or deliver a copy to his last known residence within 15 days.
  - Give 2 copies to OIC, who retains one and sends the other to the clerk.
  - For children under 18, provide another copy to a parent/guardian.

- **Offenders 18 and over.** The offender may pay the fine or request a hearing within 21 days. If found not responsible at the hearing, he is discharged. If responsible, he must pay fine.

- **Offenders under 18.** In addition to the $100 civil fine:

  - The parent/guardian of a child must file a certificate with the clerk that shows the child completed the drug education program within 1 year of the date of the offense. The program must provide 4 hours of classroom instruction and 10 hours of community service. 94C, § 32M.
  - If the program has not been completed, 94C, §§ 32L and 32N direct the clerk to conduct a hearing with the offender, parent/guardian, and enforcing officer to determine whether the fine should be increased to $1,000. The clerk must consider the parties' ability to pay, the offender's ability to participate in a program, and the availability of a suitable program. § 32L states that the child and parents are *both* liable for paying the $1,000 fine. *In addition* to the increased fine, § 32M empowers the police to file a delinquency complaint.

- **Disposition of fines.** Any civil penalties collected for marijuana go to the town or city where the offense occurred.

The key marijuana crimes mentioned in this chapter are:

- **Possession of marijuana (Class D).** 94C, § 34. Officers may arrest on probable cause. See 94C, § 41. Penalty: HC NMT 6 months; and/or Fine of $500.

- **Distribution, possession with intent to distribute, manufacturing, or cultivation of marijuana (Class D).** 94C, § 32C. Officers may arrest on probable cause. See 94C, § 41. Penalty: HC NMT 2 yrs; and/or Fine NLT $500, NMT $5,000.

- **Paraphernalia sale, manufacture, or possession with intent to sell.** 94C, § 32I. For possession/manufacture with intent to sell to anyone under 21, or an actual sale to a person 18-20, officers may arrest in presence. See 94C, § 41. Penalty: HC NLT 1 yr, NMT 2 yrs; and/or Fine NLT $500, NMT $5,000. For an actual sale to a buyer under 18, felony arrest. Penalty: SP NLT 3 yrs, NMT 5 yrs; and/or Fine NLT $1,000, NMT $5,000.

Multiple offenders may be charged and/or fined if officers determine that they participated in illegal activities. Furthermore, officers do not need to identify all the individuals involved in order to take enforcement action. *Comm. v. James*, 30 Mass. App. Ct. 490 (1991).

Identification of marijuana. For civil offense purposes, marijuana may be identified by sight and odor. This is necessary because Commonwealth drug labs refuse to analyze noncriminal quantities. On the other hand, for anything beyond low level criminal possession or distribution, officers should submit the marijuana and/or concentrate for laboratory analysis. *Comm. v. MacDonald*, 459 Mass. 148 (2011) (a trained police officer's opinion that a substance is marijuana — with its distinctive odor and appearance — is typically sufficient, by itself, to prove the identity of the drug).

Synthetic marijuana (aka K-2, Spice) is always Class C. This was discussed in *Chapter 20*. 94C, § 31.

Marijuana Possession & Cultivation

Adults 21 and over in public.

- **1 ounce, with 5 grams of concentrate, is legal.** It is legal for people age 21 or over to publicly possess, use, purchase, or process up to 1 ounce of marijuana, provided that there are no more than 5 grams of marijuana concentrate. 94G, § 7(a)(1). This means the police may not detain a person with a small amount of marijuana who appears to be 21 or over, is not consuming it in public or a prohibited area, and is not engaged in illegal distribution.

  "Marijuana concentrate" is defined as "the resin extracted from any part of the plant of the genus Cannabis and every compound, manufacture, salt, derivative, mixture or preparation of that resin but shall not include the weight of any other ingredient combined with marijuana to prepare marijuana products." 94G, § 7(g).

- **Possession of more than 1 ounce but less than 2 ounces.** $100 civil fine and forfeiture of the excess marijuana. In short, an adult may walk away with an ounce. 94G, § 13(e).

- **Possession of over 2 ounces of marijuana.** Crime. 94C, § 34.

- **Medical marijuana exception.** Generally, a medical cardholder may possess and transport up to 10 ounces of marijuana plant material or the equivalent amount of concentrate (1.5 ounces). This is considered a 60-day supply for patients. 935 CMR 501.003. The suspect must present his card on demand to a police officer, who may look up a cardholder's status in CJIS.

  It is possible for a physician to approve more or less than 10 ounces. 935 CMR 501.010(9). Officers may check CJIS to determine a patient's 60-day supply, since it will indicate whether a higher or lower amount was authorized.

- **No conspiracy against buyer.** Adults are allowed to purchase marijuana for their own use. 94G, § 7(a)(1). Adult buyers may not be charged with conspiracy if they buy from an illegal dealer — because their behavior *is* legal. *Comm. v. Doty*, 88 Mass. App. Ct. 195 (2015).

It is illegal for minors under 21 to possess any marijuana privately or publicly.

- **2 ounces or less.** $100 civil fine. 94C, § 32L.[1]

- **Internal possession.** The definition of possession under 94C, § 32L includes "having cannabinoids . . . in the urine, blood, saliva, sweat, hair, fingernails, toe nails or other tissue or fluid of the human body." This means, for example, that a 20 year old may be issued a civil ticket if she admits to being "high on weed" but possesses no more actual marijuana.

- **School suspension or expulsion possible if behavior on school grounds or at school-sponsored event.** 71, § 37H. See Department of Elementary & Secondary Education, Advisory Opinion on Question 2 (dated December 29, 2008) at doe.mass.edu/lawsregs/advisory/122908q2.html. Also see 94G, § 2(d)(3) (kindergarten and grades 1–12, no possession or consumption activities on their grounds).

- **Over 2 ounces.** Crime. 94C, § 34.

- **Medical marijuana exception.** A minor may be a qualifying medical marijuana patient. Cannabis Control Commission (CCC) regulations do not prohibit any minor under the age of 21 from purchasing or possessing marijuana, provided they have a valid registration card. 935 CMR 501.105(6). In order to become a cardholder, someone under the age of 18 must be certified by two physicians (one of them a pediatrician) and have a parent or guardian as a caregiver. For minor cardholders age 18–20, officers should allow them to possess a 60-day supply of marijuana (10 ounces or 1.5 ounces of concentrate). Minor cardholders under 18 may only possess or use in the presence of their registered caregiver. Officers should insist on contacting a parent or guardian before allowing them to leave on their own with marijuana.

- *Cultivation.* A juvenile who cultivates 12 or fewer plants in his residence is subject to a civil penalty of $100 and must attend the 94C, § 32M drug awareness program. If under 18, the parent is notified under 94C, § 32N. A juvenile under 17 at the time of the offense who fails to attend the program within one year may be the subject of a juvenile complaint. 94G, § 13(h). If a juvenile grows more than 12 plants, it is a crime under 94C, § 32C.

---

1 94G, § 2(b) keeps the current decriminalization law, found in Chapter 94C, for minors under 21.

Adults 21 and over at home (inside their primary residence).

- **Manufacturing.** There is a complicated relationship between "manufacturing" marijuana products under Chapter 94G versus 94C. First, the ability to personally manufacture marijuana products is limited by 94G, § 2(c), which states: "Unless done pursuant to a marijuana product manufacturer license issued by the [Cannabis Control Commission], this chapter does not authorize a person to manufacture marijuana or hemp by means of any liquid or gas, other than alcohol, that has a flashpoint below 100 degrees Fahrenheit." Therefore, any person, who lacks a commercial license, may not use butane, propane, or other gases or liquids, except alcohol, to create marijuana concentrate.

  The improper manufacturing behavior defined by 94G also satisfies the definition of criminal manufacturing under 94C, § 1 — *except* § 1 excludes manufacturing activity "by an individual for his own use." Therefore, if officers find a person has manufactured marijuana [i.e., created concentrate in violation of 94G, § 2(c)] for his own use, there is no available criminal penalty. Officers should simply confiscate the manufactured marijuana under their forfeiture authority in 94C, § 47.[2]

  On the other hand, if the person has manufactured marijuana concentrate for more than himself, whether or not he intends to sell it, then he is outside the protection of 94G and 94C. He should be charged with 94C, § 32C (manufacturing a Class D drug). Strict enforcement is vital because illegal, unlicensed manufacturing creates a public safety danger from fire and explosion.

- **Possession & cultivation.** Adults may possess 10 ounces or less of marijuana plus any marijuana produced by cultivating and processing 6 plants per adult, but no more than 12 plants per household, regardless of the number of adults living in the home. 94G, § 7(a)(2).

  - *Outdoors or indoors.* Homegrows are not limited to outdoor spaces. They may be indoors too. 94G, § 7(a)(2) (approves "marijuana plants cultivated on the premises" without any further definition of the term "premises").

  - *Landlord restrictions.* Landlords may prevent tenants from smoking marijuana on the premises, but they may *not* prevent them from ingesting marijuana products (e.g., edibles) *unless* allowing them to do so would cause the landlord to violate federal law (e.g., subsidized housing regulations; college and university guidelines). See 94G, § 2(d)(1). Landlords may forbid cultivation activities by their tenants. 94G, § 2(d)(1) allows a person who owns, occupies, or manages property to prohibit or regulate the "display, production, processing, manufacture, or sale of marijuana and marijuana accessories."[3]

  - *Medical marijuana implications.* Medical marijuana cardholders who allege financial and/or transportation hardship may obtain authorization from the CCC to grow enough plants to obtain 10 ounces of marijuana on a continuous 60-day cycle. Those who receive a hardship cultivation registration may grow the marijuana at their own residence or that of their caregiver. It must be done in an enclosed, locked

---

[2] This is the same approach recommended for underage possession of paraphernalia or accessories.
[3] While technically this statute does not forbid "cultivation," the words "production" and "processing" should incorporate any cultivation activities until a court says otherwise.

area not visible to the public. There can only be one medical grow per address, unless there is proof that multiple hardship patients actually reside there.

Unlike the legalization law in 94G, medical marijuana regulations do not specify a maximum number of plants. 935 CMR 501.035(1), (8), (9).

- *Only primary residence.* No place except a primary residence may be used to grow marijuana without a CCC license. A person who grows even a small quantity in a rented storage area, his workplace, or any other location outside his primary residence commits the crime of unlawful cultivation under 94C, § 32C.

- *Only for personal use or gifting.* Without a CCC license, marijuana, in any amount, may only be grown for personal use or small scale "gifting" (1 ounce or less). Evidence that any amount is being grown for sale is a crime under 94C, § 32C. Under a hardship cultivation registration in the medical marijuana program, marijuana cannot be sold or gifted in any amount. No exceptions. 935 CMR 501.035(11).

- *Excess cultivation consequences for non-medical purposes.* If a person grows more than 6 plants, but not more than 12 plants, $100 civil fine and marijuana forfeiture of the excess plants. 94G, § 13(e). If a person grows more than 12 plants, it is a crime under 94C, § 32C.

- *Visible homegrow.* A homegrow may not be visible to the naked eye from a public place (if it is visible through binoculars or from aircraft, there is no violation). $300 civil fine and marijuana forfeiture of the visible plants.[4] 94G, § 13(a).

- *Improperly secured marijuana.* If a person possesses more than 1 ounce of marijuana in a residence, the excess must be secured by a lock: $100 civil fine and marijuana forfeiture. 94G, § 13(b). The phrase in § 13(b), "secured by a lock," is vague. Does it mean a locked house is sufficient, even if the marijuana is on the living room coffee table? How about a locked room with marijuana left on a desk? Until a court says otherwise, the author recommends that officers apply the same standard for marijuana as improper gun storage (140, § 131L). The marijuana should be in a container or cabinet secured by a key or combination. See *Comm. v. Reyes*, 464 Mass. 245 (2013).

- **Child endangerment.** Overwhelming marijuana use in the presence of young children may rise to level of child endangerment under 265, § 13L. Penalty: HC NMT 2½ yrs. Right of Arrest: Arrest for breach of peace in presence. Otherwise, complaint. *Comm. v. Paul*, 2012 WL 3154545 (Appeals Court). For more detail, see *LED's Juvenile Law, Chapter 5*.

Criminal Cultivation Investigations

For suspect not in the medical program. Officers must present evidence that the suspect does not have a medical hardship cultivation registration and either: (1) was not growing the marijuana at his primary residence; or (2) possessed more than 12 plants; or (3) sold, or

---

4 The statute does not limit the forfeiture to visible plants, but this interpretation is consistent with other sections of this law.

possessed with the intent to sell, any amount of marijuana produced by the plants. *Comm. v. Long*, 2019 WL 3770342 (SJC).

For a medical cardholder. *Comm. v. Richardson*, 479 Mass. 394 (2018): Joshua Richardson called 911 to report a violent home invasion. When the sergeant learned there was marijuana growing in the basement, he ordered everyone out and secured the premises. Richardson provided his medical marijuana hardship registration. Police got a search warrant and seized 22 plants along with other materials for a grow operation. Richardson's girlfriend told police he was not a regular marijuana user.

For unlawful cultivation with a hardship license, there must be an intent to cultivate more than the permitted amount *or* an intent to distribute.

- **There was insufficient evidence of a marijuana yield in excess of 60-day supply.** The expert in this case never personally observed Richardson's marijuana grow. In fact, he had a hard time identifying from the pictures whether the plants were even male or female.[5] His hypothetical testimony was too speculative to conclude Richardson intended to cultivate more than 10 ounces of marijuana within a 60-day period.

- **However, there was sufficient evidence of intent to distribute.** Quantity, plus other factors, established an intent to distribute. Here, the lack of drug paraphernalia helped show intent, and the girlfriend's testimony that Richardson was not a regular marijuana user. Richardson had reported an armed home invasion in the cultivation area, suggesting others knew he was a drug dealer and attempted to rob him. He also had over $2,000 on his person at the time of his arrest, despite being unemployed.

Marijuana Paraphernalia or "Accessories"

Marijuana accessories defined. Under 94G, § 1(h), they are "equipment, products, devices or materials of any kind that are intended or designed for use in planting, propagating, cultivating, growing, harvesting, manufacturing, compounding, converting, producing, processing, preparing, testing, analyzing, packaging, repackaging, storing, containing, ingesting, inhaling, or otherwise introducing marijuana into the human body." This definition mirrors the definition of paraphernalia found in 94C, § 32I.

Adults 21 and over may legally (in public or private) possess, purchase, manufacture, or obtain marijuana accessories. 94G, § 8.

Adults and commercial businesses may sell marijuana accessories to other adults without a license. If a convenience store in a city or town wants to sell bongs, pipes, dabbing implements, etc., they may immediately do so — as long as they do not sell, or possess them with the intent to sell, to someone under 21. Municipalities may restrict and/or regulate this activity with an ordinance or bylaw. 94G, § 3.

Under 21 and accessories.

- **Possession protocol.** People under 21 may not legally purchase or possess accessories [see 94G, § 2(b)], but there is no civil or criminal penalty authorized by law. This author

---

5 Female plants produce usable marijuana; male plants do not.

recommends that officers: (1) identify the minor; (2) confiscate the paraphernalia under the authority of the civil forfeiture statute, 94C, § 47(a)(6); and (3) document this police action in an incident report. If the suspect agrees to forfeit his property on the street, log the item(s) into the evidence system for destruction. If the suspect objects, the department should seek an order of forfeiture from the district court.

- **Sold or possessed with intent.** If any person (adult or minor) sold, possessed with the intent to sell, or manufactured with the intent to sell, marijuana accessories to someone under 21, the seller may be criminally charged under 94C, § 32I. Police may arrest offenders in their presence who possess accessories with intent to sell to anyone under 21, or who actually sold accessories to a minor 18–20. If the actual buyer was under 18 years old, the seller commits a felony under § 32I.

Transferring or "Gifting" Marijuana

Adults 21 and over may legally (in public or private) transfer or "gift" up to 1 ounce of marijuana to another adult — provided no more than 5 grams is concentrate. 94G, § 7(a)(4). The transfer may not be advertised or promoted to the public, and may not be for any value. This prohibition includes delayed or disguised payments, bartered gifts, or other sham transactions. Chapter 55 of the Acts of 2017 warns that any gift of marijuana or marijuana products, in any amount, in conjunction with the sale of any item constitutes criminal distribution. For any improper gift, charge distribution under 94C, § 32C.

Marijuana transfer to a minor under 21, regardless of whether the adult offender receives any payment, is illegal. The reason is that 94G, § 2(b) prohibits the knowing transfer of marijuana or marijuana products (e.g., concentrates, edibles, beverages) to people under 21.

- **Furnishing (aka "Social Host" law).** 94G, § 13(i) forbids any person of any age from "furnishing" — which is defined as intentionally <u>giving</u> anyone under 21, <u>or allowing</u> anyone under 21 to possess, marijuana, marijuana products, or accessories on property they own or control. "Allowing" means that the offender was consciously aware of the illegal possession. Penalty: HC NMT 1 year; and/or Fine NMT $2,000. Right of Arrest: Arrest for breach of peace in presence. Otherwise, complaint.

    The only exceptions are that parents and grandparents may allow their children and grandchildren to use marijuana on property they own and control. The legal sale or delivery of medical marijuana is also permitted.

- **Furnishing illegal in motor vehicle.** *Comm. v. Ellis*, 2021 WL 162599 (Appeals Court) held that a motor vehicle qualifies as "property owned or controlled" by a defendant accused of furnishing under 94G, 13(i). As a result, officers in *Ellis* properly ordered the under-21 occupants to exit to investigate furnishing based on the marijuana odor and a consent search revealing a Mason jar filled with marijuana.

- **Furnishing violation may be committed by adults and minors.** 94G, § 2(b) and § 13(i) prohibit all knowing transfers to minors. It is not limited to adults. The prohibition also includes minors who distribute to minors. See *Comm. v. Kneram*, 63 Mass. App. Ct. 371 (2005).

- **If suspect receives money or anything of value, charge criminal distribution.** 94C, § 32C.

Difficult to prove an intent to distribute based on a small quantity — especially when juveniles are dealing. *Comm. v. Humberto H.*, 466 Mass. 562 (2013) (five small bags without dealer paraphernalia in 15 year old's possession was insufficient proof of an intent to distribute). *Comm. v. Ilya*, 470 Mass. 625 (2015).

Procure or Attempt to Procure

Attempt to illegally purchase or procure marijuana or accessories. Under 94G, § 13(f), a person under 21 may not: (1) purchase or attempt to purchase; or (2) make arrangements with any person to purchase or "in any way procure"; or (3) willfully misrepresent his age; or (4) alter, deface, or falsify an ID with the intent to purchase or obtain marijuana, marijuana products, or accessories.

- **Medical exception:** A minor may be a qualifying medical marijuana patient. Cardholders age 18 to 21 do not need a parent or guardian to lawfully purchase marijuana for medical purposes. Cardholders under 18 must be with a parent or guardian caregiver.

- **Penalty and procedure:** Civil fine $100 and a drug education program. *Note:* If a minor is under 17 at the time of the offense and fails to complete a drug awareness program within 1 year, the case may be filed as a delinquency proceeding in juvenile court.

- **Commercial exemption:** Owners, employees, and agents of a licensed marijuana retailer may not be criminally charged if they *reasonably* verified that the recipient appeared 21 or older and presented a government ID containing a DOB. 94G, § 9(b).

Vehicle Offenses

Operating Under the Influence (OUI). Marijuana-induced OUI in a motor vehicle, recreational vehicle, snow mobile, watercraft, or airplane is a crime. The legal right to possess and consume marijuana is *never* a defense to OUI. 94G, § 2(a). 94I, § 7.

Open Container. Like 90, § 24I (open container of alcohol), 94G, § 13(d) prohibits possessing an open container of marijuana in the passenger compartment of a vehicle on a public way. Penalty: Civil fine $500. Unlike open container of alcohol, the marijuana version may *not* be assessed on a 90C citation. For more detail, see *LED's Motor Vehicle, Chapter 10*.

Public Consumption

No marijuana consumption in any public place. 94G, § 13(c). $100 civil fine.

- **Existing public consumption ordinances and bylaws.** According to EOPSS, local bylaws or ordinances prohibiting the public consumption of marijuana may still be enforced by officers. See 94G, § 3(a)(5) and 94C, § 32L.[6] These 32L laws typically draw a $300 civil fine versus the $100 fine permitted under 13(c). While 32L bylaws are non-arrestable, 32L ordinances may authorize arrest. In fact, Everett and Malden have consumption ordinances that permit officers to arrest violators they observe! See, e.g., Everett Ord. § 13-1.1.

---

6 See EOPSS letter dated July 9, 2018 from Secretary Daniel Bennett.

No smoking in any place where smoking tobacco is prohibited. 94G, § 13(c). $100 civil fine.

- **Marijuana bar exception.** 94G, § 13(c) exempts so-called "cannabis cafes" that have been authorized and licensed by a city or town. 94G, § 3.

- **Medical marijuana exception.** 94G, § 13(c) states that it does not apply to medical marijuana cardholders. However, 94I, § 7(D) allows communities to outlaw public *smoking* of medical marijuana. Therefore, police may penalize this activity through a bylaw or ordinance enacted under 94C, § 32L (see discussion above). However, medical cardholders are permitted to consume marijuana products (e.g., edibles) in public.

No consumption areas:

- **Property owners, occupants, or managers** may prohibit smoking, display, consumption, and/or processing (but not possession) of marijuana on their property.[7] 94G, § 2(d)(1).

- **Employers** may prohibit possession or consumption by their employees in the workplace. They may also have policies restricting employee consumption (e.g., forbidding coming to work "high" or under the influence). 94G, § 2(e).

- **Government organizations** may prohibit or regulate marijuana possession or consumption within any building they own, lease, or occupy. 94G, § 2(d)(2). This includes city and town halls, police stations, public housing and transportation authorities.

- **Preschools, kindergartens, or grades 1–12** may prohibit possession or consumption. 94G, § 2(d)(3).

- **Correctional facilities** may prohibit possession or consumption anywhere on their grounds. 94G, § 2(d)(3). *Note:* Delivering, or possessing with the intent to deliver, any drug (including marijuana) to any prisoner in a correctional institution is a felony under 268, § 28. Penalty: SP NMT 5 yrs or HC NMT 2 yrs; or Fine NMT $1,000. If a person conceals marijuana in his vehicle or on the grounds of any correctional institution with the intent that an inmate receive it, he violates 268, § 31. Penalty: SP NMT 3 yrs or HC NMT 2½ yrs.

  These laws do not apply to a police or courthouse lockup, which is not considered a correctional facility. Simply charge distribution, or possession with intent to distribute, under 94C, § 32C.

Trespass. 266, § 120 penalizes, in part, the person who remains on another person's or organization's property after being told to leave. The ejection of a person from the property may be based on the violation of a reasonable rule. The prohibition against marijuana clearly qualifies. Penalty: HC NMT 30 days; and/or Fine NMT $100. Right of Arrest: 266, § 120 warrantless arrest in presence. For more detail, see *Chapter 32*.

Protective Custody (PC)

Any person incapacitated by marijuana may be placed into protective custody and transported to an emergency medical facility for evaluation. Incapacitation means that,

---

[7] As mentioned earlier, a landlord may prohibit marijuana smoking, but not consumption on the premises (unless required by federal law).

because of the consumption of marijuana, a person has become disorderly, unconscious, in need of medical attention, or a risk to cause personal injury or property damage. 111E, § 9A. For more detail, see *LED's Criminal Procedure, Chapter 9.*

Firearms Licensing

No license disqualification. Legal marijuana activity, and illegal activity that only draws a civil penalty, no longer disqualifies a citizen from getting a firearms license. 94G, § 7(a).

Suitable person. Aside from reviewing an applicant's record, a licensing authority (LA) must assess the suitability of an applicant for an LTC or FID. An applicant's excessive consumption of intoxicating substances — even legal ones like alcohol and marijuana — may be a factor. *Ceeley v. Firearms Licensing Board*, 2011 WL 445841 (Appeals Court) (applicant properly deemed "unsuitable" for LTC based on his "long history of alcohol abuse").

Carrying a Firearm Under the Influence (FUI). 269, § 10H prohibits a person with an LTC from carrying a loaded firearm while under the influence of marijuana (or alcohol or narcotics). Penalty: HC NMT 2½ yrs; and/or Fine NMT $5,000. Right of Arrest: Breach of peace in presence. Otherwise, complaint. *Comm. v. Veronneau*, 90 Mass. App. Ct. 477 (2016) (FUI standard is diminished ability to carry a gun safely). Also see *Chapter 17*.

Return of Marijuana

Request by defendant for return of marijuana evaluated by trial judge. *Comm. v. Crowell*, 2022 WL 5287862 (Appeals Court): A search warrant led to the seizure of tens of thousands of grams of marijuana in various small containers — about one thousand THC-laden treats, "dabs," or doses; eight pounds of raw marijuana; and over $4,000 in cash. All charges were dismissed four years later with an agreement for the civil forfeiture of the cash. The defendant filed a motion for return of the marijuana and THC, arguing his agreement with the Commonwealth did not require forfeiture of the drug evidence.

When seized by a search warrant, the property is held at the direction of the court. Stolen property is returned to its owners; the rest is disposed of as the court directs, 276, § 3. Since the defendant had no license authorizing him to possess these quantities of marijuana and THC, neither the public interest nor common sense entitled him to their return.

MEDICAL MARIJUANA

Cannabis Control Commission (CCC) issues "cards" to eligible:

Patients with "debilitating medical conditions"[8] who receive certification from a Massachusetts physician for a minimum of 15 days and maximum of 1 year. 94I, §§ 2 and 12. 935 CMR 501.010. A qualifying patient may be under 18 only if he has been diagnosed by two doctors (one must be a pediatrician), and has a parent or guardian as a caregiver.

Personal caregivers who are at least 21 and agree to assist patients in obtaining, using, and in some cases, growing marijuana. They are not a patient's certifying physician. 94I § 2(J).

---

[8] Defined as ALS, HIV, MS, cancer, glaucoma, or any other "health condition" certified in writing.

Dispensary agents who are owners, agents, employees, and volunteers (at least 21) who work at a Registered Marijuana Dispensary (RMD). 94I, §§ 2(E) and 10.

Cultivators. Dispensary agents may grow marijuana on the premises in a secure space. Patients and caregivers may grow marijuana in an enclosed, locked, indoor space provided they demonstrate financial or transportation hardship. 94I, §§ 2(B) and 11.

Patients must:

Possess no more than a 60-day supply — which CCC has determined to be 10 ounces. 935 CMR 501.003. A physician can approve more or less than 10 ounces as a 60-day supply. 935 CMR 501.010(9). CJIS will indicate when a higher or lower amount is authorized.

Only use marijuana for a medical purpose and never distribute or share it with anyone.

Carry their card when possessing marijuana and notify CCC within 5 business days of any change in information or lost or stolen card. 935 CMR 501.015 and 501.020.

Personal Caregivers may:

Transport patients and marijuana to and from an RMD.

Cultivate marijuana on behalf of a patient who has obtained a hardship cultivation registration at *either* the patient's primary residence *or* the caregiver's primary residence — but not both.

Prepare and administer marijuana to a patient.

Serve only one patient. An individual may serve as a personal caregiver for only one patient at one time, except in the case of:

- An employee of a hospice provider, nursing facility, or medical facility; or
- A visiting nurse, home health aide, personal care attendant; or
- An immediate family member of more than one registered qualifying patient.

Not *receive compensation for services* (only reasonable expenses, and time is not a reasonable expense). Only hospice, personal care, and medical personnel may receive compensation in the form of their regular wages. 935 CMR 501.025.

Police Procedure

Patients and caregivers must present their registration cards "to any law enforcement official who questions [them] regarding [their] use of marijuana." 94I, § 4(b). A patient must present the registration card as well as a second ID. If the individual does not have a registration card on his person, officers can input the patient's name, date of birth, and mother's maiden name into CJIS.

Registered Marijuana Dispensary (RMD) must:

Allow access to law enforcement personnel within their jurisdiction. 935 CMR 501.105(16).

Allow CCC to inspect RMD and affiliated vehicles without prior notice. 935 CMR 501.300(1).

Report any critical incident to law enforcement <u>***and***</u> ***CCC within 24 hours.*** A written report must also be filed within 10 days to CCC. 935 CMR 501.110(6). This includes any:

- Discrepancies in inventory or diversion, theft, or loss.
- Criminal action involving the RMD or a dispensary agent.
- Sale, cultivation, or distribution that might be suspicious.
- Loss or alteration of records.
- Alarm activation that required a response by public safety personnel.
- The failure of any alarm expected to last longer than 8 hours.
- Other breach of security.

Ensure that dispensary agents carry their registration card at all times while in possession of marijuana. A dispensary agent affiliated with multiple RMDs must be registered as a dispensary agent by each RMD.

An RMD may <u>not</u>:

Dispense, deliver, or transfer marijuana to a person other than a registered patient or his personal caregiver, or to another RMD or a laboratory.

Give away marijuana, including samples.

Receive orders for marijuana in any manner other than from a registered patient or personal caregiver in person at the RMD, except in cases of home delivery, in which an order may be received by phone or through a password-protected, internet-based platform.

Fill orders for marijuana in any way other than in person at the RMD or through home delivery to a patient or caregiver who presents valid ID.

Consume marijuana on the premises, unless during a legitimate demonstration.

Sell marijuana to a patient with a cultivation registration or to his caregiver, except for seeds.

Administrative Card Revocation. Under 935 CMR 501.425, the CCC, after a hearing, may revoke a registration card to a patient, caregiver, or RMD agent.

Grounds

- Submitting false or misleading information in an application or renewal application.
- Failing to notify CCC within 5 days of a lost, stolen, or destroyed card.
- Obtaining more than the amounts allowed to a patient or caregiver.
- Using marijuana as a patient "in a manner that puts others at risk of their health, safety, or welfare, or ... fail[ing] to take reasonable precautions to avoid putting others at risk."

- Purchasing marijuana from an RMD with a hardship cultivation.
- Engaging in any other act that violates the medical marijuana regulations.

Normal procedure

- **Submit incident report.** Police should submit their incident report to CCC and request that the subject's card be revoked pursuant to 935 CMR 501.425.
- **Written notice.** CCC provides the subject with written notice and a hearing, if the subject requests one within 21 days of the notice. 935 CMR 501.505.
- **Standard of proof** is "preponderance of the evidence" (same one used for civil motor vehicle hearings).

Summary suspension. The CCC may summarily suspend any registration card upon a finding of imminent danger to public health, safety, or welfare. 935 CMR 501.450. If the subject files a written request, he receives a hearing within 14 days of summary suspension. The standard of proof is also preponderance of the evidence.

SMOKING OR VAPING TOBACCO PRODUCTS

Key Definitions

Tobacco product. 270, §§ 6 and 7 define a tobacco product as containing or derived from tobacco or nicotine and intended for human consumption. This includes cigarettes, cigars, chewing tobacco, pipe tobacco, snuff; electronic cigarettes, cigars, pipes, and electronic nicotine delivery systems (ENDS); or any other products that rely on vaporization or aerosolization (i.e., vapes); but does not include products approved by the FDA for tobacco cessation and sold exclusively for that purpose.

Electronic nicotine delivery system (ENDS) — aka vaping device. 270, § 29(a) defines an "electronic nicotine delivery system" (ENDS) to include reusable or one-time devices such as electronic cigarettes, cigars, cigarillos, or pipes; vaping pens, hookah pens, and other similar devices that rely on vaporization or aerosolization (including the liquid or gel used in a device and any component necessary to use a device, even if sold separately). An ENDS does not include an FDA-approved cessation product or medical treatment, provided it is marketed and sold exclusively for that purpose.

Misconduct	Statute	Penalty
Selling or giving a tobacco product to a person who is under 21	270, § 6(b)	*1st offense:* Fine NLT $1,000 *2nd offense:* Fine NLT $2,000 *3rd or subsequent offense:* Fine NLT $5,000
Manufacturer or retailer distributing a free sample (exception for retail tobacco stores and smoking bars)	270, § 6(c)	*1st offense:* Fine NLT $1,000 *2nd offense:* Fine NLT $2,000 *3rd or subsequent offense:* Fine NLT $5,000
Selling cigarette rolling papers to person under 21	270, § 6A	*1st offense:* Fine NLT $25 *2nd offense:* Fine NLT $50 *3rd or subsequent offense:* Fine NLT $100
Failure of retail store to post sign with law and referral information for smoking cessation programs	270, § 7	Fine NMT $50
Removing required sign from retail establishment	270, § 7	Fine $10
Selling or offering for sale a flavored tobacco product (including vaping gels and oils) or flavor enhancer (exception for smoking bars)	270, § 28	*1st offense:* $1,000 *2nd offense:* $2,000 *3rd or subsequent offense:* $5,000
Selling an ENDS (i.e., vape) with nicotine exceeding 35 mgs per ml (exception for retail tobacco stores and smoking bars)	270, § 29	*1st offense:* $1,000 *2nd offense:* $2,000 *3rd or subsequent offense:* $5,000
Retail store that sells pharmaceutical goods and services prohibited from selling tobacco products	112, § 61A	No penalty given. Administrative penalty established by local Board of Health
Knowingly selling, distributing, or importing a liquid or substance containing nicotine unless in child-resistant packaging	270, § 27	*1st offense:* Fine $250 *2nd offense:* Fine $500 *3rd or subsequent offense:* Fine $1,000
In an MBTA bus, train, or station smoking or carrying an open flame or lighted tobacco product	272, § 43A	Must issue a $25 civil ticket but, if offender continues to smoke after notice, officer may arrest and penalty HC NMT 10 days, and/or Fine NMT $100 applies
Any person using tobacco product in school facilities, grounds, or buses of a public or private *primary or secondary or vocational school*, or at a school-sponsored event	71, §§ 2A and 58	No penalty given. Student discipline and/or administrative penalty established by local Board of Health

Attorney John Sofis Scheft & Law Enforcement Dimensions present

Marijuana Consequences in Massachusetts (revised 12/31/2021)

Don't believe the hype. Legalization and medical marijuana are not invitations for youth use or adult misconduct. Know the facts . . .

Behavior	Law	Potential Penalty
Sell, or intend to sell, *any* amount of marijuana *anywhere* *Only* a business in possession of a CCC issued license may sell.	94C, § 32C	Immediate arrest & up to 2 years in jail, and/or fine up to $5,000.[1]
Illegal gift is criminal distribution Legal gift = (1) age 21-to-21 transfer; (2) 1 oz (5 grams concentrate) or less; (3) for no value — e.g., barter, delayed, sham transaction; and (4) no advertising or promotion. 94G, § 7(a)(4).	94C, § 32C	Immediate arrest & up to 2 years in jail, and/or fine up to $5,000. [Chapter 55 of Acts of 2017, § 52 warns that any gift of marijuana or products in conjunction with sale of another item is criminal.]
Sell, or intend to sell, paraphernalia to youth under 21 [This includes pipes, bongs, grow lamps, or other devices.]	94C, § 32I	Immediate arrest & up to 2 years in jail, and/or fine up to $5,000. [Actual sale to minor under 18 is a felony of up to 5 years in prison.]
Furnishing (aka Social Host law) Any person of any age may not intentionally supply, provide or allow (i.e., consciously aware of activity on property) marijuana, marijuana products, or accessories (i.e., paraphernalia) to anyone under 21 for their or another's use. Only exceptions are child or grandchild on premises owned or controlled by suspect; or sale or delivery of medical marijuana pursuant to G.L. Chapter 94I.	94G, § 13(i)	Arrest for breach in presence; otherwise complaint application. Up to 1 year in jail, and/or fine up to $2,000. [Note: *Comm. v. Kneram*, 63 Mass. App. Ct. 371 (2005) (offender may be a minor for social host violation). Also, 94G, § 2(b) prohibits any "knowing transfer" of marijuana, products, or accessories to anyone under 21 with no qualifications or exemptions. *Comm. v. Ellis*, 2021 WL 162599 (Appeals Court) (social host violation may occur in a car with under 21 driver).]
Homemade marijuana concentrate No one may process marijuana with a flammable liquid or gas to create "dabs" or any other concentrate or product. Only exceptions are products made with alcohol or CCC manufacturing license. 94G, § 2(c).	94C, § 32C	Immediate arrest & up to 2 years in jail, and/or fine up to $5,000. [Note: 94C, § 1 does not allow criminal prosecution of an individual who prepares a controlled substance for his own use only.]
Criminal cultivation of marijuana at any age • Even 1 plant is a crime if not at primary residence; or • If growing 13 or more plants at residence. 94G, § 7. [Note: *Comm. v. Richardson*, 479 Mass. 394 (2018) points out that a medical marijuana hardship cultivation registration allows enough plants (no specific number given) to grow 10 ounces for each 60-day period, *but* never to distribute or sell.]	94C, § 32C	Immediate arrest & up to 2 years in jail, and/or fine up to $5,000. *Other civil cultivation offenses:* • Visible homegrow to naked eye from public place $300 civil ticket[2] and forfeit visible plants. 94G, § 13(a); • 1–6 plants at residence legal if adult [if 7–12, then $100 civil ticket and forfeit excess plants. 94G, § 13(e)]; • 7–12 plants legal if at least 2 adults; may never have more than 12. • 1–12 plants at residence — if under 21, $100 civil ticket + education class; *if not complete class & under 17*, then delinquency. 94G, § 13(h).

[1] For any potential jail sentence, if the youth is under 18, the sentence is served at a Department of Youth Services (DYS) facility, alternative placement, or through some probation arrangement. Minors under 18 are not sentenced to adult jails. Those individuals 18 and over are considered adults and may be incarcerated.

[2] All civil tickets must be written on a city ordinance or town bylaw ticket. The law does not allow the use of a motor vehicle citation. 94G, § 13(g).

Behavior	Law	Potential Penalty
Operate under the influence of marijuana Medical marijuana and/or legal possession are no defense; no driver may be "high" to any degree that diminishes their ability to operate safely.	90, § 24	Immediate arrest & 2 years probation + education program + license suspension of *at least* 90 days and probably 1 year + fines and fees of *at least* $500. *Comm. v. Gerhardt*, SJC September 2017 ("roadside assessments" may show driver's lack of balance, reflex, and mental clarity as a result of marijuana).
Open container of marijuana in vehicle Open container: Any package with marijuana or marijuana products with seal broken *or* some contents removed or consumed found within passenger compartment (not trunk or *locked* glove box).	94G, § 13(c)	$500 civil ticket may be issued to driver and/or passengers of any age.[3] [Odor, smoke, or visible signs of use sufficient to stop vehicle. This law overrules *Comm. v. Rodriguez*, 472 Mass. 767 (2015).]
Possession of 2 ounces or less in private or public by youth under 21[4] Physical *and* internal possession are covered — i.e., "being high" is enough.	94C, § 32L	If 18, 19, or 20: $100 civil ticket. If under 18: $100 civil ticket + 4-hour drug class + 10 hours of community service.[5] *If fail to complete*, then fine increases to $1,000 and is assessed against parents too, plus case may be filed in juvenile court. See 94C, § 32N.
Criminal public possession of over 2 ounces at any age	94C, § 34	Immediate arrest & up to 6 months in jail, and/or $500 fine.
Criminal private possession • Under 21 criminal possession also if over 2 ounces in private; • 21 and over may possess up to 10 ounces in their residence; • 21 and over criminal possession if over 10 ounces in residence that was not derived from a legal homegrow. See 94G, § 7(a)(2).	94C, § 34	Immediate arrest & up to 6 months in jail, and/or $500 fine. *Other civil offense:* • Over 1 ounce (from any source) not properly secured in locked container. $100 civil ticket and forfeit unsecured excess. 94G, § 13(b).
Possession of any amount on elementary or secondary school property or at a school-related event	71, § 37H	Suspension from school and other conditions imposed by administration. This may be in addition to any other civil or criminal penalty allowed by law.
Public consumption *or* smoking marijuana where tobacco smoking prohibited §270, § 22 prohibits tobacco smoking in many public private areas — e.g., workplace, public buildings, restaurants, hotels, etc. May smoke in licensed marijuana bar.	94G, § 13(c)	$100 civil ticket [Note: City ordinance enacted under 94C, § 32L may authorize arrest in presence for public consumption and $300 fine. Town bylaw may not authorize arrest per Atty General, but may impose $300 fine.]
Consumption on private property after being warned by owner or person in control	266, § 120	Arrest if still on the premises when officer arrives; otherwise complaint application. This is trespassing, penalized by up to 30 days in jail, and/or fine up to $100.

---

[3] All civil tickets must be written on a city ordinance or town bylaw ticket. The law does not allow the use of a motor vehicle citation. 94G, § 13(g).

[4] The possession of a valid medical marijuana card changes the rules related to possession significantly. See G.L. Chapter 94I and 105 CMR 725.000 et. seq.

[5] We strongly suggest that communities offer the class and monitor the service requirement through their local diversion program or another drug prevention organization.

22 Alcohol

Section I
REGULATORY AUTHORITY & ENFORCEMENT

Chapter 138 sets out a comprehensive program to regulate alcoholic beverages. Both state and local authorities are involved. Primary responsibility for retail activity is vested in local authorities (in most towns, the board of selectmen; in most cities, an appointed commission). The state authority, the Alcoholic Beverages Control Commission (ABCC), assists in the supervision of retail activity, and directly supervises wholesale, importing, and manufacturing activities. The ABCC may be contacted at:

Alcoholic Beverages Control Commission
95 Fourth Street, Suite 3, Chelsea, MA 02150 • 617-727-3040
www.mass.gov/abcc/

Types of retail licenses. Basically, there are three types of licenses that allow for the retail sale of alcohol: Section 12 Pouring, Section 15 Package Store, and Section 14 Special Licenses.

A. Licenses

Section 12 Pouring Licenses. Retail licenses for the sale of alcoholic beverages to be drunk on the premises, called "pouring licenses," fall into five types: hotel, restaurant, tavern, club, and general-on-premise. These are further divided into four categories based on the alcoholic beverages permitted to be served: all-alcohol, wine only, malt only, or wine and malt.

- **Hours of operation.** 138, §§ 12, 33, 33A, 33B. Officers should be aware of the days and hours of operation in their community, including any "last call" requirements.

- **Posting notices of penalties.** 138, § 34D. Any drinking establishment must post a copy of the penalties for operating under the influence.

- **Refusal of entry.** A licensee may refuse entrance or service to any individual, as long as the licensee does not discriminate on the basis of race, color, religious creed, national origin, ancestry, gender, sexual orientation, or physical or mental disability. *Vaspourakan, Ltd. v. ABCC*, 401 Mass. 347 (1987) (proper to revoke license for racial discrimination).

- **Cover charges.** Under 204 CMR 2.16, the ABCC requires that a sign about the cover charge appear outside the licensed premises and that it be collected inside. Also, a receipt, permanently recorded and numbered, must be presented to each individual customer or group of customers. Licensees may not charge a minimum for the purchase of alcoholic beverages or place a minimum drinking requirement on any customer.

- **Happy Hour restrictions.** Under 204 CMR 4.00, no licensee or employee shall:

    - Offer or deliver any free drinks to any person or group;
    - Deliver more than 2 drinks to any one person at a time;
    - Sell to any person or group any drinks at a price less than the price regularly charged for such drinks during a calendar week, except at private functions;
    - Sell to any person or group an unlimited number of drinks during a set period of time for a fixed price, except at private functions;
    - Sell drinks to a person or group on any one day at prices less than those charged to the general public;
    - Sell beer or drinks in a pitcher except to at least 2 or more persons at any one time;
    - Increase amount of alcohol in a drink without proportionately increasing the price;
    - Encourage or permit any game or contest which involves drinking or the awarding of drinks as prizes.

    However, licensees *may* offer free food or entertainment at any time.

- **Service of draft beer.** No malt beverages may be sold on draft from a tap unless the brand name of the beverage is clearly displayed on the tap.

- **Gambling.** 204 CMR 2.05(1). Slot machines and gambling of any type not authorized by the legislature are prohibited. For more on gambling, see *Chapter 24. RK&E Corp. v. ABCC*, 97 Mass. App. Ct. 337 (2020) (ABCC has authority to add conditions to licenses based on the type of violation; here, a bar conducted illegal gaming with video poker machines, so ABCC forbid *all* electronic games even though they were authorized by a city permit).

- **No alcohol off the premises.** No patrons or employees may leave the premises with alcoholic beverages. Consumption must be on the premises.

Section 15 Package Store Licenses. Section 15 authorizes package store licenses. No license will be issued to a premises located within or connected to a Section 12 establishment.

- **Hours and days of operation.** 138, §§ 15, 33. Officers should be aware of the authorized hours for package stores in their community. No licensee may sell or deliver any alcoholic beverages on Memorial Day, Thanksgiving, or Christmas (or the Monday following, when Christmas is on Sunday). There are no exceptions to these holiday closings. Hours are determined by the local authority, but stores may not close later than 11:00 p.m. on Sunday.

- **Posting notices of penalties.** Any package store must post a copy of the penalties for driving with an open container of alcohol.

- **Keg restrictions.** 204 CMR 9.00. Basically, each keg must be labeled with the name and address of the retail licensee and an identifying serial number, and the licensee must record the name and address of any keg purchaser.

Section 14 Special Licenses. 138, §§ 14, 23; 204 CMR 7.04. Local licensing authorities may issue special licenses for the sale of wines and/or malt beverages to a responsible manager of any indoor or outdoor activity or enterprise (for profit or nonprofit). Special licenses for the sale of all alcoholic beverages may be issued to nonprofit organizations only. There are a variety of regulations governing temporary licenses.

B. Investigatory Authority

The ABCC and local licensing authorities have investigatory authority to ensure that liquor establishments are operating within the bounds of their licenses. 138, § 1.

Warrantless arrest authority. 138, § 56 authorizes police officers, sheriffs, and ABCC investigators to arrest any person found illegally: Selling, Exposing for sale, Exporting, Keeping for sale, Manufacturing, Importing, Storing, or Transporting alcoholic beverages or alcohol. Think of "SEEK MIST" to remember this arrest authority.

Definition of "sale." 138, § 41 states that "the delivery of alcoholic beverages in or from a building . . . or other place, except a private dwelling . . . shall be [sufficient] evidence [of] . . . a sale in prosecutions for selling liquors." The value of § 41 for law enforcers is that an exchange of alcohol is presumed to be a sale, which then triggers the officer's enhanced arrest power for sales activity under § 56. *Comm. v. Rowe*, 80 Mass. 47 (1859) (delivery of liquor to restaurant patron was proof of a sale even though the witness could not remember whether he paid for it).

Police officers may serve as agents of their local licensing authority. 138, § 56 also empowers local and State Police officers, and ABCC investigators "[to] make all needful and appropriate investigations" to enforce Chapter 138. This authority has been interpreted by the ABCC to require that police officers be appointed by their local licensing authority (in writing) *before* they inspect liquor establishments. Concentrating this specialized authority in the hands of a few designated officers promotes consistency and lessens the potential for police misconduct.

All sworn officers, whether designated or not, may take immediate action to deal with emergency situations in a liquor establishment, such as overcrowding, underage drinking, after hours service, sexual and criminal misconduct, and incapacitated patrons. However, the actual administrative process — which may result in license suspension, revocation, or fine — should be instituted only by a designated agent in accordance with local policy and procedure.

C. Basis for Enforcement

Responding to illegalities. ABCC regulation 204 CMR 2.05(2) states: "No licensee for the sale of alcoholic beverages shall permit any disorder, disturbance, or illegality of any kind to take place in or on the license premises. The licensee shall be responsible . . . whether present or not." The ABCC and local licensing boards utilize this provision to address underage drinking, drug dealing, disturbances and fights, sexual misconduct, discrimination, and any other type of illegality. *Rum Runners, Inc. v. ABCC*, 43 Mass. App. Ct. 248 (1997).

Sale or delivery of alcohol to intoxicated persons. 138, § 69 prohibits the sale or delivery of an alcoholic beverage to an intoxicated person on *any* licensed premises (including bars, restaurants, and package stores). Typically, § 69 misconduct becomes the basis of a civil lawsuit or an ABCC/local authority license suspension. *Adamian v. Three Sons, Inc.*, 353 Mass. 498 (1968) (this law protects the intoxicated person and the general public). *Douillard v. LMR, Inc.*, 433 Mass. 162 (2001).

Section II
CRIMINAL ENFORCEMENT

SELLING OR FURNISHING ALCOHOL TO PERSON UNDER 21
138, § 34

Elements

The suspect did any one of the following four acts:

- **Sold or delivered** an alcoholic beverage to a person under age 21, whether for the underage person's own use or somebody else's use (including his parents); or

- **Ordered at bar.** While a patron in an "establishment," delivered or procured to be delivered (i.e., ordered) in any public room or area, alcohol for a person the suspect knew or had reason to believe was under age 21; or

- **Bought at store.** While at a package store, brewery or winery, procured an alcoholic beverage for a person under 21, *unless* the person is the suspect's child, spouse, or ward (i.e., suspect serves as legal guardian); or

- **Furnished** alcohol to a person under 21 *unless* that underage person was the child or grandchild of the adult and possessed the alcohol on property owned or controlled by that parent or grandparent.

Furnishing Defined

"Furnishing" (aka the Social Host law) means "to knowingly or intentionally *supply . . . or allow* a person under 21 years of age . . . to possess alcoholic beverages on premises or property owned or controlled by the [offender]" — except for the children and grandchildren of the person charged.

Remember, the suspect may be charged even if he simply *allows* an underage person to possess alcohol on property he owns or controls. This covers teenage alcohol parties that are held with the knowledge of parents or other adults. It also applies to individuals under age 21 who host parties while their parents are away, since *they* are in control of the property when their friends arrive. *Comm. v. Kneram*, 63 Mass. App. Ct. 371 (2005) (19 year old boy properly incarcerated for providing alcohol to his underage friends at his parent's Newburyport home; one of his friends drove away from the house drunk and killed a 16 year old girl and injured her boyfriend). *Comm. v. Ellis*, 2021 WL 162599 (Appeals Court) (furnishing occurred in a vehicle because the under-21 driver allowed his under-21 passengers to possess marijuana in a Mason jar).

Also see *Comm. v. Militello*, 66 Mass. App. Ct. 325 (2006) (while the defendant did not own the campsite, he did control the site and, therefore, committed the crime of furnishing when he gave beer to a young boy who was not his son or grandson).

Exempt Conduct

Parents, spouses, or guardians may provide alcohol to their child, spouse, or ward. This exemption reflects a longstanding belief that these individuals should be able to allow those they care for to drink at home.

Parents or grandparents may give their children alcohol on their property. *Comm. v. Parent*, 465 Mass. 395 (2013) (police could not charge defendant with providing vodka to his 15 year old daughter at their home, but he could be charged for giving it to her 14 year old friend).

Servers 18 and over may directly handle and sell alcoholic beverages. Furthermore, owners may employ staff younger than 18, as long as they do not handle, mix, sell, or serve alcohol.

Right of Arrest

For furnishing in a home — Complaint: Confiscate alcohol, eject from premises (if appropriate) and apply for complaint (since 138, § 34 has no specific arrest authority, nor does § 41 when the exchange occurs in a dwelling).

For delivering anywhere other than a dwelling — Arrest: Although § 34 provides no right of arrest, 138, §§ 41 and 56 authorize an arrest for *any* illegal exchange outside of a dwelling.

Penalty

HC NMT 1 year; and/or Fine NMT $2,000. *Note:* § 34 conviction has no impact on the defendant's driver's license.

Incapacitation Immunity

"Good Samaritan" law for alcohol incapacitation. 138, § 34E. A person under 21 years of age who, in good faith, seeks medical assistance for someone experiencing alcohol-related incapacitation, or seeks assistance for himself, or is the subject of a request for assistance, shall not be charged under §§ 34 (furnishing, "social host"), 34A (procurement or attempted procurement of alcohol) or 34C (minor in possession) if the evidence was gained as a result of seeking medical assistance.

Note: This does not apply to adults 21 and over who host an underage party or, in some other fashion, engage in illegal conduct with minors. Incapacitation means a person who consumed intoxicating liquor is: (a) unconscious; (b) in need of medical attention; or (c) likely to suffer or cause physical harm or damage property. 138, § 1.

Notes

No need to prove suspect knew minor's age. Except for the offense of ordering at a bar, there is no need to prove the defendant knew, or should have known, the age of the youth. It is sufficient to prove the alcohol recipient was under 21. *Comm. v. Montalvo*, 50 Mass. App. Ct. 85 (2000). *Burlington Liquors v. ABCC*, 7 Mass. App. Ct. 186 (1979).

ABCC action. The ABCC or local licensing authority often uses a § 34 violation as the basis for disciplinary action. *Embers of Salisbury, Inc. v. ABCC*, 401 Mass. 526 (1988) (three day license suspension based on service to 19 year old woman).

MAINTAIN AND/OR PERMIT ALCOHOL NUISANCE
139, §§ 15 and 20

Elements

Type 1: Maintaining under § 15. The suspect:

- **Control premises.** Owned, maintained, or controlled the premises; and

- **Illegal sales.** Illegally sold alcohol there.

Type 2: Permitting under § 20. The suspect:

- **Control premises.** Owned, maintained, or controlled the premises; and

- **Permit another.** Permitted another person(s) to engage in illegal alcohol sales there (including the failure to take reasonable measures to evict the occupants as soon as it could be lawfully done).

Right of Arrest

Arrest for breach of peace in presence. Otherwise, complaint.

Penalty

Maintaining: HC NLT 3 months, NMT 1 year; and/or Fine NLT $50, NMT $100.

Permitting: HC NLT 3 months, NMT 1 year; and/or Fine NLT $100, NMT $1,000.

Related "Nuisance" Procedures

Under 139, § 14, a "nuisance" may involve illegal alcohol, prostitution, gaming, or drug activity. 139, § 16A authorizes the Attorney General, a district attorney, or chief of police to seek a civil injunction to close down a nuisance. Finally, § 19 allows for a landlord to void the lease of a tenant or occupant who maintains a nuisance, and seek a court order to force him to vacate.

Notes

Anyone who sells alcohol at an unlicensed place he controls is maintaining a nuisance.
Comm. v. Reid, 73 Mass. App. Ct. 423 (2009): When Boston police were informed about a party taking place in Mattapan, two plainclothes officers attended. They paid the cover and bought drinks with marked money from Jamaree Reid. They watched him sell alcohol to others for 1 hour. Uniformed officers raided the party. Reid was properly arrested and convicted for maintaining a nuisance under 139, § 15.

To permit a nuisance, the defendant must have at least one other person illegally sell alcohol on property under his control. Comm. v. Reid, supra. (since only Reid was illegally selling alcohol in his girlfriend's apartment, he should not have been charged with permitting a nuisance under § 20).

PROCURING ALCOHOLIC BEVERAGES BY FALSE REPRESENTATION
138, § 34A

Elements

Type 1: Person under 21

- The suspect was under age 21 and:

  - Purchased or attempted to purchase; or
  - Made arrangements with any person to purchase; or
  - Misrepresented his age; or
  - In any way, altered or falsified his identification offered as proof of age (either for his own or someone else's use);

- In order to procure a sale or delivery of an alcoholic beverage for his or someone else's use. (Notice there is no age limit for the recipient.)

Type 2: Statements or Inducement by any Person

- The suspect, regardless of his age:

  - Made a false statement about a minor's age; or
  - Induced the minor to make a false statement about his age;

- In order to procure a sale or delivery of an alcoholic beverage to a minor.

Right of Arrest

Confiscate any alcohol and false ID and apply for a criminal complaint.

ID enforcement options: § 34A essentially covers every act an underage person (and assisting adult) does to obtain alcohol, including a false ID. At the same time, there are more specialized statutes concerning IDs, which provide arrest authority. See 138, § 34B (*discussion next page*) and 90, § 24B (felony for counterfeit licenses discussed in *LED's Motor Vehicle Law, Chapter 6*). In summary, when a fake ID is involved, officers may be lenient and apply for a complaint under § 34A, arrest the offender under § 34B or, in some cases, under 90, § 24B.

Penalty

Fine $300. *Mandatory registry suspension of license or right to operate:* 180 days. The suspension applies to all violators, regardless of whether they were in a vehicle at the time of the violation.

Incapacitation Immunity

See earlier discussion in relation to 138, § 34.

Notes

ABCC and police "stings" may occur at commercial establishments and private premises. *Fran's Lunch, Inc. v. ABCC*, 45 Mass. App. Ct. 663 (1998). *BAA v. ABCC*, 49 Mass. App. Ct. 839 (2000) (ABCC learned that a common carrier violated § 34 by delivering alcohol to a 19 year old decoy during a sting operation at her home). *eVineyard Retail Sales-Massachusetts, Inc. v. ABCC*, 450 Mass. 825 (2008) (Attorney General conducted a sting operation over the internet showing that a retailer lacked adequate screening procedures, and that Federal Express did not follow their delivery guidelines for alcoholic beverages at private homes).

FALSE ID OR FAILURE TO ID
138, § 34B

Elements

Type 1: False Information. The suspect:

- Transferred, altered, or defaced an identification card or license; or
- Made, used, carried, sold, or distributed a false identification card or license; or
- Used the identification card or license of another; or
- Furnished false information in obtaining an identification card or license.

Type 2: Failure to Provide Identification. Upon request of an ABCC or local licensing agent, the suspect refused to state his name, age, and address; or stated false information.

Right of Arrest

138, § 34B warrantless arrest of any person "discovered . . . in the act of violating [this law]." *Comm. v. Jones*, 21 Mass. App. Ct. 910 (1985) (defendant subject to warrantless arrest when he gave officer a liquor purchase ID bearing the address of a vacant lot).

Penalty

For providing false information: HC NMT 3 months; or Fine NMT $200.

For failing to provide identification to an alcohol investigator: Fine NMT $500.

Registry action: Revocation of license for 1 year.

Notes

6 acceptable forms of ID. § 34B clearly states what types of IDs are acceptable to prove one's age. To defend against delivering or selling alcohol to an underage person, a licensee must reasonably rely on: (1) Massachusetts driver's license; (2) Mass. Liquor ID Card[1]; (3) Mass. ID Card; (4) passport issued by the United States or a country recognized by the U.S.; (5) passport card (which is the size of a driver's license); or (6) military ID.

ID must be checked on day of service. § 34B protects owners from liability for underage service if they checked the ID on the day of service (even if it had been checked previously). *Howard Johnson Co. v. ABCC*, 24 Mass. App. Ct. 287 (1987) (if bar had re-checked minors, they would not have been served that day because they had destroyed their false ID earlier).

ID of another may be lawfully possessed. *Retsivo v. Board of Appeal*, 2011 WL 7118834 (Superior Ct.): A police officer saw 19 year old Jessee Restivo showing his friends what appeared to be a driver's license. As the officer approached, Restivo put the license in his wallet. The officer asked Restivo for ID, and he produced his own, properly issued license. The officer then seized Restivo's wallet and found his 22 year old brother's expired license inside. Restivo said his brother gave it to him.

This license was not "false" under § 34B. As the court pointed out, if it were illegal to simply possess another license, then carrying a deceased parent's license as a memento would be a crime. This is not the intent of § 34B. It is only unlawful to *use* the license of another, and there was no evidence that Restivo had used or altered his brother's license.

MINOR IN POSSESSION OF ALCOHOL
138, § 34C

Elements

- **Under 21 and no guardian.** The suspect was under 21 years of age *and* unaccompanied by a parent or legal guardian; and

- **Possess or transport alcohol.** Knowingly possessed, transported, or carried on his person any alcohol or alcoholic beverage.

Right of Arrest & Exemption

138, § 34C warrantless arrest in presence.

Employee exemption: § 34C does not apply to people between age 18 and 21 who carry or transport alcohol during the course of their employment.

Penalty

1st offense: Fine NMT $50; *2nd or subsequent offense:* Fine NMT $150.

Registry action: License suspended for 90 days, whether or not minor driving a vehicle.

---

[1] Under § 34B, any person 21 years or older who does not have a valid driver's license may apply for a liquor purchase identification card, which is valid for 5 years and issued by the registry.

Incapacitation Immunity

See earlier discussion in relation to 138, § 34.

Notes

Constructive possession. Some court clerks insist that youths may not be charged with alcohol possession unless they are physically holding the alcohol. This is incorrect. *Comm. v. Petersen*, 67 Mass. App. Ct. 49 (2006) (court affirms *constructive* possession conviction for minor).

Transporting. Even minors who have no interest in possessing or consuming alcohol violate 138, § 34C when they drive a vehicle they know contains alcohol. The only legal exemptions for driving or, in any other way transporting alcohol (e.g., by bike, boat, or moped), are: (1) being accompanied by a parent or guardian; or (2) being at least 18 and employed to deliver alcohol. In short, someone under 21 typically commits a crime under 34C by transporting alcohol — even if the alcohol is for someone else.

Related Offense

Container of Alcohol in Passenger Compartment of Vehicle. In addition to § 34C, there is a separate offense under 90, § 24I which punishes occupants of a vehicle who possess an open container of alcohol in the passenger area. See *LED's Motor Vehicle Law, Chapter 10*.

UNLAWFUL TRANSPORTATION OF ALCOHOL
138, § 22

Elements

- **Regular citizens** may, but only for their own use and that of their family and guests, transport at any one time without a permit, the following maximum quantities: 20 gallons of malt beverages; 3 gallons of any other alcoholic beverages; or 1 gallon of alcohol.

    Exception: Any person may, without a license or permit, transport from his residence to a new residence alcoholic beverages manufactured by him for his own private use.

- **Licensees** or their employees may transport and deliver their alcoholic beverages anywhere in the Commonwealth. Each vehicle must be covered by an ABCC permit.

- **Salesmen** licensed under 138, § 19A may transport samples of up to 24 gallons of alcohol or alcoholic beverages, provided they possess a 19A permit, invoices, and delivery records.

- **Winery or brewer licensees** under 138, §§ 19B, 19C, or 19F may use a parcel service or trucking business, with an ABCC permit, to deliver to customers not in excess of 108 liters per shipment. A delivery receipt must contain certification from the recipient that he is at least 21 and from the delivery person that he observed valid ID.

- **Caterers.** A caterer may obtain a 12C license and transport and store alcohol on behalf of its customers.

Proof of Violation

138, § 22 mandates that every motorist transporting alcohol carry a vehicle permit or certified copy or be exempt. The driver must produce documentation upon request of any police officer or ABCC investigator. Failure to do so is *sufficient evidence* of a violation. *Comm. v. Dzewiacin*, 252 Mass. 126 (1925) (absence of permit sufficient, no *intent* required).

Conversion figures. 20 gallons is 2,560 ounces (oz), so officers can do the math with 10, 12, or 20 oz bottles or cans. For example, eight 30-packs of 12 oz bottles = 2,880 oz of beer. Nine 24-packs of 12 oz cans = 2,592 oz of beer. Both violations! Also, domestic beer comes in 15.5 gallon ½ kegs (no one sells full kegs). Imported ½ kegs are 13.5 gallons. This is helpful information, especially in college communities!

With respect to wine and liquor, 3 U.S. gallons equals 11.3 liters. [Conversion charts appear on Google.] A typical bottle of wine is 1 liter, so 12 bottles of wine is outside the citizen exemption under § 22.

Right of Arrest

138, § 56 warrantless arrest in presence.

Penalty

HC NMT 6 months; and/or Fine $2,500.

Administrative Action: ABCC may revoke any existing transportation permit.

Related Offenses

No hawking or peddling alcoholic beverages. As a result of 138, § 32, no license or permit holder may, by himself or through an agent, travel from "place to place" selling or peddling any alcoholic beverages from a vehicle. All sales must take place at "the licensed place of business." Penalty: HC NMT 6 months; and/or Fine NMT $200. Right of Arrest: 138, § 56, warrantless arrest in presence.

Alcohol on public school premises. 272, § 40A. See *LED's Juvenile Law, Chapter 11*.

PUBLIC DRINKING OR ALCOHOL POSSESSION
272, § 59

Elements

- **Local law violation.** The suspect must be in violation of a town bylaw, city ordinance, or any other government regulation;

- **Public drinking or possession.** That prohibits public drinking or the possession of an alcoholic beverage.

Right of Arrest

272, § 59 authorizes police officers to make a warrantless arrest for this infraction, but only if it happens within their jurisdiction.

Penalty

Offender must be sentenced in accordance with the ordinance or bylaw of the town or city where the offense occurred.

Notes

Must prove terms of bylaw, ordinance or regulation. Remember, § 59 is a procedural statute that authorizes warrantless arrest for public drinking. In court, officers must identify their underlying legal authority. The best way is to present a *copy* of the bylaw, ordinance, or regulation to the judge. *Comm. v. Bones*, 93 Mass. App. Ct. 681 (2018).

An officer may also testify about the contents of the law if it is straightforward. *Comm. v. Rushin*, 56 Mass. App. Ct. 515 (2002) (sufficient proof when officer testified about Boston's public drinking ordinance, which he frequently enforced).

Reasonable belief that an area is public will prevent a lawsuit for false arrest. *U.S. v. Diaz*, 854 F.3d 197 (2nd Cir. 2017) (New York City police officer not liable for false arrest because of his reasonable belief that a stairwell in a 4-story, 12-unit, private apartment building qualified as a public place within the meaning of the public drinking law, especially where no appellate court had ruled on the scope of this law).

Constructive possession sufficient. *Comm. v. Gomez*, 2020 WL 1816108 (Appeals Court): When Boston police officers approached five people in the courtyard of a public housing development, they found Pedro Gomez and another man sitting on a bench, a woman standing behind the bench, and two men leaning against a fence at least seven feet away. All except Gomez were drinking from small plastic cups. Gomez had a half full bottle of vodka on the ground between his legs. The bottle was visible and closer to him than any other person. This established his constructive possession of the open alcohol container in violation of a city ordinance. The search incident to arrest properly revealed an illegal handgun in his waistband.

Related Procedure

Protective Custody for Alcohol Incapacitation. 111B, §§ 8 and 10 enable officers to take a person into custody who is incapacitated by alcohol and bring him home, to the station, or to the hospital. Incapacitation means that, because of his alcohol consumption, the person is disorderly, unconscious, in need of medical attention, or poses a risk of property damage or personal injury. A detailed discussion appears in *LED's Criminal Procedure, Chapter 9*, along with other forms of protective custody for those who abuse drugs, are runaways, or have mental health difficulties.

Law Enforcement Dimensions

Part VI

PUBLIC ORDER OFFENSES

Disorderly Conduct, Disturbing the Peace, and Gambling

Chapters 23 – 24

© John Sofis Scheft, Esq.
All rights reserved

23 Public Order

Police officers frequently deal with public disturbances involving a wide variety of conduct. The question arises: In a free society, how do officers determine what conduct is acceptable and what is unlawful and properly suppressed? Any discussion of public order begins with 272, § 53. Written long before the Revolutionary War in 1699, much of this statute's archaic language survives to this day:

> "[C]ommon street walkers, both male and female, common railers and brawlers, persons who with offensive and disorderly acts or language accost or annoy persons of the opposite sex, lewd, wanton and lascivious persons in speech or behavior, idle and disorderly persons, disturbers of the peace, keepers of noisy and disorderly houses, and persons guilty of indecent exposure may be punished . . . ."

Over the years, numerous court decisions have drawn six distinct offenses from this language. They are: (1) disorderly conduct; (2) keeper of a disorderly house; (3) disturbing the peace; (4) lewd and lascivious conduct; (5) annoying accosting another sexually; and (6) indecent exposure. This chapter breaks down the first three crimes. The other three offenses, because of their sexual nature, were dealt with in *Chapter 10*.

DISORDERLY CONDUCT 272, § 53

Elements

Disorderly conduct is mentioned but not defined by § 53. Past court decisions such as *Comm. v. Juvenile*, 368 Mass. 580 (1975) define this crime.

- **Cause or risk.** The suspect purposefully caused *or* recklessly created a risk;

- **Public reaction.** Public inconvenience, annoyance, or alarm;

- **Misconduct.** By one of the following types of conduct (*hint*: think "FACT"):

  - <u>F</u>ighting; or

  - <u>A</u>gitated or tumultuous behavior; or

  - <u>C</u>reating a hazard or physically offensive condition by any act that served no legitimate purpose; or

  - <u>T</u>hreatening to use force.

Right of Arrest

272, § 54 warrantless arrest in presence in public.

Special student policy: 272, § 53 holds that elementary and secondary school students under 18 may not be arrested or even charged with disorderly conduct or disturbing the peace (or interrupting an assembly under 272, § 40) for conduct anywhere on school grounds or at a school-related event. This limitation does not apply to anyone 18 and over on school grounds or to off-school behavior by juveniles.

Penalty

1st offense: Fine NMT $150.

2nd or subsequent offense: HC NMT 6 months; and/or Fine NMT $200.

Alternative disposition: 272, § 57 allows the court to discharge an individual upon the payment of the "expenses of prosecution." The defendant must conform to "good behavior" for NLT 6 months and NMT 2 yrs.

Notes

The suspect must intend or recklessly risk public inconvenience, annoyance, or alarm. *Comm. v. Papadinis*, 23 Mass. App. Ct. 570 (1987).

This public impact may occur on public or private property. *Comm. v. Lopiano*, 60 Mass. App. Ct. 723 (2004) (misbehavior at privately owned motel parking lot was still likely to affect visitors and other members of the public).

- **Secluded public location.** *Comm. v. Cadigan*, 2011 WL 5924571 (Appeals Court): Kenneth Cadigan was riding on an MBTA bus to a shelter. Police received a call about an altercation on the bus. The public element of disorderly is satisfied even if the disturbance takes place in a secluded location, so long as some members of the public are likely to be affected. The MBTA bus was filled with 20 or more people traveling to the shelter.

- **Police station.** *Comm. v. Collins*, 36 Mass. App. Ct. 25 (1994) (highly intoxicated defendant "went crazy" in the booking area trying to head butt officers; the court found this misconduct was likely to affect citizens visiting or in custody; officers may safely apply the *Collins* holding to justify disorderly charges for any citizen who behaves in a rambunctious manner in the station).

- **Private property affecting public place.** Disorderly behavior may occur on purely private property — if it affects or is likely to affect persons in a nearby public place. For these situations, "nothing less than conscious disregard of a substantial and unjustifiable risk of public nuisance will suffice." *Comm. v. Mulvey*, 57 Mass. App. Ct. 579 (2003).

In *Mulvey*, the defendant was living at his mother's house. When the police served him with a restraining order, Mulvey screamed at the officers. The confrontation took place 30 feet up a private driveway, which was shielded from public view by a fence.

There was no evidence that a crowd, inquisitive neighbors, or passersby saw or heard the disturbance. Nor was there any evidence to establish that people could have seen or heard the defendant from any place of public access, such as a nearby sidewalk, publicly used path or road, shopping area or other neighborhood facility. This is why his disorderly conviction was overturned.

Compare *Comm. v. Cabrera*, 2022 WL 4487908 (Appeals Court) (a vehicle passenger witnessed — on a third-floor balcony over the street — the defendant punching his girlfriend in the face; the driver stopped and his passenger called 911; by violently hitting his girlfriend in public view, the defendant recklessly created a risk of public alarm). *Comm. v. Rogers*, 2014 WL 2974914 (Appeals Court) (citizen called 911 to report a disturbance at the defendant's home and, although there was no evidence that a crowd had gathered, the area was "thickly settled" so members of the public were likely to be affected).

- **Presence of police does not prove public element.** As *Mulvey* noted, "the theory behind criminalizing disorderly conduct rests on the tendency of the actor's conduct to provoke violence in others, [and] one must suppose that police officers, employed and trained to maintain order, would be least likely to be provoked." Consequently, police presence, by itself, does not turn an otherwise private outburst into disorderly conduct.

Disorderly prohibits four separate acts: (1) conduct that involves force or violence; (2) threats of force or violence; (3) tumultuous behavior, which might not involve physical violence, but which causes a great commotion; or (4) conduct that creates a hazard or physically offensive condition for no legitimate purpose. *Comm. v. Alegata*, 353 Mass. 287 (1967).

Offensive language alone is typically _not_ disorderly. The leading case is *Comm. v. Juvenile*, 368 Mass. 580 (1975). The defendant yelled at clothing store employees and security, calling them "fucking pigs." A crowd of 100 people gathered to watch the outburst. He was escorted from the store, then came back and continued his tirade. The episode lasted 40 minutes! Despite this scene, the SJC overturned the defendant's conviction because it was based on his rude language alone, which infringed on his First Amendment right to speak freely.

Don't these facts seem to be the ultimate disorderly? Yet the SJC wanted to send a message to officers: Pay attention to the suspect's *actions*. Usually physical movement accompanies rude speech — e.g., a menacing gesture, blocking an entrance, approaching people aggressively. This information should appear in the police report.

"Fighting words" directed at a citizen _is_ disorderly. Fighting words exist only if "the person addressed would [most likely] make an immediate violent response." *Gooding v. Wilson*, 405 U.S. 518 (1972).

- **Vulgar terms or gestures, standing alone, are generally not fighting words.** *U.S. v. McDermott*, 971 F. Supp. 939 (E.D. Pa. 1997) ("fuck" and "bullshit" by themselves not considered fighting words).

- **Fighting words do include racial or ethnic slurs, or derogatory remarks about sexual orientation, religious beliefs, or highly personal characteristics.** *Gilles v. Davis*, 427 F.3d 197 (3d Cir. 2005) (speaker called to woman in crowd who identified herself as a lesbian Christian: "Christian lesbo," "do you lay down with dogs?" and "are you a bestiality lover?").

At the same time, police officers are expected to "exercise a higher degree of restraint than the average citizen." *Lewis v. City of New Orleans*, 415 U.S. 130 (1974).

- *Greene v. Barber*, 310 F.3d 889 (6th Cir. 2002) ("police officers . . . may not exercise their authority . . . in response to real or perceived slights to their dignity"). *Thurairajah v. City of Fort Smith*, 925 F.3d 979 (8th Cir. 2019) (drive-by "fuck you" to officer was not disorderly).

- Compare *Comm. v. Richards*, 369 Mass. 443 (1976) (intoxicated defendants called officers "motherfucking pigs" and wrestled with police as a hostile crowd gathered; while opinion that police are "pigs" was protected expression, their behavior was clearly disorderly).

- *Abraham v. Nagle*, 116 F.3d 11 (1st Cir. 1997) (although the defendant had the right to protest an arrest by yelling, "This isn't South Africa; you're White racist cops," he was properly arrested for physically interfering with the arrest of his friend). *Nieves v. Bartlett*, 139 S.Ct. 1715 (2019).

Tumultuous behavior. Tumultuous behavior does not have to be physically violent, but it must involve "riotous commotion" that constitutes "a public nuisance." *Comm. v. Zettel*, 46 Mass. App. Ct. 471 (1999).

- **Tumultuous behavior may include the refusal to obey a proper police order.**

    - *Comm. v. Marcavage*, 76 Mass. App. Ct. 34 (2010): Salem officers received multiple complaints from the crowd on Halloween about the defendant, who was using a megaphone and "getting in people's faces" to preach his religious message. A police supervisor ordered the defendant and another group to stop using megaphones. The defendant resumed his loud tirade. Police warned him and said they would confiscate his megaphone the next time. Fifteen minutes later, the defendant was at it again, and officers attempted to get his megaphone. The defendant held on tightly and began shoving. His disorderly arrest did not infringe on his First Amendment right of free expression or religion. The officers were not regulating his verbal content, just his method — which had caused a significant public disturbance.

    - *Comm. v. Sinai*, 47 Mass. App. Ct. 544 (1999): The defendant refused to pay a parking fee at the beach, screamed at the attendant and officers, attracted a crowd of 20 onlookers, and caused traffic to be rerouted.

    - *Comm. v. Jones*, 2012 WL 739092 (Appeals Court): Police responded to a call and found Dwayne Jones outside a bar, screaming and punching his hand. Police learned that he was upset about a $14 cover charge. Jones called the officers "fucking spic ass niggers." He refused to calm down. A crowd gathered and traffic slowed. Noisy behavior that attracts a crowd is common in cases of tumultuous behavior.

    - *Comm. v. Williams*, 2022 WL 627812 (Appeals Court): After pursuing and losing sight of two vehicles drag racing on Route 107 in Saugus, Trooper Lamusta found the cars at a gas station in Lynn. He told the driver of one car to stay put and then approached Gawayne Williams and his three passengers in the other vehicle. Williams presented his driver's license upon request, but rather than getting the registration, he reached behind his back, near his waist, out of the trooper's sight. Williams refused to comply with orders to keep both hands where the trooper could see them.

The trooper ordered Williams to exit for a frisk. He refused and held the car door closed to prevent Trooper Lamusta from opening it. After eventually getting out, Williams would not cooperate with a frisk. He did not move as directed towards the back of the vehicle to get away from a rear seat passenger who was engaging verbally with and distracting the trooper. Williams took a fighting stance and called out to a group of 20 onlookers to record the interaction.

The male passenger got out of the vehicle and bear-hugged Williams to pull him away from Trooper Lamusta. The trooper told Williams he would be arrested for disorderly conduct if he continued to resist, but the behavior persisted. Trooper Lamusta then arrested Williams. But only when he activated his Taser did Williams submit to custody.

Refusing to obey police orders to show his hands, exit the vehicle, and comply with a frisk was tumultuous behavior. It exposed the police and public to danger by reducing the ability of police to maintain order.

- **Tumultuous behavior does *not* occur just because a citizen argues or speaks obnoxiously.** Below are examples of improper arrests:

  - *U.S. v. Pasqualino*, 768 F.Supp. 13 (D. Mass. 1991): Defendant's arrest for yelling and swearing in a hotel was improper; although his display did attract the attention of other guests, it did not rise to the level of "riotous commotion."

  - *Nuon v. City of Lowell*, 768 F.Supp.2d 323 (2011): An officer responded to an "unwanted guest" call, which he resolved. Vesna Nuon, a visitor legitimately on the premises, began to yell at the officer that he should leave. The officer was going, but decided to remain, obtain Nuon's identification, and run a warrant check (negative results). After these activities, the officer was again leaving but, before he reached his cruiser, Nuon yelled: "You're a coward, hiding behind your badge, get lost." The officer asked Nuon's friend to get him inside, which made Nuon yell more ("You can't tell me what to do . . ."). The officer came onto the porch and took Nuon into custody.[1]

Disorderly should be rare for a psychiatric patient. *Comm. v. Accime*, 476 Mass. 469 (2017): Richie Accime was brought by ambulance to the hospital against his will. Accime said if anyone put their hands on him, he would "fuck them up." Other patients were watching through a window, so the officers re-routed them to other areas. Accime, who was 6'4" and 270 lbs, took off his shirt. He began pacing with clenched fists. Between three and six officers pepper-sprayed him. Only then did he agree to be restrained on a stretcher.

There was no evidence that Accime was aware his behavior affected anyone outside his room. It was witnessed mostly by hospital staff and public safety personnel. A patient's resistance to detention and medication is not uncommon. For this reason, criminal charges of disorderly conduct should be rare. If not, police risk criminalizing mental illness inside the very treatment centers where help is sought during a crisis.

This decision does not mean that a mental health patient can *never* be disorderly. The SJC acknowledged the outcome would have been different if Accime had struck a member of the staff or had intentionally or recklessly disrupted other patients or hospital operations.

---

[1] This case resulted in civil liability in federal court for "false arrest."

A hazard or a physically offensive condition is typically disorderly.

- **Hazards.** *Comm. v. Buffong*, 2012 WL 612556 (Appeals Court) (Tyrone Buffong allowed his dog to run to the end of its leash, snapping and growling at passersby; the officer told Buffong to control his dog, then to wait for animal control; Buffong refused and was arrested).

- **Physically offensive acts** include throwing a stink bomb, strewing garbage or other substances, urinating in public, or other conduct. *Comm. v. Juvenile*, 368 Mass. 580 (1975).

- **Peeping Tom.** The crime of disorderly applies to a Peeping Tom,[2] who causes "a physically offensive condition" by invading the privacy of persons where they are most entitled to feel secure — in their home. *Comm. v. LePore*, 40 Mass. App. Ct. 543 (1996). *Comm. v. Cooper*, 100 Mass. 345 (2021) (holding a cell phone above the divider of a bathroom stall to take a photo of the person on the toilet was "offensive" for disorderly conduct).

There must be "no legitimate purpose" for creating the hazard or offensive condition.

- *Feigenbaum* **case.** Until *Comm. v. Feigenbaum*, 404 Mass. 471 (1989), this requirement was not really a concern. In *Feigenbaum*, about 300 people engaged in a political protest at Otis Air Force Base. They blocked traffic entering and exiting the base. After several warnings, police began to arrest the protesters, including Joel Feigenbaum, for disorderly. Feigenbaum clearly did not engage in fighting, threats, or tumultuous behavior. Therefore, the Commonwealth had to prove that he caused public inconvenience by creating a hazardous condition which *served no legitimate purpose*. The SJC acquitted Feigenbaum because, while his blocking traffic was a hazard that caused public inconvenience, his actions were not shown to have been undertaken without *a legitimate purpose*.

  The SJC did not attempt to explain what might constitute a "legitimate purpose." Instead, police officers and courts are left to examine the *motivations* of protesters to decide whether their behavior is legitimate. Calling on officers to make these subjective judgments may result in inconsistent police responses to political protests, depending on the point of view represented. Officers should rely on alternative charges (e.g., trespassing or disturbing the peace) during passive political protests.

- *Finamore* **case.** *Finamore v. Miglionico*, 15 F.4th 52 (1st Cir. 2021): Cedar Street in the Town of Douglas was treated for years as a public way where it passed over a piece of property owned by Michael Finamore. Two Superior Court decisions established that Cedar Street is a public way.

  Lieutenant Miglionico and two other officers were called to Cedar Street when Finamore started to block it. The Lieutenant arrived to find Finamore had already stretched an orange plastic snow fence across the street at the northern boundary of his property and was doing the same at the southern boundary. The town administrator and highway superintendent also arrived. Lieutenant Miglionico directed Finamore to remove the fence and warned him that he would be arrested if he failed to do so. Finamore refused.

---

2 *Comm. v. LePore, supra.* explained that this term is an allusion to the Peeping Tom of Coventry, who popped out his head as the naked Lady Godiva passed, and was struck blind for it!

A crowd had gathered. People were yelling for Finamore to open the street. Lieutenant Miglionico conferred with the town administrator and superintendent to confirm Finamore had no authority to block Cedar Street. He again ordered Finamore to remove the fence. When he refused, Lieutenant Miglionico arrested Finamore on charges of disorderly conduct and disturbing the peace.

When the charges were dismissed in the local district court, Finamore filed suit in the United States District Court against the Lieutenant and other town officials.

- *The arrest for disorderly conduct was proper:* (1) Finamore was informed that blocking the street was causing public inconvenience; (2) he had stretched the fencing across the street at a particularly dangerous location, which Finamore later agreed posed a traffic hazard; and (3) the act served no legitimate purpose because a court had ruled that Finamore did not control the street.

- *The arrest for disturbing the peace was also justified:* (1) Finamore obstructed the street entirely, which most people would find unreasonably disruptive; and (2) local residents were present, demanding that Finamore stop disturbing their right to pass. See discussion about disturbing in this chapter.

- *Since the arrests were made with probable cause, there was no false arrest, false imprisonment, or malicious prosecution.*

- *Finamore did make an interesting argument that merits consideration given the Commonwealth's de-escalation requirement.* Finamore suggested that police should not have arrested him, even if he had committed this crime, but should have directed town officials to remove the barriers. The U.S. Circuit Court responded that arrest only required probable cause and an arrestable crime, even a minor one. Officers were *not* required to balance the costs and benefits to determine if arrest was necessary. *Atwater v. City of Lago Vista*, 532 U.S. 318 (2001).

- **Bosk case.** In *Comm. v. Bosk*, 29 Mass. App. Ct. 904 (1990), at 2:00 a.m., a state trooper used radar to catch the defendant speeding. Bosk refused to accept the citation and demanded to see the radar unit. The trooper denied his request, informing the defendant of his right to a hearing. Bosk got out of his car and approached the trooper, yelling that he wanted to see the radar. The trooper repeatedly told him that it was not safe to be in the road and to get back in his car. Bosk stood in the traffic lane and vehicles were forced to change lanes to avoid striking him. Finally, the trooper told Bosk that if he did not comply with her order, she would arrest him for disorderly.

  Bosk argued that his outburst was First Amendment free speech. The court disagreed because the trooper arrested Bosk for his conduct, not his message. Bosk also argued that his traffic protest had a legitimate purpose similar to the protesters in *Feigenbaum*. The court rejected this comparison by pointing out that Bosk, unlike Feigenbaum, risked danger to himself and others. Also see *Comm. v. Molligi*, 70 Mass. App. Ct. 108 (2007).

Related Issue: Begging and being homeless

No longer may arrest a person for being homeless. It was standard police procedure before 1967 to sweep "undesirables" off the street. *Comm. v. Alegata,* 353 Mass. 287 (1967) ended that practice in Massachusetts. Depending on the situation, officers may resort to protective custody or a mental health detention under 123, § 12. These noncriminal interventions may be necessary, but the best response is typically referral and transport to community services.

Peaceful panhandlers protected by the Constitution. *Benefit v. Cambridge,* 424 Mass. 918 (1997) established that peaceful begging is allowed by the First Amendment "because people are free to ignore or walk away from the beggar's request for money or attention." The SJC noted that there is "ample authority . . . to deal with beggars who transgress peaceful limits." Also see *Thayer v. City of Worcester,* 144 F.3d 218 (2015).

Illegal to employ or permit minor under 15 to beg. 272, § 58 prohibits a parent or other person from *employing* a minor under 15 to beg on their behalf. It is also illegal if a parent or caregiver simply *permits* the minor to beg. Penalty: HC NMT 6 months; or Fine NMT $200. Right of Arrest: Complaint. Also, file a mandatory 51A report with DCF. See *Chapter 14.*

KEEPER OF A DISORDERLY HOUSE
272, § 53

Elements

The prohibition against a keeper of a disorderly house appears in § 53 but is explained in past court decisions. *Comm. v. Rivers,* 307 Mass. 225 (1940). *Comm. v. Davenport,* 84 Mass. 299 (1861).

- ***Controls premises.*** The suspect completely or partially controls or manages the premises;

- ***Knowledge.*** Knows that the place has become disorderly;

- ***Habitual disorder.*** Because of habitual:
    - Noise that disturbs the public peace of the neighborhood;
    - Drinking alcoholic beverages;
    - Gambling;
    - Prostitution; or
    - Other unlawful gatherings.

Strategy & Right of Arrest

Strategy. Charging a keeper of a disorderly house is best done after repeat visits to a home concerning loud parties, underage drinking, and the like. It holds owners or other residents accountable for curbing their guests' disruptive behavior. Document warnings to eliminate a claim by the owner/resident that he or she was unaware of the problem.

Right of Arrest. 272, § 54 warrantless arrest in presence in public, which is rare for this offense. Typically, the charge will be initiated by complaint following a series of incidents.

Penalty

HC NMT 6 months; and/or Fine NMT $200.

Alternative disposition: See previous discussion of disorderly conduct.

DISTURBING THE PEACE
272, § 53

Elements

The elements of disturbing the peace are best defined in *Comm. v. Canty*, 65 Mass. App. Ct. 1113 (2006).

- **Objectively annoying conduct.** The suspect engaged in conduct that most people would find annoying or unreasonably disruptive;

- **Intentional.** The suspect's behavior was intentional and not the result of a mistake or accident;

- **Victim annoyed.** The suspect did, in fact, annoy or disturb at least one person.

Right of Arrest

272, § 54 warrantless arrest in public.

Penalty

1st offense: Fine NMT $150.

2nd or subsequent offense: HC NMT 6 months; and/or Fine NMT $200.

Alternative disposition: See previous discussion of disorderly conduct.

Special student policy: See previous discussion of disorderly conduct.

Notes

Intentional behavior that is objectively annoying. This standard protects people from being arrested for conduct that bothers the overly sensitive, since the activity must "tend to annoy all good citizens." *Comm. v. Orlando*, 371 Mass. 732 (1977).

- **Context is critical: Time, place, & manner.** A person yelling downtown during the day is acceptable. A person yelling in the middle of the night in a residential neighborhood is a different story because it is directed at a "captive" audience. *Boston v. Back Bay Cultural Association*, 418 Mass. 175 (1994). *Comm. v. Williams*, 2017 WL 1048125 (Appeals Court) (in the early evening hours of a summer day on a busy street, officers saw a group of people watching a heated argument, which ended upon their arrival; it did not provide a reasonable suspicion that Williams was disturbing the peace or that he was armed and dangerous; the police did not have a reason to detain or frisk him as he walked away).

- **Noise is not required.** *Comm. v. Britto*, 2011 WL 2120154 (Appeals Court): The victim was walking on a bike path with her husband and two children. Robert Britto was sitting on a fence. The family walked past. When the victim looked back, Britto was completely naked. Although Britto made no sounds or gestures while he was undressing and exposing himself, his conduct qualified as a disturbance. His convictions for disturbing the peace *and* open and gross lewdness were proper.

- **Standard not vague.** Although defendants argue that disturbing the peace is vague, the SJC notes that a more specific standard is impractical because what is illegal "necessarily varies according to its location and timing." In the court's opinion, a person's "common sense" will "define the proscribed conduct." *Comm. v. Orlando, supra.*

Conduct affects someone, including unidentified 911 caller. The crime must have a victim. A 911 call proves that a citizen was annoyed or disturbed, so officers do not need to identify a specific complainant. *Comm. v. Piscopo*, 11 Mass. App. Ct. 905 (1981) (defendant was member of a group that was yelling loudly and throwing beer bottles on a street in a residential neighborhood; fact that officers were dispatched proved that upset citizens had notified 911).

DISORDER DURING PUBLIC MEETINGS

Preferred Police Response

Public boards, commissions, committees, and town meetings have a person in charge. This leader (often referred to as the chair or moderator) is legally responsible for preserving order. Police officers assigned for security at a meeting should follow the directions of the chair. This does not mean that officers should delay intervening when violence or true threats happen,[3] but it does mean that officers should look for guidance from the chair when there is a lesser type of disturbance.

State law gives strong authority to the chair:

- No person may speak to the people assembled without permission from the chair.

- Any person at a meeting must be silent at the request of the chair.

- After a warning, if a person continues to be disruptive, the chair may order him or her to leave.

- If the person refuses to leave, the chair may authorize a police officer to remove him or her.

    - *39, § 17 applies to town meetings:* "No person shall address a town meeting without leave of the moderator, and all persons shall, at the request of the moderator, be silent. If a person, after warning from the moderator, persists in disorderly behavior, the moderator may order him to withdraw from the meeting, and, if he does not withdraw, may order a [police officer] . . . to remove him and confine him in some convenient place until the meeting is adjourned."

---

3 It goes without saying that officers will take charge when a fist fight starts, a chair gets thrown, a death threat is launched, property is defaced, etc.

- **30A, § 20(g) applies to other meetings of public bodies:** "No person shall address a meeting of a public body without permission of the chair, and all persons shall, at the request of the chair, be silent. No person shall disrupt the proceedings of a meeting of a public body. If, after clear warning from the chair, a person continues to disrupt the proceedings, the chair may order the person to withdraw from the meeting and if the person does not withdraw, the chair may authorize a [police officer] to remove the person from the meeting."

Police officers should be prepared to prompt the chair in how to follow the law. Many chairpersons or moderators may not understand the law or have experience controlling misbehavior. Officers should be ready to walk them through the steps authorized by law:

- **Step 1 — seek good behavior.** If a person refuses to comply with direction from the chair to sit down or be silent, an officer may approach the potential violator and address the chair: "Mr. Chairman (or Madam Chairman), would you like the person to sit down and be quiet?" Upon getting an answer, the officer can suggest that it would be better to comply and remain in the meeting, than be removed by the chair.

- **Step 2 — persuade the citizen to leave.** If Step 1 does not work, the officer should prompt the chair with: "The gentleman (or lady) refuses to remain silent, Madam Chairman, would you like them to leave the meeting?" Upon getting an affirmative answer, the officer should try to persuade the person to leave immediately as the chair directed.

- **Step 3 — order the citizen to leave.** If this fails, the officer can prompt the chair with: "The gentleman (or lady) refuses to leave the meeting, Mr. Chairman, would you like them to be removed from the meeting?" On getting an affirmative response, the officer will say to the person that they have made their point, and that leaving without the officer's assistance will be better than the alternative — physical removal and potential arrest.

- **Step 4 — escort and/or arrest the citizen.** Continued verbal and/or physical disruption constitutes the crime of <u>disturbing a public meeting under 272, § 40</u>.[4] Officers have a right to arrest for this breach of peace in their presence. See *Comm. v. Hoxey*, 16 Mass. 385 (1820) (misbehavior in violation of a town moderator's direction is a breach of peace; SJC declares that "the business transacted by the citizens, at th[e]se meetings, [is] the foundation of our whole civil polity").

    In addition to 272, § 40, arrest or charge <u>criminal trespass under 266, § 120</u>. The legal basis: Once a person has been ordered by the chair to leave, their refusal to go constitutes "remaining without right" under § 120. *Comm. v. Lapon*, 28 Mass. App. Ct. 681 (1990).

---

4 272, § 40 states: "Whoever willfully interrupts or disturbs an assembly of people meeting for a lawful purpose shall be punished by imprisonment for not more than 1 month or by a fine of not more than $50; provided, however, that an elementary or secondary student shall not be adjudged a delinquent child for an alleged violation of this section for such conduct within school buildings or on school grounds or in the course of school-related events."

This protocol recognizes that the chair — not the police officer — should be the judge of whether speech or other misconduct disrupts the meeting. That role is given to the chair by law. This is important because, on issues of public or personal concern, citizens often have heated opinions and may become unruly. Public meetings typically accommodate some harsh rhetoric and gestures, and the chair is the best person to decide how far it should go.[5]

At the same time, the police — not the chair — decide whether to arrest or apply for a criminal complaint. In the context of a public meeting — where the chair is given explicit statutory authority to command silence and order attendees to leave — the disturbance that triggers an arrest for 272, § 40 need not be nearly as extreme as the type of street disruption required for disorderly conduct or disturbing the peace under 272, § 53.

A case on point is *Comm. v. Bohmer*, 374 Mass. 368 (1978). Peter Bohmer entered two separate classrooms at the Massachusetts Institute of Technology (MIT) and interrupted each professor several times because he wanted to make an unauthorized announcement to students. His friend tried to pass out brochures. Bohmer was convicted. On appeal, the SJC found that 272, § 40 did not infringe on citizens' First Amendment rights. It then decided that Bohmer's behavior, which admittedly was not extreme by disorderly standards, still amounted to a violation of 272, § 40.

Finally, any police intervention merits an incident report. Participation in public meetings is a civil right, so police action that terminates participation — whether by agreement, warning, escort, criminal complaint, or arrest — must be fully documented. A situation — that you thought was fairly minor at the time — may later become the subject of a civil lawsuit. Your professional interaction and documentation are the keys to preventing later lawsuits and citizen complaints.

Related Offense

Disrupting a Court Proceeding. 268, § 13 outlaws causing or participating in a "willful disruption" of any court. The term disruption is much broader than the definition of disorderly applicable to public activities. Having a stricter standard is essential in the court setting. Penalty: HC NMT 1 year; and/or Fine NMT $1,000. Right of Arrest: Arrest for breach in presence; otherwise complaint. *Comm. v. Zine*, 52 Mass. App. Ct. 130 (2001) (defendant swore at judge after probation surrender hearing).

---

5 Officers should follow the chair's direction in removing a person from a meeting unless there is good reason not to — e.g., the chair is being racially or ethnically discriminatory, or arbitrary and capricious in deciding who should be silenced or ejected. Obvious misconduct by a duly recognized chair is rare, however.

Law Enforcement Dimensions

DISORDER DURING PUBLIC PROTEST

On-Scene Response

Unlawful assembly defined. 269, § 1 defines an unlawful assembly as a group of 5 or more people who are armed with dangerous weapons, or 10 or more people, armed or not, who are "riotously or tumultuously assembled in a city or town."

- **Dispersal order.** 269, § 1 also directs that any municipal or state police officer (or mayor, alderman, selectman, justice of the peace, sheriff or deputy) shall "in the name of the Commonwealth command all persons . . . immediately and peaceably to disperse."

- **Right of arrest.** For those who fail to leave, 269, § 1 authorizes warrantless arrest in presence.

- **Penalty.** 269, § 2 penalizes those who refuse or neglect to obey the dispersal order: HC NMT 1 year; and/or Fine NLT $100, NMT $500.

An assembly must be potentially violent in order to justify a police dispersal order. Comm. v. Abramms, 66 Mass. App. Ct. 576 (2006) held that an assembly only becomes unlawful when its members have a common goal to engage in violent acts. Police must reasonably believe, based on specific conduct, that group violence is imminent. Police speculation is insufficient. Police authority should not be so broad that it undercuts the right to peaceably assemble.

Related Offense

Incite to Riot. 264, § 1 prohibits: (1) advocating, counseling, or inciting; (2) an assault on a public official, killing a person, the unlawful destruction of property, or the overthrow of the state or federal government by force, violence, or other unlawful means. Penalty: SP NMT 3 yrs or HC NMT 2½ yrs; or Fine NMT $1,000. [*Note:* Defendant is ineligible for public office or employment, or employment as a public or private school teacher]. Right of Arrest: Felony.

- **Threatening a police officer was not inciting others to riot.** *Comm. v. Manolo M.*, 486 Mass. 678 (2021): Manolo M. was with an unruly group of high school students occupying a public street and disobeying police orders to disperse. Manolo took a fighting stance and yelled at Brockton SRO Vaughn, "Mother fucker you wanna go! Let's go!" Manolo swung his fist at Officer Vaughn's head.

   The crime of inciting to riot applies to a person who "by speech or by exhibition . . . advocates . . . or incites" assaulting a public official, killing someone, or overthrowing the government. No facts presented here alleged the juvenile did any of these things. Manolo challenged Officer Vaughn, and he could have been charged with assault under 265, § 13A for that. But Manolo did not try to enlist others to attack the officer.

- **A prosecution for this offense is constitutional only when the suspect's words or actions are likely to cause others to take immediate action.** See *Brandenburg v. Ohio*, 395 U.S. 444 (1969) (the court discussed statutes like Massachusetts' 264, § 11 and how they were written between 1917 and 1920 to combat communist thoughts and political action).

REFUSING TO REMOVE A SUBSTANCE THROWN ON A PUBLIC WAY
272, § 60

Elements

- **Local law.** The suspect violated an ordinance or bylaw by throwing or placing rubbish or another substance on a sidewalk, public way or public alley;

- **Officer present.** In the presence of a police officer; and

- **Refuse to remove.** The suspect refused the officer's request to remove it.

Right of Arrest

272, § 60 warrantless arrest if suspect refuses to remove the substance and to identify himself so the officer can write him a ticket.

Important restriction: The suspect may only be held until his identity is ascertained, then he must be given a local ordinance or bylaw ticket and released. *Comm. v. Bones*, 93 Mass. App. Ct. 681 (2018) (if challenged, officer should bring a copy of the ordinance or bylaw to court so that it can be offered into evidence).

Penalty

Offender must be fined in accordance with the ordinance or bylaw.

24 Gambling

GAMING OR BETTING IN PUBLIC
271, § 2

Purpose

This is the gaming offense most likely to be used by the street officer on patrol. It is perfect for three card monte players and public crap games in the park.

Elements

- **Knowingly gambled.** The suspect knowingly:

    - Played cards, dice, or another game for money or property; or

    - Bet on "the sides or hands of those playing"; or

    - Set up or permitted such a game;

- **In public.** In a public place, on a public conveyance, or "in a private place upon which he is trespassing."

Right of Arrest

271, § 2 warrantless arrest in presence.

Penalty

For playing or betting on outcome of game: HC NMT 3 months; or Fine NMT $50.

For setting up or permitting game: HC NLT 3 months, NMT 1 year; or Fine NLT $50, NMT $100.

Notes

Special forfeiture condition. For any gambling offense, 271, § 1 requires that the offender forfeit double the value of the money or goods that he won over $5. To use this provision, the prosecution must be commenced within 18 months of the commission of the crime. *Comm. v. Novak*, 272 Mass. 113 (1930).

Law Enforcement Dimensions

REGISTERING BETS
271, § 17

Elements

The suspect knowingly:

- **Kept place for registering.** Kept "any place" in which there were books or devices for registering bets; or

- **Permitted registering.** Permitted an area to be used for this purpose; or

- **Present to help register.** Was present in any public or private place to help register bets.

Right of Arrest

Felony.

Penalty

SP NMT 3 yrs or HC NMT 2½ yrs; or Fine NMT $3,000.

Notes

Knowledge means more than mere presence. The suspect must have some connection, beyond simply being present, with the place of illegal gaming. However, 271, §§ 20 and 21 state that possessing any gaming materials or records is sufficient evidence of their use by the person in possession. *Comm. v. Murphy*, 342 Mass. 393 (1961).

Registering defined. "Registering" means recording or noting a bet on some form or media (e.g., a computer) or "committing a bet to memory." At the time of registration, the bet must be "accepted" — that is, the offender must be affording the wagerer the opportunity to take a risk on an uncertain event and, depending on the outcome of that event, the wagerer must be entitled to receive or be obligated to pay money. *Comm. v. Sousa*, 33 Mass. App. Ct. 433 (1992).

Investigator's expert testimony. Similar to drug detectives, police gaming investigators may rely on their expertise to interpret the significance of gaming items found at the scene. *Comm. v. Boyle*, 346 Mass. 1 (1963) (police officer on the gaming squad for 13 years was qualified to testify that slips were bookmaking paraphernalia).

"Any place" for violation. The violation may occur in "any place . . . , public or private." *Comm. v. Carlson*, 331 Mass. 449 (1954) (hallway of building covered by this statute). A separate statute, 271, § 1A, makes all gambling laws enforceable on any "ship or vessel . . . within the territorial limits of the Commonwealth."

USE OF TELEPHONE FOR BETTING PURPOSES
271, § 17A

Elements

- **Control telephone.** The suspect used, subscribed to, or had control of the premises containing a telephone; and

- **Knowingly accept bets.** Knowingly used, or permitted the telephone to be used, for accepting bets or reporting betting results to a booking office.

Right of Arrest

271, § 10A warrantless arrest by officers present at the scene of the violation.

Penalty

HC NMT 1 year; or Fine NMT $2,000.

Notes

Definition of a bet. The gambling statutes define a bet in comprehensive terms as the "buying or selling of pools, upon the result of a contest of skill, speed or endurance of man, beast, bird, machine, or upon the happening of any event, or upon the result of any game, competition, political nomination, appointment or election."

Proof of phone use for gambling. The phone must be used for accepting bets or for reporting gambling results. Evidence of telephone conversations heard by police in conjunction with physical evidence at the scene is sufficient. *Comm. v. Massod*, 350 Mass. 745 (1966).

Phone may be used to bet legally. If the suspect is merely assisting another by placing a legal bet for him, then he is not guilty. *Comm. v. Sousa*, 33 Mass. App. Ct. 433 (1992).

ORGANIZING ILLEGAL GAMBLING FACILITIES
271, § 16A

Elements

- **Knowingly.** The suspect knowingly:

    - **Organized, managed or financed;** or

    - **Received payment from;**

- **4 people.** At least four persons;

- **Support for lottery or betting.** Who provided facilities or services for the conduct of illegal lotteries or the registration of bets.

Right of Arrest

Felony.

Penalty

SP NMT 15 yrs; and/or Fine NMT $10,000.

Notes

Proof of syndicate unnecessary. This felony punishes the manager of at least four persons who perform illegal gaming services or provide him with proceeds from those activities. It is *not* necessary to show that the defendant specifically organized a gambling syndicate. *Comm. v. Vitello*, 367 Mass. 224 (1975).

Persons supervised do not include wagerers. § 16A specifically states that the four people may not be basic wagerers. They must help provide gambling services.

ILLEGAL LOTTERY
271, § 7

Elements

- ***Promote.*** The suspect was involved, in any way, in setting up or promoting;
- ***Lottery.*** A lottery.

Right of Arrest

Felony.

Penalty

SP NMT 3 yrs or HC NMT 2½ yrs; or Fine NMT $3,000.

Notes

Illegal lottery defined. Except for the state lottery, all others are illegal in Massachusetts. A lottery involves: (1) the payment of a price; (2) for the possibility of winning a prize; (3) depending upon luck or chance. *Mobil Oil v. Attorney General*, 361 Mass. 401 (1972).

A pyramid scheme is a lottery because the odds of winning are determined by chance. *Comm. v. Stewart-Johnson*, 78 Mass. App. Ct. 592 (2011): Margarita Stewart-Johnson and her husband became involved in a money-making venture involving the Cape Verdean community. There were 15 players at each table divided into four levels. Eight players were at the "appetizer" course, four at "soup and salad," two at "entrée," and one at "dessert." Each player had to pay an entrance fee of $1,000 to $5,000 to the person enjoying dessert. The remaining players would be split into new tables and advance to the next course. The "soup and salad" players had to recruit new "appetizer" participants. This game was a pyramid scheme. Each person was supposed to leave the table with eight times what he or she initially paid. The defendants actively recruited others to join.

Here, the first two elements of a lottery were obvious. The players paid an entry fee for the possibility of winning a payoff when they reached "dessert."

The third element, chance, was also satisfied. Winning did not depend on the "skill" of the players in getting new recruits, but on when players joined. Like all pyramid schemes, it was inevitable that the pool of potential participants would become saturated, so a large group of people would never reach "dessert" and lose their entry fee. While a player may have been able to marginally improve his chances by employing "skill" in recruiting others, success or failure remained largely outside a player's control, which meant it depended on chance.[1]

271, § 7 prohibits the setting up of a lottery *and/or* promoting it. While these defendants did not initiate or manage the scheme, they clearly promoted it.

Not a lottery if no purchase necessary to play. *Comm. v. Webb*, 68 Mass. App. Ct. 167 (2007) (Webb's conviction for promoting a lottery was overturned because there was no requirement that participants pay to play, which is an element of this crime; the "free play" option on his machine was legitimate; there was no demonstrated disadvantage to those who chose free play versus those who paid).

Exemptions for gambling by nonprofit organizations. Built into the law are certain exemptions that allow nonprofit organizations to hold gambling events, provided that they follow appropriate regulations. See 271, §§ 7A, 22A, and 22B.

Related Offenses

Selling or Advertising Lottery Ticket. Under 271, §§ 9 and 11, a person cannot advertise, sell, offer for sale, or assist in selling a lottery ticket. Penalty: HC NMT 1 year; or Fine NMT $2,000. This statute does not apply to a Massachusetts lottery sales representative. Right of Arrest: 271, § 10A warrantless arrest in presence. *Comm. v. Hooper*, 22 Mass. 42 (1827).

Making or Selling False Lottery Ticket. 271, § 12 penalizes making, possessing with intent to sell, or receiving anything of value for a false lottery ticket. Penalty: SP NMT 3 yrs.

Promoting Foreign Lottery. 271, § 15 penalizes a person who "is concerned in any way" with setting up, promoting or managing a "foreign" lottery — that is, a lottery outside the Commonwealth. § 16, in similar fashion, forbids someone from selling, or possessing with intent to sell, a foreign lottery ticket. Penalty for both: HC NMT 1 year; or Fine NMT $2,000.

---

[1] The fact that money invested in an enterprise may be subject to risk does not create a lottery. If so, this would render many legitimate businesses lotteries! Pyramid schemes exhibit distinctive elements that distinguish them from legitimate businesses, such as shuffling money among participants without affecting collective wealth, and the fact that pyramid schemes are doomed to fail.

Law Enforcement Dimensions

CRIMES RELATING TO THE MASSACHUSETTS LOTTERY
10, § 30

Introduction

Massachusetts sponsors a lottery through the Lottery Commission of the Treasurer's Office, located at 150 Mount Vernon Street, Dorchester, MA 02125. Telephone: 781-849-5555.

Elements

- **Fraudulent intent.** With intent to defraud;

- **Alter or forge.** The suspect made, altered, forged, uttered, passed or counterfeited;

- **Massachusetts lottery ticket.** A state lottery ticket or share.

Right of Arrest

Felony.

Penalty

SP NMT 3 yrs or HC NMT 2 yrs; or Fine NLT $100, NMT $500.

Related Offenses

Prohibited sales. 10, § 29 prohibits three types of sales. First, it is illegal to sell a lottery ticket or share "at a price greater than that fixed by the commission." Second, no person, other than a licensed lottery sales agent, may sell tickets or shares. However, anyone may give tickets or shares as a gift. Third, no ticket or share may be sold to any person under age 18. However, a person age 18 or over may purchase a ticket or share and give it as a gift to someone under 18. Penalty for all three violations: Fine NLT $100, NMT $500. Right of Arrest: Complaint.

Impersonation of Lottery Commission Employee. 10, § 30A. Penalty: HC NMT 1 year; or Fine NLT $400. Right of Arrest: Complaint.

Attempt to Secure Sales License or Employment by Promises or Payment. 10, § 30A. A person may not pay (or promise) money, property or services in an effort to secure a license to sell lottery tickets or to secure employment with the Lottery Commission. Penalty: SP NMT 3 yrs or HC NMT 2½ yrs; and/or Fine NMT $5,000. Right of Arrest: Felony.

Law Enforcement Dimensions

CRIMES RELATING TO MASSACHUSETTS CASINO GAMBLING
G.L. Chapters 23K & 271

Introduction

Massachusetts has approved casino gambling, which is licensed by the Gaming Commission located at 101 Federal Street, 12th Floor, Boston, MA 02110. Telephone: 617-979-8400.

23K, § 38 punishes willfully interfering with the Commission or making a false statement to its agent. Penalty: SP NMT 5 yrs or HC NMT 2 ½ yrs; and/or Fine NMT $25,000.

Casino Operations

23K, § 37 punishes:

- Conducting, operating, or permitting any game or gaming device in violation of Chapter 23K. Penalty: SP NMT 5 yrs or HC NMT 2½ yrs; and/or Fine NMT $25,000 (if a business entity, NMT $100,000).

- Improperly employing an unlicensed or unregistered individual in a casino. Penalty: HC NMT 6 months; and/or Fine NMT $10,000 (if a business entity, NMT $100,000).

- An unlicensed or unregistered employee working in a casino. Penalty: HC NMT 6 months; and/or Fine NMT $10,000.

- A gaming licensee who, without permission, displays a gaming device or receives compensation for carrying on a game. Penalty: HC NMT 2½ yrs; and/or Fine NMT $25,000 (if a business entity, NMT $100,000).

- Operating a game or device after the person's gaming license has expired. Penalty: HC NMT 1½ yrs; and/or Fine NMT $25,000, (if a business entity, NMT $100,000).

- A gaming licensee who knowingly fails to exclude from their establishment a person on the Gaming Commission's excluded persons list. (See discussion below.) Penalty: HC NMT 1 year; and/or Fine NMT $5,000 (if a business entity, NMT $100,000).

- Willfully evading or failing to report, pay or truthfully account for a license fee or tax imposed by Chapter 23K. Penalty: SP NMT 5 yrs or HC NMT 2½ yrs; and/or Fine NMT $100,000 (if a business entity, NMT $5,000,000).

23K, § 45 requires the Commission to create a list of who is excluded from gaming establishments based on whether: (1) a person has been convicted of a crime of moral turpitude, or punishable by more than 6 months in jail, or involving a gaming violation in any state; (2) a person has violated or conspired to violate Chapter 23K by failing to disclose a gaming establishment interest or willfully evading fees or taxes; or (3) a person's reputation would adversely affect the public's trust in the gaming industry.

Cheating and Swindling

23K, § 39 punishes cheating, helping another person, or using a device in a gaming establishment. Penalty: Based on amount. $75,000 or more: SP NMT 10 yrs or HC NMT 2½ yrs; and/or Fine NMT $1M for person, NMT $10M for business. $10,000 – $75,000: SP NMT 5 yrs or HC NMT 2½ yrs; and/or Fine NMT $500,000 for person, NMT $5M for business. $1,000 - $10,000: SP NMT 3 yrs or HC NMT 2½ yrs; and/or Fine NMT $100,000 for person, NMT $1M for business. Less than $1,000: HC NMT 2½ yrs; and/or Fine NMT $10,000 for person, NMT $100,000 for business. Each episode or transaction may be a separate count.

23K, § 40 punishes possessing a cheating and swindling device or game. Penalty: HC NMT 2½ yrs; and/or Fine NMT $10,000 (if business NMT $100,000). *Note*: Possession of a device or game within a gaming establishment constitutes sufficient evidence.

23K, § 41 punishes manufacturing, distributing, selling, or servicing a gaming device for the purpose of cheating or stealing from a person in a gaming establishment. Penalty: SP NMT 5 yrs or HC NMT 2½ yrs; and/or Fine NMT $25,000 (if business NMT $150,000). Forfeiture: § 42 seizure and forfeiture of any device or game. Commission entitled to forfeiture share.

Underage Gambling

23K, § 43 punishes:

- Anyone under 21 who plays, wagers or collects winnings in a gaming establishment. Penalty: Fine NMT $1,000.

- A gaming licensee or employee who knowingly allows a person under 21 to play, wager, or collect winnings in a gaming establishment. Penalty: 1st offense: HC NMT 1 year; and/or Fine NMT $10,000 (NMT $500,000 for business); 2nd or subsequent offense: HC NMT 2 yrs; and/or Fine NMT $50,000 (NMT $1M for business).

- A person who knowingly plays, wagers or collects winnings for a person under 21. Penalty: HC NMT 6 months; and/or Fine NMT $1,000.

Games at Non-Licensed Location

271, § 8 punishes owning or controlling any building and permitting a lottery, raffle, or other game of chance outside of a gaming establishment licensed under Chapter 23K. Penalty: HC NMT 1 year; or Fine NMT $2,000. Right of Arrest: 271, § 10A warrantless arrest in presence.

Law Enforcement Dimensions

Part VII

THEFT OFFENSES

Larceny by Stealing, Deceiving or Embezzling, Robbery, Special Forms of Larceny, Shoplifting, Receiving Stolen Property, Forgery, & Uttering

Chapters 25 – 30

© John Sofis Scheft, Esq.
All rights reserved

25 Larceny

LARCENY
266, § 30

Summary

266, § 30 is the general larceny statute, which mentions the three ways to engage in this crime: (1) stealing; (2) larceny by false pretense; or (3) embezzlement. However, § 30 does not define these terms. Instead, case law defines the elements of each form of larceny.

Elements

Type 1: Stealing. *Comm. v. Anthony*, 306 Mass. 470 (1940) defines stealing as:

- The suspect unlawfully took and carried away;
- The money or property of another;
- With the intent to permanently deprive that person.

Type 2: Larceny by False Pretense. *Comm. v. Leonard*, 352 Mass. 636 (1967) defines it as:

- The suspect knowingly made a false statement of fact;
- That the victim relied on as being true; and
- Caused the victim to give the suspect money or property.

Type 3: Embezzlement. *Comm. v. Snow*, 284 Mass. 426 (1933) defines embezzlement as:

- The suspect was entrusted with the property of another; and
- Took the property, hid it, or converted it to his own use;
- With the intent to permanently deprive the owner.

Right of Arrest

If the suspect steals a firearm, trade secret, or the most common situation, property valued in excess of $250: 266, § 30 warrantless arrest on probable cause.

If suspect steals property valued at $250 or less: 276, § 28 warrantless arrest in presence. Otherwise, complaint.

Penalty

If the property is a firearm, trade secret, or the value of the property is more than $1,200: SP NMT 5 yrs; or HC NMT 2 yrs and Fine NMT $25,000.

If the value of the stolen property (other than a firearm or trade secret) does not exceed $1,200: HC NMT 1 year; or Fine NMT $1,500.

Protection of elders and the disabled. If victim 60 yrs of age or older, or disabled, and if the value of the property is over $250: SP NMT 10 yrs or HC NMT 2½ yrs; and/or Fine NMT $50,000. If value of property $250 or less: HC NMT 2½ yrs; and/or Fine NMT $1,000. *Note:* Felony threshold is $250, not $1,200.

Notes

Property Subject to Larceny

Larceny involves taking property. 266, § 30 defines property as money, any financial documents or deeds, any electronically stored data, any owned animal, possessions of all types, or trade secrets. *Comm. v. Catalano*, 74 Mass. App. Ct. 580 (2009). Even contraband may be stolen! *Comm. v. Ridge*, 37 Mass. App. Ct. 943 (1994) (defendant convicted of larceny because he took cocaine from his accomplice).

The value of the stolen property determines an officer's right of arrest and potential penalty. However, the value of the property is *not* an element of the offense. Once the amount exceeds $1,200, it is unnecessary to determine the exact value of the stolen articles since the felony has already been proven. *Comm. v. LaFontaine*, 32 Mass. App. Ct. 529 (1992).

- **In some cases, a suspect can steal property at more than one time pursuant to a single scheme.** If a single scheme occurs, then officers may consider the total value of all the property obtained. *Comm. v. Donovan*, 395 Mass. 20 (1985).

- **On the other hand, distinct larcenies may be presented in multiple counts.** *Comm. v. Murray*, 401 Mass. 771 (1988) (employee appropriately charged with 180 counts for 180 incidents involving forged checks from his employer). Officers may choose how to proceed. *Comm. v. Aldrich*, 88 Mass. App. Ct. 113 (2015) (defendant appropriately charged with two counts when he stole the same property at two different times and locations — once at the victim's home and again during booking at the station when an officer's back was turned).

Certain types of theft, however, are not subject to prosecution as larceny because they do not fall within the definition of property under the statute.

- **Intellectual theft** (e.g., plagiarism, movie or song piracy, etc.) is governed by federal copyright law. *Comm. v. Yourawski*, 384 Mass. 386 (1981).

- **Using property or services without payment is not larceny.** *Comm. v. Rivers*, 31 Mass. App. Ct. 669 (1991) (defendant's use of a landfill without paying the town was not larceny). *Comm. v. Geane*, 51 Mass. App. Ct. 149 (2001) (the defendant contractor failed to pay his subcontractors for their work; since he stole their services — but not their actual, tangible property — it did not qualify as a larceny).

The property must belong to another. However, the Commonwealth does *not* have to prove who owned or held the property, as long as it proves the defendant did not. This is helpful because, at times, officers may know the suspect stole property but be unable to specifically identify its rightful owner. See 277, § 25 (identity of owner need not be alleged if property is described with sufficient certainty). *Comm. v. Souza*, 397 Mass. 236 (1986).

It is a defense to larceny if the defendant honestly, but mistakenly, believed that he had a right to take the property. *Comm. v. Liebenow,* 470 Mass. 151 (2014) (defendant took metal pipes that belonged to a contractor on a private construction site; he argued that he honestly believed they were abandoned scrap metal; the prosecutor had to prove that, at the time of removal, the defendant knew he was wrongfully taking someone else's property). *Comm. v. Larmey,* 14 Mass App. Ct. 281 (1982).

Larceny occurs when the victim lacked the mental capacity to consent. *Comm. v. St. Hilaire,* 470 Mass. 338 (2015): The defendant induced an elderly woman, who lacked the mental capacity to consent, into conveying her home to him shortly before her death. By its very nature, larceny is taking another person's property *without consent*. Since the victim did not have the mental capacity to consent, the defendant was guilty.

The police are considered a victim of larceny if they had possession of the property taken, including evidence. *Comm. v. Aldrich,* 88 Mass. App. Ct. 113 (2015).

Type 1: Larceny by Stealing

Unlawfully took and carried away. Taking and carrying away (known legally as "asportation") occurs if the suspect physically transfers another's property to his control.

- **Transfer may be momentary and/or involve slight movement.** *Comm. v. Dyous,* 79 Mass. App. Ct. 508 (2011) (victim realized he left his ATM card and returned to the machine; he found Dyous holding his card and $200 cash; Dyous' control of the card and cash satisfied the asportation element because he was removing them from the ATM booth).

- **Removing property from building not required.** *Comm. v. Vickers,* 60 Mass. App. Ct. 24 (2003) (defendant took 16 pairs of shorts to a back corner of the store, where she placed them inside her beach bag; when confronted by security, she attempted to flee; her bag contained a pair of pliers like those often used to remove security sensors). *Comm. v. Bermudez,* 2016 WL 1618213 (Appeals Court) (defendant sat on a couch in a college library for an hour scanning the room before he walked over to a recently vacated desk, grabbed an unattended laptop, and put it in his backpack; when he realized he was being followed by a group of students, he shoved the laptop at the owner and ran out of the library).

Intent to deprive permanently. The suspect must intend to permanently deprive the owner. *Comm. v. Farrier,* 2013 WL 140447 (Appeals Court) (defendant took all his girlfriend's clothes from her apartment; although he left a note saying he was going to wash them, he never returned anything, and his girlfriend later found items in a dumpster behind her apartment).

- **Misplaced items are stolen when the suspect takes possession with the intent to keep them for his own use** even though he "knows or has the reasonable means of . . . ascertaining, by marks on the goods or otherwise, who the owner is." *Comm. v. Titus,* 116 Mass. 42 (1874).

- Taking property with the intent to return it and claim a reward is also larceny. *Comm. v. Mason*, 105 Mass. 163 (1870).

- **A person who steals a container or truck intends to steal its contents,** even though the contents were unknown to him at the time. *Comm. v. Schraffa*, 2 Mass. App. Ct. 808 (1974).

Possession of recently stolen property proves larceny if the defendant cannot explain why he has the items. What constitutes a "recent" theft has not been defined. It depends on the facts. *Comm. v. Defrancesco*, 2012 WL 5381435 (Appeals Court) (defendant used stolen checks within three hours after the break-in). *Comm. v. Rousseau*, 61 Mass. App. Ct. 144 (2004) (possession of stolen camcorder within 10 days of theft considered recent).

Circumstantial evidence may be sufficient proof. *Comm. v. Cheromcka*, 66 Mass. App. Ct. 771 (2006) (witnesses saw Cheromcka take money each day from a container used to collect money for sodas at the bus depot. After she left, her replacement began turning in money. Her supervisor realized Cheromcka never had! This was enough evidence to convict).

Type 2: Larceny by False Pretense (LFP)

The heart of LFP is lying to convince the victim to part with money or property. The false fact must be a key reason for the transaction. *Comm. v. Khan*, 92 Mass. App. Ct. 487 (2017): Each of the four victims received telephone calls from an individual who claimed that the victim's grandchild was in jail and needed money for bail. The caller directed the victims to send cash via FedEx to addresses in Lowell. The defendant provided a friend's address, attempted to accept deliveries in person, and lied to police about not opening a package. He was properly convicted.

- **Promise to perform.** A promise to complete a task does not qualify as a false pretense unless it can be proven that the suspect *never intended* to carry out his promise. *Comm. v. Fisher*, 2016 WL 1177899 (Appeals Court): On March 1, John and Deborah LaPaire entered into a contract with Kevin Fisher to have the siding on their home replaced. John stressed that he needed the project done by the end of the month for insurance purposes. Fisher assured him that he would get it done in a week and that weather would not delay the job. They signed a contract, and John paid Fisher $3,481. Fisher did not begin work.

  A week later, Fisher asked for more cash to purchase materials. Deborah gave him $500. The work still did not begin. John phoned and emailed Fisher several times, and Fisher eventually told him he would begin April 22 or refund the money. That date came and went without work or a refund. Fisher's phone and website were now disconnected.

  The evidence showed that Fisher did *not* intend to perform the work when he took the LaPaires' money. He verbally assured John he would start immediately and weather would not affect his work. Yet, he did nothing after receiving the money. Instead, he shut down his phone and website, and became difficult to locate.

  Compare *Comm. v. Long*, 90 Mass. App. Ct. 696 (2016): Damien Long prepared an estimate to do home improvement work for a married couple. He cashed their deposit check, bought some supplies, performed a few days of minimal work that was not to the homeowners' satisfaction, and abandoned the job. A week later, he slipped an invoice under their door, claiming that they owed *him* money. In this case, Long could not be convicted of LFP. Long's actions showed poor performance, which is not a crime. The court refused to assume fraudulent intent based *solely* on the fact that Long failed to finish the work or refund the money he received.

- **Lying about use for loan.** *Comm. v. Bethune*, 96 Mass. App. Ct. 1112 (2019): Allan Bethune owed $75,000 in personal loans to acquaintances. He asked a friend twice to lend him $50,000 for "a deal he had to get into." The victim provided a check and Bethune promised to provide paperwork the next day, which he never did. He used all the money to pay down personal loans and other bills. Three years later, he had not repaid the victim. It was clear Bethune had lied about the purpose of the loan because he believed it was the only way to get money from the victim.

- **Lying about repaying loan.** *Comm. v. Enagbare*, 2016 WL 3030894 (Appeals Court): The 90 year old victim's son noticed that his father had constantly been writing checks to his neighbor, Kim Enagbare. The victim refused to discuss the matter, so the son confronted Enagbare, who said the payments were a loan she would repay when she got a tax refund.

  The payments continued at an alarming rate, totaling $25,000 in a three month period. The victim was increasingly withdrawn and fearful, especially when the subject of Enagbare came up.

  Even though the victim later testified that his payments to Enagbare were gifts, there was strong evidence that Enagbare had promised to pay him back. After all, she told his son the money was a loan; she had acknowledged the victim wanted to be paid back; and the victim was known to be extremely frugal. These facts established LFP.

- **Ponzi or pyramid scheme.** The "Ponzi" or "pyramid scheme" is defined as a "fraudulent investment scheme in which money contributed by later investors generates artificially high dividends for the original investors, whose example attracts even larger investments." *Comm. v. North*, 52 Mass. App. Ct. 603 (2001). The Ponzi scheme may also be charged as an "illegal lottery" under 271, § 7. See *Chapter 24*.

- **Accepting government subsidies to give to someone else.** *Comm. v. Alvarez*, 90 Mass. App. Ct. 158 (2016) (defendant applied for and accepted subsidized housing, but let his undocumented niece live in the apartment instead of him; even though he paid the rent every month, he stole from the Boston Housing Authority because it could have rented the apartment to someone else for more money).

- **While a seller's exaggeration is insufficient for LFP, an obviously fraudulent opinion about the value of an item for sale will support a criminal case.** For example, in *Comm. v. Quinn*, 222 Mass. 504 (1916), the defendant, a real estate broker, blatantly misrepresented the value of land used as collateral for a real estate transaction in order to get the victim to buy. In contrast, a dealer's statement that his used car was in "good" condition was an opinion. *Briggs v. Carol Cars*, 407 Mass. 391 (1990).

- **A victim's mental disability is a relevant consideration in deciding whether the representation was false.** *Comm. v. Reske*, 43 Mass. App. Ct. 522 (1997) (sales manager sold six new pickup trucks to a mentally impaired customer at four to six times the normal profit margins; this was obvious, criminal exploitation and not just a lucky deal).

Comm. v. Christopher, 2018 WL 2727709 (Appeals Court): Kathryn Christopher was convicted of LFP. Her 88 year old victim began suffering from dementia. Christopher met the victim through her job as a home care coordinator in Belmont. When the victim was admitted to a psychiatric hospital, Christopher falsely represented herself as the victim's niece. She had the victim sign a mortgage, alleging it was to make the victim's home handicap accessible. Instead, Christopher used the money to pay her children's college tuition.

- **False credit.** 266, §§ 33 and 34 point out that larceny by false pretense occurs when a person, with intent to defraud, falsely obtains credit. *Comm. v. Duddie Ford, Inc.*, 409 Mass. 387 (1991) (salesman misrepresented customers' income, employment history, and trade-in values so the customers could secure credit to buy cars).

- **Special kind of misrepresentation: Obtaining property by trick.** Officers sometimes question whether they have the authority to pursue fraudulent games and fortune telling. In this situation, consider 266, § 75 which outlaws fraudulently obtaining anything of value "by game, sleight of hand, pretended fortune telling or by any trick or other means [, or] by the use of cards or other implements or instruments." Apply the proper penalty from 266, § 30. *Comm. v. Jenks*, 138 Mass. 484 (1885).

LFP may involve excessive charges or false representations about work performed. *Comm. v. Watterson*, 99 Mass. App. Ct. 746 (2021): Daniel Watterson was a licensed plumber and oil burner technician. He was convicted of larceny for two service calls.

- <u>Case 1:</u> **Mr. and Mrs. Thomas were over 60 years of age. Watterson came to the house when the Thomas' furnace would not work.** He looked at the furnace and said he needed a part that would cost between $100 and $150. Mr. Thomas provided his credit card number to pay for the part. Watterson returned the next day with a credit card slip made out for $250, which Mr. Thomas signed. It took 30 to 45 minutes to install the part.

    Watterson then provided Mr. Thomas with an updated slip that included, in addition to the $250, a charge for $1,500. The homeowner objected and said the furnace had not cost as much. Watterson said, "Well, flat rate." Mr. Thomas told him not to charge the credit card. The heat stopped working ten minutes later. Watterson charged the card.

    When Mr. Thomas got his regular plumber in, the repair took 45 minutes and cost $296. The city plumbing inspector visited and found Watterson's charges excessive. There was also testimony that: (1) Watterson told a work acquaintance that he looked at people's possessions to see how they were living when pricing his jobs; and (2) if there were complaints, he told customers to call his boss even though it was his own business.

- <u>Case 2:</u> **Watterson responded to the DeOliveira home on a no heat call.** He spent 25 minutes with the oil burner, then handed over an invoice for $500. When Mr. DeOliveira protested, Watterson said it was his flat rate for replacing "the firing assembly."

    Watterson was paid, but the next day the heat was not working. A different serviceman was called and repaired the problem in minutes. When shown the invoice from Watterson, the technician laughed. There is no such thing as a firing assembly. The only new part he saw in the burner was a $3.25 nozzle. Mrs. DeOliveira made several requests for Watterson to provide an itemized bill, which he never did.

Watterson was properly convicted of LFP. He lied about replacing a firing assembly. He charged a grossly excessive amount for a repair that failed the next day. In addition, he did not provide the requested description of his work or parts used.

Suspects must know they are lying. *Comm. v. Mattier*, 474 Mass. 227 (2016) (defendant submitted a claim to One Fund Boston on behalf of his aunt for injuries alleged to have occurred during the Boston Marathon bombings — even though his aunt died 13 years earlier).

- **Circumstantial proof of knowledge.** *Comm. v. Leonard*, 352 Mass. 636 (1967) (defendant owned company that submitted false invoices to a state agency; he was very involved in day-to-day operations, so his claim that he did not see the actual invoices was rejected). *Comm. v. McCauliff*, 461 Mass. 635 (2012).

- **Willful blindness.** "Willful blindness" describes the defendant who claims he lacked knowledge, but the facts suggest "a conscious course of deliberate ignorance." *U.S. v. Hogan*, 861 F.2d 312 (1st Cir. 1988). *Comm. v. Mimless*, 53 Mass. App. Ct. 534 (2002) (defendant psychiatrist extravagantly billed Medicaid for services not provided, and then said he just never understood his secretary's billing practices).

Manner and method of communication. The statement may be oral or written. In addition, the misrepresentation may be communicated directly or indirectly through an accomplice or innocent agent. *Comm. v. Leonard*, 352 Mass. 636 (1967) (an innocent agent, the defendant's wife, filled out the invoices to overbill the Commonwealth).

A false pretense does not have to be a verbal statement, it may also be *implied*. *Comm. v. Cheromcka*, 66 Mass. App. Ct. 771 (2006) (submission of credit card bills by business manager implied that she had checked if they were for official purposes).

The suspect does not need to intend to deceive a particular person. It is sufficient if he intended for somebody to rely on his false representation. *Comm. v. Camelio*, 1 Mass. App. Ct. 296 (1973) (the defendants, a doctor and an attorney, falsified reports of "accident" victims and received money from an insurance company).

The suspect's lie must be a key reason why the fraudulent transaction happened. *Comm. v. Burton*, 183 Mass. 461 (1903).

- **The false statement does not have to be the only reason.** This is important in cases where victims have mixed motives for helping the offender — e.g., a long term friendship with the suspect that was part of the reason she gave money when he lied about being evicted from his apartment.

- **The victim's naiveté or carelessness is no defense either.** *Comm. v. Drew*, 19 Pick 179 (1837) (LFP is designed "to protect the weak and credulous from the wiles and stratagems of the artful and cunning"). *Comm. v. Farmer*, 218 Mass. 507 (1914) (elderly woman bilked out of $80,000 based on defendant's preposterous representation about having access to a valuable collection of Shakespeare's original works).

Unlike other forms of larceny, the intent to permanently deprive is _not_ an element of LFP. Once the suspect lies and receives the victim's money, LFP is complete. At this point, any restitution does not undo the suspect's guilt. *Comm. v. Mimless*, 53 Mass. App. Ct. 534 (2002).

- *Comm. v. Hildreth*, 30 Mass. App. Ct. 963 (1991): The defendant engaged in "conspicuous but fanciful telephone conversations" to well-known persons such as Donald Trump! Through these charades, he brought about many investments over a 28-month period involving different people and financial institutions. The defendant later said, when caught, that he had begun paying back his victims. It was too late.

- *Comm. v. Catalano*, 74 Mass. App. Ct. 580 (2009): The fact that a defendant makes several small payments on an account will not nullify proof of her intent to steal if it is obvious that she never intended to repay the outstanding debt. Here, the defendant opened several accounts in other people's names and accumulated several thousand dollars of debt for utility services over an 11-year period.

Type 3: Embezzlement

Embezzlement is the breach of a relationship of trust in order to permanently deprive the owner of money or property. *Comm. v. Caparella*, 70 Mass. App. Ct. 506 (2007). While money is usually the object, personal property may be too. *Comm. v. Drew*, 2014 WL 2558219 (Appeals Court) (victim's expensive "rock crusher" embezzled).

Generally, the offender's intent to permanently deprive is inferred from his hiding the money. *Comm. v. Schick*, 2011 WL 5975294 (Appeals Court): As bar manager, Kathleen Schick was responsible for collecting money generated by the sale of lottery tickets and delivering the proceeds to the finance manager for deposit. The net total she entered on her spreadsheet was less than the amount on the machine reports. This was sufficient evidence that Schick had falsified her spreadsheet tallies and kept the difference.

- **Demanding return of property.** The owner does not have to demand the return of the property in order to establish embezzlement, but it helps to prove this crime. *Seelig v. Harvard Cooperative Society*, 355 Mass. 532 (1969).

- **Loans.** While an unrestricted loan cannot be embezzled (although it may be obtained by a false pretense), money advanced for a specific reason, and then used for an unauthorized purpose, is embezzled. *Comm. v. Anthony*, 306 Mass. 470 (1940).

Claim of right. If the suspect had "an honest and reasonable claim" to the money, it negates his criminal intent. *Comm. v. Carson*, 349 Mass. 430 (1965).

Failure to comply with an organization's financial controls is evidence of embezzlement. The fact that some transactions were authorized is no defense. *Comm. v. Trott*, 2018 WL 1884878 (Appeals Court): Richard Trott signed four checks for $2,500, $5,500, $18,000, and $10,000 drawn on a Disabled American Veterans (DAV) account. Trott made these checks payable to the Disabled Veterans Association of Cape Cod (DVACC) — an account he opened without authorization. He then withdrew money from the DVACC account and deposited it in his personal account. It was not necessary to prove that every transaction was unauthorized. Trott did have some discretion in spending, but it was strictly limited to emergencies.

Venue

Stealing & embezzlement. 277, § 58 provides that larceny may be prosecuted in any county where the defendant had possession of the stolen property. *Comm. v. Lepper*, 60 Mass. App. Ct. 36 (2003).

Larceny by false pretense. 277, § 59 allows the charge of Larceny by False Pretense to be prosecuted in any county where the false pretense was made, written, or used; or in any county through which the property was transported or received by the defendant. *Comm. v. Price*, 72 Mass. App. Ct. 280 (2008) (venue proper in Norfolk county where numerous victims received the fraudulent phone calls, even though the calls originated and the money was exchanged in Suffolk county).

General venue rule for all Chapter 266 crimes. Under 266, § 60B, if theft or other property crimes that could be tried together were committed in different counties, or fall under the jurisdiction of different courts, they may all be prosecuted together in any court that has jurisdiction over at least one of the crimes.

ATTEMPTED LARCENY
274, § 6

Elements

- **Specific intent.** The suspect had a specific intent to commit a larceny; and
- **Overt act.** Committed an overt act towards its commission; and
- **Failure.** Did not succeed because he failed or was interrupted.

Right of Arrest

276, § 28 warrantless arrest in presence, regardless of the value of the property. Otherwise complaint. [*Note:* This crime must be charged under the general attempt statute, 274, § 6.]

Penalty

HC NMT 2½ yrs; and/or Fine NMT $300.

Notes

Specific intent. Specific intent means that the suspect consciously intended to steal, obtain by a false pretense, or embezzle. See earlier discussion of specific intent in *Chapter 1*.

Overt act. Aside from an intent to steal, the suspect must engage in an "overt act." The act does not have to make the crime inevitable. For example, a pickpocket is guilty of attempted larceny for putting his hand in another person's empty pocket! *Comm. v. McDonald*, 5 Cush. 365 (1850).

At the same time, it must be a real step toward carrying out the crime. *Comm. v. Green*, 66 Mass. App. Ct. 901 (2006): Rolfe Green committed attempted larceny when he deposited a fraudulent check into his "business" account. He claimed the $320,000 check was given to him by the Ritz Carlton Hotel for a consulting project. The Ritz Carlton had no record of the check, which was not printed from the hotel's computer. The hotel had also been closed for renovation at the time the check was supposedly issued. The defendant's overt act was depositing the check.

PUBLIC & POLICE RESPONSIBILITIES FOR RECOVERED MONEY, GOODS, OR ANIMALS

Procedures for Recovery of Lost Money, Goods, or Animals — 134, §§ 1–7

Obligations of finder. Any person who finds lost money or goods *with a value of $3 or more* or *a "stray beast,"* and who does not know the owner, must, within *2 days*: (1) report it to the OIC of the police station within the town where the property was found; or (2) place an advertisement in a newspaper published within the town where the property was found; or (3) post notice in two public places within the town, but only if there is no police station to receive the report.

Rights of owner. The owner of the money, property, or animal shall receive them back if he or she appears *within 3 months* after the stray animal is found, or *within 1 year after the money or property are found*; and pays all reasonable expenses incurred by the finder.

Rights of finder. The finder may keep the money and/or goods if he or she complies with the notification rules, and is not contacted by the owner within 1 year of the find.

The finder may sell the stray animal at public auction if he or she is not contacted by the owner within 3 months of the find; and provides notice at least 4 days before the auction in 2 public places in the town where the animal was found. *However*, if the animal is not auctioned and the owner appears *within 1 year of the find*, then the finder must give back the animal when the owner pays the reasonable expenses. Even if the animal has been sold, the finder must pay the owner the auction price, minus reasonable expenses.

Police Obligated to Secure & Restore Stolen Property — 266, § 48

Following the arrest of a principal or accomplice to larceny or robbery, an officer must: secure the property; "annex a schedule" of items found; and upon conviction, return the property to its owner. *Comm. v. Carroll*, 360 Mass. 580 (1971).

26 Robbery

UNARMED ROBBERY
265, § 19

Elements

- **Force or fear.** The suspect by force or fear;

- **Theft from person.** Took money or property from the victim or his immediate control.

Right of Arrest

Felony.

Penalty

Basic offense: SP Life or any term of years.

If the victim is 60 years old or older: 1st *offense:* SP Life or any term of years. 2nd *or subsequent offense:* SP NMT Life (Mandatory minimum 2 yrs).

ARMED ROBBERY
265, § 17

Elements

- **Weapon.** The suspect was armed with a dangerous weapon when he;

- **Force or fear.** By force or fear;

- **Theft from person.** Took money or property from the victim or his immediate control.

Right of Arrest

Felony.

Penalty

Basic offense: SP Life or any term of years.

While masked: If offender wore a disguise, mask, or had his "features artificially distorted": 1st *offense:* SP NLT 5 yrs, NMT Life. 2nd *or subsequent:* SP NLT 10 yrs, NMT Life.

©Law Enforcement Dimensions – *All rights reserved.*

Lesser Included Offense

Larceny from the person. 266, § 25. Robbery requires indictment and trial in superior court. The district attorney's office usually will choose to keep unarmed robbery in district court, and ask the police to file a new complaint application for this lesser included offense. See discussion in *Chapter 27*.

Notes

1st method: Force. The victim must simply be aware that force is being used to take the property. The victim does not have to resist or be afraid. *Comm. v. Zingari*, 42 Mass. App. Ct. 931 (1997) (purse snatching is robbery; pickpocketing is larceny).

2nd method: Fear. Robbery may be completed without force if the victim turns over property due to an assault. *Comm. v. Lashway*, 36 Mass. App. Ct. 677 (1994).

- **What constitutes sufficient fear depends on the victim's vulnerability.** *Comm. v. Gaulin*, 75 Mass. App. Ct. 73 (2009) (elder was badgered by defendant, who asked her for a loan and then came back later to rob her; the court admitted evidence of another elderly couple nearby who feared the defendant because she had repeatedly bothered them for money).

- **Fear can exist despite the victim's denial that he was afraid.** *Comm. v. Joyner*, 467 Mass. 176 (2014) (after a convenience store robbery, the victim insisted that he had not been afraid; however, he handed money to a masked robber with a gun who demanded "all the fucking money"; other indicators were the victim's avoiding eye contact with the robber and his nervous behavior and fast speech).

- **It is sufficient if the victim is afraid for another.** *Comm. v. Davis*, 70 Mass. App. Ct. 314 (2007): Mark Davis robbed a bank. The teller was not afraid because he was behind bulletproof glass, but there was a female customer next to Davis, which scared the teller. A robbery victim's fear may be based on his or her concern that someone else might be hurt.

The exact point at which force or fear happens is irrelevant, so long as it is connected to the theft. *Comm. v. Rajotte*, 23 Mass. App. Ct. 93 (1986) (defendant took money from restaurant kitchen; employee interrupted his exit; at that point, defendant used force to escape). *Comm. v. Cruzado*, 73 Mass. App. Ct. 803 (2009).

In *Comm. v. Dedrick*, 33 Mass. App. Ct. 161 (1992), the defendant managed to grab an undercover officer's revolver. Since he was not armed when he took the officer's gun, the defendant insisted that he did not commit armed robbery. The court said that the crime of armed robbery is based on the potential danger that arises from the possession of a weapon at any point. Interestingly, the court ruled that the gun he used to rob the officer was also the property that he stole.

The suspect must take the money or property from the possession or control of the victim. The separation of money or property from the victim, even if brief in time, constitutes robbery. *Comm. v. Martin*, 467 Mass. 291 (2014).

Suspect may form the intent to steal during an attack. *Comm. v. Sanabria*, 2016 WL 3004749 (Appeals Court): Manuel Sanabria asked his former girlfriend to drive him to church. When she pulled into the parking lot, he put her in a headlock and beat her mercilessly with a rock. The victim pleaded with him to stop and offered her car, cell phone, and $400 in her purse. Sanabria drove off with these items. Sanabria was guilty of armed robbery even though he formed the intent to steal during the assault.

Protective concern, not ownership, required. Victims do not have to "own" the property taken, they must simply have a "protective concern" toward it. *Comm. v. Grassa*, 42 Mass. App. Ct. 204 (1997) (police officer had protective relationship to an unknown citizen's car when the defendant brandished a screwdriver and drove away). *Comm. v. Mavredakis*, 430 Mass. 848 (2000) (Kentucky Fried Chicken manager was a victim of armed robbery even though he did not own the money in the restaurant cash register).

Value of property irrelevant. Unlike larceny (266, § 30) the value of the stolen items is irrelevant to the crime of robbery. *Comm. v. Weiner*, 255 Mass. 506 (1926).

Dangerous weapon for armed robbery. A dangerous weapon is an instrument that is or <u>appears</u> capable of causing serious bodily injury or death.

- **Deceptive weapon device.** 265, § 58 makes possessing a fake gun qualify as being armed for robbery. *Comm. v. Powell*, 433 Mass. 399 (2001) (harmless wooden object looked enough like a gun under the defendant's coat to qualify for armed robbery).

- **Claim of unseen weapon may be sufficient.** A victim may "take the offender at his word" and believe his claim that he possesses a weapon, even though the victim never sees it. *Comm. v. King*, 69 Mass. App. Ct. 113 (2007): While robbing a convenience store, King threatened the clerk that if he got up, he would shoot him. The clerk never saw a weapon, but it was reasonable to infer that King had one, especially since he had time to discard it before he was caught.

- **On the other hand, a suspect may not be convicted if he could not have had a weapon even though he claimed he did.** In *Comm. v. Howard*, 386 Mass. 607 (1982), the defendant had his right hand in his jacket and stated to the victim, "Walk straight, look down, and don't try anything foolish or I'll pull the trigger." Although the defendant's comments implied that he had a gun, the victim never saw a gun and the defendant had no opportunity to dispose of a weapon because the police suddenly arrived and arrested him. Therefore, because it was proven conclusively that the defendant did not have a weapon, he could not be convicted of armed robbery in spite of his bluff.

- **A victim need not be aware of the perpetrator's actual weapon.** If it can be proven that the offender possessed a weapon at the time he took the money or property by force or fear, armed robbery is the proper charge. *Comm. v. Knight*, 16 Mass. App. Ct. 622 (1983).

No need to produce weapon. There must be proof that a weapon was used, but the particular weapon does not have to be produced at trial. *Comm. v. Salone*, 26 Mass. App. Ct. 926 (1988).

Victim's superior weapon does not preclude armed robbery charge. *Comm. v. Grassa*, 42 Mass. App. Ct. 204 (1997) (victim had gun; robber had screwdriver only).

Intent to use the object as a weapon not required. In *Comm. v. Tevlin,* 433 Mass. 305 (2001), Scott Tevlin assaulted a 74 year old woman in a supermarket parking lot. She resisted, and Tevlin knocked her down, stomped on her stomach twice, and ran with her purse. He argued that he never intended to use his sneakers as a weapon, but the SJC pointed out that his intent did not matter because he did use them as a weapon to complete the theft.

An accomplice must know that the perpetrator is armed with a dangerous weapon in order to be convicted of armed robbery. Knowledge is often inferred if the robbery occurs in public under circumstances where the accomplice must have known that his partner would need a weapon to persuade the victim to surrender property quickly without resistance. *Comm. v. Semedo*, 456 Mass. 1 (2010).

Claim of right. Since robbery requires proof that the perpetrator intended to steal, it is a defense if the offender honestly and reasonably believed that the money he took was owed to him. This legal principle, however, never excuses the use or threat of force. Even though a jury might be persuaded to acquit a defendant of robbery, it must still convict him of crimes associated with any assault or use of a weapon. *Comm. v. Newhook*, 34 Mass. App. Ct. 960 (1993) (defendant might not have been guilty of robbery, but he was still guilty of ABDW for cutting the victim while getting his money). *Comm. v. Vives*, 447 Mass. 537 (2006).

Masked armed robbery. This aggravated crime does not require that the suspect conceal all his facial features. It is enough if recognition is deliberately obscured. *Comm. v. Lavin*, 101 Mass. App. Ct. 278 (2022) (even if only one robber is masked, any accomplice should be charged with masked armed robbery if there is evidence that he knew the principal perpetrator would be both armed *and* masked). On the other hand, it is insufficient proof if the suspect's actions do not reveal an intent to hide a facial feature. *Comm. v. Santos*, 41 Mass. App. Ct. 621 (1996) (wearing baseball hat and sunglasses on a sunny day).

Property taken in robbery may not be the basis for a separate larceny charge. *Comm. v. Baldwin*, 52 Mass. App. Ct. 404 (2001).

Related Offenses

Unarmed Assault with Intent to Rob. 265, § 20. Penalty: SP NMT 10 yrs. Right of Arrest: Felony. *Comm. v. Ramos*, 6 Mass. App. Ct. 955 (1978).

Armed Assault with Intent to Rob or Murder. 265, § 18. Penalty: SP NMT 20 yrs. Right of Arrest: Felony. *Comm. v. Perry*, 6 Mass. App. Ct. 531 (1978).

Stealing by Confinement, Injury, or Threat. 265, § 21 punishes a person who intends to steal or commit any other felony in a building or depository and engages in highly dangerous conduct — confining, injuring, threatening, compelling someone to disclose the means to open a depository, or putting any person in fear. Penalty: SP Life. Right of Arrest: Felony. *Comm. v. McGhee*, 470 Mass. 638 (2015).

27 Specialized Larceny

LARCENY FROM THE PERSON
266, § 25

Elements

- **Take.** The suspect took and carried away;

- **Money or property.** Money or property which may be the subject of larceny;

- **Person or control.** From a person or from that person's immediate control;

- **Intent.** With the intent to permanently deprive that person.

Right of Arrest

Felony.

Penalty

SP NMT 5 yrs or HC NMT 2½ yrs.

Notes

The offender must steal — without force or fear — property from the victim or from an area within her immediate control. Comm. v. Subilosky, 352 Mass. 153 (1967) (theft from cash drawers supervised by bank manager constituted larceny from the person). Compare *Comm. v. Heaps*, 2013 WL 319507 (Appeals Court) (caregiver's theft of a supermarket gift card from elder's home was *not* larceny from the person; there was no evidence the victim was near the item at the time of theft; better charge would have been larceny from a building).

Lesser included offense of unarmed robbery. The big difference is that robbery involves force or fear. Comm. v. Glowacki, 398 Mass. 507 (1986).

Pickpocketing vs. purse snatching. Ordinary pickpocketing is larceny from the person, even if the victim learns what is happening, because no intimidation is involved. On the other hand, purse snatching is regarded as robbery. Comm. v. Davis, 7 Mass. App. Ct. 9 (1979).

Value of property irrelevant. Similar to robbery, the value of the property stolen does not affect an officer's right of arrest (since any theft is a felony).

LARCENY FROM A BUILDING
266, § 20

Elements

- **Take.** The suspect took and carried away property;

- **Building.** From a building, ship, vessel, or railroad car; and

- **Property of another.** The property belonged to another person; and

- **Intent.** The suspect did so with the intent to permanently deprive.

Right of Arrest

Felony.

Penalty

SP NMT 5 yrs or HC NMT 2 yrs; or Fine NMT $500.

Notes

***A key benefit:** This offense is <u>always</u> a felony regardless of the value of the goods stolen.* Thus, officers can use their felony arrest power. *Comm. v. Lattimore*, 6 Mass. App. Ct. 870 (1978) (no need to prove value of TV stolen since larceny from a building is a felony).

No need for vacant or unoccupied building. In *Comm. v. Willard*, 53 Mass. App. Ct. 650 (2002), the fact that a husband and wife were sleeping upstairs did not prevent the defendant from committing larceny from a building. At the time of his B&E, the husband and wife were asleep and not supervising their property. They were relying on the security provided by their locked doors and windows. Consequently, their property was "under the protection of the building." The difference between larceny from a person and larceny from a building is how the property is safeguarded. *Comm. v. Green*, 92 Mass. App. Ct. 325 (2017).

Also see *Comm. v. Scher*, 2016 WL 1658780 (Appeals Court) (law school student placed his laptop computer and other items in his locker; surveillance footage showed David Scher was the culprit; the victim relied on the locker and building to safeguard his possessions while he was away; this was larceny from a building).

Shoplifting is not larceny from a building. While shoplifting is, in a literal sense, larceny from a building, this felony is not the proper charge when retail merchandise is taken. *McDermott v. W.T. Grant Co.*, 313 Mass. 736 (1943). Instead, officers should rely on the shoplifting statute, 266, § 30A, or on the general larceny statute, 266, § 30. See *Chapters 25* and *28*.

Definition of building. A "building" is defined in 143, § 1, as "a combination of any materials, whether portable or fixed, having a roof, to form a structure for the shelter of persons, animals, or property."

Related Offense

Stealing from Trucks, Trailers, or Freight Containers. Similar to larceny from a building, 266, § 20B penalizes theft from a truck, tractor-trailer, trailer, or freight container. Penalty: SP NMT 5 yrs or HC NMT 2 yrs; or Fine NMT $500. Right of Arrest: Felony.

LARCENY BY CHECK
266, § 37

Summary

Larceny by check means that the offender wrote, cashed, or passed a check — even though he knew he did not have sufficient funds. *Comm. v. Klein*, 400 Mass. 309 (1987).

Elements

Type 1: Attempted larceny by check

- The suspect — with intent to defraud — wrote, cashed, or uttered[1], any check or order for payment;

- To a bank or other financial institution;

- With the knowledge that there was insufficient funds.

Type 2: Actual larceny by check

- And the suspect obtained money or property or services.

Right of Arrest

Attempted larceny by check in any amount: Complaint.

Actual larceny by check $250 or under: Complaint.

Actual larceny by check over $250: 265, § 30 warrantless arrest on probable cause.

Penalty

For attempted larceny: HC NMT 2½ yrs; and/or Fine, which varies depending upon the value of the check. If more than $1,200: NMT $25,000; if less than $1,200: NMT $300.

For actual larceny where money, property, or services obtained: If value more than $1,200: SP NMT 5 yrs; or HC NMT 2 yrs and Fine NMT $25,000. If value does not exceed $1,200: HC NMT 1 year; or Fine NMT $1,500.

---

1 To "utter" means to present the check. For more on the definition of uttering, see *Chapter 30*.

Notes

Failure to pay the amount of the check and associated costs — 2 days after notice — can prove fraudulent intent. *Comm. v. Littles*, 477 Mass. 382 (2017) (overwhelming evidence the defendant wrote checks with intent to defraud because her account had been closed for a long time).

- **2 days' notice is not an element of the offense, but it provides evidence of an intent to defraud.** In fact, when officers get involved in a case of larceny by check, they should make sure that the person harmed gives notice (preferably in writing) before they take action.

- **Intending to repay is not necessarily a defense.** *Comm. v. Ohanian*, 373 Mass. 839 (1977).

Providing a bad check is attempted larceny if no goods or services are received. *Comm. v. Green*, 72 Mass. App. Ct. 678 (2008): Russell Goren's printing company owed $35,000 in rent. Goren delivered two checks to the landlord totaling $8,000. The checks were drawn on a closed account. Goren Printing left the premises. Discussions with Goren were unproductive, and the landlord reported the bad checks to police. Under 266, § 37, the proper charge was attempted larceny. The bad checks did not induce the landlord to part with any property, to reduce Goren's rent, or to allow his company to occupy the premises for a longer period.

Jurisdiction. *Comm. v. Adelson*, 40 Mass. App. Ct. 585 (1996): A Massachusetts court had jurisdiction over larceny by check, even though the victim received and cashed the checks in Arizona: (1) the goods exchanged for the check were received in Massachusetts; (2) the checks were written here; and (3) they were presented to a Mass. bank for insufficient funds.

Related Offense

Bank Officer and Employee Misconduct to Facilitate Bad Checks. 266, § 53A (Felony).

CONCEALING LEASED OR RENTED PROPERTY
266, § 87

Elements

- ***Lease/rent.*** The suspect leased or rented personal property;

- ***Intent.*** With the intent to "place such property [or part of the property] beyond the control of the owner"; and

    - **Concealed** or aided in the concealment of the property; or

    - **Failed to return** property 10 days after the lease or rental agreement expired; or

    - **Sold,** conveyed, or pledged the property without the owner's written consent.

Right of Arrest

Complaint (typically). However, 276, § 28 warrantless arrest in presence.

Penalty

HC NMT 1 year; and/or Fine NMT $1,000. *Mandatory restitution* to the owner for "any financial loss."

Notes

§ 87 must be used to prosecute people who rent or lease property and fail to return it. *Comm. v. Geane*, 51 Mass. App. Ct. 149 (2001) (§ 87 correct charge, not larceny, for theft of rental property).

Under § 87, it is sufficient evidence of the suspect's intent if he: (1) presented materially false information about his name, address, and place of employment at the time he obtained the property; or (2) failed to return the property within 10 days of notice.

Proper notice. § 87 defines proper notice as actual notice or a written demand by certified mail to the address on the rental or lease agreement.

Obligation to report a stolen leased or rented motor vehicle. An adjunct statute, 266, § 87A, mandates that the owner or lessee of a leased or rented motor vehicle make a report to the police if the vehicle is stolen or "placed beyond his control." See *LED's MV Law, Chapter 12*.

FRAUDULENTLY PROCURING FOOD OR ACCOMMODATIONS FOR CREDIT
140, § 12

Summary

This law prohibits obtaining services from a hotel, motel, or restaurant (aka "the chew and screw") without paying. Under 140, § 12, it is proof of the suspect's intent to defraud if he "refuses to pay on demand" or, at a hotel, engages in a "false show of baggage," or removes items without permission while owing money.

Elements

Type 1: Procuring from a Hotel or Motel

- Without paying, the suspect obtained food, entertainment, or accommodations from a hotel, motel, or other lodging house;

- With the intent to cheat or defraud the owner (unless, at the time, the suspect had an "express agreement for credit").

Type 2: Procuring from a Restaurant

- Without paying, the suspect obtained food and/or beverage from a "common victualler" (a licensed restaurant);

- With the intent to cheat or defraud the owner.

Right of Arrest

Arrest for breach of peace in presence. Otherwise, complaint.

Penalty

For procuring from hotel or motel: If the value of the food, entertainment, or accommodation exceeds $100: HC NMT 2 yrs; or Fine NMT $600. If the value is $100 or less: HC NMT 1 year; or Fine NMT $1,000.

For procuring from restaurant: Regardless of the value of the food or beverage obtained, the penalty is HC NMT 3 months; or Fine NMT $500.

Related Procedure

Authority of innkeeper to eject visitor. 140, §§ 12A–D. See *Chapter 32* on trespass.

INSURANCE FRAUD
266, § 111A

Elements

- ***Intent to defraud.*** The suspect intended to defraud a licensed insurance company by:

    - **Presenting** or procuring the presentation of any written document; or

    - **Preparing** or procuring the preparation of any written document;

- ***False claim information.*** Containing materially false information in connection with or in support of any claim under a policy.

Right of Arrest

Felony.

Penalty

SP NMT 5 yrs or HC NLT 6 months, NMT 2½ yrs; and/or Fine NLT $500, NMT $10,000.

Notes

Materially false information. The term material means that the false information was, or might have been, a significant factor in processing the claim. It is not necessary that the false information actually affected the outcome, only that it could have. *Comm. v. Driscoll*, 91 Mass. App. Ct. 474 (2017): Bryan Driscoll's car crashed into a stone wall. His insurance did not cover single vehicle collisions, but did cover animal strikes. Driscoll filed a claim asserting that he hit a "bison or moose," which caused him to swerve into the stone wall.

However, no animal was found at the scene; no hair, blood, or fur was found on his vehicle; and the presence of a bison, moose, or buffalo so close to Boston was highly unlikely. This was sufficient evidence of a false claim.

Written document. *Comm. v. Williams*, 63 Mass. App. Ct. 615 (2005) (the defendant truck driver's false statements to an insurance adjuster, which were later transcribed, satisfied the written requirement of this offense).

Related Offenses

Fraudulent Motor Vehicle Claims. 266, § 111B, and ***Procuring Patients/Clients for Insurance Fraud.*** 266, § 111C. See *LED's Motor Vehicle Law*, Chapter 5.

CREDIT OR DEBIT CARD OFFENSES
266, §§ 37A–C

Summary

Credit or debit card crimes fall into four major categories: (1) crimes committed by non-cardholders prior to any actual use; (2) crimes involving fraudulent use; (3) crimes committed by valid cardholders; and (4) merchant illegalities.

Penalty

Two statutes delineate the various crimes. 266, § 37B presents misdemeanors, while § 37C sets forth felonies. As each offense is discussed below, the section where the crime appears is noted and whether the offense is a Felony (F) or Misdemeanor (M). This informs officers of the possible sanction.

- *For § 37B misdemeanors:* HC NMT 1 year; and/or Fine NMT $2,500.

- *For § 37C felonies:* SP NMT 5 yrs or HC NMT 2½ yrs; and/or Fine NMT $10,000.

Right of Arrest

Regardless of the card offense, §§ 37B and 37C state that any violator may be arrested without a warrant if the officer is lawfully at the place of the violation.

Definitions

266, § 37A presents definitions that apply to these offenses.

- **Credit or Debit Card.** Any instrument or device or code number, whether known as a credit or debit card or by any other name, issued by an issuer, with or without fee, for the use of the cardholder in obtaining money, goods, services, or anything else of value on credit or by debit.

- **Issuer.** The issuer is the business organization or financial institution that issues a debit or credit card, or agents appointed to issue a debit or credit card.

- **Falsely Embosses.** The completion of a credit or debit card, without the authorization of the named user, by adding any of the matter, other than the signature of the cardholder, which an issuer requires to appear on the card before it can be used.

- **Receives or Receiving.** Acquiring possession or control or accepting as security for a loan.

Crimes by Non-Cardholders Prior to Any Actual Use of Cards

Lying on Card Application. No person may lie about his identity or financial condition on a card application. § 37B (M).

Stealing a Card. No individual may take a card from the person, possession, custody, or control of another, without the cardholder's consent. § 37B (M). [Also may charge Larceny, 266, § 30(1).]

Buying a Card. It is illegal for a person to buy a card from a person other than the issuer (e.g., Mastercard or Visa) or someone authorized by the issuer. This would be illegal whether or not the suspect knows the card is stolen. § 37B (M). [If the person buys a card which he *knows* is stolen, he can be charged with the offense below or with receiving stolen property under 266, § 60.]

Selling a Card. Other than the issuer or someone authorized by the issuer, a person may not sell a card. § 37B (M).

Possessing or Receiving a Stolen, Lost, Mislaid, or Mistakenly Delivered Card. A person may not possess a stolen, lost, mislaid, or mistakenly delivered card. Nor may a person receive, sell, or give one of these cards to someone other than the issuer or cardholder. § 37B (M). The government must prove the suspect knew the card was stolen, lost, etc. The possession of a card in someone else's name with the true cardholder's signature allows the factfinder to "infer" the suspect's knowledge. Knowledge is presumed if the suspect is found in possession of cards issued in the names of four or more other persons. In either situation, the defendant may offer an explanation, but the factfinder may choose to disregard it.

Appropriating a Lost, Mislaid, or Mistakenly Delivered Card. No person may retain a lost, mislaid, or mistakenly delivered card which he finds and which does not belong to him. § 37B (M).

Possessing an Incomplete Card. A person may not be in possession of one or more "incomplete" cards. A card is "incomplete" if it has not been embossed with cardholder information. Someone with an incomplete card is typically involved in serious fraud. § 37C (F).

Possessing 4 or More Falsely Embossed Cards. A person found in possession of 4 or more falsely embossed cards is presumed to have falsely embossed them and can be charged. § 37C (F).

Counterfeiting or Embossing Cards. Unless authorized, an individual may not make, alter, or emboss a card or something which purports to be a card of an issuer. § 37C (F).

Possessing Equipment for Forging or Counterfeiting Cards. It is unlawful to possess machinery, plates, or devices which are designed to produce cards that are not authorized by an issuer. § 37C (F).

Signing a Cardholder's Name to an Unsigned Card. A person can be charged for signing a cardholder's name to an unsigned card. § 37B (M). [He can also be charged with Forgery, 267, § 1, and, if he uses the card, Uttering, 267, § 5.]

Crimes Involving the Fraudulent Use of Cards

Posing Without Authority as a Cardholder. A person may never, without the consent of the cardholder, represent that he is the cardholder and obtain anything of value. Nor may a person represent that he is the holder of a card which has not been issued, and obtain anything of value. For value received that is $1,200 or under, § 37B (M). For value over $1,200, § 37C (F). [A person could also be charged with larceny or attempted larceny, depending on whether he completed the transaction.]

Using a Stolen, Lost, Mislaid, or Mistakenly Delivered Card. By far the most common offense, this occurs when a person uses or attempts to use a stolen, lost, mislaid, or mistakenly delivered card to obtain anything of value. For value received that is $1,200 or under, § 37B (M). For value over $1,200, § 37C (F). [If the card is stolen, the person can also be charged with appropriating a card, previously mentioned. If the person actually uses the card by signing a different name from his own, and presents it to a cashier, he can be charged with Forgery and Uttering, 267, §§ 1 and 5. Remember, the sales slip and/or purchase order are forged and uttered, not the card. In most instances, the card has been stolen.]

Using an Illegally Bought Card. A person may not use or attempt to use a card that was bought from anyone other than the issuer. For value received that is $1,200 or under, § 37B (M). For value over $1,200, § 37C (F).

Using a Forged Card. No person may use or attempt to use a card which is counterfeit, altered, or falsely embossed for the purpose of obtaining anything of value. For value received that is $1,200 or under, § 37B (M). For value over $1,200, § 37C (F). [Consider larceny, attempted larceny, forgery, or uttering charges.]

Receiving Anything of Value With an Improper Card or by False Representation. This offense penalizes the person who receives anything of value (whether or not he or she actually used the card) that was obtained with a stolen, lost, mislaid, mistakenly delivered, illegally bought or sold, expired, or revoked card. Additionally, a person may not falsely represent that he is the holder of a card. For value received that is $1,200 or under, § 37B (M). For value over $1,200, § 37C (F). [Again, receiving stolen property is an alternative charge depending on the facts.]

Crimes by Valid Cardholders

Using an Expired or Revoked Card. For value received that is $1,200 or under, § 37B (M). For value over $1,200, § 37C (F). The Commonwealth must prove that the cardholder had "knowledge" of the revocation or expiration by showing that the cardholder had been advised, either orally or in writing.

Falsely Reporting Lost or Stolen Card. § 37B (M).

Crimes Committed by Merchants

Merchant Knowingly Furnishing Anything of Value for Invalid Card. If a merchant furnishes, or directs his employee to furnish, anything of value upon the presentation of a card which he knows is stolen, lost, mislaid, mistakenly delivered, illegally bought or sold, forged, revoked, or expired, he can be charged. For furnishing value in an amount of $1,200 or under, § 37B (M). For furnishing value in an amount over $1,200, § 37C (F).

Merchant Knowingly Fails to Furnish Anything of Value Listed on a Record of Charge. A merchant gets penalized for knowingly submitting a charge slip to the card issuer with a price that exceeds the level of goods and/or services that he actually furnished. If the difference between what was furnished and what is represented to the issuer is $1,200 or less, then § 37B (M). If over $1,200, then § 37C (F). [Larceny by false pretense may also apply in this situation.]

Merchant Raising Record of Charge. A merchant may not raise, or direct his employee to raise, the total amount of the purchase price indicated on the sales slip or record of charge after the cardholder has signed it. The same penalty structure applies as in the previous offense.

Notes

Misrepresentation of card ownership <u>insufficient</u> proof without owner's testimony or some other proof. *Comm. v. Liotti*, 49 Mass. App. Ct. 641 (2000): Liotti attempted to use a credit card that belonged to another person. He initially said that he was the card owner. However, while Liotti managed to provide the true owner's telephone number, he could not come up with the owner's mother's name. In addition, the store clerk noticed that Liotti's signature on the receipt did not match the signature on the card.

Even so, the Commonwealth failed to establish that Liotti used the card *without authorization*. Evidence that Liotti falsely identified himself as the cardholder did not prove that Liotti obtained the credit card without the owner's consent. Testimony from the owner was needed.

Each card owner must testify that charges were unauthorized. *Comm. v. Madeux*, 2016 WL 2864460 (Appeals Court) (both mother and father had to testify their son was not allowed to use their card; it was inadmissible hearsay for mother to say father had not approved either).

A child who uses his parents' card without permission may be charged. *Comm. v. Madeux, supra.*: A mother noticed that her credit card bill included more charges than usual, including charges for items (such as DVD rentals) that she had not made. She realized her card had been missing. There were 81 purchases that neither she nor her husband had authorized, totaling $6,000. They confronted their son, who said he was sorry. This was sufficient evidence of unauthorized use.

Once police lawfully obtain cards, they may retrieve information from the magnetic strip without a warrant. U.S. v. Bah, 794 F.3d 617 (2015) (scanning the cards to read virtual data does not involve a physical intrusion; cardholders do not have a reasonable expectation of privacy in the magnetic strips because they are routinely read by third parties — such as gas stations, restaurants, and grocery stores — to facilitate financial transactions).

Posing without authority and using the credit card are two separate offenses. Posing covers misrepresenting oneself as the card owner. Improper use requires knowing that the card has been stolen. Each crime has a different element. *Comm. v. Ford*, 2019 WL 4927050 (Appeals Court) (defendant stole victim's wallet at Boston University Law School, then was seen on surveillance video about two hours later using the victim's credit card at Nordstrom Rack).

Identity fraud is a lesser included offense. *Comm. v. Thompson*, 89 Mass. App. Ct. 456 (2016): Two victims called police after discovering several unauthorized purchases on their credit cards. One discovered a purchase from Coach.com that was shipped to a New Hampshire address. The other victim's statement included charges from a New Hampshire Turnpike EZ Pass and merchandise from Backcountry.com.

A New Hampshire detective visited the shipping address. Brenisha Thompson answered the door and told the detective she had received a Coach purse, but thought it was from her former boyfriend. She also said that the boyfriend had asked her to make extra money by receiving items in the mail and re-shipping them elsewhere. The detective obtained shipping records from UPS and FedEx for Thompson's address, and found a delivery from Backcountry.com. The purchase had been made with one of the victim's credit cards.

Although Thompson's conduct satisfied the elements of both identity fraud and credit card fraud, she could not be convicted of both crimes. The elements of identity fraud are also elements of credit card fraud, and in this case, there was no way Thompson could have committed the credit card fraud without committing the identity fraud. Thus, identity fraud was a lesser included offense.

Out-of-state offender may be convicted in Massachusetts if she failed to obtain consent from the cardholder here. This kind of jurisdictional issue is likely to appear with increasing frequency as criminals exploit our digital and virtual interconnectedness to prey on victims. *Comm. v. Thompson, supra.* (the defendant used the two Massachusetts victims' credit cards to make purchases online and had the goods sent to her address in New Hampshire; she could be charged with and convicted of credit card fraud in Massachusetts because that is where she violated her duty to obtain consent from the cardholders to use their cards, and it is where the victims suffered the detrimental effects of her conduct).

Law Enforcement Dimensions

IDENTITY FRAUD
266, § 37E

Elements

Type 1: Posing as another without authorization. The suspect:

- **Posed.** Posed as another person *or* obtained the identifying information of another;

- **Unauthorized.** Without that person's authorization; and

- **Fraudulent intent.** The suspect did so for the fraudulent purpose of:

    - Obtaining or attempting to obtain money, credit, goods, services, or anything of value; or
    - Obtaining or attempting to obtain any ID card or other evidence of this person's identity; or
    - Harassing another.

Type 2: Possessing tool to access account. The suspect:

- **Possessed.** Possessed a tool, instrument or other article adapted, designed or commonly used for accessing a person's:

    - Financial services account number or code,
    - Savings account number or code,
    - Checking account number or code,
    - Brokerage account number or code,
    - Credit card account number or code,
    - Debit card account number or code,
    - Automated teller machine number or code,
    - Personal identification number,
    - Mother's maiden name,
    - Computer system password,
    - Electronic signature, or
    - Unique biometric data that is a fingerprint, voice print, retinal image or iris image of another person,

- **Intent to steal.** With intent to commit larceny or with the knowledge that another person intends to use the information to commit larceny.

Right of Arrest

266, § 37E warrantless arrest on probable cause.

Penalty

HC NMT 2½ yrs; and/or Fine NMT $5,000. *Mandatory restitution:* The offender must provide restitution for any financial loss sustained by a victim, including costs incurred in correcting credit, lost wages, and attorneys fees.

Definitions

266, § 37E defines the following terms:

- **Harass:** Maliciously engage in an act directed at a specific person or persons that would cause a reasonable person to suffer substantial emotional distress.

- **Personal identifying information:** Any name or number used, alone or in conjunction with other information, to assume another person's identity, including any name, address, phone number, driver's license, social security number, workplace, employee ID, mother's maiden name, bank account or credit card number, or computer password.

- **Pose:** To falsely represent oneself, directly or indirectly, as another person.

- **Victim:** Any person or entity who has suffered financial loss as a direct result of the commission or attempted commission of this crime.

Mandatory Police Report & Jurisdiction

Report within 24 hours of request. A police officer shall accept a victim's report and provide a written incident report, if requested, within 24 hours.

Broad jurisdiction to receive report. Victims may file their report in any county where they reside; or where the owner or license holder maintains their personal information or place of business; or where the breach of security occurred, in whole or in part.

Notes

Evidence must show that suspect impersonated someone _without authorization_. Comm. v. Giavazzi, 60 Mass. App. Ct. 374 (2004): The defendant presented two checks at Fleet Bank. The checks were payable to Mario Jaramillo from an account maintained by Jaramillo's employer. The checks were endorsed "Mario Jaramillo." The defendant gave the teller three forms of photo identification — a UPS employee card in the name of Jaramillo; a resident alien ID card with Jaramillo's name but the defendant's picture; and a New Jersey driver's license, again with Jaramillo's name but the defendant's photo. Convinced that the alien ID and driver's license had been altered, bank personnel notified police. They charged the defendant with ID fraud.

There was no evidence that the defendant stole either the checks or the identification, or that Jaramillo's signatures endorsing the checks were not genuine. While the defendant impersonated Jaramillo, there was no evidence that he did so "without authorization." This problem could have been cured by Jaramillo's testimony, but the prosecutor never called him as a witness.

Lack of authorization may sometimes be proven by circumstantial evidence. Comm. v. Catalano, 74 Mass. App. Ct. 580 (2009): Paula Catalano opened five separate accounts in other people's names to receive several thousand dollars in utilities from NSTAR. One account was in the name of her nephew, Scott Dolan. When Dolan received a collections notice, he reported it to police. At the time, Dolan was an 18 year old senior in high school, living with his family. At no point did he reside with Catalano. Even though Dolan was never asked by the prosecutor if he had authorized Catalano to use his information, the answer was obvious given: (1) his young age; (2) his status as a student; (3) his separate living address; and (4) his report to police. *U.S. v. Harris*, 791 F.3d 772 (2015).

The suspect must obtain the victim's personal identifying information with the intent to pose as that person. *Comm. v. Whooten,* 2016 WL 2619649 (Appeals Court): Shortly after Roy Whooten and his girlfriend broke up, she began dating someone else. Whooten accused his ex-girlfriend of violating his restraining order by sending him texts and emails. In reality, Whooten created the texts and emails, which he sent by accessing her email account. This was identity fraud. He posed as her to create false evidence.

His behavior toward her new boyfriend, however, was insufficient. Whooten pretended that other people, who did not exist, heard her boyfriend say unkind statements about his ex. Impersonating someone who does not exist is not identity fraud. *Comm. v. Mattier*, 474 Mass. 261 (2016).

Intent to get "something of value" must be financial. *Comm. v. Escobar*, 479 Mass. 225 (2018): When Emilia Escobar was stopped for driving with an excessively loud exhaust, she falsely told the trooper that her name was Ana Escobar, gave a false date of birth, and said she did not have her license with her. The trooper checked with the RMV and learned Ana Escobar's license was suspended. The trooper issued a citation in Ana Escobar's name. Escobar should not have been charged with identity fraud because avoiding criminal prosecution is not "something of value" under § 37E. Instead, something of value is limited to things that can be exchanged for financial payment.

OBTAINING COMPUTER SERVICES BY FRAUD 266, § 33A

Elements

- **Fraudulently obtain or attempt.** The suspect may not fraudulently obtain, or attempt to obtain, or aid another in obtaining;

- **Computer service.** Any commercial computer service (meaning any use or access to computers, systems, programs, or networks provided for monetary compensation);

- **Various methods.** By:
    - False representation; or
    - Unauthorized charging to the account of another; or
    - Installing or tampering with any facilities or equipment; or
    - Any other means.

Right of Arrest

Complaint.

Penalty

HC NMT 2½ yrs; and/or Fine NMT $3,000.

Notes

Destruction of property statute applies to computer records. 266, § 127 now states that "the words 'personal property' ... shall also include electronically processed or stored data, either tangible or intangible, and data while in transit." Thus, viruses and other computer mischief can be prosecuted as malicious or wanton destruction of property.

Venue for computer crimes. The crimes described in 266, §§ 33A, 120F, and 127 (when the personal property involved is electronically processed or stored data) may be prosecuted and punished in any county where the defendant was physically located at the time of the violation, or where the electronic data was physically located at the time of the violation.

UNAUTHORIZED ACCESS TO COMPUTER
266, § 120F

Elements

Knowingly unauthorized access. The suspect may not, without authorization, knowingly:

- Access a computer system by any means; or
- After gaining access to a computer system by any means, and knowing that such access is not authorized, fail to terminate access.

Note: "The requirement of a password or other authentication to gain access shall constitute notice that access is limited to authorized users."

Right of Arrest

Complaint.

Penalty

HC NMT 30 days; and/or Fine NMT $1,000.

Notes

Each log-in to another's account is a separate charge. *Comm. v. Piersall*, 67 Mass. App. Ct. 246 (2006): Christopher Piersall gained unauthorized access to his ex-wife Doris' computer. After obtaining her password, Piersall logged onto her email. He sent emails to Doris' fiancé. The printouts had 13 different dates, indicating that Piersall had printed them on 13 different days. The court noted that expert testimony is needed to prove a correlation between the dates indicated and unauthorized entry into the system. In any case, Piersall was properly convicted of 13 counts, because he logged onto her account 13 different times.

OTHER SPECIAL FORMS OF LARCENY

Counterfeit Merchandise or Services — 266, § 147

Elements. (1) The suspect willfully manufactured, used, displayed, advertised, distributed, or possessed with the intent to distribute; (2) any item or service bearing or identified by a "counterfeit mark" (which is the unauthorized reproduction of any trademark or design). *Comm. v. Pierre*, 71 Mass. App. Ct. 58 (2008) (indications that the defendant possessed the counterfeit CDs for sale included: price labels, cellophane packaging, shipment boxes, customer lists, and merchandise variety; also, the statute presumes that possession of more than 25 counterfeit items demonstrates an intent to sell or distribute).

Penalty. If it is a 1st offense and the violation involves 100 or less items, or a total retail value of $1,000 or less: HC NMT 2½ yrs. If the violation involves more than 100 but fewer than 1,000 items, or has a retail value of more than $1,000 but less than $10,000, or is a 2nd offense: SP NMT 5 yrs. If the violation involves 1,000 or more items, or the retail value is $10,000 or more, or the items pose a threat to public safety, or it is a 3rd or subsequent offense: SP NMT 10 yrs. In addition, the offender is punished by a fine of 3 times the retail value of the counterfeit items or services. All counterfeit items and implements will be seized for forfeiture.

False Representation of Military Status — 272, § 106 (aka "stolen valor")

Type 1: Active member or veteran. The suspect knowingly: (1) fraudulently represents by selling, manufacturing, or using military gear, ID, or a uniform; (2) that he or she is an active member or veteran of the U.S. Navy, Army, Air Force, Marines, or Coast Guard (including armed forces reserves and National Guard); and (3) obtains money, property or tangible benefits from the fraudulent representation.

Type 2: Medal. The suspect knowingly: (1) fraudulently represents that he or she received the Congressional Medal of Honor, Distinguished Service Cross, Navy Cross, Air Force Cross, Silver Star, Purple Heart, Combat Infantryman Badge, Combat Action Badge, Combat Medical Badge, Combat Action Ribbon, or Air Force Combat Action Medal; and (2) obtains money, property, or tangible benefits from the fraudulent representation.

Right of Arrest. Arrest for breach of peace in presence. Otherwise, complaint.

Penalty. HC NMT 1 year; and/or Fine of $1,000.

Commentary. This law is likely to survive a First Amendment challenge because it requires that the offender receive a tangible benefit from his deception. At the same time, the "benefit" requirement makes this law inapplicable to situations where someone lies about military service in order to achieve psychological status.

Fiduciary Embezzlement — 266, § 57

Definition. A fiduciary is a legally recognized individual who must act responsibly for the benefit of another.

Elements. (1) The fiduciary was a guardian, conservator, trustee, executor, or administrator; and (2) fraudulently diverted; (3) money, goods, or property possessed for the benefit of a person, public organization, or charity.

Right of Arrest. Felony.

Penalty. SP NMT 10 yrs; or HC NMT 2 yrs and Fine NMT $2,000.

Unlike general embezzlement, fiduciary embezzlement does not require an intent to permanently deprive. *Comm. v. DeGennaro,* 84 Mass. App. Ct. 420 (2013): Peter DeGennaro was a building contractor. Charlene Connors was his bookkeeper. David and Sylvia Ghafari met with DeGennaro to discuss the construction of a new home. They wrote him checks for a total of $48,500. DeGennaro told them that their money would stay in an escrow account. Both DeGennaro and Connors wrote checks from the account until it reached a negative balance. No construction occurred. When the Ghafaris demanded the return of their money, DeGennaro refused.

DeGennaro was a fiduciary. He occupied a position of trust created by a written instrument. He was guilty of embezzlement despite his claim that he did not intend to deprive his customers permanently of their money. Connors was his accomplice.

Money Laundering — 267A, § 2

Type 1: Transport or possess. (1) The suspect knowingly transported or possessed money or property derived from criminal activity; (2) with the intent to facilitate criminal activity.

Type 2: Transaction to conceal. (1) The suspect engaged in a transaction involving money or property known to be derived from criminal activity; (2) to facilitate criminal activity; or conceal the nature, location, or ownership of property; or avoid a monetary report required by federal law under the Currency and Foreign Transactions Act, 31 U.S.C. § 5311. See *Comm. v. Braune,* 481 Mass. 304 (2019).

Type 3: Manage. (1) The suspect directed, financed, planned, managed, or controlled; (2) the transport of, or transactions in, monetary instruments or property; (3) known or reasonably believed to be derived from criminal activity.

Right of Arrest. Felony.

Penalty. *1st offense:* SP NMT 6 yrs; and/or Fine NMT $250,000 or twice the value of the property transacted, whichever is greater. *2nd or subsequent:* SP NLT 2 yrs, NMT 8 yrs; and/or Fine NMT $500,000 or 3 times the value of the property transacted, whichever is greater.

Immunity for reporting, 267A, § 3. Financial institutions are not liable for furnishing reports and information requested by law enforcement pertaining to money laundering. They are also protected if they choose to initiate contact and disclose information to law enforcement. None of the disclosed information is considered a public record.

Forfeiture, 267A, § 4. All proceeds from money laundering are subject to forfeiture.

Public Assistance Fraud — G.L. Chapter 18

Unlawful EBT purchases. With respect to the Department of Transitional Assistance (which distributes public assistance or "welfare" payments to indigent people), 18, § 5I forbids the use of direct cash assistance funds (which are provided on electronic benefit transfer cards) to purchase alcoholic beverages, lottery tickets, marijuana products, or tobacco products. The recipient of the public assistance must reimburse the Department directly for these illegal purchases.

Unlawful EBT sales. Under 18, § 5J, an individual or store owner is prohibited from knowingly accepting an electronic benefits card for alcohol, lottery tickets, marijuana products, or tobacco. Penalty: *1st offense:* Fine NMT $500; *2nd offense:* Fine NLT $500, NMT $2,500; *3rd or subsequent offense:* Fine NLT $2,500.

Stealing. 18, § 5K punishes anyone who embezzles, steals or obtains by fraud any funds or property provided by the Department of Transitional Assistance, or who knowingly receives, conceals, or retains funds. Penalty: If funds amount to $100 or more, SP NMT 5 yrs or HC NMT 2½ yrs; and/or Fine NMT $25,000. If the funds amount to less than $100, HC NMT 1 year; and/or Fine NMT $1,000.

False statements. 18, § 5B punishes anyone who, in order to obtain support, knowingly makes a false representation or knowingly fails to disclose any material fact affecting eligibility or level of benefits to the Department of Transitional Assistance. Penalty: HC NMT 1 year; or Fine NLT $200, NMT $500. *Comm. v. Wright*, 88 Mass. App. Ct. 82 (2015) (when the defendant applied for public benefits, she did not list her husband as a household member or account for his income; she was charged with both larceny by false pretense and public assistance fraud).

Usury — 271, § 49

Elements. (1) In exchange for loaning money or property; (2) the suspect, directly or indirectly, contracted for or received an amount for interest and expenses; (3) which exceeded an annual return of 20% upon the sum loaned.

Right of Arrest. Felony.

Penalty. SP NMT 10 yrs; and/or Fine $10,000.

Usury is the legal term for "loansharking." It is designed to protect debtors from outrageous demands by lenders. *Begelfer v. Najarian*, 381 Mass. 177 (1980). *Levites v. Chipman*, 30 Mass. App. Ct. 356 (1991) (lender could not be prosecuted because he complied with the Attorney General notification procedures). Usury also does not apply to any loan regulated by federal law.

28 Shoplifting

BASIC SHOPLIFTING
266, § 30A

Elements

- **Intentional.** The suspect intentionally;

- **Six prohibited acts.** Engaged in one of six prohibited acts:

  1. **Take.** Took, carried away, transferred, or caused to be carried away or transferred; or

  2. **Conceal.** Concealed upon his person or otherwise; or

  3. **Manipulate price tag.** Altered, transferred, or removed price tag(s) and attempted to purchase alone or in concert with another for less than the full retail value; or

  4. **Switch container.** Transferred from one container to any other container; or

  5. **Ring up false price.** Recorded less than the actual retail value; or

  6. **Remove shopping cart.** Removed a cart from premises without merchant's consent.

- **Intent to deprive.** And, as a result, intended to deprive the merchant of all or some part of the retail value of the merchandise or to permanently take a shopping cart.

Right of Arrest

266, § 30A warrantless arrest upon probable cause for all violations. Under § 30A, a merchant or employee's statement constitutes probable cause.

Penalty

For goods with a retail value of $250 or more: HC NMT 2½ yrs; and/or Fine NMT $1,000.

For goods with a retail value of less than $250: 1ˢᵗ *offense:* Fine NMT $250; 2ⁿᵈ *offense:* Fine NLT $100, NMT $500; 3ʳᵈ *or subsequent offense:* HC NMT 2 yrs and/or Fine NMT $500.

Restitution. *Comm. v. Henry,* 475 Mass. 117 (2016) (the restitution amount is the owner's wholesale cost for the goods, not their retail price, unless the owner can prove that the goods were already sold to someone or would have been).

Charging Issues

Police may only charge shoplifting if retail value less than $250. § 30A states: "If the retail value of the goods obtained is less than $250, this section shall apply to the exclusion of § 30 [the general larceny statute]." Police may charge larceny when shoplifting involves goods worth $250 or more.

Shoplifting is never larceny from a building. *McDermott v. W.T. Grant Co.*, 313 Mass. 736 (1943) (shoplifting is not larceny from a building because merchandise is protected by store employees, not the building).

If force or fear is used, shoplifting becomes robbery. *Comm. v. Rogers*, 459 Mass. 249 (2011): Daniel Rogers and two friends were "professional" shoplifters. The three were shoplifting at CVS when Cristian Giambrone, a store clerk, saw Rogers stealing toothpaste. Rogers ran from the store. Giambrone caught Rogers and flung him against a wall. Rogers stabbed Giambrone (who died) and another clerk. It became armed robbery when Rogers used a weapon to escape.

Venue

Any court having jurisdiction over at least 1 shoplifting event may hear other related cases — even though offender committed them within the jurisdiction of other courts. 266, § 60B.

Merchant Civil Recovery & Liability Protection

Merchants are limited in the civil damages they may seek from shoplifters. Under 231, § 85R½, merchants and their agents or attorneys may seek payment from offenders who steal, attempt to steal, or damage merchandise or the property of customers or employees.

The merchant may only collect actual and additional damages. Actual damages is the amount necessary to fix or replace missing or damaged items. Additional damages are limited to a maximum of $50 when the value of the stolen or damaged property is less than $50; a maximum of $250 if the property value is more than $50 but less than $250; and a maximum of $500 if the property value exceeds $250.

For example, if a shoplifter broke an electronic appliance worth $100, the merchant could seek $100 as actual damages and $250 in additional damages. The maximum recovery would be limited to $350.

Police significance: Some retail merchants now threaten to call police unless the suspect signs a legal release and pays a fee of $500 or more, regardless of the value of the stolen property. While merchants may seek a recovery, § 85R½ states that "any person who solicits payment that exceeds [these guidelines] shall be subject to a [criminal] fine of $500."

Merchants protected against civil liability. Under 231, § 94B, merchants are immune from civil liability if they reasonably detain a suspected shoplifter on their premises pending the arrival of police. § 94B insulates merchants from retaliatory civil suits from disgruntled shoplifters or those reasonably suspected of shoplifting.

Notes

Retail merchandise must be the object of the theft. This term refers to products or goods offered for sale directly to consumers.

Shoplifting is complete when merchandise is concealed. The statute was drafted this way to allow merchants to call police before offenders leave their store. "Conceal" means to cover or hide an item to prevent its discovery. *Comm. v. Davis*, 41 Mass. App. Ct. 901 (1996) (although the defendant had not left the store, shoplifting proven by his tearing off the magnetic sticker from a video camera, and carrying the goods past the cash registers into an unsecured hallway; finally, he had only $3 and no credit cards at the time of his arrest).

Comm. v. Vaillancourt, 2014 WL 2179350 (Appeals Court) (defendant shared a shopping cart with her friend, who was later found in possession of stolen items; both friends wore matching outfits to confuse store employees; both entered the dressing room together a number of times, carried empty personal bags, and remained inside one stall for 20 minutes; they exited the store moments apart carrying the bags, which appeared fuller; the defendant was not caught with stolen clothes in her possession, but had the opportunity to discard them once her friend called on her cell phone to say she had been caught).

Business customs. Proof that the items were shoplifted may be inferred from the store's business customs. *Comm. v. Torrealba*, 316 Mass. 24 (1944) (manager properly testified that no items found in the defendant's possession appeared on the store's register tapes, which meant they had not been paid for).

Rely on the motor vehicle exception, consent, or inventory to search shoplifter's vehicle. In any investigation, officers should ask the suspect: "Did you come with anyone? How did you get here? Where did you park your car?" The goal is to learn about a potential vehicle and accomplices who may still be in the area. Once officers locate a vehicle, they can typically employ one of three search options. *U.S. v. Caroline*, 791 F.2d 197 (1986) (defendants seen traveling to different stores; they entered and exited their car between stops; this pattern of activity provided probable cause to search their car under the motor vehicle exception).

Officers may request consent to search if they have a reasonable suspicion that evidence may be located inside a vehicle. *Comm. v. Torres*, 424 Mass. 153 (1997). The fact that a suspect is in custody does not prevent him from consenting, but it does make it harder for police to show that his consent was voluntary. For this reason, officers should request consent prior to arresting the shoplifter. *Comm. v. Gonzalez*, 60 Mass. App. Ct. 903 (2003).

Finally, officers may conduct an inventory of any vehicle that is lawfully towed under department policy. The best approach: If a vehicle is parked in a store or mall lot, ask the property owner/manager whether she wants the vehicle removed. The owner/manager will typically agree because the person is no longer a legitimate customer. *U.S. v. Cartrette*, 2012 WL 6734788 (4th Cir.) (shoplifter's vehicle properly towed from Walmart parking lot). Compare *State v. Huddleston*, 173 Ohio App. 3d 17 (2007) (removal policy must come from the property owner and not the police). *Comm. v. Oliveira*, 474 Mass. 10 (2016) (there was no sign indicating that the lot was only for customers, and officers consulted the store manager about vehicle removal *after* they began their inventory).

AGGRAVATED SHOPLIFTING
266, §§ 30B, 30C & 30D

Type 1: Theft Device (266, § 30B)

- **Theft detection (TD) devices**, such as electronic or magnetic detectors, are applied to merchandise to expose shoplifters. It is illegal to intentionally possess, manufacture, or distribute a tool or device to deactivate or remove a TD. It is also illegal to remove a TD with the intent to steal the merchandise; *or*

- **Theft shielding (TS) devices** are items, such as laminated or coated bags, intended to shield merchandise from theft detectors. It is illegal to intentionally manufacture or distribute a TS, or to possess a TS with the intent to commit or aid a theft.

Type 2: Return Receipt (266, § 30C)

- **With the intent to cheat or defraud a retailer;**

- **The suspect possessed, uttered, altered, or reproduced** a sales or return receipt, price ticket, or universal product code label.

Type 3: Organized Crime (266, § 30D)

- **While acting in concert with two or more people within a 180 day period;**

- **The suspect stole, embezzled, or obtained by fraud** retail merchandise worth over $2,500 in order to re-sell the merchandise.

Right of Arrest

All three offenses: Felony.

Penalty

Type 1 — detection or shielding device: SP NMT 5 yrs or HC NMT 2½ yrs; and/or Fine NMT $25,000.

Type 2 — return receipt: SP NMT 5 yrs or HC NMT 2½ yrs; and/or Fine NMT $10,000.

Type 3 — organized retail crime: SP NMT 10 yrs. If over $10,000: SP NMT 15 yrs. The leader, organizer, supervisor, manager, or financer of the organization faces a higher penalty: SP NMT 20 yrs, and/or Fine NMT $250,000 or five times the retail value of the merchandise, whichever is greater.

Venue

Any court having jurisdiction over at least 1 of these crimes may hear other related cases — even though the offender committed them within the jurisdiction of other courts. 266, § 60B.

29 Receiving Stolen Property

RECEIVING STOLEN PROPERTY
266, § 60

Elements

- **Stolen or fraudulently obtained.** The suspect possessed property that was originally stolen, embezzled, or obtained by fraudulently pretending to be a legitimate business;
- **Knowledge.** The suspect knew that the property was stolen or fraudulently obtained; and
- **Possession.** The suspect bought, received, possessed, or aided in its concealment.

Right of Arrest

If value of goods received over $250 or 2nd offense regardless of value: 266, § 60 warrantless arrest on probable cause.

If value of goods $250 or less: Complaint and confiscate stolen property.

Penalty

1st offense and the value of the property is less than or equal to $1,200: HC NMT 2½ yrs; or Fine NMT $3,000.

2nd or subsequent offense regardless of value; or the value of the property is more than $1,200: SP NMT 5 yrs or HC NMT 2½ yrs; and/or Fine NMT $5,000.

Venue Rules & Limitations Period

Offenders may be prosecuted where the goods were stolen or received. 277, § 58A. *Comm. v. Parrotta*, 316 Mass. 307 (1944) (prosecution for goods received in Suffolk County and stolen from Middlesex County properly brought in Middlesex).

In addition, any court having jurisdiction over at least 1 of these crimes may hear other related cases — even though the offender committed them in other counties or within the jurisdiction of other courts. 266, § 60B.

The 6 year statute of limitations begins on the initial concealment date. However, the limitations period starts again from the date of any later act to further conceal the property. *Comm. v. Ciesla*, 380 Mass. 346 (1980).

Notes

Element 1: There must be proof that property was stolen.

- **No need to prove <u>identity of owner</u>.** Must only prove that property was stolen from someone. *Comm. v. Cromwell,* 53 Mass. App. Ct. 662 (2002): At 4:20 a.m., Cromwell was stopped by officers, who thought he had something hidden under his arm. He was sweating profusely with cuts on his hand. The officers searched Cromwell, which yielded a screwdriver, a radar detector, a car radio stuffed in his waistband, and a leather case with 20 compact disks. The radio had gouge marks, consistent with being pried out of its holder. The defendant was arrested, saying: "You got me, just take me in."

  A check of cars nearby did not show any signs of a break-in, and there were no identifying marks of ownership on any items. The police never did locate the owners of the radar detector, radio, or CDs. Still, Cromwell's conviction was upheld because there was no doubt that these items had been stolen from someone and did not belong to him. *Comm. v. Budreau,* 372 Mass. 641 (1977).

- **No need to prove <u>identity of thief</u>.** It is unnecessary to show who the actual thief was, or that the suspect received goods directly from him. *Comm. v. Grossman,* 261 Mass. 68 (1927).

- **Origin of property irrelevant.** Whether the property was stolen in Massachusetts or another state is irrelevant. As long as the suspect knowingly received stolen goods in the Commonwealth, he can be charged here. *Comm. v. White,* 123 Mass. 433 (1877).

- **Exemption to proof that property was stolen — <u>police stings</u>.** Under § 60, the police may conduct a sting with an undercover officer or informant in which they tell their suspect that he is getting stolen property. The suspect cannot later offer the technical defense that the property furnished to him by police was not actually stolen from someone!

Element 2: Suspect must know or believe that the property was stolen.

- **His negligent failure to inquire about the source of the goods is not enough.** *Comm. v. Dellamano,* 393 Mass. 132 (1984).

- **However, his later knowledge is sufficient.** Even if the suspect did not know that the property was stolen at the time he received it, he is guilty if he subsequently learns this and still decides to keep the property. *Commissioner v. Treadway,* 368 Mass. 155 (1975).

Commonsense factors that prove the suspect knew the property was stolen:

- **Carrying goods in a suspicious manner.** *Comm. v. Cromwell,* 53 Mass. App. Ct. 662 (2002) (walking on street in the predawn hours with a car radio in his pants). *Comm. v. Hernandez,* 2014 WL 6863408 (Appeals Court) (riding one bike and pulling another at 2:00 a.m.).

- **Unrealistically low price paid for goods.** *Comm. v. Santucci,* 13 Mass. 933 (1982).

- **Cash payment required.** *Comm. v. Santucci, supra.*

- **Markings (price tags, etc.) indicating true ownership of goods.** *Comm. v. Munoz*, 7 Mass. App. Ct. 871 (1979) (boxes of ladies' clothing found in defendant's apartment; boxes had labels addressed to the owners and contained a supplier's packing slip). *Comm. v. Hernandez*, 2014 WL 6863408 (Appeals Court) (defendant possessed medication that had a shipping label with someone else's name and address).

- **Location for transfer, type of seller, and/or storage of goods inconsistent with a legitimate sale.** *Comm. v. McGann*, 20 Mass. App. Ct. 59 (1985).

- **Substantial presence in area where stolen items obviously dealt.** *Comm. v. Matheson*, 328 Mass. 371 (1952) (joint occupancy of apartment where goods trafficked openly). Compare *Comm. v. Scarborough*, 5 Mass. App. Ct. 302 (1977) (merely riding as a passenger in an automobile with stolen goods in trunk insufficient to infer knowledge).

- **Suspect's prior record, fencing activities, or course of dealing with the thief.** *Comm. v. Imbrugalia*, 377 Mass. 682 (1979).

- **Implausible explanation for source of goods.** *Comm. v. Quish*, 356 Mass. 718 (1969) (defendant walking with new office equipment; when confronted by police, he claimed he found the goods in an alley).

- **Possession of many stolen items.** *Comm. v. Smith*, 3 Mass. App. Ct. 144 (1975).

- **Possession of recently stolen property.** This factor, by itself, may prove a suspect's knowledge. The term "recently" has no fixed meaning. Whether property is considered recently stolen depends on its type, size, appearance, marketability, and any other relevant circumstances. *Comm. v. Sandler*, 368 Mass. 729 (1975) (property stolen 13 to 21 months prior not considered recent, but property stolen two to eight months before was considered recently stolen). *Comm. v. Spence*, 2018 WL 911399 (Appeals Court) (gold ring pawned by defendant three hours after it had been stolen).

- **Failure to keep records in the ordinary course of business, or to possess a receipt.** *Comm. v. Leonard*, 140 Mass. 473 (1886).

- **Suspect's admission.** *Comm. v. Cromwell, supra.* (when confronted by police, defendant spontaneously declared, "You got me, just take me in").

- **Fleeing the scene and discarding items.** *Comm. v. Borja*, 2012 WL 2308130 (Appeals Court) (defendant's minivan backed into another car and sped off; police activated lights and siren which caused the defendant to throw brand new clothes out of the passenger window; store employees later identified some of the discarded items and confirmed that they had not been properly sold that day).

Element 3: Receive, buy, or conceal the property. The suspect does not have to personally benefit, although typically he does. *Comm. v. Bean*, 117 Mass. 141 (1875) (receiver, who was doing a personal favor for another, was guilty). *Comm. v. Dias*, 14 Mass. App. Ct. 560 (1982).

The value of the stolen property determines the right of arrest and potential punishment. The value of the property may be proven by its owner's testimony. *Comm. v. Stevenson*, 2012 WL 751734 (Appeals Court).

One may not be convicted of both stealing <u>and</u> receiving the same goods. *Comm. v. Haskins*, 128 Mass. 60 (1880).

However, one may be convicted of receiving goods, even though the evidence would have proven larceny. *Comm. v. Corcoran*, 69 Mass. App. Ct. 123 (2007): Daniel Corcoran tricked Nancy Stevens, a 79 year old woman, into letting him into her Rhode Island home by pretending he was interested in buying it. He made several visits to the house, and induced Stevens to show him her jewelry. Shortly after, Stevens noticed some jewelry missing, but did not immediately report it. A few months later, Stevens visited a gift shop in Massachusetts and saw her jewelry for sale. She called police, and the store owner identified Corcoran as the man who sold him the jewelry.

Corcoran was charged with receiving stolen property, but not larceny, in Massachusetts. While an individual may not be convicted of both stealing and receiving the same property, this does not prevent a prosecutor from choosing to pursue a receiving charge on evidence that also supports a larceny conviction. Here, Corcoran could not be charged with larceny because Massachusetts lacked jurisdiction, since the theft occurred in Rhode Island. Proceeding on an indictment for receiving stolen property was a good strategic decision.

30 Forgery, Uttering, & Counterfeiting

FORGERY
267, § 1

Elements

- **Knowingly.** The suspect, with intent to injure or defraud, knowingly;
- **Alter.** Made, altered, or forged;
- **Legal document.** A document or record of apparent legal significance.

Right of Arrest

Felony.

Penalty

SP NMT 10 yrs or HC NMT 2 yrs.

UTTERING
267, § 5

Elements

- **Knowingly.** The suspect, with intent to injure or defraud, knowingly;
- **Offer.** Uttered and published as true;
- **Forged document.** A forged or altered document or record of apparent legal significance.

Right of Arrest

Felony.

Penalty

SP NMT 10 yrs or HC NMT 2 yrs.

Notes

Forgery typically committed in three ways: (1) produce a phony legal document that appears to be genuine; (2) falsely make out part of a genuine document — e.g., by forging a signature on a check; (3) significantly alter part of a genuine document — e.g., by adding a zero so the check pays $1,000 instead of $100. *Comm. v. Segee*, 218 Mass. 501 (1914).

Forgery encompasses the use of any means to alter a document. *Comm. v. Ray*, 69 Mass. 441 (1855) (defendant had a printer engrave a railroad ticket; fact that forged document did not contain his handwriting was irrelevant). The crime does not need to be "in the mind of the one whose hand holds the pen." *Comm. v. Levin*, 11 Mass. App. Ct. 482 (1981) (signature of deceased individual was forged on an insurance application at the direction of the defendant).

Forgery relates to the document itself, not its contents. Making a false statement in a document can be a separate crime, but it is not the offense of forgery. For example, in *Comm. v. Apalakis*, 396 Mass. 292 (1985), the government charged a registry examiner with forgery because he falsely certified (by making certain notations and signing his designated code number) that applicants had passed their driver's tests. He used this scheme to receive payoffs from aliens and others who desired licenses.

The SJC ruled that Apalakis' conduct did not constitute forgery. The defendant never purported to be anyone but himself. As the SJC remarked: "Telling a lie does not become forgery because it is reduced to writing." Conviction for forgery would have been appropriate if, for example, the defendant had signed his supervisor's signature to certify a license application. Of course, he was appropriately convicted for violating 268, § 6A, which punishes a public official who knowingly files a false report. See *Chapter 35*.

Documents subject to forgery and uttering.

- 267, § 1 specifies legal documents that can be forged and uttered:

    - Record or document of "any public officer" (including a town or court clerk, notary public, or justice of the peace) that "may be received as legal proof";
    - Deed;
    - Will;
    - Insurance policy;
    - Power of attorney;
    - Promissory note;
    - Check, money order, credit card, or traveler's check;
    - Certificate of title, stock certificate, or endorsement on a bill of exchange; or
    - Any evidence or muniment of title to property (see explanation below).

    In short, forgery must involve a document of legal significance.

- **Muniment of title to property.** In *Comm. v. Murphy*, 59 Mass. App. Ct. 571 (2003), the defendant argued that the bank signature card he used to open a fictitious checking account was not covered by the forgery and uttering statutes. The court disagreed: A bank signature card is a "muniment of title to property." A muniment is defined as "documentary evidence by which one can defend title to property or a claim to rights." These definitions clearly include a bank signature card, which is evidence of title to an account. *Comm. v. Upshaw*, 2016 WL 7333522 (Appeals Court) (trust document is a muniment that gives a person or group responsibility for managing money or property).

Intent to defraud. Altering a document alone is not forgery — unless done with a specific intent to defraud.

- **Typically, the victim must testify that the forgery was unauthorized.** *Comm. v. Hutchinson*, 1 Mass. 7 (1804) (victim may testify that the signature was not genuine *or* authorized).

- **Still possible to prove forgery without victim testimony.** Although preferable, it is not necessary to present the victim in all cases.

  - *Defendant must plead a defense of authorization.* In *Comm. v. O'Connell*, 438 Mass. 658 (2003), the defendant was charged with forging and uttering five checks totaling $11,000 — based on the theory that he had forged his father's signature on the checks, which he made payable to himself. Video surveillance at the banks proved that the defendant had presented the checks for payment. In addition, the signatures on the checks were conclusively shown not to be his father's. The banks also obtained an affidavit from his father confirming the forgery. However, the father later refused to testify, and the affidavit he signed for the bank was inadmissible hearsay at trial.

    O'Connell argued that the prosecution never proved that he had not been authorized to sign his father's name to the checks. The SJC ruled that it is the defendant's responsibility to raise an authorization defense by notifying the prosecutor before trial. It is only after the defendant properly presents this defense that the Commonwealth must prove the absence of authority. Since O'Connell failed to raise this issue before trial, he was prevented from arguing it.[1]

  - *Circumstantial evidence may prove lack of authorization.* **Comm. v. Sutton**, 2013 WL 308976 (Appeals Court) (defendant cashed a check payable to himself and drawn on the account of a company called Solutions at Work; the defendant never worked for Solutions; and the Solutions comptroller testified that he keeps all company payroll checks in his office and had never seen a check that looked like the one presented by the defendant). *Comm. v. Goldsmith*, 249 Mass. 159 (1924).

- **The intent to defraud any person or institution is sufficient.** In *Comm. v. Analetto*, 326 Mass. 115 (1950), the defendant insisted that the intended recipient of a government check had given him permission to sign his name and cash the check. Even if his story was true, it still constituted forgery because the defendant intended to defraud the bank and the government. *Comm. v. O'Connell*, 438 Mass. 658 (2003).

- **No person or institution has to be deceived.** *Comm. v. Stephenson*, 65 Mass. 481 (1953) (it is no defense that the forged signature did not even closely imitate the genuine signature — as long as the defendant signed with the intent to deceive).

---

[1] This rule is established in Mass. Rule of Criminal Procedure 14(b)(3): "If a defendant intends to rely upon a defense based upon a . . . claim of authority . . . he shall [in a timely fashion] notify the prosecutor in writing of such intention and file a copy of such notice with the clerk. If there is a failure to comply with the requirements of this subdivision, a . . . claim of authority . . . may not be relied upon as a defense. . . ."

- **The forged document does not need to be presented for payment.** *Comm. v. Carroll*, 122 Mass. 16 (1877) (forging a mortgage discharge is a criminal offense, even though the mortgage has already been paid).

Bank procedure for forged check. A customer who makes a timely complaint that a check drawn on his account was not authorized is entitled to have the bank re-credit the account for the entire amount of the stolen or forged check. *Stone & Webster v. First National Bank*, 345 Mass. 1 (1962). 106, §§ 4-401(a) and 4-406(f).

However, there is a procedure that the customer must follow before his or her account is re-credited. First, the bank requires the customer to go to the local police department. The bank awaits notification by the police that a report has been filed. The customer returns to the bank and signs an affidavit of forgery, certifying that the customer did not sign the check and that it was unauthorized. The bank re-credits the account.

Proof of forgery at trial. The forgery must be proven by: (a) the witness who saw the defendant make out the document; or (b) if there is no witness, proof that the forgery matches the defendant's writing.

- **The questioned document can be compared to a known sample of the defendant's writing** — for example, the defendant's signature on his license, registration, or booking sheet. *Comm. v. DiStasio*, 297 Mass. 347 (1937).

- **Police and prosecutor can seek a sample of the defendant's handwriting** (known legally as an "exemplar"). *Comm. v. Nadworny*, 396 Mass. 342 (1985). If the comparison does not present an obvious match, then authorities should use a handwriting expert. *Comm. v. Murphy*, 59 Mass. App. Ct. 571 (2003).

- **Possession of forged document strong proof that the suspect was the one who forged or caused it to be forged.** It is also strong proof if the suspect possesses other forged documents. *Comm. v. Levin*, 11 Mass. App. Ct. 482 (1981).

- **Records from a bank's data management system are generally admissible evidence.** *Comm. v. Perez*, 89 Mass. App. Ct. 51 (2016).

"Uttering" means fraudulently offering a forged document as genuine. The offender must know he presented a forged document — although he does not have to know the specific way in which it was forged. *Comm. v. Bond*, 188 Mass. 91 (1905).

Circumstantial evidence may prove knowledge for uttering. *Comm. v. Burrell*, 2018 WL 817839 (Appeals Court): The fact that the last valid check issued from a payroll account was number 5028 suggested that the later-numbered checks the defendant tendered (numbers 5089, 5092, 5102, and 5111) were not validly issued. The checks were drawn on an account opened less than one week prior, and appeared to cover less than a one-week pay period. The way the defendant cashed the checks demonstrated that he knew they were forged. Rather than deposit them into an account, he tendered each of them for cash at three different branches of the same bank on the same morning.

It is not uttering to knowingly cash a check for insufficient funds. Instead, charge larceny by check under 266, § 37 only. See discussion in *Chapter 27*. *Comm. v. Bonilla*, 89 Mass. App. Ct. 263 (2016).

Convictions for forgery and uttering possible. Frequently, it is proper to charge both forgery and uttering based on a single document. *Morey v. Comm.*, 108 Mass. 433 (1871). However, both offenses must be proven. *Comm. v. Gomez*, 2014 WL 5285597 (Appeals Court) (there was undeniable evidence that the defendant stole and forged the checks, but insufficient evidence that he was the one who cashed — i.e., uttered — them at the supermarket).

Claim of right: No defense. A suspect's belief that he is owed money is no excuse. The prohibition against forgery and uttering seek "to preserve the general integrity of commercial documents . . . [which is] crucial in a mercantile society." *Comm. v. Geane*, 51 Mass. App. Ct. 149 (2001) (defendant was a contractor who gave his customer several forged invoices supposedly from his subcontractors; although the invoices did reflect legitimate charges, it was still criminal for the defendant to pass them off as real to the customer).

Jurisdiction. *Comm. v. Upshaw*, 2016 WL 7333522 (Appeals Court) (Massachusetts courts could hear the defendant's uttering case because the forged trust document was executed in Massachusetts, and all of the defendant's activities with regard to his Iowa abandoned property claim were conducted here).

Related Offenses

Forge or Utter Vehicle Documents. 90, § 24B (felony). *LED's Motor Vehicle Law, Chapter 6.*

Forge or Utter Prescription. 94C, § 33 (felony). See *Chapter 20.*

Forge or Utter Admission Tickets. 267, §§ 2 and 6 (felonies). Covers forging, altering or uttering any kind of ticket or pass to a performance, exhibition, contest, or railroad.

Forge Vendor Licenses. 101, § 31.

Forge Lottery Tickets. 10, § 30. See *Chapter 24.*

Forge Birth, Marriage, and Death Certificates. 46, § 30.

False Entries in Corporate Records. 266, § 67 and **Fraudulent Misrepresentation of Corporate, Partnership, or Individual Assets.** 266, § 92.

COUNTERFEITING

Preferred Enforcement Approach

State counterfeiting enforcement mostly ended when a national currency was created. Today, the Secret Service has primary jurisdiction. 18 U.S.C. § 471. Local initiative is encouraged, but it should *never* take place without *immediate* federal consultation.

United States Secret Service
10 Causeway Street, Suite 447 • Boston, MA 02222 • 617-565-5640

State law may still be used to prosecute those who counterfeit United States currency. All Massachusetts offenses listed below are <u>felonies</u> (except vending machine slugs).

Masschusetts Counterfeiting Offenses

Counterfeiting Bank Bills. Under 267, § 8, no person may engage in the act of counterfeiting, including currency and traveler's checks. Penalty: SP Life or any term of years. *Comm. v. Saville,* 353 Mass. 458 (1968) (U.S. currency covered under this section).

Possessing or Bringing a Counterfeit Bill into Massachusetts. 267, § 12. Penalty: SP NMT 5 yrs; or HC NMT l year and Fine NMT $1,000.

Uttering Counterfeit Bills. 267, § 10 punishes anyone who knowingly utters counterfeit bills. Penalty: SP NMT 5 yrs or HC NMT 1 year.

- *Comm. v. Murphy,* 70 Mass. App. Ct. 774 (2007): Murphy claimed there was insufficient evidence that he had knowledge his money was counterfeit. The court disagreed. First, he purchased many drinks and asked to buy a big steak at Pub 76 in Taunton. This showed he was intent on spending money. Second, he continued to pay for everything with new $20 bills, despite having smaller bills in his pocket. Third, he separated the $20 bills from the change he received, indicating that he was keeping track of his real vs. fake cash. Finally, he lied about receiving the counterfeit money at Pub 76, since it was clear he had brought the $20 bills with him. The evidence showed he was attempting to quickly exchange counterfeit bills for genuine ones.

- Compare *Comm. v. O'Neil,* 2017 WL 2391504 (Appeals Court): A police officer saw Laura O'Neil argue with a Dunkin' Donuts cashier, then leave in a hurry. The officer spoke to the cashier, then located O'Neil. O'Neil was holding a $20 bill that appeared "questionable." She said she got it from a pizza parlor the night before. This was insufficient evidence. Her behavior at Dunkin' Donuts could have been innocent frustration over being unable to complete her purchase. There was no evidence that O'Neil had any reason to scrutinize the recently obtained bill. A Secret Service expert on counterfeit currency testified that the "red flags" are hard to detect if someone is not looking for them. O'Neil also voluntarily allowed the officer to examine the bill and waited patiently while he called for backup, suggesting she did not suspect it was fake. Unlike *Murphy,* there was no evidence of O'Neil's possession of other, identical bills.

Counterfeit Tools. 267, § 13 prohibits making or possessing any tool, instrument, paper, or other material with the intent to create counterfeit currency. Penalty: SP NMT 10 yrs; or HC NMT 2 yrs and Fine NMT $1,000. *Comm. v. Labadie,* 82 Mass. App. Ct. 263 (2012) (computer, scanner, and printer seized from the defendant's home constituted counterfeit tools because, although they were ordinary items, they had been customized and integrated into a system for producing counterfeit money).

Use of Slugs in Machines. 266, § 75A covers any effort to use a slug or other device to obtain services that should be purchased by coin or token. Penalty: HC NMT 30 days; and/or Fine NMT $100. Right of Arrest: Confiscate slugs and apply for complaint.

Manufacture or Sale of Slugs. 266, § 75B. Penalty: HC NMT 1 year; and/or Fine NMT $500. Right of Arrest: Confiscate and complaint.

Law Enforcement Dimensions

Part VIII

PROPERTY OFFENSES

Burglary & B&E, Burglarious Tools, Trespass, Destruction of Property, Arson, False Alarms, & Fire Prevention

Chapters 31 – 34

© John Sofis Scheft, Esq.
All rights reserved

31   *Burglary and B&E*

Section I
OVERVIEW OF ELEMENTS & LAW

The purpose of the various breaking & entering (B&E) statutes is to prohibit conduct which violates a person's right to security in places they own or control. Each offense requires that the offender unlawfully enter some area under the control of another. Beyond that, the severity of the offense depends on three other factors — the nature of the place entered; the purpose of the offender for coming inside; and the time of the offense.

Consider the five key elements discussed below: (1) breaking; (2) entry; (3) property of another; (4) intent; and (5) time of offense. By learning how the law defines each element, officers will be able to analyze a given situation and apply the appropriate statute.

A. Breaking

The suspect commits a "break" by physically engaging in any act designed to enter.

- **This includes moving anything that bars the way into a building or vehicle.** Examples include: breaking a window; forcing open a door; removing a plank from a wall; or even opening an unlocked door or window. *Comm. v. Lewis*, 346 Mass. 373 (1963) (defendant committed a breaking when he opened a closed but unlocked kitchen door). *Comm. v. Stallings*, 2013 WL 1349329 (Appeals Court) (jiggling a doorknob caused it to unlock). *Comm. v. Camacho*, 2013 WL 3283728 (Appeals Court) (defendant pushed his way past front entrance even though victim held the door and verbally protested).

- **Inserting a key into a lock is a break.** *Comm. v. Labare*, 11 Mass. App. Ct. 370 (1981).

- **Entry through an opening not intended as an entrance is a break.** *Comm. v. Hall*, 48 Mass. App. Ct. 727 (2000) (entry through an open window on side of house). *Comm. v. Cextary*, 68 Mass. App. Ct. 752 (2007) (defendant climbed into a car through an open sunroof).

- **However, going through an unobstructed entrance — such as an open door — is *not* a break.** *Comm v. Tilley*, 355 Mass. 507 (1969).

The suspect also commits a break if an accomplice lets him in, or if he convinces an innocent person by trick or threat to allow him to enter. *Comm. v. Labare*, 11 Mass. App. Ct. 370 (1981) (defendant said he was "Gerry," the victim's brother, to get her to open the door to her apartment so his friends could commit a robbery; his lie was a break because it caused her to open the door). *Comm. v. Lockwood*, 95 Mass. App. Ct. 189 (2019) (break resulted when defendant's son, who was afraid of him, opened the door to run into his foster home and the defendant ran in after him). *Comm. v. Sitko*, 372 Mass. 305 (1977).

B. Entry

"Entry" is the unlawful making of one's way into a building or vehicle.

- **Entry occurs if any part of the suspect's <u>body</u> (even a hand or a foot) physically enters the interior space of a building or vehicle.** *Comm. v. Smith*, 75 Mass. App. Ct. 196 (2009) (defendant placed his foot in the doorway of the victim's apartment, preventing him from closing the door). *Comm. v. Porter*, 70 Mass. App. Ct. 901 (2007) (a locked storm door is part of the "protected enclosure," and Porter's presence between the storm door and front door constituted an entry).

- **Entry also occurs if an <u>instrument</u>, which is used to commit the intended felony, physically enters the interior of the building or vehicle.** In *Comm. v. Cotto*, 52 Mass. App. Ct. 225 (2001), William Cotto threw a bottle of gas into his enemy's apartment to avenge his brother's shooting. The sole evidence of entry was the bottle thrown through a broken window. Since the device was being used to commit the intended felony — in this case, murder — the court found that an entry, along with the obvious breaking, had occurred.

- **On the other hand, if the instrument which crosses the threshold is only used to accomplish the break, there is no entry.** The strongest crime is *attempted* B&E.

As the term "B&E" implies, the break and entry typically happen simultaneously. However, they may be separated by a period of time. *Comm. v. Glover*, 111 Mass. 395 (1873).

Officers sometimes catch the offender inside the building. *Comm. v. Wygrzywalski*, 362 Mass. 790 (1973) (defendant found in rear of hardware store when police responded to an alarm; broken pane of glass above door lock was his point of entry).

Most of the time, officers rely on circumstantial evidence to prove their case.

- *Comm. v. Willard*, 53 Mass. App. Ct. 650 (2002): A husband and wife in Quincy were awakened by a crashing noise. Officer John Horrigan arrived at 2:47 a.m. and observed a shattered glass window. Outside, in the newly fallen snow, Horrigan saw a set of footprints that circled the building, stopping at each door and window. The prints led to a Yellow Cab office nearby. Horrigan spoke with a taxi driver who had just given a man a ride. The officer discovered another witness who had seen a man "with a dark, hooded sweatshirt" running away from the building.

   Horrigan went to the address provided by the cab driver. He observed footprints in the snow similar to those outside the victims' building. He tracked them from the sidewalk to the front door, then followed wet spots on the carpet to a door on the first floor. He knocked. Willard, who was wearing wet boots, opened the door and told the officer that he had been home for over an hour. He showed the officer a light nylon jacket that he claimed to have worn that evening, but the officer noticed a dark, hooded jacket hanging up. The hooded jacket was soaking wet and the zipper cold.

   Officer Horrigan arrested Willard. As a final step, the officer contacted the witness to come to the rooming house. The witness stated that he had not seen the face of the fleeing man, but that Willard's build and sweatshirt were similar to that person. The officer's circumstantial case — quickly and carefully built — was sufficient for conviction.

- *Comm. v. Latney,* 44 Mass. App. Ct. 423 (1998): The defendant was caught by police with a lawnmower, jewelry, and cold beer. The lawnmower and jewelry belonged to the occupants of a nearby house, and the cold beer was the same brand they had stored in their refrigerator. The coldness of the beer at the time of his arrest contradicted the defendant's claim that he had stumbled on these items and not entered the house to steal them. Compare *Comm. v. Renaud,* 81 Mass. App. Ct. 261 (2012).

Fingerprints, footprints, or DNA may prove B&E. *Comm. v. Fulgiam,* 477 Mass. 20 (2017). The government must prove the prints were left at the time of the crime. *Comm. v. St. Pierre,* 2012 WL 1470299 (Appeals Court) (fresh footprint impressions at the scene of a break-in were consistent in size, sole pattern, and condition with work boots worn by the defendant at the time of his arrest). Compare *Comm. v. French,* 476 Mass. 1023 (2017) (fingerprints on glass window in public area insufficient proof that the defendant broke in).

Also see *Comm. v. Tavares,* 2015 WL 124995 (Appeals Court) (defendant's DNA was found on a hat, glove, cigarette, and beer can at the scenes of four break-ins; given the personal nature of the items found, it was most likely that he left them there himself).

GPS may prove B&E. *Comm. v. Johnson,* 91 Mass. App. Ct. 296 (2017): The victim returned from vacation to find her front door lock broken. The kitchen window and screen were open. Her jewelry boxes and a pillowcase were missing. Jamie Johnson was wearing a GPS device as a condition of his release for domestic violence. GPS data revealed that he was at the victim's home for 30 minutes while she was away. Johnson was unknown to the victim, and there was no evidence his GPS had been tampered with. This was enough to convict!

C. Property Belonging to Another

The type of property entered is an important component of the offense. The most serious violations involve homes, which are more formally known as "dwellings." As citizens, we are least tolerant of invasions into our living space. Other violations occur in less private areas, such as buildings or vehicles.

A dwelling is a place where people live. *Comm. v. Barney,* 64 Mass. 478 (1852).

- **An unoccupied apartment is a dwelling when tenants have the right to move in,** even if they have not done so. *Comm. v. Kingsbury,* 378 Mass. 751 (1979).

- **A secure common hallway may be part of a dwelling.** Since the physical features of multi-family residences vary, determining whether an area is part of the dwelling depends on the facts. *Comm. v. Doucette,* 430 Mass. 461 (1999) (defendant properly convicted of home invasion when he entered the hallway of a two-family house. Even though he never made it to the second-floor apartment of his friend — where he intended to seek revenge — the court felt that this hallway was private enough to be viewed as part of her overall home). Also see *Comm. v. Rodriguez,* 100 Mass. App. Ct. 663 (2022).

- **Even if it is not a dwelling, a hallway is still inside the building.** *Comm. v. Stallings,* 2013 WL 1349329 (Appeals Court) (defendant caught in the hallway of an apartment complex; it was irrelevant that he never entered the victim's apartment because he was charged with breaking and entering into a *building*; the hallway was part of the building).

- **"Outhouses"** such as barns are considered part of the dwelling. *Devoe v. Commonwealth*, 44 Mass. 316 (1841).

- **Occupied motel room is also a dwelling.** *Comm. v. Correia*, 17 Mass. App. Ct. 233 (1983).

- **Separate apartments within a multi-unit building count as separate dwellings.** *Comm. v. Abernathy*, 2014 WL 1697223 (Appeals Court) (defendant convicted of two B&Es when he broke into two separate apartments within the same multi-unit house).

Expanded right of self-defense in a dwelling. Because the right of privacy in the home is so highly regarded, 278, § 8A authorizes occupants to defend themselves in their homes against unlawful intruders — without having to retreat. See discussion in *Chapter 4*.

Aside from dwellings, statutes protect buildings, vehicles, and vessels. Remember, it is an element of the offense to prove the particular structure, vehicle, or vessel entered.

A structure without a roof may still be a building. *Comm. v. Rudenko*, 74 Mass. App. Ct. 396 (2009): A Home Depot employee arrived at 4:00 a.m. and noticed two snow blowers were missing. The blowers had been stored in an area enclosed on three sides by a tall, chain-link fence. An overhead door permitted passage from the roofed-in portion of the store to this area. Two gates in the fence provided access for delivery trucks. The gates were locked.

The responding officer found the defendant nearby, standing next to a pickup truck. He falsely claimed to be a Home Depot employee. One of the stolen snow blowers was nearby. The defendant and his accomplice were arrested for B&E. They argued that Home Depot's enclosure was not "a building" within the meaning of the statute. The court disagreed. The area shared a wall with the roofed-in portion and was enclosed by a fence. It was part of the building.

Property must "belong to another," but the owner's identity need not be shown. In addition to showing the type of property violated, the government must prove that it was owned or controlled by someone other than the suspect. Proof of the owner's identity is not required. The basis for a B&E crime is not that the property belonged to a particular person, but rather that it did not belong to the suspect. Officers must simply show that the suspect had no right to be on the premises or in the vehicle. *Comm. v. Kalinowski*, 360 Mass. 682 (1971).

Suspect must have no "right of occupancy" at time of entry.

- **Spouse or partner.** The issue usually arises in cases lodged against a former spouse or partner. Remember, as *Comm. v. Robbins*, 422 Mass. 305 (1996) forcefully stated: "[A] marital relationship does not preclude a conviction [for] burglary." Consider the following factors in determining whether the suspect had a right to enter:

    - The marital status of the parties (e.g., pending divorce, separation);
    - The existence of any legal orders against the suspect (e.g., 209A);
    - Extended periods of separation;
    - The names on the lease, rental agreement, or title;
    - The method to gain entry; and
    - Any acknowledgment by the suspect that he should not have entered.

- **Family member.** *Comm. v. Greene,* 461 Mass. 1011 (2012): Richard Greene moved out of state, but returned to his mother's house after she went to a nursing home. On several occasions, police arrived at the house and told Greene that his mother's guardian wanted him off the premises. His convictions for trespass and B&E were overturned due to a lack of evidence that the guardian had more control over the property than Greene.

- **Past relationship.** A past relationship may result in the suspect's reasonable belief that he had the right to enter. In *Comm. v. Fleming,* 46 Mass. App. Ct. 394 (1999), overnight counselors at a facility for the intellectually disabled received regular visits from the defendant. A supervisor became concerned that the defendant's visits violated agency policy. When told to leave, the defendant became enraged and stabbed a staff member. While the assault was a crime, a separate charge for B&E could not be sustained. The defendant's prior history entitled him to believe that he had permission to enter the facility that night.

    Compare *Comm. v. Marshall,* 65 Mass. App. Ct. 719 (2006): Defendant's history of visiting his girlfriend did not give him a "right of occupancy" on the morning that he invaded her apartment and shot her new lover. The key evidence was: (1) the defendant had given back his set of keys; (2) he had packed up his belongings and moved; and (3) he had visited the apartment on previous occasions *only* with her permission. Finally, on the morning of the shooting, the defendant pried open the back door to get inside.

- **Consensual entry does not occur when the offender hides a weapon.** *Comm. v. Mahar,* 430 Mass. 643 (2000) (defendant hid a machete and convinced his girlfriend to let him into her home; he then assaulted her).

D. Intent

Just as the type of place affects the seriousness of the offense, so too does the suspect's purpose at the time of unlawful entry. Naturally, the most serious violation involves an offender who comes inside and actually assaults an occupant. There are also offenses that regard an offender's felonious motivation as important, while less serious penalties attach when the suspect's likely purpose was the commission of a misdemeanor.

Proof of an intent to commit a felony inside a home or building.

- **Clearly, an offender's felonious intent is shown when he actually commits a felony inside.** *Comm. v. Moore,* 50 Mass. App. Ct. 730 (2001) (defendant hit victim with a weapon inside her home). *Comm. v. Poff,* 56 Mass. App. Ct. 201 (2002) (defendant broke into the house of a female acquaintance and committed an indecent A&B while she was in bed).

    Compare *Comm. v. Lee,* 460 Mass. 64 (2011) (while the defendant and his friend committed a B&E on New Year's Eve, their purpose was to "crash the party." Although his friend pulled a knife when the fracas spilled out onto the street, there was no evidence that the defendant was aware that his friend was armed at the time of the original break).

- **Intent may be demonstrated by the offender's behavior leading up to the incident.** *Comm. v. Stallings,* 2013 WL 1349329 (Appeals Court): Before breaking into his neighbor's apartment and beating him, the defendant told a coworker that he was upset that his neighbor had made a sexual move on him. The defendant said, "Next time I see him, I'll stop him." This threat demonstrated his felonious intent.

Comm. v. Johnson, 2014 WL 1356501 (Appeals Court): At 4:00 a.m., the defendant disabled a motion-activated light and damaged two doors in the garage before removing an ATV and hiding it in the woods. This demonstrated he intended more than a misdemeanor, such as taking the ATV for a joyride. He intended to steal it.

- **Unless there is contrary evidence, when a person enters a home or building — at any time of the day or night — the law presumes that he intends to steal.** Since larceny from *any* building is always a felony, a suspect automatically intends to commit a felony if he plans to steal *anything* inside a structure. See 266, § 20 discussed in *Chapter 27*. Also see *Comm. v. Soares,* 51 Mass. App. Ct. 273 (2001) (defendant inside residence during the day; he had moved jewelry boxes from the bureau to the bed — indicating his intent to steal). *Comm. v. McCarthy,* 37 Mass. App. Ct. 113 (1994) (intent to steal inferred when defendant broke into a house at night and lied that he was visiting friends). *Comm. v. Burton,* 82 Mass. App. Ct. 912 (2012) (although nothing removed, fact that defendant entered when owner was not home demonstrated his intent to steal).

Intent to commit misdemeanor less difficult to prove. In *Comm. v. Scott,* 71 Mass. App. Ct. 596 (2008), Obin Onujiogu owned a two-family house. The vacant second-floor apartment was continually broken into, but the suspects always fled before police arrived. At 6:30 a.m. one morning, Onujiogu received a call from a tenant that someone was inside the vacant apartment. He went to the house and saw Samson Scott exiting the front door. Scott did not answer Onujiogu's questions and ran when police came. He was captured later. The "intent" aspect of this crime was satisfied by Scott's intent to, at a minimum, commit criminal trespass (discussed in *Chapter 32*).

Proof of intent to commit a felony inside a motor vehicle. See discussion about 266, § 16 later in this chapter.

E. Time

Time of offense important. Nighttime offenders in homes are the most threatening because of the likelihood they will encounter occupants, who may be asleep.

Under 278, § 10, nighttime occurs one hour after sunset to one hour before sunrise on the next day. Usually, this is not contested if the facts show that the suspect clearly broke in when it was dark. However, officers should never take this element for granted. If necessary, they may present an almanac or other reference to prove the time of sunset or sunrise on the evening of the offense. *Comm. v. Bergstrom,* 10 Mass. App. Ct. 838 (1980).

Proof may also be circumstantial. *Comm. v. Bennett,* 424 Mass. 64 (1997) (prosecution proved burglary occurred at night by presenting testimony from the medical examiner estimating that the victim died between 2:00 a.m. and 5:00 a.m. when shot during a B&E; in addition, the defendant admitted to his friend that he went into the house at night).

Section II
SPECIFIC OFFENSES

AGGRAVATED BURGLARY
266, § 14

Elements

- **B&E.** The suspect:
  - Breaks and enters with intent to commit a felony; or
  - Enters with intent to commit a felony and then breaks into;

- **Dwelling.** A dwelling house;

- **Night.** In the nighttime;

- **Occupied.** While someone is inside; and

- **Weapon or assault.** The suspect:
  - Arms himself with a dangerous weapon before going into *or* while inside the dwelling; or
  - Assaults a lawful occupant inside.

Right of Arrest

Felony.

Penalty

Basic offense: SP NLT 10 yrs, NMT Life.

2nd or subsequent offense: Same penalty range except the defendant "shall not be [granted a suspended sentence] or placed on probation."

If armed with firearm, rifle, shotgun, machine gun or assault weapon: SP NLT 15 yrs, NMT Life. If 2nd offense: SP NLT 20 yrs, NMT Life.

BURGLARY
266, § 15

Elements

- **B&E.** The suspect:
  - Breaks and enters with intent to commit a felony; or
  - Enters with intent to commit a felony and then breaks into;

- **Dwelling.** A dwelling house;

- **Night.** In the nighttime; and

- **No weapon or assault.** The suspect:
  - Is not armed with a dangerous weapon while in the house; and
  - Does not assault a lawful occupant.

Right of Arrest

Felony.

Penalty

Basic offense: SP NMT 20 yrs.

2nd burglary offense — *meaning that the defendant was previously convicted of burglary under § 15 or § 14:* SP NLT 5 yrs, NMT 20 yrs.

Notes

Comparison of burglary and aggravated burglary. They are the same, except aggravated burglary requires:

- **An occupant inside the dwelling during the course of the burglary.** The victim does not have to be present in the home at the time the suspect enters, as long as the victim enters while the suspect is still there. *Comm. v. Mitchell*, 67 Mass. App. Ct. 556 (2006): Rudolph Mitchell entered the home of his ex-girlfriend while she was out. When she returned, he beat her. Among other charges, he was convicted of aggravated burglary. The victim was present during the assault; it was not relevant that she was absent at the time of entry.

- **Possession of weapon.** Aggravated burglary occurs if the perpetrator possesses a weapon, whether or not he actually uses it. Also, the perpetrator does not have to bring the weapon. He may arm himself inside the dwelling — e.g., picking up a knife on the kitchen table. *Comm. v. Hawkins*, 21 Mass. App. Ct. 766 (1986).

- **Simple assault of occupant.** The other way to commit this offense is to assault an occupant in the home. The actual assault does not have to be undertaken with a weapon. Simple assault will do. *Comm. v. Claudio*, 418 Mass. 103 (1994).

Only one conviction despite assault on multiple occupants. There can be only one conviction for aggravated burglary, regardless of how many people the perpetrator assaults inside the dwelling. *Comm. v. Gordon*, 42 Mass. App. Ct. 601 (1997) (defendant and his accomplice, armed with a sawed-off shotgun, forced their way into an apartment and frightened two adults and two children at 5:00 a.m. Because there was only one act of B&E, they could only be charged with one burglary, despite the fact that four individuals were affected).

Only one burglary per dwelling despite multiple breaks during the same episode. *Comm. v. Bolden*, 470 Mass. 274 (2014) (defendant entered a house through a rear door; when confronted by a male occupant, he hit him in the head; he then forced open the basement door and struck the female occupant; it was only one burglary despite two breaks and two assaults).

However, a defendant may be charged with multiple attempts on the same dwelling. *Comm. v. Dykens*, 473 Mass. 635 (2016) (in a single night, the defendant positioned a ladder, removed an outer screen, and smashed a glass sliding door to try to get inside the home, failing each time; each independent act was a separate charge of attempted burglary).

HOME INVASION
265, § 18C

Elements

- **Enter.** The suspect knowingly entered the dwelling place of another;

- **Aware of occupants.** While:

  - Knowing or having reason to know that one or more persons are inside; or
  - Entering without that knowledge, but then remaining inside after learning or having reason to know that one or more persons are present;

- **Armed.** While armed with a dangerous weapon; and

- **Threatened occupants.** The suspect:

  - Used force or threatened the imminent use of force upon any person in the dwelling, regardless of whether injury occurred; or
  - Intentionally caused any injury to any person in the dwelling.

Right of Arrest

Felony.

Penalty

SP NLT 20 yrs, NMT Life.

Notes

Unlike burglary, home invasion does not require a break, night entry, or felonious intent. These elements are unnecessary because a home invasion injures or scares occupants.

The home invasion offender:

- **Must be armed before entry.** Unlike burglary, a person may not be convicted of home invasion if he arms himself *after* entering the home. *Comm. v. Ruiz*, 426 Mass. 391 (1998) (defendant entered a disabled victim's apartment and demanded money; when the victim refused, the defendant grabbed one of his crutches and struck him repeatedly; while other crimes were applicable, home invasion was not an option since the defendant entered without a weapon). Compare *Comm. v. Serrano*, 2015 WL 1526072 (Appeals Court) (a two-by-four piece of wood was a sufficient weapon for home invasion; the defendant must have had it prior to entry because it was not from the apartment).

- **May use an "innocent object" as a weapon.** *Comm. v. Mattei*, 455 Mass. 840 (2010) (duct tape qualified as a dangerous weapon for home invasion because the defendant brought it into the victim's house and tried to seal the victim's mouth and nose with it). *Comm. v. Bois*, 476 Mass. 15 (2016).

- **Does not enter with consent if the occupant: (1) was unaware that the defendant was armed;** *or* **(2) was aware he was armed, but unaware he intended to commit a crime.** *Comm. v. Putnam*, 75 Mass. App. Ct. 472 (2009) (victim knew the defendant was a "troubled" substance abuser when she let him enter her house, but she did not know he was carrying a knife, which he used to attack and rape her).

- **May not claim self-defense when an occupant uses force to repel him.** *Comm. v. Doucette*, 430 Mass. 461 (1999).

Accomplice must know the principal had a weapon. *Comm. v. Gorman*, 84 Mass. App. Ct. 482 (2013): A woman reported to 911 that a man had knocked on her front door while another man in her garage pointed a gun at her. Police stopped the defendants and recovered a loaded gun. The victim identified Saquan Gorman (the man at her front door) and Jovan Gordon (the one in her garage). Although Gorman claimed he believed the home was unoccupied, he knocked and rang the bell multiple times, suggesting the two had a plan to entice an occupant into opening the door. Gordon carried a clipboard, suggesting that he planned to trick an occupant into letting him in. Since the two were seeking to rob a home, Gorman must have known that Gordon would bring a weapon to overcome any resistance.

The occupant during a home invasion:

- **Must be threatened, but does not have to be afraid.** *Comm. v. Dunn*, 43 Mass. App. Ct. 58 (1997) (once suspect threatens force, the crime is complete — whether or not he actually intends to harm the occupant, and whether or not the occupant experiences fear). *Comm v. Woods*, 94 Mass. App. Ct. 761 (2019) (it was a sufficient threat when the defendant forcibly entered the victim's apartment and told her to stay silent). *Comm. v. Cowans*, 52 Mass. App. Ct. 811 (2001) (no home invasion because there was no threat after entry).

- **Need not be lawfully present.** *Comm. v. Soto*, 2012 WL 1658373 (Appeals Court) (a person does not have to be lawfully present; here, the victim was likely a drug user who entered the apartment unlawfully before being followed inside and assaulted by the defendant).

- **May enter after the offender.** *Comm. v. Martinez*, 85 Mass. App. Ct. 288 (2014) (defendant entered a home to assault the residents; a neighbor came over to investigate, and the defendant stabbed him; he was properly charged with home invasion against the residents and neighbor, even though the neighbor was not an occupant and not present initially).

Charges based on number of occupants assaulted. *Comm. v. Antonmarchi*, 70 Mass. App. Ct. 463 (2007): Antonmarchi was angry that his ex-girlfriend went on a date. The next morning he went to her house and repeatedly knocked and rang the doorbell. When she did not answer, he climbed in through an open window. He pulled his ex-girlfriend into the bathroom and beat her boyfriend, who was hiding in the closet. Antonmarchi was properly charged with two counts. Even though there was only one entry, the intruder commits as many home invasions as the number of people he assaults.

ARMED ASSAULT IN A DWELLING 265, § 18A

Elements

- ***Entry.*** The suspect entered a dwelling;

- ***Armed.*** While armed; and

- ***Assault.*** Committed an assault on someone in the dwelling; and

- ***Intend felony.*** Had the specific intent, accompanying the assault, to commit a separate felony.

Right of Arrest

Felony.

Penalty

Basic offense: SP NLT 10 yrs, NMT Life (Mandatory minimum parole eligibility of 5 yrs).

If perpetrator armed with firearm, rifle, shotgun, or assault weapon: Identical penalty, except mandatory minimum parole eligibility of 10 yrs.

Notes

An assault in the hallway of a multi-unit apartment building — accessible only to residents and building staff — is an armed assault in a dwelling. *Comm. v. Rodriguez*, 100 Mass. App. Ct. 663 (2022).

Assault must be designed to accomplish a separate felony. The armed assault charge is not proper unless the assault was designed to accomplish another, factually distinct felony. *Comm. v. Smith*, 42 Mass. App. Ct. 906 (1997). *Comm. v. Flanagan*, 17 Mass. App. Ct. 366 (1984) (the victims ran into a bedroom and held the door shut as soon as they heard the defendant and another person smash open the front door with a baseball bat; the offenders forced their way into the bedroom and threatened occupants as they ransacked the room for pills).

Having weapon during a consensual entry does not become armed assault in a dwelling, unless the suspect entered with the intent to attack someone. *Comm. v. Fleming*, 46 Mass. App. Ct. 394 (1999) (defendant entered to visit his friends and, when told to get out, spontaneously stabbed one with a knife; this was not armed assault in a dwelling).

Self-defense is not available to the perpetrator of armed assault in a dwelling. *Comm. v. Doherty*, 394 Mass. 341 (1985).

B&E WITH INTENT TO COMMIT FELONY
266, § 16

Elements

Two offenses are covered under this statute:

Type 1: B&E Nighttime. The suspect breaks and enters;

- A building, ship, vessel, or vehicle;

- In the nighttime;

- With intent to commit a felony.

Type 2: Breaking Depository. The suspect attempts or succeeds in breaking, burning, blowing up, or otherwise injuring;

- A depository of money or other valuables;

- With intent to commit a larceny or felony.

Right of Arrest

Felony.

Penalty

SP NMT 20 yrs or HC NMT 2½ yrs.

Notes

B&E into a dwelling may be charged under § 16 because a building obviously includes a home. *Comm. v. Rocheleau*, 90 Mass. App. Ct. 634 (2016).

B&E and larceny from building may be charged if theft occurred. The applicable B&E offense and Larceny from a Building (266, § 20) do not duplicate each other. The B&E count punishes the illegal entry, while the larceny count punishes the completed theft inside. *Comm. v. Ford*, 20 Mass. App. Ct. 575 (1985).

Proof of intent to commit a felony during vehicle break.

- **Old school — charge Type 1.** *Comm. v. Hill*, 57 Mass. App. Ct. 240 (2003) provided a several variables — vehicle type, break method, items removed, offender's background — that officers can rely on in determining whether a suspect committed a vehicle break with intent to commit a felony.[1] However, *Hill* still leaves the door open for defendants to argue that, absent proof that the defendant intended to steal over $1,200 worth of property from the vehicle (the felony threshold under 266, § 30), the police and prosecutor lack proof of the defendant's felonious intent.

- **New school — charge Type 2.** This crime, in the same statute and drawing the same penalty, requires that officers only prove an attempted break and an intent to commit *any* larceny (whether successful or not). In the District Court Complaint Manual, the proper code for this Type 2 violation is 266/16/B. This is the better way to go for attempted and actual breaks into vehicles.

- **Vehicle is a depository.** Of critical importance, the term "depository" is not limited to vaults and safes; it extends to any container commonly used to safeguard money or other property. A vehicle is considered a depository, even without proof that it was used to store valuables. *Comm. v. Dreyer*, 18 Mass. App. Ct. 562 (1984) ("a locked passenger automobile reasonably can be inferred to be a depository, for it ordinarily contains a radio, a glove compartment or shelf with some contents, and a trunk usually holding at least a spare tire or tools"). *Comm. v. Tilley*, 306 Mass 412 (1940) (vehicle trunk is a depository because it is a place for storing valuables, even though, at the time the burglarious tools statute was enacted in 1853, cars with trunks were not generally in use).

B&E WITH INTENT TO COMMIT MISDEMEANOR 266, § 16A

Elements

- **B&E.** The suspect breaks and enters;

- **Day or night.** At any time of day or night;

- **Building, vessel, vehicle.** A building, ship, vessel, or vehicle;

- **Intent.** With the intent to commit a misdemeanor.

---

[1] Proving intent to commit a felony during a building break-in is, by comparison, much simpler because officers can rely on the legal presumption that anyone who breaks into a building during the day or night, absent contrary evidence, intends to steal. And anyone who intends to steal any item of any value in a building is attempting to accomplish the felony of larceny from a building, 266, § 20. *Comm. v. Soares*, 51 Mass. App. Ct. 273 (2001). As you know, there is no similar felony for larceny from a vehicle.

Right of Arrest

Arrest for breach of peace in presence. Otherwise, complaint.

Penalty

HC NMT 6 months; and/or Fine NMT $200.

Notes

The crime of trespass qualifies as the intended misdemeanor. Trespass includes an element that B&E with intent to commit a misdemeanor does not — entering or remaining on the property after being forbidden to do so. *Comm. v. Scott*, 71 Mass. App. Ct. 596 (2008).

Related Offenses

B&E of Railroad Car, Truck, Tractor, Trailer, or Freight Container. 266, §§ 19 and 20A. Right of Arrest: Felony.

B&E to Steal a Firearm. 269, § 10J outlaws a B&E; into a building, ship, vessel, or vehicle; at any time of day or night; to steal a firearm. Penalty: SP NMT 5 yrs or HC NMT 2½ yrs; and/or Fine NMT $10,000. If injury to another occurs, or the crime was done to distribute the firearm to a person prohibited from lawfully possessing one: SP NMT 10 yrs or HC NMT 2½ yrs; and/or Fine NMT $10,000. For all violations, vehicle forfeiture — with the proceeds paid to the public safety training fund. Right of Arrest: Felony.

B&E of Firearms Dealer. 269, § 10K prohibits B&E; into the building where a firearms retailer, wholesaler, or manufacturer conducts business; at any time of day or night. Penalty: SP NMT 10 yrs or HC NMT 2½ yrs; and/or Fine NMT $10,000. If intent of break is to obtain a firearm, rifle, shotgun, machine gun, or ammunition: SP NMT 10 yrs or HC NMT 2½ yrs; and/or Fine NMT $10,000. If offender actually obtains a firearm, rifle, shotgun, machine gun or ammunition and unlawfully distributes it: SP NMT 20 yrs or HC NMT 2½ yrs; and/or Fine NMT $10,000. Right of Arrest: Felony.

ENTER BUILDING/MV WITHOUT BREAK AT NIGHT; AGGRAVATED B&E DAYTIME
266, § 17

Elements

- ***Entry Method.*** The suspect:
    - Enters without breaking in the nighttime; or
    - Breaks and enters in the daytime;

- **Building, vessel, vehicle.** A building, ship, vessel, or vehicle;
- **Intent.** With the intent to commit a felony; and
- **Fear.** The owner or any other person lawfully inside is "put in fear."

Right of Arrest

Felony.

Penalty

SP NMT 10 yrs or HC NMT 2½ yrs. If armed with any gun: Mandatory minimum SP 7 yrs or HC 2 yrs.

ENTER DWELLING WITHOUT BREAK AT NIGHT; B&E DAYTIME
266, § 18

Elements

- **Entry Method.** The suspect:
    - Enters a dwelling without breaking in the nighttime; or
    - Breaks and enters in the daytime;
- **Building, vessel, vehicle.** A building, ship, vessel, or vehicle;
- **Intent.** With the intent to commit a felony; and
- **No fear.** No person lawfully inside is "put in fear."

Right of Arrest

Felony.

Penalty

SP NMT 10 yrs; or HC NMT 2½ yrs and Fine NMT $500. If armed with any gun: Mandatory minimum SP 7 yrs or HC 2 yrs.

Notes

Fear of occupant. Under 266, § 17, it is a separate element that a lawful occupant must be afraid as a result of the perpetrator's illegal entry. Therefore, this offense would not be appropriate if a suspect broke in during the day but no one was present.

***Intent* to inflict fear not required.** § 17 requires that an occupant experience fear, but the offender does not have to intend that. *Comm. v. Santana,* 81 Mass. App. Ct. 829 (2012) (defendant entered a woman's house at a time when he knew she was not going to be home; the woman's roommate heard footsteps and was scared; although the defendant retreated when he realized the roommate was home, the elements of § 17 were satisfied).

Lesser included offenses. *Comm. v. Labare,* 11 Mass. App. Ct. 370 (1981) (B&E nighttime and B&E daytime are lesser included offenses of burglary). *Comm. v. Sitko,* 372 Mass. 305 (1977) (B&E daytime is lesser included offense of B&E nighttime).

Related Offense

Daytime Entry by a False Pretense. 266, § 18A prohibits: (1) entering a dwelling (breaking is not necessary); (2) in the daytime; (3) by a false pretense; (4) with the intent to commit a felony, or with the actual result of a larceny inside. This law was enacted to combat the serious problem of con artists who pretend to be home repair contractors, municipal inspectors, even disabled motorists, in order to enter homes owned predominantly by elders. Once inside, these criminals steal money and property. Penalty: SP NMT 10 yrs; or SP NMT 10 yrs and Fine NMT $5,000; or HC NMT 2 yrs and Fine NMT $5,000. Right of Arrest: Felony.

Gap in law: No offense for simple daytime entry. No Massachusetts crime applies to the offender who simply enters during the daytime with either an intent to commit a felony or misdemeanor. The offense discussed above, 266, § 18A, requires that entry be accomplished by a false pretense (i.e., a lie to the occupant to get in the house).

But what about the offender who just walks through an open door of somebody's house during the day — perhaps to look around and decide whether to steal something? This entry is not addressed by our statutes. The best available option is trespass under 266, § 120 (see *Chapter 32*) — assuming other charges, such as larceny from a building, do not apply.

POSSESSION OF BURGLARIOUS TOOL
266, § 49

Summary

The essence of this offense is the possession of a tool for the specific purpose of breaking into a depository to steal or commit some other crime.

Elements

- **Knowingly possess.** The suspect made, mended, or knowingly possessed;

- **Tool.** A tool, machine, or motor vehicle master key;

- **Designed to break depository.** Designed to cut through or break open a building, room, vault, motor vehicle, or other depository; and

- **Intent to break and commit crime.** Which the suspect possessed with the intent to break into a depository — or to allow someone else to — for the purpose of stealing or committing any other crime.

Right of Arrest
Felony.

Penalty
SP NMT 10 yrs; or HC NMT 2½ yrs and Fine NMT $1,000.

Notes

Element 1: Possession. Like other offenses, possession may be direct or constructive. *Comm. v. Namey*, 67 Mass. App. Ct. 94 (2006) (passenger in stolen car had constructive possession of syringes, a map of the area, disguises, and several tools — including a dent puller — because they were near him in the front seat area).

More than one offender may possess the same tool. *Comm. v. Ronayne*, 8 Mass. App. Ct. 421 (1979) (joint flight from burglary supported an inference that defendants jointly possessed a tire iron, even though only one of them actually carried it).

Element 2: Ordinary tool may qualify. It is not necessary that the tool be designed exclusively for crime. Everyday items such as screwdrivers, chisels, or kitchen knives may be burglarious if possessed for an unlawful purpose. *Comm. v. Dreyer*, 18 Mass. App. Ct. 562 (1984) (coat hanger and screwdriver possessed for purpose of breaking into a car). *Comm. v. Rivera*, 91 Mass. App. Ct. 796 (2017) (screwdriver found near an attempted break-in matched pry marks on the door).

- **Gloves are not burglarious instruments,** even if worn during the crime. *Comm. v. Purcell*, 19 Mass. 1031 (1985).

- **Tool must be man-made.** Natural items, such as rocks, are not "tools" or "implements" under § 49. *Comm. v. Dykens*, 473 Mass. 635 (2016) (defendant used a big rock to bash the back door of a home).

- **Tool in need of repair may qualify.** *Comm. v. Aleo*, 18 Mass. App. Ct. 916 (1984) (dent puller, even though missing a screw, was burglarious tool).

Element 3: Tool must be capable of breaking into a depository. The term "depository" is not limited to vaults and safes; it extends to any container commonly used to safeguard money or other property. *Comm. v. Tilley*, 306 Mass. 412 (1940) (vehicle trunk). *Comm. v. Doyle*, 83 Mass. App. Ct. 384 (2013) (ATM machine).

Element 4: Tool must be possessed for the purpose of breaking into a depository and committing a crime inside. Remember, this crime is complete when a tool is possessed for this purpose, which makes it great for offenders who are intercepted before their B&E.

- **Proof of burglarious intent may be direct.** If the suspect actually used the tool, then establishing burglarious intent is less challenging. *Comm. v. Doyle*, 83 Mass. App. Ct. 384 (2013) (defendant's duffel bag contained a metal grinder that was still hot, a flashlight, crowbars, wedges, a screwdriver-type object, gloves, and a ski mask).

  However, *Comm. v. Redmond*, 53 Mass. App. Ct. 1 (2001) reminds officers that they cannot assume that any tool possessed during a B&E is automatically burglarious. There must be proof that the suspect had the item to accomplish the break. For example, if a suspect commits a B&E by walking through an unlocked door with a knife in his pocket, the knife is not a burglarious tool unless officers have proof that the suspect initially brought the knife with him to help commit the B&E, *or* that he employed it during the crime.

- **Proof of burglarious intent may be circumstantial.** *Comm. v. Rousseau*, 61 Mass. App. Ct. 144 (2004): In a state park at 1:00 a.m. (long after closing at 8:00 p.m.), police officers looked inside a truck parked near a boat ramp and saw a police duty belt, a radio, a badge, and a flashlight. Officers began to search for the occupants. Having seen the cruiser lights, John Rousseau and his partner returned to the truck and drove away. Minutes later they were stopped. Police saw several items that had not been in the truck originally — including two screwdrivers, two sets of black gloves, and a ski mask. The men could not give a sensible reason for possessing these items. *Comm. v. Faust*, 81 Mass. App. Ct. 498 (2012). *Comm. v. Squires*, 476 Mass. 703 (2017) (example of insufficient evidence of intent).

- **Proof of burglarious intent may be based on expert testimony.** *Comm. v. Garreffi*, 355 Mass. 428 (1969) (officer allowed to testify that the recovered gas mask, power drill, punches, and pry bar were "a pretty complete set of safecracker's tools").

Object of break may be any crime. While the typical goal of the offender is to steal the contents of the depository, it is sufficient if his purpose is to commit *any crime* inside.

- *Comm. v. Santiago*, 2013 WL 273264 (Appeals Court): The defendant was seen unsuccessfully trying to open the door to his neighbor's car, then retrieving a long, thin wire from a shed. When police arrived, he fled. A screwdriver was in his pocket. His intent to use the screwdriver to enter the car and commit a crime was inferred from his behavior.

- *Comm. v. Krasner*, 358 Mass. 727 (1971): An MIT student had a battering ram when he was intercepted and arrested by officers. His goal had been to enter the college president's office to stage an anti-war protest. Charged with the possession of a burglarious tool — the battering ram — the defendant argued that he did not intend to steal or damage anything. Since his tool was possessed to facilitate a crime (trespass) within a depository (the president's locked office), the SJC upheld his conviction.

Related Offense

Possession of a Tool to Disable a Theft Detection Device. 266, § 30B (felony). This law is designed to deter shoplifters. See *Chapter 28*.

32 Trespass

TRESPASS AFTER NOTICE
266, § 120

Elements

- **Enter or stay without right.** The suspect entered *or* remained without right;

- **Property of another.** On or in the dwelling, building, boat, improved or enclosed land, wharf, or school bus of another;

- **Notice.** Even though a person with lawful control had forbidden the suspect's presence:

    - Directly; or

    - With a posted notice; or

    - Through a 209A, §§ 3 and 4 or 208, § 34B court order.

Right of Arrest

266, § 120 warrantless arrest in presence.

Penalty

HC NMT 30 days; and/or Fine NMT $100.

Notes

Enter or Stay Without Right

The suspect must either enter without permission or fail to leave after being told to do so.

- **Implied license.** Under some circumstances, people may enter property to determine whether the person in control wishes to deal with them. Those individuals may also leave upon receiving a negative answer. *Comm. v. Hood*, 389 Mass. 581 (1983) (protesters had a right to see if people wanted to receive leaflets until security asked them to leave). *Comm. v. Richardson*, 313 Mass. 632 (1943) (Jehovah's Witnesses).

An implied license may extend to some parts of the property but not to others. The standard is what a reasonable person would do. *Comm. v. Krasner*, 360 Mass. 848 (1971) (while the defendant might have had access to the building where the college president had an office, he could not have reasonably believed that he could enter the actual office without permission).

- **Political protest: No defense to trespass.** Political protesters frequently argue that trespass laws violate their right to free speech under the First Amendment. This argument fails because the law of trespass does not infringe on the *content* of a person's speech, it merely limits the place where a person may communicate. *Comm. v. Wolf*, 34 Mass. App. Ct. 949 (1993). *Spingola v. Texas*, 14-03-00666-CR (2004) (Charles Spingola was speaking about abortion to a crowd on the mall of Sam Houston State University; a dean told him that university policy required that he move to a free expression area; he refused to move; he was asked five more times and then properly arrested for trespass).

If suspect refuses to answer officer's question about being invited, context may provide probable cause for trespassing. *Comm. v. Noah N.*, 2019 WL 7050137 (Appeals Court): A 25-unit apartment building at 145 Lewis Street in Lynn had been the location of many crimes of violence as well as quality of life issues. It had problems keeping trespassers out. Officer Gasca worked with the landlord on a community policing plan, including the posting of numerous "no trespass" signs that were replaced as quickly as they were removed.

On April 17, there was a shooting nearby. Officers went to 145 Lewis Street where they arrested a shooting suspect for trespassing in the building.

On April 19, an officer saw this person enter the building again, now accompanied by Noah. They emerged 20 seconds later. Officer Fountain encountered (without detaining) Noah and asked if he lived in the building. He said he did not. When asked if he had been visiting someone, Noah responded that it was none of the officer's business. He was arrested for trespassing, and a handgun was found concealed in his groin.

Probable cause existed for this arrest. Noah admitted that he did not live there; entered with someone who had been arrested for trespassing two days before; and refused to say whether he had been invited by a resident. Officers do not have to "eliminate every possibility in order to have probable cause for trespassing."

Notice

There are five ways in which property owners communicate the areas that are off limits: (1) posted sign; (2) verbal ejection; (3) privacy precautions; (4) no trespass notice; and (5) court order.

Method 1: Posted sign. The sign must be visible, but it is not necessary to prove that the suspect actually saw it. Officers may testify to the sign's location and, for maximum effect, attach a photograph to their incident report. *Fitzgerald v. Lewis*, 164 Mass. 495 (1895) (sign need not state the basis of its authority).

- **There must be proof that the defendant actually entered the posted property.** *Comm. v. Joseph*, 2019 WL 3774602 (Appeals Court): After chasing a break-in suspect for several blocks, Boston police followed him down an alley. There was a no trespassing sign posted about 15 feet up on the side of the house on the right. Officers arrested him crouching behind some boxes and charged him with trespass. Unfortunately, the prosecutor did not have the property owner testify so there was no proof that the defendant actually entered a restricted area in the alley.

- **Combination of signs and visitor policy.** *Comm. v. Monteiro*, 2020 WL 4723731 (Appeals Court): During lunch at Brockton High School, students were permitted to be in a courtyard between two buildings. Saw horses with signs reading "DO NOT ENTER" were posted at the open ends. Signs posted at the main entrance to the high school required visitors to check in at the office. If a visitor did so, they were issued an orange visitor pass. Students and staff in the courtyard wore identification badges. When Maria Monteiro and her daughter walked into the courtyard during lunch to assault a student, they knew they were trespassing because of the posted notices and school policy.

- **No trespassing sign invites police investigation, not immediate arrest.** *Comm. v. Yannick Y.*, 2020 WL 5110718 (Appeals Court): The owner of a multi-unit home had been advised to post a no trespassing sign in response to groups of juveniles hanging out on his property, and he did so. In response to an anonymous complaint about youths sitting on the stairs, gang unit members arrived, recognized the youths as gang members, and arrested Yannick and another youth for trespassing. Drugs and a firearm were found on Yannick. A third person was handcuffed, then released, when it was learned he lived at the house. That resident said he had invited Yannick onto the property. He also said his grandfather owned the property and welcomed Yannick as a guest.

  A no trespassing sign invites police to look into what permission persons have to be on the property yet, in this case, officers conducted no investigation prior to the arrests. Officers needed information specific to Yannick, not just that he was a member of a gang. Without investigating, police could not know if Yannick was a resident or had permission to be present. Since the officers lacked probable cause that Yannick was trespassing, his arrest and search (which produced a gun and drugs) was unlawful.

- **For trespassing at a public park or playground, there must be proof that the sign is based on a rule approved by the appropriate governing body.** A municipal official cannot simply decide to post a sign. *Comm. v. Einarson*, 6 Mass. App. Ct. 835 (1978).

Method 2: Verbal ejection.

- **Most obvious notice: The owner (or another person with lawful control) told suspect to leave.** For a legitimate reason, the manager of property open to the public may revoke a person's permission to stay. *Comm. v. Lapon*, 28 Mass. App. Ct. 681 (1990) (defendant was in a supermarket and insisted that he deserved a free bottle of laundry detergent; after substantial discussion, the defendant was ordered to leave; he refused and was charged with trespass). *Comm. v. Bermudez*, 2016 WL 1618213 (Appeals Court) (campus police officer properly arrested the defendant because he had no affiliation with the university and would not leave the library).

- **An order to leave also applies on government property in response to a citizen's disruptive behavior.** *Hurley v. Hinckley*, 304 F.Supp. 704 (D. Mass. 1970) held that 266, § 120 applies on government property. In this case, twenty people came to the Barnstable welfare office and, in the confined space of the office, used loud, profane, and threatening language toward the director. The protesters had already been given a reasonable opportunity to present their grievances in an orderly manner, and they were arrested when they refused to leave. This was proper. In contrast, a woman at the Somerville welfare office should not have been arrested when she insisted on making a statement to someone in charge that related to welfare, which was relevant to this agency. At that point, she had not disrupted the "business of the agency."

- **An arrest for trespassing in a police station is permitted.** *Comm. v. Compres*, 2020 WL 6132295 (Appeals Court): Josue Compres wanted to bail out his brother, a juvenile. Lieutenant Bossolt told Compres that the brother could be released only to a parent. Compres became belligerent. Officers repeatedly asked him to leave the police station, but he refused. He was warned that he could be arrested if he remained. Although given adequate notice that he must leave and the opportunity to do so, Compres refused. Officers had started physically to escort him out when the arrest occurred.

  The crime of trespass occurred before the escort began. An arrest was not required to prove trespass initially. The police could decide, during their escort, to make an arrest based on the defendant's continued physical opposition while leaving.

- **In all cases, information about any prior warnings must appear in the police report.** Police must either: (1) describe the prior incident and warning in their current report; or (2) attach a prior written trespass notice to their current report; or (3) attach the prior incident report to their current report. *Comm. v. Bailey*, 2019 WL 3330630 (Appeals Court).

- **It must be clear that the person ejected has no right to remain.** *Comm. v. Greene*, 461 Mass. 1011 (2012): Richard Greene returned to his mother's house after she went into a nursing home. On several occasions, police arrived at the house and told Greene that his mother's guardian, Paul Garbarini, wanted him off the premises. Greene was arrested for trespass. However, the prosecutor neglected to present any official document or testimony from Garbarini that he, and not Greene, had lawful control over the premises. In cases where a person makes a credible claim that he has a right to be present, officers should gather evidence to dispute his claim or decline to arrest for trespass. See *Roman Catholic Archbishop of Boston v. Rogers*, 88 Mass. App. Ct. 520 (2015).

Method 3: Privacy precautions. Notice does not require that a person in control of the premises personally warn intruders. Owners may also bar entry by securing the premises with a fence, walls, locked gates, or doors. These types of normal privacy precautions directly forbid entry. *Comm. v. A Juvenile*, 6 Mass. App. Ct. 106 (1978) (officers observed the defendant inside a stadium enclosed by a locked gate and bleachers when there was no event in progress; trespass proven even though there were no signs or official statements prohibiting his entry). *Comm. v. Scott*, 71 Mass. App. Ct. 596 (2008) (defendant had no reason to be in hallway of vacant apartment building).

Comm. v. Grayson, 96 Mass. App. Ct. 748 (2019): While fleeing from police, Deshawn Grayson ran through residential backyards. He climbed over a 5-foot-tall stockade fence, crossed the backyard, and climbed the fence on the other side. The owner of the property had "at least at the points where the defendant entered and exited the yard, forbidden entry to the yard by fences." His trespass conviction was upheld. *Comm. v. Dyette*, 87 Mass. App. Ct. 548 (2015).

Method 4: Written notice. Sometimes property owners will issue written trespass notices to those individuals they wish to bar from their premises.

- **Providing prior written notice is proof that a person knew he had no right to be present.** But, contrary to popular belief, written notice is not legally required in order to charge trespass.

- **Trespass notices should contain:** (1) the name, date of birth, and address of the person ordered off the property; (2) the name of the person and organization issuing the notice; (3) a description of the property (e.g., "The Gap Store in the Burlington, MA Mall"); and (4) the potential consequences of a violation (e.g., "If you violate this notice, the police will be called and may arrest you under the authority of 266, § 120. You may be prosecuted and receive a sentence of up to 30 days in the house of correction").

  Trespass notices must provide the subject with an official contact to request that the order be rescinded or modified. *City of Akron v. Niepsuj*, No. 21369 (2003).

- **Exemption to trespass notice: Invited visitors.** *Comm. v. Nelson*, 74 Mass. App. Ct. 629 (2009): At an apartment complex under the control of the Boston Housing Authority (BHA), Gregory Nelson was arrested for possessing a dangerous weapon. He was told not to return to BHA property and given a written trespass notice.

  Seven months later, Nelson's friend, Erica McCall, invited him to her BHA apartment. Officers on patrol found Nelson in the hallway of her building. They arrested him for violating the trespass notice.

  This case reaffirmed an old rule. *Comm. v. Richardson*, 313 Mass. 632 (1943) held that a person is not trespassing while passing through the common area at a tenant's invitation. Thus, McCall had a right to invite Nelson to her home regardless of the landlord's wishes.

  - *The Nelson case narrowed the scope of a trespass notice and re-stated two important principles concerning a landlord's authority:* (1) any individual who is the subject of a notice may only pass through the property to visit his host. He may not loiter in other areas, and he certainly may not commit criminal acts or disturb others while visiting; and (2) housing authorities (such as the BHA) retain lawful control of the common areas, and may serve as a proper complainant for criminal trespass.[1]

  - *The Nelson case probably has limited application to a college campus.* It may cover faculty and graduate housing arrangements, where occupants are tenants, but not student dorms. Dormitories and fraternities are considered "lodging houses" under 140, § 22. Owners of lodging houses retain legal possession and control. The distinction turns on the fact that a tenant acquires exclusive possession, whereas a lodger merely has use of the premises. Unlike tenants, for example, students must vacate during vacations and observe a specific code of conduct.

---

1 The housing authority is not restricted, as the defendant argued, to pursuing civil injunctions under 121B, § 32C. This statute allows a housing authority to terminate a tenant's lease if the tenant or his guest engage in any criminal activity that threatens the safety of another resident, housing authority employee, or any person residing in the immediate vicinity. Advocates for Nelson argued that this statute was the exclusive remedy for housing authorities to deal with bad behavior on their property. The court stated that this law was never intended to eliminate a landlord's recourse to criminal trespass.

186, § 17 further differentiates between students and tenants by allowing college and university officials to bypass the civil eviction process in order to oust someone from student housing.

- **Other important police cautions with trespass notices.**

  - *Do not recommend that public libraries or other obvious public forums automatically issue trespass notices.* Police officers may be called to handle a disturbance at a public library or town hall. Officers may eject a misbehaving individual at the request of a staff member and, if necessary, arrest him for trespass if he fails to leave.

    The problem arises when officers take it upon themselves to recommend that a librarian or other public official issue a trespass notice to ban the individual.

    Excluding someone from a public forum may infringe on the individual's constitutional rights. In particular, courts have recognized a First Amendment right to access knowledge through a public library. *Kreimer v. Bureau of Police for Morristown*, 958 F.2d 1242 (1992). In assessing the validity of any enforcement action, a court will examine whether the public official provided the suspect with notice and an opportunity to be heard before banning him. The reason for heightened judicial scrutiny is to ensure that access is not denied arbitrarily. See *Wayfield v. Town of Tisbury*, 925 F.Supp. 880 (D. Mass. 1996) (town resident, who had a library card, was entitled to notice and a hearing before receiving a trespass notice from the librarian — especially since his unpopular and controversial political views may have influenced the decision).

    When responding to the misbehavior of a patron at a public facility, officers should not routinely recommend that staff members issue a trespass notice. Instead, officers should advise them to consult with their agency head or legal counsel to determine what process is lawfully required to exclude the patron in the future. In all cases, fully document the incident.

  - *Be prudent in informing others about a trespass notice.* Police officers may inform people who need to know that a particular individual is the subject of a trespass notice. However, be careful not to disparage the person or provide details about the behavior that led to his expulsion. Otherwise, the individual may have grounds for a defamation lawsuit. *Burley v. Comets Youth Center*, 75 Mass. App. Ct. 818 (2009).

Method 5: Court order. While a restraining order carries its own right of arrest, 266, § 120 defines trespass to include a violation of a 209A or 208 order as an added precaution.

Special Consideration 1: Public Accommodation

Enforcement of trespass law may not discriminate. There have been several publicized cases where police have been called to deal with a person who has been ejected from a business for arguably discriminatory reasons. In these difficult situations, officers must remember the public accommodation law, 272, § 92A.

Section 92A applies to any owner, proprietor, manager, employee or agent of any public or private, licensed or unlicensed, place of business open to the public. Any of these individuals may not, directly or indirectly, discriminate on the basis of race, color, religion, national origin, sex, gender identity, sexual orientation, deafness, blindness or any physical or mental disability. Discrimination covers the decision to admit, as well as the type of treatment given to a person who has entered. The penalty is defined in 272, § 98: HC NMT 1 year; and/or Fine NMT $500.

Suggested police policy to avoid the misuse of police authority. [2] When arriving on scene, officers should:

- **Learn the reason why a manager wants to eject the suspect.**

- **Listen to the suspect and see whether he is alleging discrimination or some other improper motive.**

- **If it makes sense, attempt to de-escalate and mediate the disturbance.** Officers may use this opportunity to communicate their concerns to the owner or authorized person about a possible misuse of police authority (e.g., discrimination, financial intimidation, etc.). Officers may also suggest to the suspect that if he leaves, it does not prevent him from exploring other legal options. However, officers should refrain from giving specific guidance.

- **Remember, in these cases, the motives of the parties may not be obvious.** If it is likely that the owner or authorized person is attempting to misuse police authority, officers may decline to arrest, ideally after consultation with a supervisor. On the other hand, if the owner or other authorized person provides a legitimate basis for enforcement, he or she must communicate to the suspect, in the presence of officers, that the suspect must leave the premises.

- **Basis for trespass arrest should be documented.** Include in the incident report: (1) the reason(s) provided by the owner or authorized person to eject the suspect from the property; (2) the nature of their authority over the property (e.g., owner, manager, employee, security personnel, etc.); (3) witnessing the owner or authorized person's directive to the suspect to leave; (4) the suspect's refusal to leave; and (5) the name, address, and phone number of the owner or authorized person (i.e., the complainant).

- **Other violations.** Despite the decision not to arrest for trespassing, the supervisor and/or officers on scene are not precluded from enforcing any other applicable civil or criminal violation.

Special Consideration 2: Trespass Inapplicable to Landlord/Tenant Disputes

Officers may not arrest for trespass or forcefully intervene to attempt to resolve landlord/tenant disputes. Landlords will identify occupants who have been living on their property without permission, refusing to pay rent, or otherwise misbehaving. They will request that officers eject these trespassers. Given the frequency of these disputes, officers may be tempted to impose a legal solution. This mindset risks liability for officers and their departments.[3]

---

2 This policy is adapted from the Philadelphia Police Department's Memorandum (18-02) issued on June 8, 2018.
3 This author believes that most police officers overrate their risk of civil liability and, as a consequence, may fail to intervene in certain situations. Discussing liability here is not to worry officers, but to educate them about a tricky area of the law not often discussed.

- **266, § 120 contains two important limitations.** It states: "[Criminal trespass] shall not apply to *tenants* or *occupants* of residential premises who, having *rightfully entered* said premises at the commencement of the tenancy or occupancy, remain therein after such tenancy or occupancy has been or is alleged to have been terminated. The owner or landlord of said premises may recover possession thereof only through *appropriate civil proceedings*" [emphasis added].

- **Tenants and occupants are protected.** While there may be situations where a landlord can persuasively argue that someone is not a tenant, there are very few instances where a person living in an apartment or home does not qualify as an occupant. Even those occupants who have relied on various informal arrangements (e.g., oral agreements, paying rent to a roommate, or subletting for several months without the landlord's knowledge) are protected from arrest.

- **Civil eviction is the exclusive remedy.** Regardless of the arrangement,[4] occupants are protected, and the landlord's sole remedy is the civil eviction process set forth in Chapter 139 (referred to as "summary process").

    In fact, 186, § 14 makes it a crime for a landlord to cut off utilities or attempt to regain possession of *any property used for dwelling purposes* (except for rooms in a hotel) without participating in the judicial process. This law broadly prohibits what lawyers refer to as "self-help remedies" — e.g., locking the tenant out; removing the tenant's property; or using force or the threat of force to make the tenant move out. In addition to its potential 6-month HC sentence, the statute enables a tenant to recover three months of rent or damages (whichever is greater) and attorneys fees. Section 14 does not authorize warrantless arrests, so officers and civilians must apply for a criminal complaint.

Massachusetts police officers lack the authority to evict occupants or to assist with an eviction. This is true even when:

- An occupant, who has been living in the apartment, is not listed on the lease or rental agreement;
- The lease states that the landlord has the right to "retake" the premises;
- There is documented proof that the tenant has not paid rent;
- The tenant signed an agreement that he or she would leave by a certain date;
- The landlord terminated the lease and issued a "Notice to Quit."

Ordering a tenant or occupant to vacate the premises is, in effect, an eviction — and only deputy sheriffs are authorized to do this by a written court order known as an "execution."[5] *Soldal v. Cook County*, 506 U.S. 56 (1992). *Radvansky v. Olmsted Falls*, 395 F.3d 291 (6th Cir. 2005) (detective liable for recommending that a landlord change the locks while a tenant was away; other officers engaged in a false arrest when they took the tenant into custody). *Kimball v. Town of Provincetown*, 158 F.Supp.3d 7 (2016) (police officers improperly became involved in a civil eviction by threatening to arrest the commercial tenant if he did not immediately leave).

---

4 Some leases prohibit subleasing or assigning the lease, while others require the landlord's permission to do so. Officers should *never* attempt to interpret the application of a lease to a particular living situation.

5 Sheriffs must follow a rigid set of procedures involving notice, entry, and the disposition of property. See 239, § 4.

Best practice — keep the peace. Officers must be careful not to take sides in landlord/tenant disputes. They may certainly suggest that parties work things out, use the courts, or seek mediation services (which are often the best way to resolve issues), but their major function is to keep the peace and prevent the parties from becoming violent or destroying property. *Harvey v. Plains Township*, 421 F.3d 185 (3rd Cir. 2005) (absent a court order, a police officer lacked authority to order a landlord to open the door so that a former tenant could retrieve his possessions; the officer was liable for damage to the current tenant's possessions).

Special Consideration 3: Innkeeper Authority

Innkeepers have expanded authority to deal with guests who lack the money to pay or are behaving in an obnoxious, drunken, or destructive fashion. 140, §§ 12A–D. Officers are advised to inform innkeepers of these rights.

- **Broad coverage.** This authority may be used by innkeepers of a hotel, motel, boarding house, or inn for transient occupancy. 140, § 12A.

  The statute does not define "transient occupancy," which may present a challenge when dealing with longer-term inhabitants of these establishments. The officer's decision to classify an individual as a guest versus a tenant/occupant is quite important. Innkeepers have much more authority to ask for police action against a guest than against someone who has become a tenant/occupant.

  To be consistent, the Yarmouth Police Department has adopted a policy in which occupants of a motel are no longer considered "transients" after 30 days. Other departments apply a more fact-based approach by looking at the arrangement and deciding whether it has become the subject's principal residence. The classification as a guest is an important decision because it provides an innkeeper with expanded authority.

- **Right to eject.** 140, § 12B allows an innkeeper to remove, or have removed, any guest or other person who:

  - Is unable or refuses to pay for accommodations; or
  - Is obviously intoxicated; or
  - Acts disorderly; or
  - Destroys or threatens to destroy property; or
  - Causes or threatens to cause a disturbance; or
  - Violates a rule "clearly and conspicuously posted at or near the front desk and on the inside of the entrance door to every guest room."

  If guests pay in advance, an innkeeper must refund any unused portion when they leave.

- **Right to refuse service.** 140, § 12C allows an innkeeper to refuse to admit or serve anyone for all the reasons listed for ejection. An innkeeper may also require a prospective guest to demonstrate an ability to pay, and a minor guest's parent or guardian to provide a credit card or deposit of $100 (which the innkeeper must refund if not used). Finally, an innkeeper may limit the number of persons who occupy a room.

- **Liability for hotel damage.** 140, § 12D holds a person liable for damages if that person negligently or intentionally damaged hotel property, caused injury to another, or damaged another person's property at the hotel. [*Note:* § 12D applies to any parent or guardian who has supplied their credit card or cash deposit under § 12C.]

Special Consideration 4: Homelessness

Officers may arrest a homeless person on private property. At the same time, they should understand the legal defense of "necessity." Comm. v. Magadini, 474 Mass. 593 (2016): 67 year old David Magadini was homeless. During the winter months, he tried to find shelter from the ice and snow. He had stayed at a homeless shelter, but was asked to leave and refused re-entry. Over the next several years, Magadini went onto private properties to get warm. He was served with trespass notices by three separate owners. On very cold days, he violated the notices. While police properly charged Magadini with trespass, he properly raised the necessity defense.

The SJC found that he had faced "imminent danger" during very cold nights. There was also evidence that he lacked a legal alternative to trespass, because he had been refused entry to the only homeless shelter in the area and had no friends to stay with or money. At the same time, Magadini could not claim the necessity defense for the time he entered property, in violation of a no trespass notice, on a warm day in June to use the bathroom.

The best practice is for police agencies to help develop and utilize community resources for the homeless. Arrest should really be the last resort for people in this situation.

Special Consideration 5: Beach Access

Officers who work in coastal areas know that private beach owners can become disgruntled with public use of their property.

- **Public access: Intertidal area for fishing, fowling, or navigation.** Established by law in colonial times, the public has the right to use any private beach between the high water mark and the low water mark (known as the "intertidal" or "wet sand" area) for three purposes: fishing, fowling, and navigation. This includes the right to walk or otherwise pass freely for these three activities. This right does *not* extend to recreational purposes. *Barry v. Grela*, 372 Mass. 278 (1977). *Opinion of the Justices*, 365 Mass. 681 (1974).

- **No public access: Private property above intertidal area — exception made for easements.** The public generally does not have a right to walk across privately owned property inland of the high water mark — even if they want to gain access to the intertidal area — unless a public easement (which means a right to pass) has been created.

- **Police strategies for various scenarios.**

    - *People may fish, fowl, pass in a watercraft, swim by, or walk through to engage in these activities in the intertidal area.* Explain to owners, this is legally permitted.

- *People may not be in the intertidal area if they are not engaged in these activities.* Officers should try to mediate the situation. If owners are adamant, then officers should tell people to leave. With persistent intruders, officers should consider enforcing the trespass law — preferably by complaint application.

- *People may not typically walk on private property above the high water mark.* Officers need to decide whether a public easement exists by considering: (1) any signs or barriers that permit or prohibit access; (2) if passersby have used the area in the past without objection; and (3) if the municipality or other public authority has maintained the area. On balance, if officers feel that the public reasonably has an easement, then they lack probable cause for trespass. Officers may calmly explain to owners that beach access issues can be difficult to resolve. Recommend that they consult a lawyer and/or the Office of Coastal Zone Management.

  If the conduct of any intruders is clearly unlawful — e.g., they are sunbathing on the owners' lawn, or picnicking on their beach — then officers may want to ask them to leave, seek a complaint, or (in egregious cases) arrest them.

- **When in doubt, mediate and/or seek a complaint, but don't arrest.** For a more in-depth review of applicable law, call the Office of Coastal Zone Management at 617-626-1200.

Trespass through agent. Trespass may occur if a principal offender intentionally directs an agent to enter illegally. *Comm. v. Santos*, 58 Mass. App. Ct. 701 (2003).

Trespass by drone. This emerging area is discussed in *LED's Motor Vehicle, Chapter 25*.

Trespass is not a lesser included offense of burglary or B&E. *Comm. v. Willard*, 53 Mass. App. Ct. 650 (2002).

Related Offenses

Removing or Defacing "No Trespassing" Sign. 266, § 122. Penalty: Fine NMT $25. Right of Arrest: Arrest for breach of peace in presence. Otherwise, complaint.

MV Trespass. 266, § 121A. Penalty: CMVI $250. See *LED's Motor Vehicle Law, Chapter 3*.

Obstructing Access to Medical Facility. 266, § 120E. No person may obstruct entry or exit from any medical office, clinic, laboratory or hospital — or remain inside to obstruct medical services — after court, verbal or posted notice. Right of Arrest: 266, § 120E arrest in presence. Penalty: HC NMT 6 months; and/or Fine NMT $1,000.

Impeding Access or Intimidation at Reproductive Health Facility. 266, § 120E½. Unlike the broad coverage of 266, § 120E above, § 120E½ only applies to abortion and family planning facilities, including buildings, grounds and parking areas. Right of Arrest: For impeding access, the police must issue a written "withdrawal order," which requires that the offender stay at least 25 feet from the entrance for 8 hours. § 120E½ arrest in presence during business hours. For intimidating or impeding a person or vehicle, § 120E½ arrest in presence. Penalty: A variety of penalties; all misdemeanors. Court may impose $5,000 civil fine instead.

33 Property Damage

DEFACING OR DAMAGING PROPERTY
266, § 126A

Important Police Field Tip

Massachusetts has over 40 separate statutes governing various types of property damage! Officers are better off simplifying their charging decision. Although many officers were trained to use 266, § 127 (the destruction of property statute passed by the legislature a long time ago), 266, § 126A (enacted in 1994) is far superior. Officers may effectively use § 126A in *all* situations because:

- **Warrantless arrest:** § 126A is a felony *without regard to the value of the damage*, so officers always have warrantless arrest authority on probable cause.

- **Malicious and wanton:** § 126A covers both malicious and wanton offenders with the same penalty. *Comm. v. McDowell*, 62 Mass. App. Ct. 15 (2004).

- **Damaging and defacing:** § 126A applies to offenders who damage property *or* deface its appearance (even though no damage occurs).

- **Broad coverage:** § 126A applies to *all* real or personal property, without the kinds of technical limitations that appear in other statutes. See, e.g., 266, §§ 126, 126B, 127, 127A.

Elements

- *Malicious or wanton.* The suspect maliciously or wantonly;

- *Destroy or deface.* Marked, injured, defaced or destroyed;

- *Property of another.* The real or personal property of another.

Right of Arrest

For malicious or wanton property destruction or defacement: Felony.

Recommended strategy for police discretion: Sometimes officers do not want to charge an offender with a felony, especially if it is his first offense and the damage is minor. In such a case, officers may charge § 126A for its arrest authority *and* also charge 266, § 127 as a misdemeanor alternative. During plea negotiations, or even upon conviction, the prosecutor may elect to pursue the felony under § 126A or dismiss it for the misdemeanor alternative.

Penalty

Penalty: SP NMT 3 yrs or HC NMT 2 yrs; and/or Fine $1,500 or 3 times the value of the property defaced or destroyed, whichever is greater.

Aggravated penalty if a war or veterans' memorial or gravestone is defaced: Fine $3,000 or 3 times the value of the property, whichever is greater; *and* at least 500 hours (the mandatory minimum) of court-approved community service.[1]

Restitution or performance: Offenders must either pay to repair the damage or perform the labor themselves.

Notes

Malicious is intentional. A malicious act is deliberate and hostile toward the property owner. This does not require that the suspect know the owner's identity, only that he was hostile toward the owner — whoever that might be.

- **Behavior is best indicator.** *Comm. v. Blackshear*, 2014 WL 7237122 (Appeals Court) (defendant looked around to make sure no one was watching before he scratched the victim's car; later laughing when the victim confronted him also demonstrated malice). *Comm. v. Cimino*, 34 Mass. App. Ct. 925 (1993) (the defendant rode around with his friends and took turns shooting out the windows of parked cars with a BB gun).

- **Magnitude of damage shows malice.** *Comm. v. Gordon*, 82 Mass. App. Ct. 227 (2012): James Gordon broke his own furniture first, then turned on the items in the apartment. He smashed 28 windows, a glass-top stove, and a bathroom vanity. Although Gordon told police, "I'm crazy and do this to release my rage; I didn't mean to hurt my landlords," there was sufficient evidence of malice. Gordon deliberately destroyed a considerable amount of his landlords' property, including renovated items.

- **Malice may be directed toward another.** *Comm. v. Chambers*, 90 Mass. App. Ct. 137 (2016) (when Nikki Chambers' downstairs neighbor, Mary Louise Brown, blocked her car in the driveway, Chambers kicked the front door to Brown's apartment, shattering the doorframe; Chambers' malice toward Brown was sufficient, even though the owner of this rental property was someone else).

Wanton is reckless. A malicious actor intends his conduct and the harm, while a wanton actor does not intend the harm caused by his reckless conduct.

- **Example of wanton or reckless conduct.** *Comm. v. McDowell*, 62 Mass. App. Ct. 15 (2004): A drunk Neal McDowell left the party, got into his car, and backed up rapidly — striking a wooden fence and porch. Startled, he then ran over five-foot high hedges. A police car, which had been summoned by the homeowner, pulled into the driveway. McDowell smashed into the cruiser! Clearly, McDowell did not intentionally cause this "damage cluster." His behavior was reckless, not malicious.

---

1 There is also a felony crime under 272, § 73 for this type of behavior with respect to any grave or memorial. See *Chapter 16* for more detailed discussion.

- **Minor damage is no defense when the suspect's behavior was sufficiently reckless.** In *Comm. v. Faherty*, 57 Mass. App. Ct. 150 (2003), officers observed the defendant place two pennies, wrapped in paper, into a parking meter. His goal was to put the meter out of order. He argued that his "temporary blockage" did not cause any damage, since the officers successfully cleared the meter, which required no replacement parts. The court rejected the defendant's "no harm, no foul" analogy. Since a likely result of the defendant's action was breaking the meter, the fact that it was fixed easily did not excuse his behavior.

  Compare *Comm. v. Compres*, 2020 WL 6132295 (Appeals Court): When four officers arrested the defendant in the police station, an officer's uniform pocket was torn during the struggle. However, the defendant did not fight or flail. His behavior was insufficiently reckless because a reasonable person would <u>not</u> expect to cause damage.

<u>**Destroying or injuring**</u> **property must cause damage.** *Comm. v. Rumkin*, 55 Mass. App. Ct. 635 (2002) (following a motor vehicle accident, the defendant cab driver kicked the other motorist's side mirror and door, causing significant damage).

On the other hand, <u>defacing</u> property requires that the offender harm its appearance, even though no damage occurs. *Comm. v. DiPietro*, 33 Mass. App. Ct. 776 (1992) (defendant properly convicted for defacing a temple by throwing eggs against the outside wall, even though the eggs were completely washed off later).

In *Comm. v. Bath*, 2019 WL 6769680 (Appeals Court), the victim entered a convenience store. The occupants of two nearby cars, including Qwandre Bath, followed him inside. The young men immediately attacked the victim, who fought back. During the chaos, soda bottles and other merchandise were knocked all over the floor. Since their reckless behavior defaced the well-ordered displays, the youths were properly found guilty of violating § 126A. It was irrelevant that the items on the floor were not damaged and later returned to the shelves.

Urinating or defecating on police station floor is a violation of § 126A. This is the preferred charge, along with Disorderly Conduct. 272, § 53 (disorderly includes creating a physically offensive condition with no legitimate purpose). See *Comm. v. Perez Narvaez*, 490 Mass. 807 (2022) (unruly OUI arrestee urinated inside and outside his cell door; police had to call in a hazmat cleaner to deal with the mess; prosecutor should not have charged 266, § 103, vandalism by noxious substance, since urine is less toxic than the substances referenced in that statute; 266, § 126A was the applicable charge for this malicious behavior).

Property of another. § 126A covers both real and personal property of another.

- **Real property.** "All land, structures, firmly attached and integrated equipment (such as light fixtures or a well pump), anything growing on the land . . . It is distinguished from personal property which is made up of movable items . . . ."

- **Personal property.** "Movable assets (things, including animals) which are not real property." (Definitions from Dictionary.Law.com).

- **People may damage or destroy their own property, except by fire.** See 266, § 5 discussed in *Chapter 34*.

Specialized Offenses

Although § 126A is useful in all situations, there are times when officers may want to send a message to the perpetrator by charging a more specialized offense.

Places of worship. 266, § 127A (destroying or defacing). See *Chapter 16*.

Computer information. 266, § 127 states: "The words 'personal property' . . . shall also include electronically processed or stored data, either tangible or intangible, and data while in transit." Officers may want to use this particular statute if an offender maliciously or wantonly destroys data. Also see crimes concerning unlawful computer access in *Chapter 27*.

Tagging. 266, § 126B prohibits a person from either: (1) applying paint or a sticker as part of "an activity commonly known as tagging"; *or* (2) joining a group with the intent to tag. Right of Arrest: § 126B warrantless arrest on probable cause.

Motor vehicles. Damage to motor vehicles is best charged under 266, § 28 (Felony). § 28 is the larceny and damage to a motor vehicle statute covered in *LED's Motor Vehicle Law, Chapter 12*.

Library property. 266, § 99A prohibits the concealment of library materials worth more than $250, and the destruction *or* "willful alteration" of library records or catalogs. Penalty: SP NMT 5 yrs; and/or Fine NLT $1,000, NMT $25,000. § 99A also prohibits failing to return materials that were properly checked out within 30 days (Fine NLT $100, NMT $500); or giving false information when checking out materials (Fine NLT $100, NMT $1,000). Offenders must pay replacement costs. 266, § 100 punishes *any* act to destroy or deface any materials or property inside a library. Penalty: HC NMT 2 yrs; and/or Fine NLT $100, NMT $1,000. Right of Arrest: 266, § 100 warrantless arrest on probable cause. In § 100, the statement of a library employee, age 18 and over, that a person is in violation constitutes probable cause to arrest. The activation of an electronic anti-theft device is also probable cause.

Turf, timber, plants, crops, flowers. 266, § 113. One may not willfully cut down, dig up, or carry away the turf, timber, plants, crops, or flowers of another person without permission. Penalty: HC NMT 6 months; or Fine NMT $500. Right of Arrest: Arrest for breach of peace in presence. Otherwise, complaint. *Comm. v. Smith*, 17 Mass. App. Ct. 918 (1983) (driving van on a golf course for over 300 yards and digging up 96 feet of turf). *Comm. v. Byard*, 200 Mass. 175 (1908) (tree warden convicted for gross negligence that caused injury to trees).

34 Arson, False Alarm, & Fire Prevention

ARSON
266, §§ 1 and 2

Elements

- **Burn.** The suspect set fire, burned, or caused to be burned; and

- **Malicious.** Did so maliciously by:
  - Setting the fire on purpose; or
  - Intentionally engaging in an act that created a strong likelihood that a portion of the structure would be burned.

- **Designated structure.** The structure is defined under:
  - § 1: Any occupied or unoccupied dwelling, or any structure that results in the burning of a dwelling; or
  - § 2: Any occupied, unoccupied or vacant public building, or any other structure not included in § 1.

Right of Arrest

Felony.

Penalty

For structures in § 1: SP NMT 20 yrs or HC NMT 2½ yrs; and/or Fine NMT $10,000.

For structures in § 2: SP NMT 10 yrs or HC NMT 2½ yrs.

Enhanced penalty for injury to firefighter: 265, § 13D½ authorizes a separate penalty in the event a firefighter is injured in the performance of his duty. The penalty is SP NMT 10 yrs; or HC NMT 2½ yrs and Fine NMT $1,000.

Notes

Charring is sufficient evidence of burning. Some portion of the structure must be on fire, but it does not have to be consumed. Charring the structure is enough for conviction. *Comm. v. McIntosh*, 10 Mass. App. Ct. 924 (1980).

Arson occurs when a suspect intentionally sets a fire that a reasonable person would know is likely to burn the structure. *Comm. v. Pfeiffer*, 482 Mass. 110 (2019): Following an argument with her boyfriend, Melissa Pfeiffer set a bag of his clothes on fire inside their apartment. Pfeiffer then changed her clothes and fled the building, locking the exterior door, without calling for help or warning the occupants in other units. One person died and multiple people were injured.

While Pfeiffer may not have intentionally burned the apartment building due to her impulsive rage and mental limitations, it did not matter because, undeniably, a reasonable person would have known that lighting a bag of clothes on fire creates a strong likelihood that some portion of the dwelling will be burned. Pfeiffer was guilty on this basis.

- **Behavior committed after the fire can help prove a suspect's malicious intent.** Here, Pfeiffer ran from the apartment and locked the door, showing her intent to delay anyone from discovering, reporting, and extinguishing the fire.

- **At the same time, it is not arson if the fire is caused by accident, negligence, or mistake — even if the suspect makes no attempt to extinguish or report the fire.** However, the SJC did say in *Pfeiffer* that the failure to extinguish or report could result in a conviction for involuntary manslaughter if someone died in the ensuing fire. See *Comm. v. Levesque*, 436 Mass. 443 (2002) (homeless couple in Worcester started an accidental fire in a warehouse; this was not arson; but they failed to report it to the fire department even though they had the time and the means; six firefighters died trying to locate them in the burning building; they were guilty of manslaughter). See *Chapter 6* for more on manslaughter.

Applicable structures. It is important to be aware of the type of structure burned, because that will decide the potential penalty faced by the suspect.

- **§ 1 applies to any "dwelling house,"** which includes an apartment house, hotel, dormitory, hospital, institution or "other buildings where persons are domiciled." This broad definition is further extended by the statutory language: "or an adjacent structure . . . or a building whose burning result[s] in a [dwelling house] being burned." Thus, if a felon sets fire to a tool shed next to a house, but the house gets charred, then the offender faces prosecution under § 1, even though he did not set out to burn the house. Finally, a separate charge of arson is properly brought for each dwelling burned.

- **§ 2 applies to any other building or structure** (not included under § 1).

- **Occupied or unoccupied for § 1. Occupied, unoccupied, or vacant for § 2.** Under both §§ 1 and 2, it does not matter whether the building is occupied at the time of the fire. However, only § 2 explicitly applies to vacant buildings. *Comm. v. Anolik*, 27 Mass. App. Ct. 701 (1989) (evidence that there was electrical service and that the building contained furniture, kitchen items, and food at the time of the fire was sufficient to establish that it was a dwelling).

Does not matter who owns or occupies the building. The fact that the suspect burns his own dwelling or building is no defense to arson. Ownership or occupancy of a building is irrelevant whenever a structure is maliciously burned.

Evidence often circumstantial. Arson can be difficult to prove. Often investigators end up piecing together a circumstantial case based on motive, opportunity, and other factors.

- *Comm. v. Jacobson*, 19 Mass. App. Ct. 666 (1985): The defendant's failure to pay property and income taxes on time was relevant to his motive to burn his house, especially in view of his increased insurance coverage and misleading statements to investigators.

- *Comm. v. Carlton,* 43 Mass. App. Ct. 1997 (1997): Carlton was upset that the owner of an inn did not award him a large electrical repair contract. An empty gas can belonging to Carlton was found near a bulkhead leading into the cellar where the fire was ignited with an accelerant. Shortly after the fire broke out, Carlton was seen suspiciously passing the inn *twice* in his car at a slow rate of speed. Carlton showered and washed all his clothes, including his sneakers, shortly before he was arrested, although he lied and claimed he had showered earlier. Some of the material used to ignite the fire consisted of paper circulars that bore the name and address of his housemate.

- *Comm. v. Iago I.*, 77 Mass. App. Ct. 327 (2010): Permissible for investigator to testify that the juvenile's nickname, "Nano," was found spray painted on the walls of buildings near five suspicious fires, prior to the large fire in an abandoned building in this case. This evidence showed a relevant "pattern of conduct."

- *Comm. v. Choy,* 456 Mass. 146 (2010): When firefighters responded and removed the defendant from the burning house, she did not appear upset and displayed no visible signs of injury. The fire had been intentionally set with gas throughout the house. Gas residue was found on the defendant's sweatpants. The defendant also told police that she resented her parents because they prevented her from seeing her boyfriend.

- *Comm. v. Brown*, 2019 WL 438559 (Appeals Court): The defendant removed her roommate's animals from the apartment minutes before living room couch intentionally set on fire.

Expert testimony from arson investigator frequently indispensable proof. *Comm. v. Ward,* 14 Mass. App. Ct. 37 (1982) (expert allowed to testify about two points of origin).

ARSON OF PERSONAL PROPERTY
266, § 5

Elements

- **Willfully burn or counsel.** The suspect acted willfully and maliciously:

  - To set fire to, burn, or cause to be burned; or
  - To counsel or aid in the burning of;

- **Property, trees or conveyance.** One of the following items:

  - Any personal property of another valued at more than $25; or
  - Any kind of tree, lumber, or crops; or
  - Any boat, motor vehicle or other conveyance, whether it belonged to the suspect or another.

Right of Arrest

Felony.

Penalty

Basic offense: SP NMT 3 yrs; or HC NMT 1 year and Fine NMT $500.

Enhanced penalty for injury to firefighter: SP NMT 10 yrs; or HC NMT 2½ yrs and Fine NMT $1,000.

Notes

Sufficient evidence of vehicle arson. *Comm. v. Balboni*, 89 Mass. App. Ct. 651 (2016): Police discovered a burning vehicle late at night. A gasoline can was found beside the truck. Samuel Doxsey had a motive. The truck belonged to a person who, he had just been told, sexually assaulted his sister. Doxsey used his credit card to purchase gasoline, which he pumped into a container one hour before the fire, at a gas station in Lexington, where the fire occurred, although he lived in New Hampshire. An expert testified that the fire originated and burned intensely in a part of the truck where electrical malfunction was unlikely.

NEGLIGENTLY ALLOW FIRE DAMAGE
266, § 8

Elements

Type 1: Set Fire on Property of Another

- The suspect was *not* a tenant; and

- Set or increased a fire upon another person's land; and

- That person's property was injured.

Type 2: Negligent Spread of Fire

- The suspect negligently or willfully suffered any fire on his *own* land that extended beyond the property limits; and

- As a result, the woods or property of another person were injured.

Note: Probably the most common instance for this offense involves the caretaker or property owner starting a fire to burn trash and allowing it to spread onto a neighbor's property and cause damage.

Right of Arrest

Arrest for breach of peace in presence. Otherwise, complaint.

Penalty

HC NMT 2 yrs; or Fine NMT $1,000. *Special condition:* Town where fire occurred may sue, within 2 years, the offender and recover civil damages for cost of extinguishing the fire.

Related Offense

Injury or Destruction of Wood by Fire. Under 266, § 7, a person may not recklessly injure another person's "growing or standing wood" by setting fire or by increasing a fire already set. Penalty: HC NMT 2 yrs; or Fine NMT $1,000. Right of Arrest: Complaint. In addition, the § 7 offender is subject to an enhanced penalty if a firefighter is injured: SP NMT 10 yrs; or HC NMT 2½ yrs and Fine NMT $1,000.

ATTEMPTED ARSON
266, § 5A

Elements

- **Willfully attempt to burn.** The suspect willfully and maliciously:

    - Attempted to burn; or
    - Counseled or assisted another in an attempt to burn;

- **Any structure or property.** Any structure or property covered by 266, §§ 1, 2 and 5.

Attempt Defined

266, § 5A broadly defines an attempt as "the placing or distributing of any flammable, explosive or combustible material . . . or any device in or against any building, structure or property . . . in an arrangement . . . with the intent [to] <u>eventually</u> . . . burn."

Comm. v. Ali, 7 Mass. App. Ct. 120 (1979): The defendant placed a can of turpentine in a closet for use as an accelerant at a later date. The two or three week time span between this placement and the scheduled burning of the building constituted attempted arson. The use of the word "eventually" in § 5A was meant to include all acts of preparation, even those fairly distant from the anticipated arson. *Comm. v. Hunter*, 18 Mass. App. Ct. 217 (1984) (evidence of motive is typically powerful in these cases: here, the defendant faced serious financial difficulties; he had over-insured his building and knew his policy was about to be canceled for nonpayment).

Right of Arrest

Felony.

Penalty

SP NMT 10 yrs or HC NMT 2½ yrs; or Fine NMT $1,000.

BURNING INSURED PROPERTY
266, § 10

Elements

- **Willfully.** The suspect willfully; and

- **Fraudulently burned.** With intent to defraud an insurer;
    - Set fire to, burned, or caused to be burned; or
    - Counseled or aided in the burning of;

- **Property.** A building or personal property belonging to himself or another;

- **Fire insurance.** Which, at the time, was insured against loss by fire.

Right of Arrest

Felony.

Penalty

SP NMT 5 yrs or HC NMT 2½ yrs.

Notes

Failure to extinguish fire. The intent to defraud need not precede the fire. A suspect may be convicted under § 10 for an accidental fire that he intentionally failed to extinguish or report. *Comm. v. Cali*, 247 Mass. 20 (1923).

Suspect as beneficiary is relevant, but not required. The fact that the suspect is a beneficiary of the insurance policy is relevant, but it is not an element of this offense. *Comm. v. Kaplan*, 238 Mass. 250 (1921).

Persuasive indicators. *Comm. v. Lanagan*, 56 Mass. App. Ct. 659 (2002) (experiencing financial distress and increasing homeowners' insurance; moving valuable property from the home and placing it in storage before the blaze, then claiming to have "lost everything" afterwards; finally, defendant's explanation for fire inconsistent with real cause). *Comm. v. Asherowski*, 196 Mass. 342 (1907) (only suspect-owner had key and no evidence of forced entry; store goods were stacked at center of blaze; and insurance claim was exaggerated). *Comm v. Walter*, 10 Mass. App. Ct. 255 (1980) (defendants inside their store shortly before the fire, and they had shown a "peculiar" concern for when their neighboring shop owners were closing).

Dual convictions. A person may be convicted of arson of a dwelling or other building *and* arson with intent to defraud an insurance company. The reason is that each offense has one or more distinct elements. *Comm. v. Anolik*, 27 Mass. App. Ct. 701 (1989).

HINDERING A FIREFIGHTER
268, § 32A

Elements

- **Willfully hinder.** The suspect willfully obstructed, interfered with, or hindered;
- **Firefighter.** A firefighter or fire force in the lawful performance of their duty.

Right of Arrest

Felony.

Penalty

SP NMT 5 yrs or HC NLT 30 days, NMT 2½ yrs; and/or Fine NLT $100, NMT $1,000.

Notes

Citizen's mixed motives no defense. *Comm. v. Joyce,* 84 Mass. App. Ct. 574 (2013): When Fire Chief William Pearson arrived at a house fire, police informed him that Shawn Joyce had re-entered to save his pets. Pearson found Joyce in the kitchen and ordered him to leave. Joyce said "F-U." Pearson attempted to push him out the door. Police had to help. The struggle delayed Pearson in his duty to assess the fire and ensure the safety of everyone. Joyce deliberately obstructed a firefighter. Although he claimed he was only trying to save his pets, Joyce was not frantically looking for them when Pearson entered. In any case, mixed motives are not a defense to this crime.

FALSE FIRE ALARM
269, § 13

Purpose

This statute is written expansively to cover any false alarm. Thus, there is no restriction on the method used — e.g., it could be a bogus phone call or a prank scream.

Elements

- **No legitimate reason.** Without reasonable cause;
- **False report of fire.** The suspect made or circulated a false fire alarm.

Right of Arrest

Arrest for breach of peace in presence. Otherwise, complaint.

Penalty

HC NMT 1 year; and/or Fine NLT $100, NMT $500.

TAMPERING WITH FIRE ALARM
268, § 32

Elements

- **Fire, police, motorist signal.** With a fire or police signal system, or a motorist emergency signal system on a state highway;

- **False report or tamper with.** The suspect, without authority:

    - Opened signal box for purpose of, or succeeded in giving, a false alarm or call; or
    - Injured or defaced in any way the box; or
    - Opened or tampered with the box or any parts inside or connected to it.

Right of Arrest

For fire or police signal: 268, § 32 warrantless arrest in presence. *Note:* This statute only covers a false fire alarm involving a "signal box." If the false alarm is generated by another means, officers must use 269, § 13.

For motorist signal: Arrest for breach of peace in presence. Otherwise, complaint.

Penalty

Tamper police/fire signal: HC NMT 2 yrs; and/or Fine NLT $500, NMT $1,000.

Tamper motorist call box: Fine NLT $100, NMT $500.

PREVENTION & SAFETY CODE ENFORCEMENT

Purpose

After 100 people perished at the Station Nightclub in Rhode Island in 2003, fire safety officials in Massachusetts developed laws and procedures to prevent fires at entertainment venues.

Dangerous Condition on Premises — 148, § 34A

- ***Offense description.*** Any owner, lessee or other person having control or supervision of any "assembly use group building" (defined in state building code) may not cause or permit a dangerous condition to exist at any time.

- ***Dangerous condition.*** 148, § 34A defines a dangerous condition as:
  - Any blocked or impeded entrance or exit; or
  - Fail to maintain or shut off any mandated fire protection system; or
  - Storage of any flammable or explosive without a proper permit; or
  - Use of any firework or pyrotechnic device without a proper permit; or
  - Exceeding the occupancy limit established by the local building inspector pursuant to G.L. Chapter 143.

- ***Right of arrest.*** Arrest for breach of peace in presence. Otherwise, complaint. *2nd offense:* Felony.

- ***Penalty.*** HC NMT 2½ yrs; and/or Fine NMT $5,000. *2nd or subsequent:* SP NMT 5 yrs or HC NMT 2½ yrs; and/or Fine NMT $25,000.

- ***Civil alternative.*** Under 148A, any local or state code enforcement officer empowered to enforce the state building code (780 CMR) or fire code (527 CMR) may give a citation with an assessment or warning. The citation may require that the violation be corrected within 24 hours. Offenders must pay the fine within 21 days or request a hearing.

Removal of Fire Protection Devices — 148, § 27A

- ***Offense description.*** No owner, lessee, or other person having control or supervision of a building may: (1) shut off, disconnect, obstruct, remove, or destroy; (2) any part of any sprinkler system, water main, hydrant, or other device used for fire protection or carbon monoxide detection alarm; (3) without first obtaining a permit from the head of the local fire department. Exceptions are made for emergency situations. *Comm. v. Grafton*, 93 Mass. App. Ct. 717 (2018), (defendant had to prove he got fire permit before disabling system).

- ***Right of arrest:*** Complaint.

- ***Penalty.*** HC NMT 1 yr and/or Fine NMT $1,000.

Code Violation Causing Death — 148, § 34B

- **Offense description.** No person may: (1) recklessly; (2) violate the state building code or fire code; and, as a result, (3) cause serious bodily injury or death to any person. *Comm. v. Zhan Tang Huang*, 87 Mass. App. Ct. 65 (2015).

- **Right of arrest.** Felony.

- **Penalty.** SP NMT 5 yrs or HC NMT 2½ yrs; and/or Fine NMT $25,000.

Repeat Code Violation — 148, § 34C

- **Offense description.** No person may:

    - Commit a second or subsequent violation of the state building code or fire code (including any incorporated specialized codes); or
    - Violate any lawful order of the Fire Marshal, the head of a fire department, or a state or local building inspector; or
    - Continue to violate any code or order after receipt of notice.

- **Notice.** Under 148, § 34C, notice may be provided by in-hand service, by posting it conspicuously at the premises, or by issuing a citation under Chapter 148A.

- **Right of arrest.** Arrest for breach of peace in presence. Otherwise, complaint.

- **Penalty.** HC NMT 1 year; and/or Fine NMT $1,000.

Sale of or Give Away Novelty Lighter — 148, § 60

This law prohibits manufacturing, offering for sale, selling, giving away, or transporting a "novelty lighter." A novelty lighter has "physical or audio features" (other than its flame) that make it "appealing or attractive to a child under the age of 10" (e.g., its shape is a cartoon character, animal, musical instrument, or gun). The law does not apply to lighters manufactured before 1980 or ones imprinted with a logo, decal, or artwork that does not resemble a novelty lighter.

- **Right of Arrest.** Confiscate lighters as evidence. Complaint.

- **Penalty.** HC NMT 1 year; and/or Fine NLT $500, NMT $1,000.

Law Enforcement Dimensions

Part IX

OBSTRUCTION OF JUSTICE OFFENSES

Witness Interference, False Reports, Impersonation of Officer, Bribery, Perjury, and Court Default

Chapter 35

© John Sofis Scheft, Esq.
All rights reserved

35 Obstruction of Justice

WITNESS INTERFERENCE & OBSTRUCTION OF JUSTICE
268, § 13B

Elements

- ***Directly or indirectly.*** The suspect, directly or indirectly, willfully:

  - **Threatened, attempted or caused physical, emotional, economic, or property injury;** or
  - **Promised, offered, or conveyed "anything of value";** or
  - **Misled;** or
  - **Intimidated;** or
  - **Harassed.**

- ***Another person*** who is or was:

  - <u>A witness or potential witness</u> at any stage of a criminal investigation or other criminal proceeding;
  - <u>Aware of information</u>, documents or objects that relate to a violation of a criminal statute or the conditions of bail, probation, or parole; or
  - <u>Attending</u> (or making known his intention to attend) a *civil* proceeding or *criminal* proceeding; or
  - <u>Police officer</u> — including a federal agent or investigator; or
  - <u>Judicial or corrections official</u> — including a judge, clerk, court reporter, court interpreter, court officer, probation or parole officer, prosecutor, victim–witness advocate, defense attorney, or corrections officer; or
  - <u>Juror</u> or grand juror; or
  - <u>Family member</u> of any person protected by this law.

- ***With the intent <u>or</u> with reckless disregard to:***

  - **Impede, obstruct, delay, harm, punish, or "otherwise interfere" with any civil proceeding or any criminal investigation or proceeding** (including a criminal investigation, grand jury, trial, or any other criminal proceeding, probate court proceeding, juvenile proceeding, land proceeding, clerk's hearing, court-ordered mediation, or any other civil proceeding); or
  - **Harm or retaliate against any protected person or a member of their family** for participating in any of the proceedings described in this law.

Right of Arrest

Felony.

Penalty

Basic offense: SP NMT 10 yrs or HC NMT 2½ yrs; and/or Fine NLT $1,000, NMT $5,000.

If misconduct involves any crime punishable by SP life or related parole: SP NMT 20 yrs or HC NMT 2½ yrs; and/or Fine NMT $10,000.

Definitions

- **Investigator** refers to "an individual or group officially authorized by federal, state or local law to investigate, prosecute or defend any violation of federal or state law."

- **Harass** means to "engage in any act directed at a specific person or group of persons, which seriously alarms or annoys them and would cause a reasonable person to suffer substantial emotional distress [including the use of any electronic communication device]."

Venue

A § 13B offender may be prosecuted in the county where the criminal investigation or proceeding occurred, or where the illegal conduct took place. All violations may be brought in district or superior court. 218, § 76.

Notes

The bottom line for police officers — 3 major uses of § 13B.

1. **Lying to officer.** The law prohibits any person from — directly or indirectly — misleading a police officer with the intent to interfere with a criminal investigation.

2. **Intimidating potential witness.** An offender may not — directly or indirectly — threaten or intimidate even a potential witness, with the intent to interfere with any criminal investigation or court proceeding.

3. **Influencing potential witness.** On the other hand, an offender may not — directly or indirectly — offer or provide "anything of value" to even a potential witness in an effort to interfere with any criminal investigation or court proceeding.

Lying to Officer

Mislead. The SJC defined the term "mislead" in *Comm. v. Figueroa*, 464 Mass. 365 (2013), a case where the defendant was convicted for lying to his parole officer about his whereabouts on Halloween night. Mislead means:

1. Knowingly making a false statement; or
2. Intentionally leaving out information to create a false impression; or
3. Deliberately recommending that authorities rely on a false written statement, photograph, or other item.

To qualify as misleading, the statement must be a lie or incomplete in a way that "reasonably could lead investigators to pursue a materially different course of investigation." *Comm. v. Paquette*, 475 Mass. 793 (2016): Raymond Paquette hosted a party at his father's house. Two guests, Patrick Bousquet and Tyler Spath, got into an argument in the kitchen. Bousquet hit Spath over the head with a glass bottle, slicing open Spath's head and neck. A larger fight erupted, and Paquette told everyone to go home. As Spath left for the hospital, Paquette told him not to tell anyone he was there.

State Police troopers interviewed Paquette twice. During the first interview, Paquette said he hosted the party, but that he was outside picking up beer cans at the time of the fight. He said he "saw a bunch of commotion" and ran inside after the fight was over.

Police continued their investigation and arrested Bousquet. Several guests placed Paquette in the kitchen at the time of the fight, attempting to mediate the verbal argument between Bousquet and Spath.

When Paquette was interviewed the second time, the troopers told him what the other partygoers said. Paquette insisted that he was on sleep medication and had been "blackout drunk" during the party.

Paquette was charged with two counts of misleading a police officer. However, under § 13B, the term misleads only includes lies that "reasonably could lead investigators to pursue a materially different course of investigation."

- **Material means significant or important.**

- **Witnesses ordinarily have no obligation to disclose information to police. However, if they do speak, they must tell the truth.**

- **Paquette's statements at the first interview were misleading.** The investigation was still in its early stages, and Paquette lied about the location of the fight and misrepresented that he did not know the identities of those involved. Paquette's statements reasonably could have influenced the investigation in a significant way.

- **His statements at the second interview were *not* misleading.** At that point, the police had already conducted an extensive investigation, and Bousquet had been arrested. Paquette's false information would not have led them to pursue a different investigation. Compare *Comm. v. Gomez*, 2017 WL 3122324 (Appeals Court) (immediately following a motor vehicle accident, the intoxicated defendant told the only witness to leave the scene; when police arrived, he told them that "the other guy" was driving, but gave evasive answers to officers' questions about the driver's identity; these misrepresentations were "made to send the police off course").

- **Federal law is better.** Under 18 U.S.C. § 1001, making a materially false statement to a federal law enforcement officer is a crime regardless of its possible effect on the investigation. *U.S. v. Phillipos*, 849 F.3d 464 (1st Cir. 2017).

Document extra effort. *Comm. v. Condon*, 99 Mass. App. Ct. 27 (2020): After failing to find David Condon during a week-long sexual assault investigation, Detective Ulrich interviewed him by telephone. At the end of the conversation, he asked Condon where he currently lived. Condon provided a fake address. Even though Detective Ulrich searched for the non-existent address, the Appeals Court said that the fake info was not misleading because it did not cause the police "[to] think about . . . the case in a materially different manner." While the detective wasted some time and effort as a result of Condon's lie, he was still able to obtain an arrest warrant.

The lesson from this case: Investigators should document the extra work that resulted from the offender's lie, especially any false leads that they pursued. In short, the defendant's lie has to significantly impact how the investigation is conducted.

§ 13B does not cover an "attempt to mislead" a police officer. *Comm. v. Larsen*, 2018 WL 5304456 (Appeals Court): An intoxicated woman fractured her skull in the holding cell. Surveillance video showed the woman being pushed by someone and falling. In his incident report, Officer Larsen wrote that the woman walked into the cell but then charged forward as he was closing the door. He placed his arm out to stop her. She walked into his hand, lost her balance, and fell backwards.

During his interview with the investigating officer, Officer Larsen repeated the information in his report. Although Larsen's statements were false and intended to mislead, they could not have affected the course of the police investigation because the investigating officer had already viewed the surveillance video.

His lies could not be prosecuted as an *attempt* to mislead either, because that crime is not defined in § 13B.

Proof of defendant's motive for lying not required. *Comm. v. Fortuna*, 80 Mass. App. Ct. 45 (2011).

Retracting false statement does not nullify original crime. *Comm. v. Caminero*, 2015 WL 4249147 (Appeals Court) (defendant was still guilty of misleading a police officer even though she voluntarily told police that, two days earlier, she had lied to officers about her brother's whereabouts after an arson in which he was a suspect).[1]

No violation if:

- **Subjective comment or general denial.** *Comm. v. Morse*, 468 Mass. 360 (2014): Steven Morse was driving a motorboat when it struck a kayak and killed an 11 year old boy. He admitted to police that he drank beer, but denied consuming other substances that impaired him. Although police later discovered that Morse had also smoked marijuana before the collision, there was no 13B violation because officers did not ask him a factual question (Did you consume any other drug?). Instead, they asked whether he was "impaired" by another drug. It is difficult to prove that someone's opinion is a lie. Furthermore, the court found Morse's simple answer — "no" — was a denial of guilt, not a fabrication designed to send the police off course. After his response, the police were in the same position they would have been in if he had remained silent.

---

1 Interestingly, the perjury *per se* statute, 268, § 1, does protect a witness who retracts an earlier lie. See discussion later in this chapter.

- **Sham investigation.** *Comm. v. Occhiuto*, 88 Mass. App. Ct. 489 (2015): Nicholas Occhiuto was the target of a drug investigation. A cooperating witness, "Olive," agreed to buy heroin from Occhiuto with marked money. During the transaction, Occhiuto and his partner stole the money from Olive and drove away.

  Police developed a ruse to get the men to the station and obtain information from them. They had Trooper Millet stop the car on the pretext that he had observed a road rage incident. He frisked the men and confiscated the money. When they became angry, Millet gave them a receipt and told them they could go to the State Police barracks to complain. They did.

  Lt. Hughes invented a sham investigation into Trooper Millet's conduct. Occhiuto agreed to be interviewed. Hughes and FBI Special Agent Wood asked him about the stop and removal of money. Then Agent Wood asked, "Now, just for our clarification, so we can show in court if we have to — where did you get your money from . . . so we can prove this is your money?" Occhiuto said he earned it working "under the table." He refused to identify his employer. This lie resulted in his indictment under 13B.

  However, 13B only applies to investigations that *may* result in prosecution. The investigation of Trooper Millet was a sham designed solely to incriminate Occhiuto. Occhiuto knew nothing about the real drug investigation, so he could not have intended to lie about it.

- **Swallowing drugs.** *Comm. v. Tejeda*, 476 Mass. 817 (2017) (swallowing is not misleading under 13B; it is concealing evidence under 13E). See 268, § 13E later in this chapter.

Intimidating Potential Witness

Persons furnishing information to law enforcement protected.

- **Direct interference.** *Comm. v. Fragata*, 480 Mass. 121 (2018) (defendant snatched victim's cell phone and later choked her to prevent her from calling 911).

- **Indirect threat to victim.** *Comm. v. King*, 69 Mass. App. Ct. 113 (2007): Michael King robbed a convenience store at gunpoint. King said to the clerk: "If I see you on the evening news, I'm coming back to kill you and your family." King argued that this threat was only designed to prevent media, not police involvement! However, § 13B covers direct and *indirect* threats. King's media reference recognized that his robbery would be news *only if* the victim called police. His goal was to prevent any investigation. *Comm. v. Carvalho*, 88 Mass. App. Ct. 840 (2016).

- **Threat to intermediary.**

  - *Civilian. Comm. v. Valentin V.*, 83 Mass. App. Ct. 202 (2013): Fred and Valentin were both under suspicion for stealing an Xbox from school. At a meeting with school officials, Valentin referred to Fred as a "snitch" and stated that he was "going to get him." Valentin made the threat with the intent that school administrators communicate it to Fred. His remarks were designed to interfere with the investigation.

  - *Law enforcement. Comm. v. Gomez*, 2014 WL 5347625 (Appeals Court): Julio Gomez attacked a woman and tried to force his penis into her mouth. The woman's son and his boyfriend witnessed the attack and called police. Gomez was arrested. He looked up from the street at the witness' apartment and angrily told an officer: "If it was one of those homos that called police, I'll take care of them." While Gomez's statement may have been motivated by anger over his arrest, he should have expected that the officer would communicate his threat to his potential targets so they could protect themselves.

Witnesses in civil court also protected. *Comm. v. Arrocho*, 2020 WL 2130607 (Appeals Court): DCF was involved with Roberto Arrocho's family for a year prior to a decision to take away his child. After a hearing, Arrocho left a voice mail for a DCF employee who had appeared in court. Arrocho said that DCF had messed him up, and he was having "homicidal and suicidal thoughts" and would "see" the DCF employee "soon." His intent to intimidate could be inferred.

If defendant _intends_ to intimidate, the crime occurs — whether or not the victim is afraid.

- **Civilians.** *Comm. v. Rivera*, 76 Mass. App. Ct. 530 (2010): While on patrol, an officer observed three men standing around a fourth man on the ground. He appeared to have been assaulted. As the officer approached, Rivera, who was one of the three males, said: "We were just joking around." Then Rivera turned to the victim and yelled in a "hard" voice: "We were just joking around, right?" The victim was transported to the hospital for minor injuries. He agreed to cooperate, saying that he was not afraid of Rivera.

  The victim's personal reaction is irrelevant. The issue is "whether the defendant acted or spoke with the intent to impede, obstruct, or interfere with a criminal investigation." In *Rivera*, the *goal* of the defendant had been to scare the victim. That's enough.

- **Police officers.** *Comm. v. Wood*, 2012 WL 3052901 (Appeals Court): Sergeant Horton and Officer Brady were ordered to appear in court for a probation matter involving Derrick Wood. In the courthouse, Wood yelled at the officers: "You're fucking me over. You guys are bitches. Why are you doing this to me? You'll get yours." These officers were witnesses. The fact that Wood tried to frighten them was enough for conviction.

A defendant may possess more than one intention. *Comm. v. Rosario*, 83 Mass. App. Ct. 640 (2013): Angel Rosario, who had a pending trial for stabbing Joseph Alvarado, was at the courthouse for a probation meeting. Knowing that Alvarado was also there for an unrelated offense, Rosario waited for an hour after his meeting. When Alvarado passed by him, Rosario mimicked shooting a gun and said, "You're going to die."

Rosario argued that his threat was a result of longstanding animosity toward Alvarado for dating his girlfriend, but the court believed Rosario's threats were, at least in part, designed to affect Alvarado's testimony against him. Mixed motives are enough for witness intimidation.

Intimidation depends on the surrounding circumstances, not just the words spoken.

- **Civilians.** *Comm. v. Nordstrom*, 100 Mass. App. Ct. 493 (2021) (defendant's voice was loud and she refused to take "no" for an answer when she demanded the victim recant his allegation of sexual assault).

  Comm. v. Frazier, 2021 WL 1561358 (Appeals Court): Raymond Frazier attended the sexual assault trial of his brother. Frazier sent the female victim a Facebook message:

"U fuck my bro life up u lied in court what kind of peace [sic] of shit are you stop spreading [sic] your legs." Especially given its sexually explicit language, this message was intimidating. *Comm. v. Middleton* 100 Mass. App. Ct. 756 (2022).

- **Police officers.** *Comm. v. Casiano*, 70 Mass. App. Ct. 705 (2007): While waiting in court, David Casiano pointed his cell phone camera at a police officer who was testifying against him on drug charges. He pressed buttons as if he were taking pictures. When the officer confiscated the camera, Casiano said that he had already emailed the pictures over the internet. The officer worked undercover and believed that if his picture was posted on the internet, he and his family would be in danger. He checked the internet for several days. It was irrelevant whether pictures were actually taken, so long as the threat was credible and designed to intimidate this police witness.

The intimidation must be designed to affect an actual or potential investigation.

- **Sufficient.** *Comm. v. Nicholson*, 2012 WL 1658372 (Appeals Court): Less than two hours after Detective Michael McAuliffe questioned Michael Nicholson's wife about a criminal investigation, Nicholson telephoned the detective and said: "If I come down there this afternoon, I may not be fuckin' happy with you . . . you better have your fighting suit on." McAuliffe was concerned enough to issue a "be on the lookout" alert to other officers.

    Nicholson drove to the station that afternoon, passed several empty public parking spots, entered the area where officers park their private vehicles, and used his cell phone to take photographs. He drove off quickly when officers approached him. Clearly, Nicholson's words and actions were intended to intimidate McAuliffe during an investigation.

- **Insufficient.** *Comm. v. Hickey*, 2012 WL 2093338 (Appeals Court): Robert Hickey rear-ended a car with his pickup truck. He became agitated and uncooperative when confronted by police, who told him: "Calm down or you're going to get arrested." The police took Hickey to the hospital and went back to the station. Hickey was belligerent with medical personnel, so police were called back. When officers told Hickey to calm down, he responded: "What, they sent five of you . . . I'll take all you fucking guys!" He got up and pointed his finger in an assaultive manner. He was arrested for intimidation of a witness.

    The police were at the hospital in response to Hickey's disruptive behavior. Since his threat was not connected to the investigation of his vehicle accident, it could not be the basis of a 13B charge. Disorderly conduct would have been a better option because Hickey engaged in tumultuous behavior in the hospital.[2]

The defendant does not have to be the first aggressor. *Comm. v. Coggeshall*, 2019 WL 1492685 (Appeals Court): The 19 year old victim had accused Joseph Coggeshall's nephew of rape. While walking home, the victim saw Coggeshall following her in his truck. She lost sight of the truck, then Coggeshall appeared in front of her and would not let her pass. He told her his nephew did not rape her. The victim unsuccessfully tried to push past Coggeshall, then kicked him in the groin. Coggeshall responded by punching her in the eye. As she lay on the ground, Coggeshall again yelled that she should say it was all untrue. Even though the victim used force first, Coggeshall was guilty of witness intimidation.

---

2 For more on disorderly conduct, see *Chapter 23*.

Restraining order violation may result in a separate charge of intimidation. This occurs when the defendant violates the order with the goal of convincing the victim to alter her testimony or refuse to testify. *Comm. v. Braun*, 2013 WL 1294126 (Appeals Court).

Threat to bring post-verdict legal action may be intimidation. *Comm. v. Simeone*, 2014 WL 5347627 (Appeals Court) (defendant told the victim he was going to sue her when the assault case against him was over; this demonstrated an intent to obstruct her from testifying; if made in a threatening manner, statements about suing the victim after the criminal case ends are not protected by the First Amendment).

Outcome of underlying criminal case irrelevant. Even if the defendant is acquitted after the witness testifies, the government may still go forward on the 13B charge. This rule recognizes that intimidation of *any* witness deters other citizens from coming forward and threatens the integrity of the system. *Comm. v. Wiencis*, 48 Mass. App. Ct. 688 (2000).

Intimidation includes retaliation for past participation. *Comm. v. Cathy C.*, 64 Mass. App. Ct. 471 (2005). *Hrycenko v. Comm.*, 459 Mass. 503 (2011).

Out-of-state conduct is still intimidation if it pertains to a Massachusetts proceeding. *Comm. v. Nurse*, 2015 WL 3618136 (Appeals Court) (defendant claimed he was out of state when he sent text messages and voicemails; the victim received these in Connecticut; this was still witness intimidation because the defendant knew he faced serious charges in Massachusetts for invading the victim's home).

Consider less serious crime. *Comm. v. Ramos*, 2013 WL 4029209 (Appeals Court): After Nilton Ramos was handcuffed and placed in the back of a cruiser, he said to an officer: "I'm going to shoot you motherfuckers as soon as I get out!" The police wisely used their discretion and did not charge Ramos with the 13B felony. Instead, they added a charge of threat to commit a crime to his original charge of disorderly conduct.

Caution: Officers must avoid witness interference too.

- **Intimidation.** *Comm. v. Teixeira*, 76 Mass. App. Ct. 101 (2010): The defendant was charged with malicious destruction of property after a night of drinking. One witness was a police officer's niece. The officer learned from his brother that his niece was afraid because the defendant said something to her. The officer, accompanied by his partner, approached the defendant the day before trial and said: "You fuck with my family and we will kill you; I will make you disappear" and, "If nothing happens at trial tomorrow, you're going to have to deal with us every day."

    Needless to say, the court was concerned about the officer's threat to kill, and his implied threat that the defendant's acquittal would lead to continuing police harassment. Ironically, this officer likely violated the same witness intimidation law that the defendant was charged with.

    Police officers must not intervene in cases involving family members. It is a conflict of interest because an officer's professional judgment may be compromised by his family loyalty. In *Teixeira*, the officer would have been wise to refer the matter to a detective at the outset.

- **Influence.** *Comm. v. Ruano*, 87 Mass. App. Ct. 98 (2015): A police officer lost his temper when he believed the victim's car was blocking his SUV. He pushed the victim with his vehicle. The next day, after learning the victim reported the incident to police, the officer asked him to recant. He said he was in danger of losing his job and pension, and that he had two daughters. He told the victim that if he recanted, the victim "could make 200 plus friends," "have the key to the city" and "if he got in trouble, he could get out of trouble." They shook hands. Clearly, the officer offered something of value in exchange for the victim's changed testimony.

Witness Protection Program

A statewide witness protection program is administered by the Executive Office of Public Safety & Security (EOPSS). The five-member board includes the Secretary of EOPSS (who serves as chair), Attorney General, State Police Colonel, one chief of police and a designated district attorney. District attorneys apply for resources — including armed escorts, relocation, and housing expenses. Three or more members of the board must approve. However, exigent circumstances justify certain temporary measures by a prosecutor prior to the board's approval. 263A, § 1.

Related Offenses

Disclosure of Witness Protection Participant. 263A, § 13. No one may disclose anyone's participation in the witness protection program in a way that poses a risk of harm. Penalty: HC NMT 2½ yrs; and/or Fine NMT $5,000. Right of Arrest: Arrest for breach of peace in presence. Otherwise, complaint.

Distribution of Grand Jury Testimony. 268, § 13D. No one may distribute, or possess with the intent to distribute, a grand jury transcript with the intent to obstruct a criminal proceeding or witness. Penalty: SP NMT 5 yrs or HC NMT 2½ yrs; and/or Fine NMT $5,000. Right of Arrest: Felony. Under 13D, a judge may issue a protective order to prevent counsel from giving a grand jury transcript to the defendant if necessary to protect a witness or victim.

TAMPERING OR DESTRUCTION OF EVIDENCE
268, § 13E

Elements

- *Attempt or actually alter, destroy, or conceal.* The suspect knowingly attempted or actually altered, destroyed, or concealed;

- *Evidence.* Any written or tangible (i.e., physical) evidence;

- *Intent to affect court.* With the intent to impair a current or future court, grand jury, or official state proceeding.

Right of Arrest

Felony.

Penalty

When the evidence relates to a violation of a criminal statute: SP NMT 10 yrs or HC NMT 2½ yrs; and/or Fine NMT $25,000.

When evidence relates to an ethics or campaign finance violation, or civil enforcement by the Attorney General: SP NMT 5 yrs or HC NMT 2½ yrs; and/or Fine NMT $10,000.

Notes

The evidence does not have to be admissible. 13E states that the prosecution does *not* have to prove that the evidence – which was altered, destroyed or concealed by the defendant – would have been admissible in court. The prosecutor simply must show that the item affected was evidence (i.e., proof of the underlying criminal matter at issue).

Intent proven by suspect's actions. *Comm. v. Martinez*, 98 Mass. App. Ct. 545 (2020): Jose Martinez, a court officer, was arraigned on 11 charges relating to sexual assaults. He called a fellow court officer and asked him to find a cell phone that Martinez kept in the courthouse, then smash the phone and throw it into the river. Instead, the court officer reported Martinez's call. The cell phone held images of Martinez's penis and the breasts and genitals of unknown women.

Martinez admitted to making the call to the court officer, but said his intent was to spare his family embarrassment, not destroy evidence. The jury was free to disbelieve Martinez, who lied to investigators about the existence of the phone and asked a fellow employee to get rid of it. In the past, Martinez had repeatedly shown the images to others at the courthouse even though his wife also worked there.

<u>Never</u> choke a suspect who swallows drugs; charge 13E and provide medical assistance. Restraint techniques that involve squeezing the trachea, windpipe, or throat area to stop a suspect from swallowing drugs are very dangerous and illegal. See 6E, § 14(c) ("[a] law enforcement officer shall not use a chokehold"; notice that there are no exceptions to this police standard) and § 1 (definition of chokehold). Instead, when officers have probable cause that a suspect swallowed a controlled substance, they should:

- **Arrest the suspect for the underlying drug crime <u>and</u> for concealing evidence under 13E.**

- **Request that emergency medical services (EMS) evaluate the suspect's condition.**

Venue. A prosecution under 13E may be brought where the official proceeding was or would have been, or where the misconduct took place.

TAKING OR DISSEMINATING IMAGES OF VICTIMS
271, § 51

Type 1: Recording image

- **First responder.** A law enforcement officer, firefighter, EMT, or other person whose usual duties include rendering assistance at a crime, accident, or emergency scene;

- **Official duty.** Responded to or was present at the scene of a crime, accident, or emergency;

- **Took a photograph or digital image of a victim.** Took a photograph or digital image of a victim, *unless* done in the performance of duty *or* with permission.

Type 2: Disseminating image

- **First responder.** A first responder (same definition);

- **Showed another person.** Transmitted, disseminated, or made available to another person without proper permission.

- **A victim's image.** An image of a victim of a crime, accident, or emergency.

Exemptions

- **BWC.** A bodyworn or vehicle camera was properly used.

- **Official duty.** Recording or disseminating the image was part of the officer's official duty.

- **With permission.** The recording was made or disseminated with the permission of the victim or the victim's immediate family member, which is defined as "a spouse, child, step-child, adopted child, sibling, step sibling, adopted sibling, parent, step-parent, legal guardian, adoptive parent, grandparent or grandchild."

Right of Arrest

Complaint, unless a breach of peace in presence.

Penalty

HC NMT 1 year; and/or Fine NMT $2,000.

FALSE REPORT TO PUBLIC SAFETY DISPATCH
269, § 14B

Elements

Type 1: False Information

- **Willful.** The suspect willfully and maliciously communicated with *or* caused a communication;

- **PSAP.** To a PSAP (an emergency 911 dispatch center);

- **False.** Concerning information that the suspect knew *or* had reason to know was false;

- **Emergency response.** Which resulted in the dispatch of emergency services to a nonexistent emergency *or* to the wrong location of an actual emergency.

Type 2: Silent Calls

- **Willful.** The suspect willfully and maliciously made *or* caused to be made;

- **3 silent calls.** 3 or more "silent calls";

- **PSAP.** To a PSAP (an emergency 911 dispatch center);

- **3 responses.** Which resulted in the dispatch of services 3 or more times.

Right of Arrest

1st *offense:* Complaint. While certainly a breach of the peace, this violation will probably never occur in the actual presence of an officer.

2nd *or subsequent offense:* Felony.

Penalty

1st *offense:* HC NMT 2½ yrs; or Fine NMT $1,000.

2nd *or subsequent:* SP NMT 10 yrs or HC NMT 2½ yrs; and/or Fine NMT $5,000.

Definitions

- **Emergency response services:** Police, fire, EMS, "private safety department or other public safety agency."

- **PSAP:** A facility "assigned the responsibility of receiving 911 calls and, as appropriate, directly dispatching emergency response services or . . . relaying emergency 911 calls to other public or private safety agencies . . . ." It is not required for the caller to dial 911 — a business line is sufficient. The crime must involve a PSAP, but not a particular line.

- **Silent Call:** "[A] call or other communication made to a PSAP in which the initiating party fails to provide information regarding his identity or location or the nature of the emergency." *Note:* The fact that the 911 system automatically shows an address or phone number is *not* considered communication from the initiating caller.

FALSE REPORT OF CRIME TO POLICE
269, § 13A

Elements

- ***Intentionally make or cause.*** The suspect intentionally made, or caused someone to make;

- ***False crime report.*** A false report of a crime to the police.

Right of Arrest

If the report is made directly to an officer in the field, arrest for breach of peace in presence. However, a false report called in by phone would not satisfy the in presence requirement, so a complaint application is the only option.

Penalty

HC NMT 1 year; and/or Fine NLT $100, NMT $500.

Notes

Substantially inaccurate. *Comm. v. Fortuna*, 80 Mass. App. Ct. 45 (2011) decided that § 13A requires a "substantially inaccurate" account of a crime — not just an untrue detail about it. See *Comm. v. Salyer*, 84 Mass. App. Ct. 346 (2013) (defendant gave police a copy of a threatening email she claimed was sent by her ex-boyfriend; she obviously fabricated the email because her ex-boyfriend's email address for the past 10 years was misspelled). *Comm. v. Dahdah*, 2014 WL 470358 (Appeals Court) (defendant falsely told police that a Burger King manager had grabbed his arm and twisted it behind his back; witnesses stated that the manager never touched the defendant and that they heard the defendant threaten to lie about the manager if he called police).

Related Offenses

False Report of the Location of a Dangerous Item. 269, § 14 (felony). *Chapter 19.*

False Fire Alarm. 269, § 13 (misdemeanor: complaint). *Chapter 34.*

False Call from a Fire Alarm, Police Signal, or Motorist Highway Signal. 268, § 32 (misdemeanor: § 32 warrantless arrest in presence); *Chapter 34.*

False Statement Concerning Vehicle Theft. 268, § 39 (misdemeanor: complaint). See *LED's Motor Vehicle Law, Chapter 12.*

Law Enforcement Dimensions

IMPERSONATION OF A POLICE OFFICER
268, § 33

Elements

- **Pretend to be officer.** The suspect pretended to be a police officer; and

- **Behave as if an officer.** "Acted as such or required a person to aid or assist him in a matter pertaining to the duty of such officer."

Right of Arrest

Arrest for breach of peace in presence. Observing this conduct in the field would clearly qualify as a breach of peace. Otherwise, complaint.

Penalty

HC NMT 1 year; or Fine NMT $400.

Other Officials Covered

In addition to police officers, § 33 also penalizes impersonating a justice of the peace; notary public; sheriff or deputy; medical examiner; constable; probation officer; or investigator of the Registry of Motor Vehicles, Department of Public Utilities, Alcoholic Beverages Control Commission, Bureau of Special Investigations, or Department of Revenue.

Notes

The impostor must pretend <u>and</u> act like a police officer. *Comm. v. Widberg*, 2015 WL 5009275 (Appeals Court) (defendant told the victim he needed to ask her some questions, followed her, and said he was a Boston police officer in an attempt to get her to stop and pay attention). The same standard applies to the federal version of this crime. 18 U.S.C. § 912.

Actual police officer, who deliberately misrepresents her authority or jurisdiction, commits this crime. *Comm. v. Nordstrom*, 100 Mass. App. Ct. 493 (2021): When Danelle French and Hilma Nordstrom arrived without notice at the victim's house, they identified themselves as police officers. They were not in uniform and showed no identification. The victim invited them in. French and Nordstrom talked about a sexual assault the victim had reported to police involving an assailant who was, in reality, French's brother and Nordstrom's son. They argued with the victim that he should now recant his previous allegation.

At trial, Nordstrom admitted that she lied about being a police officer. French testified that she was, in fact, a military police officer. But this was no defense because French knew she had no investigative authority or jurisdiction whatsoever. Both women presented themselves at the victim's door as though they had authority to act as police officers in this particular investigation. Their lie persuaded the victim to allow them to enter his home and talk about his victimization by their family member.

Related Offenses

Disguise with Intent to Hinder an Officer. 268, § 34 penalizes the person who *"disguises* himself with the intent to obstruct . . . or to intimidate, hinder or interrupt an officer . . . in the lawful performance of his duty." Penalty: HC NMT 1 year; or Fine NMT $500. Right of Arrest: Complaint — although, if it occurred in the presence of an officer, an arrest could be made for this obvious breach of peace. *Comm. v. Healey*, 17 Mass. App. Ct. 537 (1984) (absent some type of physical disguise, a suspect may not be charged with this offense).

Unlawful Possession of Badge. 268, § 35 prohibits unauthorized individuals, "with the intent to assume an official character," from making or simply possessing "a badge or thing in the likeness of an official badge" of a police officer, firefighter or other town officer. Penalty: Fine NMT $50. This penalty is too low in the author's opinion. Right of Arrest: Arrest for breach of peace in presence. Otherwise, complaint.

FALSE WRITTEN REPORT BY PUBLIC OFFICER
268, § 6A

Elements

- **Public employee.** The suspect was a police officer or other government employee; and
- **Official duty.** In the course of his official duties;
- **Knowingly filed.** The suspect knowingly executed, filed or published;
- **False report.** Any written report with false information of a *material* nature.

Right of Arrest

Complaint.

Penalty

HC NMT 1 year; and/or Fine NMT $1,000.

Notes

False statement must be clear. *Comm. v. Kelley*, 35 Mass. App. Ct. 745 (1994) (the government claimed that a police officer lied in his report to cover up illegal activity by a tow company, but the meaning of his report was ambiguous and equally consistent with innocence). *Comm. v. McHugh*, 2021 WL 5236603 (Appeals Court) (the jury could consider the victim's injuries — a seven day hospital stay to treat bruises and abrasions on his face, seven broken ribs, and a fractured vertebra — and conclude that the police officer defendant learned of the extent of the victim's injuries and wrote his report to cover up his unreasonable use force during the off-duty arrest and the involvement of a co-defendant in the assault on the victim).

False statement must be "material" or significant. *Comm. v. Garvey*, 99 Mass. App. Ct. 139 (2021) (officer's report contained false statements that the victim blocked access to an intoxicated subject and bumped the officer several times; these false statements were material to understanding whether the officer was justified in using OC spray and her baton).

An officer may not excuse his filing of a false report on the grounds that he was following orders. *Comm. v. Luna*, 418 Mass. 749 (1994) (defendant police officer included false statements in his search warrant affidavit in connection with a murder investigation; the officer could not defend his blatantly illegal action on the basis that his superiors directed him to do this).

BRIBERY
268A, § 2

Elements

Type 1: Accepting a bribe

- A public employee may never, *with corrupt intent*, ask, demand, or agree to receive;
- Anything of value;
- In exchange for performing an official favor, committing fraud on a public agency, or promising to take official action or inaction.

Type 2: Offering a bribe

- A person may never, *with corrupt intent*, give, offer, or promise;
- Anything of value;
- To a public employee;
- For the purpose of influencing the official to act or fail to act, or to commit a fraud on any government agency, in violation of his lawful duty.

Right of Arrest

Felony.

Penalty

SP NMT 10 yrs or HC NMT 2½ yrs; and/or Fine NMT $100,000. Upon final conviction, defendant is not allowed to hold any state, county, or municipal office.

Notes

Offering or accepting bribe. The law punishes both the person who offers the bribe and the official who accepts it. The bribe does not have to come from a private party. A public employee may bribe another public employee. *Comm. v. Wooldridge*, 19 Mass. App. Ct. 162 (1985) (police officer bribed another officer).

- **No defense that bribe not accepted.** The fact that the police do not take the bribe is no defense. *Comm. v. Ellerbe*, 430 Mass. 769 (2000) (police found cocaine in defendant's vehicle; she said: "What can I do to make this go away? I'll give you $10,000 if you let me go").

- **No defense that bribe could not affect outcome of case.** In *Comm. v. Corey*, 10 Mass. App. Ct. 873 (1980), the defendant offered a bribe to an officer to get him to drop a case involving a minor who had been arrested with a case of beer outside his liquor store. The defendant was convicted even though, at the time of his offer, it was impossible for the officer to alter the outcome because he had already filed his report.

Corrupt intent. The direct or indirect offer *to provide* something for certain official action (or inaction) indicates corrupt intent. A public employee's agreement *to receive* something of value does too. The item offered or accepted does not have to be money. Anything of value qualifies. *Comm. v. Gallo*, 2 Mass. App. Ct. 636 (1974) (home improvements). *Comm. v. Qualter*, 19 Mass. App. Ct. 970 (1985).

DEFAULT FROM A COURT APPEARANCE
276, § 82A

Elements

- **Released.** The suspect was released on bail or personal recognizance by a judge, magistrate, or bail commissioner; and

- **Notice.** As a condition of release, was informed of the date and time on which he was required to appear in court; and

- **Failed to appear.** He failed to appear in court without sufficient excuse.

Arrest Procedure

Whenever a defendant defaults, a warrant issues on the underlying charge(s). At that point, some courts automatically issue an additional 82A complaint for failure to appear. If a particular court does not do that, then officers should apply for one when they bring the suspect to court on the default warrant.

Penalty

If defendant charged with misdemeanor: HC NMT 1 year; and/or Fine NMT $10,000.

If felony charge: SP NMT 5 yrs or HC NMT 2½ yrs; and/or Fine NMT $50,000.

Condition: "A term of imprisonment [for an 82A violation] shall be consecutive to any other imprisonment for the offense for which the prisoner failed to appear."

Notes

§ 82A is perhaps the most underrated charge in the court system. Defendants often benefit from being absent — witnesses become unavailable, victims lose interest, evidence gets lost. By taking out § 82A complaints against those who default, police ensure that, if all else fails, they are able to go forward on a criminal offense that carries a potential jail sentence.

Released on bail or recognizance. This offense applies to every defendant because it covers those released on bail as well as those granted recognizance. "Personal recognizance" means that a person is released on his own promise to appear, without having to post any money.

Informed of date and time of appearance. The defendant must have been informed of the date and time to appear in court. This can usually be shown by obtaining a copy of the bail receipt signed by the defendant. For a case already before the court, the docket should reflect that the defendant was informed.

"Without sufficient excuse" means the absence was deliberate. The government must prove the suspect's absence was deliberate. While an accident or illness might be legitimate, it is not an excuse if the defendant feared the outcome of his trial.

82A is a separate crime and must be proven. *Sclamo v. Comm.*, 352 Mass. 576 (1967) (judge simply ordered defendant to serve a year in jail when defendant said, "I just kind of took off," in response to the judge's demand that he explain his absence from court; this was improper; the defendant was entitled to a trial). *Comm. v. Coleman*, 390 Mass. 797 (1984).

PERJURY
268, §§ 1, 1A, and 2

Purpose & Summary

The goal of our legal system is justice. The crime of perjury preserves the integrity of our system. Three statutes convey four ways to commit perjury: (1) lie under oath; (2) make inconsistent statements (known as "perjury *per se*"); (3) lie in a document; or (4) get someone else to lie under oath (known as "subornation of perjury").

Elements

Type 1: Spoken Perjury

- The suspect knowingly;
- Made a false statement during testimony under oath in court or another hearing; and
- The falsehood was "material," meaning that it reasonably tended to affect the determination of a relevant issue or the outcome of a proceeding.

Type 2: Perjury Per Se

- The suspect knowingly (and not as a result of a good faith mistake);
- Gave two obviously inconsistent statements about a material issue during the course of a criminal proceeding concerning a violent crime. [*Note:* The government does not have to prove which statement is false. Also, the witness may avoid perjury if he admits to lying *before* it affects the criminal proceeding or *before* it has or will be exposed.]

Type 3: Written Perjury

- The suspect knowingly made a material false statement;
- In a written document signed "under the penalties of perjury."

Type 4: Subornation of Perjury. The suspect convinced another person to commit perjury in one of the ways mentioned above.

Right of Arrest

Felony.

Penalty

Perjury during a trial of a capital crime: SP Life or any term of years.

Any other case: SP NMT 20 yrs or HC NMT 2½ yrs; and/or Fine NMT $1,000.

Notes

Knowing and material falsehood. The suspect must *know* he is lying. The false statement must be significant to the trial, hearing, or document. It is not necessary that the false statement *actually* affect the outcome, only that it had the potential to do so. *Comm. v. Kelley*, 33 Mass. App. Ct. 934 (1992). *Comm. v. Cerveny*, 373 Mass. 345 (1977) (statements made on forms signed by the defendant under the penalties of perjury were materially false because they were intended to fix per diem rates for nursing homes; his lies increased the amount of money his business got).

Type 1: Spoken perjury. 268, § 1 requires that verbal perjury be given under oath. The offense applies to judicial proceedings (including the grand jury) and to hearings before investigative and legislative bodies. *Comm. v. Giles*, 350 Mass. 102 (1966). It does not apply to sworn statements given in the course of prosecutorial investigations. *Comm. v. Dawson*, 399 Mass. 465 (1987) (police officer, accused of stealing cocaine from the evidence locker, repeatedly lied in a transcribed statement given under oath to a State Police lieutenant in the District Attorney's office; this did not qualify as perjury).

Type 2: Perjury per se. Before, if a witness made contradictory statements under oath, prosecutors had to determine which one was false in order to charge perjury. This legal loophole allowed witnesses to make statements that canceled each other out — fulfilling their obligation to testify while avoiding being labeled a "snitch." Now, perjury *per se* penalizes testimony involving obviously inconsistent statements on an important issue.

Type 3: Written perjury. A written statement must contain a written declaration that it is signed "under the penalty of perjury." *Galvin v. Town Clerk of Winchester*, 369 Mass. 175 (1975). The document does not have to be handwritten. *Comm. v. Zhan Tang Huang*, 87 Mass. App. Ct. 65 (2015).

Type 4: Subornation of perjury. Subornation occurs when the defendant successfully persuades someone else to commit perjury. *Comm. v. Borans*, 379 Mass. 117 (1979).

Level of proof required. A person can be convicted of perjury based on the testimony of a single witness, but only if there is additional, independent evidence. *Comm. v. Knowlton*, 50 Mass. App. Ct. 266 (2000) (police officer properly convicted of multiple counts of perjury stemming from a dispute with a neighbor that escalated into a legal feud).

Defendant previously acquitted of underlying charge. The fact that a defendant has been acquitted will not prevent the government from prosecuting him in a separate trial for perjury committed during his initial trial. However, this approach should be undertaken cautiously, since judges have been warned of "the danger of [prosecutorial] harassment . . . in the guise of a trial for perjury." *Comm. v. Mitchell*, 15 Mass. App. Ct. 577 (1983).

Related Offenses

Attempt to Persuade Another to Commit Perjury. 268, § 3. Penalty: SP NMT 5 yrs or HC NMT 1 year. In *Comm. v. Senior*, 454 Mass. 12 (2009), the defendant was engaged in a continuing neighborhood dispute. One day the defendant was driving his car when he became involved in a shouting match with his neighbor. The defendant's business associate was with him.

Later that day, the defendant went to the police station, handed an officer a brick and claimed that his neighbor used it to shatter his car window. An officer observed the damaged window and cuts on the defendant's hands consistent with broken glass. The neighbor was arrested and charged with ADW and malicious destruction of property. Prior to trial, the defendant had three conversations with his business associate to try to get him to testify falsely and corroborate his story. Instead, the associate reported the defendant's efforts to get him to lie under oath. The neighbor's case was dismissed, and the defendant was convicted of attempted perjury.

Written Perjury Concerning Stolen Motor Vehicle. 268, § 39. This species of perjury is discussed in *LED's Motor Vehicle Law, Chapter 12*.

Subject Index

This quick index is in alphabetical order and designed to help you locate a topic easily.

209A 13-4, 13-15
258E 13-24
911 35-12

A

Accessory After the Fact 2-5
Accomplice 2-1
Alarm
    false fire 34-7
    tampering with 34-8
Alcohol
    criminal enforcement 22-4
    giving to people under 21 22-4
    identification, false 22-8
    possession 22-9
    public drinking 22-11
    unlawful transportation 22-10
Animals
    confinement 8-2, 8-4
    cruelty to 8-1
    devocalization 8-5
    fighting 8-7
    sex with 8-6
Annoying & Accosting Sexually 10-3
Annoying Communications 15-6
Arson 34-1
    attempted 34-5
    burning insured property 34-6
    negligent burning 34-4
    personal property 34-3
Assault 4-1
    catalogue of assault crimes 4-13
    dangerous weapon 4-3
    with intent to rape 9-12
Assault & Battery 4-5
    catalogue of A&B crimes 4-13
    child, aggravated 14-7
    civil rights violation 16-5
    dangerous weapon 4-9
    domestic 13-29
    elder 14-7
    indecent on child under 14 9-14
    indecent on person 14 and over 9-13
    on intellectually disabled person 14-12
    on public employee/officer 5-1
Attempt 2-7
Attempted
    escape 5-13
    larceny 25-9
    murder 6-5

B

B&E 31-1
    daytime 31-15
    entry 31-2
    intent to commit misdemeanor 31-13
    nighttime with intent to commit felony 31-12
    of firearms dealer 31-14, 17-27
    to steal firearm 31-14, 17-27
BB guns 17-16
Bias-free Policing 16-9
Body Armor 17-27
Bomb Threat 19-5
Bribery 35-16
Breastfeeding 10-7
Burglarious Tools 31-16
Burglary
    aggravated 31-7
    unarmed 31-8

C

Child
    abuse reporting 14-1
    endangerment 14-11
Civil Rights 16-1
    assault & battery 16-5
    bias-free policing 16-9
    interfering with 16-1
    injunctions 16-8
Cocaine 20-1, 20-15, 20-18

Computers
    obtaining services by fraud 27-14
    unauthorized access 27-15
Conspiracy 2-9
Counterfeit
    currency 30-5
    drugs 20-22
    merchandise 27-16
Court
    default 35-17
    disruption of 23-12
Credit Card Crimes 27-7
Crime Scene Photos
    improper dissemination 1st responder 35-11
Criminal Harassment 15-1
Cruelty to Animals 8-1
Cultivation, Marijuana 21-2, 21-4, 21-5, 21-11, 21-12

D

Dangerous Weapons
    carrying 18-1
    definition of 4-3
Default from Court 35-17
Disabled Protection 14-2, 14-7
Disorderly Conduct 23-1
Disorderly House 23-8
Disturbing the Peace 23-9
Dispatch
    false calls 35-12
Domestic Violence (209A coverage) 13-1
    officer on scene responsibilities 13-4
    violation of restraining order 13-17
Drinking in Public 22-11
Drug(s) 20-1
    conspiracy 20-28
    counterfeit 20-22
    distribution concepts 20-10
    distribution offenses 20-15
    fraudulently obtaining 20-25
    inducing minors to distribute 20-24
    marijuana (see Marijuana)
    paraphernalia, selling 20-19
    possession concepts 20-5
    possession offenses 20-8
    protective custody for adults 20-9
    protective custody for children 20-24
    school & park zone 20-22
    stealing 20-26
    trafficking 20-17

E

Elder Abuse 14-2, 14-7
Electrical Weapon (aka "stun gun") 17-15
Embezzlement 25-8
Enticing Child 7-6
Electronic Enticement 7-8
Entry (see B&E)
Escape 5-12
    escape attempt 5-13
    escape from DYS 5-13
Evidence Tampering 35-9
Explosives 19-1
Extortion 3-5

F

False
    911 call 35-12
    arrest 5-10
    filing false report 35-13
    fire alarm 34-7
    impersonation and identity 27-12
    name or SSN 5-10
    reports by police officer 35-15
Fingerprints 26-4, 31-3
Firearms
    alien rights 17-20
    carrying in a vehicle 17-25
    carrying on campus 17-23
    carrying under the influence 17-23
    community guns 17-28
    discharging w/in 500 ft. of bldg. 17-24
    exemptions 17-18
    fake gun 4-3, 26-3
    nonresidents 17-20
    proof it works 17-9
    "Red Flag" order 17-6
    sales to minors 17-28
    stealing 17-27
    storage 17-26
    trafficking 17-28
    transporting 17-28
    unlawful possession 17-6

Firefighter
    hindering 34-7
Fire Prevention 34-9
Fireworks 19-7
First Complaint in Sexual Assault 9-18
Force
    standard for use of 5-6
Forgery 30-1

G

Gambling
    licensed casino 24-7
    organizing services 24-3
    public 24-1
    registering bets 24-2
    using phones 24-3
    Ponzi/pyramid scheme 24-4, 25-5

H

Hate Crimes 16-8
    bias indicators 16-2
Harassment
    criminal 15-1
    Prevention Orders (HPO) 13-24
Hijack 19-5
Hoax Device/Substance 19-1
Home Invasion 31-9
Hypodermic Needles 20-20

I

Identity Fraud 27-12
Incest 12-13
Impersonation of Police Officer 35-14
Indecent A&B 9-13
    child under 14 9-14
    person 14 and over 9-13
    public safely personnel 9-17
Indecent Exposure 10-6
Innkeepers
    defrauding 27-5
    rights of 32-9
Insurance Fraud 27-6
Interception of Oral Communication 15-7
Interfering with Police Officer 5-3
Intimidating a Witness 35-1

J

Joint Venture (see Accomplice)

K

Keeping Disorderly House 23-8
Kidnapping 7-1
    parental 7-3
Knives
    possession of 18-1

L

Larceny
    by check 27-3
    embezzlement 25-8
    false pretense 25-4
    from a building 27-2
    from person 27-1
    special forms 27-16
    stealing 25-3
Lewd & Lascivious 10-1
Littering 23-14
Loansharking 27-18
Lottery 24-4

M

Mandatory Reporting 14-1
Manslaughter 6-5
Marijuana
    cultivation (see Cultivation)
    distribution 20-10
    medical (see Medical Marijuana)
    recreational regulation 21-1
Mayhem 4-15
Medical Marijuana 21-10
Money Laundering 27-17
Murder 6-1

N

Narcotics (see Drugs)
Nuisance 22-6

O

Obscene Communications 15-6
Obscene Material (see Pornography)

Obstructing Access
    medical facility 32-11
    reproductive health facility 32-11
Obstruction of Justice 35-1
Open & Gross Lewdness 10-7

P

Parental Kidnapping 7-3
Perjury 35-18
Pickpocketing 27-1
Pimping 11-4
Police Dog
    mistreat 8-7
Ponzi/Pyramid Scheme 24-4, 25-5
Pornography
    depicting children 12-1
    dissemination to minors 12-11
    possession 12-7
Possession
    concepts 20-5
    of alcohol 22-9
    of drugs 20-8
    with intent to distribute 20-11
Prisoner (see Escape)
    sex with inmate 9-10
Property
    destruction of 33-1
    malicious 33-2
    wanton 33-2
Prostitution
    inducing minor 11-5
    permitting use of premises 11-6
    pimping 11-4
    pimping minor 11-5
Protective Custody
    adult w/drugs 20-9
    minors w/drugs 20-24
Public Assistance
    fraud 27-18
Public Drinking 22-11

R

Rape
    aggravated 9-1
    aggravated statutory 9-8
    aggravated under 16 9-6
    assault with intent to 9-12
    drugging for intercourse 9-11
    public safety personnel 9-10
    rape 9-1
    rape of child under 16 9-6
    statutory 9-7
Receiving Stolen Property 29-1
Reckless
    A&B 4-5
    endangerment to child 14-11
    involuntary manslaughter 6-2
Refusal to Assist Officer 5-5
Rented Property
    concealing 27-4
Resisting Arrest 5-6
Restraining Orders 13-4, 13-15
    enforcement of out-of-state 13-10
    violation of 13-17
Robbery
    armed 26-1
    unarmed 26-1

S

Secret
    interception of oral communication 15-7
    sexual surveillance 10-10
Self-Defense 4-17
    spray 17-17
Shoplifting 28-1
Smoking 21-13
Solicitation of a Felony 2-12
Stalking 15-1
    criminal harassment 15-1
Statute of Limitations 1-10
Statutory Rape 9-7
Suffocate or Strangle 13-31

T

Threat to Commit a Crime 3-1
Tobacco
    selling or giving to minor 21-14
Trespassing 32-1
    beach access 32-10
    homelessness 32-10
    innkeeper 32-9
    landlord/tenant 32-7
    no trespass notices 32-2
    public accommodation 32-6

U
Uttering 30-1
    false prescription 20-25
    legal document 30-2
Usury 27-18

V
Vaping 21-13

W
Welfare (see Public Assistance)
Witness Intimidation 35-1

No entries for Q, X, Y, and Z